EXPLORING PREHISTORY

How Archaeology Reveals Our Past

SECOND EDITION

PAM J. CRABTREE

New York University

DOUGLAS V. CAMPANA

New York University and National Park Service

Boston   Burr Ridge, IL   Dubuque, IA   Madison, WI   New York
San Francisco   St. Louis   Bangkok   Bogotá   Caracas   Kuala Lumpur
Lisbon   London   Madrid   Mexico City   Milan   Montreal   New Delhi
Santiago   Seoul   Singapore   Sydney   Taipei   Toronto

Higher Education

Published by McGraw-Hill, an imprint of The McGraw-Hill Companies, Inc., 1221 Avenue of the Americas, New York, NY 10020. Copyright © 2006, by The McGraw-Hill Companies, Inc. All rights reserved. No part of this publication may be reproduced or distributed in any form or by any means, or stored in a database or retrieval system, without the prior written consent of The McGraw-Hill Companies, Inc., including, but not limited to, in any network or other electronic storage or transmission, or broadcast for distance learning.

Some ancillaries, including electronic and print components, may not be available to customers outside the United States.

This book is printed on acid-free paper.

3 4 5 6 7 8 9 0 VNH/VNH 0 9

ISBN   978-0-07-297814-8
MHID   0-07-297814-7

Vice president and editor in chief: *Emily Barosse*
Editorial director: *Phillip A. Butcher*
Senior sponsoring editor: *Kevin Witt*
Developmental editor: *Gabrielle Goodman White*
Project manager: *Anne Fuzellier*
Production supervisor: *Randy Hurst*
Designer: *Jeanne M. Schreiber*
Art editor: *Robin Mouat*
Photo research coordinator: *Alexandra Ambrose*
Photo researcher: *David Tietz*
Compositor: *GTS-LA*
Cover image: *© Nathan Benn/Corbis*
Typeface: *10/13 Palatino*
Printer: *Von Hoffmann Press*

Library of Congress Cataloging-in-Publication Data

Crabtree, Pam J.
    Exploring prehistory: how archaeology reveals our past / Pam J. Crabtree, Douglas V. Campana.—2nd ed.
        p. cm.
    Rev. ed. of: Archaeology and prehistory.
    Includes bibliographical references and index.
    ISBN 0-07-297814-7 (sofcover: acid-free paper)
        1. Prehistoric peoples. 2. Antiquities, Prehistoric. 3. Anthropology, Prehistoric. I. Campana, Douglas V. II. Crabtree, Pam J. Archaeology and prehistory. III. Title.

GN740.C727 2005
930.1—dc22   2005043796

www.mhhe.com

EXPLORING PREHISTORY

How Archaeology Reveals Our Past

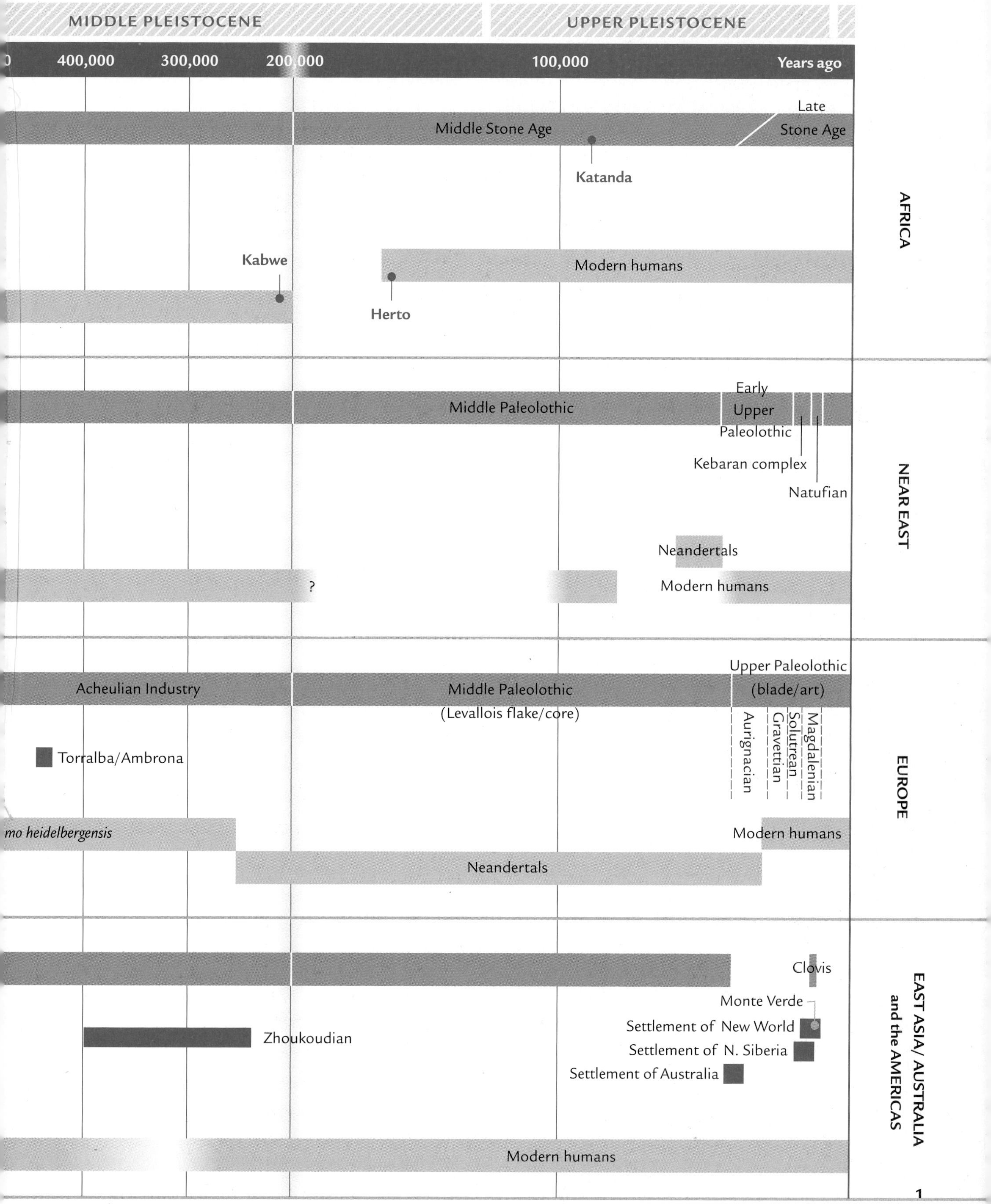

| 400,000 | 300,000 | 200,000 | 100,000 | Years ago |

AFRICA

Middle Stone Age

Late
Stone Age

Katanda

Kabwe

Modern humans

Herto

NEAR EAST

Middle Paleolothic

Early
Upper
Paleolothic
Kebaran complex
Natufian

Neandertals

?

Modern humans

EUROPE

Acheulian Industry

Middle Paleolothic
(Levallois flake/core)

Upper Paleolothic
(blade/art)

Aurignacian
Gravettian
Solutrean
Magdalenian

Torralba/Ambrona

mo heidelbergensis

Modern humans

Neandertals

EAST ASIA/ AUSTRALIA and the AMERICAS

Clovis

Monte Verde

Zhoukoudian

Settlement of New World

Settlement of N. Siberia

Settlement of Australia

Modern humans

1

To Mike, Tom, and Robby, with love.

ABOUT THE AUTHORS

PAM J. CRABTREE, who received her Ph.D. in Anthropology from the University of Pennsylvania in 1982, is an associate professor in the Center for the Study of Human Origins of the Anthropology Department at New York University, where she has worked since 1990. Professor Crabtree was an assistant professor of anthropology at Princeton University from 1985 to 1990 and a research fellow at the Museum Applied Science Center of the University of Pennsylvania from 1982 to 1984. She has written many scholarly articles on zooarchaeology and animal domestication and coedited *Animal Use and Culture Change* (with Kathleen Ryan). She has also edited *Medieval Archaeology: An Encyclopedia*, and she coedited *Ancient Europe: Encyclopedia of the Barbarian World 8000 B.C.–A.D. 1000* (with Peter Bogucki). Professor Crabtree has conducted archaeological research in England, Ireland, Germany, India, the West Bank, and the United States. She is currently engaged in an archaeological study of forts of the French and Indian War period in the Delaware Water Gap area on the New Jersey–Pennsylvania border. Professor Crabtree is a member of the Hopewell Township (New Jersey) Historic Preservation Commission.

DOUGLAS V. CAMPANA is a research associate in the New York University Anthropology Department and an archeologist with the National Park Service. He is a member of the Northeast Region Archeological Program based at Valley Forge National Historical Park, Pennsylvania. He received his Ph.D. in Anthropology from Columbia University in 1981. Dr. Campana has published scholarly articles on Near Eastern prehistory and bone tool technology, and he edited *Before Farming: Hunter-Gatherer Society and Subsistence*. He has conducted research in Israel, the West Bank, and Europe; his research has been sponsored by the National Science Foundation, the Wenner-Gren Foundation, and the National Geographic Society. Dr. Campana has directed archaeological excavations throughout the Mid-Atlantic states, including the excavation of a portion of Washington's Revolutionary War encampment at Valley Forge National Historical Park.

Although Dr. Campana is a federal archeologist, the positions and conclusions expressed in this text are his own and do not reflect any official position of the National Park Service, the Department of the Interior, or the government of the United States. Dr. Campana is not involved in the administration of NAGPRA or the decisions involving the Kennewick remains.

BRIEF CONTENTS

CONTENTS

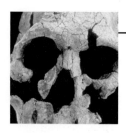

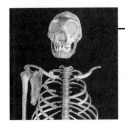
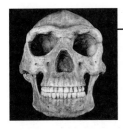

CHAPTER 6

The Middle Paleolithic and the Appearance of the Neanderthals   93

PART 2 THE ORIGINS OF MODERN HUMAN SOCIETY   107

CHAPTER 7

The Appearance of Modern Humans   110

CHAPTER 8

Late Paleolithic Cultures of the Near East and Africa   122

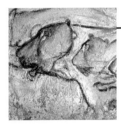
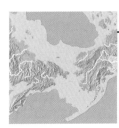

PART 3 POST-PLEISTOCENE ADAPTATIONS
How Did Human Societies Change at the End of the Ice Age?   184

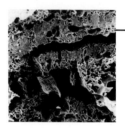

CHAPTER 13

The Mesolithic Period in Europe   188

CHAPTER 14

Post-Pleistocene Adaptations in the Americas: The Development of the Archaic   202

CHAPTER 21

CHAPTER 22

CHAPTER 23

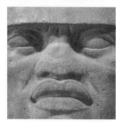

CHAPTER 24

Complex Societies in Mesoamerica 351

CHAPTER 25

Cities, States, and Empires in the Andes 369

CHAPTER 26

Middle Range and Complex Societies in North America 386

CHAPTER 27

The Future of Archaeology   404

ACKNOWLEDGMENTS

Writing an introductory textbook in archaeology is a daunting undertaking, and this project could not have been completed without the help of many friends, colleagues, and family members. Many people helped us complete this project, and we would like to thank all of them. First, we are grateful for the support of our colleagues at New York University and the National Park Service who have provided help and encouragement throughout the project. In particular, we would like to thank Jim Boyle and Heather Heineman, who researched the permissions for many of the figures that are included in this text. We owe a special debt of gratitude to Terry Harrison, Richard Lesure, Francis McManamon, and Bernard Wailes, who read and commented on various chapters in the first edition. Special thanks are due to Laurie Tedesco, who went above and beyond the call of duty. We would also like to thank the late Professor John Rowe, who supplied the drawing for Figure 25.7, and the many other colleagues who provided photographs and line art that are used in this text. Randall White, Susan Antón, Anthony Marks, Rob Blumenschine, Ian Kuijt, Yun Kuen Hee and Richard Klein have all provided new illustrations that have been included in the second edition of this text, and we are grateful for their assistance.

This text has benefited from the comments and suggestions made by many reviewers whose helpful and insightful suggestions have improved the content and presentation of this text in many ways:

Second Edition Reviewers

John W. Arthur, University of South Florida

Michael Heckenberger, University of Florida

John Kantner, Georgia State University

Randy McGuire, Binghamton University

Eleanorea Reber, University of North Carolina, Wilmington

Mark Schurr, University of Notre Dame

First Edition Reviewers

David Bernstein, State University of New York at Stony Brook

David Carlson, Texas A&M University

Christopher DeCorse, Syracuse University

James Enloe, University of Iowa

Michael Jochim, University of California, Santa Barbara

Mary Lou Larson, University of Wyoming

Deborah Olszewsky, University of Pennsylvania

Alan Orborn, University of Nebraska, Lincoln

Rene Peron, Santa Rosa Junior College

Gerald Schroedl, University of Tennessee

Tammy Stone, University of Colorado at Denver

Our editorial and production staff has been wonderfully supportive and patient throughout the long development of the first and second editions of this textbook. The second edition of this text would not have been possible without Kevin Witt, Sponsoring Editor from McGraw-Hill Higher Education, and our developmental editor, Gabrielle Goodman White. Many thanks also to the rest of our book team from McGraw-Hill: Marketing Manager Dan Loch, Project Manager Anne Fuzellier, Designer Jeanne Schreiber, Art Editor Robin Mouat, Photo Researcher Alexandra Ambrose, Supplements Producer Michele Borrelli, and Media Producer Shannon Gattens.

Finally, we want to thank our family and friends for their support throughout the long process of writing and revising this textbook. Special thanks go to our sons, Michael, Thomas, and Robert Campana, for their patience and understanding.

Pam J. Crabtree
Douglas V. Campana
February 2005
Pennington, NJ

PREFACE

Students usually first encounter archaeology during their freshman or sophomore year in college, since archaeology is rarely taught in high schools. By that time, however, many students already have some preconceived ideas about what archaeologists do for a living. We might envision archaeologists exploring ancient Egyptian tombs, searching for traces of early human activity in East Africa, or studying Maya ruins in the jungles of Guatemala. The romance of discovery is unmistakable. But, what are archaeologists really looking for? How do they know where to dig? How do they interpret what they find? *Exploring Prehistory: How Archaeology Reveals Our Past* is designed to answer these questions by providing a concise, yet comprehensive introduction to world prehistory. In addition, we introduce students to many of the archaeological methods, techniques, and theoretical models that archaeologists use to reconstruct the past.

Exploring Prehistory is the second edition of *Archaeology and Prehistory*, which was originally published in 2001. We have given our book a new title to better reflect its unique, integrative approach: to present a survey of prehistory that explores selected archaeological methods in context with specific topics so that students can see why, when, and where these techniques are applied.

WHAT ARE PREHISTORY AND ARCHAEOLOGY?

Prehistory is the chronicle of all that human beings accomplished before the advent of written records. While humans and their direct ancestors have lived on earth for about six million years, it was just over 5000 years ago that writing was developed. During the many millennia before writing was invented, prehistoric humans spread to every continent except Antarctica. They developed farming and permanent villages; they even built cities that housed complex, class-stratified societies. In this text, we will trace human history in many different parts of the world, from its earliest beginnings up to the appearance of writing.

Archaeology is the collection of methods, techniques, and analytical procedures that scholars use in their attempt to understand the events that took place in the past. These events are evidenced today by material remains buried in the earth, from simple fragments of pottery and stone tools to elaborate burial sites and temples. To study these remains, archaeologists make use of ideas, methods, and techniques derived from geology, biology, chemistry, physics, the social sciences, and other fields, as well as techniques developed by archaeologists themselves. We will explore the techniques archaeologists use to understand and interpret the past in the absence of written records.

APPROACH

Most traditional textbooks on world prehistory include a few brief introductory chapters on archaeological methods and then go on to recount a detailed world prehistory, paying very little attention to how archaeologists actually study the past. Textbooks on archaeological methods tend to be cookbooks, with very few examples of how these methods are applied in the real world.

Our approach is very different. We wrote *Exploring Prehistory: How Archaeology Reveals Our Past* so that students could really begin to understand how archaeologists do their work. We believe that students need to understand that archaeological methods are not simply a bag of scientific tricks. The methods used by archaeologists are designed to answer specific questions about how real people lived in the past. In *Exploring Prehistory*, we integrate relevant aspects of archaeological method into every chapter in the text. We do this in boxes titled Archaeology in Practice. For example, our chapter on the earliest human ancestors (Chapter 2) includes an Archaeology in Practice box on the methods used to date these very early sites. Our chapter on the earliest farmers in the Old World (Chapter 16) includes Archaeology in Practice boxes describing how archaeologists try to distinguish early domesticated or farm animals and plants from their wild relatives. The chapter on complex societies in South America (Chapter 25) includes an Archaeology in Practice box on the preservation of organic materials such as the beautiful textiles that have been recovered from many prehistoric sites in Peru.

Complementing the Archaeology in Practice boxes, many chapters include a Case Study box focusing on a major archaeological issue of a site discussed in the chapter. These Case Studies are set in a broad archaeological context to allow students to understand why the sites are important. For example, Chapter 12 includes a Case Study on the site of Lake Mungo in Australia, which first revealed that the Australian continent had been settled by hunter-gatherers more than 25,000 years ago. A Case Study in Chapter 19 describes the spectacular discoveries of Sir Leonard Woolley at the Royal Cemetery at Ur in southern Mesopotamia, while another (Chapter 26) describes the achievements of Native Americans in the great Mississippian sites of Cahokia in Illinois and Moundville in Alabama.

In the second edition, we also give students an expanded introduction to some of the questions and ideas that are the subject of current debate for working archaeologists with a new series of boxes called On the Cutting Edge, described in the next section.

New to this Edition

- ORGANIZATION: In this second edition, we have a new organization streamlined into four Parts: Part 1, Archaeology of the Human Ancestors: What Does Archaeology Tell Us about Ancient Human Societies?; Part 2, The Origins of Modern Human Society; Part 3, Post-Pleistocene Adaptations: How Did Human Societies Change at the End of the Ice Age?; and Part 4, How and Why Did Cities and States Develop?

- NEW TIMELINES: A unique Master Timeline covering all periods, geographical areas, and

major events discussed in the book appears on the inside front and back covers. In addition, each Part opens with its own specific timeline for handy, "big picture" reference.

- THE ARCHAEOLOGIST'S TOOLKIT: In a substantially revised Chapter 1, we have a special new feature that gives students an early overview of the basic methods used in archaeological excavation.

- NEW CHAPTER: For more extensive coverage of complex societies, we have written a new Chapter 22 devoted to the origins of complex societies in China.

- ON THE CUTTING EDGE BOXES: These boxes address contemporary theoretical issues and debates in archaeology. In Chapter 7, for example, we examine the controversy surrounding the origins of modern human behavior. In other On the Cutting Edge boxes, we examine the role of human sacrifice in early Egypt (Chapter 21) and examine the effect of the war in Iraq on the archaeology of Mesopotamia (Chapter 19).

- KEY TERMS: At the end of each chapter we include a list of all the boldfaced key terms and the pages on which they appear.

- FURTHER READING: Each chapter includes a short annotated list of references that students and instructors should find helpful in searching for additional material on the respective chapter contents. Selected readings include easy-to-read, accessible articles and books.

- QUESTIONS FOR DISCUSSION: Each chapter now concludes with several open-ended questions that are designed to explore the concepts introduced in the chapter.

- BIBLIOGRAPHY: A new, comprehensive Bibliography organized chapter-by-chapter appears at the end of the text.

- GLOSSARY: A new, alphabetically organized Glossary appears at the end of the text and provides capsule definitions of important terms and sites.

NEW CONTENT

Archaeology is a rapidly growing field, and no basic textbook can provide an exhaustive survey of all of world prehistory. In *Exploring Prehistory,* we have chosen to focus on the major issues, questions, and controversies that archaeologists and prehistorians have tackled in the past and which continue to occupy their attention today. We will introduce students to such "big picture" questions as:

What can archaeology tell us about the lives of human ancestors?

When did modern humans first appear, and how did they spread throughout the world?

How did human hunter-gatherers respond to the climatic changes that took place at the end of the Ice Age, and why did certain peoples begin to practice agriculture at about that time?

How and why did cities and states develop in both the Old World and the Americas?

Although our organization is essentially chronological, we begin with a stand-alone introductory chapter. Chapter 1 offers a brief history of earlier thoughts about human antiquity and about the ways in which the discipline of archaeology developed in both the Old World and the Americas, as well as a basic introduction to archaeological data. We examine the kinds of questions that archaeologists ask about the past. A new feature in this chapter is "The Archaeologist's Toolkit," described above.

Part 1 focuses on the archaeology of human ancestors. We begin with an overview of the fossil evidence for human evolution (Chapter 2) and then examine the beginnings of the archaeological record and the earliest archaeological sites in Africa (Chapter 3). Both chapters have been substantially updated to reflect recent archaeological and fossil human discoveries. We examine the ways in which archaeology can be used to study the behavior of early human ancestors, creatures who were very different, in terms of both biology and behavior, from ourselves. Chapters 4 and 5 center on the movement of ancient humans out of Africa and into the subtropical and temperate areas of the Near East,

East Asia, and Europe. We focus on the ways in which simple stone tools were made and used, and on the questions raised by evidence of hunting and scavenging in the archaeological record and by the evidence of the first controlled uses of fire. The new edition includes a discussion of the important new discoveries at Dmanisi and the evidence for hearths from the site of Gesher Benot Ya'acov in Israel. The final chapter in Part 1 (Chapter 6) is devoted to the archaeology of the Neanderthals, one of the most intriguing issues in all of world prehistory.

Part 2 begins with the critical question of where, when, and how modern humans first appeared (Chapter 7). In an attempt to answer this important question, we draw on evidence from archaeology, molecular biology, and human skeletal remains, including the recently discovered fossils from Herto Bouri. An Archaeology in Practice box is devoted to the molecular evidence for human evolution. We discuss the latest archaeological evidence for the replacement of the archaic Neanderthals by anatomically modern humans. Chapters 8 and 9 examine the archaeology of late Pleistocene modern humans in Africa, the Middle East, and Europe. An On the Cutting Edge box considers whether modern hunter-gatherers can serve as appropriate models for prehistoric hunter-gatherer behavior. The chapter on late Pleistocene art (Chapter 10) includes new images from Grotte Chauvet, a cave site that was discovered in 1994. Chapters 11 and 12 examine the initial human colonization of North America and Australia. Chapter 12 also includes new data in later Australian and Tasmanian prehistory. An On the Cutting Edge box addresses the question of why Tasmanians stopped fishing in later prehistory.

Part 3 examines the changes that human societies experienced at the end of the Ice Age, just over 11,000 years ago. In Chapter 13 we describe techniques—for example, pollen analysis—that archaeologists use to study past environments. Chapters 13 and 14 examine the ways in which hunter-gatherer societies in Europe and North America responded to the climatic changes at the end of the Pleistocene. In this edition, the Archaeology in Practice box on radiocarbon recalibration appears earlier in the book (Chapter 14), and all dates in Parts 3 and 4 are now presented as corrected radiocarbon dates.

Until the end of the Pleistocene, all humans everywhere in the world made their living by some combination of hunting, fishing, and plant collecting. Farming was unknown. Beginning about 11,000 years ago, human beings began to experiment with planting crops and keeping animals. Farming developed independently in several areas of the world, including the Near East, Southeast Asia, West Africa, Mesoamerica, highland South America, eastern North America and New Guinea. Chapter 15 provides a basic introduction to the study of agricultural origins. Chapter 16 outlines the beginning of farming in the Eastern Hemisphere and includes new information on early cattle domestication in sub-Saharan Africa and on early plant domestication in New Guinea. Chapter 17 examines the beginnings of farming in the Americas and includes new information on maize and squash domestication from the important site of Guilá Naquitz in Oaxaca, Mexico. A new Archaeology in Practice box on the study of phytoliths (plant silica bodies) has also been added to Chapter 17. The final chapter in Part 3 (Chapter 18) examines the consequences of the "agricultural revolution," including population growth, the development of new technologies, and the increasing incidence of certain diseases. A new On the Cutting Edge box examines the relative roles of migration and the adoption of domestic plants and animals by indigenous hunter-gatherers in the spread of farming to Europe.

One of the most interesting consequences of the beginnings of farming is the development of complex, urban societies. Extensive archaeological research in both the Eastern and Western Hemispheres has shown that agriculture provided the economic basis for the development of urban societies such as the Maya of Central America and the Egyptians of North Africa. We examine how and why these large-scale, class-stratified societies developed in Part 4.

Part 4 begins with the origins and growth of urban societies in the Old World. The chapter on Mesopotamia (Chapter 19) includes a new Archaeology in Practice box on aerial photography and landscape reconstruction. The chapter on the Indus Valley (Chapter 20) has been updated to reflect recent archaeological discoveries. Our chapter on ancient Egypt (Chapter 21) has been expanded to include complex urban societies in other parts of Africa. We have included a section on the archaeology of Nubia, Egypt's rival to the south, and a discussion of the beginnings of urbanism in the Inland Niger Delta in Mali. Our new chapter on the origins of complex societies in China (Chapter 22) includes an Archaeology in Practice box that describes some of the techniques used to explore subsurface archaeological remains prior to excavation, and we show how these techniques have been used to explore early Chinese tombs. In addition to extensive updating, our chapter on Europe (Chapter 23) also includes a new Archaeology in Practice box on the analysis of metal artifacts.

We have expanded our coverage of complex societies in the Americas. Chapter 24 includes new information on the archaeology of Aztec daily life. Chapter 25 includes a discussion of the Wari citadel of Cerro Baul, where a brewery for *chicha* (maize beer) has been recently discovered. Our chapter on North America (Chapter 26) includes a new case study of the Mississippian center at Moundville in Alabama, as well as a new section on the archaeology of the pueblos in the American Southwest.

The final chapter in our text (Chapter 27) explores the future of archaeology. We consider such questions as the looting and the destruction of archaeological sites, the issues of archaeology and nationalism, and the ways in which archaeological data have been used for political purposes. A new On the Cutting Edge box explores the controversy surrounding Kennewick Man and the relationship between archaeologists and Native Americans in North America. These are some of the critical ethical questions that surround archaeology today.

LEARNING FEATURES

In addition to the new features described above, *Exploring Archaeology* retains the following features from the first edition to enhance learning and make the presentation more engaging:

Chapter Outlines: Each chapter opens with a convenient, page-referenced list of the section titles in the chapter.

Maps: In every chapter, maps help students locate the major sites discussed in the chapter and provide a sense of the prehistoric landscape and landforms.

Key Terms: All key terms are boldfaced and defined within the text. In addition, all the key terms are defined in the new Glossary at the end of the book.

Conclusions: Each chapter ends with a Conclusion section that succinctly synthesizes the chapter content.

SUPPLEMENTAL RESOURCES

The Online Learning Center at www.mhhe.com/crabtree2 provides interactive resources to address the needs of a variety of teaching and learning styles. For every chapter, students and instructors can access chapter outlines, sample quizzes, crossword puzzles using key terms, and more. For instructors specifically, the Online Learning Center offers a downloadable Instructor's Resource Manual with essay topics, suggestions for videos to accompany the course, and classroom activities that can be used to extend the material presented in each chapter.

In addition, instructors also receive an Instructor's Resource CD-ROM (IRCD) containing the Instructor's Resource Manual and Test Bank.

EXPERIENCE ARCHAEOLOGY FIRSTHAND

We hope that this text will spark your interest in archaeology, and we encourage you to become a volunteer on an archaeological excavation. The best way to learn about archaeology is to experience it firsthand. Both of us decided to become archaeologists after working as volunteers on archaeological excavations while we were undergraduates. Doug Campana's first archaeological experience was working as a volunteer on the early Paleolithic site of 'Ubeidiya in Israel (see Chapter 4), while Pam Crabtree first worked as a volunteer at the excavation of the medieval city of Winchester in England. The Archaeological Institute of America publishes an annual "Archaeological Fieldwork Opportunities" Bulletin on its website. Other fieldwork opportunities are often published on university websites.

1

EXPLORING THE PAST

THE DISCOVERY OF THE ICEMAN

In October 1992, the cover of *Time* magazine, a space usually reserved for celebrities and politicians, displayed the face of a man about whom virtually nothing was known, not even his name, and who had died more than 5000 years ago (Figure 1.1). The discovery of the Iceman, as he was called, generated a press sensation. Scores of newspaper and magazine articles and several books on the Iceman soon appeared, including one denouncing the find as a fraud. Most scientists, however, are quite convinced that he is genuine. The body was discovered in September 1991, high in the Tyrolean Alps between Italy and Austria. The summer had been warm, and a deposit of dust on the glacier resulted in an unusual degree of melting. The Iceman's frozen body, entombed in the glacial ice for millennia, was finally released. German tourists hiking through the pass came upon his remains just poking through the ice. Had they not found him, within a few days he would have been covered with a fresh fall of snow and returned once more to the glacier.

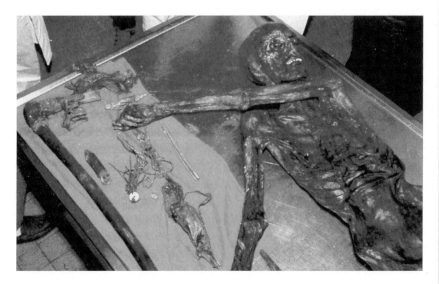

FIGURE 1.1   The 5000-year-old body of the Iceman, recovered from a glacier in the Tyrolean Alps.

FIGURE 1.2   A copper axe and a flint knife, a few of the numerous items in the Iceman's equipment.

Why should the Iceman, whose possessions were humble in the extreme, who hailed from a time scarcely known to the average person, have aroused such excitement? Much was made of the claim that the Iceman was the oldest completely preserved human, but, in truth, some Egyptian mummies are older. For some Europeans, surely, the fact that the Iceman was himself a European provided a tie to their past. Most likely, though, he was so interesting because he was a common man, the antithesis of the pharaohs of Egypt or the emperors of China. Possibly, he was a shepherd, not so different from the Tyrolean shepherds of today. He carried with him only the equipment that served him in his everyday life. His garments, equipment, and weapons buried with him in the ice told of an ordinary man.

The methods of archaeology tell us all we know about who the Iceman was. (Physical anthropologists and biologists study the man's body itself.) The Iceman carried with him a metal axe (Figure 1.2), at first believed to be bronze because it closely resembled the axes found in sites dated to the early Bronze Age of the region (starting about 2200 B.C.). When samples from the Iceman, however, were dated using radiocarbon (to be discussed in detail in Chapter 9), he was found instead to have died between 3500 and 3000 B.C.—the early Copper Age. The blade of the axe was analyzed chemically; it turned out to be copper. Its flanged form, though, was unusually sophisticated for that early date. The early Copper Age from this part of the Alps is so poorly known that the local occurrence has not even been given a name. The closest analog to the flanged axe comes from a nearby cemetery at Remedello, Italy, but about 500 years later. The rest of the Iceman's equipment has even fewer parallels, and much of it is unique, because objects of wood and leather are very rarely preserved. It was a remarkable set of equipment. His leather clothing, although crudely patched, perhaps by the Iceman himself, had been finely stitched together, by a practiced hand, from the contrasting skins of several animals. His shoes were well-made, grass-insulated against the cold, and he wore a fur-lined cap on his head. He carried his supplies in a wood-framed backpack, including a quiver filled with arrows, a few of which still had feathers attached. Around his waist he wore a leather pouch that contained some flint tools and tinder for fire making. He had a birch-bark container as well, blackened on the inside as if it had contained fire. Very likely, the Iceman was making himself a new bow when he met his death, for he carried an unfinished longbow made from yew, the best wood known for that purpose. There were other items as well, some 20 in all. Particularly interesting are some bits of fungus threaded on a thong. Known to have antibiotic value, they perhaps served as a first-aid kit. The sophistication of the Iceman's clothing, his tools, and his evident knowledge of the natural world all came as a surprise.

In 2001, the Iceman made the news again. New X rays of his body revealed evidence that had been missed before. An arrowhead was deeply embedded under his left shoulder. Furthermore, a deep stab wound was found in his right hand (Dickson et al. 2003). Even more recently, DNA analyses by Thomas Loy of the University of Queensland indicate that the blood of four different individuals were on the Iceman's weapons and clothing, suggesting he may have been in a battle. Was the Iceman murdered while defending himself? This question is still being debated.

The European Copper Age, or Chalcolithic, is known only from archaeology. All that we know of the people of the European Copper Age comes from the material traces they left behind. **Archaeology** means, literally, the study of ancient things; it refers in practice to the study of the material remains created by past human beings. Archaeologists use a wide range of techniques to puzzle out the past, and they enlist the aid of many specialists from other fields. Archaeology is more, though, than the collection of methods and techniques needed to uncover individual facts about the past. Archaeology provides a variety of ways for integrating these isolated facts into a broad picture of the world of the past and a framework for understanding how that world developed and changed.

In Europe, the people of the Copper Age did not write. Indeed, we can only speculate about what sort of language they may have spoken. More than 2000 years would pass before the epics of Homer would mark the beginning of written history in Europe. The events of the Copper Age are the stuff of prehistory, as are all the events in which humans participated before the advent of written records. **Prehistory** (as archaeologists use the word) is the sum of all that we know of the activities of humans before the beginning of written history. Prehistory ends at different times in different parts of the world. Some regions, such as China, have a long tradition of written records extending back for almost 4000 years. In other areas of the world, such as Poland and Scandinavia, the earliest written records do not appear until about A.D. 1000. Archaeology is the means by which we have gained almost all our knowledge of prehistoric times.

ARCHAEOLOGY

Written records are available for only a minute fraction of past human societies. Writing is the exception rather than the rule. For most of humanity's time on earth, all that is left to us are material remains: stone tools and potsherds, skeletons and animal bones, trash pits, structures, stains in the soil. Yet the material vestiges of past human behavior tell us much about how these ancient human societies subsisted, developed, and interacted, and even, through careful inference, something of their ideas and beliefs.

Archaeology, as noted earlier, is the study of the material remains of past societies. If we are to understand the forces that shaped human society, we must try to interpret these remains, to understand what they were and how they came to rest

Differing Attitudes toward the Dead

Most Americans and Europeans greeted the discovery of the Iceman with wonder, curiosity, and fascination, as he provided a glimpse of life in an almost unknown past. Few people objected to the widespread publication of his image. Austria and Italy vied with each other for the right to study him, preserve his remains, and put him and his possessions on public display.[1]

The 1996 discovery of the almost complete skeleton of a man near Kennewick, Washington, however, provoked a very different response. When a radiocarbon age determination showed him to be about 9000 years old, Native American groups soon claimed him. According to their traditions, their people had been in America since the beginning of time. Clearly, therefore, this man was one of their ancestors. They demanded his immediate reburial and condemned any further study as disrespectful of the dead.

A number of scientists objected strenuously to the Native Americans' claim. They said that the Kennewick Man differed physically from living Native Americans and that there was no clear cultural link between the ancient man and modern Native American peoples. They insisted instead that Kennewick Man belonged to all people, not just Native Americans, and that the reburial of the Kennewick bones would deprive science of invaluable evidence about the ancient world.

The conflict over the fate of the Kennewick skeleton became the subject of an extended legal debate that will most likely reach the Supreme Court. Whatever the Court's decision, though, it is unlikely that either the scientists or the Native Americans will change their views.[2]

Such profound differences in worldview are a reflection of the gulf between European and Native American cultural and religious traditions. Europeans have been concerned primarily about those individuals from the past who lived after the historical beginnings of the Christian or Jewish faiths. When, for instance, a medieval Jewish cemetery was excavated in the city of York, England, the chief rabbi of Britain oversaw the reburial of the bodies. On the other hand, pagans, such as early Anglo-Saxons, are not generally reinterred, and some are displayed in the British Museum today. Native Americans, however, view their culture and religion as deeply rooted in an indefinite past. They have objected strenuously to museums or other institutions that have put any Native American remains or ceremonial objects on public display.

Archaeologists today must always be cognizant and sympathetic to the sensibilities of the modern people among whom they work. This is rarely an easy course to follow. Scientific goals and conclusions are sometimes deeply at odds with strongly held religious beliefs and cultural traditions. For example, those whose religious beliefs teach the special creation of humanity will surely discount the evidence for human evolution as it is presented in this text.

---

[1]The Iceman ultimately came to the South Tyrol Museum of Archaeology in Bolzano, Italy, established especially to house him.

[2]The full story of the Kennewick controversy is recounted in the final chapter of this book.

---

where they were found, and to infer from them human behavior, social organization, and the relationship between early humans and their environment. It is a bit like a detective story in which an unseen crime must be pieced together from often elusive clues. Like Sherlock Holmes, the archaeologist must exercise careful logic in interpreting the archaeological data and then formulate likely **hypotheses** (tentative explanations designed to account for a set of facts) to explain what is observed. These hypotheses must then be tested against further observations so that unsatisfactory explanations can be eliminated. Archaeologists try, in the end, to arrive at the most likely explanation for events in the past.

THE ISSUES AND PROBLEMS OF PREHISTORY

This text will concentrate on the prehistoric periods around the globe and on archaeology as it is applied to the study of prehistory. Many of the crucial events that have shaped humanity and human society have left behind no record other than stone tools, some food remains, and the skeletons of our predecessors. Prehistoric archaeologists find themselves with some fascinating and challenging problems to solve. Some of the most important issues are the following:

- Who were our earliest human ancestors? What were their lives like? Did they hunt for their food, or did they obtain it by scavenging kills left behind by more powerful carnivores? How were early human societies organized? We will address these questions in Chapters 2 through 6.

- How, when, and where did modern humans evolve? How did they come to replace more ancient forms of human beings, and when and how did they spread throughout the world? These questions will be addressed in Chapters 7 through 12.

- How did human populations respond to the climatic changes at the end of the Ice Age? These questions will be addressed in Chapters 13 and 14.

- When, where, and why did farming replace hunting and gathering? When did the first permanent villages appear in the Old World and in the Americas? Chapters 15 through 18 will address these issues.

- Can we trace the development of the great civilizations of the Old World? How did the pre-Columbian civilizations of the New World develop? These questions will be addressed in Chapters 19 through 26.

Today, archaeologists believe they have some answers to some of these questions, but many basic problems are yet unresolved. Many alternative hypotheses have been offered concerning these issues, and much lively (and sometimes rancorous) debate continues among archaeologists. There is much work for the future.

The methods and archaeological viewpoints to be discussed in this book are primarily those developed in the West, specifically Europe and North America, in the wake of the explosive growth in the natural sciences during the eighteenth and nineteenth centuries. In the early twentieth century, the political dominance of the West led to the adoption of Western archaeological practices and prehistoric frameworks throughout much of the world. Some peoples outside Europe, however, held quite distinctive views of their own most ancient times. The Chinese, in particular, have recorded their own history for millennia, and even in the earliest writings they took notice of the material remains from bygone ages. Chinese historical writings were sometimes supplemented with detailed descriptions (with a distinctly archaeological flavor) of objects belonging to ancient periods. Like the ancient Greeks, the early Chinese were aware that their own use of metals was preceded by a time when people depended on stone tools. (Early Chinese society will be discussed in greater detail in Chapter 22.)

The modern-day search for our early human ancestors, however, surely found its impetus in the scientific and humanistic developments in Europe during the eighteenth and nineteenth centuries. In the late nineteenth and early twentieth centuries, Western scholars journeyed to Africa, Southeast Asia, and China in search of the antecedents of humanity. They took Western science with them, particularly the methods of geology and the concepts of biological evolution. National scholars in Africa and Asia by and large accepted these ideas. The methods of European archaeology and the prehistoric framework originally developed for Europe came to be applied in many areas of the world. Archaeologists soon came to realize, though, that the prehistory of most of the world could not be forced into the European mold. Today, archaeologists from China, Japan, Africa, Latin America, and elsewhere are hard at work refining the unique prehistories of their regions; in so doing, they are expanding the horizons of scientific archaeology as a whole.

THE HISTORICAL GROWTH OF ARCHAEOLOGY IN EUROPE

Until a few hundred years ago, almost no one could conceive of the great antiquity of human presence on the earth. The medieval European universe, for example, was short-lived and firmly centered, both physically and philosophically, on the earth and humanity. For European Christendom, the world

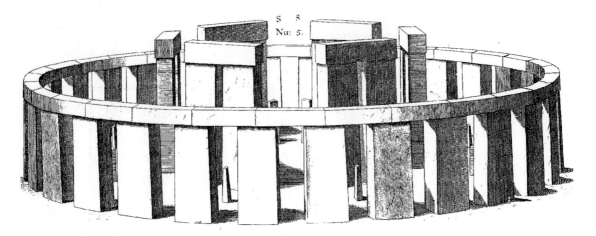

FIGURE 1.3   Seventeenth-century architect Inigo Jones's interpretation of Stonehenge as a Roman temple.

began shortly before the creation of Adam and Eve, and Armageddon lay not very far in the future. In the sixteenth and seventeenth centuries, new astronomical discoveries brought a better understanding of the size and complexity of the physical universe, but, in the popular mind at least, the life span of this universe was derived from a reading of the Bible. In 1636 the Irish archbishop James Ussher calculated, on the basis of the text of the Bible, that the world had been created in 4004 B.C. Together with the works of classical antiquity, the Bible provided all that was known of history.

During the seventeenth century, however, scholars began to examine the world of nature ever more closely. As the telescope had revealed the universe, the invention of the microscope opened up the world of the very small. The sciences of chemistry and physics were developing, and the earth's array of plants and animals began to be classified. This growing interest in the natural world also drew the curiosity of many to the mysterious monuments scattered across the European countryside—earthworks, stone chambers and rings, and standing stones. Among the most well-known of these ancient monuments were the standing stones that make up Stonehenge. Seventeenth-century scholars attributed the building of Stonehenge to the Celts or Britons or other peoples known from the classical writers. In 1620

the royal architect Inigo Jones concluded that Stonehenge was a Roman temple (Figure 1.3). John Aubrey (1626–1697) was the first to undertake a detailed study of the great stone circle: "The celebrated antiquity of Stonehenge . . . I affirm to have been temples, and built by the Britons [the inhabitants of Britain at the time of the Roman conquest of the island in the first century A.D.]" (Aubrey in Daniel 1967: 37). Aubrey believed Stonehenge was the work of Druid priests living in Britain before the Roman conquest of the island. This myth was popularized in the eighteenth century and remains embedded in popular culture even today. Neo-Druids congregate at Stonehenge on the summer solstice (June 21) to celebrate this popular myth. Stonehenge, in fact, far antedates the Britons; its earliest phases were probably erected before 2000 B.C. (For an up-to-date review of the archaeology of Stonehenge, see Chippendale 2004.)

Medieval farmers frequently encountered stone axes in their fields; such things were usually attributed to magic, leprechauns, or the action of lightning. The sixteenth-century voyages of discovery brought a better answer: These objects were stone tools made in the absence of metals, not unlike the tools and weapons used by many native New World and Pacific Island peoples. Still, the true antiquity of these stone tools could not be imagined. Not until the nineteenth century, in fact, was it possible to appreciate how very old these objects were. In 1802 the Danish archaeologist Rasmus Nyerup could still lament:

> Everything which has come down to us from hea-thendom is wrapped in a thick fog; it belongs to a space of time we cannot measure. We know that it is older than Christendom but whether by a couple of years or a couple of centuries, or even by more than a millennium, we can do no more than guess (Nyerup in Daniel 1967: 36).

For this fog to be lifted, the chronology of the earth had to be recast, and the evidence for this new chronology was to come from the developing science of geology.

THE NEW GEOLOGY

Today we take it for granted that the many meters of consecutive rock layers that make up the earth's crust (seen clearly in places like the Grand Canyon) were laid down layer by layer over many ages. At the start of the eighteenth century, this concept was not so clear. The prevailing idea at that time was that the rocks of the earth had precipitated all at once from a world-encircling ocean, perhaps the Great Flood of Noah.

The key figure in refuting this explanation was the Scotsman **James Hutton** (1726–1797). Hutton would not accept that the geological features of the earth were laid down by the Great Flood. Instead, he argued, v [James Hutton refutes the] t work on the earth [idea that the Great Flood created geological features.] volcanic activities [ ] ie past. This view w [Uniformitarianism – his principle] n principle, or **uni** [that we must look to processes] earth, according to [still at work on earth today] plifted and eroded, [soil erosion/volcanic activity] [to understand the past.] entary rock had bee [ ] a from the sediment carried from the uplands to the sea, a process that may be observed today. The layers of rock are immensely thick, and such processes are very slow. The earth, therefore, must be far older than the 6000 years calculated by Ussher.

Most scholars of Hutton's time, however, saw the appearance and disappearance of fossil species in the rocks as the result of a series of catastrophes, which, like the Great Flood, had swept away the living species, after which new species would appear.

This theory, known as **catastrophism,** was more in keeping with the early nineteenth-century world-view; Hutton's ideas were practically forgotten.

Between 1830 and 1833, however, **Charles Lyell** (1797–1875) published a textbook, *Principles of Geology,* that revived the uniformitarian principles introduced by Hutton, but which was bolstered by much additional evidence. Lyell argued his position extremely convincingly; the textbook saw many editions, and the uniformitarian view of geology came to be practically universally accepted. By the mid-nineteenth century most scientists had come to accept the deep antiquity of the earth, an earth shaped by the slow, gradual effects of ordinary geological processes—the erosion of the rocks and soil by wind and water and the slow buildup of sediments by rivers and streams. Among those scientists was **Charles Darwin** (1809–1882). During the 1830s Darwin signed on as natural history officer aboard the HMS *Beagle* and began his famous voyage of discovery down the coast of South America and through its offshore islands. (Darwin had read Lyell's book before embarking.) During this trip he made the crucial wildlife observations that would lead to his publication of *On the Origin of Species* in 1859 (for a more detailed discussion, see Eiseley 1958). The mechanism proposed by Darwin for the evolution of new species, natural selection, proceeded by the extremely slow accumulation of minute changes; only the time depth provided by Lyell's geology could make evolution possible.

HUMAN ANTIQUITY

During the nineteenth century, the evidence for the true antiquity of humans began to pile up (Daniel 1959; Daniel and Renfrew 1988; Grayson 1983). In 1797, **John Frere** (1740–1807) recognized that humans had lived on earth for a very long time, based on his discoveries at Hoxne, Suffolk, in eastern England. Many flint tools, including chipped flint axes (Figure 1.4), and the bones of extinct animals were found buried in a layer some 4 m (12 ft.) below the ground surface. As Frere noted:

> The situation in which these weapons were found may tempt us to refer them to a very remote period indeed, even beyond that of the present world (Frere in Daniel 1967: 47).

FIGURE 1.4 A drawing of a flint handaxe found by John Frere at Hoxne, Suffolk, in 1797, which he realized came from the remote past.

Could humans really have lived at the same time as extinct animals? In the 1830s, at a cave known as Kent's Cavern in England, flint tools were found together with the bones of extinct animals, sealed beneath a layer of limestone that had been deposited by the percolating water in the cave. The scientific establishment of the time, however, would not accept the contemporaneity of the tools and extinct animal bones. It could not be proved that the limestone layer had not been broken and the tools introduced much later than the fossil bone. Yet, further associations of flint tools and ancient animals continued to come to light. In 1832 the Frenchman **Jacques Boucher de Perthes** (1788–1868) found a flint **handaxe,** a stone tool, in a gravel pit at Abbeville in the Somme Valley. Over the years Boucher de Perthes collected thousands of stone artifacts, found in the company of the bones of mammals long extinct in Europe, such as mammoths and rhinoceroses.

The turning point was an excavation conducted by **William Pengelly** (1812–1894). Pengelly was a natural science teacher and a talented amateur geologist. In 1846 he decided to reexamine the finds from Kent's Cavern; he became convinced that the simple stone tools were indeed contemporary with the bones of extinct animals, implying that humans had lived at the same time as those prehistoric beasts. He could not, however, convince the members of the English scientific societies, who pointed out that the cave had been extensively disturbed by the earlier excavations. Their minds were no longer closed, however, and Pengelly was given an opportunity to prove his point. In 1858 Pengelly undertook the excavation of Brixham Cave, near Windmill Hill, Torquay, in southwest England. His work was closely observed by a group of prominent scientists, including Charles Lyell, from the Royal Society (a highly influential, learned scientific society) and the Geological Society of London. The cave contained an unbroken floor of stalagmite. Pengelly broke through the floor, and beneath it were stone tools in the company of the bones of mammoth, woolly rhinoceros, cave bear, cave lion, and other ancient mammals. The learned societies were convinced; ancient humans had lived at the same time as extinct animals. Later that year two of Pengelly's observers visited Abbeville. They came back assured that Boucher de Perthes's observations too were correct. In 1859 these conclusions were presented to the Royal Society. Many questions were still unresolved, but from then on, most scientists would accept the antiquity of humanity.

What, though, of Stonehenge, the stone tombs, and the many objects of bronze and iron found scattered throughout Europe? These things were obviously far later than the stone tools in the Somme gravels and the English cave sites, but they too could not be accounted for within the time of written history. Scandinavia was particularly rich in such finds, and by the early 1800s many such artifacts had been collected to form the core of the Danish National Museum. **Christian J. Thomsen** (1788–1865), the first curator of the museum, had an idea about how this large collection could be organized logically. Thomsen had experience in organizing ancient coins in chronological order. When dates were not present on the coins, stylistic similarities suggested which coins were closest in time. He applied the techniques he had learned to the objects in the museum. Thomsen grouped the objects into those of stone, bronze, and iron.

He went further, however, and suggested that they represented three successive ages: the Stone Age, the Bronze Age, and the Iron Age. Thomsen recognized that bronze and stone objects, for instance, might continue to be made in the Iron Age. He used stylistic similarities among the objects, as he had with coins, to sort out which of them were likely to be contemporary. This straightforward ordering of Scandinavian antiquities became known as the **Three Age System** and was soon extended to much of Europe north of the Alps.

Thomsen was assisted in his research and later succeeded by **Jens Worsaae** (1821–1885), who is now recognized as one of the founders of the discipline of archaeology. Worsaae examined the burial mounds and other ancient sites of Denmark. It was Worsaae who recognized that a bronze or an iron object found in isolation would do little to unravel the chronology of prehistory. It was critically important to observe which kinds of objects were regularly found together and which were associated with particular burial practices and monuments. Groups of objects usually found together could be assumed to be contemporary, and if one group of objects was found to overlie another, the overlying group was clearly later in time. When the successive groups of artifacts were taken all together, a pattern emerged that could be interpreted as gradual change. Worsaae's careful excavations established the chronological validity of the Three Age System. He was able to show that sites and burials containing artifacts only of stone were older than those that also contained bronze artifacts. Worsaae published his work in 1843. He was far ahead of his time; only many years later would an appreciation of his methods reach beyond Scandinavia to the rest of the world. Many problems remained, but today the emergence of scientific dating methods has done much to clarify the chronology of the European Bronze and Iron Ages (see Chapter 23).

THE BEGINNINGS OF ARCHAEOLOGY IN THE AMERICAS

While the beginnings of archaeology in Europe were closely linked to growing European nationalism, the beginnings of archaeology in the Americas were linked to colonialism and the relationships between Europeans and Native American peoples. In the wake of Columbus's voyages, and the European explorers, conquerors, and settlers that followed, the fate of the native peoples of the Americas was inextricably caught up in the course of European history. Native American peoples, for the most part, were never afforded the opportunity to write down their own history, and most of the newly arrived Europeans assumed that the native peoples knew no history. Today, scholars realize that this view was not accurate. Many nonliterate Native American groups had rich traditions of oral history; the literate Maya (Chapter 24), we now know, recorded historical events for future generations.

Still, archaeology as it developed in the Americas, and as it has been practiced until recently, has had a fundamentally European perspective. Although change is on the horizon (see Chapter 27, "The Future of Archaeology"), the role of Native American perceptions and insights has been relatively minor. American archaeology has its academic roots in the European scientific developments we have just discussed. Seen less positively, Native Americans have been viewed largely as they appear to European eyes.

The first Europeans to encounter Native American peoples had considerable difficulty fitting them into the traditional European worldview, since American Indians held no obvious place in either classical history or religious teaching. Some speculated that they were the descendants of the Ten Lost Tribes of Israel. Others saw the American natives as scarcely human and thus rationalized the Europeans' right to displace them from their lands. In Mexico and Peru, the Spanish conquerors sought to consolidate their own colonial power and suppress the native religion. They did what they could to cut off the native peoples' contact with their history by destroying their monuments and burning their texts. In North America, Native Americans were commonly viewed as simple, unchanging savages, and many years of strife and warfare between the colonists and natives exacerbated such beliefs.

Not all Europeans, however, shared these attitudes toward Native Americans. An exception was surely Thomas Jefferson, who would ultimately become president of the United States.

Jefferson was a member and eventually president of the American Philosophical Society. He shared the society's interest in scientific debate, including the ongoing controversy over the nature of the ancient mounds found in many areas of eastern America. In 1784 Jefferson undertook the excavation of several of the burial mounds he found on his Virginia plantation. He took note of the distinctive layers in the soil and how some graves overlay others, indicating a long series of burials over time. Most important, Jefferson excavated these mounds to try to learn something of the Native American past.

Thomas Jefferson sometimes has been called the father of American archaeology. As Willey and Sabloff (1980: 38) have pointed out, however, he was a parent without intellectual offspring. Very little notice was taken of his archaeological endeavors. In the climate of the times, it is not likely that many European colonists would have favored research that demonstrated the antiquity of Native Americans' claim to the land. The most impressive ancient features on the North American landscape, the great mounds of the Ohio Valley, were assumed to be the work of a vanished Mound Builder people, who had been driven away by the savage Indians. Throughout the nineteenth century, a majority of scholars stereotyped Native American cultures as uniformly simple and unchanging. Even the achievements of the Inca and Aztec civilizations were explained away as simply the products of Spanish exaggeration, intended to heighten the glory of their conquest.

Eventually, the accumulation of evidence would sweep away that point of view. A series of travelers and explorers penetrated the jungles of the lowland Maya homeland and brought home stirring tales of their adventures and magnificent images of the hidden, ancient cities they found there. These popular accounts suited the public tastes of the time and were read avidly. New scientific expeditions of discovery were mounted, and by the end of the nineteenth century a variety of surveys and studies of the antiquities of Central and South America had been completed or were under way.

Archaeology, in close association with anthropology, continued to develop in the United States during the late nineteenth century. It was recognized that much of the diversity of Native American culture was fast disappearing, in part because in the late nineteenth and early twentieth century American Indians were not permitted to speak their native languages in school. In 1879 the Smithsonian Institution formed the Bureau of Ethnology (later called the Bureau of American Ethnology) to record the vanishing languages and traditions. Archaeology was seen as a part of those studies, but archaeological findings were interpreted largely as projections of modern Native American societies into the past. Only in the twentieth century have archaeologists recognized the depth, diversity, and complexity of the North American archaeological record. Nineteenth-century efforts to describe and classify Native American antiquities gave way to the establishment of prehistoric sequences and chronologies (Willey and Sabloff 1980), and more recently, to attempts to explain the events of American prehistory.

THE FIELD OF ARCHAEOLOGY TODAY

Archaeology as it is practiced today is broad and varied. Archaeologists study a wide range of ancient peoples and work in a broad variety of settings, from universities and museums to federal and state governments and private companies. All the different varieties of archaeology, however, share a basic premise: that the material remains left behind by people in the past can be interpreted to yield an understanding of past human behavior.

In America archaeology has developed as part of the broader discipline of **anthropology.** In the late nineteenth and early twentieth century, the new social science of anthropology was growing up, and early anthropologists saw themselves in a race against time to record native languages, traditions, and religious practices. They approached their topic along four fronts, which were to become the four major branches of American anthropology. American **cultural anthropology** began with the **ethnography** of Native American peoples—the detailed recording of these peoples' societies and lifeways. **Anthropological linguistics** started with comparative studies of Native American languages, and **physical anthropology** involved comparative anatomical studies of the people themselves. American **anthropological archaeology** was concerned with the material remains of the Native Americans' predecessors. All these fields have since grown far from their original roots as the discipline of anthropology has evolved. Today, cultural anthropologists study contemporary human societies around the world; biological anthropologists study human evolution, primate biology and behavior, and modern human biological adaptations; and anthropological linguists are interested in languages and the social context of language throughout the world.

Until about 35 years ago, most American archaeologists, particularly those interested in prehistory, were trained as anthropologists and held appointments in college and university departments of anthropology. While most U.S. archaeologists are still trained as anthropologists, the majority of American archaeologists today work outside the academy. Since the early 1970s, federal environmental legislation has required that any federally funded construction include environmental impact statements describing the effects that the new construction will have on existing archaeological resources. Later legislation was directed specifically toward the preservation and protection of archaeological resources, and similar laws were enacted by the states. More recently, the Native American Graves Protection and Repatriation Act (NAGPRA) was enacted to help protect Native American cultural heritage. These topics will be discussed further in Chapter 27. As a result of these laws, many archaeological surveys and excavations have been conducted in advance of highway, bridge, and building construction in the United States. For example, the Five Points site (Figure 1.5), a nineteenth-century immigrant neighborhood in downtown New York City, was discovered and excavated in advance of construction carried out at the New York federal courthouse building. These explorations reveal much about the day-to-day lives of the people whose neighborhood was popularized in the 2002 film *Gangs of New York*. Unfortunately, the finds recovered from these excavations were stored in Building 7 of the World Trade Center and destroyed

FIGURE 1.5 Excavations on the site of a new courthouse at Foley Square in lower Manhattan exposed the remains of tenements that were part of the infamous Five Points neighborhood. The excavation was done by Historic Conservation and Interpretation (HCI) in 1991; artifact analysis and interpretation were completed by John Milner Associates under contract to the U.S. General Services Administration.

in the attacks on September 11, 2001. Today, many archaeologists are employed within cultural resource management (CRM) divisions of federal, state, and local government agencies, within similar CRM departments of large private engineering and architectural firms, or within independent archaeological firms providing their services to government agencies under contract.

In Europe the development of archaeology took a somewhat different path. Archaeology grew up as part of the desire to understand local cultural and national origins. As we saw earlier, it grew up too in the company of the developing natural sciences of geology and paleontology. As a result, depending on the period of interest, most European archaeologists see themselves closely linked with the disciplines of history and geology, and they frequently hold university appointments in these departments. Many European universities now include independent departments of archaeology

FIGURE 1.6 The site of Lothal in northwest India. The excavation of this important Indus Valley site was sponsored by the Indian government in the 1950s.

that accommodate archaeologists with a diversity of interests. This same interest in local culture history and national origins has encouraged the growth of archaeology in Latin America, Africa, and South and East Asia, especially in the postcolonial period. In India, for example, the end of British colonial rule in 1947 was followed by an explosive growth in indigenous Indian archaeology. A striking example is the excavation of the major port city of Lothal (Figure 1.6) in northwest India by the Indian archaeologist S. R. Rao between 1954 and 1958. (For a more complete discussion of Lothal and the Indus Valley civilization, see Chapter 20.) As in America, in many other nations today, much archaeology is conducted following the mandates of archaeological preservation laws.

In North America until about 20 years ago, archaeologists who studied literate societies were found in departments of classical archaeology, biblical archaeology, Egyptology and Assyriology (the studies of ancient Egypt and Mesopotamia, respectively), art history, and history. In recent years, however, North American archaeologists have applied the methods and techniques of prehistoric archaeology to historically documented societies. Historical archaeologists in North America study the changes that have occurred in the New World since Columbus's voyages 500 years ago. They have used archaeology, for example, to provide new insights into the lives of enslaved African Americans in the antebellum South (Orser 1990). In the Old South, many slaves were prevented from learning to write, and the available historical records were written mostly by and about the white planters. Archaeological evidence can provide unique information about the daily lives of enslaved people and about the institution of slavery itself.

In Europe the methods and techniques of prehistoric archaeology have been used to cast new light on historical periods such as the early medieval Dark Ages. The collapse of the Western Roman Empire in the fifth century A.D. led to profound changes in settlements, farming technologies, and trade. For much of the Roman Empire, there are very few documents that provide information about daily life after the end of Roman rule. Archaeological excavations of Dark Age sites, such as the early Anglo-Saxon site of West Stow (Figure 1.7) in eastern England (West 1985), have provided information about post-Roman settlements and subsistence practices in the former Western Roman Empire.

GOALS OF ARCHAEOLOGICAL INTERPRETATION

Medieval and historic North American archaeologists share both methods and approaches with prehistoric archaeologists. Like prehistoric archaeologists, they are interested in using material remains to study the ways humans lived in the past and to explore changes in human societies through time and space. Today, archaeologists generally share five goals for research and interpretation. First, *they aim to build a time and space framework for the past.* Archaeologists want to answer the basic who, what, where, and when questions of human prehistory. Second, *archaeologists try to understand how humans lived in the past.* What kinds of houses did they build? What kinds of food did they eat? How did they make their living? Third, *archaeologists want to be able to answer the why questions of human prehistory,* that is, to try to explain why change takes place in human societies. These first three goals have formed the basis of archaeological research for more than 30 years. Two additional goals have come to the forefront in recent years. The first is the goal of *understanding the nature of the archaeological record itself.* Archaeologists want to understand the relationship between material remains, such as pieces of pottery and house foundations, that are discovered through excavations and the actual prehistoric behavior that produced those remains. Second, *archaeologists are interested in preserving the past for the future.* Each of these goals will be examined in detail as follows.

RECONSTRUCTING CULTURE HISTORY: ARCHAEOLOGY AS HISTORY WITHOUT WRITING

During the early years of the discipline, archaeologists were concerned primarily with gathering the data needed to fill in the vast span of time before writing began—to develop histories without written records. In Europe much of the early impetus for research came from the desire to know more about national and cultural origins. In Scandinavia, as we have seen, the formation of the Danish National Museum led Thomsen and Worsaae to undertake their pioneering work. The antiquities of Denmark in particular were of interest to the museum; the goal was a better understanding of the origins and early history of the Danish people. Nationalistic motivations played a strong role in the development of archaeology in Germany, Italy, and England as well. At the same time, the discovery of ancient stone tools, fossil humans of archaic form (to be discussed in Chapters 2 through 6), and the general intellectual climate following Darwin's *On the Origin of Species* soon led many archaeologists into a search for human origins. While anatomists and paleontologists studied the fossil humans themselves, archaeologists concentrated on the objects those early humans made and what those objects could tell us about the lifeways of early humans and the relationships among the peoples who made them. Archaeologists sought, and have continued to seek, the origins of new technologies and the beginnings of major changes in social life: the first stone tools, the earliest use of fire, the beginning of farming, the first cities. The finding of a new, earlier date for an invention or event still captures the popular

FIGURE 1.7 The early Anglo-Saxon village of West Stow. Excavations carried out at this Dark Age site provided information on day-to-day life in Britain after the collapse of the Western Roman Empire. The photograph shows reconstructions of the early Anglo-Saxon houses that were built between the fifth and seventh centuries A.D.

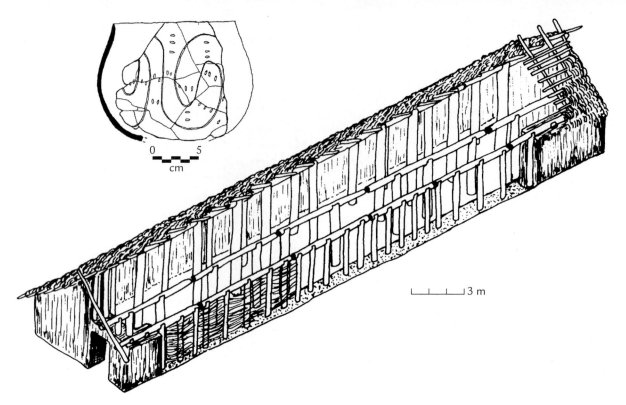

FIGURE 1.8 An example of an archaeological culture: the Linear Pottery culture of central Europe. Large rectangular timber houses and pottery marked with curvilinear designs are typical of the Linear Pottery culture.

imagination, but today archaeologists agree that it is far more important to try to understand *how* and *why* such changes occurred.

Culture history is the chronicle of the changes that occur within an archaeological culture over time. In Europe in the early twentieth century, the eminent prehistorian V. Gordon Childe used the term **archaeological culture** to denote widespread and regularly associated occurrences of archaeological finds. For example, the Linear Pottery, or Linearbandkeramik culture, the material remains of the earliest farmers of central Europe, is characterized by distinctive pottery with curvilinear decorations; rectangular, timber longhouses; the cultivation of emmer wheat; and livestock husbandry, principally cattle (Figure 1.8). Commonly, an archaeological culture can be subdivided into a number of successive periods based on relatively minor temporal changes in the constellation of characteristics that typify the culture. One archaeological culture may also succeed and replace another. Culture history chronicles these kinds of changes.

Anthropologically trained archaeologists working in the Americas have preferred to avoid the restricted usage of the term *archaeological culture* because it conflicts with anthropology's broader definitions of culture. The concept of culture is central to anthropological research. Although it has been defined in numerous ways, **culture** refers to the system of values, beliefs, customs, behaviors, and artifacts that the members of a particular society share and that allows those individuals to cope with their world and with each other (Bates and Plog 1990: 7). Although this terminology is still widely used in Old World archaeology, an archaeological culture, which is defined on the basis of artifacts and features alone, is not necessarily the same thing as a system of shared beliefs and values.

THE INVESTIGATION OF PREHISTORIC LIFEWAYS

By the 1950s archaeologists in both the Old World and the Americas had established a temporal and

FIGURE 1.9 Organic materials preserved from the Swiss lake dwellings include wooden items, textiles, and plant foods.

spatial framework for prehistory. A sequence of successive archaeological periods had been developed, and the location and geographic extent of various archaeological culture areas had been delineated. At the same time, there was great interest in both the Old and New Worlds in interpreting what life had been like in ancient times. Such interpretations were stimulated initially in Europe by the mid-nineteenth-century discovery of the Swiss lake villages. In 1853 an uncommonly dry year led to an unusual lowering of the Swiss lakes' waters, revealing remarkably well-preserved wooden structures built on pilings. These proved to be the dwellings of late Stone Age and early Bronze Age farmers, dating from approximately 4000 to 1500 B.C. The water had preserved a wealth of materials that normally would have disappeared: wooden utensils, basketry, matting, ropes, fishnets, balls of linen thread, and fabrics, as well as plant foods such as wheat and barley, hazelnuts, and apples (Figure 1.9). These things provided a rich visual image of daily village life.

American archaeologists working in the southwestern United States enjoyed some similar advantages. The prehistoric pueblo dwellers of the Southwest had lived in a desert climate that also preserved much of their organic **material culture,** notably plant foods and basketry (Figure 1.10). Even more important, the direct descendants of these peoples lived on in the area (see Chapter 26). Much in the prehistoric culture that might not have been interpretable otherwise became comprehensible when compared with modern practices. The prehistoric sites, for example, contain features that are similar to kivas, subterranean religious structures still in use today. This interpretive approach, the projection of the present into the past, is known as **direct historical analogy.** It is meaningful only if a direct historical relationship can be demonstrated between a historically known and a prehistoric people. For most of prehistory, there are no such links.

In the early 1950s, the British archaeologist J. G. D. Clark investigated the waterlogged site of Star Carr, in East Yorkshire, England. Star Carr was a campsite of hunters who lived at the very end of the Stone Age. Clark's work went beyond the simple description of the way of life of these hunters to attempt to sort out how they functioned within their

FIGURE 1.10   Coiled baskets recovered from Broken Roof Cave in Arizona.

investigation of the natural resources available within the region of an archaeological site and an analysis of the exploitation of those resources. A number of Higgs's own students have followed his lead, but the paleoeconomic approach frequently has been criticized for assuming that the subsistence economy was the major factor in shaping prehistoric societies. Paleoeconomic approaches often take no account of religion, ideology, social structure, and other noneconomic variables that may also play important roles in governing past human behavior.

Today, all archaeologists would agree that human societies are much more than economic and technological systems. An effort to gain an understanding of social life, religion, and ideology is critical in the study of prehistoric societies. For example, archaeologists have used differences in house forms, burials and grave goods, and even diets to study differences in social status. In an archaeological study of medieval nunneries, Roberta Gilchrist (1994) showed that wealthy medieval nuns feasted on venison, porpoise, and crane, while poorer religious women ate chicken, goose, and conger eel, supplemented by bread, beer, and vegetables. Gilchrist's study also showed that gender is an important structuring principle for premodern social systems. She found significant differences between nunneries and male monasteries that reflect differences between male and female roles in medieval society.

ARCHAEOLOGY AS THE STUDY OF CULTURE CHANGE

Archaeologists must do more than reconstruct the ways of life of a particular historical period. They need to understand how and why lifeways changed in the past. The approaches that archaeologists have taken to the study of culture change have varied dramatically over the past 50 years (see Trigger 1989). This section presents a brief historical overview of differing approaches to the study of culture change and the ways those changes are explained by archaeologists.

The process of fitting a particular site or group of sites into a wider context lies at the heart of

natural environment. A major goal of the excavation was the recovery of the well-preserved organic remains, which an interdisciplinary team of botanists and zoologists helped analyze. One of Clark's major aims was the interpretation of the subsistence pattern of the Star Carr hunters—the range of foodstuffs on which they lived and the means used to procure them (Figure 1.11). J. G. D. Clark trained many students while at Cambridge University. He and his work have been a major factor in shaping British archaeology today. The results of Clark's work at Star Carr will be discussed in greater detail in Chapter 13.

Eric Higgs, one of Clark's students, focused even more directly on the **paleoeconomy** of prehistoric societies. Higgs's method involved a detailed

FIGURE 1.11 *Life* magazine (from the 1950s) illustration of daily life at Star Carr.

archaeological interpretation. Even within the framework of culture history, archaeologists attempted to explain why cultures change. Until the 1950s archaeologists explained change in essentially historical terms—in terms of the movement of peoples from one region to another or the exchange of ideas between one group and another. The wholesale replacement of the artifacts and features typifying one archaeological culture with an entirely different set was often interpreted as evidence of the **migration** or movement into the region of people with new traditions. For example, during the first few hundred years A.D., the stone-tool-using hunters of much of southern Africa were largely displaced by the southward migration of iron-using farmers, probably related to today's Bantu speakers. Most of the changes that are observed in archaeological cultures are less pervasive. A new trait—a technological innovation or a new artistic style, for example—may appear within a region. If the new technology or artistic style is known from an earlier time in an adjacent region, the acquisition of the new trait is usually ascribed to **diffusion.** Diffusion

is the spread of cultural traits, such as artistic styles or technological methods, from one culture to another. Diffusion may mean that some new item of material culture, such as a pottery style or a metal-working technique, may be introduced bodily from an outside source, perhaps through trade. Diffusion might also occur if new individuals with a special skill, such as skilled potters, should enter the group, perhaps through a marriage. Finally, if no outside source for a new trait or technology is apparent, its appearance may be attributed to **independent invention.**

During the 1950s and 1960s, archaeologists became increasingly dissatisfied with historical explanations of culture change. All the culture-historical "explanations" were essentially descriptive; they provided little insight into how and why a new trait developed, or why it should be accepted from an outside source. Why should a culture develop in a particular way? Why, too, did some unrelated cultures come to follow similar courses of development? Anthropologist Julian Steward (1955) suggested that the answer lay in the complex relationship between a culture and its environment. He termed the study of this relationship **cultural ecology,** an extension of the biological study of ecology that examines the mutual relationships among various organisms and their environments. Culture change, Steward argued, could come about as a given culture adapts to changes in the environment. Change arises through the interplay of the culture (as determined by its previous history), its physical habitat (climate and geography), the animals and plants on which it depends, and the influence of neighboring cultures.

The 1950s and 1960s saw several major archaeological projects that incorporated a broadly ecological approach. These projects were also distinguished by their explicit problem orientation. The excavators set out to answer a specific set of questions. For example, several projects focused on the investigation of the beginning of farming in the Old and New Worlds. The Iraq-Jarmo Project, directed by Robert Braidwood, investigated a wide range of archaeological sites in Iraqi Kurdistan (northern Iraq). This region, because of its topography, its climate, and the availability of the wild ancestors of sheep, goats, wheat, and barley, was a very likely location for the appearance of the earliest Old World farmers. Braidwood's research will be discussed in some detail in Chapters 15 and 16. In highland Mexico Richard S. MacNeish undertook the Tehuacán Archaeological-Botanical Project. This project investigated the beginnings of food production in the New World, as well as the ways in which the landscape was utilized, both seasonally and over the longer term (see Chapter 17). Both Braidwood's and MacNeish's projects brought together large teams of geologists, biologists, and archaeologists to lend their particular insights to the research. While these projects set out to attempt to explain the process by which agriculture came into being, they were far more successful in describing how early farmers functioned in relation to their environment.

Ecological approaches continue to play a major role in archaeological interpretation. Today, the environment is defined broadly to include not just the physical and the biological environments but also the social environment—that is, the relationships with other people. Modern ecological explanations emphasize the interrelations between humans and their environment. Archaeologists investigate the effects of human behavior on the environment as well as environmental constraints on human behavior.

Archaeology as a Science

Is archaeology a science? In the 1960s the American archaeologist Lewis Binford, introducing what has come to be known as the **New Archaeology,** contended that archaeology, as a part of anthropology, should be a science, and that archaeological research should follow the methods of science (Binford 1962). This view of archaeology was most fully articulated as an explicitly scientific approach by P. J. Watson, S. LeBlanc, and C. Redman (1971, 1984). Julian Steward had called for archaeologists to look beyond the goals of culture history and to begin to investigate the *processes* by which cultures changed. Binford took up this cause. He further argued that if archaeologists were to discover the reasons cultures function as they do and why cultures change, they must try to find broadscale regularities in the way cultures function and develop. Binford and others argued that the ultimate goal of archaeological research should be the formulation of **covering laws,** similar to the laws of physics, to explain ancient human behavior and the process of culture change.

If archaeology were to develop such a set of laws, that is, to take on a theoretical structure similar to that of the physical sciences, then archaeological research would have to be conducted according to the rules of scientific method. The use of the scientific method was not simply a matter of incorporating the findings of other scientific disciplines, such as scientific dating methods, into archaeological interpretation. The use of the scientific method, as recommended by the new archaeologists, required archaeologists to begin research by formulating hypotheses (models) to explain past human behavior. They then had to develop research designs to test those hypotheses against real archaeological data.

Only hypotheses that could withstand repeated rigorous testing could be accepted as theory. The application of scientific methods to study the processes of culture change has been termed the **processual approach** to archaeological interpretation.

In attempting to understand how and why cultures change, processual archaeologists often viewed human cultures as systems of behaviors that allowed humans to adapt to the constraints of their natural and social environments. Processualists emphasized the dynamic relationship between human cultures and their environments, and cultural changes were often seen as adaptive responses to changes in the biological, physical, or social environments.

While the goals of the New Archaeology were admirable, in practice, archaeologists found it difficult to develop meaningful general laws to explain past human behavior. As yet we have no archaeological equivalent of the laws of thermodynamics. Archaeology today is probably no closer to uncovering significant cultural covering laws than it was when the goal was first conceived. Human societies are too varied, and the limitations of the archaeological record have proved a much higher hurdle than was once hoped.

Contemporary Approaches to Archaeological Interpretation

While many contemporary archaeologists continue to rely on a processual approach to archaeological interpretation, others have grown increasingly wary of the optimistic outlook of the New Archaeology. Processual models and hypotheses have been drawn, for the most part, from the natural sciences, particularly from ecological models for animal behavior. Such models, it is argued, are too simplistic to explain how and why human cultures change. Culture provides humans with a wider range of available responses to change than is available to other animals. On the other hand, the cultural beliefs or values of a specific human group may restrict and shape that group's response to a new situation. Further, processual models do not allow for the effect on a society of the sometimes unpredictable and idiosyncratic actions of individuals.

Reaction to the limitations of the processual approach led to the beginnings of the **postprocessual movement** in archaeology approximately 20 to 25 years ago. While archaeologists recognize that the processual approach brought scientific rigor to archaeological method, some contemporary archaeologists are not satisfied with processual explanations for cultural change. They argue that the processual approach failed to appreciate the dynamic roles that ideology and social and political structures can play in the process of social transformation. Moreover, the postprocessualists argue that the processualists viewed human societies as made up of a series of "faceless blobs" (Tringham 1991), rather than seeing societies as made up of individual actors. Members of different political factions, different social classes, and even different genders may think and act in very different ways. In order to understand how and why cultural changes come about, archaeologists must begin to examine the social, political, and economic diversity that characterized ancient societies. In order to do this, postprocessual archaeologists have drawn on social theories that were developed by cultural anthropologists and scholars in other social sciences and the humanities. Today, postprocessual archaeologists are drawing alternative models for the interpretation of culture change from perspectives as diverse as feminist theory, literary criticism, and Marxist economic interpretations (see, for example, Hodder and Hudson 2003). In addition, many archaeologists have tried to combine processual and postprocessual approaches in an attempt to create a more holistic picture of ancient peoples and their societies.

THE ARCHAEOLOGICAL RECORD

All the structure of interpretation we have discussed—culture history, explanation of culture change, descriptions of ancient lifeways—rests on a fundamental foundation: the discovery, recording, and decoding of the archaeological record. Survey, excavation, cataloging, the analysis and interpretation of finds, as well as the integration of data from history, geology, biology, and other fields, are the essential first steps that archaeologists must pursue in their attempt to understand the past.

The attention of the general public is often captured by spectacular discoveries such as the Iceman or a gold-filled tomb, but the vast bulk of archaeological research is focused on the prosaic. The gradual accumulation of archaeological knowledge is the result of extensive preparation, patient and persistent fieldwork, and careful analysis of what is found. Discoveries are not usually made purely by chance. Our knowledge of the prehistoric past is built by asking and answering many limited research questions. Archaeologists undertake surveys and excavations with well-defined research goals in mind. Research is usually designed to address a specific hypothesis or competing hypotheses about events in the past. An archaeologist, usually with the assistance of others in the sciences and humanities, must interpret the data that result from fieldwork and decide whether these data provide new insight into his or her research goals. Such interpretation can be very difficult and must be approached in the full light of peer review and criticism.

Wresting an understanding of the past from what remains in the earth can be a daunting task. Nearly all our knowledge of the prehistoric past comes from the study of ordinary things, usually small fragments of such materials as stone tools and pottery that have been preserved because of their chemical stability. Almost everything that was made or used by humans in the distant past has disappeared. Except under the most fortuitous circumstances (in the extreme aridity of a desert or a perennially waterlogged peat bog, for instance), organic materials such as wood, hides, horn, and fabric soon rot away. Most metals corrode and are gone as well. Bone, too, can sometimes disintegrate, depending on the nature of the soil. The skeletons of ancient humans, though, are sometimes preserved, as are the bones of the animals they ate. Stone tools have been preserved in vast numbers, and they are by far the most common finds from early prehistory. Pottery, which was first invented about 14,000 years ago, is a common find in later archaeological sites. Whole vessels are rare; most pottery is found broken into small fragments. All these things

together can provide only a dim reflection of the lives of ancient humans, but this is the evidence that is available to prehistoric archaeologists. The challenge for the archaeological detective is to extract from these data as much understanding as is possible of the world of the distant past.

Artifacts, Ecofacts, and Features

Before we can move on to our discussion of archaeology and prehistory, we must define some of the fundamental terms used by archaeologists. The basic unit of archaeological analysis is the **artifact,** which is any object made, modified, or utilized by humans. A stone axe, a pottery vessel, a bronze sword, and a marble statue are all artifacts. The Iceman's copper axe and his bow, arrows, and quiver are artifacts as well (Figure 1.12). Broadly speaking, a stone tomb or a discarded soup bone is also an artifact. In practice, however, archaeologists frequently use the term *artifact* to refer to a portable, intentionally manufactured or used object. Artifacts are sometimes found singly, but more commonly, artifacts of varying kinds are found grouped together. Any such group of artifacts found together, and which appear to have been deposited together, is known as an **assemblage.** Sometimes an artifact grouping was intentional, as in the case of offerings that were placed with a body in a grave. These might include, perhaps, a bronze dagger and a distinctive pottery vessel used for a food offering, as well as personal items of adornment on the body, such as pins, bracelets, and earrings. Other assemblages are unintentional, such as those in a trash pit, which might include food wastes, broken pottery fragments, and other worn-out and cast-off items. Another example of an unintentional assemblage is the small objects, such as coins, pins, and bits of pottery and glass, that frequently accumulate beneath the wooden floor of a house.

Ecofacts (a term introduced to archaeology in the 1960s) are those remains deriving from the natural environment that, while not intentionally made or manufactured by humans, become incorporated into archaeological deposits. They can provide information about past environments or ways of life. Ecofacts include the products of human

FIGURE 1.12 The Iceman's arrows and quiver.

activities such as the preparation and consumption of food. Food wastes may include animal bones or charred plant fragments and seeds. The analysis of these materials can provide insight into what was eaten, as well as how it was obtained, prepared, and distributed. For example, the contents of the Iceman's intestinal tract indicate that he ate einkorn (a primitive wheat) that was ground to make flour for bread (Figure 1.13). Other ecofacts may enter the deposit purely accidentally. Pollen may be blown in by the wind or carried in on people's feet. Pollen found in the Iceman's intestinal tract indicates that he died in the late spring. Various kinds of insects and small mammals such as mice may take up residence in people's houses. Pollen, insect remains, and the bones of small mammals can yield much valuable information about climate, local plant and animal communities, and the degree to which the local environment has been altered by human interference.

Features are the immovable products of human activities that are affixed to or embedded in the landscape. Buildings are features, as are trenches and earthworks. Smaller features include such things as burials, hearths, and stone pavements. The soil discoloration left behind by the rotting away of a timber post (a post mold) or the filling in of a storage pit are also features. Movable artifacts are frequently, but not necessarily, included within features. Archaeologists expend a good deal of effort in working out the spatial, functional, and chronological relationships among archaeological features.

Sites

Artifacts, ecofacts, and features found together constitute an archaeological **site.** A site is a rather loosely defined entity that may range from a few stone flakes scattered on the ground to an entire ancient city. It is an area where artifacts and features indicate that human activity has taken place. There are a multitude of types of sites. Some sites result from only a short period of human activity, such as a butchery site where a game animal was cut up for transport, leaving behind only some waste bone and a few worn-out stone tools. Another site might represent an encampment of a few days or weeks, including, perhaps, debris from the making of stone tools, some food remains, traces of a hearth, or a ring of stones where a tent was pitched. Sometimes a favored camping place was revisited time after time, creating a cluster of superimposed and partially overlapping campsites. Other sites are

FIGURE 1.13 Grains of einkorn wheat, an example of an ecofact.

formed by long-term, continuous or nearly continuous occupations. In settled villages dwellings are built and abandoned, walls constructed and torn down or weathered away, and new structures built over the rubble of the old dwellings and the refuse of the previous inhabitants. Layer by layer these sites grow thicker, the older occupations buried below the more recent. The great artificial mounds, called tells, of the Middle East, often many meters high, were formed in just this fashion. At the base may lie a tiny farming village; above it many layers, or **strata,** of refuse, decaying walls, and silt were deposited through hundreds or thousands of years of occupation. The superimposed strata in an archaeological site are frequently compared to a layer cake, but this comparison is an oversimplification. The disentangling of the complicated relationships among the strata in a site, the art and science of **stratigraphic analysis,** is one of the principal preoccupations of the field archaeologist. In this analysis, the sequence of events that created the site can be worked out.

Understanding How the Archaeological Record Was Formed

The Archaeology in Practice box reveals some of the difficulties that archaeologists face in trying to interpret complex archaeological sites. Most archaeological sites result from a combination of human activities and natural processes such as sedimentation. Archaeologists must be able to distinguish traces of human activity from deposits that result from geological or biological processes. In addition, archaeologists seek to identify the human behaviors that produce specific combinations of artifacts, ecofacts, and features. The American archaeologist Lewis Binford has been in the forefront of the development of a series of theories that are intended to explain specific archaeological phenomena. These theories, known as **middle-range theories,** are designed to serve as bridging arguments, establishing relationships between the archaeological record and the dynamic behavioral processes that produced it. Hypotheses and data can be drawn from a variety of sources, including experiments and the observations of modern peoples. The field of **ethnoarchaeology,** the study of the behavior of

modern peoples and of the material remains of that behavior, has developed as part of the search to develop middle-range theories that can establish links between the static archaeological record and the dynamic behaviors that produced those material remains.

An example of such research had been carried out by C. K. Brain, a specialist in the study of archaeological animal bone remains. Working in South Africa, Brain (1967, 1981) examined the bone remains of domestic goats that had been eaten by Hottentot herders and discarded outside their camp. These bones were later scavenged by numerous dogs. Brain found that the dogs destroyed certain kinds of bones and left others, producing a distinctive pattern of bone survival. Brain could then hypothesize that similar patterns of animal bones found in the archaeological record might also be the result of carnivore scavenging. These observations have been of great importance. Carnivores may have actually created certain sites that had been attributed to the activities of early human ancestors. Brain's research will be discussed further in Chapter 2.

PRESERVING THE PAST

One of the biggest challenges facing all archaeologists today is the preservation of the world's archaeological heritage. Each archaeological site is unique and contains information that may not be available anywhere else. Every year, hundreds of sites are damaged and destroyed as a result of development, vandalism, and looting. For every one site that is excavated by a team of professional archaeologists, many are destroyed, and the information that they contained is lost forever. Archaeologists have an obligation to preserve the world's archaeological heritage for future generations.

This obligation can take a number of different forms. At the most basic level, archaeologists work to pass laws that protect archaeological sites and to end the trade in artifacts that have been removed illegally from archaeological sites. In addition, archaeologists have a responsibility to educate the public about our shared past. All archaeological excavation involves destruction. If archaeologists fail to publish and publicize their results, they are no better than the looters and pot hunters who destroy

ARCHAEOLOGY IN PRACTICE

Stratigraphy and Stratigraphic Analysis: How Do Archaeologists Reconstruct the Sequence of Events at an Archaeological Site?

Archaeologists are often asked how they trace the sequence of events that occurred at an archaeological site. How do they know that one building or structure was built before another? How can they be sure that two buildings were in use at the same time, or that one grave is older than another? The answers to these questions depend on detailed stratigraphic analyses, the critical interpretation of the layers and features that make up an archaeological site. In practice, this interpretation involves many complexities and subtleties, but the fundamental principles involved are simple and straightforward.

The simple **principle of superposition of strata,** first widely applied by geologists in the eighteenth century, states that if the strata in a geological deposit are piled up like the layers in a cake, the oldest must be at the bottom. Archaeologists also use this principle, but the deposits in an archaeological site may derive from a wide variety of sources. An individual stratum or layer may be distinguished by its distinctive color, texture, and composition. Often inclusions such as pebbles or charcoal help define strata. A fine greenish clay stratum, for instance, may be easily distinguished from a layer of coarse yellow sand. Frequently, however, stratigraphic boundaries are difficult to perceive, and they can tax the skill of the field archaeologist in following them.

Some of the strata are purely geological in nature. The underlying soil or bedrock is, of course, of geological origin. Later, the debris of human activities may be covered by soils and silts carried by natural agencies such as the wind and running water. Soils and deposits near the tops of hills may be washed down by rainstorms to collect in the hollows of the landscape (slope-wash). Fine silts may be carried by the wind to cover broad areas of the landscape, including archaeological sites. The most dramatic of natural deposits to cover or intrude on archaeological sites are the products of volcanic eruptions, such as ash and pumice. Pompeii, magnificently preserved by the fall of ash from nearby Mount Vesuvius, is the most famous of such sites, but others will be discussed in this text.

Archaeologists are most interested in the deposits of anthropogenic origin—the products of human activities. Humans disturb natural soils (and older archaeological deposits) in a multiplicity of ways. Holes and pits may be dug for food storage, trash disposal, and burials. Trenches and pits may be dug during construction activities. Those features cut through earlier strata, and the soils they contained (including artifacts) may be displaced. Later, when dwellings are occupied, debris from everyday life accumulates, including artifacts and food remains. Some of those deposits may be trampled into dirt floors; other trash may be spread around dwellings or be carried to trash dumps (middens). Fireplaces or hearths for heating and food preparation, often containing charcoal and food remains, are another such localized deposit. When a structure is abandoned, it may be intentionally destroyed and the rubble spread around to make a base for a new structure. If a site is no longer occupied, the forces of rain and wind may accomplish that dispersal. Many sites show alternating phases of occupation and abandonment, with strata of human origin alternating with naturally deposited silts or sands.

Archaeological sites that are repeatedly reoccupied or occupied for a long time will contain many interdigitated layers, small localized deposits (called lenses), and features (Figure 1.A). Some strata may extend across the site; others may be very limited in extent. At the start of an excavation, archaeologists frequently dig a small test trench to ascertain the nature and duration of the occupation and the sequence of occupations, from earliest to latest. A **stratigraphic cross section** of the test trench is prepared to serve as a guide for further excavation. This is a carefully prepared measured drawing, supported by photographs, of one or more of the vertical faces of the trench. The face is made as clean, flat, and vertical as possible so that subtle changes in the stratigraphy may be seen and recorded. Distinctive characteristics of each of the strata and lenses, such as color, texture, and inclusions, are noted on the cross section. These data may prove helpful in correlating (provisionally, at least) the stratigraphy in different parts of the site. Because test trenches are frequently misleading, good judgment must be exercised in their placement and interpretation. The earliest, the latest, or intermediate phases of occupation might not be represented in the place where a particular test is dug. If, for example, the eastern portion of a large site was occupied during the earliest and latest phases of occupation and

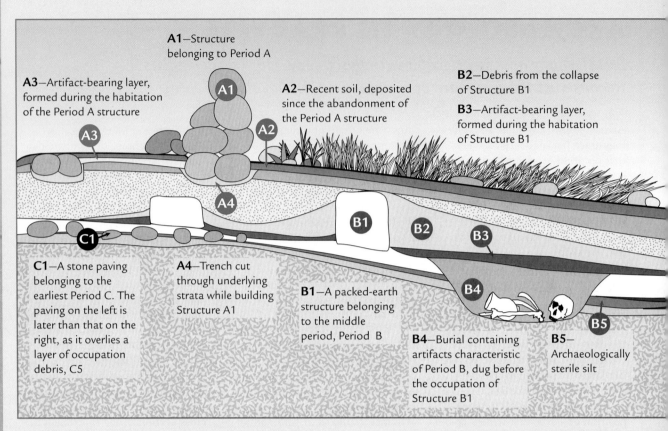

A1—Structure belonging to Period A

A3—Artifact-bearing layer, formed during the habitation of the Period A structure

A2—Recent soil, deposited since the abandonment of the Period A structure

B2—Debris from the collapse of Structure B1

B3—Artifact-bearing layer, formed during the habitation of Structure B1

C1—A stone paving belonging to the earliest Period C. The paving on the left is later than that on the right, as it overlies a layer of occupation debris, C5

A4—Trench cut through underlying strata while building Structure A1

B1—A packed-earth structure belonging to the middle period, Period B

B4—Burial containing artifacts characteristic of Period B, dug before the occupation of Structure B1

B5—Archaeologically sterile silt

FIGURE 1.A A simplified, imaginary cross section of an archaeological site, illustrating some of the typical strata and features that are encountered. Three main periods of occupation are represented: A, B, and C. A structure belonging to the latest phase, Period A, still stands at the surface.

the western portion was occupied only during the middle and latest phases, tests placed in these different areas would give quite different impressions of the site's contents. A small test can easily be misplaced within the boundaries of a feature or into soil that was disturbed in ancient times, leading to difficulties in interpretation. Only when a reasonably extensive area of the site is excavated can these difficulties usually be resolved.

Archaeologists today often attempt to expose large areas of a site to try to trace activity areas and to interpret functional relationships within the site. The occupants of a dwelling may manufacture their pottery in an area nearby, use these vessels to cook their food on a hearth within the house (where a few broken fragments fall through the floor), and dispose of broken pottery, along with food remains, in a trash pit out of the way of daily traffic. They may bury their dead in a grave adjacent to their dwelling or even beneath its floor. All these activities produce distinctive features and artifacts. A structure, burial, or hearth might belong to any of the periods of occupation represented at a site. A functional interpretation of the features and artifact distributions within a site is meaningful only if we are certain that the features and artifacts were actually in use at the same time. Within an individual site, archaeologists need to determine which of the various deposits and features are contemporary. They must be sure that artifacts and features interpreted as a unit were found within the same or demonstrably contemporary strata, a procedure known as maintaining **stratigraphic control.** Archaeologists must follow stratigraphic distinctions over broad areas and find ways to correlate the stratigraphic cross sections in different parts of the site, which is rarely easy to do. The excavators need sharp eyes and a sensitive touch to follow subtle color and texture changes and to expose a single layer over a broad horizontal area. This work is guided by constant cross-checking against vertical cross sections that are preserved at the margins of the excavated area.

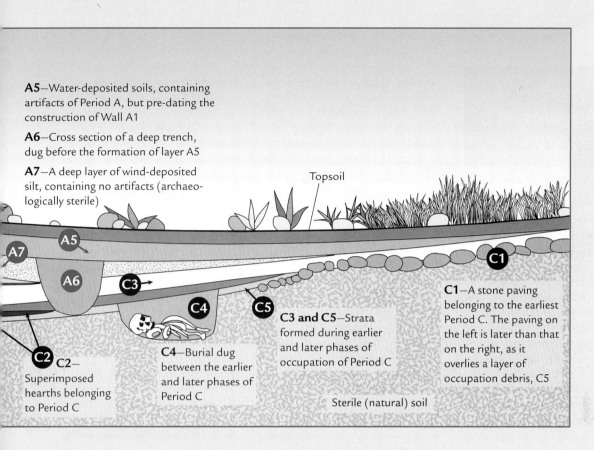

A5—Water-deposited soils, containing artifacts of Period A, but pre-dating the construction of Wall A1

A6—Cross section of a deep trench, dug before the formation of layer A5

A7—A deep layer of wind-deposited silt, containing no artifacts (archaeologically sterile)

Topsoil

A5

A7

A6

C3

C4

C5

C1

C3 and C5—Strata formed during earlier and later phases of occupation of Period C

C4—Burial dug between the earlier and later phases of Period C

C1—A stone paving belonging to the earliest Period C. The paving on the left is later than that on the right, as it overlies a layer of occupation debris, C5

C2 **C2**— Superimposed hearths belonging to Period C

Sterile (natural) soil

Features and artifacts that are found within the same layer are said to be associated, and, if they are not greatly displaced from their original locations, can be assumed to be contemporary. Great care must be taken, however, to ensure that the artifacts found in a layer are not intrusive. Many processes can result in the intrusion of younger or older artifacts into an archaeological deposit. Pits, ditches, and burials from later periods penetrate the strata laid in earlier times, carrying more recent materials downward and bringing earlier materials upward. Burrowing animals, such as mice, rats, and porcupines, do the same. Often these problems can be controlled for by careful recording of the features and the locations of animal burrows.

Geological forces can also move artifacts. Very ancient archaeological sites may have been subjected to the same geological forces that have modified the rest of the earth's surface. Archaeological strata may have been eroded, or even folded or tilted. Alternating periods of freezing and thawing may have churned the soil. Stream actions, in particular, can mix artifacts from many different strata and locations, creating artifact associations that have little to do with human activities. The stratigraphic interpretation of such sites often requires a thorough knowledge of soil formation processes and the geology of wind- and water-laid sediments. It has been especially difficult to unravel the complicated relationship between geologic forces

and human activities that formed the sites associated with our earliest human ancestors. We shall return to this problem in Chapters 2 and 3.

An Archaeologist's Toolkit

The Archaeology in Practice boxes in each chapter of this text will introduce a range of methods used in the analysis and interpretation of archaeological data. In this chapter, for example, the methods used in stratigraphic analysis have been described in detail. However, before interpretation can begin, archaeologists must locate, assess, and excavate archaeological sites. Excavation is the most important way that archaeologists collect new data. Since all excavation involves destruction, archaeologists have developed standardized ways of recording and preserving archaeological data.

The first challenge is the location of archaeological sites. Many important sites have been discovered by accident, as a result of construction or agricultural activities. Others are discovered as a result of systematic reconnaissance or field survey. In the United States, federal environmental laws require archaeological surveys to be conducted in advance of any construction that involves federal money. Archaeological reconnaissance can be conducted in a number of different ways. Old maps and photographs may show the location of walls and other archaeological features. Aerial photographs (see Archaeology in Practice, Chapter 22) may reveal the location of sites and features that are not visible at ground level. Systematic field surveys can also identify possible archaeological sites. Archaeologists walk across the landscape and note the location of artifacts, such as pottery and stone tools, that may reveal the location of buried sites. Field surveys are often conducted shortly after agricultural fields have been plowed, since plowing may bring buried artifacts to the surface.

Once a possible site has been identified, its location must be recorded in relation to a published map. Today, many archaeologists use GPS (global positioning system) technology to record the precise location of their sites. Archaeologists often use test trenching to evaluate the archaeological potential of possible sites. A **test trench** is a small (often one meter square) excavation designed to reveal the stratigraphy at the site (Figure 1.B left). Test trenches can reveal the nature and depth of the archaeological deposits, but since they are very small excavations, they provide very little information about the distribution of artifacts and features across a site. As a result, test trenching is often followed by open-area excavation.

In an **open-area excavation,** a large portion of the site is excavated to reveal the spatial relationships between artifacts, ecofacts, and features (Figure 1.B right). Test trenches can serve as guides to the stratigraphy, so that the site can be excavated stratigraphically—that is, one layer at a time. The goal of excavation is to remove the soil around artifacts but to leave them in place so that their spatial relationships to other artifacts and to features can be determined. Trowels, brushes, and even dental picks are used during excavation. Plans and photographs are used to record the precise locations of artifacts and features before they are removed and cataloged. These data are crucial for archaeological interpretation, since the context in which an object is found is as important as the object itself. For example, a pottery vessel found in or near a grave may mean something very different than a pot discovered in a hearth. Coins, beads, small bones, and other small artifacts and ecofacts are easily overlooked during excavation, so all the soil removed during excavation is carefully sifted through fine screens.

Careful record keeping is the key to successful excavation. Maps, plans, photographs, and other records can preserve archaeological data long after the site has been fully excavated.

FIGURE 1.B Methods of excavation. Left: a one-by-one meter test trench at the site of Salibiya I in the West Bank. Right: an open-area excavation at the Valley Forge, Pennsylvania, National Historic Park.

archaeological sites. Since many excavations today are funded by public monies, archaeologists have an obligation to share their research with the taxpayers who funded it. Moreover, an educated public is more likely to support archaeology and historic preservation legislation. We will return to these important issues in Chapter 27.

CONCLUSION

Although archaeologists study many different time periods and work in many different areas of the world, all archaeologists share common goals and methods. Archaeologists are interested in reconstructing culture history, studying the ways people lived in the past, and understanding why human cultures change through time. Modern archaeologists also seek to understand the complex nature of the archaeological record and to preserve our common cultural heritage for future generations. In the following chapters, we will begin to explore our common human past, starting with the earliest human ancestors who appeared in Africa more than 6 million years ago.

KEY TERMS

Anthropological archaeology   11
Anthropological linguistics   10
Anthropology   10
Archaeological culture   14
Archaeology   3
Artifact   20
Assemblage   20
Boucher de Perthes, Jacques   8
Catastrophism   7
Covering laws   18
Cultural anthropology   10
Cultural ecology   18
Culture   14
Culture history   14
Darwin, Charles   7
Diffusion   17
Direct historical analogy   15

Ecofacts   20
Ethnoarchaeology   22
Ethnography   10
Features   21
Frere, John   7
Handaxe   8
Hutton, James   7
Hypotheses   4
Independent invention   17
Lyell, Charles   7
Material culture   15
Middle-range theories   22
Migration   17
New Archaeology   18
Open-area excavation   26
Paleoeconomy   16
Pengelly, William   8
Physical anthropology   11
Postprocessual movement   19

Prehistory   3
Principle of superposition of strata   23
Processual approach   19
Site   21
Strata   22
Stratigraphic analysis   22
Stratigraphic control   24

Stratigraphic cross section   23
Test trench   26
Thomsen, Christian J.   8
Three Age System   9
Uniformitarianism   7
Worsaae, Jens   9

QUESTIONS FOR DISCUSSION

1. Today many public school districts are debating the roles of evolution and creationism in the science curriculum. Creationists accept the Bible literally and argue that the world is only a few thousand years old. Can you see parallels between creationist thought and the catastrophist theories of the eighteenth and nineteenth centuries?

2. Native American views of the past are based, to a large extent, on oral traditions that are passed down from generation to generation. What role has oral tradition played in your family's and community's views of the past? How well do these oral traditions correspond to what is known from written history?

3. Archaeologists attempt to understand the past from the material evidence left behind by ancient people. What kinds of such evidence do you think might give us some insights into the daily lives of these people, their relationships with one another, or their cultural or religious beliefs?

FURTHER READING

Dickson, James H., Klaus Oeggle, and Linda L. Handley
   2003   The Iceman Reconsidered. *Scientific American* 288 (5): 70–79.
   This article presents an up-to-date review of the status of the Iceman. It is well illustrated and readable.

Hodder, I. and James Hudson
   2003   *Reading the Past: Current Approaches to Interpretation in Archaeology.* 3rd ed. Cambridge: Cambridge University Press.
   A contemporary view of the interpretation of the archaeological record. This book is the most accessible introduction to the postprocessual movement in archaeology.

Trigger, Bruce G.
   1989   *A History of Archaeological Thought.* Cambridge: Cambridge University Press.
   A detailed and authoritative history of archaeology, focusing on the changing approaches to the interpretation of the archaeological record.

PART 1

ARCHAEOLOGY OF THE HUMAN ANCESTORS

What Does Archaeology Tell Us about Ancient Human Societies?

Questions about human origins and human evolution have intrigued scholars for more than a century. This part of the text examines the role that archaeology can play in the study of our earliest human ancestors. Chapter 2 begins with a brief history of research on human origins in Africa, highlighting the discovery of the Taung child by Raymond Dart and Louis Leakey's work at Olduvai Gorge. This is followed by a brief overview of the earliest-known human ancestors, the australopiths. These early human ancestors walked upright, but they did not leave an archaeological record because they did not manufacture or use stone tools.

Chapter 3 examines the archaeological record of early human behavior at East African sites, including Olduvai Gorge in Tanzania and Koobi Fora in Kenya. We consider how these ancient sites are excavated, how they are dated, and what can be learned about early human behavior from the study of simple stone tools and butchered animal bones.

More than 1 million years ago, human ancestors began to move out of Africa and into the subtropical and temperate regions of the Old World, including East Asia, Southeast Asia, the Near East, and Europe. *Homo erectus/ergaster*, a human ancestor that initially appeared in Africa about 1.8 million years ago, was the first ancient human to migrate widely outside Africa. While fossils of *Homo erectus* are rare, many early archaeological sites have been found in Asia, North Africa, the Middle East, and Europe (Chapters 4 and 5). These sites allow us to trace the spread of humans out of Africa and to examine the role that fire played in this expansion. Stone tools allow us to study the technological capacities of these early humans, and butchered animal bones can shed light on how they made a living. Were these early humans big-game hunters, or did they survive by scavenging, or by some combination of scavenging and hunting? Sites such as Torralba and Ambrona in Spain have traditionally been seen as evidence for large-mammal hunting by *Homo erectus,* with important implications for archaic humans' use of language, technological sophistication, and social cooperation. Modern reanalyses of these sites have challenged traditional ideas about "man the hunter."

In Chapter 6, we examine the most intriguing and enigmatic of all archaic humans, the Neanderthals. The chapter begins with a history of the discovery of Neanderthal fossils. In the remainder of the chapter, we focus on the role that archaeology can play in studying Neanderthal behavior, including Neanderthal burials and the question of whether the Neanderthals were hunters or scavengers.

TIMELINE

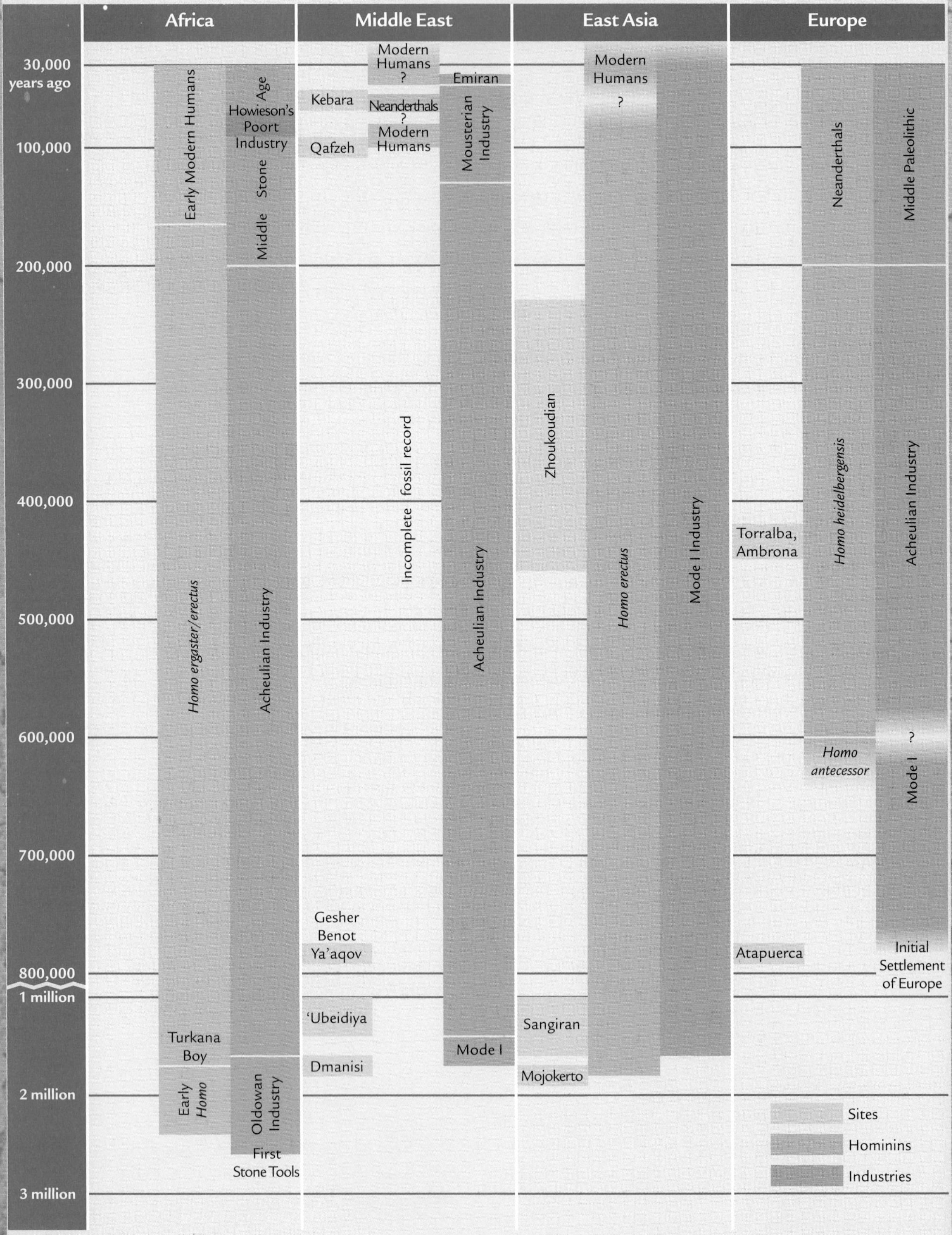

	Africa	Middle East	East Asia	Europe
30,000 years ago		Modern Humans ? — Emiran — Kebara — Neanderthals ? — Modern Humans — Qafzeh	Modern Humans ?	
	Early Modern Humans	Howieson's Poort Industry		Neanderthals — Middle Paleolithic
100,000		Middle Stone Age		
200,000	Homo ergaster/erectus — Acheulian Industry	Mousterian Industry		
300,000		Incomplete fossil record	Zhoukoudian	Homo heidelbergensis — Acheulian Industry
400,000				Torralba, Ambrona
500,000		Acheulian Industry	Homo erectus — Mode I Industry	
600,000				Homo antecessor — Mode I ?
700,000				
800,000		Gesher Benot Ya'aqov		Atapuerca — Initial Settlement of Europe
1 million	Turkana Boy	'Ubeidiya — Mode I — Dmanisi	Sangiran — Mojokerto	
2 million	Early Homo — Oldowan Industry			
	First Stone Tools			
3 million				

Legend:
- Sites
- Hominins
- Industries

2

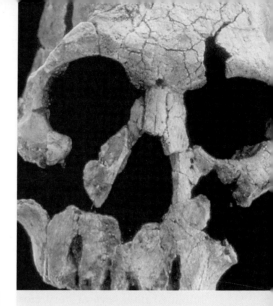

SETTING THE STAGE

Who Were the Earliest Human Ancestors?

In February 2001, a team of French and Kenyan scientists announced the discovery of the "Millennium Man," a possible human ancestor they named *Orrorin tugenensis* and dated to about 6 million years ago (Semut et al. 2001). A year later, a different research team working in Chad announced the discovery of *Sahelanthropus tchadensis* (Brunet et al. 2002), another possible human ancestor dated between 6 and 7 million years ago. These two fossils represent the earliest known human ancestors, and their discovery has deepened our understanding of human evolution (Wong 2003).

Most of this chapter deals with the earliest members of the human family who inhabited Africa between about 6 and 2.5 million years ago. These early human ancestors did not make or use stone tools and therefore did not leave an archaeological record. Although this topic is not, strictly speaking, archaeological, we must understand the nature of these early human ancestors to appreciate the pattern and tempo of early human evolution and the relationship of these early human ancestors to the later humans who did make and use stone tools. This text will begin where human evolution began, in Africa. Although the earliest human ancestors have only been discovered within the past few years, it will be easier to understand the significance of these fossils if we follow the trail of African discoveries beginning in the 1920s. First, though, we must make clear how modern humans are classified among the animal species of today.

HUMANS AS PRIMATES AND HOMININS

Humans are members of the order **Primates,** which also includes the prosimians (lemurs, tarsiers, lorises, aye-ayes, and indris), the Old and New World monkeys, and the apes. The apes include the lesser apes—gibbons and siamangs—and the great apes—orangutans, gorillas, and chimpanzees—who are humans' closest living relatives. The line that would lead to *Homo sapiens,* known as the Hominini, or **hominins,** split off sometime between 6 million and 8 million years ago. The hominins include modern humans and the immediate ancestors of humans, plus several very closely related forms. While quite a number of early hominin fossils are now known, there are no unquestioned fossils at all available of the early ancestors of the gorillas and chimpanzees, and very few fossils of either hominins or great apes dating to between 6 million and 8 million years ago have been recovered.

How should a hominin be defined? It is not difficult to set down how modern humans differ from the other primates. Modern humans are **bipedal;** that is, they walk upright on two legs. Theories for the origins of bipedalism are varied; they include freeing the hands for using tools or carrying objects, or even for a wider range of climbing activities. Modern humans also possess large brains, which provide the capacity for language and culture. A large brain and erect posture are reflected by the human skeletal form. Of great importance to human paleontologists, scientists who study fossil human skeleton remains, are the less obvious differences in the shape of the teeth, because teeth are among the most common fossils. In contrast to humans, male and female great apes often differ markedly, with the males having large, projecting canines. Human canines in both males and females are very small. These characteristics, though, represent the end point of human evolution. How would we recognize a primitive hominin who was not far removed from the common ancestor of chimpanzees and humans? Did all the uniquely human traits develop together, or did different traits develop at different times? At the start of the twentieth century, most scientists were convinced that it was the enlargement of the brain, with the consequent growth of

human intelligence, that was the primary event that preceded and led to all the other human evolutionary changes. It was also generally believed that the earliest human ancestors would be found in Asia. *Pithecanthropus*—the so-called Java Man—had been found by Eugene Dubois in 1891 in what is now Indonesia (see Chapter 5). Beginning in the 1920s, however, a remarkable series of discoveries made in Africa would radically challenge these views.

AUSTRALOPITHECUS AND THE SOUTH AFRICAN DISCOVERIES

Raymond Dart, an anatomy professor at the University of Witwatersrand, South Africa, had an avid interest in fossils. In 1924 Dart learned of a nearby limestone quarry at a place called **Taung** (Figure 2.1) that had been producing many interesting fossils; he made an arrangement with the quarry owner to be allowed to study them. In the box of fragments sent to him, Dart soon made a riveting discovery. It was a very small skull embedded in limestone, rather like that of a chimpanzee but yet definitely not a chimpanzee. After painstakingly freeing the skull from the limestone matrix, Dart found that the skull was indeed unique. It was the skull of a child; the deciduous (milk) teeth were still in place, with the permanent molars just coming in. The teeth, especially the canines, were very different from those of an ape. Apes and monkeys have large canines, but the canines in this skull

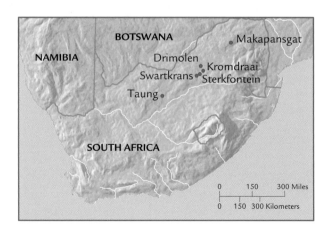

FIGURE 2.1 Map of southern Africa showing locations of australopith sites.

FIGURE 2.2 The Taung child: The first *Australopithecus africanus* fossil, discovered by Raymond Dart in 1924.

were small, more like those of humans. The face was flatter too, and the forehead was higher than those of apes or monkeys. Most striking of all, however, was the position of the foramen magnum, the hole at the base of the skull through which the spinal cord passes. In apes and monkeys, as in most quadrupeds, the foramen magnum is near the back of the skull, but in the Taung fossil, the foramen magnum was directly beneath the skull. Unlike the skull of a quadruped, which is in front of its body, this skull had been balanced vertically above the vertebral column. The Taung child, Dart concluded, had walked erect.

Dart quickly published his discovery. He named it *Australopithecus africanus* (Figure 2.2), which means "southern ape of Africa." Dart asserted that *Australopithecus* was on or close to the human ancestral line. In the public eye, the Taung child was an immediate sensation, but the scientific world greeted Dart's claims with skepticism. There were numerous problems. The fossil did not fit the early twentieth-century ideas of what an early human ancestor should look like. The Taung fossil had a very small **cranial capacity,** the volume enclosed within the braincase. It has been estimated that if the Taung

child had grown to be an adult, it would have had a cranial capacity of only about 440 ml, compared with an average of about 1350 ml for modern humans. Dart's analysis suggested that upright walking had preceded the expansion of the brain, contrary to the notion prevalent in the 1920s. In any case, the Taung skull was immature, and because immature skulls of humans and apes are rather similar, many scientists argued that this skull might have been a young ape rather than a young hominin.

Eventually, though, new specimens were found that helped support Dart's position. In 1936 Robert Broom, a Scottish physician who had gained prominence for his paleontological studies of African reptiles and mammals, made a major find at the cave of **Sterkfontein,** near the site of Taung. The Sterkfontein skull was very similar to the one from Taung, but this specimen was mature; it was clearly not an ape. Still, few workers felt comfortable placing these fossils on the human family line, and Broom's finds the next year confused the situation even more. He discovered another hominin site at **Kromdraai,** about a kilometer from Sterkfontein. The Kromdraai fossils were quite different from the previous finds. The Taung and Sterkfontein skulls were lightly built, or gracile; the Kromdraai skull was much more robust, with bony attachments for much larger chewing muscles. The cheek teeth (the molars and premolars) were much larger than those of Taung and Sterkfontein (Figure 2.3). The robust forms may have had a very different diet from the gracile **australopiths.** (Australopith is a general term for hominins other than *Homo*.) The large teeth and strong chewing muscles of the robust australopiths would have been well adapted to the consumption of tough plant materials such as tubers and seeds. The gracile forms probably had a more generalized, omnivorous diet, similar to that of chimpanzees. Today, the robust forms are generally assigned to a separate genus and species, *Paranthropus robustus.*

After the Second World War, Broom and his assistant, John T. Robinson, resumed work at these sites, which yielded many more fossils. Broom soon found further specimens of the robust form both at Kromdraai and at another nearby site, **Swartkrans.** Sterkfontein produced a nearly complete gracile skull

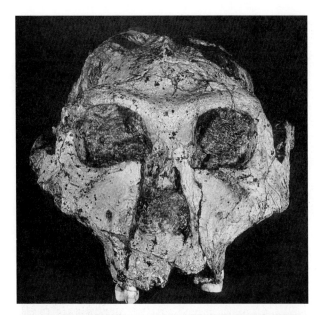

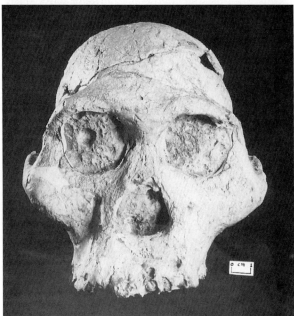

FIGURE 2.3 Robust and gracile australopiths.

All the South African sites are caves, dissolved into the limestone bedrock. The caves were never actually occupied by hominins; instead, the hominin bones, along with the bones of many other animals, fell or were washed into the caves through long vertical shafts in the caves' roofs. Later, the surface above the caves eroded away, exposing the caves' contents. The stratigraphy of these sites is difficult to interpret, and the fossils are encased in a hard limestone concretion, called **breccia**, that forms in caves. It is difficult to date the South African sites; the best evidence for the relative age of these sites is provided by the kinds of extinct animals associated with the hominin fossils. (See the Archaeology in Practice box later in this chapter.) The animal bones suggest that the *Australopithecus africanus* sites are the earliest, with Makapansgat perhaps as old as 3 million years. The *Paranthropus robustus* sites of Kromdraai and Swartkrans are younger, possibly 2 million years old or less (Delson 1988).

THE LEAKEYS AND OLDUVAI GORGE

Because the South African sites have been so difficult to interpret and date, much recent research has focused on other areas of Africa. Many of the finds of the past 40 years have come from the **Great Rift Valley** of East Africa, which runs from Mozambique in the south to the Red Sea in the north, enclosing Olduvai Gorge in Tanzania, Lake Turkana, and ending in the Afar Triangle of northern Ethiopia (Figure 2.4). The Great Rift Valley is a giant geological fault; the land to the east of the rift is slowly pulling away from the rest of Africa. At the time when the early hominins were evolving, the Rift Valley contained numerous volcanoes, which frequently showered the landscape with pumice and ash. These ashfalls have been a boon to paleontologists. Volcanic rock can be dated in absolute terms by a scientific dating method known as potassium-argon (K-Ar) dating (which will be discussed in detail later). **Tuffs,** layers formed from falls of volcanic ash, serve as chronological markers for the fossils contained within them or between them. The land of the Rift Valley has been in constant motion. In some areas, such as at Olduvai, the land was uplifted. Fast-running rivers cut deep canyons through the sediments, revealing deposits laid down over mil-

and additional bones, including a pelvis, vertebrae, and part of a femur. Additional gracile australopiths were discovered by Dart in 1948 at the cave of **Makapansgat.** In the 1990s additional *Paranthropus robustus* specimens were discovered at the South African cave of **Drimolen** (Keyser 2000), about 7 km north of Sterkfontein. In all, nearly 150 early hominin fossils have been recovered in South Africa.

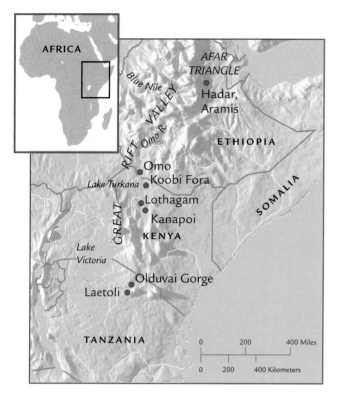

FIGURE 2.4 The Great Rift Valley in East Africa, showing the locations of the most important archaeological and paleontological sites.

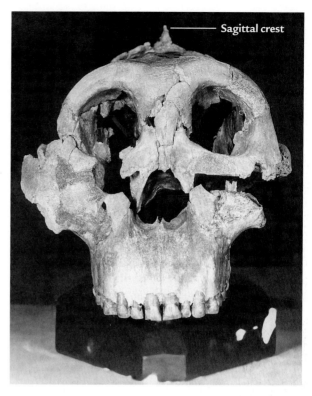

FIGURE 2.5 *Zinjanthropus—Paranthropus boisei.* An extremely robust australopith fossil, discovered by Mary and Louis Leakey at Olduvai Gorge.

lions of years. In other areas, the sediments were tilted and deformed by the moving rift, bringing ancient deposits to the surface where their contents could be revealed by erosion. The geology of the Great Rift Valley is complex but interpretable, and vast areas within it are littered with fossils.

Paleontologist Louis Leakey and archaeologist Mary Leakey first began their search for early humans at **Olduvai Gorge,** Tanzania, in the early 1930s. Louis Leakey was convinced that the earliest human ancestors were to be found in Africa. Olduvai Gorge was an ideal place to look for them. The gorge is a deep valley cut down through the sediments laid down by an ancient lake. Animals of many kinds had visited the shores of the lake, and many had died there. Fossil bones of all sorts had eroded from the beds at Olduvai. So had stone tools, including very simple forms—stone flakes and pebbles with just a few flakes knocked off—which came from the lowest beds. Yet for all their conviction and many years of searching, the Leakeys found only a few hom-

inin fragments. Only in 1959 did Mary Leakey happen upon the first major hominin find at Olduvai. It was a relatively complete, although fragmentary, skull of a robust australopith, even more robust than the ones from South Africa. Louis Leakey named it *Zinjanthropus boisei;* today it is usually classified as **Paranthropus boisei,** but the original specimen is commonly referred to as Zinj (Figure 2.5). Zinj's cheek teeth were even larger than those of the South African robust fossils, and the chewing muscles must have been larger too. Running front to back at the top of the skull was a high bony ridge, the sagittal crest, to which enormous temporal muscles used in chewing had been attached.

Paranthropus boisei appeared even farther from the human line than the South African fossils, but it provided a crucial piece of evidence: a firm, geophysically derived date. The shores of the ancient Olduvai lake had been showered at intervals by falls of volcanic ash from the nearby volcano, Mt. Ngorongoro. The Zinj skull was found in the lowest bed at Olduvai

Gorge, Bed I, sandwiched between ashfalls dated at 1.8 million years ago below and 1.7 million years ago above. It was clear now that by 1.75 million years ago there were at least two, perhaps three, different kinds of hominins. A common ancestor for these forms had to be sought farther back in time.

AUSTRALOPITHECUS AFARENSIS: LUCY AND THE FIRST FAMILY

American anthropologist Donald Johanson, together with French geologist Maurice Taieb, found a possible human ancestor at **Hadar,** in the Afar Triangle of Ethiopia, during the 1970s. The Hadar deposits hold many well-preserved fossils that can be closely dated through a variety of geological and physical methods (described later). An exceptional series of hominin fossils have been recovered from Hadar.

The best-known find from Hadar dates from about 3.18 million years ago. It is the partial skeleton of a small australopith, nicknamed Lucy, after a popular Beatles song of the 1960s. The skull is only fragmentary, but about 40% of the body skeleton was recovered. Since the right and left sides of the body are symmetrical, enough bone was recovered to permit a quite complete reconstruction of how Lucy's skeleton appeared (Figure 2.6). Lucy stood about 1 m (3.5 ft.) tall and walked upright. Generally similar to that of the South African gracile australopiths, Lucy's cranial capacity was even smaller (about 400 ml). A number of other features appear more primitive: The canine teeth, for example, are larger than those of the South African gracile australopiths. Many additional fossils, including numerous skull fragments, have been recovered from Hadar. Lucy and many of the other Hadar hominins have been placed into a separate species, *Australopithecus afarensis,* which was probably ancestral to the other later australopith forms.

Shortly after the discovery of Lucy, another very important find was made at Hadar: A collection of nearly 200 hominin bones, all belonging to *A. afarensis,* were found together, in circumstances suggesting that they may have all died together as a group. At least 13 individuals are represented, including four children. How they were killed is not clear, although the excavators speculate that they may have been caught in a flash flood. This group

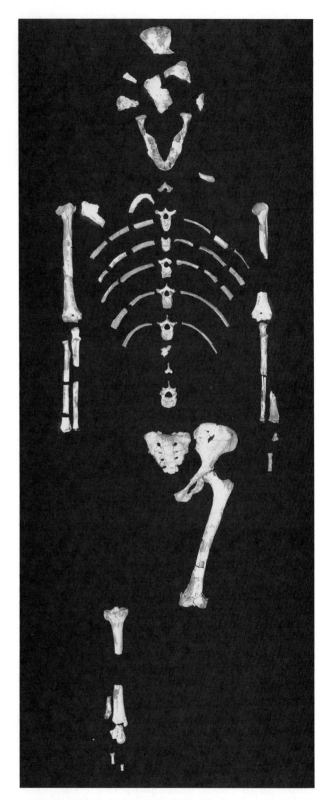

FIGURE 2.6 Lucy—*Australopithecus afarensis.* One of the most complete australopith skeletons, Lucy appears to have stood 1 m (3.5 ft.) tall and walked erect.

has come to be called the First Family, although whether the individuals were actually related is not known. Dating to about 3.2 million years ago, the find provides the earliest evidence for the range of variation that was present within an early hominin population. Including Lucy, the Hadar adult australopiths vary greatly in size, from about 1 m, or 3.5 ft. (Lucy), to about 1.5 m (5 ft.) tall. Some of this variation may be accounted for by a considerable size difference between the sexes.

THE LAETOLI FOOTPRINTS

While Johanson and his team were at work at Hadar, Mary Leakey had begun excavating a new site, **Laetoli,** in Tanzania. Laetoli is quite early, dating to about 3.7 million years ago. Several hominin fossils were found, similar to the *A. afarensis* finds from Hadar. Initially, the assignment of the Hadar and Laetoli hominins to the same species was questioned because the two sites are widely separated geographically, but a number of new fossil finds from areas lying between Hadar and Laetoli indicate that *A. afarensis* was widely distributed in East Africa. Laetoli, however, has preserved other fossil information in addition to animal and hominin bones. An extremely unusual and fortuitous series of events during the formation of the Laetoli deposits created a matrix in which thousands of animal footprints have been preserved. A nearby volcano produced a series of ashfalls, which, when wet by the rain, formed a cementlike mud in which the tracks were impressed. Soon after the mud dried, another ashfall sealed the layer, preventing the tracks from being washed away again. In 1975 a unique discovery was made. Among the multitude of animal tracks were the footprints of at least two, probably three, bipedal hominins, one larger than the others, probably walking together (Figure 2.7). The trail of footprints extends in a straight line across the level ground for nearly 25 m (80 ft.). It is assumed that they were made by *Australopithecus afarensis*. Their gait was much like that of modern humans. The shape of the prints is humanlike too, with the big toe pointing farther forward than in the apes. The Laetoli tracks capture a moment of hominin behavior of nearly 4 million years ago;

FIGURE 2.7 The footprints of an erect-walking hominin, discovered by Mary Leakey and her colleagues in a volcanic ash deposit at Laetoli.

they also prove conclusively that these hominins easily walked erect (Hay and Leakey 1982).

A clearly bipedal hominin that is even older than *A. afarensis* has recently been discovered in Kenya at the sites of Kanapoi and Alia Bay (M. Leakey et al. 1995). ***Australopithecus anamensis*** have been dated to between 3.9 and 4.2 million years ago. The tibia (shin bone) of this species indicates that it walked upright, and the fossils share many other similarities with *A. afarensis*. The lower jaws of *A. anamensis* are nearly parallel, more like those of modern apes. As a result, these fossils have been placed in a separate species, although they are clearly ancestral to the later *A. afarensis*.

FIGURE 2.8 Arm bones from *Ardipithecus ramidus*, found at Aramis, near Hadar, in Ethiopia. Dating to 4.4 million years ago, *A. ramidus* shares some features with both the hominins and the apes such as the chimpanzee.

EARLIEST ANCESTORS

In 1992 and 1993, T. White, G. Suwa, and B. Asfaw uncovered a group of fossils that are even earlier than *Australopithecus anamensis*. Found at Aramis, near Hadar, and dating to around 4.4 million years ago, these fossils include some teeth, some skull fragments, and several arm bones. The Aramis specimens appear even more primitive than *A. afarensis*, and some of the dental and other characteristics approach those found in apes such as the chimpanzee. The forward position of the foramen mag-

num, however, suggests that this species may be an early hominin. The discoverers initially proposed the name *Australopithecus ramidus* for these finds (Fig. 2.8). *Ramidus* means root in the Afar language; the name was suggested because these fossils seem to be very near the root of the hominin line (White et al. 1994). These fossils have recently been reclassified as **Ardipithecus ramidus** (White et al. 1995).

An earlier form of *Ardipithecus*, **Ardipithecus kadabba**, was recently discovered in the Middle Awash region of Ethiopia (Haile Selassie 2001, 2004). These fossils date between 5.2 and 5.8 million years ago. *Ardipithecus kadabba* is considered a hominin because its canine teeth are smaller than the canine teeth seen in modern and fossil apes. It is not known whether the species was bipedal.

As noted at the start of this chapter, two new fossil hominins, **Orrorin tugenensis** and **Sahelanthropus tchadensis**, were recently discovered in Kenya and Chad. These specimens extend the record of human ancestors back to about 6 million years ago. These fossils are very close to the time when the chimp and human lines diverged, and their status as human ancestors is still a matter of debate among anthropologists (Wolpoff et al. 2002). For example, *Sahelanthropus* (Brunet et al. 2002) has many chimplike features, but its canines show wear on the tips, like those of modern humans. Some anthropologists would include *Orrorin* and *Sahelanthropus* within the *Ardipithecus kadabba* taxon (Haile Selassie 2004), creating a single long-lived and variable early hominin ancestor. The early hominin fossil finds are summarized in Figure 2.9.

THE BRANCHING TREE OF HOMININ EVOLUTION

How do the australopith fossils relate to the human ancestral line? In a number of ways (particularly the dentition), the earlier gracile forms seem more like modern humans than do the later robust types. Most anthropologists consider *P. robustus* and *P. boisei* to be side branches of hominin evolution and not direct ancestors of modern humans. In 1985 a new fossil, discovered on the west bank of Lake Turkana, shed considerable light on the evolution of the robust australopiths. Known as the Black Skull (KNM-WT

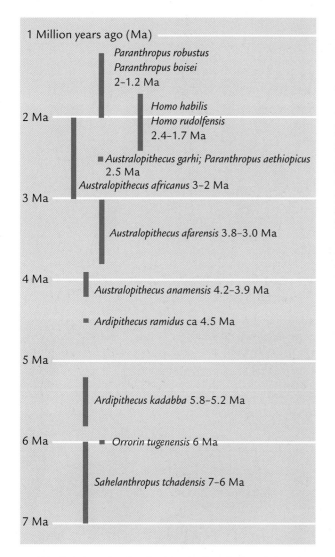

FIGURE 2.9 — Timeline contents:

1 Million years ago (Ma)

Paranthropus robustus
Paranthropus boisei
2–1.2 Ma

Homo habilis
Homo rudolfensis
2.4–1.7 Ma

■ *Australopithecus garhi; Paranthropus aethiopicus*
2.5 Ma
Australopithecus africanus 3–2 Ma

Australopithecus afarensis 3.8–3.0 Ma

Australopithecus anamensis 4.2–3.9 Ma

■ *Ardipithecus ramidus* ca 4.5 Ma

Ardipithecus kadabba 5.8–5.2 Ma

■ *Orrorin tugenensis* 6 Ma

Sahelanthropus tchadensis 7–6 Ma

FIGURE 2.9 The fossil record of early hominins.

FIGURE 2.10 KNM-WT 17000: the Black Skull—*Paranthropus aethiopicus.* A very early robust form.

THE EARLIEST MEMBERS OF OUR GENUS, *HOMO*

Louis Leakey never accepted the australopiths as human ancestors. He was convinced that more humanlike fossils would be found, and in the early 1960s several new fossil skull fragments came to light from the lower beds of Olduvai. Leakey believed that the fossils filled this gap. He considered these fossils very primitive humans, and he and his colleagues gave them the name **Homo habilis** (handy man). The average cranial capacity of the skulls was about 640 ml, larger than the australopiths, but this estimate was in doubt because the fossils were very fragmentary and in poor condition. Very few other anthropologists accepted Leakey's attribution of the fossils to *Homo*. Better evidence was needed.

Richard Leakey, Louis and Mary Leakey's son, began work in 1969 at a site near Lake Turkana (formerly Lake Rudolf) in Kenya, known as **Koobi Fora.** Koobi Fora is a very large, well-preserved site that has produced many thousands of fossils, including numerous hominins. In 1972 Richard Leakey announced the discovery of a new skull of unique importance. Known as KNM-ER 1470, this

17000, its museum accession number), the nearly complete cranium dates from about 2.5 million years ago (Walker et al. 1986). The skull bears a combination of traits reminiscent of *Australopithecus afarensis* and robust features much like those of *P. robustus* and *P. boisei.* The antiquity of the Black Skull indicates that the divergence of the evolutionary line leading to the robust australopiths took place very early. The Black Skull itself (Figure 2.10) has been given the name **Paranthropus aethiopicus.** It is unlikely that *A. africanus* evolved into the robust forms. It remains an open question whether *Australopithecus africanus* is ancestral to later humans (Figure 2.11).

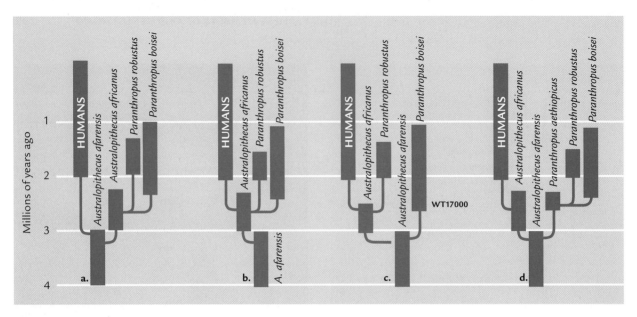

FIGURE 2.11 Four possible family trees that have been proposed for the early hominins. Courtesy of Frederick E. Grine.

skull was relatively complete, although it was badly fragmented and required painstaking reconstruction. It was strikingly different from the australopiths, with a notably higher, more rounded braincase, and a much larger cranial capacity of 775 ml. Today, most anthropologists accept KNM-ER 1470, along with a number of other more recent finds from Koobi Fora and elsewhere, as representative of the genus *Homo*. There is, in fact, considerable diversity in the group of fossils now assigned to early *Homo*. Some specimens, such as KNM-ER 1470, possessed relatively large brains, and rather large teeth as well. Others had smaller brains and also smaller, human-sized, teeth. Some workers today recognize two species of early *Homo: Homo habilis,* which includes the finds from Olduvai Gorge, and **Homo rudolfensis,** which includes KNM-ER 1470 and similar fossils (Figure 2.12).

The dating of the deposits at Koobi Fora has been an issue of critical importance for the understanding of the early stages of human evolution. Potassium-argon dating has been applied to the volcanic tuffs present at the site, and comparative studies of the associated animal species have also played an important role. At present, the best estimate for the age of KNM-ER 1470 is about 1.9 million years.

Most anthropologists think that *Australopithecus afarensis* is ancestral to *Homo habilis* and *Homo rudolfensis*. However, *Australopithecus afarensis* disappeared about 3 million years ago, and the earliest

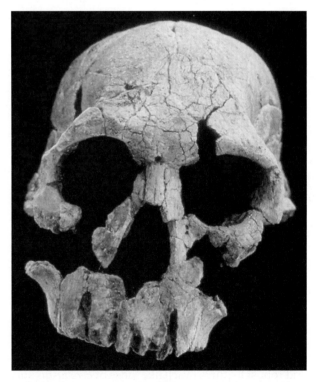

FIGURE 2.12 KNM-ER 1470: *Homo habilis (rudolfensis)*. An early human skull from Koobi Fora.

fossils of *Homo* date to about 2.3 to 2.4 million years ago. Several species of australopiths are known from the period between 3 and 2 million years ago. These include *Australopithecus africanus* and a recently discovered species, **Australopithecus**

ARCHAEOLOGY IN PRACTICE

Dating the Earliest Hominins

Which fossil hominin came first? The dating of fossil finds is critical to any understanding of human evolution; earlier fossils may potentially be ancestral to later fossils. Placing them in chronological order is a matter of **relative dating.** A variety of physical and chemical methods have also permitted scientists to assign actual calendar dates to archaeological and fossil deposits. This process is known as **absolute dating.** Together, these methods have permitted paleontologists and archaeologists to construct a temporal framework for the early fossil hominins. Unfortunately, for this early time period, there are no methods currently available that can be used to date the fossils themselves. Instead, the fossils must be dated indirectly, by determining the dates of the geological strata in which they lie. More often than not, even this is not possible, so the date of a fossil is usually estimated by dating deposits that lie above or below the fossil. The fossil may be presumed to be younger than a dated deposit lying below it and older than a dated deposit found above it (Figure 2.A). If datable deposits can be located both above and below a fossil, its date can be fixed within well-defined limits.

Depending on the geological circumstances and time frame involved, certain absolute dating methods may be amenable to a given site, while others may not be applicable. In practice, each of the physical dating methods has potential sources of error, so cross-checking by using several dating methods is the best course of action. In some instances no absolute dates are possible; for these sites relative dating techniques may help fix their place in time. The following discussion introduces the basic principles behind the most important methods used to date the early hominin sites.

ABSOLUTE DATING

Radiometric Clocks

Fixing an absolute date depends on finding a suitable clock. A variety of physical and chemical processes can be called on to serve as clocks. These processes all consist of measurable changes that occur in a regular way over an extended period of time. Among the best such clocks are those that depend on changes in the atomic nucleus. Nuclear processes are virtually unaffected by environmental variables, such as temperature and pressure, that might otherwise affect the rate of ticking of the clock. Most of the clocks so far devised depend on the spontaneous radioactivity of certain atoms, known as radioactive **isotopes.** Most chemical elements found in nature include several isotopic forms, some of which may be radioactive. The nuclei of radioactive isotopes may also gradually break down to produce other chemical elements, known as daughter nuclei. The radioactivity of a given isotope and the rate at which a nucleus breaks down can be precisely determined. The period of time required for one-half of the nuclei of a radioactive isotope to break down (to form daughter products) is known as its **half-life.** All the radiometric dating methods in use measure just how much of a specific radioactive isotope in a sample has broken down since the sample was formed; the more that has broken down, the older the sample. The actual technique for measuring this quantity takes a number of forms, depending on the method used.

Potassium-Argon Dating

The **potassium-argon dating method** (Aitken 1990) is one of the most important for the dating of the early hominin sites and provides an illustration of the basic principles of radiometric dating. The very long half-life of potassium-40 (1.25 billion years) permits the dating of very ancient rocks, while advances in analysis techniques have made it possible to obtain dates younger than 100,000 years. The potassium-40 isotope makes up about 0.01% of naturally occurring potassium, which is found in substantial quantities in igneous rocks such as volcanic lavas, ashes, and tuffs. As the potassium-40 decays, a small

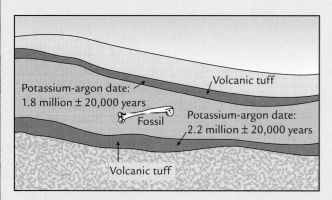

Figure 2.A The fossil bone must be older than 1.8 million years and younger than 2.2 million years. Estimated age is about 2 million years.

Within the figure:
Potassium-argon date: 1.8 million ± 20,000 years
Volcanic tuff
Fossil
Potassium-argon date: 2.2 million ± 20,000 years
Volcanic tuff

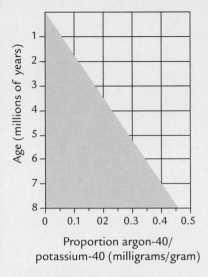

Figure 2.B   The principle of potassium-argon dating. The more argon-40 accumulated in the sample, the older it is. Source: After Aitken 1990: 121

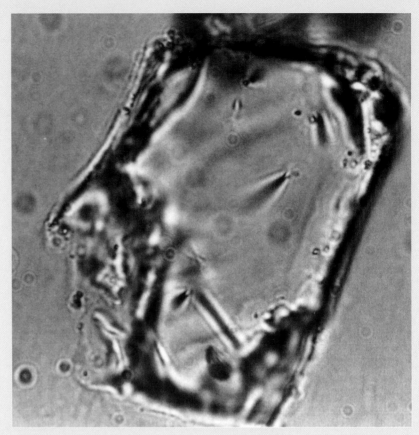

Figure 2.C   Fission tracks.

proportion (about 0.06% every million years) is converted into the inert gas argon-40. The argon gas remains trapped within the structure of the mineral crystals until the rock is melted, releasing the argon gas. This occurs during a volcanic eruption; at that time the potassium-argon clock is "set to zero." As soon as the rock solidifies, the argon begins accumulating again. In principle, to ascertain the date of the volcanic eruption, it is necessary to determine only how much potassium-40 is present and how much argon-40 has accumulated in the intervening span of time (Figure 2.B). The argon-40 gas is released by melting the rock sample and is measured in a mass spectrometer, a sensitive instrument for separating atoms of differing weights.

Potassium-argon dating is straightforward, but if reliable dates are to be obtained, the samples used must be uncontaminated by older or younger inclusions. The method is further complicated because some minerals may leak argon gas and therefore give an incorrect age. For example, argon loss initially led to anomalously young dates for the *Australopithecus afarensis* fossils from Hadar.

Since the 1990s, the $^{40}Ar/^{39}Ar$ ("argon-argon") dating method has replaced conventional potassium-argon dating (Deino et al. 1998). The technique is more precise and accurate than traditional potassium-argon dating, because the potassium and argon content of the sample are measured in the same mass spectrometer experiment. In order to date a sample, the material is irradiated so that a portion of the potassium-40 is converted to argon-39 by bombardment with fast neutrons. The $^{40}Ar/^{39}Ar$ method allows single crystals to be analyzed, as long as they contain measurable quantities of argon-40. The method has been used to date the *Australopithecus afarensis* fossils from Hadar and the *Ardipithecus kadabba* fossils from Ethiopia.

Fission-Track Dating

Fission-track dating (MacDougall 1976) is an alternative method that has also been used to date the early hominins. It is a more limited method in that it is practical for only a few minerals, of which zircon is the most frequently used. These minerals include small quantities of uranium-238 as an impurity. In addition to being radioactive, uranium-238 will occasionally spontaneously fission, forming two smaller daughter atoms. As the two atomic nuclei recoil from one another, they disrupt the structure of the mineral crystal, leaving behind fission tracks that can be made visible by appropriate chemical treatment. When viewed under the microscope, the fission tracks appear as short, dark lines scattered over the crystal's surface. If the crystal is heated, the tracks anneal, causing them to disappear. The number of fission tracks, therefore, is proportional to the time elapsed since the mineral was last heated. The technique can be used to date igneous rocks such as lava that contain suitable mineral grains. The age is proportional to the ratio of the number of fission tracks to the amount of uranium-238 present. The age of the sample is determined by chemically etching the fission tracks to make them visible and counting them under a microscope (Figure 2.C). The amount of uranium-238 present is found by irradiating the sample in a nuclear reactor to induce a known proportion of the uranium atoms to fission, and then counting the newly formed fission tracks.

Geomagnetic Reversals

The earth's magnetic field is not static; the magnetic poles of the earth are in constant movement. The past location of the magnetic poles can be found through the examination of rock formations. When volcanic rock solidifies, or when a sedimentary rock hardens, magnetic particles in the rock that had aligned themselves with the earth's magnetic field become frozen in position. The rock acquires a weak magnetic field that may be used to determine the orientation of the earth's field in the past.

The earth's magnetic poles wander continuously. In addition, at irregular intervals, the magnetization of rock formations indicates that the earth's poles have abruptly exchanged positions, with the North pole becoming the South pole and vice versa. These interchanges are termed **geomagnetic reversals**. Through the use of radiometric dating methods, such as potassium-argon dating, the dates of many of these reversals have been determined. The pattern that has emerged is of extended epochs (or chrons) during which the field is either normal (as it is today) or reversed. These epochs are interrupted by short periods (called events, or subchrons) during which the field temporarily has the opposite polarization. Figure 2.D shows

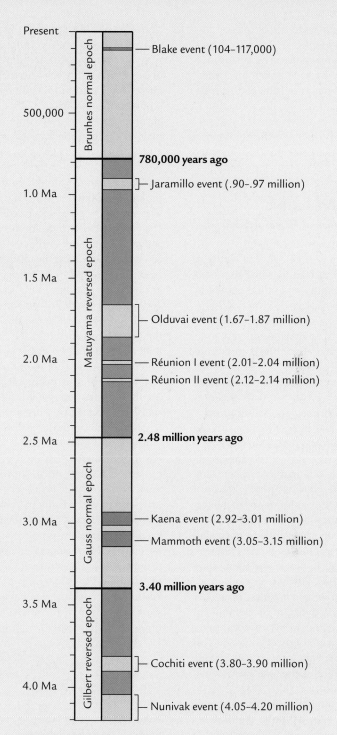

Figure 2.D Major geomagnetic reversals. Source: Based on data in Aitken 1990 and Butler 1992.

the major reversals of interest to archaeologists.

Geomagnetic reversals do not directly provide a date for a site. If the orientation of the earth's magnetic field during the formation of a site can be determined, however, it can help resolve difficult situations where the dates provided by absolute dating methods are ambiguous or in conflict.

RELATIVE DATING

Correlation of Faunal Assemblages

The animals that inhabit a given location change over the course of geological time as some species become extinct and others evolve to take their place. Paleontologists have long used the associated group of animals found at a site, the **faunal assemblage,** to help temporally correlate rock strata found at different locations. Two strata containing very similar types of fossils can usually be presumed to be close in age. During the age of mammals, the Cenozoic, animal species evolved rapidly, so a distinctive faunal assemblage can often be quite accurately placed within the evolutionary sequence. Only areas that are not too distant geographically and have similar environments, however, may be expected to have supported similar faunas. Further, an isolated area may have seen a course of evolution different from that of other areas. With the environment taken into account, however, faunal correlations have proved very useful for tying together the early hominin sites.

A number of African archaeological sites dating to the time of the early hominins have provided assemblages of animal bones that can be used as chronological guides. The site of **Omo** in Ethiopia, studied under the direction of F. C. Howell, has produced an extensive sequence of animal bone assemblages as well as a number of hominin remains.

The sequence of deposits at Omo can also be anchored in time through the potassium-argon dating of key strata. Olduvai Gorge and Hadar have also produced good animal bone sequences with some absolute dates. Several kinds of animals, including horses, elephants, and, particularly, various types of pigs, appear, diversify, and become extinct in turn. At any given time period, the faunal assemblage at a site can be expected to include a characteristic group of species that differs from that of earlier or later periods. The various species of pigs have proved to be particularly important temporal indicators. Today, three species of pigs remain in sub-Saharan Africa: the bushpig, the giant forest hog, and the warthog. About 1 million years ago, 10 different species were to be found, 7 of which are now extinct. About 2 million years ago, yet another set of pig species was present, and so on back through the last several million years. Figure 2.E, derived from the sequence proposed by H. B. S. Cooke (1985), shows the associations of pig species characteristic of each distinctive faunal period. Horses and elephants can also be used to produce similar temporal associations of species (Cooke 1983). The strata at Omo, Olduvai Gorge, Hadar, and a number of other African sites have been correlated through the application of these faunal data.

DATING IN PRACTICE

How Were the Earliest Hominins Dated?

None of today's physical dating methods were available when the South African australopith fossils were first discovered. The approximate dates of Taung and Sterkfontein were estimated on the basis of the species of animals found at the sites. Even today, the dating of the South African sites has proved difficult because

there are no volcanic deposits suitable for potassium-argon dating. The animal species present in the South African sites differ from those in East Africa, but the group of species present at Makapansgat, Taung, and Sterkfontein is different from those found in Kromdraai and Swartkrans. The faunal evidence suggests that Makapansgat, Taung, and Sterkfontein (the *A. africanus* sites) were roughly contemporary, while Kromdraai and Swartkrans (the *A. robustus* sites) were later in time (Cooke 1966: 106; see also White and Harris 1977). Faunal correlations with East African sites have proved very uncertain because the environments of the two areas are quite different, and it is possible that some species survived longer in South Africa.

In East Africa the potassium-argon method has provided dates for a number of key strata (primarily volcanic tuffs), and these dates have frequently been cross-checked through the application of fission-track dating, determinations of geomagnetic polarity, and faunal correlations. The dating of the fossil finds at Hadar provides an example (Johanson and Edey 1981). A key date was provided by the potassium-argon dating of a volcanic ash dated at 2.8 ± 0.04 million years that overlay the principal australopith finds. This date was confirmed by a fission-track date of 2.7 ± 0.23 million years. Another basalt layer below the fossils was at first potassium-argon dated to about 3 million years, but because of the nature of the test material this dating was doubtful. The magnetization of the basal layer indicated that it was laid down during a period when the earth's poles were reversed. This occurred between 3 million and 3.1 million years ago (the Mammoth event) and, previously, between 3.4 million and 3.8 million years ago (at the end of the Gilbert reversed epoch). The later date of 3 million years was

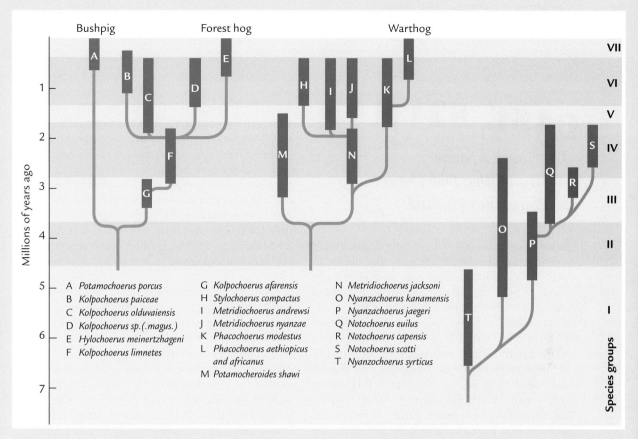

Figure 2.E The temporal relationship among the various species of pigs found in East Africa during the Pliocene and Pleistocene, as proposed by H. B. S. Cooke (1985). Several distinct chronological groups of species can be distinguished. A similar scheme, differing only in details and some of the species names, has been proposed by J. M. Harris and T. D. White (1979).

initially accepted, making Lucy and the other *A. afarensis* fossils about 2.9 million years old. The fossil pigs in the assemblage, however, seemed too primitive for that date. Cooke (1978) thought an age of 3 million to 3.5 million years was more likely. The basalt layer, therefore, probably formed in the earlier period of geomagnetic reversal, about 3.75 million years ago.

The dating of the *Homo habilis (rudolfensis)* fossil KNM-ER 1470 at Koobi Fora is another example of the difficulties encountered in absolute dating. KNM-ER 1470 had been found below a volcanic stratum, known as the KBS tuff, that served as a critical chronologi-cal marker. The first potassium-argon dates for the KBS tuff placed it at about 2.6 million years old. The *Homo habilis (rudolfensis)* skull, therefore, would have had to be older, perhaps 2.9 million years old. That would have been far too old for *Australopithecus africanus* to be a human ancestor. The other animal species in the deposit, particularly the fossil pigs, however, suggested that it was considerably younger, correlating with deposits from Omo of about 2 million years of age. The reexamination of rock samples from the KBS tuff complex revealed that they were contaminated by older minerals; new potassium-argon determinations of carefully puri-fied samples have given a date of 1.88 ± 0.02 million years ago (Feibel et al. 1989), and KNM-ER 1470 is now dated to about 1.9 million years.

CASE STUDY

The South African Australopiths: Did They Hunt, or Were They Hunted?

Stone tools have never been found associated with the South African australopiths except in sites in which early *Homo* may also have been present. Still, the earliest hominins may have used tools made from other materials: wood, bone, teeth, or horn. This was the suggestion of Raymond Dart, based on his investigations of the South African australopith sites. The use of bone tools by the australopiths has proved very difficult to verify, and Dart's suggestion was widely challenged. Further, Dart coupled his hypothesis with some rather startling assertions concerning australopith behavior. The australopiths, he said, were violent, aggressive hunters, violent not only toward their prey but also toward each other. Dart's evidence for this scenario and its refutation by the careful observations and experiments of C. K. Brain (1981) are detailed below.

The South African sites at which *Australopithecus africanus* has been found—Taung, Sterkfontein, and Makapansgat—contained no stone tools associated with the fossil hominins. Instead, each of these cave sites held large quantities of fragmentary animal bones belonging to a variety of species. Earlier researchers had interpreted similar deposits as the work of large carnivores, notably hyenas, but on the basis of his experience and some limited research, Dart rejected hyenas as likely bone-collecting agents. At an early stage in his researches, Raymond Dart became convinced that the South African bone accumulations came into the caves as the result of hominin activities. The deposit at Taung, he noted, was similar to known archaeological sites belonging to early modern humans (Dart 1929: 648). Dart reasoned that the animal bones must have been brought into the caves for a purpose. At Makapansgat the proportions of the various skeletal parts recovered were markedly different from their proportions in a complete animal skeleton, suggesting to Dart that certain bones had been selected for use as tools. He thought he could identify pointed tools made by twisting and cracking long bones, scoops and spatulate bone tools, and composite tools made by forcing one bone into another or by wedging stone fragments into the ends of bones. Dart envisioned uses for practically all the bone that was found at Makapansgat. He termed this technology the **osteodontokeratic** (bone, tooth, and horn) industry.

Among the bones from Taung, Sterkfontein, and Makapansgat were numerous baboon skulls. Dart noted that many of these skulls, as well as six australopith skulls, bore depressed fractures, as if they had been struck on the head. Dart concluded that these fractures must have been caused by violent attacks by the australopiths, and, in the absence of stone artifacts, that the weapon used must have been a large animal bone, possibly an antelope humerus (upper arm bone). Examining the bone collection from Makapansgat, Dart observed that there was a high proportion of antelope skulls present, but very few neck vertebrae or tailbones. This suggested to him that the game animals had been intentionally decapitated and that the australopiths were headhunters. Dart reasoned that the australopiths were:

> Confirmed killers: carnivorous creatures that seized living quarries by violence, battered them to death, tore apart their broken bodies, dismembered them limb from limb, slaking their ravenous thirst with the hot blood of victims and greedily devouring livid writhing flesh (Dart 1953: 209).

The idea that the human lineage is innately violent soon penetrated into popular culture. Dart's lurid view of early hominin behavior was popularized by science writer Robert Ardrey in a best-selling book *African Genesis* (1961). Stanley Kubrick's classic 1969 film *2001: A Space Odyssey* opens with a series of scenes of violent, club-wielding australopiths.

Dart's enticing hypotheses, however, have not stood up to closer scrutiny. A series of observations and experiments, primarily the research of C. K. Brain presented in his 1981 book *The Hunters or the Hunted?*, have shown that some of Dart's fundamental premises were incorrect.

Dart was convinced that the bone accumulations were the work of hominins and that large carnivores had played no part. Later research has shown, however, that large carnivores such as hyenas and leopards can and do carry meat into their lairs, resulting in large accumulations of food bone. A number of observers have reported bone accumulations by African hyenas. Particularly interesting are the observations made by G. Ilani (1975) of a striped hyena den in the Negev Desert of southern Israel. Within the den were hundreds of skulls of domestic dogs, camels, donkeys, sheep, and goats, including two human skulls, presumably from a nearby Bedouin cemetery. On the basis of his own observations, Brain has demonstrated that leopards too will collect the bones of their prey in feeding lairs. Vegetarian porcupines also collect bones, which they chew to wear down their incisors. Any or all of these animals may have contributed to the South African bone assemblages.

What of the fractures and depressions in the animal and hominin skulls? Brain points out that fossil bones frequently become deformed and marked from the pressure of stones in the deposit in which they lie and that such markings can easily imitate the results of injuries. Since the nature of the deposit is unknown for all the fossils showing depressions, the actual cause of these markings cannot be demonstrated. The question is largely moot for the site of Taung. The Taung cave, from which the hominins were recovered, was destroyed by mining operations in the late 1920s, so the exact context of the Taung fossils is unknown. Recently, however, geological examinations of the Taung area and of the sediments adhering to the fossils have indicated that the geological history of the Taung cave was more complicated than Dart realized and that the hominin fossils actually came from a later time period than the game they had presumably hunted. Further, Brain was able to examine a preserved block of limestone breccia from Taung containing a number of baboon skulls and other bones. He confirmed that the bones had been damaged by gnawing and that they were very likely the food bone accumulation of a large carnivore such as a leopard.

What of the odd distribution of bone types at Makapansgat, attributed by Dart to conscious selection by hominins? Brain's observations of the food remains left behind by Hottentot goat herders provide an alternative explanation. The Hottentots butcher and eat numerous goats, scattering the bones in the area of their huts, where they are gnawed on by dogs. Brain noted that many of these bone fragments look like bone tools, even though the Hottentots deny that they ever made bone tools. The wear that appeared on the pseudotools that Brain collected apparently came from the abrasion of the bone fragments in the sand as they were trodden underfoot. Over two years Brain collected several thousand discarded goat bones from the Hottentot villages. By counting the numbers of each of the different skeletal parts present (femurs, humeri, mandibles, etc.), it was possible to determine the minimum number of goats that must originally have been present, and from that number to calculate how many of each kind of bone should have been found had all the bones been preserved. The proportions of bone types that actually remained after the Hottentot butchers and the ravaging dogs had done their work proved to be markedly different from the proportion that had originally existed. Mandibles (lower jaws) were the best preserved; most of them still remained. Most other bones fared far more poorly. The sample should have contained 1224 caudal vertebrae (tailbones), but there were none. Unchewable bones survived best; young, soft bones survived the worst.

When Brain compared the Hottentot data to the bone assemblage from Makapansgat, the similarity was immediately apparent. Although minor differences existed, in general, those skeletal parts found in large numbers in the modern goat bone sample were also common in Makapansgat. Conversely, those bones that had been destroyed in the goat bone sample were also missing from Makapansgat. The most likely explanation for the bone collection at Makapansgat, therefore, is that it was probably collected, and greatly modified, by the activities of large carnivores.

The events at Sterkfontein have proved more difficult to interpret, largely because the collections of animal bones from the site may have been biased and incomplete. The great majority of specimens from the site are skulls, with very few other skeletal parts represented. Nevertheless, the collection is remarkable. The most common animals at the site were baboons, followed in turn by *Australopithecus africanus,* and then by large carnivores such as saber-toothed cats. Brain's reexamination of the skulls supposedly damaged by violent blows showed little that could not equally be attributable to compressional effects, and the preponderance of skulls strongly suggests that Sterkfontein too is a collection created by large carnivores.

How did so many baboons and hominins find their way into the Sterkfontein deposit? Clues may be found in the examination of other South African hominin sites. The cave of Swartkrans, which contained both *Paranthropus robustus* and fossils of early humans, shows some interesting similarities to Sterkfontein. Skulls are preponderant in the lower layer of Swartkrans, where nearly all the hominins were found. Baboons and hominins are the most common species and about equally frequent. Large herbivores follow, and large carnivores are also common. The distribution of skeletal parts at Swartkrans, as at Makapansgat, and frequent evidence of carnivore gnawing make it clear that this collection of bones was created by the activities of large carnivores. The bone assemblage in the *Paranthropus robustus* site of Kromdraai shows many similarities to that of Swartkrans, although the bones are very fragmentary and the case is not so clear.

Brain concludes, therefore, that the australopiths in Sterkfontein, Swartkrans, and Kromdraai did not inhabit the sites where they were found but rather were dragged there as food by large carnivores, such as leopards, saber-toothed cats, or perhaps hyenas. Rather than being the vicious predators envisaged by Dart, the australopiths were instead the prey of more powerful creatures. How did the bones end up in the caves? Brain presents an intriguing hypothesis (Figure 2.F). Today the openings to limestone caves are frequently surrounded by groves of trees that grow readily because of the abundance of groundwater.

FIGURE 2.F   The Swartkrans leopard hypothesis: A leopard has carried an australopith into a tree to protect it from scavengers such as hyenas. Later, the remains will fall to the ground, and the bones will be washed into the cave. Source: After Brain 1981.

Leopards often carry their prey onto the branches of trees, where they can feed undisturbed by hyenas. Brain speculates that leopards may have carried the unfortunate australopiths up into the trees growing above the Swartkrans shaft and that their remains ultimately dropped down into the cave. Brain supports this hypothesis by a fascinating piece of evidence. The skull of an australopith child from Swartkrans shows two holes pierced through it, 33 mm (1.3 in.) apart. This spacing exactly fits the canine teeth of a leopard also found in the deposit.

garhi, which dates to about 2.5 million years ago (Asfaw et al. 1999). Anthropologists disagree, often vociferously, about which, if any, of these species may be ancestral to early humans.

CONCLUSION

Brain himself found a few convincing bone tools at Swartkrans, but they could well have been made by early humans rather than australopiths. With the appearance of the genus *Homo,* stone tools also appear in large numbers. As will be discussed in Chapter 3, scatters of stone artifacts and the waste products from their manufacture are the surest signs of the presence of humans. A number of archaeological sites, including concentrations of stone artifacts, animal bones, and sometimes hominin fossils, have come to light at Olduvai, at Koobi Fora, and elsewhere in Africa. Unlike the South African australopith sites, these sites are much more likely to be the result of early human activities: places where animal foods, obtained through scavenging or hunting, were butchered, possibly shared, and consumed. The interpretation of these sites has been the subject of much controversy, but they provide the first clues to the lifeways of our earliest ancestors. The nature and interpretation of these sites will be the subject matter of Chapter 3.

KEY TERMS

Absolute dating 41	Fission-track dating 42
Australopith 33	Geomagnetic
Ardipithecus kadabba 38	reversals 43
Ardipithecus ramidus 38	Great Rift Valley 34
Australopithecus	Hadar 36
afarensis 36	Half-life 41
Australopithecus	Hominins 32
africanus 33	*Homo habilis* 39
Australopithecus	*Homo rudolfensis* 40
anamensis 37	Isotopes 41
Australopithecus garhi 40	Koobi Fora 39
Bipedal 32	Kromdraai 33
Breccia 34	Laetoli 37
Cranial capacity 33	Makapansgat 34
Drimolen 34	Olduvai Gorge 35
Faunal assemblage 44	Omo 44

Orrorin tugenensis 38	Primates 32
Osteodontokeratic 46	Relative dating 41
Paranthropus	*Sahelanthropus*
aethiopicus 39	*tchadensis* 38
Paranthropus boisei 35	Sterkfontein 33
Paranthropus robustus 33	Swartkrans 33
Potassium-argon dating	Taung 32
method 41	Tuffs 34

QUESTIONS FOR DISCUSSION

1. Examine the different phylogenetic trees in Figure 2.11. What are the differences between the various trees? Which phylogenetic tree do you find most convincing and why?

2. How did the discovery of the Taung child (*Australopithecus africanus*) in the 1920s revolutionize the study of human origins?

3. Why do you think that bipedalism developed so early in the course of hominin evolution?

FURTHER READING

Aitken, M. J.
   1990 *Science-Based Dating in Archaeology.* London and New York: Longman.
   An up-to-date, concise summary of the principles, applications, and limitations of the physical dating methods currently in use in archaeology. Recommended for the advanced student.

Delson, Eric, Ian Tattersall, John A. Van Couvering, and Alison S. Brooks, eds.
   2002 Encyclopedia of Human Evolution and Prehistory, 2nd ed. New York: Garland.
   An authoritative and up-to-date reference work on human evolution and prehistoric archaeology.

Klein, Richard G.
   1999 *The Human Career: Human Biological and Cultural Origins,* 2nd ed. Chicago: University of Chicago Press.
   A valuable overview of human evolution and archaeology, written by a recognized authority in the field.

Wong, Kate
   2003 An Ancestor to Call Our Own. *Scientific American* 288 (1): 54–63.
   This article discusses the discovery of Sahelanthropus *and its relationship to* Orrorin, Ardipithecus, *and later fossil hominins.*

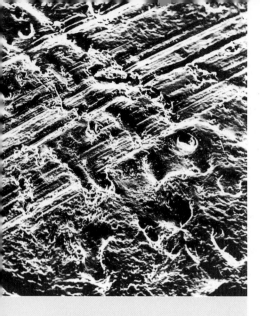

3

THE EARLIEST ARCHAEOLOGICAL SITES

The First Stone Tools

How do archaeologists recognize the earliest archaeological sites? The earliest, simplest sites have presented archaeologists with a major challenge. How can we distinguish the evidence for specifically human activities from the remains left by other animals, such as the bone accumulations of scavenging carnivores, or from natural accumulations created by running water or other geological forces?

Human fossils are uncommon discoveries, and when they are found they make front-page news. In 2003 Robert Blumenschine and his colleagues (Blumenschine et al. 2003) described the discovery of a new human ancestor at Olduvai Gorge in Tanzania. The fossil, designated OH 65, included a complete maxilla (upper jaw) and lower face of a member of the genus *Homo*. It was found with stone tools and butchered animal bones dating between 1.79 and 1.84 million years ago. An analysis of the tools showed that some were made from stones that could be found locally, but others were made from materials from far away. This indicated that these early humans were traveling long distances, occupying not just one shore of the ancient Olduvai lake but moving to the other side as well, carrying their tools with them.

Much of what we know about the behavior of these human ancestors comes from the archaeological record and is based on painstaking analysis of artifacts, ecofacts, and archaeological sites.

For most archaeologists, the first appearance of stone tools and butchered animal bones marks the beginning of the archaeological record—the record of specifically human activities. Stone tools within an archaeological site are one clear marker that the site resulted, at least in part, from human rather than nonhuman activity. The evidence, however, for the use of the simplest stone tools by our remote human ancestors is usually quite ambiguous and difficult to

50

FIGURE 3.1   A chimpanzee making use of a tool. The twig is used to fish for termites through an opening in the termite mound.

interpret. How do archaeologists determine that a stone object is really an artifact made and utilized by humans?

Fifty years ago, anthropologists thought that tool use was a unique attribute of humans and their immediate ancestors. An early archaeology textbook bore the title, *Man the Tool-Maker* (Oakley 1950). Observations of primates in the wild conducted since the 1960s have shown that chimpanzees, and even some orangutans, also use tools (Figure 3.1). Chimpanzees use tools for subsistence activities. They use sticks to "fish" for termites, and some West African chimp populations use stones and anvils to crack nuts (Boesch and Boesch-Ackermann 2000). The common ancestor of both humans and chimpanzees may have used some rudimentary tools.

Stone tools, stones that are deliberately fractured to produce sharp cutting edges, first appear about 2.6 million years ago, nearly 3.5 million years after the first possible human ancestors have been recognized in the fossil record. Butchered animal bones showing distinctive cut marks also appear at about this time, indicating that early stone tools were used to obtain meat, fat, and marrow from animal carcasses.

THE BEGINNINGS OF THE ARCHAEOLOGICAL RECORD

The oldest stone tools known at present have been found in Ethiopia, from deposits near Hadar, dating to about 2.5–2.6 million years ago (Semaw 2000; Semaw et al. 2003). The tools are older than any known fossils of early *Homo;* the earliest fossils of the genus *Homo* date to about 2.4 million years ago. It is possible that *Australopithecus garhi* was the earliest African stone tool maker. *A. garhi* has been dated to about 2.5 million years ago. In the Bouri Formation in Ethiopia, butchered animal bones have been found near the *A. garhi* fossils. It is likely, however, that most of the early East African stone tools were made by members of the genus *Homo.*

In South Africa the picture is even more complex. The site of Swartkrans has produced both stone tools and a number of animal bones that appear to have been used as tools. The bones show evidence of grinding, and they may have been used to dig into termite mounds (Backwell and d'Errico 2001; d'Errico and Backwell 2003). It is not clear whether these tools were made by *Paranthropus robustus* or early *Homo.*

THE EARLIEST FORMS OF STONE TOOLS

The simplest stone tools can be difficult to distinguish from fragmented stones resulting from natural geological processes. Two lines of evidence indicate to the archaeologist that a specific object is the result of human activity. The first is *location:* If no known natural process can account for the occurrence of an object in the place where it is found, the archaeologist may suspect that the object, even an unworked stone, was brought there by human agency. It is not always easy, though, to determine whether or not natural forces (notably water action and the activities of animals) played a role in the location of artifacts. The importance of this problem will be discussed later in this chapter.

The second line of evidence that an artifact is of human origin is the degree to which a natural object, such as a stone nodule, has been *modified.* If an artifact has clearly been *intentionally changed,* for example, by removing a series of flakes from a flint nodule, the archaeologist may conclude that it is a product of human activity. When the degree of modification of a stone is minimal, it can be very difficult to ascertain whether the object was the product of natural agencies or intentional manufacture. As the degree of modification is increased (as more flakes are removed), the archaeologist may be more confident that the object is of human origin.

An assemblage of stone tools made and used together is termed a **lithic industry,** from the Greek word for stone, *lithos.* The earliest lithic industries generally resemble that found in the lowest level at Olduvai Gorge, Bed I, where several important archaeological sites have been discovered. This industry is named the **Oldowan** (after an alternate name for Olduvai). The Oldowan is typified by the assemblage from the site DK (the K stands for *Korongo,* meaning "gully" in Swahili), which lies near the base of the long sequence at Olduvai Gorge (Figure 3.2), in Bed I, and dates to approximately 1.8 million years ago. DK will be discussed in some detail later in this chapter.

The DK stone tool assemblage includes both flakes and cores. Numerous flakes, both of basalt and quartzite, are found in the assemblage, and some of these show signs of utilization. Experiments by archaeologist Nicholas Toth have demonstrated that flakes such as these would have been quite suitable for butchering animals, and traces of wear on flakes of similar age from Koobi Fora do suggest that they were used for cutting meat (Toth 1987; Keeley and Toth 1981). The cores include unifacially-flaked

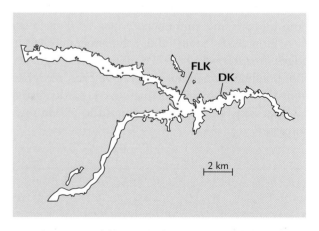

FIGURE 3.2 Olduvai Gorge, Tanzania. The circles mark archaeological sites. Source: After M. Leakey 1971.

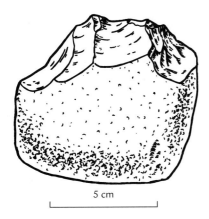

5 cm

FIGURE 3.3   A typical chopping tool made from a basalt pebble from the site of DK, Olduvai Gorge.

choppers and bifacially-flaked **chopping tools** (Figure 3.3), chipped, for the most part, from locally available basalt pebbles (see Archaeology in Practice box, this chapter). A few were made from quartzite. It is not clear whether these cores were actually used as tools, or whether they are simply leftovers from the production of sharp flakes (Toth 1985). Some pebble tools, flaked in several directions to form intersecting edges, are classified as **polyhedrons,** while others made on flattened pebbles are termed **discoids.** Other tools have been classed as **scrapers.** All these artifacts are crude and grade from one form into another. Rather enigmatic artifacts found in the Oldowan are **spheroids**—pebbles flaked over their entire surface to a roughly spherical form. The functions of these objects are unknown, but many of these tools show edges that are chipped and battered from use. Simple flake and core industries, like the Oldowan, are often referred to as **Mode I industries.** The Oldowan represents the earliest part of the **Paleolithic** (paleo means "old," lithic means "stone") or Old Stone Age.

THE NATURE OF THE EARLY ARCHAEOLOGICAL SITES

The lower layers of Olduvai Gorge and the approximately contemporary deposits at Koobi Fora have produced a variety of sites that include artifacts and bones evidencing hominin activity. Attempts to understand and interpret the nature of these sites

have proved challenging and frequently controversial. The true nature of the earliest African archaeological sites has been the subject of intense debate.

When the archaeological deposits at Olduvai Gorge and Koobi Fora were first discovered, archaeologists attempted to interpret them in terms of modern human behavior. Those sites containing concentrations of artifacts and animal bones resembled archaeological sites from later periods that have ordinarily been interpreted as **base camps**— areas occupied by a human group for a period of weeks or months in which a variety of domestic activities took place. Were the similar-appearing sites at Olduvai and Koobi Fora very early examples of base camps?

Some widespread scatters of artifacts had clearly accumulated over a long period of time and had often been redistributed by geologic factors such as erosion. The artifacts and bones in many of the accumulations, however, were concentrated in thin layers and showed little evidence of having been eroded or moved by running water. The excavators, therefore, accepted these deposits as relatively undisturbed evidence for human behavior. Mary Leakey interpreted sites containing the bones of a single animal associated with a small number of artifacts as **butchery** or **kill sites.** Sites that included a concentration of artifacts associated with the bones of a number of different animals, usually representing several species, were interpreted as **living floors.** If these interpretations are accepted, further inferences about early human subsistence and social behavior may follow.

THE INTERPRETATION OF PROTOHUMAN BEHAVIOR

What do the earliest archaeological sites tell us about early human behavior? In the 1970s the early African archaeological sites were widely accepted as primarily the product of protohuman activity, but what function did these sites serve? The interpretation that had gained the most widespread acceptance, advanced by archaeologist Glynn Isaac (1978), was known as the **food-sharing hypothesis.** According to the food-sharing hypothesis, the well-preserved artifact and bone concentrations at

ARCHAEOLOGY IN PRACTICE

The Basics of Working Stone

Stone artifacts (along with bones) are without doubt the most important evidence available for the archaeology of early humans. Unlike many of the materials that may have been used by early hominins, stone is practically indestructible. Early archaeological sites often include artifacts left from every stage of the procurement, manufacture, and use of a stone implement. Archaeologists can recover the raw materials from which the objects were made, waste products from the manufacture process, and the stone tools themselves in every stage, from new, through modification and reuse, to final discard.

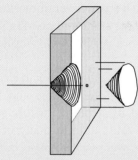

When a projectile such as a BB strikes a pane of plate glass, the force of the impact spreads out as a conical wave, known as the cone of percussion. The glass fractures along this cone, dislodging a conical fragment, and leaving behind a conical hole in the glass. The same effect occurs when a sharp blow is delivered to a homogeneous material such as flint.

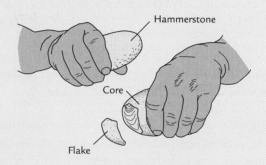

The simplest form of stone working is direct percussion. A nodule of a homogeneous stone such as flint or basalt is struck with a hammerstone to remove a flake or a series of flakes. The stone from which the flake was removed is known as a core. Both the flakes and the core may be used as tools or further worked into other artifacts.

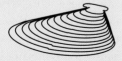

As ripples spread from a rock thrown into a pool of water, ripples may form along the plane of fracture, radiating away from the point of impact. The surface formed resembles a clamshell. This kind of breakage is known as conchoidal fracture.

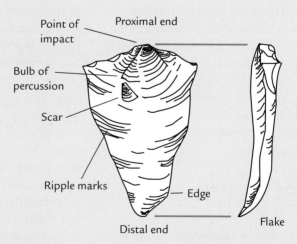

A typical flake, showing some of the terms used to describe it.

Figure 3.A The basic principles of stone flake production.

Through many years of analysis, ethnographic observations, and experimentation, archaeologists now know much about the processes of stone tool manufacture.

Initially, early humans must have made use of whatever stone was conveniently at hand that was suitably sized and shaped for a hammer, pounder, or the like. No one knows how early humans learned that certain types of stone could be flaked, yielding useful fragments with sharp cutting edges. It is evident, however, that the special suitability of certain types of stone was recognized early on and that these stones were intentionally sought out as tool-making materials.

A stone appropriate for being made into flaked stone tools must possess certain characteristic properties: It must be hard enough to produce effective cutting edges; it must break relatively easily when struck with a sharp blow; and it must be sufficiently homogeneous that the breakage can be controlled to produce thin flakes. Stones such as slate or calcite that break, or cleave, along well-defined **planes of cleavage** (planes along which the rocks split easily) or that tend to shatter when struck are far more difficult to work. Usually, stones that are deficient in any of these

properties were only used when better materials were not readily available.

By far the most widely used materials for the manufacture of flaked stone tools belong to a closely related group of fine-grained siliceous stones that includes chalcedony, jasper, flint, and chert. These materials generally were deposited from silica-containing groundwaters into the seams and hollows of limestone bedrock. Erosion may reveal seams of blocky **tabular chert,** while **flint nodules** commonly accumulate in the beds of streams where they may readily be collected. Flint and its relatives exhibit excellent properties for flaking, or knapping. Their constituent mineral, silica, is very hard, and flint edges will cut or scratch almost all other natural materials, including bone. They break very easily when struck with a hammer, yielding large, thin flakes. A skilled flint-knapper can easily control the character of the flakes produced because good-quality flint is very homogeneous. Instead of breaking irregularly or along cleavage planes, flint fractures along a cone, or portion of a cone, radiating from the point of impact (Figure 3.A). Concentric ripple marks usually form so that the surface resembles a seashell. This phenomenon is called

conchoidal fracture (from the Greek word for mussel, *konché*).

At its simplest, a stone striker, known as a **hammerstone,** may be used to detach a flake, or a few flakes, from one side of another stone, such as a flint nodule or a basalt pebble. The stone from which the flakes are detached is called the **core.** It may serve as a source of flakes, or it may itself be used as a **core tool.** A pebble with only a few flakes removed from one side is said to be **unifacially** worked and is called a chopper (Figure 3.B). The core may then be turned over and flakes struck from the opposite side, using the surface from which the flake was detached as a **striking platform.** The ridge between the two opposing sets of flakes forms a sharp edge. Such tools are said to be **bifacially** worked, and they are sometimes distinguished from choppers as chopping tools.

First blow:
A flake is detached

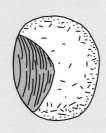
Unifacial chopper

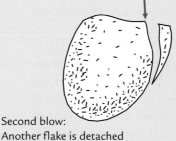
Second blow:
Another flake is detached
from the opposite side of the core

Bifacial chopping tool

Figure 3.B The earliest stone tools: choppers and chopping tools.

Olduvai and Koobi Fora were evidence for home bases, to which protohuman hominins, presumably hunter-scavengers and gatherers, carried meat and other foods for consumption. The most prominent examples of such sites included FLK at Olduvai (the Zinjanthropus floor) and FxJj 50 at Koobi Fora. In its most elaborated form, the food-sharing hypothesis envisaged the hunters (probably males) sharing their quarry with other members of their social group, including juveniles and females, who presumably also contributed to the diet through the gathering of vegetal foods and small animals. Features characteristic of modern human societies, therefore, such as family organization and the sexual division of labor, were seen as having their roots in this very early period.

Archaeologists believed they were justified in creating this scenario because they perceived a trail of similar archaeological evidence leading backward from the present into the past. Concentrations of artifacts and food refuse can be observed accumulating around the camps of modern hunter-gatherers. Similar features are commonly found in relatively recent archaeological contexts, such as in Native American sites in North America or in late Stone Age sites in Africa or Europe. That these latter-day sites represent encampments has not been questioned. Sites such as DK and FLK strongly resemble these later campsites, and they were initially accepted by their excavators as similar in nature. The bone refuse within the sites, including the skeletal remains of a wide variety of animals, large and small, was assumed to be primarily the result of hominin activities. These hominins clearly ate meat, and since the food remains were concentrated at what appeared to be a home base, the hominins very likely shared the meat among the members of their group.

In the early 1980s, Lewis Binford (1981) sharply criticized the food-sharing hypothesis. Much of his criticism, and most of the extended debate that followed, has centered on the site **FLK** at Olduvai Gorge, where the Zinjanthropus fossil was found. FLK is one of the most fully studied of the living floor sites. Binford challenged the interpretation of FLK along two lines. First, according to Binford, the *integrity* of FLK as an undisturbed archaeological site had not been established, and

further, the period of time during which the deposit at FLK had accumulated (the *resolution* of the site) was unknown. Therefore, the relationships among the artifacts and the bones were suspect. Second, Binford performed a statistical analysis of the animal bones based on the preliminary data included in Mary Leakey's 1971 report. Binford concluded that the assemblage of types of animal bones did not resemble what would be expected of a hunter's refuse, but rather that of a hominin "scavenging the kills and death sites of other predator-scavengers for abandoned anatomical parts of low food utility" (Binford 1981: 282). In effect, Binford turned the humanlike depiction of the food-sharing hypothesis on its head, and instead describes the FLK hominins as, at best, marginal scavengers.

HOW WERE THE OLDUVAI AND KOOBI FORA SITES FORMED?

Many of Binford's points were well taken, but the implications of the food-sharing hypothesis as well as the character of the Olduvai and Koobi Fora sites had been coming under close scrutiny well before the publication of Binford's critiques. The most crucial question to be resolved was whether or not these sites had been formed by the activities of hominins. Several alternative explanations were possible:

◆ The sites may have been created by natural forces, particularly the action of running water.

◆ The accumulations of artifacts and bones may have been accidental associations that built up over a very extended period of time.

◆ The accumulations of bones may have been created by scavenging carnivores and later utilized by hominins.

◆ The bone and artifact accumulations may have been created by hominins and later acted upon by scavenging carnivores.

Taphonomy is the study of the processes by which bones and artifacts finally become incorporated into a site and of the factors that modify the composition of those assemblages. Figure 3.4 illustrates some of the processes that probably influenced the buildup of the combination of bones and artifacts that eventually

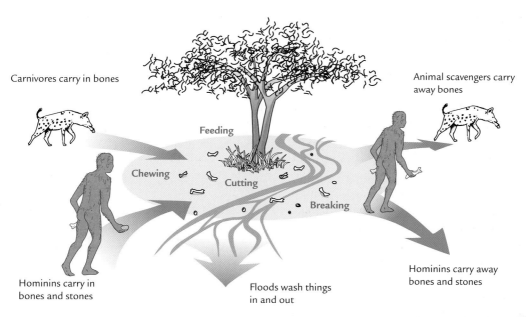

Carnivores carry in bones

Animal scavengers carry away bones

Feeding

Chewing

Cutting

Breaking

Hominins carry in bones and stones

Floods wash things in and out

Hominins carry away bones and stones

FIGURE 3.4 A variety of processes result in the adding, rearrangement, modification, and removal of bones and artifacts at an archaeological site. Source: Adapted from an illustration by Isaac 1983.

characterized the Olduvai and Koobi Fora sites. In the 1970s a number of archaeologists began detailed taphonomic studies of these sites. From this work (Kroll and Isaac 1984; Bunn 1982; Bunn and Kroll 1986), the following points may be drawn:

◆ Although the sites had been moved about slightly by gently moving water and covered by waterborne deposits, none of the sites showed any geological evidence of water that moved swiftly enough to account for the observed accumulation.

◆ The densities of artifacts and bones are much greater in the site areas than in surrounding areas.

◆ The layers containing artifacts and bones are quite thin, generally less than 10 cm (4 in.), and many fragments of stone tools and pieces of animal bone can be fitted back together (see the Archaeology in Practice box in Chapter 4), indicating that those bones were deposited at the same time and that the stone tools were manufactured on the spot. For example, at the 2.34-million-year-old site of Lokalalei 2C in Kenya, 60 stone cores could be refitted (Roche 1999).

◆ The degree of weathering on the bones indicates that they were exposed on the surface for varying times up to about 10 years. There are differing opinions as to whether this represents the time during which the site was occupied (Potts 1988) or the time it took for a very brief occupation to be completely covered (Bunn and Kroll 1986), but the period of accumulation appears to have been short in geological terms.

Taken together, this evidence makes a good case that the Olduvai and Koobi Fora sites and other early Oldowan sites were not chance phenomena, long-term accumulations, or accidental water-laid deposits. Who, then, created them?

WHO CREATED THE SITES? THE ROLES OF CARNIVORES AND HOMININS

As discussed in Chapter 2, scavengers such as hyenas are known to have collected accumulations of food bones in their dens. Could these sites have been primarily the product of scavenging carnivores such as hyenas? Richard Potts (1988) examined this possibility in some detail. When the assemblage of animal bones from the Olduvai sites was compared with that recovered from a known hyena den, there were some similarities, but there were also differences, notably in the proportions of the ends versus the shafts of bones. Bunn and Kroll (1986) noted that at FLK the proportion of gnawed bones is far lower than that observed in carnivore accumulations. Further, the presence of stone artifacts points unambiguously to hominin involvement; it is rather difficult to picture early hominins confronting scavenging carnivores in their den to obtain a few remaining scraps of food. The weight of the evidence, therefore, seems to point to the Olduvai and Koobi Fora sites as primarily the result of hominin activities, and today most investigators accept this interpretation.

If hominins carried the animal bones (and, presumably, the surrounding meat and/or marrow) into the sites, how did they obtain them? There is clear-cut evidence that both hominins and carnivores acted on the bone assemblage. The initial assumption, underlying the food-sharing hypothesis, was that hominins hunted the animals, or at least most of them. Binford's assertion, on the contrary, was that carnivores killed the animals and hominins merely collected the scavenged remnants. The implications of these opposing interpretations were in marked contrast:

- If hominins were the primary hunters, large portions of meat were being brought to the sites—too much for a single meal, but enough to be shared among the other members of the social group.

- If, on the other hand, only the meat-stripped remnants of carnivore kills were being carried in by the hominins, all that would be available would be some scraps of meat and the marrow that could be obtained by cracking open the long bones—enough to feed a single individual. There would be no food sharing.

Does the truth lie at either of these extremes, or somewhere between? Differences of opinion are almost as numerous as there are scholars in the field. Lewis Binford still holds to his interpretation based primarily on the published data. Other workers have extended the analyses of the Olduvai and Koobi Fora animal bones. These more detailed studies include a complete analysis of the fauna from FLK by H. T. Bunn as well as studies by several workers, including Bunn, R. Potts, P. Shipman, and R. Blumenschine, of **butchery marks** appearing on the bones. These butchery studies have provided the primary evidence for the relative roles of hominins and carnivores.

CUT MARKS ON BONE: BUTCHERY AT OLDUVAI AND KOOBI FORA

When hunters or herders skin an animal for its pelt, dismember it, or remove meat for food, cuts and scrapes are left on the bones. Bone may be intentionally broken too, most often for the removal of marrow. Blumenschine (1995; Blumenschine and Selvaggio 1988) has identified a class of marks known as **percussion marks** that result from the use of a hammer stone to break open a bone for marrow extraction (Figure 3.5). Archaeologists have long been aware that cut marks on bones and the way bones are fragmented can yield clues to the activities that produced the bone assemblage.

In addition to butchery there are, of course, other sources for the marks found on bone surfaces, and sometimes those marks can be quite difficult to distinguish from cuts. Such marks include certain natural features of the bone, marks left by rootlets on the bone surface, scratches caused by

FIGURE 3.5 Percussion marks on an animal bone from Olduvai.

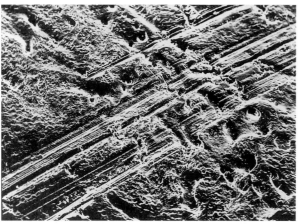

a.

b.

FIGURE 3.6 Bone marks: a. SEM of cut-marked bone; b. SEM of bone gnawed by a carnivore.

trampling on the bone, and marks left during the course of excavation. Of particular interest are the tooth marks left behind when carnivores gnaw on bones.

Henry Bunn (1983) examined the animal bones from FLK (and some roughly contemporary sites at Olduvai and Koobi Fora), relying for the most part on observations at low magnifications. He observed that several hundred of the bones bore cut marks on their surfaces. A methodologically different approach had been taken by Richard Potts and Pat Shipman (1981), who chose to study a sample of about 20 cut-marked bones from several Olduvai sites using the scanning electron microscope (SEM). Bones were also experimentally cut and scored in a variety of ways, and the results documented with the SEM. Their goal was to establish a set of criteria for unambiguously identifying cut marks (Figure 3.6). Shipman (1986) has since followed up on this work with an SEM study of about 200 bones from Olduvai with cutlike markings. Shipman's criteria for accepting a mark as a stone tool cut are considerably more conservative than those of Bunn.

Not too surprisingly, Bunn, Shipman, and Potts reached some quite different conclusions about the meaning of the Olduvai bones. All these investigators, however, agree that many of the bones show unambiguous cut marks from stone tools as well as numerous tooth marks from carnivore gnawing. In

several cases tooth marks and cut marks overlap—sometimes the tooth marks came after the cuts; in other cases, the tooth marks were there first.

Were these early hominins hunters, or did they scavenge the meat brought down by other carnivores? It is clear that both carnivores and hominins had access to the bones. Sometimes the carnivores had them first; at other times carnivores chewed the bones after the hominins left them. Even more complex scenarios are possible. The bones may have been defleshed by carnivores; humans may have removed the flesh scraps and marrow; and then carnivores may have further ravaged the bones (Selvaggio 1998). Unfortunately, the cut-mark evidence is ambiguous, and it has been interpreted in diametrically opposing ways.

Bunn and Kroll (1986) emphasize the frequent cut marks they found on the shafts of meaty bones, as well as the presence of cuts around the ends of bones. The marks near the ends of bones, they argue, indicate that the bones were cut apart (presumably for transport away from a carcass) and that the cuts on the bone shafts indicate that substantial portions of meat were available on the bones. The cut marks seen on upper limb bones are especially significant, since these regions are usually devoid of flesh at carnivore kill sites (Domínguez-Rodrigo 2002). This evidence implies that the hominins had access to the meat before it had been consumed by

CASE STUDY

The Interpretation of Early Hominin Behavior: The DK Controversy

In 1962 Mary Leakey undertook the excavation of the site **DK** in Bed I of Olduvai Gorge. The site lies below a volcanic tuff dated to 1.75 million years ago and rests on a layer of lava. DK contains numerous stone artifacts, mostly of basalt, plus a wide variety of animal bones. Stone artifacts and bones were found throughout the deposit.

A unique feature at DK, however, sets it apart from all the other very ancient sites. As reported by Mary Leakey (1971), a rough circle of blocks of basalt about 4 m (13 ft.) in diameter lay on the old soil surface (Figure 3.C). Most of these stones were 10 to 15 cm (4 to 6 in.) in diameter, and some of the stones were piled in heaps about 30 cm (12 in.) in height. Some stone was also scattered within the circle. The circle, in fact, was not immediately recognized, and a portion of it was destroyed before the excavators realized what it was. The positions of the removed stones had all been previously recorded, however, so the plan of the entire circle could be restored.

Mary Leakey suggested that the piles of stone at DK may have anchored wooden poles or branches to form a crude shelter or windbreak. The circle was very reminiscent of features commonly found in sites of much later periods, and, as illustrated in the Olduvai site report, the present-day Okombambi people of Namibia build branch and grass shelters held down by a ring of stones at the base. If the DK circle had been found in a late Stone Age site, its acceptance as an architectural feature would likely be unquestioned.

The Reinterpretation of DK

Today, few archaeologists accept the DK circle as representing an ancient structure. The controversy surrounding the site, however, illustrates the difficulty of interpreting the behavior of the earliest hominins and shows how greatly a scientist's preconceptions can influence his or her interpretation of what is observed. Lewis Binford (1981: 254), in particular, has vigorously challenged Mary Leakey's interpretation of DK on two grounds. First, Binford questions whether DK, among other sites, can realistically be considered a living floor. The designation "living floor" implies a relatively undisturbed site including the remains from a brief, well-defined period of occupation. Binford argues that the deposits at DK probably built up over a long period of time. Binford's principal evidence for this contention is the large number of crocodile teeth found in the site. DK was located on a lake margin. The teeth were gradually shed by the crocodiles living in the lake; a long period of time must have passed for the more than 4600 teeth found at DK to have accumulated. Binford concludes, therefore, that the interpretation of DK as a living floor cannot be supported by the evidence. Second, Binford argues that the interpretation of the stone circle as human-constructed was influenced by the excavator's acceptance of the DK deposit as primarily the product of human activity. The South African windbreaks that had been offered as parallels were created by modern humans, not early members of the genus *Homo* who lived nearly 2 million years ago. It is problematic to project the behavior of modern humans onto *Homo habilis*,

other carnivores, and therefore the early hominins were either hunters or they scavenged meat so aggressively that they drove away other animals before they had an opportunity to eat their kill (Bunn 1991). This process has recently been termed "power scavenging" (Bunn 2001). Shipman (1986), on the other hand, argues that the proportion of cuts near the ends of bones is too low to indicate the regular disarticulation of the limb bones. She suggests instead that bones were largely free of meat

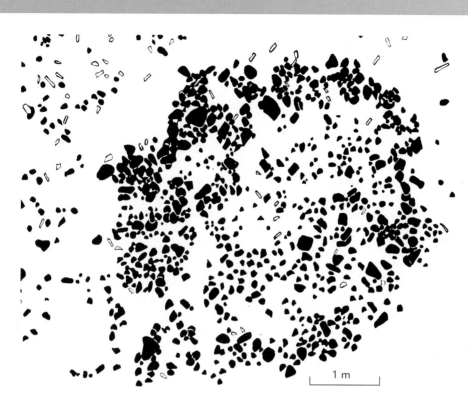

FIGURE 3.C   The circle of basalt stones at DK, Olduvai Gorge. Source: After M. Leakey 1971, Figure 7.

especially since *H. habilis* lacked fire. Fire, which can be used for warmth, protection from predators, and the preparation of food, is one of the principal features of modern human campsites. Without fire for protection, the concentration of food in a home base would have been very attractive to predators; it might have been a very dangerous place indeed for early humans.

Binford offers no alternative interpretation of the circle, which he concedes is enigmatic. One alternative, suggested by Richard Potts (1984: 345), is that the stones were thrust up from the underlying lava layer by the action of tree roots. This possibility is yet to be investigated. Although Binford had no alternative explanations, his critique has been strongly influential. While archaeologists remain sharply divided about his specific conclusions, they generally agree that the interpretation of early sites must include a broad range of alternatives and that any hypotheses put forward must be rigorously tested against the evidence. Moreover, we cannot assume that ancient hominins behaved the same way as anatomically modern humans do.

when they were obtained—that is, the bones were scavenged.

Potts (1988) takes an intermediate position. He argues that hominins scavenged from carnivores' kills at a fairly early stage, while there was still substantial meat available. Potts (1988: 202, 218) points out that not all the marrow-bearing bone was smashed to obtain the last bit of nourishment and enough food was left to attract carnivores back to the bones.

While the cut marks and tooth marks on bones have provided some intriguing evidence, how this evidence can be applied to the hunting-versus-scavenging controversy remains to be resolved. It is clear that hominins had begun to eat meat; less clear is how it was obtained and just how much meat was available. The assumption that these early hominins were either hunters or marginal scavengers is probably an oversimplification. They may have both hunted and scavenged as the opportunity presented itself, or they may have scavenged aggressively enough to obtain carcasses with a substantial amount of meat. The disentangling of these complex possibilities has proved extremely difficult. Nevertheless, the shift to a higher protein diet may have provided the energy needed for cranial expansion and increased body size (Milton 1999).

EXPLAINING THE SITES: ALTERNATIVE HYPOTHESES

Regardless of how they were obtained, animal carcasses appear to have been transported by hominins to limited locations, where they were further processed. Why were certain locations chosen? It is difficult to find much in the setting of the archaeological sites that sets them apart from the surrounding area. One possibility is that these locations were shady or even that hominins could climb into groups of trees for their protection from competing carnivores (Isaac 1983). Still, dangerous carnivores would likely be attracted to the accumulations of bone in such areas. It is possible that early humans worked cooperatively to defend localities that offered water, trees, and food resources from predators (Rose and Marshall 1996).

Richard Potts (1984) has suggested instead that the availability of stone for the making of tools determined the site locations. Suitable stone would have been difficult to transport; instead, according to his hypothesis, it would have been cached at various locations on the landscape. The carcasses, however acquired, would then be brought to the caches for processing. This activity would be carried out as expediently as possible, and the site would be abandoned before competing carnivores put in their appearance. Potts's hypothesis accounts

for the overlapping of tooth and cut marks, and it also helps explain the occurrence of the bones of many other animals surrounding the main skeleton at the so-called butchery sites. According to Potts's scenario, the discovery of the large carcass would have led the hominins to bring the needed stone tools to the location. These tools were then left there, and other animals were brought to the spot for butchery. The **stone cache hypothesis** has been criticized as crediting these hominins with an unlikely degree of foresight and planning (Binford 1985). Potts (1988) has countered that it is merely a matter of remembering where the caches of stone are. Alternatively, early humans may have carried stone tools with them while foraging. Chimps have been observed carrying tools to foraging sites, and some Oldowan assemblages include tools made of nonlocal materials (Plummer et al. 1999). Early humans may have carried cores and struck off flakes as needed for cutting and slicing tasks.

SUCCESSFUL SCAVENGERS?

The interpretation of the animal bone data offered by Bunn and Kroll suggests that early sites were indeed created by hominins who hunted and obtained substantial amounts of meat through aggressive scavenging. Binford's and Shipman's views suggest that meat was obtained from scavenged carnivore kills. Some archaeologists have seen scavenging as marginal activity, unlikely to provide the abundance of food resources that might have encouraged food sharing. Recent studies, however, have shown that under certain conditions natural mortality can provide scavengers with large amounts of meat.

Robert Blumenschine (1986, 1987) has carried out extensive studies of the activities of scavengers in the modern Serengeti and Ngorongoro. His work has made clear that an abundance of scavenging opportunities can be found in the woodlands bordering lakes and streams, the kinds of environments in which the Olduvai and Koobi Fora sites were located. Food resources vary depending on the time of year. During the dry season, starvation leaves numerous carcasses accessible to scavengers. Lions kill large animals, mostly during the dry season, and sometimes abandon their carcasses for extended periods of time. These resources would have been available to early hominins, but at some risk on the open plain. A safer resource, available all year round, would have been the carcasses of mid-sized animals that leopards frequently store in trees, where they are hidden from competing scavengers such as hyenas and vultures. As pointed out by Blumenschine and Cavallo (1992), hominins could have exploited these opportunities, filling out their normally vegetarian diets with meat and marrow during the dry season, when suitable plants were less available. By beating out competitors, they might well have carved out a niche that could provide them, as scavengers, with sufficient surplus to make food sharing possible.

CONCLUSION

Although archaeologists may disagree on the interpretation of the very early archaeological sites, the archaeology of early humans has revealed several important aspects of their behavior. It is clear that early humans made and used stone tools. One way these early stone tools were used was to remove meat from animal carcasses. This use demonstrates that meat played a role in the diet of these early humans. Finally, it is clear that the behavior of these early humans differed from the behavior of both modern humans and nonhuman primates such as chimpanzees. It is only through detailed archaeological investigations that we can begin to reconstruct the behavior of the ancient hominins.

KEY TERMS

Base camp 53
Bifacially 55
Butchery marks 58
Butchery site 53
Chopper 53
Chopping tool 53
Conchoidal fracture 55
Core 55
Core tool 55
Discoid 53
DK 60
Flint nodule 55

FLK 56
Food-sharing hypothesis 53
Hammerstone 55
Lithic industry 52
Kill site 53
Living floor 53
Mode I industry 53
Oldowan 52
Paleolithic 53
Percussion marks 58
Plane of cleavage 55

Polyhedron 53
Scraper 53
Spheroid 53
Stone cache hypothesis 62

Striking platform 55
Tabular chert 55
Taphonomy 56
Unifacially 55

QUESTIONS FOR DISCUSSION

1. Do you think that early members of the genus *Homo* were hunters, active scavengers, or passive scavengers? Why?

2. How can the study of chimp and other primate tool use contribute to our understanding of tool use by early hominins?

3. Compare and contrast the food-sharing hypothesis and the stone cache hypothesis. What kind of evidence is used to support each model?

FURTHER READING

Blumenschine, R. J., and J. A. Cavallo
1992 Scavenging and Human Evolution. *Scientific American* 267 (4): 90–96.
The authors argue that early hominins may have succeeded as efficient scavengers rather than as hunters.

Domínguez-Rodrigo, Manuel
2002 Hunting and Scavenging by Early Humans: The State of the Debate. *Journal of World Prehistory* 16 (1): 1–54.
An up-to-date review of the subject. The author argues that early hominins had access to fleshy carcasses before other carnivores had access to them.

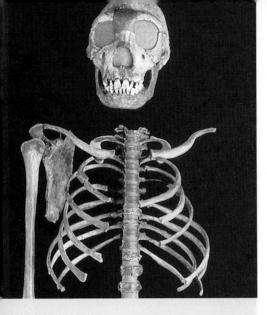

4

HOMO ERGASTER AND THE LOWER PALEOLITHIC IN AFRICA AND THE NEAR EAST

At about 1.81 million years ago, the earth's climate changed. That time marks the beginning of the **Pleistocene** epoch, commonly known as the "Ice Age," a period marked by low global temperatures and substantial climatic oscillations. In the northern latitudes, the Pleistocene is characterized by a series of cold phases or **glacials,** when ice sheets covered much of Europe and North America, and warmer phases known as **interglacials.** During the colder phases, much of the earth's water was trapped in the glacial ice, leading to lower worldwide sea levels.

In Africa, the home of early hominins, the climatic changes associated with the beginning of the Pleistocene were not as marked. However, the period around 1.8 million years ago is characterized by increasing aridity in southern and eastern Africa. Savanna grasslands expanded at the expense of woodland and forest. A number of large African carnivores, including saber-toothed and false saber-toothed tigers, became extinct at the beginning of the Pleistocene. Some archaeologists (Marean 1989) have suggested that the extinction of these large carnivores may have limited scavenging opportunities for early members of the genus *Homo* in Africa.

At this time a new hominin species appeared in Africa (Rightmire 1990). This species was originally identified as *Homo erectus* because of its similarities to early Pleistocene fossils initially found in Java in the nineteenth century (see Chapter 5). Today, however, many anthropologists use the name *Homo ergaster* for the African and Near Eastern fossils[1]. Unlike *Homo habilis* and *Homo*

---

[1]In this text, we will use the term *Homo erectus* in its broadest sense, including both *Homo erectus* and the fossils that some anthropologists call *Homo ergaster*.

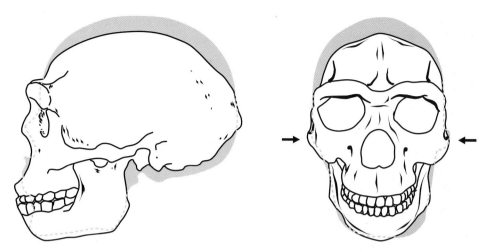

FIGURE 4.1 Skull shape of *Homo erectus* (front) compared with *Homo sapiens* (rear). Arrows point to location of greatest breadth of *Homo erectus* skull.

rudolfensis, which were small hominins with relatively short legs and long arms, *Homo ergaster* had a taller and more modern body. Although this species possessed a brain considerably smaller than that of modern humans, it was larger than the brains of earlier African hominins such as *Homo habilis.* The top of the thick-boned skull was flattened rather than rounded. A heavy bar surmounted the eye sockets; behind the orbits of the eyes the skull was markedly narrower (constricted) compared with modern humans (Figure 4.1). When viewed from behind, the widest part of the skull of *Homo erectus* is set much lower than in modern humans, again due to the smaller brain size. The cranial capacity ranges from 650 to 1250 ml, compared to an average of 1350 ml for modern humans. The face projects forward, and the heavy lower jaw lacks a chin. The teeth of *Homo erectus* are also larger than those of modern humans.

Until recently, little was known of the stance, stature, or appearance of early *Homo erectus* in Africa. Most of the fossil finds were skull fragments, with only a few bones from below the neck to provide clues. Then, in the summer of 1984, a group of investigators led by Richard Leakey, working in a deposit approximately 1.6 million years old at **Nariokotome III** near Lake Turkana, Kenya, uncovered the skeleton of a young boy. Soon nicknamed the Turkana Boy, it proved to be the most complete specimen of *Homo erectus*[2] yet discovered (Walker and Leakey 1993). The skeleton lacked only its hands and feet (Figure 4.2).

The teeth and limb bones indicate that the boy was approximately 11 years old. He died among the reeds growing in the still, shallow water at the banks of a lake or slow-moving river. Little evidence survives to indicate how he died; nothing on the bones suggests that he was attacked by an animal. No tools or other artifacts were found with the body. The only clue to possible ill health was some

---

[2]The Turkana specimen was originally identified as *Homo erectus,* but today many scholars consider it *Homo ergaster.*

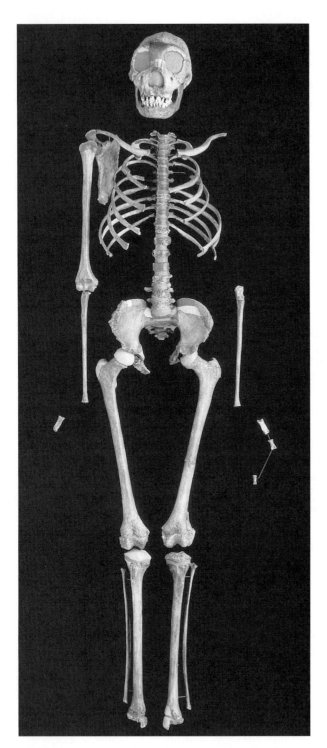

FIGURE 4.2 The Turkana Boy—Nariokotome III—
Homo ergaster (originally *H. erectus*).

resorption of the jawbone around his teeth, the result of periodontal infection. Without modern antibiotics, infections of this kind can lead to very serious consequences, even death. Usually, when the earliest humans died, their bodies fell prey to the same fate as those of any other animal, to be consumed by scavengers, the bones destroyed or scattered far and wide. The circumstances of the Turkana Boy's death must have resulted in the rapid burial of the body, hiding it from the view of scavengers. The body lay facedown in the water, where it was soon covered with silt. Apart from some trampling and water transport of the bones, the skeleton suffered little disturbance until very recently—when the bones were discovered, a large tree was growing among them.

The Turkana Boy possessed a low, sloping skull without a forehead, which housed a brain about two-thirds the size of a modern human's brain. The postcranial (body) skeleton, however, although differing in some details, was much like that of modern humans. Had the boy grown to be an adult, he would have been quite tall, perhaps 180 cm (6 ft.) in height. Comparison of this complete skeleton with the other, more isolated, finds of limb bones from Africa shows that his height was not atypical—as a group *Homo ergaster/Homo erectus* was much taller than the preceding *Homo habilis* (around 150 cm, or 5 ft., in height). The Turkana Boy's tall and slender body type, which maximizes the ratio of heat-radiating surface to body bulk, would have been well adapted to coping with the heat of the tropics. Some modern African peoples have similar body builds. Some of the details of the boy's pelvis and femurs (thigh bones) retain some traits characteristic of earlier hominins, but the overall configuration suggests that he was a very effective walker and runner, perhaps better at those activities than modern humans. Physically, *Homo erectus* was well equipped to be an effective hunter, gatherer, or active scavenger.

THE ACHEULIAN INDUSTRY

No stone tools were found with the Turkana Boy, but at about this same time (about 1.6 million years ago), a new form of stone tool appeared in Africa alongside the simple flakes and choppers that typified the Oldowan stone industry. The Oldowan tools had required little more than a moment's thought and a few blows from a hammerstone to produce the sharp cutting edge needed to butcher an animal. The new tool, the **handaxe,** was very different (Wynn 1995). A handaxe is a large stone tool, usually oval, with a flattened cross section (see Figure 4.3a). The tool was made by removing a series of flakes from both sides of a stone core to produce a length of relatively straight cutting edge. Usually, one end was relatively pointed; the other, more rounded so that it could be held in the hand. Early archaeologists called these tools handaxes, because they presumed that the tools were unhafted hacking implements held in the hand.

The first truly standardized tool form, the handaxe was the result of a definite, preconceived idea in the mind of its maker. Planning and considerable stoneworking skill were required to make a handaxe. Most important, the making of handaxes became a tradition, passed from maker to maker, down through the millennia. With the appearance of the handaxe, culture—the transmission of shared ideas from generation to generation—becomes evident as a dominant force in the shaping of human development.

The handaxe is the hallmark of the **Acheulian industry** (Clark 1994), named after the **type site** at Saint-Acheul, a suburb of Amiens in northern France, where the industry was first described. (A site that gives its name to an industry is known as a type site.) At first, handaxes were irregular and crudely made. Over the many thousands of years during which they were made, they gradually became thin, symmetrical, and skillfully crafted, and they were made in a wide variety of forms. Some of this variation can be explained by the raw materials used in handaxe production (see McPherron 2000). At the start of the Acheulian industry, other large forms usually accompanied the handaxes. Some typical forms, such as **trihedral picks** and **cleavers,** are shown in Figure 4.3. Tool types characteristic of

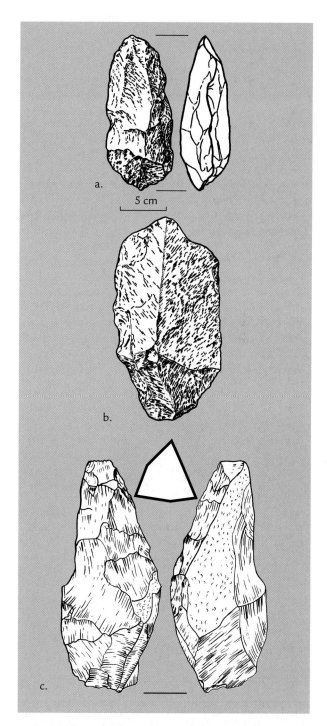

5 cm

FIGURE 4.3 Acheulian industry tools: a. Acheulian handaxe (basalt) from Olduvai Gorge; b. Acheulian cleaver (quartzite) from MNK, Olduvai Gorge; c. trihedral pick (basalt) from 'Ubeidiya, Israel.

ARCHAEOLOGY IN PRACTICE

Experimental Archaeology: How Were Stone Tools Made and Used?

For almost the entirety of human existence, stone has been the primary raw material for the manufacture of weapons and tools. Before the discovery of metallurgy, much of the history of technology consisted of the development of new ways to shape and use stone. Archaeologists, therefore, have a great interest in understanding these processes. Today, however, with only rare exceptions, the knapping, or flaking, of stone to produce useful objects has become a lost art.

Fortunately, the art was not completely unknown. In the late nineteenth century, the English antiquarian John Evans was interested in trying to replicate the handaxes he had seen coming from archaeological sites. At that time at Brandon in eastern England, workers were still mining and knapping flint (Figure 4.A). They were shaping the flints into gunflints—small, square fragments of flint that were fixed into the mechanism of flintlock pistols and muskets.

Evans observed and described the gunflint workers' techniques, and he applied what he observed to an attempt to replicate ancient stone tools. Over the years since Evans's time, a number of archaeologists have concentrated on replicating the techniques by which stone tools were made. Sometimes ethnographic sources have provided some clues. Although stone tools had long since ceased to be made in Europe and the Americas, some Pacific Islanders still made and used stone implements though the eighteenth and nineteenth centuries. A few rare groups even continued to make them in the twentieth century. Nicholas Toth and his co-workers (Toth et al. 1992) were able to observe a group of New Guinea highlanders making and using stone axes for woodcutting, using techniques much like those that must have been used throughout the Old and New Stone Ages (Figure 4.B).

More often, the experiments are a matter of guessing the most

Figure 4.A Nineteenth-century flint workers at Brandon, England, making flints for use in firearms. Such flints were used to create the spark that fired a flintlock musket or pistol.

Figure 4.B New Guinea highlanders making stone axes.

likely practical technique. The results of these trials are then compared with the ancient artifacts to see how closely the finished products match in form, sequence of flake removal, and details of flake characteristics. Sometimes the flakes removed during the manufacture of an ancient stone tool can be found and fitted back together. This provides another source of evidence for the sequence of flake removal that the experimenter needs to duplicate. If the match is very close, the experimental technique may be much like that used in the past.

In recent years the **refitting** of artifacts, particularly lithics (stone tools), has become an increasingly important archaeological technique (Figure 4.C). Although the technique is simple, it is not easy. Reassembling a lithic jigsaw puzzle demands the extensive examination and painstaking manipulation of large assemblages of artifacts. Artifact refitting can yield information about past behavior that goes well beyond the reconstruction of flint-knapping techniques. Reassembling the trimming flakes onto a stone core, for instance, illustrates the sequence of flake removal from the core. If a core and its trimming flakes are all found in a single area of the site, that area may represent the workshop area where a stone tool was made. (Depending on what is found, it might also represent an area in which waste materials were dumped.) Sometimes cores and flakes and finished tools that can be refitted, or **conjoined,** are found in separate areas of a site. This might represent the separation of areas of stone tool manufacture and use, or the circulation or exchange of artifacts within an encampment. Artifact refitting can also yield very valuable information about the processes by which a site was formed. Broad scatters of conjoinable artifacts, especially

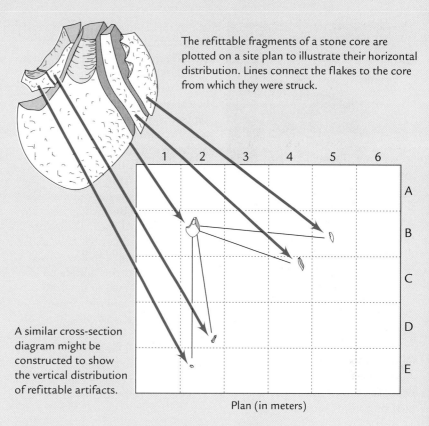

The refittable fragments of a stone core are plotted on a site plan to illustrate their horizontal distribution. Lines connect the flakes to the core from which they were struck.

A similar cross-section diagram might be constructed to show the vertical distribution of refittable artifacts.

Plan (in meters)

Figure 4.C The technique of artifact refitting.

if they are distributed through several vertical layers, are strong evidence that the site was disturbed after it was originally deposited. Conversely, provided that site stratigraphy is clear and unambiguous, conjoinable artifacts spanning two or more artifact scatters are a strong indication that the scatters were formed contemporaneously.

Archaeologist Nicholas Toth has performed some interesting experiments in attempting to duplicate and use some of the characteristic Oldowan and early Acheulian stone tools found in the earliest African sites (Toth 1987). Toth made choppers and chopping tools as well as Acheulian-like handaxes. He noted that the ancient tools were asymmetrical in the way that the flakes were removed from the core. This is a result of which hand held the core

and which hand held the hammerstone. Comparing these tools with his experiments, Toth determined that the ancient African hominins were predominantly right-handed, just as people are today.

Toth then used these tools, as well as the flakes produced in making them, to butcher a wide variety of animals ranging from goats and sheep through wildebeests, up to the butchery of an elephant. He found that simple, unretouched flakes were most effective for cutting up a large animal carcass. Toth suggested that too much emphasis has been placed on core tools, and that the importance of simple flakes in these early sites must be taken into account. Choppers do serve well, however, for breaking up bones, and Toth found that an Acheulian handaxe was effective

Figure 4.D Nicholas Toth butchering a large game animal using a handaxe he replicated. The animal died of natural causes.

in disarticulating the joints of very large animals (Figure 4.D).

Experiments like these can show that certain types of stone implements were usable for a variety of butchery tasks, but they do not prove that the ancient tools were actually used in these ways. Further evidence can come from the marks left by tools on the ancient bones, as was discussed in Chapter 3. The use of stone tools for various tasks may also leave distinctive wear patterns on the tool itself. These patterns can sometimes tell how, and on what material, a tool was used. Some specialists concentrate on experiments designed to determine the distinctive patterns of microscopic chipping, scratches, and polish left on the edges and surfaces of flint tools when the tools are used to cut meat, work wood, dig in the earth, and so on. They can then apply those observations to prehis-

toric artifacts, and sometimes it has been possible to determine how the ancient tools were used. Although most of the African Oldowan and Acheulian tools were made of basalt, which is too coarse-grained for such analysis, a few finer-grained tools did show wear consistent with cutting meat, working wood, and cutting vegetation (Toth 1987).

the Oldowan persisted, such as choppers, spheroids, and polyhedrons. The true function of the Acheulian handaxe is not really known; it may have served as a weapon, a chopper, or a digging tool. When archaeologists have looked closely, they have found that Acheulian sites contain numerous flakes along with the large tools. Flakes would have been produced during tool manufacture, but would also have served as very effective cutting implements in themselves.

The Oldowan and Acheulian industries make up the Lower (or Early) Paleolithic, the earliest part of the Stone Age. The Acheulian industry was to be one of the longest-lasting and one of the most geographically widespread technological traditions in all of prehistory. The earliest Acheulian assemblage known so far was found at the base of the deposits at **Konso-Gardula** in Ethiopia, dated to 1.6 million years ago (Asfaw et al. 1992). The industry persisted for almost 1.5 million years, giving way to

new forms of stone tools only within the last 200,000 years. Today, archaeologists have found Acheulian stone artifacts throughout all of Africa, most of western Europe, and much of western Asia as well.

THE CONTROL OF FIRE

Some scant, but tantalizing, evidence suggests that *Homo erectus* may have achieved an important technological breakthrough even before expanding out of Africa. The control of fire (although not necessarily the ability to create it) would have greatly improved human chances to thrive and expand in the harsher, colder world north of sub-Saharan Africa.

The recognition of the earliest use of fire in the archaeological record is not easy. The remnants of burning—charcoal, ashes, burned bones, or burned and baked soil—may be found but may be the result of natural fires, which occurred frequently. The least ambiguous evidence for the control of fire is a constructed hearth, but hearths do not appear until relatively late in the archaeological record. Burned clay was found at the Oldowan site of **Chesowanja,** Kenya, dated to 1.4 million years ago, in a concentration that might represent a hearth, with a skull belonging to *Paranthropus boisei* nearby (Gowlett et al. 1981). This fire, though, might have been the result of natural causes.

Clearer evidence comes from Swartkrans Cave, South Africa, although here too, some archaeologists suggest that the burning may have resulted from natural causes (Klein 1999: 350). Swartkrans is estimated to date between 1 million and 1.5 million years ago. Although no hearths have been found, one of the layers does contain evidence of fire. Of nearly 60,000 animal bones found in the layer, 270 bones, mostly of antelope, were burned (Brain and Sillen 1988; Sillen and Brain 1990). Experiments indicate that the bones were heated to the temperatures found in campfires. The only hominin found in the layer containing burned bones was *Paranthropus robustus,* but earlier deposits in the cave contain fossils of both *P. robustus* and *Homo erectus.* The burned bones were scattered through many different levels, indicating that fires were a repeated occurrence. The evidence does not indicate, though, whether the fire was used for heat, cooking, or protection from predators, or which of the hominins used the fire.

WHEN AND WHY DID HOMININS EXPAND OUT OF AFRICA?

Prior to about 1.8 million years ago, hominin fossils and archaeological sites are known only from the continent of Africa. Shortly after the appearance of *Homo ergaster/erectus,* archaeological sites appear in the Middle East and Southeast Asia for the first time. Anthropologists sometimes refer to this event as Out of Africa 1. (Out of Africa 2 describes the spread of modern humans out of Africa beginning about 100,000 years ago and will be discussed in Chapters 6 and 7). The dispersal process was probably somewhat sporadic (Bar-Yosef and Belfer-Cohen 2001: 19) and probably took place over hundreds of thousands of years.

The reasons why early humans moved out of Africa remain elusive. One possibility is that the larger brains and bodies of *Homo ergaster/erectus* required a richer diet, including more meat and possibly more thoroughly processed tubers and other plant foods. In order to obtain a richer diet, early humans may have needed a lower overall population density, leading to geographic expansion. As noted, another possibility is that scavenging opportunities in Africa decreased with the extinction of several large carnivore species at the beginning of the Pleistocene (Marean 1989). Whatever the reasons for human expansion out of Africa, recent archaeological research has shed new light on some of the earliest sites outside Africa.

One of the most remarkable sites discovered in the past 20 years is the site of **Dmanisi** (Wong 2003) in the Republic of Georgia (formerly part of the Soviet Union). The site was initially explored as a paleontological site, but in the early 1990s the excavators uncovered a mandible (lower jaw) of what was then described as *Homo erectus* (Gabunia and Vekua 1995). The site also yielded an Oldowan (also termed a Mode 1) stone tool industry composed of flakes and choppers and many butchered animal bones. No handaxes were found at the site. Since the site is dated to about 1.7 million years ago (Gabunia et al. 2001), it is likely that these early humans left Africa before the appearance of the Acheulian industry. Recent excavations at Dmanisi have yielded the remains of three hominin crania (Gabunia et al. 2000; Vekua et al. 2002). These skulls show striking similarities to the early *Homo ergaster* fossils from Africa, particularly the Turkana Boy (WT15000), and some researchers now classify the Dmanisi specimens as *Homo ergaster.*

Another early Middle Eastern site is **'Ubeidiya,** dated to about 1.4 million years ago; it lies within the Jordan Rift Valley, just south of the Sea of Galilee (Figure 4.4). Geologically, the Jordan Rift Valley is a continuation of the Great Rift Valley of Africa. The conditions in the Jordan Rift Valley 1.4 million years ago were much like those in Africa. The region of the present Jordan Valley was then filled with a number of freshwater lakes, providing an environment that could support large herds of

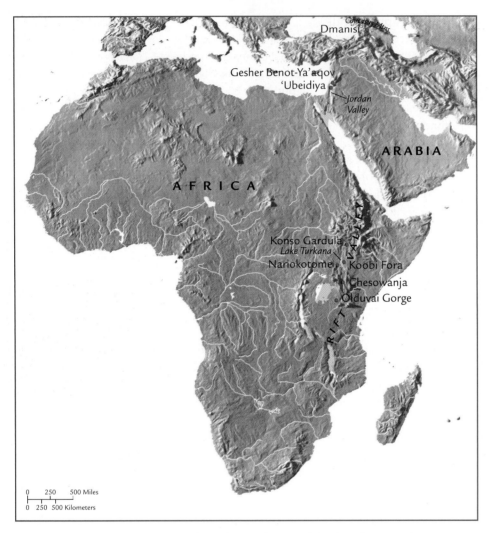

FIGURE 4.4   The major archaeological sites discussed in this chapter. The arrow traces the initial expansion of *Homo erectus* out of Africa and into the Middle East.

animals. With an abundance of game animals, the Jordan Valley would have been attractive to early humans. 'Ubeidiya may be one of the first stops of *Homo erectus* along the route out of Africa. The site was discovered by accident when the land was graded to plant a vineyard. Numerous fossil bones were uncovered, including a few tiny fragments of hominin skull. Numerous pebble tool artifacts were also found. The fauna indicated that the site dated to the earliest part of the Pleistocene. Excavated first by the Israeli archaeologist M. Stekelis and later by his student O. Bar-Yosef of the Hebrew University of Jerusalem, 'Ubeidiya has proved to be

a remarkable site. 'Ubeidiya lies in a portion of the Rift Valley that has experienced marked geological shifting and folding since the archaeological layers were deposited. Today, the strata at 'Ubeidiya are tilted nearly perpendicular to their original position (Figure 4.5). This odd circumstance had one advantage for the excavators: A horizontal trench could expose a long series of strata.

The deposits at 'Ubeidiya indicate that people camped near the shore of a lake that occupied the Jordan Valley at the time. Fifteen layers yielded major assemblages of artifacts and animal bones. Some of the layers consist of very compact expanses of large pebbles and cobbles separated from adjacent layers by layers of silt. The bones and artifacts lie among the cobbles. The bones of many species of fish, amphibians, birds, and mammals have been found at 'Ubeidiya. The 80 or so species of mammals range in size from rodents to hippopotamuses and elephants. The large assemblage of animal bones provides the means for dating the site. The range of species present correlates well with European assemblages of known age—between 1 million and 1.4 million years ago. The many species present indicate that this is a naturally accumulated fossil assemblage rather than the remains of human hunting, although some of the large deer, bovines, and hippos appear to have been butchered and eaten by the human inhabitants of 'Ubeidiya, because stone-tool cut marks are visible on some of the bones.

The earliest layers at 'Ubeidiya contain stone tool assemblages resembling those of the African Oldowan, including choppers made from flint, polyhedrons, and limestone spheroids, as well as flakes. The later layers include **bifaces,** made mostly from basalt but also of limestone and flint. Bifaces are tools that are produced by removing flakes from both sides of a stone core. These assemblages, with thick bifaces and heavy trihedral and quadrahedral (four-sided) picks, are characteristic of the early Acheulian (Bar-Yosef and Goren-Inbar 1993). In recent years a few bifaces have been found in the lower levels at 'Ubeidiya (Bar-Yosef and Belfer-Cohen 2001: 24).

THE LATER ACHEULIAN IN THE NEAR EAST: GESHER BENOT YA'AQOV

Handaxe-using peoples probably followed the northward route up the Rift Valley and through the extension of the rift that forms the Jordan Valley. Many later Acheulian sites have been found in the areas of Southwest Asia bordering the Mediterranean Sea, particularly Israel, Jordan, Lebanon, and Syria. Many of these sites are scatters of stone tools on the surface, but several deep Acheulian deposits have been found in the caves and rock shelters common in the mountainous regions of Israel, Lebanon, and Syria. Only a very few Acheulian sites are known in Iraq, Iran, and the Arabian Peninsula, but to some extent this is due to

FIGURE 4.5 A tilted stratum at 'Ubeidiya.

the limited research that has been conducted in those areas.

Somewhat later in time is the site of **Gesher Benot Ya'aqov** (meaning "Bridge of Jacob's Daughters," in Hebrew), located north of the Sea of Galilee in the Jordan Valley of Israel (see Figure 4.4). Gesher Benot Ya'aqov, although its strata have been tilted by geological movements, includes several occupations that seem relatively intact. Preserved organic remains are extremely rare in the oldest archaeological sites. Gesher Benot Ya'aqov is a unique exception. In this Lower Paleolithic site, wood, seeds, fruits, and bark are found in abundance. The site has recently been dated to about 780,000 years ago (Verosab et al. 1998). Like 'Ubeidiya, the site represents an occupation along the shores of a lake that occupied the Jordan Valley at that time. As at 'Ubeidiya, the layers at Gesher Benot Ya'aqov have been tilted, to about a 45-degree angle. Seven archaeological occupations were found, yielding assemblages that included

FIGURE 4.6 Gesher Benot Ya'aqov elephant skull with wooden log.

Acheulian basalt bifaces and cleavers. The cleavers were made using a distinctive technique first seen in Africa. The assemblage as a whole seems to have African affinities; perhaps Gesher Benot Ya'aqov was an encampment of a group of people moving up the Rift Valley from Africa.

The artifacts appear to lie in their original locations. Among these artifacts the excavators found the skull of an early straight-tusked elephant, lying bottom-side up in the deposits. The entire base of the skull had been removed. Fragments of the skull were scattered around it. Beneath the skull lay an oak log about 1 m (3 ft.) long (Figure 4.6). A large basalt core, 32 cm (13 in.) long, and a basalt boulder were also found beneath the skull. A number of basalt handaxes lay nearby. On the basis of the condition of the deposits, the excavators do not think it is likely that the skull came to the site by natural means. They offer the possible explanation that the elephant's skull was deliberately opened to extract its brain, a very desirable food. The log may have been used to turn the skull base-side up, and the boulder and core used to prop it up while it was being broken open (Goren-Inbar et al. 1994).

Another remarkable find at Gesher Benot Ya'aqov was a fragment of a plank of willow wood. This object, a small piece about 25 cm (10 in.) long of something originally larger, appears to have been intentionally flattened and polished on one side. If this object is what it seems, the range of Acheulian technology may have included wood and other perishable materials not often preserved in archaeological sites.

Most recently, the excavator of Gesher Benot Ya'aqov, Naama Goren-Inbar, and her colleagues have discovered a series of hearths at the site (Goren-Inbar et al. 2004). The presence of these hearths indicates that the early hominins at the site were able to control fire.

CONCLUSION

In this chapter we have discussed the appearance of *Homo erectus* (or *H. ergaster*) in Africa. *Homo erectus*'s new technologies, including the probable control of fire, facilitated the movement of early humans out of Africa. They were able to settle much of the subtropical and tropical and even some of the temperate zones of Asia. The Acheulian handaxe industry appeared in Africa shortly thereafter, to become the most widespread and long-lasting pre-historic technological tradition. The earliest emi-grants from Africa appear to have been users of simple choppers and chopping tools. Later, they were followed into western Asia and Europe by people who made and used handaxes. The colder climate of Europe presented a significant challenge. Just when early humans reached western Europe remains an open issue. The earliest settlement of eastern Asia and Europe will be discussed in the following chapter.

KEY TERMS

Acheulian industry   67

Bifaces   73

Chesowanja   71

Cleavers   67

Conjoined artifacts   69

Dmanisi   71

Gesher Benot Ya'aqov   73

Glacials   64

Handaxe   67

Homo erectus   64

Homo ergaster   64

Interglacials   64

Konso-Gardula   70

Nariokotome III   65

Pleistocene   64

Refitting   69

Trihedral picks   67

Type site   67

'Ubeidiya   71

QUESTIONS FOR DISCUSSION

1. How do refitting studies contribute to our under-standing of early human behavior and site forma-tion processes?

2. Why do you think that early hominins first left Africa about 1.8 million years ago?

3. In what ways are 'Ubeidiya and Dmanisi similar to the early African sites from Olduvai Gorge and Koobi Fora? What are the differences?

FURTHER READING

Clark, J. Desmond
1994   The Acheulian Industrial Complex in Africa and Elsewhere. In *Integrative Paths to the Past: Paleoanthropological Advances in Honor of F. Clark Howell*, edited by R. S. Corruccini and R. L. Ciochon, pp. 451–469. Englewood Cliffs, NJ: Prentice Hall.
An excellent overall review of the Acheulian industry and the principal Acheulian sites.

Gabunia, L., S. Antón, D. Lordkipanidze, A. Vekua, A. Justus, and C. C. Swisher III
2001   Dmanisi and Dispersal. *Evolutionary Anthropology* 10: 158–170.
An account of the fossil hominins and archaeological evidence from Dmanisi, written by several members of the Dmanisi scientific team.

Toth, Nicholas, Desmond Clark, and Giancarlo Ligabue
1992   The Last Stone Ax Makers. *Scientific American* 267 (1): 88–93.
A description of the making and use of stone axes by New Guinea highlanders using techniques much like those of the Stone Age.

Vekua, A., D. Lordkipanidze, G. P. Rightmire, J. Agusti, R. Ferring, and G. Maisuradzeb
2002   A New Skull of Early *Homo* from Dmanisi, Georgia. *Science* 297: 85–89.

Wong, Kate
2003   Stranger in a New Land. *Scientific American* 289 (5): 74–83.
A very readable and well-illustrated account of the excavations at Dmanisi.

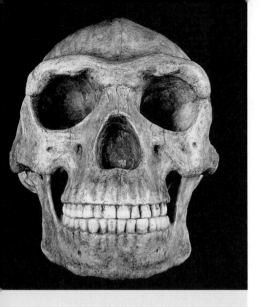

5

THE LOWER PALEOLITHIC IN ASIA AND EUROPE

Historically, the first fossils of *Homo erectus* were uncovered in Asia, long before any such finds had been made in Africa. They were the result of nineteenth-century science's search for a so-called missing link—an intermediate fossil form between modern humans and their presumed apelike ancestors. In the last quarter of the nineteenth century, our knowledge of early human fossils was meager at best. Several Neanderthals (a form of fossil human that lived about 200,000 to 30,000 years ago, see chapter 6) and some fossils of anatomically modern humans were all that had been found. Scientists, however, had become convinced of the reality of evolution, including human evolution. Somewhere, it was argued, might be found the fossils of the common ancestor of humans and the apes. Anatomists argued that such a creature should be intermediate in form between modern humans and the great apes, and even gave it a name: *Pithecanthropus,* literally, "ape-man."

In the 1890s a young Dutch anatomist, Eugene Dubois, set off with the express purpose of finding the ape-man, or "missing link." Convinced that the most likely place to find him was in the tropics, Dubois succeeded in getting himself posted as a doctor in the Dutch army in Sumatra and later in Java. In Java he began a series of excavations at the site of **Trinil,** on the Solo River (Figure 5.1). Amazingly, within a year and among a stream of fossil mammal finds, he found what he was looking for. Dubois found the top portion of a humanlike skull, but it was far too thick and robust to be that of a modern human. Later, at some distance from the skullcap, he found a human femur, or thighbone (Figure 5.2). The femur, though, was very much like that of a modern human. Dubois was convinced that both fossils came from a single individual, and that individual must have walked erect. He named his discovery *"Pithecanthropus erectus,"* the erect-walking ape-man.

At first, Dubois's ideas were met with skepticism and even derision. Few scholars accepted his claim that the Java fossils were

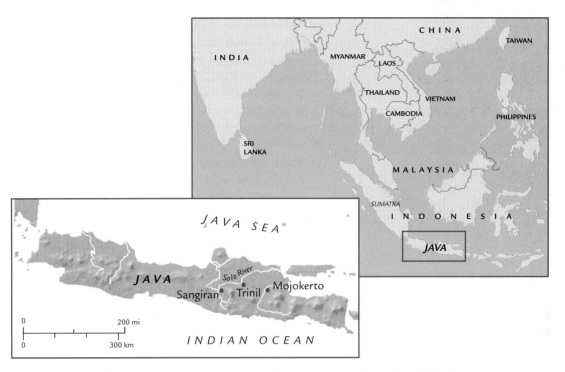

FIGURE 5.1   The island of Java in Indonesia, where Eugene Dubois found the first evidence of *Homo erectus* (originally named *Pithecanthropus erectus*) at Trinil on the Solo River. Later discoveries at Mojokerto and Sangiran have recently been dated to as early as 1.8 million years ago.

an intermediate form between apes and humans, and many doubted that the fossils were actually associated with one another. Discouraged, Dubois withdrew from academic society and for many years refused to show or discuss his finds. Fortunately, other scholars eventually followed up his work in Java. Other fossil-bearing sites were discovered in Java at **Mojokerto** in 1936 and at **Sangiran** in the 1970s. These fossils have been assigned to *Homo erectus*, broadly defined. Dubois's *Pithecanthropus* is now also assigned to the species *Homo erectus*, and Dubois is universally recognized as the discoverer of *Homo erectus*.

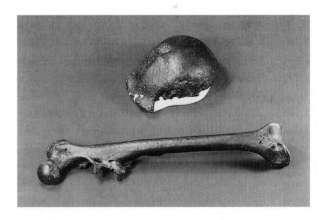

FIGURE 5.2   Trinil *Homo erectus* fossils.

FIGURE 5.3   Recent excavations at Sangiran. Courtesy of Susan Antón.

THE INITIAL HUMAN SETTLEMENT OF JAVA

The Mojokerto fossils from Java have been dated to 1.8 million years ago, making them the oldest known examples of *Homo erectus* outside Africa (Swisher et al. 1994). These dates, however, are derived from the geological formations in which the fossils are believed to have been found. Unfortunately, the locations of the original find spots are somewhat uncertain, so some doubt has been cast on the accuracy of the dating. Recent excavations at Sangiran have provided more precise dates for the initial human settlement of Southeast Asia. Strata that have produced highly fragmented remains of *Homo erectus* have been dated from 1.66 to about 1 million years (Sémah et al. 2000; see also Antón 2003). Unfortunately, only a few Mode 1 stone tools have been recovered from the excavations (Figure 5.3). These early dates imply that within a paleontologically imperceptible time after the first appearance of *Homo erectus* in Africa, the species had spread from its homeland across the breadth of the Old World, traversing the Middle East, India,

and Indonesia en route to Java (Figure 5.4). (It is important to note that although Java is an island today, it was connected to the Southeast Asian mainland at various times during the early Pleistocene. Early hominins, therefore, would not have needed boats or other watercraft to settle Java.) This interpretation has received some support by finds of simple stone tools at Riwat, Pakistan, possibly dating to about 1.9 million years ago. These recent finds are still being evaluated. (For up-to-date reviews of the movement of *Homo erectus* out of Africa, see Larick and Ciochon 1996 and Tattersall 1997.)

STONE INDUSTRIES WITH AND WITHOUT HANDAXES: THE MOVIUS LINE

Acheulian-like handaxe industries spread to cover Southwest Asia and as far east as the Indian subcontinent. Ultimately, the Acheulian industry reached most of western Europe. Handaxe industries, however, have not been found in eastern Europe or in Russia north of the Caucasus. The Acheulian seems never to have reached eastern Asia. Instead, a broad area of the Old World came to be dominated by industries lacking in handaxes (Figure 5.5). In eastern Europe and southern Russia, these industries are Oldowan-like, while distinctive chopper–chopping tool or Mode 1 industries are found in China, Southeast Asia, and Indonesia. The abrupt demarcation between areas with handaxes and those without handaxe industries was first noted by American archaeologist Hallam Movius in the 1940s. This boundary has come to be called the **Movius Line.** Despite a half-century of continued research and reevaluation, this basic distinction still appears valid. However, the recent discovery of Acheulian-like handaxes in South China may force archaeologists to move the Movius Line somewhat further east. The handaxes were discovered at Bose and date to about 800,000 years ago (Yamei et al. 2000).

The archeological evidence suggests that the earliest wave of emigrants from Africa (eventually reaching Java) did not make handaxes. A later wave of handaxe makers overtook them, and handaxe industries spread into western Europe and as far east as India. Why did handaxes spread no

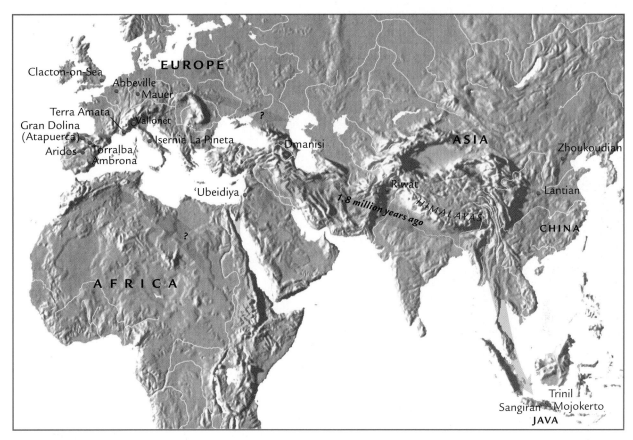

FIGURE 5.4 The spread of *Homo erectus* from sub-Saharan Africa into North Africa, across Asia, and into Europe. *Homo erectus* may have appeared in Java as early as 1.8 million years ago. The major sites discussed in this chapter are also indicated.

farther? Several hypotheses have been offered to explain the phenomenon of the Movius Line (Schick 1994):

- It has sometimes been suggested that eastern Asia lacked suitable raw materials for making bifaces and that therefore the Acheulian tradition was lost. However, this lack of materials cannot really be demonstrated for the vast area of Asia.

- Perhaps other raw materials were used instead of the stone handaxe in the east, especially if stone suitable for biface production was hard to obtain. Bamboo would have been readily available and could have been fashioned into tough, sharp cutting and stabbing implements.

- Perhaps at the time of the spread of the Acheulian industry, geographical barriers such as mountains or rain forests cut these peoples off from the populations to the east. According to this scenario, western and eastern populations continued to develop separately.

- It is unknown whether *Homo erectus* possessed any spoken language. If, as is likely, this species did not, then the transmission of the Acheulian tradition must have depended on nonverbal demonstration and observation. Toth and Schick (1993) have suggested that the handaxe-making tradition may have been lost if, during early humans' spread out of Africa, suitable materials for making bifaces were to be unavailable for more than a generation.

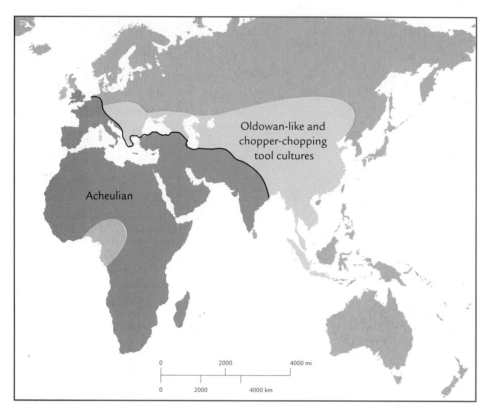

FIGURE 5.5   The Movius Line, the demarcation between areas with handaxes and those without, first proposed by archaeologist Hallam Movius in the 1940s. Source: After Schick 1994.

BEYOND THE MOVIUS LINE: THE LOWER PALEOLITHIC OF EAST ASIA

Late Acheulian sites appear as far east as Pakistan and India, where handaxe industries, fashioned largely from quartzite, are found in several deeply stratified sites. On the Indian subcontinent, Acheulian sites are found as far north as Nepal.

A vast area of Asia, however, including most of China and Southeast Asia (and extending west as far as eastern Europe) lies beyond the boundaries of the Acheulian industry (see Figure 5.5). In China and Southeast Asia, the stone assemblages consist of flakes and simple core tools, termed chopper–chopping tool complexes.

By far the most important of the Chinese Lower Paleolithic sites, and the earliest discovered, is **Zhoukoudian,** near Beijing (Figure 5.6). (The discovery of Zhoukoudian and a description of the site, its inhabitants, and their material culture are discussed subsequently.) More recently, other important sites have come to light, notably the **Lantian** area in central China, which has produced both *Homo erectus* fossils and an assemblage of quartz and quartzite artifacts.

DRAGON BONES, ZHOUKOUDIAN, AND THE DISCOVERY OF PEKING MAN

According to traditional Chinese medicine, dragon bones, when finely powdered and brewed into a tea, were a cure for fever, dysentery, malaria, and numerous other diseases. In the early twentieth century, these so-called dragon bones could be found readily in the apothecary shops of China. Farmers discovered the ancient bones and brought them to the shops for sale. As paleontologists working in

FIGURE 5.6   Zhoukoudian cave site.

China were aware, the bones were, in reality, fossils of ancient birds and mammals. One place from which large numbers of dragon bones were known to have come was called Chicken Bone Hill (Zhoukoudian), near Beijing. By the 1920s the richness of the site led paleontologists, headed by J. G. Andersson, to begin excavating it for the ancient mammal fossils to be found there. Then, in 1926, two teeth were found. They were turned over to Davidson Black, a Canadian anatomist, of the Peking Union Medical College, for identification. Black identified them as definitely hominin. On the basis of the associated fauna, Black realized that the teeth were proof of the antiquity of humans in China. Encouraged by the finds, and with Black in charge of the hominin studies, the excavation of Zhoukoudian was renewed in earnest. Another tooth was found, and Black named the fossils *Sinanthropus pekinensis,* roughly, "Chinese

man of Peking." (Today, we would classify these specimens as ***Homo erectus pekinensis***). Finally, in 1929, a skull was found. In the years that followed, until 1937 when the excavations were halted by the events leading up to World War II, many more fossils were found representing at least 40 individuals that became familiar to the public as Peking Man.

Zhoukoudian was the first, and remains the most important, early hominin site in China. The Zhoukoudian sites are actually a number of limestone caves, just west of Beijing (see Figure 5.4). The most important is Locality 1, Lung Ku Shan (Dragon Bone Hill). This is a very large cave including more than 40 m (130 ft.) of deposits. It is estimated that the cave was occupied for about 200,000 years, between 460,000 and 230,000 years ago. New ESR dates (see Archaeology in Practice box, this chapter) from Zhoukoudian indicate that

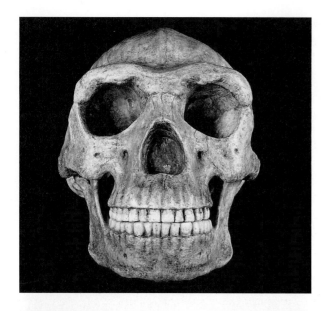

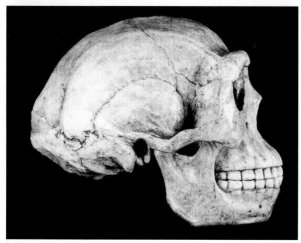

FIGURE 5.7   *Zhoukoudian H. erectus* skull.

the youngest layers bearing *Homo erectus* fossils date to about 300,000 years ago (Grün et al. 1997). It was initially excavated in the 1920s and 1930s under the direction of the Chinese archaeologist Pei Wenzhong. Younger Chinese scholars studied the site anew during the 1970s (Wu Rukang and Lin Shenlong 1983). Fourteen skulls plus many teeth and other bones belonging to about 45 individuals were recovered from this cave. They all belonged to the Chinese variety of *Homo erectus* (Figure 5.7). Below the neck they were fully erect and not very different from modern humans. The Zhoukoudian

skulls were much like those from Java, with a thick skull, a receding chin, and heavy bars above the eyes, but the brain size was larger, averaging about 1075 ml. Far more skulls than postcranial bones were found at Zhoukoudian, and many of the skulls had their bases broken in, perhaps to extract the brains. This circumstance led the excavators to infer that the inhabitants of the Zhoukoudian cave were probably headhunters and likely to have been cannibals as well. Some scholars, however, have questioned this interpretation and prefer to attribute the breakage to the activities of other carnivores, such as hyenas, whose bones are also found in the cave (see Binford and Stone 1986).

Vast numbers of animal bones were recovered from the sites, including many deer. It remains a matter of some contention what proportion of these bones may have been left by the carnivores who also occupied the cave, particularly in the earliest phases, but many, surely, were the food remains of the human occupants. It is not known whether they hunted or scavenged this game. Very large numbers of charred hackberry seeds were also recovered. They too may have been a food source.

Zhoukoudian is located in northern China; thus the cave dwellers there would have experienced very cold winters. The cave is one of the earliest sites with possible evidence for fire. The excavators found four thick layers of what appeared to be ashes in the cave, ranging from 1 to 6 meters in depth. Recent chemical analyses of these layers (Weiner et al. 1998) identified no residues characteristic of wood ash in the sediments. The presence of large numbers of burned bones and associated stone tools suggest that the hominins at Zhoukoudian may have used fire, but the presence of hearths or campfires cannot be conclusively proved.

The stone tools at Zhoukoudian include no handaxes. Instead, the industry includes choppers (Figure 5.8) and numerous flakes, which were often retouched into other tools. Quartz, flint, and sandstone were used. Many flakes were made by striking a core directly with a hammerstone. Another technique, characteristic of Zhoukoudian, was to place the stone to be flaked on a larger stone, which served as an anvil. The stone to be flaked was then struck with a hammerstone, knocking off flakes that

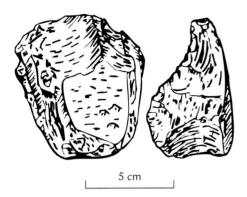

5 cm

FIGURE 5.8   Chopper from Zhoukoudian.

had bulbs of percussion at both ends. This technique is called **bipolar percussion.** The stone industry at Zhoukoudian slowly changed during the long history of occupation at the site. Bipolar percussion becomes increasingly common in the latest levels at Zhoukoudian.

The fossils found at Zhoukoudian were a treasure trove of information about early humans in China. Unfortunately, during the turmoil of the Second World War, the ancient bones disappeared under mysterious circumstances as they were about to be loaded on board a ship that was to take them to the United States for safekeeping. The story of the discovery, disappearance, and renewed search for the Peking Man fossils is a fascinating one and is described in detail in *Peking Man,* by Harry L. Shapiro, from which much of this account has been drawn.

THE INITIAL SETTLEMENT OF EUROPE

The research and discoveries of pioneers such as Pengelly and Frere in Britain and Boucher de Perthes in France helped establish the antiquity of humanity, but just when Europe was initially settled is still an open question. Some scholars would date the first entry of humans into Europe as early as 2 million years ago, or even before. The evidence for such early settlement, however, is very sparse and contested. Numerous sites throughout western Europe have potentially early dates (before 500,000 years ago), but most are surface finds, stratigraphically insecure, or poorly dated (Gamble 1994).

Absolute dating has proved a problem for very early sites in western Europe. Potassium-argon (K-Ar) and argon-argon dating are the most reliable dating techniques for sites of this age, but they are dependent on the presence of volcanic deposits that can be related to the archaeological sites. Only a few such sites are found in Europe. The site of **Isernia La Pineta,** in central Italy, is one of the best-dated early sites (see Figure 5.4). A volcanic tuff there directly overlies an archaeological level containing stone tools and animal bones. The tuff has been K-Ar dated to 730,000 years. (Some authors argue, however, on the basis of faunal evidence, that the site should be dated to after 500,000 years ago.)

The dating of most other early sites has depended on a combination of faunal correlations and paleomagnetic studies, which attempt to place the site within the known sequence of geomagnetic reversals (see Chapter 2). Such data are open to a broad range of interpretations, so the dates of such sites are frequently debatable. A particularly controversial site is the cave of **Vallonet,** near Nice on the southern coast of France. The stone tools there are simple choppers and flakes, and the fauna is similar to that of the late Villafranchian (early Pleistocene). The magnetic polarity of the deposits, however, is normal. Because of the primitive character of the lithics and the fauna, the excavator (H. de Lumley) has advocated dating the site to the time of the Jaramillo event, a brief magnetically normal period during the Matuyama epoch, 900,000 years ago. Other scholars, however, would place the site much later in time.

THE EARLIEST INHABITANTS OF EUROPE: THE GRAN DOLINA SITE, SPAIN

Spain, just across the Strait of Gibraltar from North Africa, was likely a way station on one of the probable routes of early humans into Europe. Numerous early sites have been found in Spain, but, for the most part, they have been unstratified surface finds. The cave site of **Gran Dolina** (Figure 5.9), in the Atapuerca mountain range, northern Spain, is an exception. It contains a long stratigraphic sequence with a potentially early date and is rich in artifacts, fauna, and human remains.

FIGURE 5.9   Atapuerca area, showing Gran Dolina.

At the end of the nineteenth century, during the construction of a railroad, a deep cut was made through the limestone beds at Atapuerca, revealing a number of caves and cavities filled with sediment. The importance of those caves was not recognized at the time. From 1978 onward, however, a number of excavations have been undertaken in the area. Excavation began at the cave of Gran Dolina in the 1980s (Carbonell et al. 1995; Carbonell and Rodriguez 1994; Bermudez de Castro 2004). Gran Dolina contains more than 16 m (50 ft.) of stratified deposits, divisible into 11 distinct geological layers. Five of these layers contain bones, both human and animal, as well as stone tools. The stone assemblages of the three upper layers include bifaces, but the lower two include only pebble cores and flakes, a Mode 1 industry.

The lowest layer in which artifacts were found contained only three quartzite cores and two flakes, although it also held the bones of bears, deer, and rhinoceroses, as well as other smaller animal species. A layer about 4 m (13 ft.) higher proved considerably richer in artifacts. By the time this layer,

known as TD6 or the Aurora stratum, had been completely excavated in 1996, a total of 86 hominin remains from at least six different individuals had been recovered. About 250 stone artifacts were found as well, including cores and flakes of limestone, quartzite, sandstone, and flint. There were no bifaces. The bones of numerous mammals, large and small, were also recovered.

When the first human fossils were recovered from the Aurora stratum in 1994, they were initially identified as a very early form of **Homo heidelbergensis**. *Homo heidelbergensis* is the name first given to a mandible (lower jaw) found at **Mauer,** just outside Heidelberg in Germany. Today, the taxon is used to describe a number of European and African hominins of the Middle Pleistocene (roughly 800,000 to 300,000 years ago) Age that have somewhat larger cranial capacities than are seen in the Asian *Homo erectus* fossils but that retain other primitive features of the face and teeth (Rightmire 1998).

The discovery of several facial fragments at Gran Dolina in 1995 led the excavators to suggest that the Atapuerca remains might represent a new, earlier species of hominin. The facial remains revealed a primitive dentition but a relatively modern face. The excavators named the hominin *Homo antecessor* (Bermúdez de Castro et al. 1997) and suggested that it might be ancestral to both Neanderthals (Chapter 6) and modern humans (Chapter 7).

The Gran Dolina site has been dated through a combination of faunal associations and paleomagnetic measurements. The long stratigraphic section within the cave has provided a long series of samples for paleomagnetic dating. Paleomagnetic studies (Parés and Pérez-Gonzales 1995) indicate that the rich upper stratum was laid down near the time of the Brunhes-Matuyama geomagnetic reversal (see Chapter 2). This would date that stratum to older than 780,000 years and would make the Gran Dolina fossils among the oldest in Europe. More recent ESR and uranium series dates suggest an age range of between 780,000 and 857,000 for the TD6 layer at Gran Dolina.

THE LATER LOWER PALEOLITHIC IN EUROPE

The archaeological data from Atapuerca indicate that parts of southern Europe were initially occupied during the later part of the Lower Pleistocene. Prior to 500,000 years ago, it is likely that the settlement of Europe was intermittent and limited to those regions south of the Alps (Roebroeks 2001). After 500,000 years ago, Europe saw a large influx of settlers, and parts of central and western Europe were occupied for the first time. Many of those settlers in the western portion of Europe carried with them the Acheulian industry. A second group of sites is lacking in handaxes. The assemblages in that group, dominated by flakes, are termed **Clactonian,** after the site of Clacton-on-Sea, in southern England. The Acheulian and Clactonian appear to be separate industries.

Acheulian sites are widespread in France, Spain, southern England, and northern Italy (Gamble 1999). A second Atapuerca site, Sima de los Huesos or "chasm of the bones," has yielded more than 4000 hominin fossils representing at least 28 individuals,

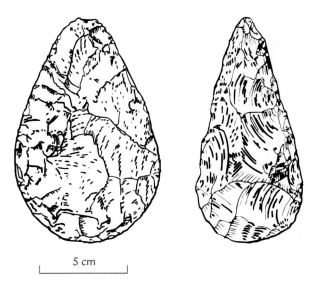

FIGURE 5.10 Characteristic handaxes from the French Middle Acheulian (left, from Commont's Workshop, in the Somme Valley) and Upper Acheulian (right, from La Micoque, a cave site in the Dordogne).

with an Acheulian handaxe. The site appears to be a location where early humans deposited corpses. The estimated date of the site is 400,000 to 500,000 years ago (Bermúdez de Castro et al. 2004).

A notable group of sites is found in the Somme Valley in northwest France, including Abbeville, excavated by Boucher de Perthes, and St. Acheul, for which the Acheulian is named. Historically, the French Acheulian sequence has been divided into Lower, Middle, and Upper Acheulian (Figure 5.10), but this sequence cannot readily be extended to the rest of western Europe. Moreover, these divisions do not correspond to the Early, Middle, and Late Acheulian of the Near East and Africa.

THE LEVALLOIS TECHNIQUE

In the course of the Middle Acheulian, a special technique became increasingly important. In the **Levallois technique** (named for a Paris suburb), a stone core was specially shaped (prepared) so that, ultimately, a flake or series of flakes could be struck from it that would be essentially preformed to the desired shape, requiring little further

ON THE CUTTING EDGE *The Human Family "Bush"*

Forty years ago, the human family tree really looked like a tree. Most anthropologists saw human evolution as a gradual process of change that led from *Homo habilis* to *Homo erectus* and ultimately to modern *Homo sapiens*. The main focus of debate was whether the Neanderthals (see Chapter 6) represented a stage of human evolution between *H. erectus* and modern humans or whether they represented a side branch of the family tree that died out 30,000 to 40,000 years ago. New discoveries in Africa, Asia, and Europe have led scholars to revise this picture, so that the human family tree now looks more like a bush (Figure 5.A).

This change can be seen clearly in the study of human ancestors from the Lower and Middle Pleistocene. Fossils that were once lumped into the *Homo erectus* taxon are now divided both geographically and chronologically. Many anthropologists now term the early African fossils, such as the Nariokatome boy, *Homo ergaster*. Some scholars restrict the term *Homo erectus* to the Lower and Middle Pleistocene fossils from East and Southeast Asia. Later hominin fossils from Europe and Africa are often classified as *Homo heidelbergensis* and distinguished by their larger cranial capacities. As Figure 5.A shows, Pleistocene human evolution may have involved a series of speciation events in different parts of the world.

The new human family tree, or family bush, poses some interest-

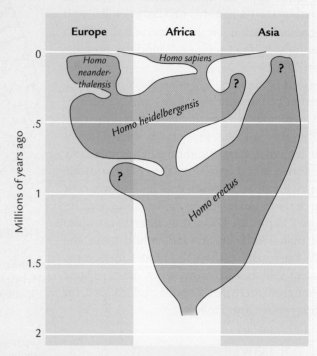

FIGURE 5.A   The family tree of the genus *Homo* (after Rightmire 1998).

ing challenges for archaeologists. The first and most fundamental question is: Who made the tools and artifacts that we find in archaeological sites? Very few sites have produced both substantial numbers of stone tools and hominin fossils; Dmanisi and Gran Dolina are notable exceptions. Important archaeological sites such as Torralba and Ambrona have produced no human remains, and rich fossil-bearing localities such as Sangiran have produced few stone tools. It is clear that the earliest hominins outside Africa, at sites such as Dmanisi, Sangiran, and Gran Dolina, used a simple Mode 1 technology and may have left Africa before the appearance of the Acheulian. The questions then are: Who made the Acheulian tools, and were these tools made by more than one species of human ancestor? While we cannot yet answer these questions, they are important for archaeologists to bear in mind. If *Homo erectus, Homo ergaster, Homo heidelbergensis,* and *Homo antecessor* are really different species of human ancestors, then it is possible, or even probable, that they had different technologies, diets, and ways of life.

working (Figure 5.11). The use of the technique implies considerable forethought and knowledge of the worked material. Prepared-core techniques become increasingly important through the Middle and Upper Paleolithic.

ACHEULIAN LIFEWAYS: ELEPHANT HUNTERS OR SCAVENGERS? THE EVIDENCE FROM TORRALBA AND AMBRONA

At the twin sites of **Torralba** and **Ambrona** in central Spain, Acheulian handaxes and other artifacts lie amid the bones of dozens of elephants, as well as horses, deer, wild cattle, and other large animals. The sites appear to date to sometime between the Early and Middle Acheulian, perhaps 420,000 to 450,000 years ago. First discovered and partially excavated in 1909, the sites were studied by F. C. Howell and L. Freeman over a number of seasons between 1961 and 1981. The excavations were extensive; over 1000 sq m (0.25 ac.) at Torralba and about 2800 sq m (0.7 ac.) at Ambrona were excavated. At both sites, which were originally wet or were even marshlands, numerous archaeological strata point to a lengthy series of events.

The finds at Torralba and Ambrona were highly suggestive. At Torralba stone tools and flakes were associated with the partial skeleton of an ancient elephant, and at Ambrona elephant bones and tusks were also accompanied by stone tools. Fragments of apparently worked wood were also found. Bits of charcoal were scattered in the deposits. A particularly intriguing and enigmatic feature at Ambrona is a linear arrangement of elephant bones, with limb bones lined up end to end and other bones lying perpendicular to the alignment (Figure 5.12).

In keeping with the views current in the 1960s and 1970s, Howell and Freeman initially interpreted the finds at Torralba and Ambrona as evidence for the killing and butchering of elephants by bands of Lower Paleolithic big-game hunters. A number of imaginative reconstructions were put forward. One scenario, picked up in the popular press, pictured bands of ancient hunters, armed with torches, driving a herd of elephants into the marsh to be slaughtered.

Using the Levallois technique, a series of flakes requiring little or no further shaping could readily be struck from a stone core. Before the first desired flake was struck from the core, the core was prepared, or pre-shaped, in a very standardized way:

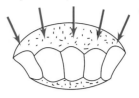

1. A series of flakes are removed from around the periphery of the core. (The arrows indicate the direction and point of impact of the blow used to detach the flake).

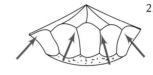

2. The core is then turned over, and a second series of flakes are struck on the other side of the core, converging at the center.

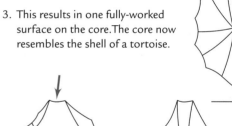

3. This results in one fully-worked surface on the core. The core now resembles the shell of a tortoise.

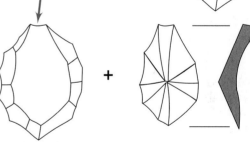

4. A carefully placed blow at the edge of the core detaches a characteristically shaped Levallois flake.

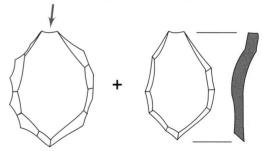

5. Subsequent blows detach further fully formed Levallois flakes, until no more can be made. The core is then said to be exhausted.

FIGURE 5.11   The Levallois technique.

FIGURE 5.12 Elephant bone alignment at Ambrona.

Lewis Binford, in the same 1981 volume in which he attacked the interpretation of the Olduvai Gorge living floors (Chapter 3), leveled a similar set of criticisms at the interpretation of Torralba and Ambrona (Binford 1981). He questioned the assumption that the bone accumulations at these sites were primarily the result of human activities. Considering the long period of time during which these deposits accumulated, he proposed that the animals may have met their deaths there naturally and that the role of humans may have been marginal. In a later publication, Binford (1987) made some further suggestions concerning Torralba. Using previously published data, he statistically reanalyzed the relationships among stone tool types and the various animal bones. On the basis of this analysis, Binford came to the conclusion that not only were the elephants at Torralba not hunted, but the archaeological evidence there pointed to, at most, the opportunistic scavenging of animal leftovers. This conclusion was bolstered by some studies of the Torralba bones that pointed to only a very low frequency of butchery marks.

Binford's assessment was widely accepted. P. Villa, in her 1990 study of the site of **Aridos,** near Madrid, accepted the characterization of Torralba as a highly disturbed site but questioned Binford's conclusion that only marginal scavenging was involved. Aridos (actually two adjacent sites) is a more recently excavated Acheulian site, quite similar to Torralba and Ambrona. At Aridos, too, elephant bones are closely associated with an assemblage of stone tools (Figure 5.13). Many of the stone artifacts could be refitted, indicating that they resulted from a single episode. The lithics found at the site appear to represent the remains from the manufacture and resharpening of tools used by a small group of humans specifically for butchering the elephants there. Whole carcasses seem to have been involved, not just leftovers.

In his review of the Torralba and Ambrona sites, Freeman (1994) readily admits that the early interpretations of these sites had been overdrawn. He argues, however, that Binford's statistical analysis of his data is invalid, because the data Binford used were flawed and because the methods were inappropriate. Freeman also argues that the deposition at Torralba and Ambrona did not occur continuously over a long period but instead represented a series of discrete events, separated by lengthy

FIGURE 5.13 Plan showing location of elephant bones (in outline) at Aridos, Spain. Lines show refitted artifacts.

hiatuses. Further, he states that contrary to some analyses, a substantial number of bones bear gross butchery marks and quite a few of the lithics could be refitted.

In short, Torralba and Ambrona do not seem too different in nature from Aridos (and recall as well Gesher Benot Ya'aqov, Chapter 4). Real evidence for big-game hunting is lacking, but these sites clearly indicate that the Acheulian people regularly butchered and ate elephants, even if they may not have hunted them.

TERRA AMATA: A HUNTERS' ENCAMPMENT?

While Torralba, Ambrona, and Aridos appear to be butchery sites, the site of **Terra Amata** in southern France has been interpreted as an Acheulian habitation. According to the excavator, Henri de Lumley, the site of Terra Amata preserves the remains of a series of wooden huts. These would be the earliest-known structures in Europe. This interpretation, however, has been seriously questioned; the data from the site present numerous difficulties. Terra Amata, however, is a rare example of an in-place Acheulian encampment in the open air, rather than within a cave. It remains, therefore, one of the most important Acheulian sites in Europe.

The digging of Terra Amata was, in fact, an example of urban rescue archaeology. A large apartment building was under construction in downtown Nice in southern France. In the alleyway named Terra Amata, after which the site is named, the builders came upon a sandy beach deposit containing Acheulian artifacts. Once the importance of the find was appreciated, the construction work was halted, and in 1966 Henri de Lumley, with the help of a large crew of volunteer workers, began a major archaeological salvage excavation. Today, the site is preserved in a museum in the building's lower floor. Over a period of five months, more than 200 cu. m (262 cu. yds.) of soil were excavated.

The site is dated to 230,000 ± 40,000 years ago, based on thermoluminescence dating of burnt flints (see the Archaeology in Practice box). At that time the Mediterranean Sea level was much higher than it is today. Although the site is now inland, a series of ancient beaches were found at Terra Amata; the inhabitants of the site occupied the youngest of the beaches, not far from the Mediterranean shore.

When the excavation was completed, de Lumley (1969) distinguished 21 separate Acheulian living floors at Terra Amata, 4 on a sandbar, 6 near the shore, and 11 on an inland dune. According to de Lumley's reconstruction, these floors held evidence for a series of oval huts, ranging in length from 8 to 15 m (26 to 49 ft.) and from 4 to 6 m (13 to 20 ft.) in width, outlined by stakes driven into the sand. Ash and organic material filled the interior of the structure. Large holes within some of the huts suggest that sturdy poles may have been used to support the roof. Each hut had a hearth at its center, with a little wall on the northwest side, probably to act as a windbreak.

Animal bones found at Terra Amata include those of elephants, deer, wild cattle, and wild boar; the fragments of a rhinoceros jaw; plus some rabbit bones. A few shellfish were also found. At the time of the excavation, it was assumed that these animals were the prey of the Terra Amata big-game hunters. Whether the animals were acquired by hunting or scavenging is not known.

De Lumley interpreted the superimposed huts (particularly the 11 found on the dune) as very brief seasonal encampments, perhaps yearly visits to the spot by the same group of individuals. This interpretation has since been called into question. In particular, P. Villa (1983) has cast doubt on whether the site can really be divided into distinct living floors, based on a refitting study of the Terra Amata lithics (see Chapter 4, Archaeology in Practice box). Lithics that frequently were vertically separated by up to 30 cm (12 in.), often across different levels, could be refitted. Trampling, geological processes, and movement by animals are some of the possible causes of the up-and-down movement of artifacts (see Chapter 1). The deposits at Terra Amata might also have been more finely divided vertically than was really justifiable. The thickness of the levels there was frequently only a few centimeters; segments of different levels might also have inadvertently been confused.

De Lumley's interpretation of the site as a series of well-defined structures has also been questioned, as only a few actual stake holes were found and recorded, rather than the many suggested by early site descriptions (Villa 1994: 54–55). The site data have been published only in a preliminary fashion. A real assessment of the site must await the final publication of the data.

THE DISTRIBUTION OF EARLY HUMANS IN EUROPE

The earliest humans seem never to have reached beyond southern and central Europe. Premodern humans probably did not possess the skills and technology needed to cope with the harsh environments of Scandinavia and the northern borders of Europe. In addition, the occupation of the temperate latitudes (north of 40 degrees north latitude)

ARCHAEOLOGY IN PRACTICE

Dating the Past: Thermoluminescence (TL) and Electron Spin Resonance (ESR)

Potassium-argon dating methods are limited to sites that include or are in close relationship with volcanic deposits (see Chapter 2). Radiocarbon dating methods (Chapter 9) are limited to relatively recent times (later than 60,000 to 70,000 years ago). Archaeologists have long been in need of dating methods applicable to a wider variety of sites and suitable for dating deposits formed between 100,000 and 1 million years ago.

Two new methods have come into use to fill this need. **Thermoluminescence (TL) dating** is an absolute dating technique applied originally to the dating of pottery. The underlying principle can also be applied to the dating of burnt flint, and this newer application is becoming increasingly important. **Electron spin resonance (ESR) dating** is a closely allied measurement technique. These methods can be used to date materials as old as 500,000 years and can sometimes be extended as far back as 1 million years.

From the time they are first formed, the mineral crystals within a ceramic fragment or within a piece of flint receive a constant low-level flow of radiation from adjacent minerals and deposits. Some minerals can absorb the energy from this radiation in the form of entrapped electrons within their crystal structure. This energy accumulates slowly over time, and if the rate of accumulation can be determined, it can serve as an absolute clock. Thermoluminescence and ESR dating are alternative techniques for measuring the energy trapped in the crystal grains. When a ceramic object is fired or when a flint is heated in a fire, the energy entrapped in the crystals is released; in effect, the mineral clock is set to zero. The energy then begins to accumulate anew.

Thermoluminescence dating measures the energy trapped in crystal grains by the slow heating of the mineral within a highly sensitive light sensor. As the crystal heats up, the stored energy is released as a pulse of light, superimposed on the normal red-hot glow of the sample. The age of the sample is proportional to the amount of light released.

ESR directly measures the number of electrons trapped in the crystal. The sample is placed in a magnetic field and exposed to a high-frequency electromagnetic field. Under these conditions the electrons will precess, or spin rather like tops, and at a certain combination of frequency and field strength, they will suddenly resonate with the electromagnetic field, drawing power from it, which can be measured. In this case the age of the sample is proportional to the amount of energy absorbed from the electromagnetic field.

Both TL and ESR dating present many practical difficulties. Both depend on accurate measurement of the amount of radiation reaching the sample as well as an accurate measurement of the sensitivity of the sample to radiation. Various physical and chemical effects complicate the measurements. When these methods are used to date burned flint, one must be certain that the sample was sufficiently heated in antiquity to set the clock to zero.

---

was probably limited to the warmer, interglacial periods (Dennell 2003).

Archaeologists still have much to learn about the lifeways of Lower Paleolithic people in Europe. It is unclear whether these early inhabitants were hunters or scavengers. However, the recent discovery of three wooden throwing spears from lakeside deposits at Shöningen in Germany indicates that hunting may have played an important role in Lower Paleolithic subsistence in Europe. The spears date to about 400,000 years ago and are the oldest known hunting weapons. Bones of wild horses were found in the same deposits, and it is possible that these throwing spears were used to hunt wild horses (Thieme 1997). The role of plant foods in the diet is also unknown, owing to the absence of preserved plant materials. Although these early Europeans may have constructed simple shelters, their degree of seasonal mobility is also unknown. Did they move their campsites on a seasonal or periodic basis, or did they occupy a single site for an extended portion of the year? Sites such as Terra

Amata have provided some clues, but the interpretation of this excavation has been controversial. These topics all await further research.

CONCLUSION

Archaeological data indicate that early humans had reached the Middle East and Southeast Asia well before 1 million years ago. Acheulian industries never reached eastern Asia. In East and Southeast Asia, increasingly sophisticated chopper and flake industries persisted throughout the Middle Pleistocene. While southern Europe appears to have been colonized somewhat later than the Far East, new data from Gran Dolina suggest that this colonization may have begun before 780,000 years ago. The earliest emigrants from Africa, who penetrated as far as Southeast Asia, were followed by handaxe makers, who would reach western Asia and Europe. In those regions, the Acheulian industry dominated until the appearance of the Middle Paleolithic industries about 130,000 years ago.

KEY TERMS

Aridos 88	Mojokerto 77
Bipolar percussion 83	Movius Line 78
Clactonian 85	"Pithecanthropus
Electron spin resonance	erectus" 76
(ESR) dating 91	Sangiran 77
Gran Dolina 83	Terra Amata 89
Homo antecessor 85	Thermoluminescence (TL)
Homo erectus	dating 91
pekinensis 81	Torralba and
Homo heidelbergensis 84	Ambrona 87
Isernia La Pineta 83	Trinil 76
Lantian 80	Vallonet 83
Levallois technique 85	Zhoukoudian 80
Mauer 84	

QUESTIONS FOR DISCUSSION

1. What would early humans have had to do in order to adapt to the colder climates of Europe and Asia?

2. Do you think that early humans in Europe were hunters or scavengers?

3. Why do you think the Acheulian industry is limited to Africa and parts of Europe?

FURTHER READING

Bermúdez de Castro, J. M., M. Martinón-Torres, E. Carbonell, S. Sarmiento, A. Rosas, J. van der Made, and M. Lozano
2004   The Atapuerca Sites and Their Contribution to the Knowledge of Human Evolution in Europe. *Evolutionary Anthropology* 13: 25–41.
An up-to-date review of the important excavations at the Atapuerca sites.

Dennell, R.
2003 Dispersal and Colonisation, Long and Short Chronologies: How Continuous Is the Early Pleistocene Record for Hominids Outside East Africa? *Journal of Human Evolution* 45: 421–440.
A very useful consideration of how and why early hominins first left Africa about 1.8 million years ago. The article includes a comprehensive bibliography.

Gamble, Clive
1999   *The Paleolithic Societies of Europe.* Cambridge: Cambridge University Press.
An important new book that examines the nature of Paleolithic societies in Europe from 500,000 years ago until the end of the Upper Paleolithic.

Larick, Roy, and Russel L. Ciochon
1996 The African Emergence and Early Asian Dispersals of the Genus *Homo. American Scientist* 84 (6): 538–551.
A clear discussion of the possible causes for the movement of Homo *from Africa into Asia.*

Schick, Kathy D.
1994 The Movius Line Reconsidered: Perspectives on the Earlier Paleolithic of Eastern Asia. In *Integrative Paths to the Past: Paleoanthropological Advances in Honor of F. Clark Howell*, edited by R. S. Corruccini and R. L. Ciochon, pp. 569–596. Englewood Cliffs, NJ: Prentice Hall.
A clear overview of the geographical relationships between handaxe and non-handaxe industries during the Lower Paleolithic. Various hypotheses are offered to explain why handaxe industries never reached beyond the Movius Line.

Tattersall, Ian
1997   Out of Africa Again . . . and Again? *Scientific American* 276 (4): 60–67.
A concise and up-to-date discussion of the evidence for repeated waves of hominin migration out of Africa into Asia and Europe.

6

THE MIDDLE PALEOLITHIC AND THE APPEARANCE OF THE NEANDERTHALS

The name "Neanderthal" conjures up vivid and varied images in the popular imagination. The popular image of the Neanderthal is a rather brutish form of cave-dwelling subhuman with limited intellectual powers. Neanderthals have also been subjects of popular works of fiction, including Jean Auel's *Clan of the Cave Bear.* This novel paints a more sympathetic portrait of the Neanderthals, depicting them as capable of, among other things, caring for the infirm and elderly members of their community. Auel's work of fiction is based on data recovered from the excavations of Shanidar Cave in Iraq. In this chapter we will examine the archaeological record of Neanderthal behavior. We begin, however, with the initial discovery of Neanderthal fossils 150 years ago.

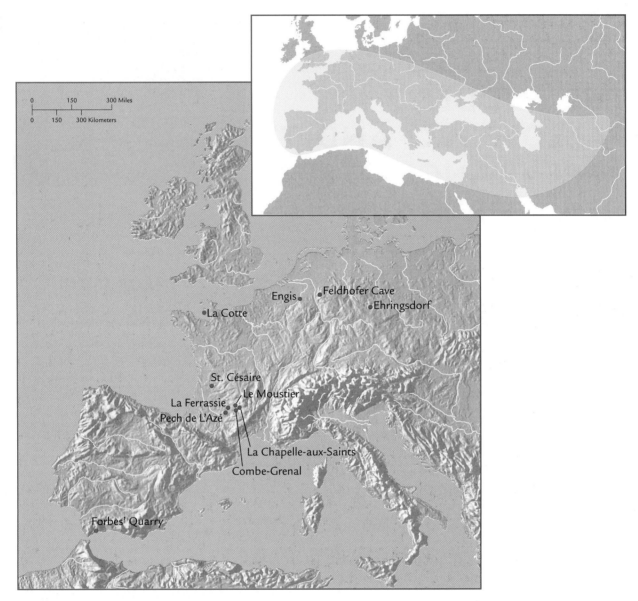

FIGURE 6.1 The location of the sites mentioned in this chapter. St. Césaire will be discussed in Chapter 8. The light shading on the smaller map shows the region inhabited by the Neanderthals.

HUMANS UNLIKE OURSELVES: THE DISCOVERY OF THE NEANDERTHALS

In the year 1830, in the **Engis** cave in Belgium, the skull of a young child with an anatomy quite unlike our own came to light (Figure 6.1). Although its excavator was convinced of the skull's antiquity, the scientific community took little notice. A similar skull, that of an adult, was found by military builders at **Forbes' Quarry, Gibraltar,** in 1848. As with the Engis discovery, few were interested in the meaning of this skull; Western science was not yet ready to accept the antiquity of humanity. By 1856, though, just three years before Darwin would publish *On the Origin of Species,* scientific ideas about human evolution were beginning to change. In that year workers quarrying for limestone in a German grotto called **Feldhofer** happened upon the skull and the skeleton of a strange, robust human, with thick ridges over his eyes and thick, curved limb bones. The valley, the Neander Tal (Neander Valley) near Düsseldorf, where the cave is located, would give its name to these new humans. Unlike the Engis and Gibraltar skulls (now known also to be **Neanderthals**), the Feldhofer fossils created an immediate sensation. The bones had been delivered to a local schoolteacher, who recognized their importance and engaged an anatomy professor from the University of Bonn to help study them. Together they presented their findings to the scientific world, with the conclusion that these bones represented a form of human of the greatest antiquity. Their conclusions were by no means generally accepted, but the debate about the nature of the Neanderthals, which continues to this day, had begun.

To date, the remains of several hundred Neanderthal individuals have been found, although usually an individual is represented by just a few bones. A small number of fairly complete skeletons have been found. The Neanderthal anatomy is markedly different from that of modern humans (Figure 6.2). Although different individuals show considerable variation, in general, Neanderthal skulls have thick, bony ridges over each eye and a low, sloping, rather than upright, forehead. The lower jaw lacks a chin. The face projects forward and must have been dominated by a remarkably large, broad nose. The limb bones are thick and robust and often slightly curved to support a powerful, muscular physique. The skull, however, encloses a brain as large as or slightly larger than that of modern humans.

Could such beings have been the ancestors of modern humans? In 1913, when the French paleontologist Marcellin Boule set out to describe the Neanderthals, such an idea was very difficult to accept. Boule based his study primarily on the most complete Neanderthal skeleton so far discovered, an individual found in 1908 at **La Chapelle-aux-Saints** in central France. The portrait Boule reconstructed was hardly flattering. Boule painted

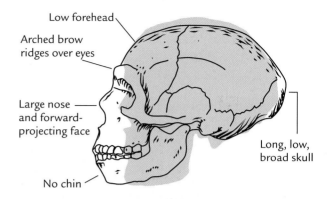

FIGURE 6.2 A Neanderthal skull, showing its distinctive anatomical features, including the low, sloping forehead; massive brow ridges; projecting face; and absence of a chin. Shading shows modern human skull (top). Reconstruction of the face and upper body of the Neanderthal male from La Ferrassie (bottom).

the Neanderthals as more apelike than human, with bent knees, a slouching posture, and a forward-thrusting face. Such a creature surely could not have been in the direct line of human ancestry. Today, we realize that the posture and gait of the Neanderthals were not very different from our own.

ARCHAEOLOGY IN PRACTICE

The Pleistocene and Its Chronology

The environment of the Neanderthals was the Ice Age world of the Pleistocene epoch. The Pleistocene began about 1.6 million years ago and ended about 10,000 years ago, at the end of the last great glaciation. The Pleistocene epoch was characterized by a series of episodes of worldwide cold climate, known as **glacials,** during which average tem-peratures were considerably lower than today (perhaps 6 to 8 degrees Celsius, or 11 to 14 degrees Fahrenheit). Current evidence indicates that as many as 30 such episodes occurred during the Pleistocene epoch, alternating with extended periods when temperatures were as high as or higher than those to-day, periods known as **interglacials.**

During the cold phases, great glaciers covered much of north-ern Europe, the northern portion of Eurasia, and northern North America as far south as New York State. Glaciers grew in the high mountain ranges as well, notably the Alps.

The movements of the glacial ice left distinctive features on the

Age in years	Oxygen isotope stage	Alpine glaciation		Some key sites					North American galciation
				Africa	Europe	Asia	Australia	Americas	
10,000	1	HOLOCENE	UPPER PALEO.					Monte Verde	HOLOCENE
	2	WÜRM			Grotte Chauvet		Upper Swan		WISCONSAN
	3				La Chapelle-aux-Saints				
75,000	4		MIDDLE PALEO.						
	5	RISS-WÜRM		Klasies River					SANGOMON
		INTERGLACIAL		Mouth					INTERGLACIAL
	6								
200,000				Kabwe					
	7	RISS							ILLIONOISAN
250,000									
	8								
	9					Zhoukoudian			
	10	MINDEL-RISS							YARMOUTH
	11	INTERGLACIAL			Torralba/				INTERGLACIAL
	12				Ambrona				
	13								
	14								
600,000	15		LOWER PALEOLITHIC						
	16								
	17	MINDEL							KANSAN
	18								
750,000	19								
	20				Gran Dolina				
	21	GÜNZ-MINDEL							AFTONIAN
	22	INTERGLACIAL							INTERGLACIAL
900,000									
		GÜNZ							NEBRASKAN

Figure 6.A The Alpine and North American glacial chronology, which was in wide-spread use until recently.

landscape. European geologists in the early twentieth century could identify the traces left behind by the advances of the Alpine glaciers. These great glaciations were named after the Alpine valleys where the evidence was found: the Günz (the earliest), the Mindel, the Riss, and the Würm (the latest). The Neanderthals first appear in Europe between the Riss and the Würm and are replaced by modern humans well before the Würm comes to an end. Until recently the Alpine sequence of glaciations (and related sequences elsewhere in Europe) had formed the chronological framework for European prehistory during the Pleistocene. Archaeological sites were tied to the glacial and interglacial periods by means of a wide variety of geological phenomena and observations. These correlations always proved extremely difficult because the geological record is, unfortunately, very incomplete. Figure 6.A presents an approximate chronology of the Alpine and North American Pleistocene glaciations. The Alpine glacial terminology appears in many older publications, and some workers continue to use those terms as a matter of convenience.

A NEW CHRONOLOGY: DEEP-SEA CORES AND OXYGEN ISOTOPE RATIOS

A new approach has provided geologists and archaeologists with a far better understanding of the climatic fluctuations of the Pleistocene. Terrestrial geology has preserved evidence from just the last few glaciations; deep-sea cores, however, provide a record of sediments accumulated throughout the Pleistocene. Deep-sea cores indicate a long series of cold-warm oscillations during the Pleistocene epoch (Figure 6.B).

The mechanism by which deep-sea cores have captured a record of ancient temperatures is quite indirect, but it has proved very reliable. Consistent results have been

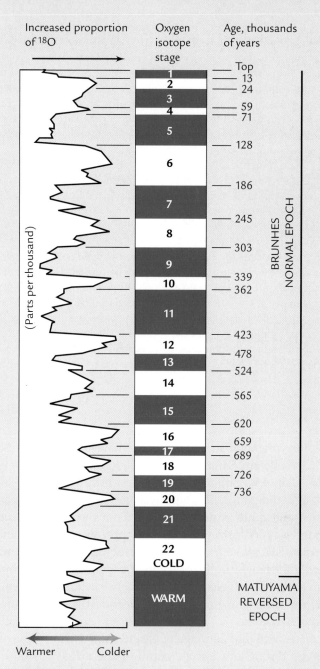

Figure 6.B The oxygen-isotope stages for the Pleistocene and their approximate dates.

obtained from hundreds of cores. The deep-sea cores take samples of the calcitic ooze made up of the skeletons of marine microorganisms that settled to the ocean floor in a constant rain throughout the Pleistocene. When these organisms were alive, they absorbed oxygen

from the ocean water. When they died and settled to the bottom, that oxygen was incorporated into the sediment. Oxygen occurs in several forms, or isotopes. The lighter isotope, oxygen-16 (^{16}O), is the common form; the heavier isotope, oxygen-18 (^{18}O), is much rarer.

97

The ^{16}O isotope, being lighter, tends to evaporate from the surface of the oceans more readily than does the heavier form. During glacial periods, water containing an excess of ^{16}O evaporates from the oceans and becomes trapped in the glaciers, leaving the oceans enriched in ^{18}O; therefore a higher percentage of ^{18}O is incorporated into the marine microorganisms. During warm periods, glacial water runs into the oceans, raising the proportion of ^{16}O. This change too is reflected in the microorganisms. Sediments relatively rich in ^{18}O, therefore, indicate a colder climate; sediments with a higher proportion of ^{16}O indicate a warmer climate.

A record of climatic oscillations without a time scale would be of little use. Fortunately, the ocean sediments preserve a record of the orientation of the earth's magnetic field at the time of their deposition. This sequence can be correlated with the sequence of the earth's magnetic reversals, which have been well dated by absolute dating techniques, such as potassium-argon dating (see Chapter 2, Archaeology in Practice box).

Today, the preferred chronological framework for the Pleistocene is expressed in terms of the fluctuations seen in the deep-sea cores. Each distinctive period of warm or cold climate is referred to as a numbered **oxygen isotope stage,** which may be further divided into substages. In general, each major glacial–interglacial oscillation is represented by a cold stage and a warm stage. The exception is the Late Pleistocene, which is represented by more stages because the data are better. In the time between the human fossils at Gran Dolina (see Chapter 5), 780,000 years ago, and today, at least eight major glacial–interglacial cycles have occurred. The earliest Neanderthals appeared in Europe during isotope stage 7, which began 250,000 years ago (the latter part of the Riss glaciation). They disappeared during isotope stage 3, ending 30,000 years ago, in the midst of the Würm glaciation (see Figure 6.B).

While the deep-sea core studies have greatly improved our knowledge of the Pleistocene climate, it remains difficult to tie individual archaeological sites into the new chronology. Absolute dating methods such as thermoluminescence and electron spin resonance (see Chapter 5, Archaeology in Practice box) will gradually change this picture.

Boule's interpretation may have been skewed by the La Chapelle-aux-Saints Neanderthal, known as the Old Man, who suffered from severe arthritis. More likely, though, Boule (who was an excellent anatomist and quite aware of the fossil's arthritic condition) was led astray by his own preconceptions. Scientists, strive as they may for objectivity, are inevitably caught in the conceptual framework of their time. Nevertheless, Boule's reconstruction became the dominant image of the Neanderthals for decades to come.

Humans with the full range of Neanderthal features lived throughout Europe south of the areas covered by the glaciers. They have been found in the Near East (in Israel and Iraq) and as far east as Uzbekistan in Central Asia. Today, most biological anthropologists think that *Homo heidelbergensis* is the ancestor of the European Neanderthals. The Neanderthals may be descended from a population represented by fossil finds at **Ehringsdorf,** near Weimar, Germany, dated to 230,000 years ago (Stringer and Gamble 1993: 66). These fossils, including a skull, show the characteristic Neanderthal features, such as heavy brow ridges, but in a less extreme form than in later Neanderthals. During the Neanderthals' long existence, the earth's climate oscillated from warm to cold several times. The Neanderthals developed in a world growing increasingly cold and harsh. Their stocky bodies and short limbs were probably an adaptation helping them conserve body heat under those challenging conditions. The short and stocky bodies of the Inuit who live in Alaska, northern Canada, and Greenland are a modern-day example of such an adaptation. The Neanderthals survived an extended period of severely cold climate and continued into a time of milder temperatures. The last Neanderthals, who lived about 28,000 years ago, saw the world growing cold again.

MIDDLE PALEOLITHIC ARCHAEOLOGY: THE MOUSTERIAN INDUSTRY

As the Neanderthal people came to dominate the European landscape, the characteristic stone tools found in the associated archaeological sites gradually changed. The Acheulian industry, typified by bifacially flaked handaxes made on stone cores, was replaced by another industry, known as the **Mousterian,** in which most of the stone tools were

FIGURE 6.3 The site of Le Moustier (Dordogne), France, the type site for the Mousterian stone tool industry.

made from large, thick flakes. Traditionally, this shift denotes the end of the Lower Paleolithic period and the beginning of the **Middle Paleolithic.** The Mousterian is named for the stone tool industry discovered in the nineteenth century within the cave of **Le Moustier,** near Les Eyzies in the Dordogne region of southern France (Figure 6.3). In 1908, in another shelter just below Le Moustier, a skeleton of an adolescent Neanderthal was found. Until recently it had appeared the Neanderthal people and the Mousterian stone tool industry were invariably interlinked—Neanderthals were often referred to as possessors of a Mousterian culture. Today, it is clear that the reality was more complex. In Europe some later Neanderthals have now been shown to have used more advanced types of stone tools. In the Near East, as in Europe, Neanderthals

are associated with Mousterian artifacts, but recent evidence shows that another form of human—the early anatomically modern humans—was using Mousterian stone tools as well. (These issues will be discussed in greater detail in Chapter 7.)

THE BORDES TYPOLOGY OF MIDDLE PALEOLITHIC STONE TOOLS

The Mousterian stone tool industry remains a primary source of evidence for the activities of the inhabitants of Europe and adjacent areas during the long duration of the Middle Paleolithic. While the Acheulian industry includes only a limited variety of stone tool forms, the Mousterian includes many more types of stone artifacts. An artifact **typology** is the systematic classification of those artifacts according to clearly defined characteristics. The French archaeologist François Bordes (1968, 1984) systematized the typology of the Mousterian industry in the early 1960s, and his typology continues in use today. Bordes subdivided the Mousterian stone artifacts into 63 distinctive tool types (Bordes and de Sonneville-Bordes 1970). Many of these tool types were various kinds of **scrapers:** flakes **retouched** into a number of shapes by the removal of a series of small flakes from one or more edges. The tools presumably were used for tasks such as scraping hides but might have served many other purposes. Other types included several kinds of points and knives, **borers** (pointed stone tools suitable for making holes), and **burins** (tools with a sharp facet suitable for cutting or engraving materials such as wood or bone). **Notches** were tools with a notch retouched into an edge, perhaps for shaping wood. **Denticulates** were flakes heavily retouched to have a saw-toothed edge. Levallois flakes and points were also tabulated.

Bordes quantified the proportions of different tool types he found in the Middle Paleolithic assemblages. He also constructed proportions (indexes) that reflected the technological characteristics of the assemblage. One standard measure was the **Levallois Index,** essentially the proportion of artifacts in the assemblage made using the Levallois technique. Bordes used the proportions of artifact types and the indexes he devised to compare a large

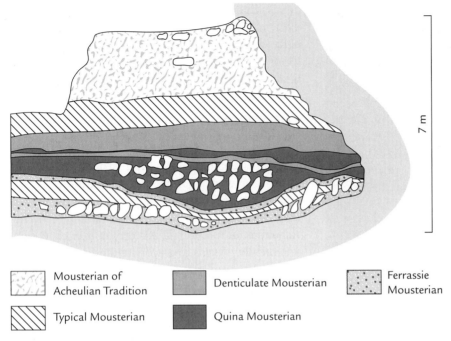

7 m

| | Mousterian of Acheulian Tradition | | Denticulate Mousterian | | Ferrassie Mousterian |

| | Typical Mousterian | | Quina Mousterian |

FIGURE 6.4 Diagram of stratigraphic section from Combe-Grenal, showing the stratigraphic positions of the various Mousterian variants.

number of French Middle Paleolithic stone tool assemblages. He found that tool proportions were not random but instead clustered into five distinctive groups. Bordes named these groups the Typical Mousterian, Denticulate Mousterian (with many denticulates and notches), Mousterian of Acheulian Tradition (includes handaxes, in greater or lesser proportion), and a Charentian Group, divided into two subgroups after the sites where they were found: Quina Mousterian (with a high proportion of Levallois artifacts), and Ferrassie Mousterian (with a low proportion of Levallois artifacts).

EXPLAINING THE VARIABILITY IN MOUSTERIAN ASSEMBLAGES: TRIBES, ACTIVITIES, AND TOOL MANUFACTURE

These groups were not geographically separated, nor were they separated in time. Instead, at cave sites such as **Pech de L'Azé** and **Combe-Grenal** (Figure 6.4), strata bearing the different Mousterian groups interdigitate, seemingly at random. Bordes interpreted the differing groups of Mousterian artifacts as the products of distinct, separate tribes of Mousterian people, coexisting in the French countryside, but scarcely interacting. It is hard to imagine such distinctive groups living together in close proximity for many millennia while maintaining their individual identities. Bordes, however, stressed the conservatism of primitive societies: "If one supposes that a Mousterian of Acheulian tradition man married a Quina woman, she might have gone on using the thick scrapers to which she was accustomed, but we doubt that her daughters would have done the same" (Bordes 1972: 147).

Bordes's viewpoint was immediately challenged. Lewis and Sally Binford (Binford and Binford 1966) subjected the data from some of Bordes's excavations, as well as data from Sally Binford's own excavation in the Near East, to a series of statistical analyses. From these analyses they produced a number of groups of artifacts, called factors, that tended to be correlated. They interpreted the various factors as representing differing activities. The different Mousterian assemblages, they suggested, were the result of whether the site was a base camp (where people slept, ate their meals, and carried on routine activities) or a hunting camp or work camp (where food or other raw materials were procured). The Binfords' interpretation drew fire in its turn. Bordes did not accept the Binfords' site classification as applicable to southwest France; he believed a wide range of activities took place in the sites. Others questioned the Binfords' statistical methods and their functional interpretation of the correlated groups of artifacts. The debate continued for some years.

Recently, a new approach has been offered to account for some of the variability in Mousterian stone assemblages. Departing from the conventional typology of Bordes, Harold Dibble (Dibble and Roland 1992) has focused instead on **lithic reduction sequences.** Stone tool types are not fixed, according to Dibble's research, but instead pass through a number of forms during the extended history of their use. As a scraper, for instance, is dulled by use, its edge must continually be resharpened by retouching. Over time the shape of the tool changes, and a large side scraper may eventually be reduced to become a small transverse scraper. Mousterian toolmakers did not, therefore, set out to make a specific kit of scrapers with preconceived forms. The proportion of tool forms in an assemblage has much to do with how those tools were made, used, and reused over time.

THE CULTURE OF THE MIDDLE PALEOLITHIC

For the Neanderthal people living in Europe during the height of the Ice Ages, life must have been very hard indeed. For much of the year, plant foods must have been scarce or nonexistent. At times the Neanderthals' diet must have consisted almost entirely of animal foods, either hunted or scavenged. To the south and east, the Neanderthals living near the Mediterranean in what is now Israel and in the mountains of what is now northern Iraq enjoyed somewhat less challenging conditions. Archaeologists generally agree that the Neanderthals were successful hunters of small to medium-large animals. Philip Chase (1986, 1988) has studied the

animal bone remains from the site of Combe-Grenal, France, closely. Many of the horses eaten at Combe-Grenal were in the prime of life. Large, meat-bearing bones, often with marks of butchery, are common in the assemblage. The ages at death of the animals and the butchery marks on the bones strongly indicate that the Mousterian inhabitants of this cave were hunting rather than scavenging horses (Chase 1986). The animal food remains found in European sites are dominated by the bones of red deer, wild cattle, horses, and reindeer. In the Near East, fallow deer, gazelle, and wild sheep and goats are the common food animals.

Mary Stiner's (1994) work on Mousterian faunas from Middle Paleolithic sites in west central Italy sheds important new light on Neanderthal subsistence practices and ecology. Stiner found that Neanderthals, like modern humans, obtained food both by hunting and by scavenging. However, she found that after about 55,000 years ago there was a shift toward ambush hunting, focusing on prime-age adults. What is most interesting is that this change in foraging behavior does not correspond to a change in stone tool technology or to the replacement of one human form by another.

Whether the Neanderthals successfully hunted very large mammals, such as mammoth and hippopotamus, or simply scavenged them when they were available is an open question. A site that seems to illustrate at least one, perhaps exceptional, example of the hunting of large mammals has been found at **La Cotte de Sainte-Brelade,** on the Isle of Jersey in the English Channel. Found beneath a rock cliff, two large piles made up from the bones of numerous mammoths and woolly rhinos have been interpreted as the result of a Middle Paleolithic hunting drive (Scott 1980). Another find suggesting the hunting of large mammals is a spear made of yew wood, 2.5 m (8 ft.) long, found beneath the skeleton of an elephant at the early Middle Paleolithic site of **Lehringen,** Germany.

Middle Paleolithic open-air sites are rare. Most of the sites discovered so far have been within caves and rock shelters, and archaeological exposures of horizontal surfaces in these sites have been limited. With the exception of a few sites at the very end of the Middle Paleolithic, shelters and other

CASE STUDY

The Excavations in Kebara Cave, Israel

The cave of Kebara, in the limestone hills overlooking the coastal plain of northern Israel, has been in use by humans for more than 60,000 years. In recent times, until it was first investigated by archaeologists in the 1920s, the cave had been used by local pastoralists for penning their sheep and goats. The top several meters of the site, containing extensive remains from more recent periods, were excavated almost completely in the 1930s. Beneath lay Levalloiso-Mousterian deposits. In 1982 Israeli archaeologist Ofer Bar-Yosef and French anthropologist Bernard Vandermeersh began an interdisciplinary study of the cave, a project that included many other scholars as well (Bar-Yosef et al. 1992).

A principal goal of the excavation was a clarification of the absolute dating of the Middle Paleolithic of the region. Better dating was crucial for understanding the temporal relationship between the Neanderthal and more modern-appearing hominins in the area, both of whom produced Mousterian industries. (This issue will be discussed in detail in Chapter 8.) Other goals were studies of the distribution of the features, artifacts, and animal bones in the site, and of the processes that formed those deposits. The excavators also hoped to find new human fossils.

The excavation continued through nine field seasons. During this time many excavation units and soundings were placed in the cave. At the center of the cave, an area of about 12 sq m (130 sq ft.) was excavated with the greatest of care. This entire area was excavated horizontally, following the site's stratigraphy as closely as possible. A number of circular hearths containing charcoal and ashes were exposed. The positions of the many flint artifacts and animal bones were carefully recorded. Other Middle Paleolithic hearths were revealed in the carefully prepared stratigraphic cross sections elsewhere in the cave. The excavation was capped by the discovery in a deep sounding of a Neanderthal burial of great importance (Figure 6.C).

As had been the case elsewhere, the hearths contained no stones or other trace of structure. They were merely roughly circular deposits of charcoal, usually less than a meter across—fires built from oak wood and grasses. Above the charcoal was a layer of white ash, which appeared

structures are unknown. Mousterian sites typically consist of scatters of stone tools and chipping debris along with bones from the animals eaten there. Many sites include hearths, presumably for protection and warmth, and perhaps for cooking food. These were simply large scatters of charcoal and ash without any additional structure. Constructed hearths with stone walls appear only at the very end of the Middle Paleolithic. In addition to the stone tools, hearths and animal-bone food remains are the only significant evidence of everyday life during the Middle Paleolithic.

In the Near East the Middle Paleolithic is typified by a variety of the Mousterian, known as the **Levalloiso-Mousterian,** that includes many Levallois flakes and points. Recent excavations in the cave of **Kebara,** in northern Israel, have produced one of the broadest exposures of a Mousterian site to date and have also provided new insights into the nature of the Neanderthals.

THE ISSUE OF NEANDERTHAL BURIALS

No human fossil from before the Middle Paleolithic shows any signs of having been intentionally buried, although Sima de los Huesos may have served as a dumping ground for carcasses. Early hominin remains are generally sparse and fragmentary, because they were preserved by the same processes that preserved any other animal fossil. Middle

FIGURE 6.C Neanderthal burial from Kebara Cave in northern Israel.

was not occupied. No animal bones were in the hearths, but carbonized seeds, particularly wild peas, were found among the charcoal. Kebara, therefore, contains evidence for the consumption of both animal and plant foods.

The burial in the deep sounding proved to hold the most complete Neanderthal skeleton yet discovered. The burial was dated by thermoluminescence and electron spin resonance to between 64,000 and 59,000 years ago. Although the skull was missing, the lower jaw and hyoid bone remained. Because the hyoid bone anchors the muscles of the tongue, it plays a role in the ongoing debate over whether or not Neanderthals were fully capable of speech. The Kebara hyoid, the first Neanderthal specimen discovered, was shaped much like that of modern humans, suggesting that the anatomy of the Neanderthal throat could probably have supported speech.

The Kebara Neanderthal was intentionally buried; the wall of the burial pit could clearly be discerned. The body of a male, lying on his back, appeared to have been placed intact into his grave shortly after death. Only later, after the body had decayed, was the skull removed. The manner of removal argues that humans, rather than animals, removed the skull. Their purpose, of course, remains unknown.

to have been spread about after the fire was extinguished. The hearths were ranged toward the front of the cave. Against the back wall of the cave was what appeared to be a refuse dump of artifacts and animal bones—gazelles, deer, horses, wild cattle, and many others, including even a few bones of rhinoceroses. Many of the bones were burned or showed cut marks from butchery. The evidence indicates that the human inhabitants of the cave consumed this game, although carnivores such as hyenas clearly ravaged the bones during the intervals when the cave

Paleolithic human remains, especially Neanderthals, are far more common and often more complete. In part, this is because at least some Neanderthals were quickly interred beneath the earth, and thus protected from scavengers and other natural processes that scatter and destroy bones. Because burials were made in caves, they were preserved where they could readily be found by archaeologists.

One of the first Neanderthals discovered, at Le Moustier, appeared to have been purposely buried. The find at La Chapelle-aux-Saints may also have been a burial. Seven burials were found in 1934 at the nearby site of **La Ferrassie.** Sometimes interpreted as a family cemetery, the graves included a man and woman, two children, and three infants.

The skull of one of the children was buried separately from the body, under a stone.

Although Neanderthal burials have been a subject of controversy (Gargett 1989), most prehistorians accept that these people did bury at least some of their dead. A more difficult question is what Neanderthal burials imply about these people's concepts of religion and ritual. Stringer and Gamble (1993: 160) argue that these burials were not related to symbolic behavior at all but were merely "corpse disposal." One Neanderthal burial difficult to fit into this description is the child's grave at **Teshik-Tash,** Uzbekistan. This burial was surrounded by a ring of goat horns driven point-down into the ground.

The huge cave of **Shanidar** in the Zagros mountains of Iraq, excavated in the 1950s by Ralph S. Solecki, has produced one of the largest samples of Neanderthal individuals found so far in any site (Solecki 1971; Trinkaus 1983). In all, nine Neanderthals were found in the cave. Four of them met their deaths beneath giant boulders falling from the roof of the cave. The remaining five were purposefully buried. One of these burials, Shanidar IV, seemed quite remarkable.

As Shanidar Cave was excavated, numerous soil samples were collected. Later, these samples were subjected to a **palynological** (pollen) **analysis** by specialist Arlette Leroi-Gourhan (1975). Pollen is resistant to decomposition and can provide much information about past environments and the human uses of plants (see Chapter 13). The pollen produced by flowering herbs and trees is quite distinctive in shape and can often be identified as to species. The plant species found in the Shanidar Cave samples that Leroi-Gourhan analyzed were all very consistent, with the exception of two samples that were quite different. Those samples contained very large numbers of flower pollen, many of them grouped into clumps, indicating that they must have come from complete blossoms. Those samples (and later a third) proved to have come from the soil beneath the Neanderthal burial, Shanidar IV. Solecki and Leroi-Gourhan concluded that Shanidar IV must have been laid to rest in a grave lined with flowers. Their interpretation has been questioned, and the presence of the flower pollen has been attributed to contamination, perhaps borne on workers' clothing.

If the evidence for flowers in the grave of Shanidar IV is accepted, it demonstrates a concern among the Neanderthals for the dead (or at least for the individual buried in that grave). Another of the Shanidar Neanderthals, Shanidar I, shows that these people could also show concern for the living. The Neanderthals lived a very harsh existence; many skeletons show signs of broken bones and other wounds. Life had been especially hard for Shanidar I. At some time, a blow to his body had damaged his right arm so badly that it withered away. The lower arm and hand either dropped off or were amputated. He was blind in one eye, and his legs were partially crippled. Yet this unfortunate individual probably lived into his forties—old age for a Neanderthal. It is difficult to imagine how this man could have survived the rigors of life for so long had he not been cared for by others. While the Shanidar Neanderthals may well have shown compassion, interpersonal violence was likely also a part of life. One of the ribs of another Shanidar Neanderthal shows a partially healed wound, probably caused by a thrusting weapon that may well eventually have cost him his life.

THE MIDDLE PALEOLITHIC–MIDDLE STONE AGE IN AFRICA

Neanderthals, strictly speaking, have not been found in Africa. Middle Paleolithic sites, however, are widespread across northern Africa. South of the Sahara, a similar time span is filled by assemblages belonging to the African **Middle Stone Age.** A number of human fossils from this time have been found in Africa, most notably **Kabwe (Broken Hill),** from Zambia (formerly Northern Rhodesia, leading to the name Rhodesian Man). The skull, with massive brow ridges, in some ways resembles the Neanderthals, but today most scholars place it closer to the line leading to modern *Homo sapiens*. Elsewhere in Africa, early modern *Homo sapiens* appear to have been the makers of the Middle Stone Age industries (see McBrearty and Brooks 2000). (This topic will be discussed in greater detail in Chapter 7.)

In North Africa the Acheulian was followed by a Mousterian industry similar to those of Europe and the Near East. At some time, perhaps as early as 70,000 years ago, the Mousterian was then replaced by a distinctive North African industry known as the **Aterian.** The Aterian stone tools possessed distinctive tangs (narrowed projections at the base) to facilitate hafting. Just who made the Aterian industry is not yet clear, but at the site of **Dar-es-Sultan,** Morocco, Aterian artifacts are associated with robust but modern-looking humans (Stringer and Gamble 1993: 131).

South of the Sahara, in broad regions of central and west Africa, the Acheulian industry developed into a characteristic African Middle Stone Age industry called the **Sangoan,** named after

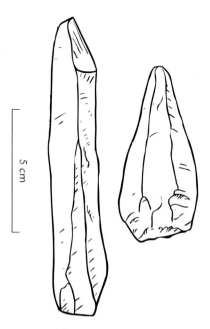

5 cm

FIGURE 6.5   Middle Stone Age tools from the Klasies River Mouth, South Africa.

Sango Bay in Uganda. The Sangoan shows a very clear likeness to the Acheulian and is typified by large core scrapers and large, bifacially worked core tools, particularly a slender picklike form. Until recently the Sangoan industry was thought to be relatively late, dating to after 50,000 years ago. New date estimations, however, place the beginning of the Sangoan, at least at some sites, as early as 100,000 years ago, making it contemporary with the other industries discussed in this chapter. The Sangoan industry has sometimes been described as an adaptation to a forest environment, but this connection has never been clearly demonstrated. Since human fossil evidence is lacking, the makers of the Sangoan industry are unknown.

In South Africa, however, a new Middle Stone Age industry (sometimes called **Pietersburg**) appears that shows a complete break with the preceding Acheulian. Although numerous sites have been investigated, some with very deep deposits and long archaeological sequences, very little is known of the transition to this new industry. One of the best-known of these sites is **Klasies River Mouth** on the southern coast of South Africa (Figure 6.5). The new industry appears with initial occupation of

the site, dated to greater than 120,000 years ago. It is a flake-blade industry, with characteristic long, parallel-sided flakes struck from specially made cores. This industry persisted at Klasies River Mouth for perhaps 80,000 years. The site is rich in animal bone remains, indicative of the hunting and/or scavenging of a wide range of species (Klein 1976; Binford 1984). Shellfish were also gathered throughout the occupation, the earliest example of exploitation of marine resources.

Human remains recovered at Klasies River Mouth have been interpreted as *Homo sapiens sapiens*—modern humans. Even earlier modern humans have recently been discovered in East Africa, at Herto, Middle Awash, Ethiopia (White et al. 2003). This very early appearance of modern human forms is of great importance to our understanding of how anatomically modern humans spread throughout the Old World. Klasies River Mouth will be discussed in more detail in the following chapter.

CONCLUSION

For much of the latter part of the Pleistocene, until about 30,000 years ago, Europe and the Middle East were occupied by the Neanderthals, a form of human distinctly different from ourselves. They made and used stone tools that were quite different from and more varied than those of the preceding Acheulian. Neanderthals began to intentionally bury their dead, but what this implies about their worldview has been the subject of much debate. In the meantime, by about 100,000 years ago, modern *Homo sapiens sapiens* began appearing in southern Africa. In the next chapter, we examine the replacement of the Neanderthals by anatomically modern humans.

KEY TERMS

Aterian   104
Borers   99
Burins   99
Combe-Grenal   100
Dar-es-Sultan   104
Denticulates   99

Ehringsdorf   98
Engis   94
Feldhofer   95
Forbes' Quarry,
   Gibraltar   94
Glacials   96

Trinkaus, Erik, and Pat Shipman
1992 *The Neandertals: Of Skeletons, Scientists, and Scandal.* New York: Vintage Books.
This book presents a detailed history of the discovery of the Neanderthals and shows how interpretations of Neanderthal behavior and phylogeny have changed through time.

Wong, Kate
2000 Who Were the Neanderthals? *Scientific American* 282 (4): 98–107.
An up-to-date summary of recent research on the Neanderthals and their relationship to anatomically modern humans.

QUESTIONS FOR DISCUSSION

1. How have Neanderthals been portrayed in film and literature, and how do these portrayals compare to the archaeological record of Neanderthals' behavior?

2. Why do you think that Neanderthals buried their dead?

3. What can some tool technology tell us about Neanderthal behavior?

FURTHER READING

Mellars, P.
1996 *The Neanderthal Legacy: An Archaeological Perspective from Western Europe.* Princeton, NJ: Princeton University Press.
An important book on the archaeology of the Neanderthals in Europe.

Stringer, Christopher, and Clive Gamble
1993 *In Search of the Neanderthals.* New York: Thames and Hudson.
A readable introduction to the archaeology and physical anthropology of the Neanderthals, written by two of the foremost authorities on the subject.

PART 2

THE ORIGINS OF MODERN HUMAN SOCIETY

Part 2 examines the problem of the biological and cultural evolution of early modern humans. Since modern humans were the first hominins to inhabit the Arctic and sub-Arctic regions of both the Old World and the Americas, the chapters in this part examine the subsistence practices and settlement patterns of early modern humans in Eurasia, as well as the peopling of the Americas and Australia. Chapter 7 examines the molecular, fossil, and archaeological evidence for the appearance of early modern humans. Chapters 8 and 9 examine the archaeological evidence for early modern human settlement and subsistence in the Near East, Africa, and Europe. Chapter 10 focuses specifically on the art of the Upper Paleolithic and its implications for communication, social organization, and religion. In Chapter 11, we examine the migration routes that modern humans may have used to enter the New World, as well as new evidence for the dating of the earliest human settlement in the Americas. Chapter 12 examines the initial Pleistocene colonization of Australia and the subsequent development of hunter-gatherer societies in Greater Australia.

TIMELINE

	Africa			Middle East			East Asia	
10,000 years ago						Natufian		
	Nelson Bay Cave		Late Stone Age	Ein Gev I		Kebaran		
20,000								
					Anatomically Modern Humans	Ahmarian and Levantine Aurignacian (Early Upper Paleolithic)		
30,000								
40,000						Emiran		
50,000		Anatomically Modern Humans	Age				Modern Humans	Mode I Industry
					Neanderthals			
60,000					Kebara			
			Stone					
70,000			Howieson's Poort		?	Middle Paleolithic (Mousterian) Industry		
80,000			Middle					
							?	
90,000	Katanda				Anatomically Modern Humans			
							Late *Homo erectus*	
100,000				Qafzeh				

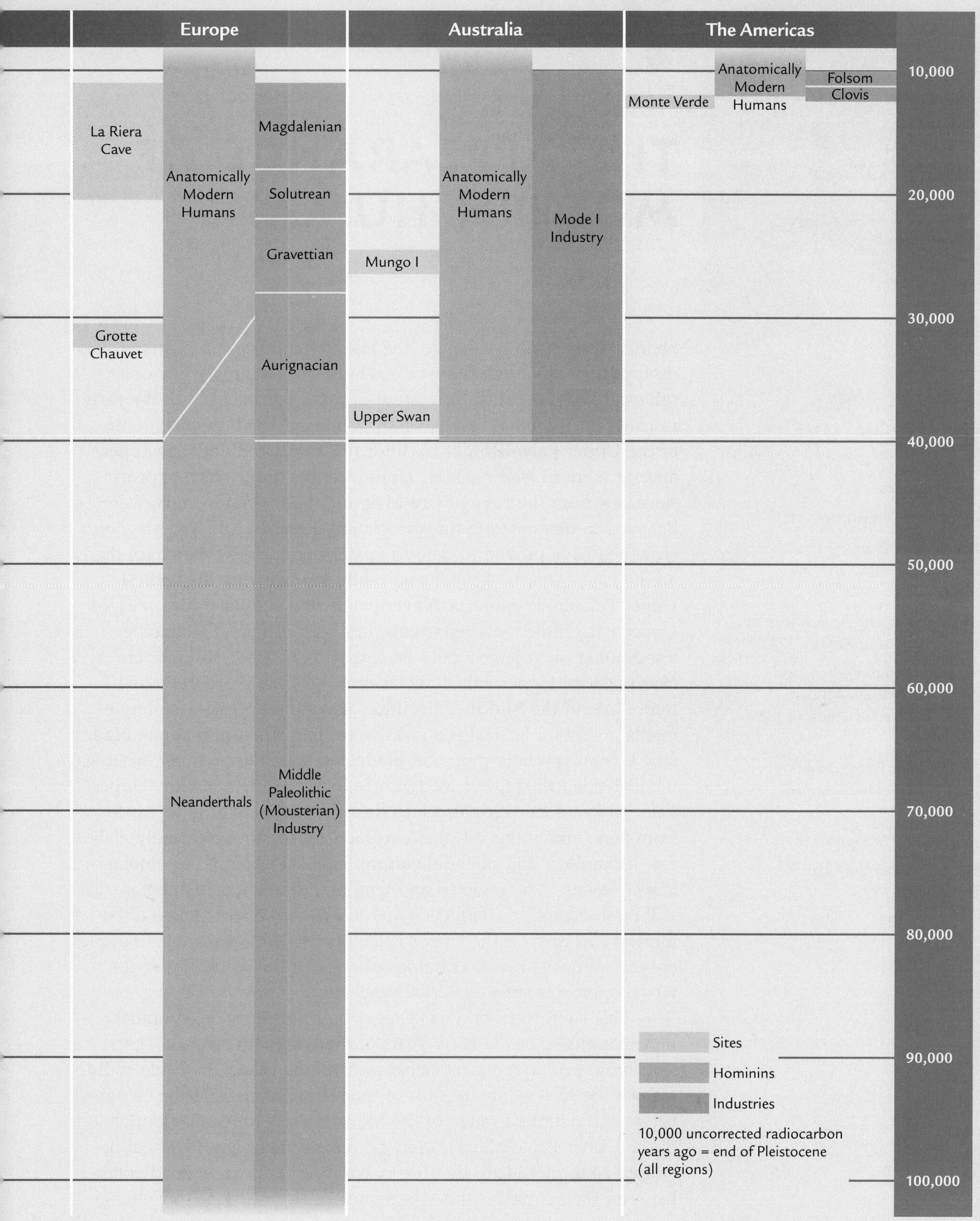

	Europe	Australia	The Americas

Europe | Australia | The Americas

10,000

La Riera Cave

Magdalenian

Anatomically Modern Humans

Anatomically Modern Humans

Monte Verde

Anatomically Modern Humans

Folsom
Clovis

Solutrean

20,000

Mode I Industry

Gravettian

Mungo I

Grotte Chauvet

30,000

Aurignacian

Upper Swan

40,000

50,000

60,000

Middle Paleolithic (Mousterian) Industry

Neanderthals

70,000

80,000

Sites

90,000

Hominins

Industries

10,000 uncorrected radiocarbon years ago = end of Pleistocene (all regions)

100,000

7

THE APPEARANCE OF MODERN HUMANS

Shortly after 28,000 years ago, the last of the European Neanderthals disappeared. Anatomically modern humans, essentially like ourselves, took their place. In western Europe, where much of the early research on Paleolithic archaeology was conducted, the beginning of the **Upper Paleolithic** is traditionally associated with the appearance of modern *Homo sapiens*. Until recently, the modern-appearing skeletons from the cave of **Cro-Magnon**, discovered in 1868, were believed to demonstrate this association. Recently, the Cro-Magnon skeletons have proved to date to a later period (see following); there are no *Homo sapiens* skeletons currently known from the earliest Upper Paleolithic contexts. Nevertheless, the sudden appearance of Upper Paleolithic tools represents a radical change of technology, a technology that later would be clearly associated with modern *Homo sapiens*. Upper Paleolithic assemblages are far more varied than those of the Middle Paleolithic. A wide range of stone implements, many for specialized tasks, were retouched from stone **blades** struck from specially prepared **blade cores.** Blades are long, narrow, parallel-sided flakes, at least twice as long as they are wide. Upper Paleolithic assemblages also include large numbers of tools made from bone and antler. All these artifacts reflect an increasingly elaborate technology and material culture. Upper Paleolithic assemblages display many more regional and temporal differences than before, as will be discussed in Chapters 8 and 9. Art, virtually nonexistent before, arrives early in the Upper Paleolithic. The most notable examples are the spectacular cave paintings of western Europe (Chapter 10), which appear as early as 32,000 years ago.

This swift transition has caught both scholarly and popular imaginations since the early years of the twentieth century. The slouching, primitive Neanderthal pictured by Marcellin Boule could scarcely be seen as an ancestor of modern humans, and the contrast between the limited range of the Mousterian culture and the richness of the Upper Paleolithic strongly reinforced that view. Fictional literature soon picked up the theme, building on the imagined conflict between the simple Neanderthals and the sophisticated, technologically superior modern humans who replaced them. Modern fiction, notably Jean Auel's *Clan of the Cave Bear,* has continued this tradition, albeit with more sympathy for the cultural and emotional capacities of the Neanderthals.

EARLY THEORIES ON THE ORIGINS OF MODERN HUMANS

When and where did anatomically modern *Homo sapiens* originate? During the early years of the twentieth century, the predominant view was that modern humans must have arrived from outside Europe and that the Neanderthals had little, if any, role in modern human ancestry. Some scholars, such as Boule, saw the Neanderthals as so different that the divergence of modern humans from the Neanderthal line must have occurred far in the past. Others, such as the American anthropologist W. W. Howells (1976), argued that the split occurred much more recently and that modern humans and the so-called classic Neanderthals both derived from more generalized, although Neanderthal-like, ancestors.

A few scholars held a very different view. Ales Hrdlicka (1927) and, later, Franz Weidenreich, contended that certain anatomical traits seen in the fossil evidence suggested that the races of modern humans found in Europe, Asia, and Africa could be traced backward to the earliest inhabitants of those areas. According to this model, which emphasized regional continuity, the Neanderthals were direct ancestors of the modern human inhabitants of Europe, while the modern human inhabitants of East Asia and Africa found their roots in the peoples represented at Zhoukoudian and Kabwe, respectively. Milford Wolpoff (1989) championed another version of this perspective, known as the **multiregional hypothesis.** Wolpoff emphasized the unity of modern *Homo sapiens.* He proposed that, while the African, Asian, Australian, and European populations evolved simultaneously, sufficient interbreeding always occurred among these groups to maintain *Homo sapiens* as a single, if variable, species.

THE BIOCHEMICAL EVIDENCE

In recent years new fossil evidence, new absolute dates, and new biochemical evidence have strongly challenged the multiregional hypothesis. One of the most important new lines of research has been developed by molecular biologists, using a body of data totally separate from the fossil and archaeological evidence. In 1987 Rebecca Cann, Mark Stoneking, and Allan Wilson published a study comparing the mitochondrial DNA (see the Archaeology in Practice box) from 147 individuals from around the world (Cann et al. 1987). A statistical analysis of these data led them to conclude that the most likely origin for modern *Homo sapiens* lay in Africa. Later studies involving larger samples led them to suggest that all modern humans have descended from an ancestral population that spread out from Africa about 200,000 years ago. In the opinion of these molecular biologists, the preexisting populations of Europe and Asia, including the Neanderthals and the Asian representatives of *Homo erectus*, played no role at all in the ancestry of modern humans. This scenario, known as the **Out-of-Africa model**[1], was readily accepted by those anthropologists who had reached similar conclusions based on the fossil evidence (Stringer and Andrews 1988). More recently, however, the statistical methods used in these DNA studies have been questioned, and the proposed dating has been questioned as well. According to critics, the data can be interpreted to support points of origin other than Africa, and if Africa was the origin, the date of departure might be early enough to represent the initial spread of the hominins into Europe and Asia. While these issues

---

[1]The model is sometimes referred to as Out-of-Africa 2 to distinguish it from the initial movement of *Homo ergaster*/*Homo erectus* out of Africa during the early Pleistocene.

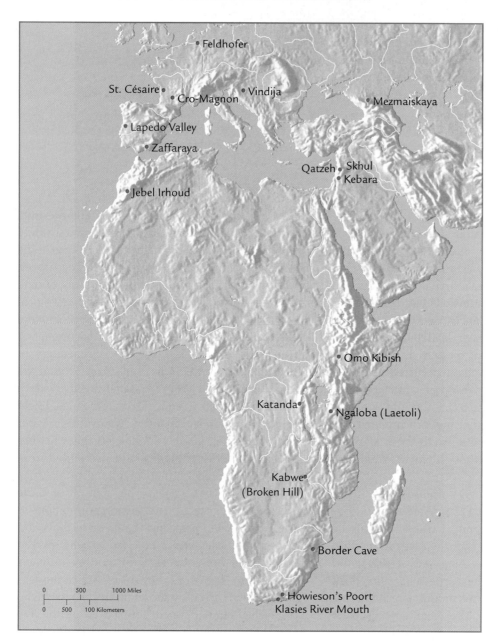

FIGURE 7.1   Location of sites mentioned in this chapter. The cave of Tabun is immediately adjacent to Skhul.

remain unresolved, recent analyses of mitochondrial DNA (mtDNA) recovered from Neanderthal skeletons have cast additional doubt on the multiregional model.

In 1997 a team of German and American researchers (Krings et al. 1997) reported their analyses of mtDNA extracted from the Neanderthal type specimen from Feldhofer Cave in Germany. They found that the Neanderthal mtDNA was outside the range of variation of modern humans and concluded that Neanderthals contributed little, if anything, to modern human mtDNA. Three years later, another team of researchers (Ovchinnikov et al. 2000) reported the extraction and sequencing of mtDNA from a second Neanderthal individual, a 29,000-year-old infant from **Mezmaiskaya Cave** (Figure 7.1)

ARCHAEOLOGY IN PRACTICE

Biochemical Evidence of Heredity and the Molecular Clock

How closely related are the living populations of modern humans? In recent years techniques for the analysis of DNA have provided a new, quantitative measure of how closely any two individuals are related. DNA (deoxyribonucleic acid) is the molecular basis for heredity. In DNA four different bases are strung together in a multitude of different ways. These combinations constitute the genetic code, which in turn determines the characteristics of an organism. Mutations are random changes in the base sequences of DNA. Mutation introduces new variation into a population and can lead to evolutionary change.

The millions of genes that determine the characteristics of an individual are enclosed in the nucleus of each cell. Outside the nucleus cells also contain structures known as mitochondria. Each mitochondrion contains its own genome of only 37 genes. While the DNA in the nucleus of the cell is derived from the fusion of sperm and egg during fertilization, **mitochondrial DNA (mtDNA)** is inherited from the mother alone.

Observations have indicated that mutations occur frequently in mitochondrial DNA. Consequently, this DNA provides a good measure of how closely two individuals are related. The farther back in time

they descended from a common maternal ancestor, the more different their mtDNA will be. Since all humans are related, ultimately, all modern people must share a common maternal ancestor at some time in the past. The question is how far back in time this common ancestor is to be found.

Mitochondrial DNA appears to mutate at a fairly constant rate. It can be used, therefore, as a kind of molecular clock. Presumably, the older the population, the more time it would have had to accumulate genetic variation. So, the more variable a population's DNA, the farther back in time it diverged from its common ancestor. The difficulty lies in calibrating the clock. Rebecca Cann and her coworkers used two events with established dates to do this. The mtDNA of humans and chimpanzees, which diverged about 5 million years ago, are about 25 times more different than the variability seen in modern human populations. At the other end of the scale, Australian and New Guinea aboriginals, who reached those areas about 50,000 to 60,000 years ago, are only about one-third as variable as are modern humans as a whole. These considerations suggest that modern humans diverged from a common maternal ancestor roughly 200,000 years ago.

Recently, the mitochondrial DNA studies have been joined by new studies of certain genes found within the nuclear DNA (Tishkoff et al. 1996). One set of studies has concentrated on genes found on the Y chromosome (Dorit et al. 1995), making it possible to track human ancestry back through the paternal as well as the maternal line. The nuclear DNA studies agree rather well with mtDNA findings, suggesting that living humans descended from a common ancestor between 100,000 and 200,000 years ago.

The mtDNA data can also be used to construct family trees, using a statistical technique known as cluster analysis. Individuals with the greatest similarity are first grouped together; these groups are in turn linked to other groups, and the process is repeated until all the individuals are linked to a common ancestor. When this was done, individuals with the most closely similar mtDNA generally came from the same geographic region, and the pattern suggested that the earliest ancestor of modern humans came from Africa. The conclusion seemed clear: About 200,000 years ago (give or take 100,000 years) modern humans migrated out of Africa, completely displacing the preexisting inhabitants of Europe and Asia.

in the Caucasus of Georgia. That individual's mtDNA was also outside the range of variation of modern humans. Moreover, the Mezmaiskaya mtDNA is strikingly similar to the mtDNA from the Feldhofer specimen, even though Feldhofer is located approximately 2500 km (1550 mi.) from Mezmaiskaya.

FOSSIL EVIDENCE: THE APPEARANCE OF MODERN HUMANS IN AFRICA

The evidence from mtDNA is supplemented by a rich record of fossils from Africa, the Near East, and Europe (see Figure 7.1). Fossil evidence that has gradually accumulated is interpreted today as demonstrating the early evolution of African *Homo*

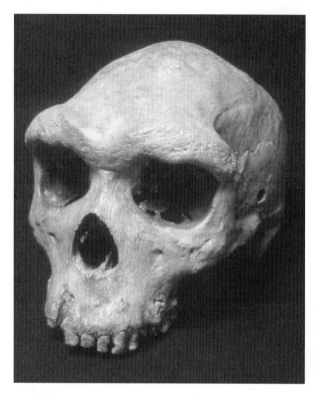

FIGURE 7.2   Kabwe (Broken Hill) skull, formerly known as Rhodesian Man.

erectus into anatomically modern *Homo sapiens*. The Kabwe (Broken Hill) skull from Zambia appears to date to near the beginning of this process, perhaps 200,000 years ago (Figure 7.2). This robust skull is problematic, with a mixture of *erectus*-like and more modern features. Limb bones found nearby somewhat resemble more modern *Homo sapiens*. Some scholars (Stringer and Gamble 1993: 127) would group the skull with *Homo heidelbergensis* (Chapter 5) and consider it a possible ancestor of both the Neanderthals and modern humans.

Fossil skulls dating to between 200,000 and 100,000 years ago that are regarded as transitional to modern *Homo sapiens* have been found in several parts of Africa. **Omo 2,** from Omo Kibish in Ethiopia, dated to about 195,000 years ago, is particularly notable. The rear of this skull resembles *Homo erectus,* but the face looks quite modern, with practically no brow ridge. A rather similar specimen was found at **Jebel Irhoud** in Morocco, although the dating is not so certain. A skull from the site of

Ngaloba, Laetoli, Tanzania, dating to about 130,000 years ago, was found along with Middle Stone Age artifacts. This skull also has a mixture of ancient and modern features, but housed a fully modern-sized brain.

Recent excavations at **Herto Bouri**, a series of localities in the Herto Member of the Bouri Formation in the Middle Awash region of Ethiopia, have revealed a series of hominin fossils that appear to be directly ancestral to anatomically modern humans. The one immature and two adult hominins have been dated to between 160,000 and 154,000 years ago. While there is considerable diversity among contemporary hominins, the Herto specimens are clearly morphologically intermediate between earlier African specimens like Kabwe and later anatomically modern humans from Klasies River Mouth (see following; White et al. 2003: 745). Associated artifact assemblages are transitional between the Acheulian and the African Middle Stone Age (Clark et al. 2003). Both Levallois flakes and Acheulian bifaces and cleavers were recovered. The artifact assemblages and fossil hominins from Herto provide a crucial link between earlier African fossils and artifact traditions and later anatomically modern humans from Africa.

The earliest modern humans appear nearly 200,000 years ago in Africa. An anatomically modern skull and long bones found at **Omo Kibish,** not far from the spot where Omo 2 was found, may date to about 195,000 years ago (McDougall et al., 2005). At Dar-es-Sultan in Morocco, a modern-looking skull was found in association with Middle Stone Age Aterian artifacts (Chapter 6). Modern-appearing humans' fossils have been found in the Middle Stone Age levels of **Border Cave** in Natal, South Africa, but it is possible that those fossils may be intrusive from later deposits.

Of great interest is the series of skull fragments and limb bones from Klasies River Mouth, South Africa (mentioned in Chapter 6). These fragments, which closely resemble those of modern humans, are associated with the Middle Stone Age assemblages at the site and date from 70,000 to 120,000 years ago (Rightmire and Deacon 1991). The site is rich in animal bone remains indicative of the hunting and/or scavenging of a wide range of species.

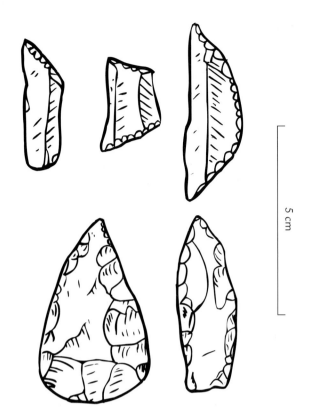

5 cm

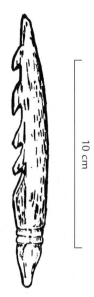

10 cm

FIGURE 7.3   Typical tools, including microliths, of the Howieson's Poort industry.

FIGURE 7.4   Example of a finely worked bone point from Katanda, Zaire.

Klasies River Mouth, which is very near the coast, provides the earliest example for the exploitation of marine resources (Klein 1979). Although no evidence for fishing was recovered, seals made up a substantial part of the diet, and shellfish were also gathered throughout the occupation.

The elongated flake-blade Pietersburg-like Middle Stone Age stone industry at Klasies River Mouth somewhat resembles the blade industries that make their appearance with the Eurasian Upper Paleolithic (see Chapters 8 and 9), although no direct relationship is likely. This stone industry persists through the entire Middle Stone Age occupation of the site complex, except for a brief interruption that occurred about 70,000 years ago. For a short time, the flake-blade industry was displaced by an industry that included very small stone blades, often trimmed into tiny geometric forms known as **microliths** (very tiny stone tools). This industry, called **Howieson's Poort,** is known from a number of sites in the region (Figure 7.3). The Howieson's Poort industry is by far the earliest known occurrence of a microlithic stone industry; it anticipates by 50,000 years the microlithic assemblages that would characterize the Epi-paleolithic and Mesolithic cultures of the Near East and Europe (Chapters 13 and 16). The makers of the Howieson's Poort industry are unknown, as no associated human remains have been found.

Even more unusual are the finds made by Alison Brooks and John Yellen at some Middle Stone Age sites at **Katanda,** in the Upper Semliki Valley, Zaire (Brooks et al. 1995; Yellen et al. 1995). In close association with Middle Stone Age artifacts, these sites contained a series of finely worked bone points, many with barbs along one or both edges (Figure 7.4). In general form and sophistication of manufacture, these bone points resemble artifacts typical of the European Upper Paleolithic of 15,000 years ago. Surprisingly, thermoluminescence and electron spin resonance measures have dated the deposits to approximately 90,000 years ago. Numerous bones of large catfish were

CASE STUDY

Skhul, Qafzeh, and Kebara: Anatomically Modern Humans and Neanderthals in the Levant

In the period between the First and Second World Wars, a series of excavations was conducted in the Near East that did much to establish the prehistory of the area. The research done by the British archaeologist Dorothy Garrod, along with an international, interdisciplinary team, in the Mount Carmel region of northern Israel was particularly important. Garrod excavated a number of caves and rock shelters in the Wadi Mughara (Valley of the Caves) near the coast of the Mediterranean. The deposits in these caves spanned much of the Paleolithic and helped define the sequence of archaeological industries of the Levant (Garrod and Bate 1937). Two of these caves, the **Mugharet es Skhul** (the cave of the kids) and the **Mugharet et Tabun** (the cave of the oven) contained Middle Paleolithic layers filled with artifacts belonging to the Levalloiso-Mousterian industry (Chapter 6). Both caves also contained a number of human skeletons. The cave of Skhul held the remains of 10 individuals, including a child, apparently intentionally buried. Several lay in what is known as a flexed posture,

with their knees drawn up to their chests. One male held the jaw of a wild boar in his arms. In the cave of Tabun, a skeleton of a woman was found, plus a separate large jawbone.

All these skeletons had features more or less reminiscent of the European Neanderthals, but the fossils differed greatly from one another. The Skhul skeletons, particularly, looked far more like modern humans than did those from Tabun. All, however, were associated with Mousterian tools. Initially, the entire group of Mount Carmel skeletons was regarded as a highly variable Neanderthal population.

The cave of **Qafzeh,** near Nazareth, was also initially excavated between the wars by the French archaeologist René Neuville. Neuville found five skeletons in the Middle Paleolithic Mousterian levels, but he died before the data could be published. In the 1960s Bernard Vandermeersch took over the excavation of the cave. The remains of 24 more individuals were found. Among them was a burial of a young woman with a 6-year-old child buried across her feet. Another child was buried with the skull of a deer, complete with antlers. The Qafzeh skeletons, accompanied by Mousterian tools, looked very much like the skeletons from Skhul.

Vandermeersch undertook an extensive study of the Qafzeh remains (Vandermeersch 1981). He demonstrated that the Qafzeh people (and the very similar Skhul population) were actually early anatomically modern humans rather

found along with the bone points. The people at Katanda probably camped there to fish in the nearby streams—perhaps the bone points served as fishing implements. If the early dates hold true, the Katanda sites may provide evidence for much greater technological sophistication at this early time than had previously been thought possible. Recently, Brooks, the excavator of Katanda, and McBrearty (2000) have argued that many of the characteristics traditionally associated with the European Upper Paleolithic, such as worked bone and blade tools, actually appear much earlier in the African Middle Stone Age (See On the Cutting

Edge: Debating the Origin of Modern Human Behavior).

New finds and new much earlier dates assigned to African stone industries strongly support Africa as the original home of modern *Homo sapiens*. New absolute dates have also changed our picture of the relationship of modern *Homo sapiens* to the Neanderthals in the Near East.

The relationship between modern humans and the Neanderthal people in the Levant remains very unclear. It is difficult to imagine such dissimilar groups living side by side, producing essentially the same material culture. Although the stone tool

FIGURE 7.A Early modern human skull from Qafzeh, northern Israel.

beyond the limits of radiocarbon age determination (Chapter 9). Some scholars assumed that because the Skhul and Qafzeh people were closer to modern humans, they must necessarily be later than the Neanderthals of Tabun. Israeli zoologist Eitan Tchernov (1981, 1989) argued otherwise. On the basis of his studies of the small mammal remains found in the deposits, Tchernov argued that the Qafzeh hominins were much earlier than had been supposed. This idea was greeted with skepticism, but when electron spin resonance and thermoluminescence dating became available, these methods confirmed Tchernov's inference. Qafzeh was dated by thermoluminescence to 92,000 years ago, and by electron spin resonance to between 100,000 and 120,000 years ago. Somewhat later, Skhul was found to have similarly early dates. (See Schwarcz 1994 for a summary of the dating evidence from these sites.)

At the same time, the Neanderthal skeleton from Kebara Cave was securely dated to between 64,000 and 59,000 years ago. (The excavation of the Neanderthal skeleton from the cave of Kebara in northern Israel has been described in some detail in Chapter 6.) This dating evidence means that Neanderthal people were inhabiting the Levant about 40,000 years *after* modern humans lived there. New dates for the Neanderthal layers at Tabun, on the other hand, have placed them at about the same time as Qafzeh and Skhul.

than Neanderthals (Figure 7.A). Their stone industry, however, was Levalloiso-Mousterian, essentially the same as that of other undoubted Neanderthals who also lived in the region. This finding shattered the old belief that only Neanderthals were associated with the Mousterian. Contrary to the expectations of archaeologists, two very different groups of people were making and using the same kinds of tools.

More surprises were to come. Dating of the Near Eastern Middle Paleolithic deposits had long been a problem, as their dates lay well

assemblages used by the Neanderthals and early modern humans in the Near East are quite similar, detailed studies of the stone tool assemblages and the fauna from these sites have pointed up some subtle but intriguing differences in the ways these two groups made a living (Lieberman and Shea 1994; Shea 1993). The faunal data indicate that the sites occupied by anatomically modern humans were occupied for only one season, while those occupied by Neanderthals were occupied for more than one season. On the other hand, the stone tool assemblages associated with the Neanderthals include a slightly higher percentage of projectile

(spear) points, indicating that the Neanderthals may have hunted somewhat more frequently than anatomically modern humans did. The increased intensity of hunting by the Neanderthals might have been a strategy for coping with the animal resource depletion that resulted from multiseasonal occupation of sites over a long period of time (Lieberman and Shea 1994).

The Levant is an ecological crossroads where African and European flora and fauna intermingle and alternate according to changes in climatic conditions. Perhaps Neanderthal and modern human groups alternated in the region, with Neanderthal

ON THE CUTTING EDGE *Debating the Origin of Modern Human Behavior*

DNA studies and the recent fossil finds from Herto in East Africa have provided strong evidence that anatomically modern humans evolved in Africa shortly after 200,000 years ago. An important question that remains unanswered is whether these biologically modern people behaved in the same way as later modern humans did. To phrase the question another way, "Can we see Upper Paleolithic hunting and gathering societies as the ancestors of those known to us from ethnohistory?" (Bar-Yosef 2002: 375). Archaeologists have advanced two competing theories to explain the origin of modern human behavior: 1) Modern human behavior developed in Africa along with early modern humans some time before 100,000 years ago (McBrearty and Brooks 2000). 2) Modern human behavior was the result of a "creative revolution" (Pfeiffer 1985) some time around 50,000 years ago in Africa that led to the development of modern human behavior (Klein 1995; 1999: 590) and the expansion of modern human populations throughout the world.

As noted at the start of this chapter, much of the early research on Upper Paleolithic archaeology was conducted in Europe. In Europe, the transition from the Middle to the Upper Paleolithic was marked by several significant changes in material culture, including increasing artifact diversity, standardization of artifact types, blade technology, worked bone and antler, personal ornaments and art, structured living spaces, ritual, economic intensification, an enlarged geographic range, and expanded exchange networks (McBrearty and Brooks 2000: 491; Bar-Yosef 2002: 365–369). The unresolved questions for archaeologists are when, how, and why these modern behavioral traits developed.

Richard Klein (1995, 1999) has argued that the appearance of modern behavior resulted from a mutation that led to the development of the fully modern brain. This mutation may not be apparent in the skeleton, but it led to rapid and revolutionary changes in human behavior. These changes are seen "as a cultural explosion, or as a big bang—the origins of the universe of human culture" (Mithen 1996: 152). The early modern humans recovered from sites such as Skhul and Qafzeh in the Middle East and Klasies River Mouth in Africa were, in Klein's view, anatomically modern, but not behaviorally modern. It was behaviorally modern humans who eventually replaced the Neanderthals in Europe and the Middle East some time after 50,000 years ago.

McBrearty and Brooks (2000) take a very different view of the Upper Paleolithic "revolution." They argue that many of the cultural changes that have traditionally been associated with the Middle to Upper Paleolithic transition in Europe can be seen in the African Middle Stone Age at considerably earlier dates. Moreover, they note that the African Middle Stone Age, unlike the European Mousterian, was made by anatomically modern people. McBrearty and Brooks point to evidence such as the early use of bone tools at sites such as Katanda in the Republic of the Congo (formerly Zaire) to suggest that modern behavior developed gradually in Africa. In their view, the development of modern human behavior was an evolutionary process, not a revolutionary one.

---

groups moving in during times of harsh glacial conditions in the north (Tchernov 1992).

In the Middle East, Neanderthals were ultimately replaced by anatomically modern humans some time after 50,000 years ago (Shea 2003; see Chapter 8).

FROM AFRICA TO EUROPE

In broad terms the African and Near Eastern fossil evidence and the new dates provided by thermoluminescence and electron spin resonance accord well with conclusions drawn by the DNA specialists: Modern humans left Africa about 100,000 years ago. The early modern humans living in the caves of the Levant may well have been among that first wave of emigrants.

The appearance of modern Cro-Magnon people in Europe was traditionally dated to about 32,000 years ago. However, recent redating of the Cro-Magnon specimens indicate that these skeletons do not date to the early Upper Paleolithic (Henri-Gambier 2002a, 2002b). At present, no human fossils are known from Europe from the early part of the Upper Paleolithic period. It is possible that these people did not bury their dead; instead they may have exposed dead bodies to the elements. The early Upper Paleolithic Aurignacian stone tool industry, which appears to have been made by modern humans, first appeared in Europe around 40,000 years ago (Conard and Bolus 2003). Modern Europeans appear to have entered central Europe via the Danube corridor, and they also may have spread westward across the Mediterranean. Modern humans entered western Europe at a relatively late date, possibly at first coexisting with the Neanderthals and then displacing them. Modern Europeans arrived in eastern Europe by 35,000 years ago and appear to have replaced the local Neanderthal populations by 25,000–30,000 years ago (Hoffecker 1999).

SAINT CÉSAIRE AND THE LAST NEANDERTHALS

It is clear that some Neanderthals lingered on in western Europe even as modern humans were appearing. In 1979 construction workers discovered an archaeological site near the base of a cliff called La Roche à Pierrot, near the village of **Saint Césaire** in western France (Lévêque et al. 1993). A salvage excavation was quickly organized. When the site was dug, the archaeologists (led by François Lévêque) discovered the skeleton of the most recent Neanderthal then known. Thermoluminescence dates on flints near the skeleton placed its age at about 36,300 ± 2700 years ago. The Saint Césaire skeleton was a nearly complete, tightly flexed burial. What was most remarkable, though, was the stone industry with which it was associated. All previous European Neanderthals had been found along with Mousterian tools. The Saint Césaire Neanderthal was associated with a stone industry known as the **Châtelperronian**. Actually, the Châtelperronian contains many Mousterian artifact types, including Levallois flakes and Mousterian-like scrapers and points. What distinguishes the Châtelperronian industry is the prevalence of a pointed blade implement with a curved, blunted back, known as a Châtelperron knife. Although François Bordes had argued that the Châtelperronian evolved from the

Mousterian of Acheulian Tradition (Chapter 6), the Châtelperronian had always been considered an Upper Paleolithic industry, and it had tacitly been assumed to have been the work of modern humans.

How should this surprising discovery be interpreted? For those archaeologists who held to a multiregionalist view, the Saint Césaire find lent support to the idea that the Neanderthals were independently evolving to an Upper Paleolithic way of life. Those who argued that the Neanderthals were replaced by modern humans from elsewhere saw in the Saint Césaire Châtelperronian industry an example of the last Neanderthals borrowing ideas from the modern humans with whom they were then coming into contact.

During the past 20 years, even more recent Neanderthal fossils have been discovered in Europe. Neanderthal bones dating to 32,000 years ago were found at Zafarraya in Spain (Smith 2000). A Neanderthal fossil from **Vindija** in Croatia has been dated to 28,000 to 29,000 years ago (Smith et al. 1999), and the infant from Mezmaiskaya Cave in the Caucasus is of similar age (Golovanova et al. 1999). If the appearance of the early Upper Paleolithic Aurignacian industry is, in fact, associated with the entry of anatomically modern humans into Europe, then it is possible that Neanderthals and anatomically modern humans may have coexisted for several millennia.[2]

In 1998 an even more intriguing fossil discovery was made when a child's skeleton was found in Portugal's Lapedo Valley. The 24,500-year-old skeleton appears to be a modern human, but it shares some characteristics with Neanderthals, including short lower limbs. Some anthropologists have seen the **Lapedo Child** (Figure 7.5) as a hybrid between a Neanderthal and a modern human.

---

[2]The extent of the chronological overlap is a subject of debate among archaeologists. Variation in the amount of carbon in the upper atmosphere (see Archaeology in Practice, Chapter 9) has led to some anomalies in radiocarbon dates for the period 30,000 to 50,000 years ago. It is possible that some Neanderthals and Middle Paleolithic stone tool assemblages have dates that are somewhat too young, exaggerating the extent of chronological overlap between the Neanderthals and early anatomically modern humans (Conard and Bolus 2003: 358–9; see also Pettitt 1999).

FIGURE 7.5 The Lapedo Child, seen by some as a possible Neanderthal–modern human hybrid.

CONCLUSION

Although the Neanderthals and modern humans seem to have coexisted in Europe for several millenia, shortly after 28,000 years ago the last Neanderthals were replaced by modern humans. These modern humans carried with them the more advanced tools of the Aurignacian industry, which marked the beginning of the Upper Paleolithic period (Chapter 10). The nature of this replacement remains a matter of great debate. As Erik Trinkaus, a biological anthropologist from Washington University, recently noted:

> The extinction of the Neanderthals by early modern humans, whether by displacement or population absorption, was a slow and geographically mosaic process. The differences between the two groups in basic behavior and abilities must have been small and rather subtle. (UniSci 1999: 1)

For example, recent studies of faunal assemblages from the Middle East have shown that Neanderthals and anatomically modern humans hunted a similar range of species (Kaufman 2002). Detailed studies of the animal bones recovered from Grotte XVI in southern France have revealed no differences in animal use between the Middle Paleolithic and the Upper Paleolithic that could not be attributed to climatic changes (Grayson and Delpech 2003).

While Neanderthals ultimately became extinct, recent multidisciplinary research has shed new light on the biology and behavior of this archaic form of humanity.

KEY TERMS

Blade   110
Blade cores   110
Border Cave   114
Châtelperronian   119
Cro-Magnon   110
Herto Bouri   114
Howieson's Poort   115
Jebel Irhoud   114
Katanda   115
Lapedo Child   119
Mezmaiskaya Cave   112
Microlith   115
Mitochondrial DNA
 (mtDNA)   113
Mugharet es Skhul   116
Mugharet et Tabun   116
Multiregional
 hypothesis   111
Ngaloba   114
Omo 2   114
Omo Kibish   114
Out-of-Africa model/
 Out-of-Africa 2   111
Qafzeh   116
Saint Césaire   119
Upper Paleolithic   110
Vindija   119

QUESTIONS FOR DISCUSSION

1. Why do you think that Neanderthals were ultimately replaced by anatomically modern humans? How might this replacement have taken place?

2. What do the archaeological and fossil hominin remains from Qafzeh, Skhul, and Kebara tell us about the relationship between Neanderthals and modern humans in the Near East?

3. In what ways are the Neanderthals like modern humans? In what ways are they different?

FURTHER READING

Klein, Richard G.
    1999 *The Human Career: Human Biological and Cultural Origins*, 2nd ed. Chicago: University of Chicago Press.

McBrearty, Sally and Alison S. Brooks
    2000 The Revolution That Wasn't: A New Interpretation of the Origin of Modern Human Behavior. *Journal of Human Evolution* 39: 453–563.
    These readings provide two alternative views of the origins of modern human behavior. Klein's volume also provides a comprehensive overview of human biological evolution and cultural change.

8

LATE PALEOLITHIC CULTURES OF THE NEAR EAST AND AFRICA

As we saw in the previous chapter, the relationship between archaic and early modern humans is complex. While the ancestors of early modern humans appeared in Africa 160,000 years ago, modern humans did not replace the European Neanderthals until around 30,000 years ago. The relationship between archaic and modern humans is even more complicated in the Near East, where modern humans appeared at such sites as Qafzeh and Skhul more than 90,000 years ago but Neanderthals are known from more recent sites, including Kebara and Shanidar. Moreover, there is no simple correlation between fossil humans and the kinds of artifacts they left behind. In the Middle East, both Neanderthals and early modern humans made Mousterian tools. In addition, the differences between Neanderthal and modern behavior in the Near East are subtle; early modern humans appear to have been somewhat more mobile, while Neanderthals used more spear points, perhaps indicating that they hunted more frequently (Lieberman and Shea 1994).

How and why anatomically modern humans ultimately replaced the Neanderthals in the Middle East remains a subject of intense debate. The problem is exacerbated because we have no human fossils from the Near East dated to the period between 47,000 and 20,000 years ago. However, Shea (2003) has suggested that competition between Neanderthals and anatomically modern humans may have contributed to the development of modern human behavior in the Near East. Modern humans' ultimate success may have been based, in part, on the development of projectile weapons, such as bows and arrows and throwing spears, and the ability to establish larger social networks.

In this chapter we will examine the late Pleistocene cultures of the Near East and Africa, from about 40,000 years ago to the end of the Ice Age, about 10,000 years ago. We will be looking at the archaeological record of early modern humans, although human skeletal remains are few in both areas. The stone tool industries we will discuss are termed **Upper Paleolithic** in the Near East and northern Africa, while in sub-Saharan Africa, the term **Late Stone Age** is used. In addition to examining the development of stone tool technologies in these areas, we will also look at changes in settlement patterns and subsistence strategies. That is, we will ask how these early human populations made a living by hunting, gathering, and other activities, such as fishing.

Although identifying artifacts such as spear points as hunting weapons provides some information about these early humans, examining faunal remains (archaeologically recovered animal bones) plays a crucial role in the study of prehistoric subsistence. Bones are preserved with increasing frequency in late Pleistocene sites. The ways in which animal bones can be used to reconstruct hunting practices are described in the Archaeology in Practice box.

THE UPPER PALEOLITHIC IN THE NEAR EAST

Until the 1960s excavations of Upper Paleolithic sites in the Near East had focused on a limited number of caves and rock shelters. In the past 40 years, however, our knowledge of Upper Paleolithic sites in the Near East has expanded dramatically. Many new sites have been discovered as a result of archaeological survey projects in the Negev Desert, in the Sinai, and in southern Jordan. New caves and open sites have been excavated, and artifactual and faunal materials from old excavations have been reanalyzed. These efforts have resulted in a revised picture of life in the Near East in late Pleistocene times.

During the cold phases of the Pleistocene glaciations, ice sheets covered many of the northerly parts of Eurasia and North America. Although the Near East was not covered by glacial ice, the glaciations in the northern latitudes had significant effects on the climate of the region. In general, periods of glacial advance in the northern latitudes correspond to relatively cold and dry eras in the

Levant (the regions of the Near East bordering on the Mediterranean). The period between 75,000 and 45,000 years ago was a relatively dry period in the Near East, and relatively dry conditions continued until about 32,000 years ago. The climate became more humid between 32,000 and 22,000 years ago, but very cold and dry conditions prevailed between 22,000 and 13,000 years ago.

These climatic fluctuations would have had some impact on vegetation in the Near East, although the changes may not have been dramatic. The lusher areas of the Near East are characterized by a Mediterranean climate with short, mild winters and hot, dry summers. The vegetation is a mix of trees and maquis (shrubs), including oak, pistachio, cedar, pine, cypress, olive, laurel, and juniper (Gilead 1991: 112). The more marginal areas, including the Sinai, the Negev, southern and eastern Jordan, and the Syrian desert, are generally drier, with annual rainfalls of between 100 and 350 mm (4 and 14 in.). These marginal areas are characterized by steppe and desert vegetation. During the drier phases of the Pleistocene, areas of steppe

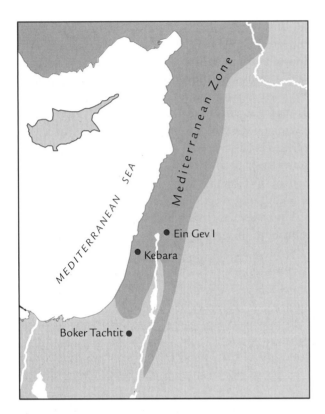

FIGURE 8.1 Location of Near Eastern sites mentioned in this chapter in relationship to the distribution of the Mediterranean climatic zone.

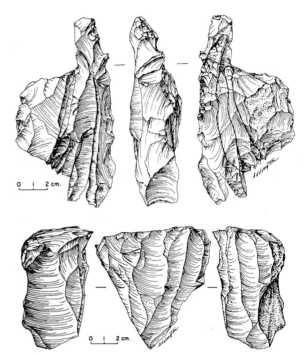

FIGURE 8.2 Levallois core from Boker Tachtit Level 1 (top) and blade core from Level 4 (bottom).

and desert may have expanded at the expense of Mediterranean forests (Figure 8.1).

Recent archaeological excavations in the Negev area suggest that the transition from Middle to Upper Paleolithic stone tool technology may have been a very gradual one in the Near East (Marks and Ferring 1988). The stone tool industry associated with this transition is often termed **Emiran** or Initial Upper Paleolithic. The site of **Boker Tachtit** (Marks and Kaufman 1983; Marks 1993), located near a spring-fed lake at the mouth of a narrow box canyon, was occupied between about 45,000 and 38,000 years ago. The occupation floors at Boker Tachtit provided evidence of core stone tool production, use, and discard. By careful refitting of the stone tool fragments, archaeologists were able to reconstruct the process by which stone tools were manufactured at the site. In the early phases of the site, points and blades were produced using a specialized Levallois technique, a typically Middle Paleolithic method of stone tool production (Figure 8.2). By the end of the occupation, blades were produced from single striking platform blade cores, a strategy that is more typical of later Upper Paleolithic sites. The Upper Paleolithic blade core technology is more efficient than the Levallois technique; that is, more cutting edge can be produced from the same amount of flint using the blade core technology. The excavator of the site, Anthony Marks of Southern Methodist University, argues that this change in stone tool technology is related to increasing mobility during the early Upper Paleolithic. As human populations moved more frequently, they would not always have had access to high-quality flint. The adoption of an Upper Paleolithic blade technology was one facet of adaptation to a more mobile way of life in the late Pleistocene.

Faunal data also suggest that Upper Paleolithic populations in the Levant were highly mobile. Daniel Lieberman (1993, 1994) has used gazelle teeth to determine the seasons at which Middle and Upper Paleolithic sites in the Near East were occupied. The cementum, or connective tissue, that surrounds

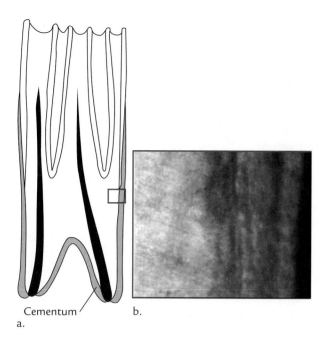

Cementum
a.   b.

FIGURE 8.3 Cementum or connective tissue in gazelle teeth forms seasonally alternating translucent and opaque bands: a. cross-section of a gazelle tooth with cementum shown in gray; b. photomicrograph showing translucent and opaque cementum bands. Studies of these bands suggest that Upper Paleolithic sites in the Near East were occupied for one season only.

gazelle teeth forms alternating translucent and opaque bands. The opaque and translucent bands alternate seasonally and reflect seasonal differences in diet (Figure 8.3). In the winter wet season, gazelles eat mainly grasses, while in the summer, their diet includes a higher percentage of browse (Lieberman 1994: 533). By examining the outermost layer of cementum, Lieberman was able to determine the season in which prehistoric gazelles were killed. Lieberman's (1993) research showed that at Middle Paleolithic sites such as Kebara gazelles were killed during more than one season, indicating that many of the Middle Paleolithic sites may have been occupied for an extensive portion of the year. Upper Paleolithic sites included the remains of gazelles that were killed during only one season, suggesting a pattern of seasonal movement.

The stone tool industries of the Near East and Europe that date between 35,000 to 40,000 and 10,000

years ago are usually termed Upper Paleolithic. Upper Paleolithic stone tool assemblages generally include large numbers of tools made on blades that are often struck from prismatic (regularly faceted) blade cores. The Near Eastern Upper Paleolithic sites that date between 38,000 and 22,000 years ago are termed early Upper Paleolithic (Gilead 1991: 121). The earliest early Upper Paleolithic stone tool assemblages from Near Eastern sites generally contain a very high proportion of blades (long, slender flakes that are more than twice as long as they are wide) and bladelets (small blades). The term **Ahmarian tradition** is used to refer to these blade and bladelet assemblages. Early Ahmarian assemblages date between approximately 38,000 and 25,000 years ago, while many scholars recognize a late Ahmarian industry dating between 22,000 and 16,000 years ago (Belfer-Cohen and Goring-Morris 2003: 8–9; see also Bar-Yosef 2002: 374). A small number of bone tools and bone ornaments have also been recovered from Ahmarian sites (Bar-Yosef 2000: 130; Kuhn et al. 2001). Other Upper Paleolithic sites have produced fewer blades and bladelets and more flakes, end scrapers, burins, and bone implements. These assemblages are termed **Levantine Aurignacian,** and their dates range from about 32,000 to about 26,000 years ago (Belfer-Cohen and Goring-Morris 2003: 8). Similar Aurignacian industries have been identified as far east as Iran and Iraq (Olszewski and Dibble 1994). The relationship between the Ahmarian and the Levantine Aurignacian is not entirely clear. However, today most scholars view the Ahmarian as a local development and argue that the Aurignacian industry was introduced from elsewhere, possibly Europe (Belfer-Cohen and Goring-Morris 2003: 11). Who developed these stone tool industries? While it is likely that both industries were made by early modern people, virtually no human remains have been recovered from any early Upper Paleolithic sites in the Near East.

A number of different lines of evidence suggest that the Upper Paleolithic population of the Near East was relatively small, especially in the core areas of Mediterranean vegetation. Surveys in the Mount Carmel area of northern Israel have revealed few Upper Paleolithic sites (Olami 1984). Most Upper Paleolithic sites are small, Upper Paleolithic levels

ARCHAEOLOGY IN PRACTICE

Animal Remains as Archaeological Evidence

Zooarchaeology (Brewer 1992; Reitz and Wing 1999), or faunal analysis, is the study of animal remains, primarily bone and shell, recovered from archaeological sites. It is one of the fastest-growing specializations in modern archaeology. Until the 1950s animal bones and shells were rarely collected from archaeological sites in a systematic way. Fine screens were not always used, so the remains of small vertebrates such as birds, fish, and rodents were often lost during excavation. In addition, excavators often saved only complete or identifiable bones, abandoning many bone fragments in the field. Animals bones were identified by zoologists, whose interests were not always the same as those of prehistoric archaeologists.

As archaeologists have become increasingly interested in the dynamic relationship between past human cultures and their environments, faunal studies have come to play a major role in archaeological analysis and interpretation. Faunal remains can provide valuable information on prehistoric subsistence strategies, hunting practices, and diets. Zooarchaeology also plays an important role in the study of animal domestication and animal husbandry practices (Chapter 16).

At the most basic level, faunal analysts can identify the animal species that were killed by prehistoric hunters. Since most archaeological animal bones have been butchered and broken, they are more difficult to identify than complete specimens. Bone fragments are identified using a **comparative collection** of modern reference specimens. Taphonomic studies (Chapter 3; see also Lyman 1994) can be used to distinguish the remains of hunted and scavenged animals from fauna that may have entered the deposit naturally.

Archaeologists want more than just a laundry list of the animal species present in an archaeological deposit; they want to know which animals were most important in prehistoric economies. A number of methods of quantification (Grayson 1984) have been developed to estimate the relative importance of the various animal species in an archaeological assemblage. The two most widely used techniques are the fragment count, or **NISP (number of identified specimens per taxon)** method, and the **MNI (minimum number of individuals).** Using the NISP method, species frequencies are based on the counts of bones identified to each species of animal.

For an assemblage that included 400 reindeer bones and 100 bison bones, the ratio of reindeer to bison would be 4 to 1. The MNI method is used to calculate the minimum number of animals that are needed to account for all the bones of a given species in an archaeological bone collection. For example, a minimum of 8 reindeer are needed to account for 8 left reindeer femurs (thigh bones). Thus, a minimum of 8 reindeer and 2 bison would also produce a reindeer-to-bison ratio of 4 to 1. Zooarchaeologists have debated endlessly over the relative merits of these two methods (see, for example, Grayson 1984; Marshall and Pilgrim 1993), but both are commonly used by faunal analysts.

Zooarchaeologists can also identify the ages of the animals that were killed by prehistoric hunters. Aging data can allow archaeologists to determine whether hunters were preying on whole herds of animals, whether they were focusing on mature adults, or whether they were killing only immature and elderly animals. Both teeth and limb bones can be used to estimate the ages of mammals. In mammals, the deciduous, or milk, teeth are replaced by permanent teeth in a known sequence. The degree of tooth wear

in cave sites are usually thin, and the area occupied is limited (Ronen 1975: 242). These data suggest that the Near East was occupied by small, highly mobile hunting and gathering bands during the Upper Paleolithic.

The early Upper Paleolithic economy of the Levant appears to be based on the hunting of a number of medium to large mammals, such as gazelles, fallow deer, and ibex. There is little evidence

for the use of small mammals, reptiles, fish, and invertebrates, although ostrich egg shells and tortoise carapaces are found in the arid regions (Rabinovich 2003). The role of plant foods in the Upper Paleolithic diet in the Near East remains unknown, but it is likely that plant foods played a significant role in the diet. Plant foods such as acorns and pistachios would have been available in the core Mediterranean areas.

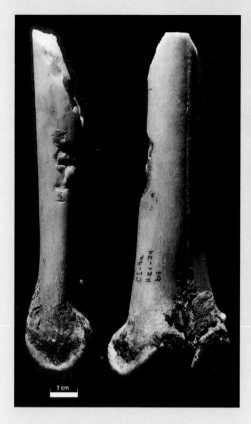

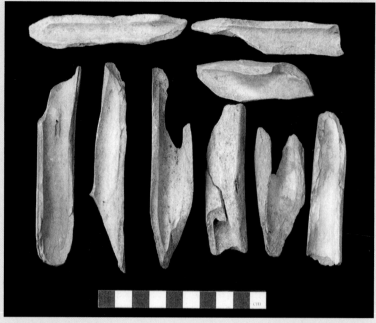

FIGURE 8.A Animal long bones broken for the extraction of marrow.

can be an approximate indicator of age in older animals. The limb bones of mature mammals can also be distinguished from those of juvenile mammals. In juvenile animals the ends of the long bones are separated from their shafts by plates of cartilage. When the animal nears bodily maturity, the plates of cartilage ossify, joining the bone ends to their shafts.

Zooarchaeologists can use a variety of techniques to determine the season or seasons in which animals were killed (Monks 1981). These data can indicate whether animals were being killed throughout the year or whether they were killed during only one season. The data have important implications for studies of settlement patterns and seasonal mobility (Lieberman 1994). In addition, large seasonal kills may have necessitated some form of meat preservation, such as drying, smoking, or freezing.

Butchery marks on bone can indicate the techniques used to dismember the carcass and to remove the meat from the bones. Limb bones may also have been broken for the extraction of marrow (Figure 8.A). In addition, careful identification and matching of the bones can allow the archaeologists to trace the distribution of a single animal across a site.

This pattern of small, mobile hunter-gatherer bands continued into the later part of the Upper Paleolithic. The term **Kebaran Complex** has been used to describe the stone tool industries from the Levant dated between approximately 19,000 and 14,000 years ago. The Kebaran Complex is named after the type site of Kebara Cave where the industry was first found in the uppermost layers. Traditionally, the Kebaran was distinguished from earlier Upper Paleolithic industries by the presence of microliths, very small stone implements that would have formed parts of **composite tools,** or tools made of more than one material. The microliths, for example, could have served as barbs for projectile points.

The site of **Ein Gev I** in eastern Israel typified the way of life of the Kebarans. The site overlooks the Sea of Galilee (Lake Kinnaret) and appears to

FIGURE 8.4 Excavations at the Kebaran site of Ein Gev I overlooking the Sea of Galilee in eastern Israel. The site appears to have been a seasonal hunters' encampment.

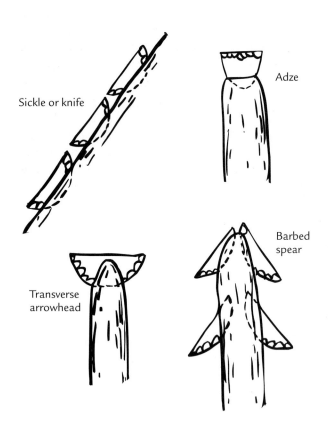

Sickle or knife

Adze

Transverse arrowhead

Barbed spear

FIGURE 8.5 Reconstructions of the various techniques for hafting backed microliths from Late Stone Age South African sites.

have been occupied on a seasonal basis by a small band of hunters (Figure 8.4). It has been suggested that the Kebarans practiced a circulating settlement pattern (Mortenson 1972), making use of a variety of different areas on a seasonal basis during the course of a single year.

About 13,000 years ago, the world's climate began to change. In the Near East, this final Pleistocene warming trend is associated with the expansion of the zones of Mediterranean vegetation. These climatic changes, which had profound effects on systems of human settlement and subsistence in the Near East, will be discussed in detail in Chapter 16.

THE LATE STONE AGE IN AFRICA

Many trends seen in the Near Eastern Upper Paleolithic are also apparent in the archaeology of the African Late Stone Age. In sub-Saharan Africa there is a great deal of continuity between the Middle Stone Age and the Late Stone Age industries, perhaps because both were made by anatomically modern humans. Late Stone Age industries generally show an overall reduction in artifact size, including a large number of microliths. These tools were often fitted into hafts or handles or used as barbs or tips for arrows (Figure 8.5). The edges of the microliths were steeply trimmed in order to blunt them so that they would not split the hafts (Phillipson 1993: 60–61). Late Stone Age industries also show increased evidence for regional diversification. During this period nearly all areas of the

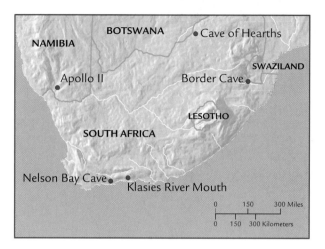

FIGURE 8.6 Location of Nelson Bay Cave in relation to other Middle and Late Stone Age sites in southern Africa.

noted in Chapter 7, the Middle Stone Age levels at Klasies River Mouth provide evidence for the use of marine foods, including molluscs, seals, and penguins. The faunal data from Nelson Bay Cave indicate that coastal resources were exploited even more effectively during the Late Stone Age (Klein 1979). The Nelson Bay faunal assemblage includes large numbers of bones of fish and flying seabirds such as cormorants, gulls, and gannets. Bows and arrows may have been used to hunt these birds. The artifactual assemblage from Nelson Bay Cave includes two types of artifacts that may have been used in fishing: stone net or line sinkers and bone gorges, small bone slivers with points on both ends, which may have been used to bait a line. The absence of fishing gear at Middle Stone Age sites such as Klasies River Mouth suggests that Middle Stone Age people may not have known how to fish (Klein 1999: 456).

Differences between the Middle and Late Stone Ages are also apparent in the hunting of terrestrial mammals. The Middle Stone Age faunal assemblage from the Klasies River Mouth is dominated by the remains of the relatively docile eland; remains of wild pigs are rare. In the Late Stone Age at Nelson Bay Cave, wild pigs, including bushpigs and warthogs, are far more common. Wild pigs are dangerous when attacked, so the intensive hunting of these animals must have required sophisticated technology such as snares and possibly the bow and arrow (Figure 8.7).

African continent were occupied, some for the first time. Clearly, some of the regional variability that is apparent in Late Stone Age industries reflects adaptation to different environments.

A number of Late Stone Age sites in South Africa have provided evidence for changes in hunting and subsistence practices. Of particular interest is the Late Stone Age site of **Nelson Bay Cave** in South Africa (Figure 8.6). The site is dated to between 19,000 and 12,000 years ago and is associated with a stone tool industry that includes many tiny bladelets and few standardized retouched tools. As

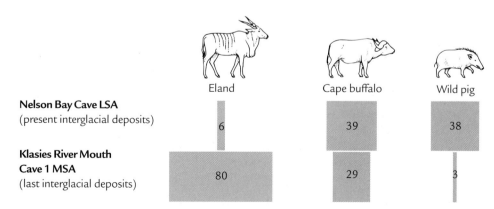

FIGURE 8.7 Comparison of MNIs from Middle Stone Age deposits at Klasies River Mouth and Late Stone Age deposits from Nelson Bay Cave.

ON THE CUTTING EDGE   *Ancient and Modern Hunters and Gatherers*

Archaeological research has shown that humans and their ancestors have lived by some combination of plant collection, scavenging, hunting, and fishing for almost all of human history. Within the past 10,000 years, however, farming has replaced hunting and gathering as the primary way of obtaining food. Today, very few hunter-gatherers remain, and those few people who continue to provide for themselves by hunting and gathering live in areas such as the Arctic that are inhospitable to agriculture. Since the 1950s both cultural anthropologists and archaeologists have sought to study the remaining hunting and gathering populations to understand how they make a living. The critical question for archaeologists studying ancient human societies is: To what extent can modern human hunter-gatherers be used as models for late Pleistocene and early post-Pleistocene hunter-gatherers?

In the early 1960s, Richard B. Lee (1968, 1979) began a program of long-term ethnographic research among the !Kung San people (formerly known as Bushmen) of southern Africa (Figure 8.B). The !Kung San subsist by hunting and gathering in the Kalahari Desert. Lee found that approximately two-thirds of the !Kung San diet was made up of vegetable foods that were collected primarily by women. The mongongo nut, which was available year-round, formed a staple of the !Kung diet. Hunting provided only about one-third of the !Kung food supply. The !Kung moved approximately six times per year to make use of plant and ani-

FIGURE 8.B   !Kung San foragers.

mal resources that were available in different areas at different seasons of the year. Lee's research showed that, at least among the !Kung, gathering played a more important role in the diet than did hunting.

Many archaeologists used the !Kung hunting and gathering practices as models for ancient hunters and gatherers. Unfortunately, the !Kung, who live in a hot, dry environment, are not necessarily good ethnographic models for ancient hunters and gatherers who lived in temperate environments such as Europe and North America. The temperate regions are characterized by warm summers and cold winters. While wild plants may be abundant in the summer and early fall, fresh plant foods are generally not available during the winter months. In the cold season in temperate regions, hunter-gatherers must rely on hunting, fishing, and/or stored plant materials. The availability of different plant and animal foods in different seasons can affect the ways hunter-gatherers organize their annual round.

In the late 1960s and early 1970s, the archaeologist Lewis Binford conducted research while living among the Nunamiut Inuit (Eskimo) in north central Alaska. He found that Nunamiut mobility patterns differed from those that had been described for the !Kung and other San foragers in the Kalahari. Binford (1980) developed two different models for the ways hunter-gatherers organize their settlement and subsistence systems. He termed these patterns foraging and collecting.

Foragers, such as the !Kung San of the Kalahari, move their campsites on a periodic or sea-

FIGURE 8.C Nunamiut hunter skinning a caribou killed during the spring migration.

sonal basis to make use of separate patches of food resources. Foragers do not generally store food; they hunt and gather nearly every day. In the Kalahari the San move their camps to make use of melons during the dry season. During the wet season, they move close to seasonal marshes that are attractive to game. **Collectors,** on the other hand, are logistically organized; rather than moving their camps on a periodic or seasonal basis, they obtain "specific resources through specially organized task groups" (Binford 1980: 10). These groups often seek large quantities of food that can serve as stores for considerable periods. An example is the Nunamiut hunting of caribou during their spring migration (Figure 8.C). Binford's notions of foragers and collectors represent the end points of a continuum of hunter-gatherer mobility strategies. Most hunter-gatherers fall somewhere in between these end points.

While archaeologists may gain insights into ancient hunter-gatherer subsistence and settlement by studying modern and historically recent hunter-gatherers, there are limits to what can be learned from these studies. Modern hunter-gatherers are *not* living representatives of the Stone Age. The San, the Nunamiut, and other modern hunter-gatherers have unique histories. For example, the Nunamiut today hunt using snowmobiles, while all Pleistocene hunters were obviously pedestrian. Historical and archaeological studies suggest that some of the San may have traded with Dutch colonists in early historic times (see Schrire 1984).

As we will see in Chapter 9, there is also faunal and artifactual evidence for increasingly sophisticated hunting technology in the Upper Paleolithic of Europe. In addition, coastal resources were increasingly exploited at some late Upper Paleolithic sites in western Europe.

CONCLUSION

In the Near Eastern Upper Paleolithic, we see the emergence of small, highly mobile bands of hunters and gatherers who made use of plant and animal resources on a seasonal basis. The contemporary Late Stone Age sites in Africa reveal an increasing sophistication in hunting and gathering technology, including the use of bird and fish resources.

KEY TERMS

Ahmarian tradition   125

Boker Tachtit   124

Collectors   131

Comparative
   collection   126

Composite tools   127

Ein Gev I   127

Emiran   124

Foragers   130

Kebaran Complex   127

Late Stone Age   123

Levantine
   Aurignacian   125

MNI (minimum number
   of individuals)   126

Nelson Bay Cave   129

NISP (number of
   identified specimens
   per taxon)   126

Upper Paleolithic   123

QUESTIONS FOR DISCUSSION

1. How has faunal analysis contributed to our understanding of the Upper Paleolithic period in the Middle East? How has it contributed to the study of the Late Stone Age in Africa?

2. The Middle East lies at the crossroad between Africa and Eurasia. To what extent can the Near Eastern Upper Paleolithic be seen as an independent development? What role did outside influences play in the Upper Paleolithic of the Near East?

3. Do we see evidence for a creative revolution in the Near East and Africa?

4. Do you think that the Upper Paleolithic inhabitants of the Near East were foragers or collectors? Why?

FURTHER READING

Gilead, I.
   1991   The Upper Paleolithic Period in the Levant. *Journal of World Prehistory* 5 (2): 105–154.
   An up-to-date and comprehensive review of the Levantine Upper Paleolithic by one of the foremost authorities in the field.

Goring-Morris, A. Nigel, and Anna Belfer-Cohen
   2003   *More than Meets the Eye: Studies on Upper Paleolithic Diversity in the Near East.* Oxford: Oxbow Books.
   An up-to-date and comprehensive review of the Upper Paleolithic in the Levant, which includes contributions from most of the scholars in the field. For the advanced reader.

Phillipson, David W.
   1993   *African Archaeology,* 2nd ed. Cambridge: Cambridge University Press.
   A comprehensive overview of African archaeology and prehistory from the earliest humans to the complex societies of the second millennium A.D.

9

THE INDUSTRIES AND CULTURES OF THE UPPER PALEOLITHIC IN EUROPE

Living in the information age, we marvel at the speed of the technological and social changes that go on around us. Today's laptop and desktop computers are more powerful than many mainframe computers that were in use just 30 years ago. We can hop on a commercial passenger jet in New York and arrive in London 6 hours later. Our family cars are made up of parts that are manufactured in a dozen different countries. At the same time, many older Americans who now take refrigerators for granted grew up in a world where ice for iceboxes was delivered in horse-drawn vans. While it is hard to imagine a world without cable television, DVDs, and video rentals, most Americans over age 55 remember their family's first purchase of a TV set. Although the nineteenth century was marked by the invention of the steam engine, railroads, the telephone, the phonograph, and the lightbulb, to name just a few examples, the speed of technological change in the twentieth century far outstripped that of the nineteenth.

The same kind of comparison can be made between the speed of change during the Lower and Middle Paleolithic periods in Europe and the more rapid and dramatic changes that took place during the Upper Paleolithic period, between about 40,000 and 10,000 years ago. The Acheulian stone tool industry lasted for more than 1 million years. Although Acheulian technology spread from Africa to Europe, the Middle East, and South Asia, the Acheulian industry remained essentially unchanged for hundreds of thousands of years. While there is clear evidence for the development of the Levallois technique during the later part of the Lower Paleolithic, the pace of technological innovation was slow at best. During the late Pleistocene, however, it appears that the rate of technological change was accelerating throughout the world. The changes can be seen in many areas of human activity, including the appearance of art (Chapter 10), improvements in hunting and foraging technology, and the spread of humans to Australia (Chapter 11) and the New World (Chapter 12). This acceleration in the rate of cultural and technological change was especially marked in Europe, because the Middle to Upper Paleolithic transition appears to correspond to the replacement of Neanderthals by anatomically modern humans. In this chapter we will examine the development of stone tool technology, subsistence practices, and settlement patterns during the late Pleistocene in Europe.

This chapter focuses on the stone tool industries that developed in Europe between about 40,000 and 10,000 years ago. In Europe, as in Asia and North Africa, these stone tool traditions are termed Upper Paleolithic. During this period we see increasing evidence for regional differences in stone tool technology, often accompanied by variations in settlement patterns, subsistence technology, and other aspects of material culture. As described in the Archaeology in Practice box, since the 1950s radiocarbon dating has provided accurate absolute dates for sites and industries of the Upper Paleolithic period.

UPPER PALEOLITHIC INDUSTRIES: GENERAL CHARACTERISTICS

When compared with the Middle Paleolithic industries that preceded them, Upper Paleolithic industries in Europe are characterized by the use of a wider range of stone tool types. Many of those tools were made on blades—long and narrow flint flakes. By definition, blades must be at least twice as long as they are wide. Blades are often removed from prismatic (regularly faceted) cores using a **punch technique** (Figure 9.1). The punch technique is one of a number of methods of **indirect percussion** used to manufacture stone tools. The hammerstone does not contact the flint core directly; instead, the hammerstone strikes a punch, usually made of bone or antler. A blade is detached at the point where the punch contacts the flint core. This technique allows a large number of long, thin blades to be removed from a single flint core. The main technological advantage of this method over the Levallois technique is that it allows the knapper to produce much more cutting edge per kilogram of flint. The blade technology makes efficient use of available resources. The blades serve as blanks for the production of a

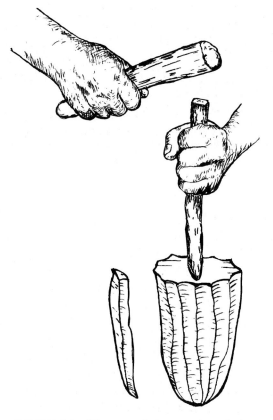

FIGURE 9.1   The use of the punch technique to remove blades from a blade core.

ARCHAEOLOGY IN PRACTICE

Radiocarbon Age Determination

The development of **radiocarbon dating** in 1949 revolutionized the archaeology of the Upper Paleolithic and later periods. Before Willard Libby (Libby et al. 1949) developed the radiocarbon dating method, there were no dating methods available that could provide absolute dates (in years before the present) for the Upper Paleolithic period. Sites and industries could often be placed in a relative sequence based on their geological context and stratigraphic position, but it was nearly impossible to determine how old those sites really were. The radiocarbon revolution provided a chronological framework that allowed archaeologists to examine the rate of technological and cultural changes during the Upper Paleolithic.

The radiocarbon dating method is based on carbon, an element that is present in all living things. The most common isotope of carbon is a light, stable isotope, carbon-12 (^{12}C); however, all living plants and animals also contain trace quantities of a heavier, radioactive isotope of carbon, carbon-14 (^{14}C). Small quantities of radioactive ^{14}C are constantly being formed in the earth's upper atmosphere when neutrons from cosmic rays strike atmospheric nitrogen (Figure 9.A). Both ^{14}C and ^{12}C combine with oxygen to form carbon dioxide, one of the most common gases in the earth's atmosphere. Carbon dioxide (CO_2) is absorbed by plants during photosynthesis, a process by which plants convert CO_2 and sunlight into food and oxygen. When plants absorb CO_2 from the atmosphere, they absorb large quantities of ^{12}C and trace amounts of ^{14}C. As these plants are eaten by animals who are, in turn, eaten by other animals, radiocarbon

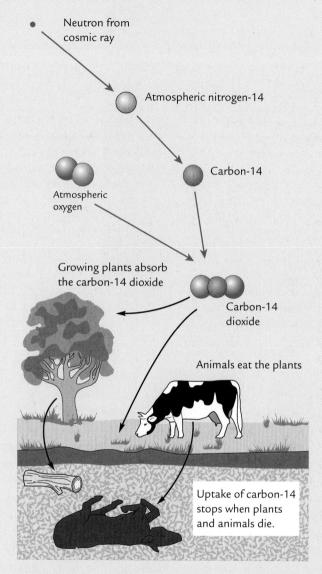

FIGURE 9.A Carbon-14 works its way through the food chain.

is spread throughout the food chain. Therefore, living plants and animals will contain the same small proportion of ^{14}C that exists in the earth's atmosphere. (The ratio of ^{12}C to ^{14}C in the earth's atmosphere is about 8 hundred billion to 1.)

When an organism dies, it ceases to take up any new radiocarbon.

The radioactive carbon that is present in the organism's tissues decays at a known rate, called the half-life, or the amount of time needed for half the radioactive atoms to decay. The half-life of radiocarbon is 5,730 ± 30 years. Thus, by measuring the amount of radioactive carbon that remains in a sample of organic material, archaeologists can estimate the amount of time that has elapsed since that organism died. This is the principle that underlies radiocarbon age determination. (See Renfrew 1973 for a detailed summary of the assumptions that lie behind the radiocarbon dating method.)

The advantage of radiocarbon dating over other methods is that it can be used on a wide range of organic materials: charcoal, wood, bone, shell, and the like. Traditional radiocarbon dating requires about 25 gr (about 1 oz.) of the organic material for laboratory analysis. The material is cleaned and then converted to a gas by burning; its radioactivity is measured over a period of 2 weeks. This measure is used to estimate the amount of radiocarbon remaining in the sample. A newer procedure known as the **AMS (accelerator mass spectrometry)** method uses an accelerator and a mass spectrometer to measure directly the amount of ^{14}C remaining in the sample (Hedges and Gowlett 1986). The AMS technique, which allows much smaller samples to be dated, has been used to date the charcoal wicks in Upper Paleolithic lamps and the charcoal used as a colorant in ancient wall paintings (Chapter 11).

With conventional radiocarbon dating techniques, organic materials as old as about 40,000 years can be dated. After about seven half-lives, the amount of ^{14}C remaining in the sample is so small that it becomes difficult to measure. The AMS technique may allow somewhat older samples to be dated, but the samples must be entirely free of modern organic contamination. Other techniques, such as electron spin resonance and potassium-argon dating, are used to date older materials.

Radiocarbon age determinations are expressed in years B.P., or before present. It is important to note that the present has been defined arbitrarily as A.D. 1950. Radiocarbon dates always include a plus-or-minus factor, for example, 2550 ± 50 years B.P., because radiocarbon dates are not absolute ages; they are statements of probability. The date of 2550 ± 50 B.P. means that there is approximately a 66% (2 out of 3) chance that the true age of the archaeological sample will fall between 2500 and 2600 years B.P. The "± 50 years" is a statistical measure known as a standard deviation.

The radiocarbon dating method works on the assumption that radioactive ^{14}C is produced at a constant rate in the upper atmosphere. Research since the 1960s has shown that the rate of radiocarbon production has changed through time, causing variations in radiocarbon dates. The problem is especially acute for dates between 30,000 and 50,000 years ago. A calibration curve has been produced to allow archaeologists to correct Late Pleistocene and more recent radiocarbon dates (see Archaeology in Practice, Chapter 23). Correction curves are not available for dates in the 30,000 to 50,000 year range, and these dates should be treated with some caution.

wide range of stone tools, including spear points and burins, tools with a sharp, chisel-shaped edge that can be used to work bone or antler.

Upper Paleolithic industries are generally characterized by a much wider use of bone and antler as raw materials. In western Europe bone spear points and antler harpoons appear for the first time during the Upper Paleolithic. The Upper Paleolithic also is characterized by an increasing use of composite tools, or tools made of more than one material. Examples of composite tools include bone spear points hafted onto wooden shafts and bows and arrows.

THE UPPER PALEOLITHIC SEQUENCE IN EUROPE

Much of the research on the Upper Paleolithic period has focused on western Europe, particularly on the Dordogne region of southwestern France. The fascination with the Upper Paleolithic cultures of southwestern France can be explained, at least in part, by historical factors. In the Dordogne region of France, the Vézère River cuts through an area of limestone caves and rock shelters that were attractive to Paleolithic people. In 1863 Edouard Lartet, a French lawyer and amateur geologist, and Henry Christy, an English banker of independent means, began a series of excavations in the Dordogne region that were to change the course of Paleolithic archaeology. They began work at a time when scholars had just begun to recognize the great antiquity of the human presence on earth. Lartet and Christy excavated many important French Upper Paleolithic sites, including La Madeleine and Laugerie-Haute; they also began excavation at the site of Le Moustier, which was to become the type site for the Mousterian industry in Europe. Lartet and Christy's pioneering work established a strong

TABLE 9.1 Major Periods of the South-west European Upper Paleolithic and Their Approximate Dates

Period	Approximate Dates
Aurignacian	40,000–28,000 B.P.
Gravettian	28,000–22,000 B.P.
Solutrean	22,000–18,000 B.P.
Magdalenian	18,000–11,000 B.P.

Note: Dates follow White (2003).

tradition of Paleolithic research in the Dordogne region that continues to the present day. Because of the wealth of archaeological data available from southwestern France, François Bordes (1968, 1984) based his typological studies of Upper Paleolithic stone tools primarily on data from France. However, recent research in eastern Europe, the Near East, sub-Saharan Africa, and eastern Asia has revealed great regional variation in late Paleolithic stone tool industries from around the world (Chapter 8). Nevertheless, the rich archaeological record from western Europe provides important information on how early modern humans coped with the cold, periglacial environments of the late Pleistocene period.

Until perhaps 35 years ago, much of the research on the European Upper Paleolithic focused on the typological study of stone, bone, and antler implements to develop a chronological sequence of Upper Paleolithic industries. The western European Upper Paleolithic sequence is briefly summarized in Table 9.1.

These industries were originally defined on the basis of a series of artifact types deemed typical of a particular period; typical tools from each period are illustrated in Figure 9.2. The **Aurignacian** period in southwestern Europe is characterized by the presence of a range of stone and bone tools, including nosed and carinated (shaped like a ship's keel) end scrapers made on thick flakes and blades, large blades with continuous retouch around their edges,

strangulated blades (with a central constriction), and bone points, including those with split bases. Typical **Gravettian** (formerly known as the Upper Perigordian) tools include gravette points, micro-gravette bladelets, tanged points, and burins made on truncations (snapped-off ends). The **Solutrean** is characterized by the presence of large, flat spear points that resemble laurel leaves in shape. Producing these points required that the flint first be heat-treated, or "cooked," for an extended period to facilitate the initial removal of flakes from the cores. The laurel leaves were shaped using a technique known as **pressure flaking,** in which a flint knapper presses a piece of a hard material such as antler or wood against the edge of the tool to detach a small, flat flake. Eyed needles also make their first appearance during the Solutrean (Stordeur-Yedid 1979). These needles may have been used to produce tailored, or fitted, clothing made of hides, skins, and leather. Sinew (animal tendons) may have been used as thread. The **Magdalenian** period is characterized by the appearance of barbed points made of antler, known as harpoons. Typical stone tools include bladelets, a variety of borers, small blades with abrupt retouch, and increasing numbers of microliths (small stone tools, generally less than 1 cm [1/2 in.] in maximum dimension).

Since the late 1960s, the focus of archaeological research has shifted away from typological studies toward questions of human subsistence and settlement. Specifically, archaeologists have tried to understand how Upper Paleolithic people made a living in the cold climates that characterized late Pleistocene Europe. Archaeologists have used paleoenvironmental data such as pollen cores and oxygen isotope analyses to reconstruct the late Pleistocene environment; faunal remains and artifacts have been used to reconstruct hunting practices; and increasingly precise methods of excavation have been used to study Upper Paleolithic settlements.

The Upper Paleolithic period in Europe was a time of full glacial conditions. The Alpine ice sheet covered much of Alpine central Europe, while the Scandinavian sheet covered Scandinavia as well as northern Germany, northern Poland, the Baltic states,

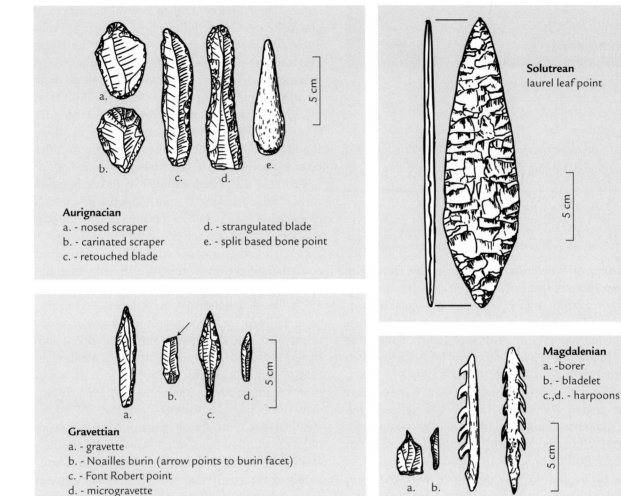

Aurignacian
a. - nosed scraper
b. - carinated scraper
c. - retouched blade
d. - strangulated blade
e. - split based bone point

Solutrean
laurel leaf point

Gravettian
a. - gravette
b. - Noailles burin (arrow points to burin facet)
c. - Font Robert point
d. - microgravette

Magdalenian
a. -borer
b. - bladelet
c.,d. - harpoons

FIGURE 9.2   Typical tools from each phase of the European Upper Paleolithic.

and parts of Russia (Figure 9.3). In general, Europe's climate was dry and very cold. In southwest France July temperatures are estimated to have been about 5° C (9° F) colder than at present (White 1985: 41). At the height of the last glaciation, about 18,000 years ago, the earth's sea levels dropped by about 100 to 150 m (330 to 490 ft.). While many parts of Europe experienced steppic or even tundralike conditions during this period, the vegetation in southwest Europe (southwestern France and northern Spain) appears to have been much more diverse. The varied topography in this region supported different plant and animal communities at different elevations. Pollen data suggest that sheltered, south-facing areas with

adequate water may have supported warm-loving trees, such as hazel and oaks, even during the glacial maximum (see, for example, Straus and Clark 1986: 371). The varied vegetation would have supported a large and diverse animal community, which, in turn, may have supported a large human population (White 1985: 49–51).

SUBSISTENCE STRATEGIES IN THE EUROPEAN UPPER PALEOLITHIC

Artifactual evidence from a wide range of European Upper Paleolithic sites suggests that increasingly sophisticated hunting technologies were developing

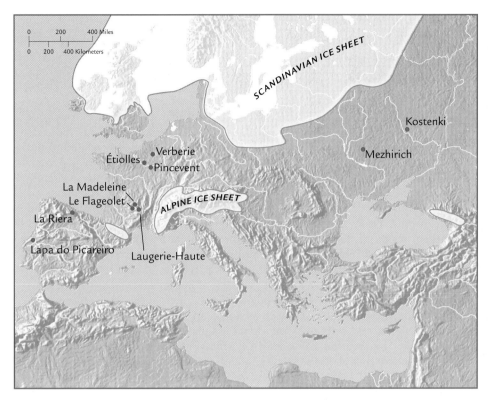

FIGURE 9.3 Extent of the Alpine and Scandinavian ice sheets and the locations of the sites mentioned in this chapter.

throughout the period. Stone, bone, and antler projectile points are common throughout the Upper Paleolithic. Spear throwers, which would have increased both the speed and the accuracy of thrown spears, appear in Upper Paleolithic assemblages by 20,000 B.P. (White 1986: 43). The presence of barbed and tanged arrowheads at Solutrean sites in Spain provides indirect evidence for the use of the bow and arrow at that time (Davidson 1974). However, zooarchaeological evidence is required to study the kinds of animals that were hunted during the Upper Paleolithic and the techniques that were used to hunt them. For example, archaeologists want to know whether large herds of animals were hunted on a seasonal basis or whether individual animals were hunted as they were encountered throughout the year.

Recent studies by Françoise Audouze and James Enloe (1991) have shown that both types of hunting can be documented in the European Upper Paleolithic. Audouze and Enloe contrasted the pattern of hunting seen at the Magdalenian site of Verberie in the Paris basin with the hunting techniques seen at the site of Le Flageolet in the Périgord region of southwestern France. Both sites are overwhelmingly dominated by the remains of reindeer; at Le Flageolet reindeer make up 95% of the animals hunted. At Verberie the large size of the reindeer kill and the ages of the animals suggest that the reindeer were killed in large numbers during the autumn migration. During the fall the reindeer would have been at their nutritional peak because the best forage would have been available during the summer months. Moreover, the reindeer would have been available at a predictable time and place during the fall migration. By killing large numbers of reindeer in the fall, the hunters at Verberie would have obtained large amounts of high-quality, fat-rich meat, which would have been stored for use throughout the winter (Audouze and Enloe 1991: 64).

The pattern of hunting seen at Le Flageolet is quite different. At Le Flageolet, many of the

CASE STUDY

Paleolithic Subsistence: La Riera Cave

The excavations at the Upper Paleolithic site of **La Riera** (Straus and Clark 1986) in northern Spain demonstrate how hunting and foraging practices changed through time. La Riera Cave is located in the Cantabrian region of northern Spain, halfway between the cities of Santander and Oviedo. The cave offered its Paleolithic inhabitants shelter and proximity to fresh water. From the cave, prehistoric people could have made use of the coastal plain, the coastal estuaries, local rivers, and the slopes and cliffs of the coastal mountain ranges. The location of La Riera Cave meant that ancient people had access to a wide variety of terrestrial and marine food resources. La Riera produced a long sequence of occupations and a large number of radiocarbon dates. Initially occupied more than 20,000 years ago, the site was inhabited during the Solutrean (20,500 to 17,000 B.P.), Lower Magdalenian (17,000 to 16,000 B.P.), Upper Magdalenian (12,400 to 11,000 B.P.), and later periods. Detailed studies of the faunal and artifactual remains from the cave reveal the ways that hunting and foraging techniques changed throughout these periods.

The principal game species throughout the occupation of La Riera Cave was red deer (*Cervus elaphus*), an animal closely related to the American elk. Beginning in the Solutrean period, there is evidence that La Riera hunters were using techniques such as drives or surrounds to capture a large number of animals of all ages and both sexes at one time. The highly fragmented state of the mammal bones indicates that they were probably used for marrow and grease in addition to meat. There is also evidence for the increasing use of marine and estuarine resources through time. Limpets and, later, marine fish such as sea bream were added to the diet during the Upper Magdalenian period. Thus the record reflects both an intensification of large mammal hunting and a diversification of the subsistence base through the addition of marine fish and shellfish. As we shall see (Chapter 16), this pattern of intensification and diversification of the subsistence base is seen in the late Pleistocene of the Near East as well. The excavators of La Riera Cave, Lawrence Straus and Geoffrey Clark, attribute these changes to a growing imbalance between population and available food resources.

reindeer that were hunted were adults, especially adult females. In the winter female reindeer are generally in better condition than the males. The high numbers of adult female reindeer at Le Flageolet suggest that the hunters at the site were hunting individual or small groups of reindeer throughout the winter, a pattern known as encounter hunting. The different patterns of hunting seen at Verberie and Le Flageolet point to the varying hunting strategies and techniques used by Upper Paleolithic hunters in Europe.

Small mammals seem to have played an increasingly important role in late Upper Paleolithic diets in southwestern Europe. For example, the late Paleolithic (11,800–12,300 B.P.) site of **Picareiro Cave** in Portugal produced small numbers of red deer and wild boar bones. Most of the faunal remains recovered from the site were the bones of rabbits (*Oryctolagus cunniculus*). The rabbits were probably caught using nets or snares and would have been an important source of meat and fat for late Paleolithic Iberian hunters (Hockett and Bicho 2000).

Meat, fish, and shellfish made up only part of the diet during the Upper Paleolithic period in Europe. While very few plant foods would have been available during the cold winter months, plant foods must have played a role in the diet during the warmer summer season. There is little clear evidence for the use of plant foods at La Riera Cave. However, the nearby early Magdalenian site of El Juyo (Freeman et al. 1988) has produced evidence of 51 different genera of plants from 21 different families. The plant remains include fragments of acorns, beechnuts, and raspberry pits.

It is difficult to assess the relative importance of animal and plant foods in the European Upper Paleolithic diet. Clearly, relatively few plant foods would have been available in the colder, drier areas of eastern Europe, especially during the coldest periods of the Pleistocene. A greater variety of plants may have been available in the summer months during the warmer periods of the Pleistocene and in areas such as southwestern France that supported a diverse mixture of grassland and forested environments.

UPPER PALEOLITHIC SETTLEMENT PATTERNS

Studies of Upper Paleolithic subsistence practices are closely related to questions of settlement patterns, or how prehistoric people distributed themselves across the landscape. In studying prehistoric settlement patterns, archaeologists want to know how sites are distributed in relationship to natural landscape features such as rivers and lakes, the sizes of sites and their locations in relationship to other sites, and how houses and other structures are distributed within the sites themselves. The rich archaeological record for Upper Paleolithic Europe allows archaeologists to begin to answer some of these questions.

As noted previously, environmental data suggest that the rich late Pleistocene environments of southwestern France and northern Spain would have supported comparatively large human populations. The varied landscape, with a mosaic of steppe and forest environments, would have supported a rich and diverse range of animal resources on which those human populations depended (White 1985: 51). For example, the site of Le Flageolet has produced the animals that lived in woodland, forest, steppe, and montane environments, including the reindeer, red deer, horse, and ibex (Boyle 1990: 276). The valley-side locations of many of the sites in southwestern France allowed hunters to make use of several different environmental zones during the course of a season or a year. These locations also provided ready access to water.

Upper Paleolithic sites in Europe vary greatly in size. Ethnographic studies of modern hunter-gatherer populations indicate that group size varies throughout the year. At certain seasons of the year, large groups of perhaps 50 to 100 people congregate to make use of seasonally available plant and animal resources. During much of the rest of the year, the population breaks up into small bands, sometimes as small as individual families. A similar pattern may be reflected in the archaeological record of the European Upper Paleolithic. Excavations at caves, rock shelters, and open sites have revealed a pattern of many small sites and a few much larger occupations. Many of the smaller sites may have been occupied by individual hunting bands on a seasonal basis. The larger sites have produced greater quantities of artwork (see Chapter 10), including beads and pendants, which are undoubtedly symbols of personal identity and group membership. The larger sites probably represent seasonal aggregation sites where large social groups came together for initiation rites, marriage ceremonies, and other ritual activities, in addition to hunting and plant collecting.

While many of the sites in southwestern France and northern Spain are located in caves and rock shelters, some of the most impressive evidence for the layout of individual settlements comes from open-air sites. One of the most famous is the site of **Pincevent** in the Paris basin (Leroi-Gourhan and Brézillon 1972). The site, which was excavated by André Leroi-Gourhan, not only has provided a wealth of new information on the structure of late Paleolithic hunters' camps but also has served as a laboratory for the development of new methods and techniques of excavation.

Excavators at Pincevent used a program of horizontal excavation. The goal of horizontal excavation is to open up a broad area of the site so that the spatial relationship of artifacts, ecofacts, and features to one another can be seen clearly. Not only was the precise location of each artifact and animal bone recorded, but also the artifacts and bones were left in place so that their relationship to each other could be seen clearly. The distribution of these artifacts was documented using both drawings and photography, and the location of each piece of charcoal and each fragment of red ochre (an iron-based red pigment) was also indicated on the plans and drawings. Once each excavation unit had been drawn

FIGURE 9.4 One of the habitations at Pincevent. The photograph illustrates how the distribution of stone tools, bones, charcoal, and other artifacts can be used to define the size and shape of the huts.

and photographed, a mold was made of the living surface using latex rubber. A plaster cast of the living surface could be made from the mold, thus preserving the spatial relationships of the artifacts even after they were removed from the ground.

The excavations at Pincevent revealed the remains of several small, circular huts (Figure 9.4). Although nothing remained of the huts themselves (they were undoubtedly made of perishable materials such as skins or hides), the stone tools and animal bones formed distinctive circular concentrations. Asymmetrical, hollow hearths were located outside the huts (Audouze and Enloe 1991: 64). These habitations would have been occupied by reindeer hunters for a short period in September and October (Enloe et al. 1994: 106). Detailed studies of the animal bones revealed how the individual reindeer carcasses were shared among the different huts (Enloe and David 1989).

Similar methods of excavation were used to document the nearby Magdalenian quarry site of **Étiolles** (Pigeot 1987) (Figure 9.5). At this site workers were manufacturing stone tools from

FIGURE 9.5 Étiolles: the use of latex rubber to make a mold of the living surface.

FIGURE 9.6 A mammoth-bone dwelling from Mezhirich, Ukraine. Note the herringbone pattern of the jawbones.

flint nodules that were up to 50 cm (20 in.) long. The difficulty of working these large cores led to an increased flexibility in stone tool manufacture. Workers needed to adapt their techniques to the shape of the raw material and the accidents of the knapping process. Detailed spatial and refitting studies have been carried out at one of the habitations at Étiolles. They reveal that the expert flint knappers worked around the central hearth, striking a large number of blades from the best cores, which had been preshaped before they reached the habitation. Farther away from the hearth, novice knappers practiced their skills on partly worked-out cores. At Étiolles detailed spatial studies allow the excavators to reconstruct the organization of stone tool production.

Some of the most spectacular evidence for Upper Paleolithic living sites has come from open-air sites in eastern Europe. Among the most unusual are the mammoth-bone dwellings found at sites on the East European Plain in the Ukraine and adjacent areas of Russia and Belarus. An example is the site of **Mezhirich** (Gladkih et al. 1984), located near the Dnieper River in the Ukraine. At least five

mammoth-bone dwellings are known from the site, and four have been excavated (Figure 9.6). These small, circular huts are between 4 and 7 m (13 and 23 ft.) in diameter, providing an interior floor area of 8 to 24 sq. m (86 to 258 sq. ft.). Inside the dwellings are the remains of hearths where bone was used as a fuel. Timber would have been very scarce in the steppe environment of the Russian plain during the Pleistocene. The foundations and walls of these huts were constructed of carefully assembled mammoth bones. The outer portion of the wall of one hut was made of 95 mammoth mandibles (lower jaws) placed chin down to form a herringbone pattern. These mammoth-bone dwellings were probably occupied during the 9-month cold season; during the summer, the inhabitants would have moved to temporary warm-season camps. Radiocarbon dates suggest that these mammoth-bone dwellings were occupied about 15,000 years ago. The presence of these huts on the Russian plain indicates that Upper Paleolithic hunters were able to adapt successfully to the cold, glacial climates of the eastern European periglacial steppes where winter temperatures may have reached −35° to −40° C (−31° to −40° F). Many

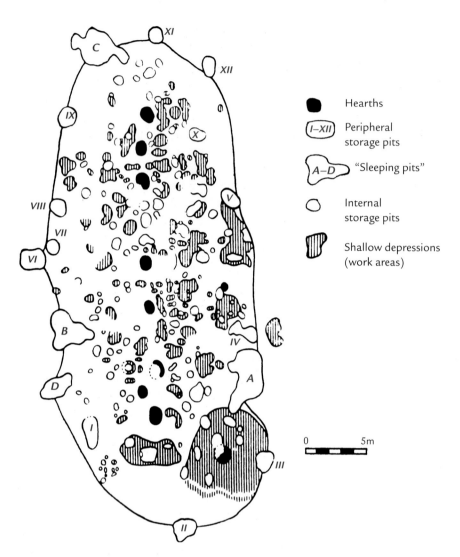

Hearths

I–XII Peripheral storage pits

A–D "Sleeping pits"

Internal storage pits

Shallow depressions (work areas)

0   5m

FIGURE 9.7   Plan of Kostenki I-1, showing location of storage pits, activity areas, sleeping pits, and the central hearths.

eastern European open-air sites have produced substantial numbers of fur-bearing animals such as Arctic hare and fox, which were undoubtedly used to make protective clothing (Hoffecker 1999: 139).

Substantial dwellings of a different form have been recovered from the site of **Kostenki I** (Klein 1973: 103) on the Don River in the eastern Ukraine. Kostenki I-1 (Figure 9.7) revealed a large complex of features covering an area of roughly 18 by 40 m (60 by 130 ft.). The outside was surrounded by a series of storage pits that appear to have been used to store mammoth bones for fuel. The feature

complex included a central line of hearths, as well as sleeping pits, internal storage pits, and work areas. It is not clear how this complex structure may have been roofed, but it appears to have housed a sizable population.

NORTHERN EUROPE AT THE END OF THE ICE AGE

Evidence from pollen analyses (see Archaeology in Practice, Chapter 13), fossil faunas, and permafrost features indicates that Europe had an extremely cold climate between 24,000 and 13,000 years ago. Although the northern European ice sheets began to decrease in size as early as 18,000 to 17,000 years ago as a result of rising summer temperatures, winter temperatures remained cold until about 14,000 B.P.

Pollen analyses, studies of fossil beetles, oxygen isotope records, and evidence of marine fauna in the North Atlantic indicate that temperatures rose rapidly in northwest Europe about 13,000 years ago. It is estimated that summer temperatures in Britain may have risen as much as 8° to 10° C (14° to 18°F) at that time. This marked climatic warming caused a rapid retreat of the glaciers. The ice sheets covering much of the British Isles began to decrease in size, and broad regions of the North European Plain became deglaciated. This late glacial warm period is termed the **Windermere interstadial;** it lasted from about 13,000 to 11,000 years ago.[1] By 11,500 years ago, birch and pine forests had replaced steppe and tundra in many areas of central, southern, and eastern Europe, but a broad zone of steppe parkland still covered much of France, southern Britain, the Low Countries, and northern Germany (Andersen and Borns 1994). The retreat of the glaciers opened new areas to human settlement.

Subsequently, however, oxygen isotope records show that there was a considerable drop in temperatures about 11,000 years ago in Europe. The causes of this rapid climatic deterioration are unknown, but changes in atmospheric circulation patterns clearly played a role. In addition, the draining of the floodwaters of Lake Agassiz (an enormous North American lake formed by glacial meltwaters) into the North Atlantic at that time may also have played a role in global cooling (Dawson 1992: 108). The result was a return to almost full glacial conditions. The decrease in temperature was most dramatic in northwestern Europe, where it is estimated that summer temperatures dropped by

8° to 10° C (14° to 18°F). Glaciers increased in size in Scandinavia, the Alps, and Siberia, as well as other parts of the world. In northern Scotland, where the ice sheets had disappeared during the Windermere interstadial, new glaciers began to form. This cold period, termed the **Younger Dryas,** lasted for nearly a millennium, although the period from 11,000 to 10,500 years ago was coldest in Europe. (The name Dryas comes from the mountain avens plant, *Dryas octopetala*, which commonly occurs in arctic plant communities and appears in many pollen cores in northern Europe at this time.) As a result of this cold spell, the forestation of Europe was halted; the forest belt moved southward, leading to an increase in tundra. For example, during the Younger Dryas, many areas of Scandinavia that had been ice-free were covered with an arctic tundra vegetation with low bushes and scattered birch trees (Figure 9.8).

The Younger Dryas period was followed by a rapid change to postglacial conditions about 10,300 years ago, marking the beginning of the **Holocene,** or Recent, period, which will be discussed in Chapter 13.

LATE PLEISTOCENE HUNTERS AND FISHERS IN NORTHERN EUROPE

As noted previously, the glacial retreat that began in the late Pleistocene opened up new areas of north central Europe to human settlement. Between 14,000 and 10,000 years ago, humans were able to resettle many parts of the Low Countries, northern Germany, and southern Scandinavia. These hunters, long dependent on reindeer, were not simply following the migrating herds northward; instead, they were finding new ways to make use of the resources becoming available in the northern environments. Recent research in northern Europe has shown that these foragers were adaptable pioneers who moved into a previously uninhabitable landscape (Fischer 1991). These late Pleistocene hunters used a simple and expedient blade technology to manufacture stone tools, which included a number of points designed specifically for hunting. There is evidence for the hunting of moose, reindeer, bear, wolverine, swan, and possibly roe

---

[1] In Scandinavia the pattern of glacial warming is more complex. An initial warm period, the Bölling interstadial (13,000 to 12,000 B.P.), was followed by a brief return to colder conditions. This brief cold snap, known as the Older Dryas stadial, extended from 12,000 to 11,800 B.P. The Older Dryas was followed by a second warm period known as the Alleröd interstadial (11,800 to 11,000 B.P.) (Dawson 1992: 79).

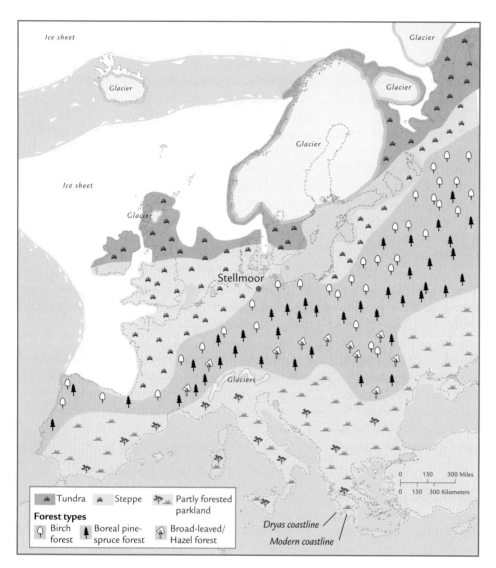

FIGURE 9.8 Europe during the Younger Dryas period showing the extent of the remaining glaciers and the vegetation zones at that time. The location of the late Paleolithic site of Stellmoor is also shown.

deer (Fischer 1991: 113). Pike bones also have been recovered from some sites, and the location of many sites along lakes and streams suggests that fishing played an important role in the economy.

Excavations at the site of **Stellmoor** in northern Germany have provided insights into the hunting techniques used by the late Pleistocene foragers. Faunal evidence suggests that the reindeer were hunted in the autumn, but that humans subsisted on dried meat and stored grease and marrow on

a year-round basis (Bokelman 1991). At Stellmoor hunters appear to have driven a herd of reindeer into a lake where they then shot them with arrows. More than 100 pinewood arrows and arrow fragments were recovered from the site. The arrows were tipped with flint and had a detachable wooden foreshaft that facilitated repairs (Bokelman 1991: 79). The site provides early evidence for the use of the bow and arrow during the late Upper Paleolithic.

Two distinct types of late Pleistocene sites have been identified in northern Europe. Residential campsites, which are located near permanent sources of freshwater, contain a central hearth surrounded by domestic refuse. Hunting camps, on the other hand, are often located on elevated spots on the landscape where game movements could be observed. The deglaciation of Europe would have opened up a large land area that was rich in food and raw materials. Population densities appear to have been low, as most sites would have housed no more than a few families, but the conditions of life may have been quite favorable for these north European pioneers (Fischer 1991: 117).

CONCLUSION

How do the settlement patterns, subsistence practices, and technological systems of the inhabitants of Upper Paleolithic Europe compare with what is known from the preceding Middle Paleolithic period? The artifactual evidence, including spear throwers and bows and arrows, suggests an increasingly sophisticated hunting technology. This impression of hunting success is confirmed by the animal bone evidence, which indicates that Upper Paleolithic people in Europe were successfully hunting a wide range of herbivores, including reindeer, bison, wild cattle, mammoth, wild swine, horse, ibex, chamois, and red deer. The settlement evidence from both eastern and western Europe indicates that Upper Paleolithic people had successfully adapted to the cold, dry climates of the late Pleistocene period. In both eastern and western Europe, the density of settlements increased in the Upper Paleolithic. In Russia Upper Paleolithic settlements extend as far north as the Arctic Circle, while Mousterian sites are found no farther north than 54° north latitude (Klein 1973: 122). Clearly, innovations such as fitted clothing must have played an important role in the successful occupation of the Arctic Zone during the Upper Paleolithic. Moreover, it is during the late Pleistocene that we see the expansion of northeast Eurasian populations into the New World, a topic we will address in greater detail in Chapter 12.

KEY TERMS

AMS (accelerator mass spectrometry) 136
Aurignacian 137
Étiolles 142
Gravettian 137
Holocene 145
Indirect percussion 134
Kostenki I 144
La Riera 140
Magdalenian 137
Mezhirich 143

Picareiro Cave 140
Pincevent 141
Pressure flaking 137
Punch technique 134
Radiocarbon dating 135
Solutrean 137
Stellmoor 146
Windermere interstadial 145
Younger Dryas 145

QUESTIONS FOR DISCUSSION

1. Why do you think that fish, birds, and small mammals played an increasingly important role in late Paleolithic subsistence?

2. How did modern human populations adapt to the cold glacial conditions of late Pleistocene Europe?

FURTHER READING

Andersen, B. G., and H. W. Borns
1994 *The Ice Age World.* Oslo: Scandinavian University Press.
A well-illustrated and authoritative account of Pleistocene geology with an extensive glossary of terms.

Gamble, Clive
1999 *The Palaeolithic Societies of Europe.* Cambridge: Cambridge University Press.
A comprehensive review of the Paleolithic societies of Europe from the initial occupation of the continent to the end of the Pleistocene. While this is undoubtedly the most comprehensive volume available in English on the Paleolithic in Europe, it is written at a high level and recommended for serious students only.

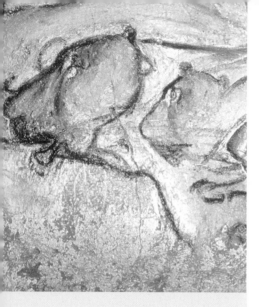

10

ART AND COGNITION IN THE UPPER PALEOLITHIC

The Upper Paleolithic art of Europe, including both cave paintings and small sculptures, represents one of the most interesting and enigmatic subjects in all of Paleolithic archaeology. While European sculptures and cave paintings are the most famous examples of Paleolithic art, it is important to note that late Pleistocene rock paintings have also been discovered in Africa and Australia. For both archaeologist and layperson alike, these works of art provide a link to the ideas, thoughts, and beliefs of the long-vanished people of the Paleolithic. Yet this feeling of communication with the past is in large measure illusory. While the paintings and sculptures of animals and symbols surely had meaning to their creators and evoke an emotional response in the modern viewer, millennia of cultural change separate the artists from us. Our intuitive reaction to this art, shaped by thousands of years of social, religious, and artistic tradition, is likely to be far afield from the artwork's meaning to its ancient makers.

How do we know that this art was produced by Paleolithic artists? How was this art produced, and how has it been preserved for tens of millennia? This chapter will seek to answer those questions. Why did the hunters and foragers of late Ice Age Europe paint naturalistic images on the almost inaccessible walls and ceilings of caves? What role did small portable sculptures and pendants play in the daily lives of their makers? What meaning did those works of art have within the cultures that produced them? This chapter will address those issues as well. While numerous hypotheses have been offered, we can probably never fully understand the intended meaning of Paleolithic art.

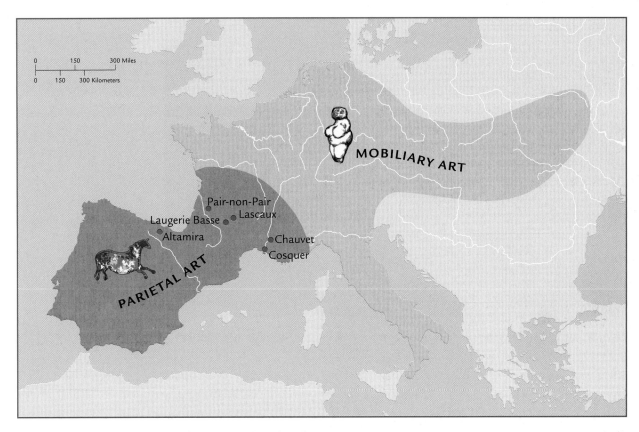

FIGURE 10.1   Location of sites mentioned in this chapter.

HISTORICAL BACKGROUND: THE DISCOVERY OF THE PAINTED CAVES

In Europe, there are two major forms of Paleolithic art: **parietal** (cave wall) **art** and **mobiliary,** or portable, **art.** Cave paintings are known primarily from three areas in western Europe—southwestern France, northern Spain, and the Pyrenean region. Small carvings and sculptures are known from a much broader area across Ice Age Europe. The locations of the major southwest European sites discussed in this chapter are shown in Figure 10.1. Parietal art includes both the paintings (Figure 10.2) and engravings or low-relief carvings (Figure 10.3) that were used to decorate the walls and ceilings of caves. Mobiliary, or portable, art includes a range of small carved or engraved objects made of bone, antler, or stone. The famous statuettes sometimes referred to as Venuses (Figure 10.4) were sculptures of women, often depicted with protruding breasts and buttocks. Other examples of mobiliary art include pendants, engraved plaques, as well as carved and decorated items such as spear throwers decorated with animal figures (Figure 10.5). Examples of mobiliary art were first recovered from archaeological sites in the mid-nineteenth century, along with stone tools and the bones of Ice Age animals. Because these small plaques and carvings were found along with Stone Age tools, their authenticity as products of Paleolithic craftworkers was never seriously questioned. The acceptance of the painted caves as the work of Paleolithic artists, however, was a longer and more complicated process.

One of the great milestones in the history of Paleolithic cave art was the discovery of painted bison on the ceiling of the Spanish cave of **Altamira** in 1879. The excavator of the cave was a Spanish nobleman, Don Marcelino Sanz de Sautuola. The previous year he had visited an

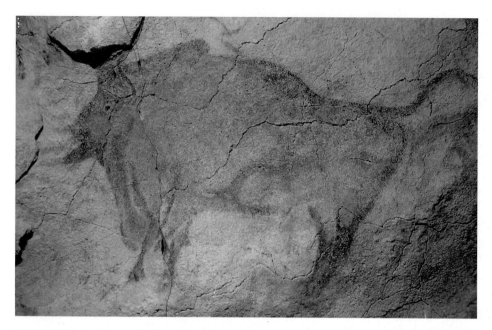

FIGURE 10.2   Naturalistic painted bison from the ceiling of the cave at Altamira (Santander), Spain.

FIGURE 10.3   Low-relief carving of a salmon from the Abri de Poisson (Dordogne), France, 105 cm (41 in.) in length.

exhibition of Paleolithic mobiliary art and artifacts in Paris. In November of 1879 de Sautuola was excavating the floor of the cave at Altamira, searching for artifacts, while his young daughter Maria was running wildly around the cave. Suddenly, she recognized the figures of a group of bison on the roof of the cave. De Sautuola rec-

ognized that the style of the bison was similar to the style of carving used on the portable art he had seen in Paris. In 1880 he published a short booklet on his discoveries at Altamira, cautiously asking whether the painted bison might be contemporary with the Paleolithic deposits from the cave floor. Unfortunately, his suggestions were greeted

FIGURE 10.4   Carved stone female figurine known as the Venus of Willendorf, Austria, approximately 11 cm (4 in.) in height.

FIGURE 10.5   Elaborately decorated spear thrower (9 cm [3.5 in.] in length by 7 cm [3 in.] in height) made of reindeer antler. The carving depicts two headless ibexes locked in an embrace (possibly playing or fighting). The heads of the two animals may have been attached separately.

with skepticism and derision by the archaeological community.

The discovery of another series of cave paintings and engravings around the turn of the twentieth century led to the eventual acceptance of Paleolithic cave art. When, in 1895, the owner of La Mouthe cave in France removed some debris, he exposed a previously unknown gallery containing painted images. Another important discovery was the painted and engraved images at the cave of Pair-non-Pair near Bordeaux. The acceptance of the authenticity of cave art in the early twentieth century led, in the first two decades of the century, to the search for and discovery of a number of painted caves in the Dordogne region of France, the Cantabrian region of Spain, and the Pyrenees.

The most spectacular find, however, was that of **Lascaux Cave** (Arlette Leroi-Gourhan 1982) in

France at the very beginning of World War II. The discovery of the cave has often been attributed to French schoolboys, who found the cave after their dog had fallen into a deep hole. In fact, the boys were using stones to test the depth of a hole created by a fallen pine tree. Once the opening had been enlarged, they slid down a tunnel of wet clay. Within the cave they were met by a spectacular array of horses, cattle, and other animals painted in bright colors along the walls and ceiling of the cave. They reported the discovery to their schoolmaster. The cave was subsequently inspected by the Abbé Henri Breuil, an important French prehistorian, whose *Four Hundred Centuries of Cave Art* (1952) remains an important sourcebook for the study of Paleolithic art in Europe. The beauty and mystery of this site for the general public led to its becoming a major tourist attraction. The popularity of Lascaux threatened the images, which had been preserved as a consequence of the naturally stable temperature and humidity in the cave. Visitors introduced dust, dampness, and fungi, causing the paintings to deteriorate. Lascaux is now closed to all but a very small number of visitors, but Lascaux II, a three-dimensional reproduction of the paintings

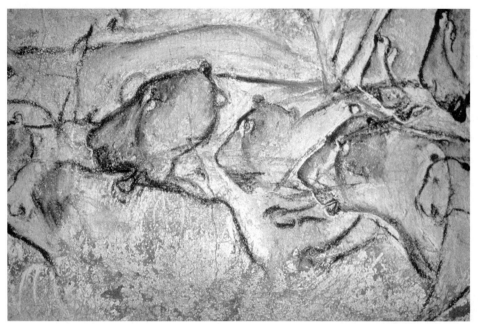

a.

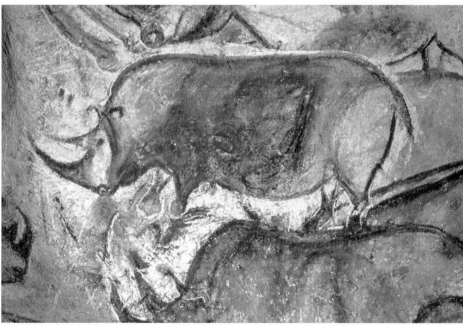

b.

FIGURE 10.6   Two images from the cave of Chauvet: a. lions hunting on the main panel in the end chamber. Scenes are rare in Paleolithic art. This one is unique. The most spectacular: b. rhinoceros in a group of 17. These animals are particularly plentiful in the Chauvet Cave. (Credit: Photographs by Jean Clottes.)

made using original techniques and completed in 1984, still attracts many tourists.

The discovery of several new painted caves in the past few years has put Ice Age art back on the front pages of newspapers around the world. For example, the discovery in 1994 of the **Grotte Chauvet** (Figure 10.6) in Vallon-Pont-d'Arc (Ardèche) in southern France revealed an unusual range of Ice Age images (Chauvet et al. 1996; Clottes and Courtin 1996). In addition to painted pictures of horses, bovids (cattle and bison), and other common animals, the Grotte Chauvet included depictions of woolly rhinos and carnivores such as cave bears and cave lions. In fact, rhinos, cave lions, mammoths, and bears make up 60% of the images from Grotte Chauvet (Clottes 1996).

Equally surprising are the early dates for the Chauvet images. Thirty-two radiocarbon dates indicate that the images at Grotte Chauvet were painted during the Aurignacian period between about 32,500 and 30,500 years ago. The dates were based on charcoal fragments and on fragments of organic material in the paint itself (see following). The cave seems to have been reused during the Gravettian period (27,000 to 26,000 years ago), but no images date from this period (Valladas et al. 2004).

The 1991 discovery of the **Grotte Cosquer** (Clottes and Courtin 1996), a painted cave near Marseilles whose entrance lies 37 m (120 ft.) underwater, has also attracted worldwide attention. At the time the cave was painted, between 19,000 and 27,000 years ago, the cave entrance would not have been underwater; the entrance was submerged as a result of rising sea levels at the end of the Pleistocene. The paintings within the cave date to two distinct periods. The earlier paintings include 46 hand outlines, while the later paintings and engravings include images of horses, ibex, bison, and deer, as well as unique representations of seals and great auks.

PARIETAL ART: THE IMAGES ON THE WALLS

The subjects represented in parietal art include both figurative and nonfigurative motifs. Most of the figures are naturalistic representations of animals,

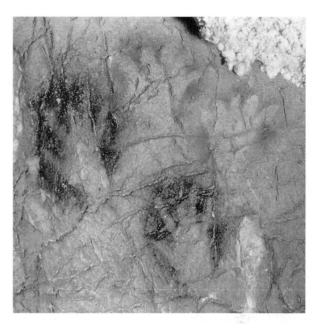

FIGURE 10.7 Hand stencils from Gargas (Hautes Pyrenées), France. Some appear to have missing digits.

including horses, wild cattle, bison, ibex, reindeer, red deer (an animal similar to the American elk), mammoths, woolly rhinos, birds, fish, and occasional carnivores such as cave lions. Horses, wild cattle, and bison are the most common images. Human figures are relatively rare; they are generally far less naturalistic than the animal images. Positive and negative images of hands have also been recovered from caves such as Gargas (Figure 10.7). Nonfigurative images include a number of signs, which range from simple fingerprints to complex quadrilateral images. Some are shaped like arrows, while others appear to resemble female genitalia.

Earth tones predominate in the cave paintings. The reds, yellows, oranges, and browns were produced using iron oxides such as hematite, limonite, and, especially, red ocher (Martin 1993: 261). Manganese dioxide and occasionally charcoal were used to produce the black pigments, while porcelain clay was used for the whites. At Lascaux, cave water, which is naturally high in calcium, was mixed with the ground mineral pigments to ensure both durability and adhesion to the cave wall surface (Arlette Leroi-Gourhan 1982: 109–110). Experiments suggest

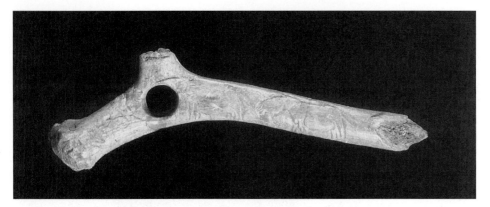

FIGURE 10.8 A Magdalenian *baton de commandement* made of reindeer antler, from the site of La Madeleine (Dordogne), France, 15 cm (6 in.) in length.

that the paint may have been applied by a number of different techniques. It may have been applied with the fingers or by using animal-hair brushes. Pieces of red ocher may also have been used as crayons. The negative hand impressions must have been produced using a spray painting technique. Experiments suggest that dry pigment could have been blown through a tube, or wet pigment could have been blown directly from the mouth.

Since paintings were often placed in remote areas of dark caves, lighting would have been a major challenge for Ice Age artists. De Beaune and White (1993) studied approximately 300 stone lamps that have been recovered from over 100 different Upper Paleolithic sites, mostly in southern France. Most of the lamps are made of limestone or sandstone, and investigations of the chemical residues remaining in the lamps indicate that they would have been used to burn animal fats (De Beaune and White 1993: 111). Experiments indicate that suitable wicks could have been made out of dried lichen, moss, or juniper twigs. Juniper twigs have been identified as one of the wick materials used at Lascaux (Arlette Leroi-Gourhan 1982: 107).

Scaffolding would have been necessary for painters to reach the upper parts of the walls and ceilings of the caves. At Lascaux recesses cut into the cave walls about 2 m (6 ft.) above the floor have been identified. The recesses were packed with clay and could have supported heavy branches that served as the foundation for a platform.

Incised designs and low-relief carvings could have been made with flint burins and other sharp flint tools. Deep engravings, such as those found on the walls of Pair-non-Pair Cave in France, could have been made with stone picks (Bahn and Vertut 1988: 91). The artists often made use of natural irregularities in the cave walls to indicate parts of the animals' bodies. For example, a bulge in the cave wall might be used to indicate a shoulder or hip.

MOBILIARY (PORTABLE) ART

Small, decorated objects were commonly made of antler, stone, ivory, and bone. Animals are often represented in mobiliary art, appearing as decorations on spear throwers and other items that would have been used for an extended period of time. Carved or incised decoration often appears on enigmatic objects termed **batons** (or *batons de commandement*) (Figure 10.8). These objects are generally made of reindeer antler and are perforated near one end. The function of these objects is unknown, but hypothesized uses range from spear-shaft straighteners to tent pegs to symbols of authority (White 1986: 47). Other engraved items include small plaques, often decorated with rows of incised dots. Microscopic examination has revealed that these dots were often made by a number of different tools, suggesting that they were made over a period of time (Marshack 1972). Traditionally, these dots have been seen as

ARCHAEOLOGY IN PRACTICE

Tools and Art Objects of Bone and Antler

Bone and antler objects form an important and very noticeable part of Upper Paleolithic assemblages. These raw materials were fashioned into new tools, weapons, and a variety of art objects, including items of personal adornment, such as beads and pendants. In addition to objects such as figurines, tools and weapons were sometimes elaborately carved. These artifacts and art objects clearly reflect a level of cultural achievement far beyond what had gone before.

Bone and antler objects probably represent only the durable remnant of a much larger body of similar tools and artworks, most of which would have been made from wood. As we have seen, woodworking in its simplest form dates back to the Lower Paleolithic. Although wooden objects are very rarely preserved, there is little reason to doubt that they formed an important part of ancient material culture.

Upper Paleolithic bone and antler objects were made, for the most part, by methods that would also have been suitable for working wood. An examination of the tool marks on these objects indicates that bones and antlers were divided into usable sections by cutting grooves into them with stone burins or gravers. Holes were made in them with stone borers, and stone scrapers were used to shape and smooth the surfaces. Gravers and burins were used to engrave patterns into bone surfaces and to shape them into artistic representations.

Bone and antler implements enjoyed an advantage over similar objects that may have been made of wood: Bone and antler are very tough and durable, and considerably harder than wood.

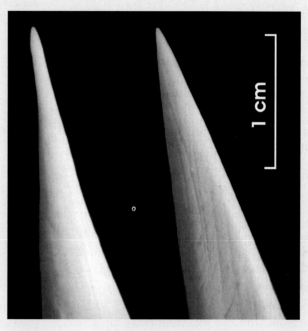

FIGURE 10.A Two methods of working bone. The point on the left has been shaved with a flint tool; the point on the right has been shaped by grinding.

Such tools could take and keep a sharp point for a long time and could be used for years. That this was the case is strongly suggested by the deep polish, the result of prolonged handling, that appears on many of these artifacts. Bone beads sometimes show a similar depth of wear and polish, as if they had been kept and handled for a very long time.

Another newer technique for working bone also made its appearance. The smooth contours and toolmarks seen on some objects, such as some beads, shows that they were shaped by grinding against an abrasive, such as sandstone. Objects could be made more efficiently by this method, and the results were smoother and more symmetrical. Eventually, in later periods, abrasive techniques would be applied to making stone objects as well (Figure 10.A).

Durable as bone implements were, flint could provide a much harder, sharper cutting edge. The advantages of both could be realized by mounting renewable flint blades in a bone haft to form a compound implement.

tally marks, perhaps representing individual kills, similar to the notches on a cowboy's gun. Alexander Marshack (1972) argued instead that the patterning of these marks showed some correlations with the phases of the moon and suggested that they may represent a primitive calendar. Whether these dots represent tally marks, a primitive calendrical system, or something entirely different remains a matter of debate.

The so-called Venus figurines are among the most well-known examples of prehistoric art. Many of these female figurines date from the Gravettian period, approximately 28,000 to 22,000 years ago. They are made from a variety of materials, including ivory, steatite, and calcite (White 1986: 114). The Venuses often have exaggerated breasts and buttocks, and some appear to be pregnant. Bahn and Vertut (1988: 138) note that the fleshier ones appear to represent "bodies worn out and altered by age and childbearing." The heads of the figurines are often small, and the legs frequently taper to a point. The function of these figures and their role in Upper Paleolithic ritual and religion remain unknown. While the Venuses have often been viewed as fertility goddesses, only a minority (17%) can plausibly be interpreted as pregnant (Rice 1981). Recent reinterpretations of the carvings on some Venus figurines indicate that they are wearing various forms of headgear, body bandeaux, and skirts. The carvings on these figurines suggest that these garments were made of plant fibers. They may have been used to signify personal and social identity.

Another important class of mobiliary objects are personal ornaments, including ivory beads and perforated teeth (Figure 10.9). The beads are often made of exotic raw materials such as fossil shells and soapstone. They were worked by polishing and abrasion to produce ornaments with particular tactile qualities (see Archaeology in Practice, this chapter). Personal ornaments are commonly found in Aurignacian contexts in Europe (White 2003: 80); however, they may have had a longer history in Africa. Christopher Henshilwood (Henshilwood et al. 2004) has recently identified a group of 39 perforated shell beads dating to about 75,000 years ago from the Middle Stone Age site of Blombos Cave in South Africa. Beads and other forms of personal adornment are especially important forms

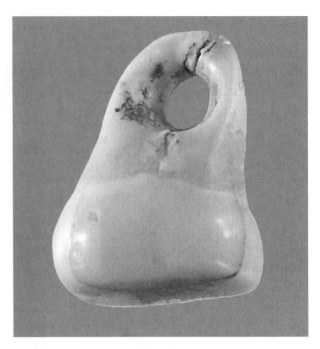

FIGURE 10.9   A human molar from Isturitz in southern France that has been perforated and used as a pendant.

of Paleolithic art, since they can be used to communicate personal and group identity.

DATING AND CHRONOLOGY

The chronological development of Upper Paleolithic art has presented several methodological challenges for archaeologists. Unlike the Middle Stone Age in Africa, where decorated bone objects are known from recent excavations in Zaire (Yellen et al. 1995), there is almost no unequivocal evidence of art or decoration in the European Middle Paleolithic (Chase and Dibble 1987). The appearance of art in the Upper Paleolithic in Europe has been seen as a kind of creative explosion (Pfeiffer 1983). Understanding the origins and development of the art of Upper Paleolithic Europe necessitates some kind of chronological framework.

While mobiliary art is usually found in archaeological layers in association with materials such as charcoal that can be dated using the radiocarbon method, it is far more difficult to date the cave paintings. Early attempts at developing a chronology for Upper Paleolithic parietal art were based

FIGURE 10.10   Horse from Lascaux (Dordogne) showing its short, smooth summer coat. In winter the horses' coats are shaggier and darker.

primarily on stylistic changes (see, for example, André Leroi-Gourhan 1968). Unfortunately, stylistic changes cannot provide an absolute chronology for artistic developments. Recent developments in radiocarbon dating (Chapter 9), including the use of the AMS method for the dating of very small samples of organic materials, are beginning to provide a more detailed chronology for the development of Paleolithic art. The radiocarbon method has been used to date the carbonized wicks remaining in lamps, the torch marks on cave walls, and sometimes even the organic materials within the pigments themselves. At least 80% of the known Upper Paleolithic art from Europe dates to the latest phase of the Upper Paleolithic period, the Magdalenian period (White 1986: 138). For example, radiocarbon dating of the charcoal remains in the Lascaux lamps indicates that the site was used about 17,000 years ago (Arlette Leroi-Gourhan 1982: 107) during the Magdalenian period. The new radiocarbon dates from Grotte Chauvet, noted previously, however, have indicated that techniques of cave painting were well developed by the earliest phases of the Upper Paleolithic period in Europe. The dates indicate that those images were painted

approximately 30,000 years ago and suggest that the traditions and techniques of parietal art were established early in the Upper Paleolithic period and then continued for approximately 20,000 years.

INTERPRETATION OF PALEOLITHIC ART

One of the most challenging tasks facing Paleolithic archaeologists is attempting to understand the function and meaning of parietal and mobiliary art. Many scholars of the early twentieth century, including the Abbé Henri Breuil, assumed that the images represented a kind of hunting magic, designed to ensure the abundance of wild game animals. There is no question that many of the images depict large herd animals, such as horses, bison, wild cattle, deer, and reindeer, that we know were hunted by Upper Paleolithic people. In addition, the images display the detailed knowledge of animal anatomy and behavior that would be expected from a foraging population. For example, Sally Casey (1995) has recognized images of animals in both their summer and their winter coats (Figure 10.10). There are several problems, however, with the interpretation of all Paleolithic art as hunting magic. While many of the images are those of large game species, large predators such as felines and bears occasionally appear in the art. Would Paleolithic hunters have wanted to face increasing numbers of predatory species? In addition, there is a difference between the species of animals most commonly painted on the cave walls and the species that were actually hunted by Paleolithic hunters. Horses, wild cattle, and bison are the species that occur most frequently in parietal art, while Upper Paleolithic faunal assemblages in southern France are dominated by the remains of reindeer, and those in northern Spain are often dominated by red deer (Chapter 9). Since the hunting magic hypothesis does not explain the range of animals depicted in Paleolithic cave art, modern scholars have sought other explanations.

One of the most innovative approaches was pioneered by the French prehistorian André Leroi-Gourhan (1968). Leroi-Gourhan began by examining the distribution of the images within the caves. He found that most of the images of horses, bison, and wild cattle were concentrated in the central areas of the caves, while images of rare animals such as bears and felines were concentrated in the more remote areas. He used these data to suggest that Upper Paleolithic painted caves had a standardized layout, much like a modern church or temple. His interpretation of the meaning of these images is far more controversial. Leroi-Gourhan suggested that these images reflected a structural opposition between males and females. Not only did he interpret the horse images as male and the bovids (cattle and bison) as female, he also interpreted many of the nonfigurative signs as male and female symbols. Arrows, for example, were seen as male. One of the problems with this interpretation is that the images of horses, bison, and cattle include both male and female animals. Why should all the horses be male symbols and all the bovids be female?

Other scholars have emphasized the role of art as a means of symbolic communication. As noted in Chapter 9, some of the largest European Upper Paleolithic sites may have served as seasonal aggregation sites (Conkey 1980) where small hunter-gatherer bands congregated to form larger social units for a short period of time. Many of the large

FIGURE 10.11   Shaft scene from Lascaux (Dordogne) showing disemboweled bison, human, and a bird on a staff.

Upper Paleolithic sites, such as Laugerie-Basse in southwest France, have produced large numbers of art objects (White 1986: 85). The art may have played a role in the ritual activities that took place at these seasonal aggregation sites.

Some cave art may have helped communicate traditional stories or myths. The famous scene in the shaft at Lascaux (Figure 10.11) suggests this interpretation. Hidden deep in a recess in the cave, the painting juxtaposes the figures of a disemboweled bison, a strange bird-headed man, and an equally enigmatic "bird on a stick" object. What this scene conveys (if indeed it is a single, unified scene) is, of course, a mystery to us.

Although conclusions drawn from analogy with modern people are always chancy, the art of the San of South Africa may provide a useful model. Ethnographic and historical studies of rock art have shown that "San rock art is best described as essentially religious in that it reflects a belief in a God or spiritual power that can be accessed by trained medicine-people or shamans for assistance in activities such as healing, rain-making, and social rituals" (Deacon 1999: 57). It is likely that Upper Paleolithic cave art in Europe was also related to religious practice.

FIGURE 10.12   Rock painting showing naturalistic animals and human figures from Makwe, near Wedza, Zimbabwe.

While we can marvel at the artistry and technical skill manifest in Paleolithic art, much of its meaning remains elusive. Detailed studies of the contexts in which particular images are found may shed some light on the symbolic and religious systems of which these images were a part. However, as Ucko and Rosenfeld (1967: 239) noted more than 30 years ago, "perhaps many Paleolithic representations were made for reasons which still totally escape the modern observer."

ROCK ART FROM OTHER REGIONS OF THE WORLD

While this chapter has focused on the parietal and mobiliary art of western Europe, rock art has been produced in a number of other areas of the world, including the American southwest, southern Africa, and Australia. While the American rock art is relatively recent (Howard 1996), there is an increasing body of evidence to suggest that the African and Australian examples may have roots in the Pleistocene. African rock art, which includes naturalistic paintings and engravings of animals and people (Figure 10.12), often appears on the walls of shallow caves and rock shelters and on rocky outcrops. It is therefore far more exposed

to the elements than is European cave art, which is located deep within the recesses of caves. Many of the extant paintings are therefore likely to be recent. More than 30,000 rock art sites are known from South Africa. While the oldest rock art is late Pleistocene in date (see following), most of the rock art was painted by San hunter-gatherers in more recent times. The engravings, however, are less susceptible to deterioration (Phillipson 1993: 74). In southern Namibia, slabs bearing naturalistic painted images of animals have been found at **Apollo 11 Cave;** these images may be 27,500 years old (Wendt 1976). Stratigraphic evidence indicates that they must date between 27,500 and 19,000 years ago. These data suggest that the South African tradition of rock art may be as old as the European.

CONCLUSION

It is important to emphasize that the rock and cave art of Ice Age Europe, prehistoric southern Africa, and Australia was produced by populations who made their living by hunting and gathering. While we may not be able to reconstruct the function and meaning of these prehistoric images, the mere survival of these artistic treasures gives us a glimpse into the rich symbolic and expressive world in which these ancient foragers lived.

KEY TERMS

Altamira 149	Grotte Cosquer 153
Apollo 11 Cave 159	Lascaux Cave 151
Batons 154	Mobiliary art 149
Grotte Chauvet 153	Parietal art 149

QUESTIONS FOR DISCUSSION

1. What role or roles do you think art played in the lives of Upper Paleolithic people in Europe?

2. Do you think that there was a "creative revolution" some time after 50,000 years ago? Why or why not?

3. Why are animals commonly portrayed in Upper Paleolithic paintings and sculpture?

FURTHER READING

Bahn, Paul G., and Jean Vertut
    1997   *Journey through the Ice Age*. Berkeley: University of California Press.
    An updated version of Bahn and Vertut's 1988 volume, Images of the Ice Age, *this new edition includes images of Grotte Chauvet.*

White, Randall
    2003   *Prehistoric Art: The Symbolic Journey of Humankind*. New York: Abrams.
    A beautifully illustrated and engaging survey of prehistoric art by one of the foremost authorities in the field.

11

THE INITIAL HUMAN COLONIZATION OF AUSTRALIA

The first 5 million years of human prehistory center on the evolution of early humans in Africa and the subsequent human settlement of Eurasia. During the late Pleistocene, humans first moved out of Aseurica (the landmass that includes Africa, Asia, and Europe) into other regions of the world. The questions of how, when, and why humans settled Australia and the New World have intrigued scholars for generations. In this chapter we will trace the movement of human populations out of Asia into Greater Australia (Australia, New Guinea, and Tasmania). Recent discoveries indicate that the initial human colonization of Greater Australia may have taken place as early as 50,000 years ago.

GREATER AUSTRALIA: THE ENVIRONMENTAL BACKGROUND

Today, Australia, New Guinea, and Tasmania are three large but separate islands in the South Pacific. In late Pleistocene times, this region was quite different in appearance. Sea levels were as much as 160 m (525 ft.) lower during the height of the last glaciation. Sea levels dropped worldwide because much of the earth's water was trapped in the large ice masses that covered northern Eurasia and North America. **Eustatic sea level changes** are variations in world sea levels that result from the growth and melting of glacial ice (Van Andel 1989; see Archaeology in Practice, this chapter). A drop of only 30 m (100 ft.) in sea level is necessary for New Guinea to be joined to the Australian continent, and sea levels were at least that low between 80,000 and 6500 B.P. (before present). When sea levels dropped 65 m (213 ft.) below the present level, the island of Tasmania was also joined to Australia. This occurred between 25,000 and 12,000 years ago and may have occurred three other times during the late Pleistocene (Cosgrove 1989). The large continent formed by the joining of Australia, New Guinea, and Tasmania is often termed Greater Australia, or **Sahul** (White and O'Connell 1982: 6). At the height of the last glaciation, the lowered sea levels would have increased the land area of the Sahul by about one-quarter, to about 10.6 million sq. km (4 million sq. mi.) (Figure 11.1).

Although world sea levels were considerably lower throughout the late Pleistocene, the Sahul region was never connected to the Southeast Asian mainland by a land bridge. This means that the crossing to Australia must have involved some form of sea craft, such as rafts or boats. The initial colonists of Australia, however, would not have sailed off into an undifferentiated open sea. The open sea between mainland Southeast Asia and New Guinea is dotted by chains of high islands, and no leg of the voyage is likely to have been longer than about 100 km (62 mi.) in Pleistocene times. Birdsell (1977) identified a series of five possible routes between the Southeast Asian mainland and Greater Australia (see Figure 11.1). The routes involved between 8 and 17 stages. The more northerly routes led to New Guinea, while the southerly routes led directly to the Australian mainland. One of these routes provides intervisibility between the islands all along the route to New Guinea, and two others are at the margins of intervisibility (Irwin 1992: 21). This intervisibility makes deliberate exploration, rather than simply accidental settlement, a real possibility. However, whether the initial colonists of Australia were purposeful settlers or simply early island-hoppers who were blown off course is a question that cannot be answered on the basis of archaeological data alone.

THE ARCHAEOLOGICAL EVIDENCE FOR THE INITIAL COLONIZATION OF THE SAHUL

When did early humans first settle Greater Australia? In the late nineteenth and early twentieth centuries, Australia was seen as having a short prehistory. It was believed to have been settled quite late, and the Australian archaeological record was seen as limited and unchanging. The arrival of humans in Australia was measured in centuries rather than millennia (Mulvaney 1964: 263). By the mid-1960s archaeologists recognized that Australia had been settled by late Pleistocene times (Mulvaney 1964). However, it was the discovery of artifacts and human remains at the site of **Lake Mungo** in New South Wales in 1968 that revolutionized the chronology of the human settlement of Australia.

The Lake Mungo finds indicated that the Australian continent had been colonized by modern humans by about 40,000 years ago. Subsequent archaeological research has identified additional early sites in the Sahul. These include the site of **Kuk** in the New Guinea highlands, where charcoal and fire-cracked rocks transported by humans have been radiocarbon dated to about 30,000 years ago (Golson and Hughes 1977), and the site of **Devil's Lair** in western Australia, where possible stone and bone artifacts and chips of nonlocal stone were found in deposits that may date to as early as approximately 33,000 years ago (Dortch 1979). More recently, charcoal fragments associated with stone tools from the site of **Upper Swan** near Perth in southwestern Australia have been dated to 38,000 years ago (Pearce and Barbetti 1981). In addition,

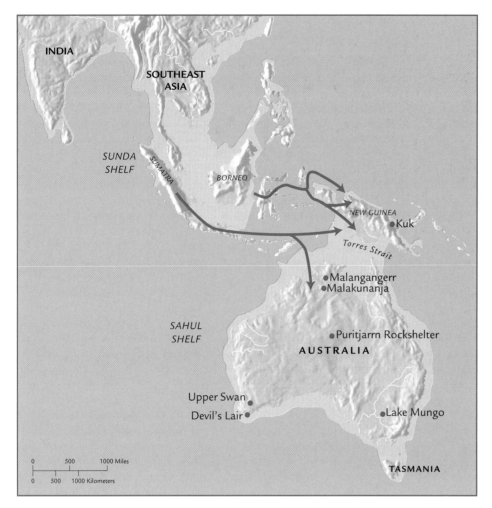

FIGURE 11.1 The Sahul region, showing the approximate coastline when sea levels were 150 m (500 ft.) lower than today, and the possible sea routes to New Guinea and Australia.

new radiocarbon dates indicate that a coastal midden site on the island of New Ireland was initially occupied by 32,000 B.P. New Ireland is near Greater Australia, but even at the height of the Pleistocene it would not have been attached to Greater Australia. The data indicate that New Ireland must have been colonized from the Australian mainland via the island of New Britain by 32,000 years ago (Allen et al. 1989).

The data from Upper Swan indicate that the areas of Greater Australia that were farthest from Southeast Asia were settled nearly 40,000 years ago. In addition, radiocarbon dates indicate that

the inland regions of Tasmania were colonized by about 35,000 years ago (Jones 1995). More recently, thermoluminescence (TL) dates have been obtained for two previously excavated sites in northern Australia, Malakunanja II and Malangangerr (Roberts et al. 1990). The TL dates suggest that humans first arrived at Malakunanja II between 45,000 and 61,000 years ago. Malakunanja II, which is located along the base of the prominent Arnhem Land escarpment in northern Australia, is likely to have been brought into use shortly after the initial colonization of the area. These TL dates, therefore, may mark the time of the initial

ARCHAEOLOGY IN PRACTICE

Changing Sea Levels: Eustacy and Isostacy

Archaeological research has revealed that hunters and gatherers who inhabited Greater Australia and other parts of the Old World during the late Pleistocene led lives very different from those of modern peoples. These Ice Age foragers also lived in a world that looked very different from the world of today. During the height of the last glaciation, sea levels were much lower than they are at present. Much of the earth's water was trapped in a number of permanent glaciers. Large ice masses covered many parts of the Northern Hemisphere, including Scandinavia, the Alps, and much of Canada and the northern United States. Smaller glaciers were located in highland areas such as central Tasmania and the Zagros Mountains of the Middle East. As a result, late Pleistocene coastlines bear little resemblance to the coastlines of today. As noted in this chapter, Australia, New Guinea, and Tasmania were all connected to form the single continent of Greater Australia or Sahul, with a land mass 25% larger than the modern region. In addition, Britain and Ireland were connected to continental Europe, and the Rhine and Thames Rivers shared a common drainage. North America and northeastern Siberia were connected to form the land mass known as Beringia (see Chapter 12).

As temperatures began to warm, starting about 18,000 years ago, the glaciers began to melt, and sea levels rose. This process is known as **eustacy** or glacio-eustatic sea level rise (Dark 2004: 48). As sea levels rose, Tasmania was separated from the Australian mainland some time around 12,000 to 10,000 years ago (Lourandos 1997: 255). At a later date, between about 8500 and 8000 B.P., the isthmus that connected New Guinea and northern Australia was breached by a series of sea channels (Mulvaney and Kamminga 1999: 261). These channels later merged to form the Torres Strait, the body of water that today separates Australia and New Guinea. In Europe rising sea levels led to the inundation of the Irish Sea and then the English Channel, severing the land link between Britain and continental Europe by about 7400 B.C. (Dark 2004: 48). As we will see in Chapter 12, Beringia appears to have been submerged by rising sea levels some time after 13,000 years ago (Hoffecker and Elias 2003: 34).

A second process known as **isostacy** or glacio-isostatic change is also responsible for changes in coastlines. The earth's crust is relatively thin and rests on top of a more viscous material that makes up the earth's mantle. When a heavy weight, such as a glacier, rests on the rocks of the earth's crust, the weight causes the crust to sink. When that weight is removed, as a result of glacial melting, the earth's crust begins to rebound. Although glaciers formed on Tasmania's central plateau during the coldest part of the late Pleistocene, about 20,000 years ago, isostacy played a minimal role in the formation of the postglacial coastline of Tasmania. Isostatic rebound is seen most clearly in Scandinavia, where sea levels are still rising 8000 years after the final melting of the Scandinavian ice sheets (Dincauze 2000: 221).

human settlement of greater Australia. Similar dates have been obtained for an archaeological site on the Huon terrace in Papua New Guinea. The site yielded a large number of waisted stone axes and appears to have been occupied at least 40,000 years ago (Groube et al. 1986). The early dates from these sites in northern Sahul led Flood (1990: 94) to suggest that the most likely time of human arrival in Australia is the period of low sea levels about 52,000 years ago. Other scholars are skeptical of the early TL dates and argue that Australia was probably colonized between 35,000 and 40,000 years ago based on the radiocarbon chronology (O'Connell and Allen 1998; see also Mulvaney and Kamminga 1999: 138–146).

While the recent radiocarbon and TL dates suggest that the Australian continent may have been settled by modern humans from mainland Southeast Asia as early as 50,000 years ago (Roberts et al. 1990), the ways human populations spread throughout this vast, environmentally diverse continent are not well understood. Today, much of New Guinea is covered with tropical rain forest, while the vegetation of Australia ranges from tropical rain

CASE STUDY

Lake Mungo

Lake Mungo is one of a series of extinct lakes, known as the Willandra Lakes, that are located in New South Wales, northwest of Melbourne, Australia. The lakes were a series of overflow basins, filled by the Lachlan River when it was in flood. Although these lakes have never been filled in **Holocene** (post-Pleistocene) times, during the Pleistocene the lakes were permanently filled. The geology of these extinct lakes was being studied by geomorphologist Jim Bowler in 1968 when he discovered burnt bones in a deposit known to be more than 20,000 years old. Bowler (Bowler et al. 1970) assumed that these were food bones burnt by early humans and marked them for future excavation by archaeologists.

Excavation of the site the following year revealed that the burnt bones were, in fact, a human cremation. Subsequent survey revealed a highly fragmented cranium about 0.5 km (0.3 mi.) from the original find. The initial skeleton, Mungo I, has been dated by radiocarbon to between 24,500 and 26,500 years ago (Bowler et al. 1972). It represents the charred and fragmented remains of a young woman. In 1974 the buried remains of an adult male, Mungo III, were discovered during additional geological surveys of the area (Bowler and Thorne 1976). Based on its stratigraphic position, Mungo III was initially dated to about 28,000–30,000 years ago. More recent radiocarbon age determinations suggest a date of between 40,000 and 43,000 years ago (Gillespie and Roberts 2000). Although even earlier dates have been suggested on the basis of ESR and other dating methods (Thorne et al. 1999), the earlier dates have not been widely accepted. Nevertheless, the Lake Mungo specimens represent the earliest skeletal remains known from the Sahul.

Additional archaeological evidence has been recovered from the Lake Mungo area, including stone tools and 16 circular patches of carbon that appear to be hearths. The hearths contained

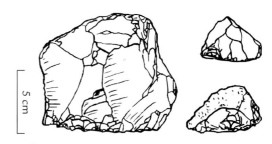

FIGURE 11.A   Choppers and flakes from the Lake Mungo excavations.

a range of faunal remains, including bird and mammal bones, freshwater shellfish, the bones of golden perch, and emu eggshells. The emu eggs would have been available in the region in late winter, while the fish and shellfish were probably caught in the late spring to summer. The excavators concluded that the site probably represents a seasonal, lakeside campsite (Bowler et al. 1970).

Most of the Lake Mungo stone tools were made of silcrete, a fine-grained stone that was available in the area. The tools include choppers that may have been used for heavy woodworking and scrapers made from flakes (Figure 11.A). The cores are shaped like horses' hooves. This industry is often described as the **Australian Core Tool and Scraper Tradition** (Lourandos 1997: 282–286).

Placing the Lake Mungo finds in a broader economic system presents a more difficult challenge (White and O'Connell 1982: 39). The differing dates for the Mungo I and Mungo III human remains suggest that the region may have been occupied, at least sporadically, over several thousand years. If the Lake Mungo hearths represent seasonal campsites, then those remains must be part of a broad range of seasonally occupied campsites in the region. Stone tool workshops and kill-butchery sites are needed to reconstruct the full range of Pleistocene subsistence activities.

forests in the northernmost areas to deserts in the west. Changes in temperature, sea levels, rainfall patterns, and oceanic currents would all have affected the environment of Greater Australia during the Pleistocene. Long-term paleoenvironmental investigations have been carried out only in a few areas, such as the Willandra Lakes region. Clearly, more archaeological and environmental research is required to reconstruct the pattern of settlement of Greater Australia.

Three differing models for the peopling of Australia have been proposed. Birdsell (1977) favored a rapid, radiational settlement of the Australian continent from a point of entry in the north. Bowdler (1977), however, argued for an initial settlement of the coastal regions, followed by the use of the Murray River system to reach inland areas such as Lake Mungo. She maintained that the initial inhabitants of Australia were adapted to a coastal way of life and that adaptations to the desert and montane regions of Australia took place considerably later (Bowdler 1977: 205). However, recent research at the **Puritjarrn rock shelter** near Alice Springs in the dry center of Australia has shown that at least some portions of the interior were settled by 22,000 B.P. (Flood 1990: 79). These data indicate that desert adaptations in Australia may have a much greater antiquity than was originally thought. Horton (1981), on the other hand, has emphasized that Greater Australia would have been a wetter continent at the time of the initial Pleistocene colonization. He argued that early settlement may have focused on the slopes and plains of eastern Australia, which are located between the east coast and the desert. With the addition of a number of large Pleistocene animals that have since become extinct, this intermediate zone would have been a highly productive environment for early hunter-gatherers. As Horton (1991: 350) notes, additional archaeological research in central Australia is needed to choose between these competing models of Australian settlement.

In general, it is likely that the Pleistocene inhabitants of Australia lived in small, geographically dispersed groups (Allen et al. 1989: 559). The accumulating evidence suggests that they may have adapted to a diverse range of environments as early as 30,000 to 35,000 years ago (Allen 1989: 153). The early inhabitants of New Britain relied on shellfish and marine fish (Allen et al. 1989) over 30,000 years ago, while the earliest inhabitants of Tasmania were hunting kangaroos and birds and collecting emu eggs at about the same time (Cosgrove 1989). The stone tools used by the early inhabitants of Greater Australia show little variability; most are simple choppers and flakes. However, the wide range of environments inhabited by these colonists provides evidence for great inventiveness and adaptability (Allen 1989).

LATER AUSTRALIAN PREHISTORY: A CONTINENT OF HUNTER-GATHERERS

While the aboriginal peoples of Australia had occupied a wide range of habitats by 30,000 years ago, archaeological research conducted since the 1960s indicates that much of the arid core of Australia was depopulated during the late glacial maximum (approximately 25,000–15,000 years ago), when the climate was significantly colder and drier than that of today (Mulvaney and Kamminga 1999: 206). During this period settlements were concentrated in areas with reliable water sources (Lourandos 1997: 193). Foraging expeditions into the arid regions were conducted from base camps in the semiarid areas with access to water.

With the advent of warmer and wetter conditions during the late Pleistocene and early Holocene, hunter-gatherer settlements expanded throughout Australia. While farming developed in New Guinea by 6000 B.P. (Mulvaney and Kamminga 1999: 87), if not earlier (see Chapter 17), Australia remained a "continent of hunter-gatherers" (Lourandos 1997) until modern times.

Although aboriginal Australians never adopted farming, there is archaeological evidence for significant social, economic, and technological changes in later Australian prehistory. Archaeological research at a number of different locations in southern Australia has produced evidence for larger and more permanent settlement after 4000 B.P. Australian hunter-gatherers built fixed facilities, such as drainage ditches and fish traps, that were designed to use smaller territories more intensively. Regionalization

ON THE CUTTING **EDGE**   *The Tasmanian Paradox: Why Did the Tasmanians Stop Fishing?*

The colonial history of Tasmania is a very sad one. The first European to encounter the island was the Dutch explorer Abel Tasman, who visited the island in 1642. At that time Tasmania was home to about 4000 hunter-gatherers. In the 1700s the island was visited by Captain Cook, who thought that it was part of the Australian mainland. The British established a penal colony on the island in the early part of the nineteenth century. At that time the British colonists attempted to extirpate the indigenous population, and the remaining Tasmanians were relocated to a reservation on an island off the coast of Tasmania, where more than half of them died within a decade. Subsequently, the surviving Tasmanians were resettled in northern Tasmania (Figure 11.B). Although the last full-blooded Tasmanian died in the later nineteenth century, her body was kept on display, against her wishes, in a museum in Hobart until 1976, when her remains were finally cremated. Today, some 6000 people can claim Tasmanian descent; most are descendants of European sealers and whalers who had children with Tasmanian women.

While the treatment of Tasmanian aboriginal people by the British colonists was appalling, archaeological research has revealed a unique Tasmanian prehistory that differs markedly from the prehistory of the Australian continent. As noted in the Archaeology in Practice section of this chapter, the land bridge between Australia and Tasmania was inundated at the end of the Pleistocene, between 12,000 and 10,000 years

FIGURE 11.B   Photograph of Tasmanian Aborigines taken in 1858. Source: Abbott Album, W.L. Gowther Library, State Library of Tasmania.

ago. Today, 200 km of open water separate Tasmania and mainland southeastern Australia. There does not seem to have been any contact between Australia and Tasmania since the end of the Pleistocene, since Holocene innovations such as the dingo and the Australian Small Tool Tradition never spread to Tasmania (Lourandos 1997: 274). The archaeological data from Tasmania reveal some interesting changes in Tasmanian technology and subsistence that have been interpreted in varying ways.

In the late 1970s, the Australian archaeologist Rhys Jones (1978) noted that at about 3500 B.P. the native population of Tasmania stopped fishing, as fish bones disappear from Tasmanian sites at this time. Bone tools (see Archaeology in Practice, Chapter 10) decrease in number during the Holocene and

also disappear at about the same time. Jones (1977: 176) suggests that a number of other technologies were lost by the Tasmanians after their isolation from Australia, including boomerangs, barbed spears, edge-ground axes, and basic hafting techniques. It should be noted, however, that only the loss of fishing technology and bone points has been documented in the archaeological record (Lourandos 1997: 277). Jones explained these losses as a kind of "devolution" that resulted from the isolation of the Tasmanian population from the wider social networks of continental Australia (Jones 1977, 1978).

Other archaeologists viewed the loss of fishing and bone working from a different perspective. For example, Allen (1979) noted that the cessation of fishing coincided with the onset of cooler and drier climatic conditions that may have led to a shift toward fattier foods such as sea mammals and away from fish. Others (e.g., Lourandos 1983) have suggested that the cooler and drier conditions of the later Holocene would have opened up opportunities for terrestrial hunting, leading to a reorganization of Tasmanian subsistence practices.

The question of the loss of fishing technology by the Tasmanians has recently been reopened by Joseph Henrich (2004). Henrich suggested that the inundation of the Bass Strait between 12,000 and 10,000 years ago would have markedly reduced the interacting pool of social learners in early Holocene Tasmania. Under these conditions complex technological skills such as fishing and bone tool production may have disappeared, while simpler technologies, such as stone tool manufacture, may have remained stable or even shown some improvement.

The debate over why the Tasmanians stopped fishing during the Holocene remains unresolved. While additional archaeological excavations might help to resolve this debate, archaeological research has been almost completely suspended in Tasmania, due to poor relations between archaeologists and the Tasmanian Aboriginal Land Council (Mulvaney and Kamminga 1999: 356).

in art styles and growing numbers of cemeteries also point to increasing territoriality in Australia during the later Holocene. In Binford's (1980) terminology (see Cutting Edge box, Chapter 8), later Holocene Australian hunter-gatherers can be seen as collectors, inhabiting base camps for substantial portions of the year.

Technological changes include the appearance of the **Australian Small Tool Tradition** (Lourandos 1997: 287–295; Mulvaney and Kamminga 1999: 230–232), beginning about 5000 B.P. Steeply retouched microliths were manufactured from high-quality raw materials, often obtained from distant sources (Figure 11.2a). Some specimens bear traces of gum or resin, indicating that they were used as part of composite tools, possibly as barbs for spearheads. In addition, small points, generally 2–10 cm in length, appear at this time (Figure 11.2b). Many of these points were shaped by pressure flaking. Another importance is the appearance of the dingo, or Australian dog. Dingos were introduced to Australia from Southeast Asia some time after 4000 B.P. The dog is the one domesticated animal that is commonly found in hunter-gatherer societies. In Australia these dogs were used for hunting and as companion animals. They may have played a role in the extinction of

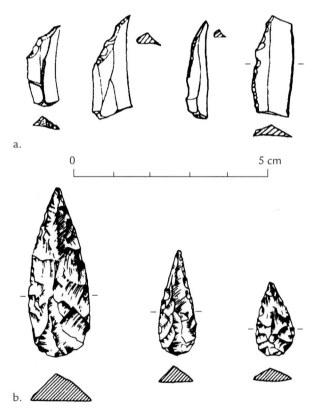

FIGURE 11.2 Tools of the Australian Small Tool Tradition: a. microliths and b. small, finely flaked points. Credit: a. H. Lourandos 1997: Continent of Hunter-Gatherers; b. J. Mulvaney and J. Kamminga 1999: Prehistory of Australia.

the Tasmanian devil and the Tasmanian tiger on the Australian mainland.

CONCLUSION

Archaeological research conducted since the 1960s clearly indicates that Greater Australia was settled by anatomically modern hunter-gatherers by 35,000 to 40,000 years ago, if not somewhat earlier. Since Australia was never connected to mainland Southeast Asia, the initial settlement of Australia undoubtedly involved the use of boats or other watercraft. A simple but flexible stone technology allowed these early colonists to inhabit a diverse range of environments for more than 30,000 years. While Australia remained a continent of hunter-gatherers until modern times, archaeological research has revealed significant social, technological, and economic innovations, including the appearance of the Australian Small Tool Tradition in later Australian prehistory.

KEY TERMS

Australian Core Tool and Scraper Tradition 165	Holocene 165
Australian Small Tool Tradition 168	Kuk 162
Devil's Lair 162	Lake Mungo 162
Eustatic sea level changes 162	Puritjarrn rock shelter 166
Eustacy 164	Sahul 162
Isostacy 164	Upper Swan 162

QUESTIONS FOR DISCUSSION

1. Why do you think that the Tasmanians stopped catching and eating fish about 3500 years ago?

2. What kind of watercraft do you think that the aboriginal Australians used to cross from Southeast Asia to Greater Australia?

3. Why do you think that Australia remained a continent of hunter-gatherers until modern times?

FURTHER READING

Lourandos, Harry
   1997   *Continent of Hunter-Gatherers: New Perspectives in Australian Prehistory.* Cambridge: Cambridge University Press.
   An ecological approach to the prehistory of Australia. Recommended for the advanced reader.

Mulvaney, John, and Johan Kamminga
   1999   *Prehistory of Australia.* Washington, DC: Smithsonian Institution Press.
   A comprehensive overview of Australian archaeology, with an excellent section on Australian art.

12

THE PEOPLING OF THE NEW WORLD

While an increasing body of archaeological evidence indicates that the Australian continent may have been colonized as early as 50,000 years ago, there is considerably less evidence for the settlement of the Americas before the last few millennia of the Pleistocene. For nearly 150 years, questions regarding the peopling of the Americas have been the subject of intense and sometimes acrimonious archaeological debate. As early as 1856, Samuel Haven, the librarian of the American Antiquarian Society, argued that the Americas had been populated from Asia (Haven 1856). This view has never been seriously challenged. In fact, it has received additional support from biological studies of Native American teeth. Turner (1989, 1994) identified certain features of tooth crowns and roots, such as shovel-shaped incisors, that he termed the Sinodont pattern. The distribution of these distinctive features suggests that Native Americans are more closely related to northern Asians than they are to Southeast Asians or Europeans. Moreover, Turner suggested that Native American and north Asian populations may have separated about 15,000 years ago. Any discussion of the settlement of the Americas therefore must begin with the late Paleolithic archaeology of northeast Asia and Alaska.

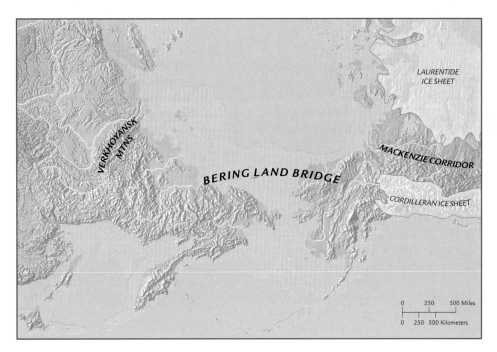

FIGURE 12.1   Beringia during the late Pleistocene.

GEOLOGICAL BACKGROUND

During the height of the last glaciation, when sea levels were considerably lower than they are today, northeast Asia was connected to Alaska by the **Bering Land Bridge** (Figure 12.1). A drop of approximately 50 m (165 ft.) in sea level below today's levels was necessary for the creation of the land bridge. Recent geological studies indicate that the land bridge would have been open throughout most of the late Pleistocene from 60,000 until after 11,000 years ago.

The term **Beringia** has been used to describe the landmass that would have stretched between the Verkhoyansk Mountain Range in eastern Siberia and the maximum limit of the Laurentide (North American) ice sheet, west of the Mackenzie River in the Canadian Yukon (Hoffecker et al. 1993; Hoffecker and Elias 2003). The nature of the environment of this landmass has been subject to serious debate among both archaeologists and environmental scientists. Some scholars have argued, based primarily on pollen data (see Archaeology in Practice, Chapter 13), that Beringia was a "dry, bleak, windswept land bridge" (Colinvaux and

West 1984: 11), which supported only sparse and scattered populations of horse, bison, and mammoth. Others used faunal data to suggest that Beringia may have been more steppelike than tundralike and could have supported a rich and diverse community of large mammals (Guthrie 1990; Hopkins et al. 1982). While debate continues over the nature of the environment of Beringia at the height of the Pleistocene glaciation, it is likely that later glacial Beringia included a mosaic of different environments, some of which could have supported human settlement (Hoffecker et al. 1993: 48; Hoffecker and Elias 2003: 34).

The pollen data do provide evidence for climatic amelioration beginning about 14,000 years ago. These improvements are part of a series of worldwide climatic changes that took place between about 14,000 and 10,000 years ago, marking the end of the Pleistocene (see Chapter 13). Pollen evidence from Alaska and the Yukon indicates an increase in birch tree pollen at that time. The reappearance of trees in river valleys and elsewhere would have provided greater access to firewood, a necessity in cold, late glacial Beringia (Hoffecker et al. 1993: 51). (See Archaeology in Practice, following, for a

ARCHAEOLOGY IN PRACTICE

Causes of Climatic Change

The climatic changes that took place at the end of the Pleistocene were worldwide, although the nature of the changes varied in different parts of the world. Europe and North America experienced some of the most dramatic changes at the end of the Pleistocene. Why did the climate change dramatically about 10,000 years ago? The changes in the world climate appear to have been triggered by alterations in the earth's orbit that led to increased solar radiation during the summer in the northern hemisphere (where most of the earth's landmass lies). A combination of eccentricities in the earth's orbit, an increase in the earth's tilt on its axis, and changes in the season when the earth is closest to the sun may have triggered the climatic changes. The changes in earth-sun geometry (Figure 12.A) began about 18,000 years ago but reached their maximum about 9000 years ago, when the solar radiation during the summer in the northern hemi-

sphere was about 7% greater than it is today (Kutzbach and Webb 1991: 191).

The effects of increased summer insolation were tempered by the effects of the slowly melting ice sheets that covered parts of Eurasia and much of northern North America. These huge ice masses reflected sunlight away from the earth's surface and also affected patterns of global air circulation. The complex interaction of these factors altered storm tracks, which influenced precipitation patterns in different areas of the world. Changes in temperature and rainfall patterns, in turn, affected the distributions of the plant and animal resources on which humans depended. Those changes are reflected in the palynological and geological records for different parts of the world.

Geological evidence indicates that sudden, major climatic changes occurred about 10,300 years ago, including, among others, changes in

the proportion of carbon dioxide in the earth's atmosphere. The amount of CO_2 rose steadily from 17,000 to 10,000 years ago and has remained at that higher level until quite recently. (Since the beginning of the Industrial Revolution, increasing industrialization and global population growth have caused the proportion of carbon dioxide in the atmosphere to begin rising once again.) It should be noted, however, that the rise in the percentage of atmospheric CO_2 (one of the so-called greenhouse gases) at the end of the Pleistocene was not nearly enough to account for the massive global climatic changes that took place at that time. Moreover, the rise in CO_2 may have been a consequence, rather than a cause, of late Pleistocene global warming (Pielou 1992: 228). Other effects include changes in the kinds of small animals (called foraminifera) found on the ocean floor, which indicate sharply rising ocean temperatures and the extinction of a large number of mammal species.

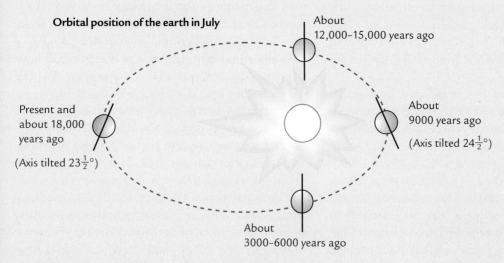

FIGURE 12.A Schematic drawing showing changes in earth-sun geometry since 18,000 B.P.

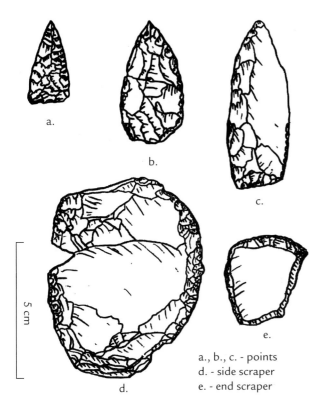

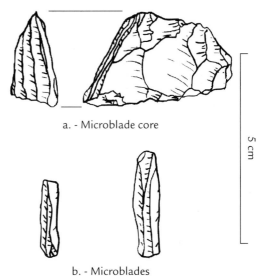

a. - Microblade core

b. - Microblades

FIGURE 12.3 Microblades and typical wedge-shaped core from sites of the Denali Complex in Alaska and late Pleistocene sites in northeast Asia.

a., b., c. - points
d. - side scraper
e. - end scraper

FIGURE 12.2 Typical tool kit of the Nenana Complex: bifacially retouched points, end scrapers, and side scrapers.

discussion of the causes of climatic change during the Pleistocene.)

THE EARLY ARCHAEOLOGICAL RECORD FROM ALASKA

The climatic improvement that marks the last four millennia of the Pleistocene appears to coincide with the initial human settlement of Beringia. Recent radiocarbon dates from the Russian far east indicate that western Beringia, including the Indigirka River basin and the Kamchatka Peninsula, was initially occupied between 14,000 and 12,000 years ago (Kuzmin 1994: 375). The colonization of Beringia is an outgrowth of the recolonization of the Siberian high-altitude mammoth steppe after the last glacial maximum about 20,000 years ago (see Goebel 1999).

The earliest archaeological sites in Alaska are found in the north-central foothills of the Alaska mountain range in the Tanana and Teklanika Valleys. (For a historical review of late Pleistocene archaeology in Alaska, see Bever 2001.) The earliest occupants appear to have entered the region between 12,000 and 11,000 years ago during an interstadial, a warm period marked by the expansion of trees in the river valleys. The river valleys served as refuges for steppe-tundra animals during the late Pleistocene and would have been attractive to bison and mammoth at a time when central Alaska was becoming increasingly forested (Powers and Hoffecker 1989: 271). The hunters' tool kit, known as the **Nenana Complex,** was based on a flake and blade core technology, including small bifacially worked projectile points, retouched blades, scrapers, wedges, and planes (Figure 12.2). The bearers of the Nenana Complex hunted sheep, bison, and elk in central Alaska and may also have taken small mammals, fish, and birds.

The Nenana Complex differs markedly from the late Paleolithic stone tool industries that were common in many parts of northeast Asia between 10,000 and 15,000 years ago. Those industries are characterized by the presence of microblades (very small blades), which were removed from small, wedge-shaped cores (Figure 12.3). The microblade industry first appears in Alaska, where it is known as the **Denali Complex,** at about 10,700 B.P. (Hoffecker et al. 1993: 52), and may represent the spread of a new population into Alaska. The earlier Nenana Complex appears to have more in common with pre-microblade Eurasian Upper Paleolithic stone tool industries.

The Nenana Complex is important not only because it appears to represent the earliest human settlement of Alaska but also because of its relationship to the peopling of the rest of the Americas. By 14,000 B.P. the melting of the continental ice sheets in northern Canada would have provided an access route for humans from Beringia to the North American Great Plains (Hoffecker et al. 1993: 47). While an ice-free corridor may well have existed between the Laurentide ice sheets that covered much of northern North America and the Cordilleran ice sheets that covered the coastal mountain ranges throughout the height of the late glacial period (25,000 to 14,000 B.P.), it probably sustained few plants and animals. Pollen data indicate, however, that by shortly after 12,000 B.P., sage, willow, grass, and poplar would have invaded this corridor, thus creating an environment that was more favorable to human settlement (Haynes 1987: 83).

CLIMATIC CHANGES: LATE GLACIAL NORTH AMERICA

The initial settlement of the American continents must be seen against the backdrop of changing environmental conditions in late glacial Beringia. Pollen and geological data indicate that similar changes were happening throughout the North American continent in the late glacial and early postglacial periods. Although there are many similarities in the patterns of deglaciation in Europe and North America, the final melting of the large North American ice sheets took about 500 years longer. The larger landmass of Eurasia in comparison with that of North America allowed for more rapid postglacial warming and therefore more rapid glacial melting (Kutzbach and Webb 1991).

In North America the glaciers began to retreat between 18,000 and 14,000 years ago. By about 14,000 years ago, the southern portions of the Great Lakes

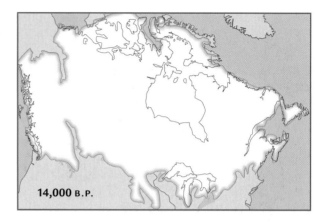

14,000 B.P.

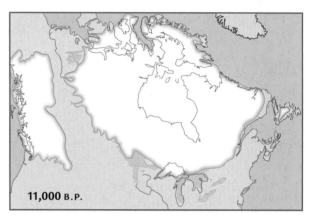

11,000 B.P.

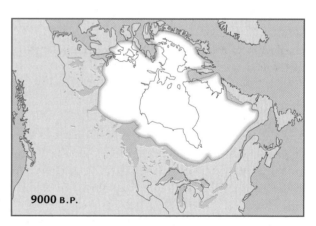

9000 B.P.

FIGURE 12.4 Views of the Laurentide (major North American) ice sheet between 14,000 and 9000 B.P., showing the extent of the ice sheet and the formation of the glacial meltwater lakes that were the precursors of the Great Lakes.

region were deglaciated, and ice-dammed lakes (eventually to become the Great Lakes) began to form between the southern ends of the lake basins and the retreating glaciers (Figure 12.4). Geological evidence indicates that significant climatic amelioration occurred in North America between 14,000 and 11,000 years ago. All sections of the North American ice sheets began to retreat. By 11,000 years ago, the coast of Maine had been deglaciated; the Cordilleran ice sheet covering the western mountains had retreated; and the Great Lakes region was largely free of ice. This period is also marked by the spread of deciduous forests, although some steppe and tundra conditions persisted in deglaciated regions in the east.

Although the evidence for the Younger Dryas event is not as marked in some regions of North America as it is in Europe, both geological and pollen evidence for this event is found in eastern North America. Glaciers advanced in both Newfoundland and Nova Scotia in the Canadian maritimes, and pollen records for the midwestern United States also show evidence for temperature decreases.

CLOVIS HUNTERS IN NORTH AMERICA

In North America the earliest well-dated archaeological sites south of Alaska are part of the **Clovis** culture. Clovis sites date to between 11,200 and 10,900 B.P. (Haynes 1992: 364). The sites are characterized by the presence of distinctive fluted points (Figure 12.5). Flutes are long, narrow flakes that are removed from both sides of spear points. They make it easier to mount the spear point into a split shaft, and they also make the point more streamlined, improving both its stability in the haft and its penetration into game animals (Haynes 1987: 91). Clovis sites have traditionally been identified by the presence of these distinctive spear points. However, with the exception of the distinctive Clovis points, there are remarkable similarities between Clovis stone tool assemblages and those of the earlier Alaskan Nenana Complex. They share many artifact types in common, including bifacially flaked projectile points, convex side scrapers, end scrapers, gravers, and wedges. Since radiocarbon dates for the Nenana Complex fall between 11,800 and 11,000 B.P. (Haynes 1992: 368), it is reasonable to

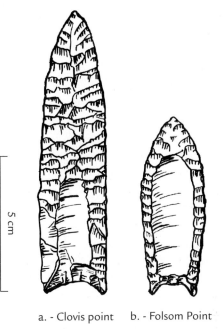

a. - Clovis point   b. - Folsom Point

FIGURE 12.5 Fluted points from the Clovis and Folsom cultures.

trace the origins of the Clovis culture to the Alaskan Nenana Complex.

Clovis points were first discovered at the site of **Blackwater Draw** near Clovis, New Mexico (Figure 12.6). At Blackwater Draw, a series of ancient springs formed a deep pond with a marshy drainage channel. The lowermost levels of the site yielded Clovis projectile points and other stone tools associated with mammoth bones. Clovis points have been associated with mammoth remains at a number of other early sites in the American southwest. For example, at the **Lehner** site in the extreme southeastern part of Arizona, Clovis points were found associated with the remains of mammoth, horse, bison, and tapir. The animals, including the mammoths, appear to have been killed and butchered on the spot. At the **Colby** site in Wyoming, limb bones, including the remains of three mammoths, were piled into stacks. These bone stacks may represent caches of meat for later use (Jennings 1989: 88).

The evidence from the American southwest suggests that the Clovis people were successful and efficient hunters of large game, including mammoth. Thirteen mammoths were killed at the

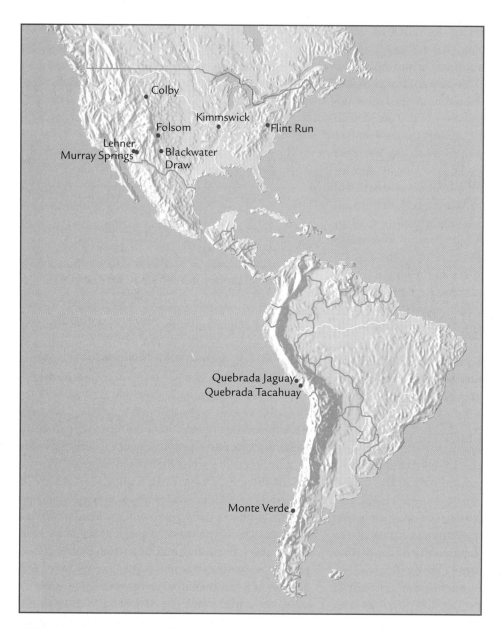

FIGURE 12.6   Locations of North and South American sites discussed in this chapter. Murray Springs is located very close to the Lehner site.

Lehner site, and eleven were killed at the nearby Murray Springs site, also in southeastern Arizona. Often the mammoth carcasses were only partially disarticulated (Fagan 1995: 83).

How were mammoths and other large game hunted by the Clovis people of the American southwest? Studies of African elephants indicate that these animals return to the same water holes

and vegetation patches on a regular basis (Fagan 1995: 82). In general, Clovis sites are located on low terraces along streams and rivers where mammoths and other large game may have obtained food and water. Several techniques may have been used to hunt mammoths. Clovis hunters may have used spear throwers; they may have stabbed mammoths directly with spears; or they may have used spears with detachable foreshafts (Fiedel 1992: 66). The stone spear point would be lashed to a bone foreshaft that would detach from the main shaft, allowing the spear shaft to be retrieved and reused. Mammoths, like all other members of the elephant family, were formidable beasts. Hunters may have waited until one animal became separated from the herd and then attacked the straggler. If the other mammoths became aware of the attack, hunters may have had to kill the whole herd (Fiedel 1992: 69). A whole herd of mammoths appears to have been killed at the Lehner site.

LATE PLEISTOCENE EXTINCTIONS

One of the most striking features of the late Pleistocene was the extinction of a wide range of large mammal species in a number of different areas of the world. In Eurasia the mammoth and the woolly rhino had disappeared by the end of the Ice Age. In North America a much larger range of megafauna became extinct, including both large herbivorous mammals, such as mammoths, horses, tapirs, and camels, and the large carnivores that may have preyed on them, including the saber-toothed tiger and the dire wolf (Figure 12.7). Australia saw the extinction of a substantial number of large marsupial mammals, although the Australian extinctions began more than 10,000 years before the North American extinctions. While the cause or causes of these great mammal extinctions remain a mystery (Pielou 1992: 265), vertebrate paleontologists and archaeologists have vigorously debated a number of theories. Most scientists would argue that the profound climatic changes that took place at the end of the Pleistocene played a critical role in the extinction of these large mammals. However, some archaeologists and paleontologists have suggested that human hunting may have caused the extinction of at least some species of Pleistocene megafauna in North America (Haynes 2002; Fiedel and Haynes 2004).

THE PLEISTOCENE OVERKILL HYPOTHESIS

The argument that human hunting played a role in the late Pleistocene extinctions is known as the **Prehistoric Overkill Hypothesis** and has been put

FIGURE 12.7 The dire wolf (*Canis dirus*) is a larger and more heavily built relative of the extant timber wolf, with much larger teeth. The dire wolf became extinct about 10,000 years ago.

forward by the paleontologist P. S. Martin (1984). Simply put, the prehistoric overkill hypothesis states that human hunters may have caused the extinction of Pleistocene large mammals such as the mammoth. Martin noted that Pleistocene extinctions were more common in Australia and the Americas, continents that were not occupied by humans until late Pleistocene times, than they were in Eurasia and Africa. In Australia 19 genera and more than 50 species have disappeared in the past 40,000 years, while in the Americas more than 70 genera have disappeared. Martin (1984: 394) argued that most, if not all, of the American extinctions have taken place within the last 15,000 years. Moreover, Martin noted that the Australian extinction events took place somewhat earlier than the American extinctions did, mirroring the earlier human settlement of the continent of Australia. He concluded that the record of late Pleistocene extinctions more closely reflects the movements and activities of humans than the late glacial climatic changes that took place between 18,000 and 10,000 years ago (Martin 1984: 396). Martin suggested that intensive hunting would have maximized the speed and intensity of the human impact on indigenous fauna while minimizing the amount of time between the initial human settlement of an area and the disappearance of its native fauna.

Although the prehistoric overkill hypothesis seems quite plausible at first glance, there are a

CASE STUDY

The Murray Springs Clovis Site

The Murray Springs site in southern Arizona is important because it illustrates how difficult it can be to distinguish the effects of human predation on large mammal populations from the effects of environmental change. The site does provide clear evidence for human hunting of mammoth, a species that did become extinct at the end of the Pleistocene. At the same time, however, detailed environmental research at the site has revealed dramatic climatic changes that may have affected the viability of mammoth populations in the American southwest.

Most of the Clovis kill sites in the American southwest are associated with mammoths. If humans did play a role in the extinction of any of the large Pleistocene mammals in North America, then mammoths would certainly have been the most likely victims of human hunting practices. In analyzing the data from the **Murray Springs** Clovis site (Figure 12.B), Haynes (1991) has recently suggested a model for the ways both

climatic change and human hunting may have led to the extinction of the North American mammoths.

The Murray Springs Clovis site is one of a number of Clovis Complex mammoth kill sites in extreme southeastern Arizona. The site was discovered in 1966, and additional excavations took place there in 1974 and 1975. These excavations yielded evidence for a mammoth kill, a bison kill, and a hunters' camp (Haynes 1991). The presence of projectile (spear) points, other stone artifacts, and **debitage** (waste flakes from stone tool production) at the mammoth kill site indicates that the mammoths were killed by human hunters. Radiocarbon dates for the Murray Springs site average 10,900 B.P. (Haynes 1992: 363), indicating that it is a very early site, contemporary with the initial widespread settlement of the North American continent. This is the kind of evidence one might use to support Martin's prehistoric overkill hypothesis.

On the other hand, geological evidence from Murray Springs and other contemporary sites indicates that there was a major drought in the southwest at that time. The dry interval dates from between 11,300 and 10,900 years ago. This drought may coincide with the Younger Dryas

number of strong arguments against this theory (Pielou 1992: 257). First, it is important to note that the Clovis period population of North America appears to have been quite low, perhaps too low to have had an effect on the populations of other animal species.

An even more compelling argument against the overkill model focuses on the chronology of large mammal extinctions in North America. The archaeologist D. K. Grayson (1991) reviewed the evidence for late Pleistocene mammalian extinctions in North America. He noted that the radiocarbon evidence shows that not all Pleistocene extinctions in North America took place between 12,000 and 10,000 years ago, the period of the widespread early human settlement of the North American continent. Large

mammals such as the short-faced bear and the American cheetah became extinct well before the appearance of the Clovis hunters. Of those species that did become extinct between 12,000 and 10,000 years ago, only two, mammoth and mastodons, have been recovered from human kill sites. Moreover, only 14 sites provide clear evidence for the hunting of mammoth and mastodonts by Clovis peoples (Grayson and Meltzer 2002), leading Grayson and Meltzer to suggest that current archaeological data do not support the Pleistocene overkill model.

Similar objections can be raised against the overkill hypothesis as it has been applied to Australia. As was shown in Chapter 11, Australia appears to have been settled by modern humans sometime between about 40,000 and 50,000 years ago. However,

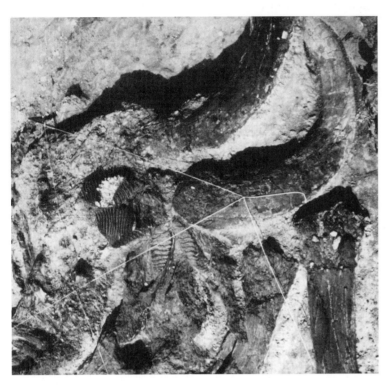

FIGURE 12.B   Excavations at the Murray Springs site, southeastern Arizona, showing the bones, tusks, and teeth of a mammoth.

climatic event in other parts of the world. It would have produced a significant reduction in the traditional watering places used by large mammals such as mammoths. The drought would have placed these large mammals under severe stress at the very time that the opportunistic Clovis hunters arrived in North America (Haynes 1991: 447). Animals under stress would have been easier prey for human hunters. The data from Murray Springs suggest that both climatic changes and human predation may have contributed to the extinction of the mammoths in North America. The extinction of at least one species of Pleistocene megafauna may have been a result of the combined effects of prolonged drought and the success of the Clovis hunters.

the wave of late Pleistocene extinctions in Australia began about 26,000 years ago and extended over a period of approximately 11,000 years (Pielou 1992: 255). The Australian data certainly do not support Martin's scenario, in which newly arrived human hunters rapidly exterminated a number of indigenous animal species.

ALTERNATIVE EXPLANATIONS FOR LATE PLEISTOCENE MEGAFAUNAL EXTINCTIONS

Most archaeologists and paleontologists reject Martin's prehistoric overkill hypothesis because it does not explain the vast majority of megafaunal extinctions that took place at the end of the Pleistocene. A variety of alternative explanations have been suggested that focus on the effect that late Pleistocene climatic changes would have had on large mammal populations. The massive climatic changes that took place at the end of the Pleistocene radically altered the range and composition of plant communities and may therefore have dramatically restricted the ranges of certain animal species. Late Pleistocene climates may have been more equable than those of today. While average yearly temperatures were relatively low during the late Pleistocene, equability means that the seasonal changes between summer and winter would have been less marked. Increasing summer temperatures in the early Holocene may have led to shifts in the vegetational communities, which in turn affected the animal populations that depended upon them (see Grayson 1991).

Dale Guthrie (1984) has developed an ecological theory to explain the megafaunal extinctions in North America based on the vegetational changes that took place at the end of the Pleistocene and the effects that those changes would have had on certain large mammal species. He argued that increasing seasonality (hotter summers and colder winters) at the end of the Pleistocene would have led to increasing zonation of plant communities. That is, some plant species that were found together during the Pleistocene were found in separate environmental zones during the early Holocene. The smaller variety of plant species in any given zone resulted in a shortened and less diverse growing season in that region, reducing the quantity and quality of plant foods available to many large mammal species. For animal species that relied on a "long growing season and a diverse vegetation to provide a balanced diet, the new Holocene buffet was ultimately a disaster" (Guthrie 1984: 290). For animals such as horses, mammoths, and mastodons, the result was extinction.

CLOVIS SETTLEMENT AND SUBSISTENCE IN THE EASTERN UNITED STATES

Although attention is often focused on the spectacular mammoth kill sites in the American southwest, Clovis sites are widespread across North and Central America. It has been suggested that these sites were occupied by groups of related, highly mobile hunting bands. In addition to the well-known kill sites, hunters' camps, base camps, and quarry sites have also been identified. Base camps are generally identified by their large size and by the presence of hearths and a greater diversity of tool types, indicating that tasks in addition to hunting and butchery took place there. Quarries include the site of **Flint Run** in northern Virginia, about 80 km (36 mi.) west of Washington, DC, which was exploited for high-quality jasper. In general, Clovis tools are made of high-quality raw materials such as flint, chalcedony, and jasper.

The subsistence practices of the Clovis hunters in the eastern parts of North America are less well

known because bone is often poorly preserved at eastern sites. At the **Kimmswick** site, approximately 30 km (18 mi.) south of St. Louis, Missouri, Clovis points were found associated with the bones of a mastodont (Graham 1981). At the time the Clovis hunters occupied the site, about 11,000 years ago, the environment would have been a deciduous woodland with open patches of grass. In the northeast, environmental studies indicate that the vegetation would have been a patchy, variable woodland offering a scattered diversity of food resources. It is likely that this varied environment was occupied by a low-density, highly mobile foraging population (Jennings 1989: 96).

FOLSOM HUNTERS

As noted, Clovis sites in the west date to between 11,200 and 10,900 B.P. About 10,900 years ago, the descendants of the Clovis hunters began to make a slightly different style of projectile point. **Folsom** points (see Figure 12.5) are characterized by longer flutes than the earlier Clovis points. Initial excavations in 1926 and 1927 at the Folsom type site in New Mexico revealed 19 Folsom points associated with 23 individuals of an extinct, long-horned species of bison, *Bison antiquus*. These excavations were the first to reveal that Native Americans occupied the North American continent at the same time as late Pleistocene fauna (Jennings 1989: 83). (The even earlier Clovis complex was not identified until 1932.)

Since mammoth became extinct in North America about 11,000 years ago, Folsom hunters in the Great Plains focused primarily on bison. Folsom sites date from between 10,900 and 10,200 years ago (Haynes 1992: 364). Reanalysis of the fauna from the Folsom type site indicates that all 23 bison were killed at the same time in early winter (Frison 1978). The animals appear to have been driven into an arroyo (dry creek), where they were then killed with spears. At other Folsom sites, herds of bison were driven over cliffs or into box canyons, which served as natural traps. The successful hunting of large numbers of bison at one time provides indirect evidence for strategic planning, for cooperation between hunters, and for an intimate knowledge of animal behavior. Other Folsom kill sites include

5 cm

FIGURE 12.8   Bifacial tools made of exotic basalt from the site of Monte Verde in south central Chile.

the remains of only a single bison, indicating that hunting strategies and techniques may have varied depending on the season, the numbers of hunters available, and other factors.

PRE-CLOVIS OCCUPATION OF THE AMERICAS: THE EVIDENCE FROM MONTE VERDE

For more than a century, archaeologists and other scholars have suggested that humans were present in North America before about 12,000 years ago. (For an up-to-date review of the evidence, see Nemecek [2000].) Various sites have been claimed as presenting evidence of a human presence in the Americas prior to the **Paleoindian** tradition. (The general term *Paleoindian* is applied to the Clovis, Folsom, and Nenana Complexes of late Pleistocene North America.) Some sites have yielded crude stone flakes, while others have included only bones that were allegedly modified by prehistoric humans. Over the years, the dating evidence, stratigraphic

position, and the nature of the artifacts from many of these sites have been challenged. The following is just one example: Alleged bone "tools" from the Old Crow Flats site in the Canadian Yukon were claimed to provide evidence for human settlement of Beringia as early as 30,000 years ago. Since the claim was first advanced, the stratigraphic position of the bones has been questioned; taphonomic analyses have shown that the so-called worked bones were likely produced by nonhuman agencies; and radiocarbon dating has shown that some of the worked bones are only about 1300 years old (Nelson et al. 1986). Moreover, the Old Crow Flats assemblage shows no similarity to any known Old World Paleolithic assemblage. Most other claims for a pre-Clovis presence in the Americas have met a similar fate (see Dincauze 1984; Lynch 1990).

The notable exception is the site of **Monte Verde** in south central Chile (Dillehay 1989, 1997, 2000). Excavations at the site have yielded artifacts and organic remains, including wood, bone, and skin, on an occupation surface that has been dated to approximately 12,500 B.P. The chipped stone artifacts include large bifaces made of basalt and quartzite (Figure 12.8). The site of Monte Verde is so important for archaeologists studying the peopling of the Americas that in January 1997 it was visited by a group of well-respected Paleoindian specialists (Meltzer et al. 1997). These scholars noted that the Monte Verde stone tools were unquestionably manufactured by humans and that the radiocarbon dates from the site are internally consistent. They concluded that the Monte Verde site was occupied by early humans approximately 12,500 years ago.

The excavations at Monte Verde have produced important details about settlement practices and subsistence patterns in late Pleistocene Chile. Since Monte Verde is a waterlogged site, organic remains, including wood and other plant material, were well preserved. The excavations at Monte Verde revealed evidence for a 20-meter-long tentlike structure with wood foundations. The body of the tent may have been made from animal hides (Dillehay 2000: 161). The inhabitants of Monte Verde collected wild potatoes, seeds, nuts, and fruits and hunted animals including mastodonts.

The evidence from Monte Verde has important implications for our understanding of the peopling of the New World. Although Monte Verde is only about 1300 years older than the oldest known Clovis sites in North America, Monte Verde is located approximately 16,000 km (10,000 mi.) south of the Bering Strait. The results of the excavations at Monte Verde "imply a fundamentally different history of human colonization of the New World than envisioned by the Clovis-first model and raise intriguing issues of early human adaptations in the Americas" (Meltzer et al. 1997: 662). The questions that these new finds raise include the following: How did early human populations reach South America from Asia? What is the relationship between the Monte Verde settlers and the later Clovis hunter-gatherers in the Americas? Clearly, these questions can be answered only by further research and by the identification of other pre-Clovis sites in the Americas.

Two recently discovered sites in Peru may shed light on the route by which some early Americans reached South America. The sites of **Quebrada Jaguay** and **Quebrada Tacahuay** are located along the south coast of Peru and are contemporary with the Paleoindian sites in other parts of the Americas, circa 11,000 to 10,000 years ago (Keefer et al. 1998; Sandweiss et al. 1998). The occupants of these sites made ample use of marine resources, including seabirds, shellfish, and small schooling fish such as anchovies and drums. The inhabitants of these coastal Peruvian sites probably used nets to catch these small fish. These coastal sites offer support for the idea that some early Americans used a coastal route to enter the New World.

CONCLUSION

Recent archaeological research has shed new light on the initial human colonization of the Americas. Archaeological research in Russia and Alaska suggests that Beringia was initially colonized about 14,000 years ago. The Clovis industry (11,200–10,900 B.P.) is the first archaeological culture known from North America south of Alaska. Moreover, recent excavations at the site of Monte Verde in Chile have indicated that humans had reached South America by 12,500 B.P. This site is more than 1,000 years older than the oldest known Clovis Complex site in North America. It raises important new questions about the initial human settlement of the Americas that can be answered only by additional research.

KEY TERMS

Bering Land Bridge   171
Beringia   171
Blackwater Draw   175
Clovis   175
Colby   175
Debitage   178
Denali Complex   174
Flint Run   180
Folsom   180
Kimmswick   180

Lehner   175
Monte Verde   181
Murray Springs   178
Nenana Complex   173
Paleoindian   181
Prehistoric Overkill
   Hypothesis   177
Quebrada Jaguay
   and Quebrada
   Tacahuay   182

QUESTIONS FOR DISCUSSION

1. How do you think that early humans traveled from Asia to Chile (Monte Verde) during late Pleistocene times?

2. What role (if any) did humans play in the extinction of North America's Pleistocene megafauna?

FURTHER READING

Dillehay, Thomas D.
2000 *The Settlement of the Americas: A New Prehistory.* New York: Basic Books.
A new account of the initial peopling of the New World, focusing on the data from Latin America. This volume includes a very readable account of the excavations at Monte Verde.

Grayson, Donald K., and David J. Meltzer
2003 A Requiem for North American Overkill. *Journal of Archaeological Science* 30: 585–593.
An up-to-date review of the Prehistoric Overkill Hypothesis.

Hoffecker, John, and Scott A. Elias
2003 Environment and Archeology in Beringia. *Evolutionary Anthropology* 12: 34–49.
This review draws on new environmental and archaeological data to examine the initial human settlement of Beringia.

PART 3

POST-PLEISTOCENE ADAPTATIONS

How Did Human Societies Change at the End of the Ice Age?

Beginning about 18,000 years ago, the earth's climate began to warm up. A period of climatic instability began about 14,000 years ago and ended with a significant rise in world temperatures at about 11,500 B.P., which marked the end of the Pleistocene. While these climatic changes were experienced throughout the world, some of the most dramatic changes in landscape took place in Europe and North America. In these two regions, areas that were previously glaciated were opened to human settlement in the post-glacial period. In addition, the post-Pleistocene temperature changes led to marked changes in flora and fauna throughout the Northern Hemisphere. In Europe and eastern North America, large areas of grassland and tundra were replaced by woodlands and forest. In parts of the American West, including the Great Plains and the Great Basin, post-Pleistocene climatic changes led to increasing desiccation and the disappearance of some well-watered habitats.

Part 3 examines the ways in which human hunter-gatherer communities responded to these dramatic climatic changes. Chapter 13 examines the ways in which Mesolithic hunter-gatherers changed their technology, subsistence patterns, and settlement systems in response to the dramatic changes in climate, flora, and fauna that characterized Europe during the early Holocene. Chapter 14 examines the ways in which Native American hunter-gatherers in both the Eastern Woodlands and the Great Basin responded to the environmental changes at the end of the Ice Age. The hunter-gatherers of the Archaic and the Mesolithic were making use of these new Holocene environments in active and creative ways.

One of the most striking developments of the early post-Pleistocene period is the beginning of farming, including both plant cultivation and animal husbandry. Since agriculture formed the economic basis for the well-known ancient urban societies in the Old and New Worlds, such as the Maya and the Egyptians, the study of agricultural origins is crucial to our understanding of the emergence and growth of urban societies in both the Eastern and Western Hemispheres. Archaeological research conducted since the end of the Second World War has shown that farming developed independently in several regions of the Eastern and Western Hemispheres, including the Middle East, Africa, China, Southeast Asia, New Guinea, southern Mexico, highland South America, and the American Midwest. In the Near East, in particular, the beginning of farming coincides with the climatic changes that took place at the end of the Ice Age. The questions of how and why early human societies began to practice farming are some of the most interesting questions that archaeologists attempt to answer. In Chapter 15 we examine some of the theories that have been proposed to explain the origins of farming. Chapter 16 explores the archaeological evidence for the beginnings of farming in the Old World, while Chapter 17 examines agricultural origins in the Americas. The final chapter in this part, Chapter 18, examines the positive and negative consequences of the beginning of farming, including population growth and increasing incidence of disease.

TIMELINE

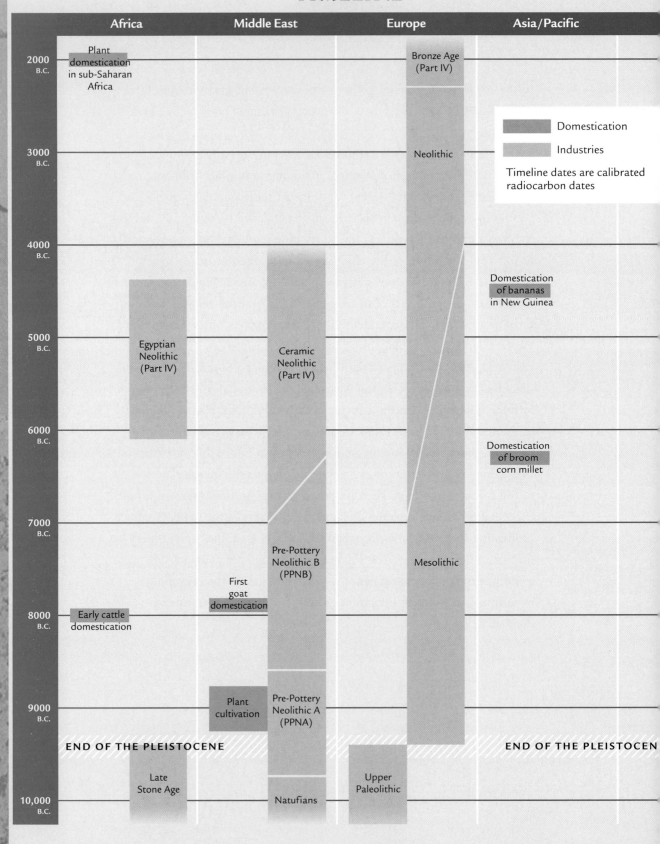

	Africa	Middle East	Europe	Asia/Pacific
2000 B.C.	Plant domestication in sub-Saharan Africa		Bronze Age (Part IV)	
3000 B.C.			Neolithic	
				Domestication of bananas in New Guinea
4000 B.C.				
5000 B.C.	Egyptian Neolithic (Part IV)	Ceramic Neolithic (Part IV)		
6000 B.C.				Domestication of broom corn millet
7000 B.C.			Mesolithic	
8000 B.C.	First goat domestication	Pre-Pottery Neolithic B (PPNB)		
	Early cattle domestication			
9000 B.C.	Plant cultivation	Pre-Pottery Neolithic A (PPNA)		
END OF THE PLEISTOCENE				END OF THE PLEISTOCEN
	Late Stone Age		Upper Paleolithic	
10,000 B.C.		Natufians		

Legend:
- ■ Domestication
- ■ Industries

Timeline dates are calibrated radiocarbon dates

North America	Mesoamerica	South America	
			2000 B.C.
Beginnings of plant domestication		Preceramic Period (Part IV)	
			3000 B.C.
		Domestication of camelids	
			4000 B.C.
	First maize		
			5000 B.C.
Archaic	Archaic		
			6000 B.C.
			7000 B.C.
	Early squash domestication at Gúilá Naquitz	Archaic hunters and gatherers	
			8000 B.C.
			9000 B.C.

END OF THE PLEISTOCENE

| Paleo-Indian | Late Pleistocene hunters and gatherers | Late Pleistocene hunters and gatherers | **10,000** B.C. |

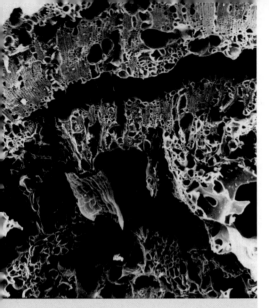

13

THE MESOLITHIC PERIOD IN EUROPE

In Europe, the retreat of the glaciers opened up many areas of central and northern Europe for human settlement (Chapter 9). The gradual reforestation of Europe created environments that were unlike any known there during the late Pleistocene. In this chapter we will examine the ways hunting and gathering populations in Europe responded to those marked environmental changes.

CLIMATIC CHANGES IN EUROPE IN THE EARLY POSTGLACIAL PERIOD

The end of the Pleistocene was marked by a rapid rise in the earth's temperatures, beginning about 9500 B.C.[1] In Europe the summers may have been as warm as those of today, although winter temperatures were still somewhat cooler. This rapid temperature rise caused significant changes in the European landscape. The melting ice caused sea levels to rise quickly between 9500 and 6000 B.C. By about 7400 B.C. the island of Great Britain became separated from the European continent.

While temperatures rose quite quickly at the end of the Ice Age, changes in vegetation, as reflected in pollen samples, took place somewhat more slowly (see Archaeology in Practice, this chapter). Gradually, the open steppe and tundra landscapes of the Pleistocene were replaced by parkland and forest vegetation. Initially, birch, a pioneer species, began to colonize areas that were previously dominated by periglacial and tundra vegetation. Later, pines and then a range of deciduous trees and shrubs, including oak, elm, linden, and hazel, came to dominate Europe's forests. These changes in vegetation led to significant alterations in Europe's animal populations. Animals such as reindeer and wild horse that prefer steppe and tundra environments were replaced by forest forms, including red deer (a large deer closely related to the North American elk), roe deer (a small deer about the size of a North American whitetail), wild pigs, and wild cattle. During the Holocene, reindeer populations were limited to the very northern reaches of Europe (primarily northern Scandinavia), while wild horses were restricted to the drier, steppic areas of eastern Europe and central Asia.

MESOLITHIC SOCIETIES IN EUROPE

The term **Mesolithic** (from *meso*, meaning "middle," and *lithic*, meaning "stone") is used to describe the postglacial hunters and gatherers of Europe.

The Mesolithic period begins with the end of the Pleistocene Ice Age about 11,500 years ago (9500 B.C.) and ends with the beginnings of farming, including agriculture and animal husbandry. The earliest European agriculture appeared in Greece, where it was introduced from the Near East about 7000 B.C., but agriculture and animal husbandry did not appear in parts of northern Europe until almost 3000 years later. For example, agriculture and animal husbandry were not adopted in Denmark until about 4000 B.C. As we shall see in Chapter 18, the spread of agriculture throughout Europe was a gradual process involving both the movement of farmers into Europe and the adoption of agricultural practices by native hunting and gathering peoples.

Mesolithic people were the last indigenous hunters and gatherers in Europe. Their sites lack the spectacular cave paintings and art objects that are found in many Upper Paleolithic sites in western Europe (Chapter 10). It is not clear why art played a less important role in Mesolithic life, but archaeologists have formed some hypotheses based on the role that art played in Upper Paleolithic life in western Europe. Paintings and sculptures are often found at Upper Paleolithic aggregation sites (see Chapter 9), locations where large numbers of people came together on a seasonal basis (Conkey 1980). Wall paintings (parietal art) may have played a role in unifying this diverse community by communicating a shared ideology. As we will see in this chapter, most early Mesolithic sites are quite small and would have been occupied by no more than perhaps a dozen families. Parietal art may not have been needed to unify the smaller and more homogeneous Mesolithic communities. It is also possible that Mesolithic art was made of perishable materials such as hides and wood and simply has not survived in the archaeological record.

By comparison with Upper Paleolithic peoples, the European Mesolithic folk were traditionally seen as impoverished. Scholars of the first half of the twentieth century viewed Mesolithic hunters and gatherers as poor foragers who eked out a meager existence in a changed and changing environment. Their lives were supposed to have been nasty, brutish, and short (see Price 1987 for a brief review

[1]With the transition from the Pleistocene to the Holocene, we will shift to the use of dates in years B.C. and A.D. We will use corrected radiocarbon age determinations throughout Parts 3 and 4 (see Archaeology in Practice, Chapter 14, for a discussion of the recalibration of radiocarbon dates).

ARCHAEOLOGY IN PRACTICE

Pollen Analysis

Palynology, or pollen analysis, is the study of pollen grains. Archaeologists are particularly interested in using pollen recovered from Pleistocene and Holocene contexts as a tool for reconstructing past human environments (Moore et al. 1991). Pollen, produced by seed plants, is part of the plant's reproductive system. Pollen grains are produced in the anthers, the male part of the flower. When pollen grains are released by plants, they are mixed in the atmosphere and ultimately fall onto land and water surfaces. This pollen rain is a reflection of the vegetation that produced it. Thus, analyzing ancient pollen helps archaeologists reconstruct past environments and climatic change.

Pollen analyses can be used in several ways by archaeologists. As noted, pollen data can be used to trace the vegetational history of a particular area. Since a region's vegetation is a reflection of temperature, rainfall, and soil conditions, changes in vegetation over time may reflect changes in climatic variables such as temperature and precipitation. Pollen analysis can also be used to assess past human impact on vegetation. As we will see in Chapters 15 to 18, the beginnings of agriculture led to significant changes in vegetation history. In addition to the introduction of cultivated crops and the weeds of cultivation, the beginning of farming was sometimes accompanied by forest clearance in areas such as northern and central Europe and eastern North America (Delacourt et al. 1998). Finally, the analysis of pollen recovered from specific features, such as pits and burials, within archaeological sites

may produce information about past human behavior. As noted in Chapter 6, pollen samples recovered from one of the Shanidar Neanderthal burials suggested that the individual had been buried with flowers.

Pollen is preserved best under conditions that inhibit microbiological activity, such as waterlogging, extreme aridity, high acidity, and an excess of salt or metal ions in the soil (Dimbleby 1985: X). Most pollen samples used for environmental reconstruction come from stratified waterlogged deposits, such as peat or lake mud, where pollen accumulates progressively through time. The dating of pollen samples, especially those from non-archaeological deposits such as lake beds, has been a persistent problem for environmental archaeologists. Radiocarbon dating (see Chapter 9) of the organic materials within a pollen core sample can provide independent dating for pollen records.

Once the pollen samples have been taken, recorded, and dried, the extraction and identification of pollen becomes a specialist task requiring laboratory facilities (Dimbleby 1985: 25). Pollen extraction (separating the pollen grains from the soil matrix) often requires the use of caustic and toxic chemicals such as hydrofluoric acid. Pollen samples are then mounted on slides so that the pollen grains may be identified and counted. Differences in the size and form of the pollen grain (Figure 13.A) are used to distinguish the pollen of different plants (Pearsall 1989: 251).

Once the identifications have been completed, pollen data are usually presented in the form of a

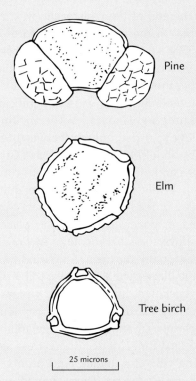

Pine

Elm

Tree birch

25 microns

FIGURE 13.A Illustrations of pollen grains of pine, elm, and tree birch. Differences in size, shape, and external morphology can be used to distinguish the pollen of different plant taxa.

pollen diagram. In a typical pollen diagram, the vertical axis is used to depict the soil depth, while the horizontal axis shows the relative or absolute abundance of different types of pollen. The soil depth reflects the relative age of the pollen samples, while the pollen abundance reflects the general prevalence of plant species in the environment. Pollen diagrams may also show the relative abundance of different groups of plants. For example, one common measure is the

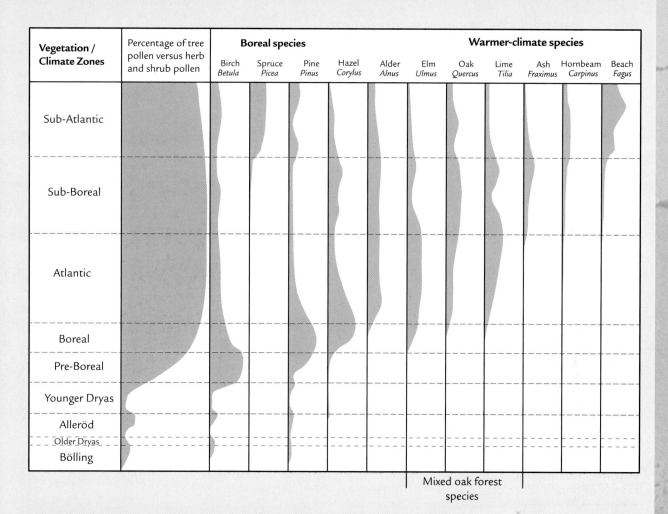

Vegetation / Climate Zones	Percentage of tree pollen versus herb and shrub pollen	Boreal species						Warmer-climate species				
		Birch *Betula*	Spruce *Picea*	Pine *Pinus*	Hazel *Corylus*	Alder *Alnus*	Elm *Ulmus*	Oak *Quercus*	Lime *Tilia*	Ash *Fraximus*	Hornbeam *Carpinus*	Beach *Fagus*
Sub-Atlantic												
Sub-Boreal												
Atlantic												
Boreal												
Pre-Boreal												
Younger Dryas												
Alleröd												
Older Dryas												
Bölling												

Mixed oak forest species

FIGURE 13.B Generalized pollen diagram showing the vegetational changes that took place in southern Scandinavia in late glacial and early postglacial times. The column on the left shows the percentage of tree versus shrub and herb pollen. Note the rapid development of forests in Europe in the early postglacial period. The Alleröd, Older Dryas, and Bölling chronological zones have recently been combined into the Windermere interstadial.

proportion of arboreal (tree) pollen to nonarboreal pollen. The relative abundance of different groups of species, such as aquatic plants, shrubs, and herbs, may also be depicted (Moore et al. 1991).

A generalized pollen diagram showing the vegetational changes in late glacial and early postglacial southern Scandinavia is shown in Figure 13.B. The column to the left shows the percentage of tree pollen in relation to the proportion of herb and shrub pollen. This diagram shows a clear increase in tree pollen beginning about 10,000 years ago. The increase in trees is a reflection of the increasing temperatures that prevailed after about 10,000 years ago. The first trees to appear are pioneer species such as birch and pine. About 8000 years ago, warm-loving mixed-oak forest species begin to replace those trees.

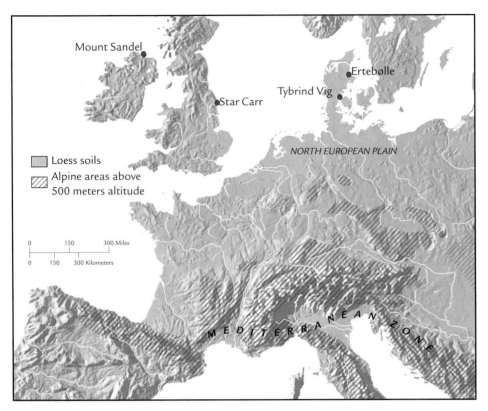

FIGURE 13.1 Map of Europe showing the four main geographic zones (Mediterranean zone, Alpine zone, loess belt, and North European Plain) and the locations of the sites mentioned in this chapter.

of the history of Mesolithic research). However, recent research on Mesolithic sites throughout Europe has radically changed our perception of these postglacial foragers. As a result of a series of important excavations that have been conducted since the end of World War II, including the sites of Star Carr and Mount Sandel (described in this chapter), archaeologists now recognize that the Mesolithic hunters and gatherers actively exploited the new postglacial environments in a variety of innovative ways (Figure 13.1).

MESOLITHIC STONE TECHNOLOGY

The stone tools used by Mesolithic peoples provide clues as to the ways these hunters and gatherers made use of the forested environments of early Holocene Europe. Two types of stone tools are commonly found in Mesolithic sites (Figure 13.2). The

first type is large, chipped stone axes made of flint. They were used to fell trees and, when mounted as adzes, to work wood. The second type is a group of small flint tools known as microliths, produced by snapping long flint blades into small geometric pieces 1 to 2 cm (0.4 to 0.8 in.) long. They were used as parts on composite tools—for example, as barbs for arrows. The advantage of the microlithic technology is that tools are easily repaired and versatile. It was "well suited to situations where the type and quantity of game are unpredictable" (Zvelebil 1986: 108).

HOW DID MESOLITHIC PEOPLES MAKE A LIVING?

For the most part, the Mesolithic hunters and gatherers who inhabited early postglacial Europe were broad-spectrum foragers who made use of a wide

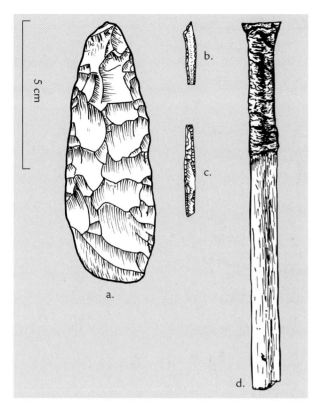

FIGURE 13.2 Typical examples of Mesolithic stone tool technology: a. large, chipped stone axes that were used for felling trees and/or working wood; b.,c. small, geometric microliths that could be used as parts of composite tools; and d. a microlith mounted as an arrow tip. The tip is mounted transversely to increase bleeding.

range of animal and plant resources, including large mammals such as deer, wild pigs, and wild cattle; birds; fish; shellfish; and plant foods such as nuts and tubers. The establishment of forested conditions in the early postglacial period (or early Holocene) created conditions favorable to forest animals such as roe deer, red deer, wild cattle, and wild pigs. Unlike reindeer, which were the primary game during the late Upper Paleolithic, these forest species do not migrate great distances. They are territorial and live within a relatively small geographical area. Moreover, deer and wild pigs reproduce rapidly; therefore, they can survive heavy annual harvesting.

As we shall see, Mesolithic peoples developed a range of new hunting, fishing, and plant-collecting technology that allowed them to forage in the diverse, forested environments of postglacial Europe. In addition, Mesolithic foragers made increasing use of technologies such as the bow and arrow that were initially developed during the late Upper Paleolithic but that were particularly useful for hunting forest game animals. When tipped with a single microlith mounted transversely, bows and arrows could be used to hunt small game. Alternatively, a group of microliths could be used as barbs on arrows that were designed to bring down large animals such as deer and wild pigs.

The foragers of Mesolithic Europe supplemented hunted meat by fishing and fowling. As we saw in Chapter 9, fishing played an increasingly important role in the economies of late Upper Paleolithic Europe. This trend intensified during the Mesolithic. In addition to the migratory species such as salmon, the rivers and lakes of postglacial Europe would have been full of fish such as carp and perch. Fish traps constructed of reeds have been recovered from waterlogged sites in northern Germany and Denmark. Boats would have been useful both for fishing and for hunting wild birds. A dugout canoe has been recovered from the site of Pesse in Holland. On the basis of the pollen associated with the find, the canoe from Pesse appears to date to approximately 8000 B.C. Parts of fish spears known as **leister prongs** provide additional evidence for fishing in lakes and streams. Two of these prongs, which are sometimes barbed on the inside edge, would have been attached to a wooden shaft and used to spear fish (Figure 13.3). Arrows with blunt, wooden heads would have been used for fowling. The blunt darts would stun the birds, which could then be collected by hunters.

Shellfishing played an increasingly important role in the later Mesolithic cultures of Denmark and northern Germany. **Kitchen middens,** shell mounds found along the coasts of Denmark and northern Germany, contain the remains of oysters, mussels, and cockles, as well as the bones of mammals, birds, and fish. Unlike earlier Mesolithic foragers, who moved on a seasonal basis to make use of various plant and animal resources, the inhabitants of coastal Germany and Denmark may have been sedentary collectors, who occupied these sites

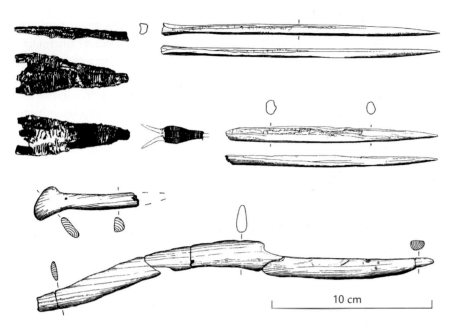

FIGURE 13.3   Preserved leisters recovered from the site of Tybrind Vig, a submerged late Mesolithic settlement in Denmark.

on a permanent basis. This increasing settlement permanence is certainly a reflection of the abundant food resources that would have been available along the coastal regions of northern Europe during the later Mesolithic period. The coastal hunters and gatherers did not have to move on a seasonal basis to make use of plants and animals that were available in different areas during different parts of the year. Adequate food resources, including shellfish, fish, game mammals, and wild birds, would have been available in the vicinity of these coastal sites on a year-round basis.

Archaeologists know less about the uses of plant foods by Mesolithic hunters and gatherers than they do about hunting, fowling, and fishing, because plant remains are often less well preserved than animal bones and marine shells. However, an increasing body of evidence, including the charred remains of seeds, tubers, and other plant parts, suggests that Mesolithic peoples made widespread and intensive use of a variety of plant foods (Zvelebil 1994). Many Mesolithic sites dated after 8000 B.C. have provided evidence for the use of hazelnuts, a storable, high-calorie food source that would have played an important role in the Mesolithic diet.

Mesolithic sites in the east Baltic areas have provided evidence for the intensive harvesting, processing, and storage of water chestnuts (Zvelebil 1994). Other plant foods, such as tubers, were also harvested by Mesolithic hunter-gatherers (Perry 1997). The presence of mattocks and hoes at many northern European Mesolithic sites suggests that these people regularly worked or interfered with the soil. There is a clear correspondence between the distribution of Mesolithic antler mattocks in the forest zone and the distribution of roots and tubers (Clarke 1976), and it has long been suggested these plant foods may have been part of the Mesolithic diet. Archaeologists are just now beginning to develop the techniques, such as scanning electron micrography of charred plant remains, to allow them to identify the charred remains of tubers and similar plant remains from archaeological sites (Figure 13.4) (see Perry 1997).

Mesolithic people appear to have taken an active role in modifying their environments by using fire to manipulate the natural vegetation. Mesolithic pollen diagrams from Britain (Mellars 1975, 1976) show the appearance of plants that favor an open habitat, suggesting that people used fire to clear the natural forest vegetation. Recent research on pollen

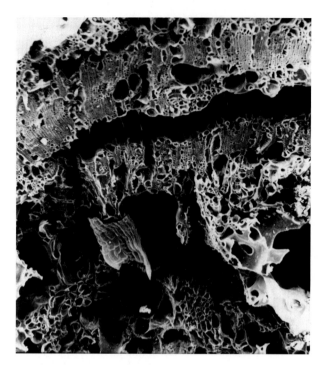

FIGURE 13.4 Scanning electron micrograph of a tuber recovered from a Mesolithic archaeological site in the Netherlands (fragment of *Beta vulgaris*, [NP3–11484: 369/30], tertiary vascular tissue).

diagrams from the Mesolithic period in both Britain (Simmons et al. 1989) and Scandinavia (Welinder 1989) has revealed episodes of vegetational change, known as disturbance phases, in which tree pollen decreases while pollen of more open vegetation, such as light-demanding herbs, increases. These disturbance episodes are often accompanied by the presence of charcoal and can reasonably be interpreted as evidence of forest clearance. This is the earliest evidence from Europe for the use of large-scale fires for land clearance.

What are the advantages of planned burning? Dense arboreal vegetation will shade out scrub vegetation such as hazel that was used both as a food source and as raw materials for basketry and mats. Planned burning can increase plant and animal food yields by between 500 and 900% (Mellars 1976: 22–26) by increasing plant resources such as hazel and by increasing the density of low-lying shrubs and berries that are attractive to deer and other wildlife. Burning would have provided additional

benefits as well. Burned soil absorbs and retains heat, causing grasses and other plants to appear two to three weeks earlier in the spring in burned-out areas. This would have been particularly advantageous for Mesolithic Europeans who lived in a strongly seasonal environment with long winters (Bogucki 1995).

MESOLITHIC SETTLEMENT PATTERNS

Mesolithic foragers were not uniformly distributed across Europe. In the Alpine regions and along parts of the Mediterranean coast, Mesolithic foragers often occupied cave sites. Along the Atlantic coast and across the **North European Plain,** the low-lying areas that were covered by the Scandinavian ice sheet at the height of the Ice Age, Mesolithic sites are often located along the shores of lakes and rivers (see Figure 13.1). Mesolithic sites are much less common in the **loess belt,** the area of central Europe that lay between the Scandinavian and the Alpine ice sheets at the height of the last glaciation. During the late Pleistocene, this area was covered by fine, windblown sediments known as loess. The loess belt was less attractive to Mesolithic foragers because the environment was relatively dry between the river systems and because the area lacked biological diversity. The coastal regions, the Alpine areas, and the North European Plain were more diverse environments, with lakes, rivers, coastal areas, and a variety of soil types. The environmental diversity was especially attractive to Mesolithic foragers because it supported a wide variety of plant and animal species.

AN EXAMPLE OF A MESOLITHIC SETTLEMENT: MOUNT SANDEL IN NORTHERN IRELAND

Most early Mesolithic settlements in northern Europe are small sites composed of between one and three round or oval huts, about 2 to 3 m (6 to 10 ft.) in diameter and marked by postholes. An example of an early Mesolithic (ca. 8000 B.C.) campsite is the site of **Mount Sandel,** located on the Bann River in Northern Ireland (Woodman 1981, 1985, 2004). Excavations at Mount Sandel revealed four hearth

CASE STUDY

Star Carr: Interpreting Mesolithic Seasonality

Ethnographic studies of modern hunter-gatherers have shown that many of these foraging peoples move their campsites on a seasonal or periodic basis to make use of different food resources that are available in different areas at different times of the year. This is a pattern that Binford (1980) has termed foraging (see Chapter 8, On the Cutting Edge). Most early Mesolithic peoples probably moved their base camps on a seasonal basis. Therefore, archaeologists who study the European Mesolithic have been interested in trying to determine the season or seasons in which these sites were occupied. The early Mesolithic site of **Star Carr** in northern England is a classic case study of the methods archaeologists have used to determine the season a site was occupied.

Star Carr (Clark 1954, 1972; Mellars 2004) is perhaps the best known of all the Mesolithic sites in Europe. The site, first excavated between 1949 and 1953 by the late Professor Graham Clark of Cambridge University, is located on a former lakeshore in the Vale of Pickering between the North York Moors and the Yorkshire Wolds. Additional excavations were conducted at the Star Carr site between 1985 and 1997 (Mellars and Dark 1998). Star Carr was occupied during the early Mesolithic and has been dated on the basis of radiocarbon to approximately 8700–8400 B.C. The site was of particular interest because the deposits were waterlogged, which allowed for the preservation of organic materials such as bone and wood.

Analysis of the animal bones recovered from the Star Carr site indicated that the Mesolithic hunters killed a range of large game animals, including red deer, wild cattle, moose, roe deer, and wild pigs. Red deer provided about 60% of the meat supply. In the initial analysis of the Star Carr site (Clark 1954, 1972), the season of occupation was determined primarily on the basis of the deer antlers present. Red deer, roe deer, and moose shed and regrow their antlers each year. Red deer, in particular, shed their antlers in April. Since the vast majority of the deer antlers recovered from the Star Carr site were still attached to their skulls, Clark and his colleagues argued that the site was occupied during the winter months. The few shed red deer antlers that were recovered indicated that the site may have been occupied until April. Moose shed their antlers in January, and since almost half the moose antlers recovered were unshed, the excavators argued that the site must have been initially occupied before January.

However, reanalyses of the mammal bones from Star Carr (Legge and Rowley-Conwy 1989) have cast doubt on Clark's interpretation. Two British archaeologists, Anthony Legge and Peter Rowley-Conwy, have argued that the deer antlers may not be a good indicator of seasonality because antler was an important raw material for toolmaking and was therefore kept for long periods. At Star Carr, antlers were used as raw material for the production of small, barbed bone points (Figure 13.C). Instead of examining antlers, Legge and Rowley-Conwy examined animal teeth, because teeth can be good indicators of age in juvenile animals. The teeth came from many jaws of young deer that must have been killed between April and August. A single moose mandible came from an animal killed in September or October. In addition, the animal bones included the remains of a very young moose that must have died shortly after its birth in May, June, or July. Legge and Rowley-Conwy concluded that Star Carr must have been occupied during the summer months rather than

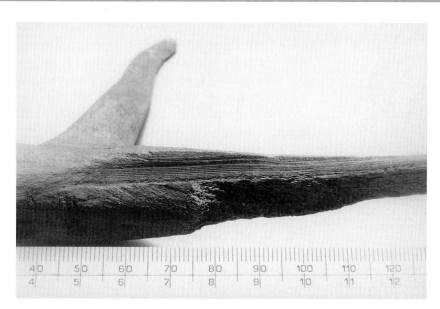

FIGURE 13.C   Early Mesolithic fragment of red deer antler from the site of No Name Hill, Vale of Pickering, near Scarborough, England. Each line results from one cutting action with a flint burin. This item has been directly dated to approximately 8700 to 9100 B.C. Similar fragments of worked antler were recovered from the initial excavations at Star Carr.

in winter. Nevertheless, their work confirms that Star Carr was occupied on a seasonal basis by a small, mobile hunter-gatherer population.

The new excavations conducted at Star Carr between 1985 and 1997 provided additional information on the seasonal use of this Mesolithic site that supplements Legge and Rowley-Conwy's analysis (Mellars 1998: 216). The charred reed remains recovered from the new excavations have tightly rolled leaf stems which indicate that these plants were burned in the early part of the growing season, most likely March or April. Carbonized fragments of aspen catkins are likely to have been burned shortly after they were shed, probably between April and June. New analyses of the birch bark resin from the original excavations show high sugar levels, suggesting that the bark was collected in late April or early May. Finally, radiographs of the roe deer lower jaws indicate that these animals were between 10 and 11 months old when they died. Since roe deer are generally born in May, it is most likely that these deer were killed in March or April. When these data are combined with Legge and Rowley-Conwy's evidence, it seems most likely that the Star Carr site was occupied by hunter-gatherers from late March or early April until June or early July.

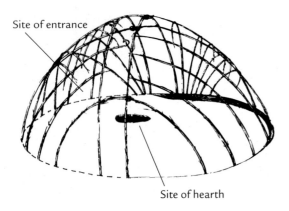

Site of entrance

Site of hearth

FIGURE 13.5   Reconstruction of a small, circular hut from the early Mesolithic site of Mount Sandel in Northern Ireland.

areas within a small hollow. Each hearth was associated with a circle of postholes (Woodman 1981: 120–121), which marked the outlines of huts that were about 5 to 6 m (15 to 20 ft.) across. The postholes were set at an angle, suggesting that the huts were dome-shaped (Figure 13.5). The postholes, which were about 20 cm (8 in.) deep, may have held sturdy saplings, which could have been bent inward and lashed together at the top (Woodman 1981: 121). Lighter branches could then have been woven into the framework, and the hut may have been covered with a lighter material, such as bark or hides.

The plant and animal remains from Mount Sandel reveal a diversified economy based on fishing, hunting, and plant collecting (Woodman 1981). Salmon run up the Bann River in summer and would have been available in June, July, and August. Eels, which were also procured by the Mount Sandel fishers, run down the Bann in the fall. Animal bones indicate that pigs were hunted in the late winter. Hazelnuts, which ripen in the fall, could have been stored for winter consumption. Thus, the plant and animal remains from Mount Sandel suggest that the site may have been occupied for a substantial portion of the year (Woodman 2004: 153). In addition, the presence of the bones of sea bass indicates that the inhabitants of Mount Sandel traveled several miles to the coast to obtain marine fish.

The subsistence and settlement evidence from Mount Sandel indicates that these early Mesolithic hunter-fisher-gatherers were collectors (Binford 1980). The site of Mount Sandel overlooks the rapids of the Bann River, where Mesolithic peoples would have fished for salmon and eels. Other critical resources, including sea bass and flint for toolmaking, were located some distance from the site and may have been obtained by a specially organized task group.

POPULATION GROWTH AND ECONOMIC TRANSFORMATIONS IN THE LATER MESOLITHIC

Both Mount Sandel and Star Carr are early Mesolithic sites that were occupied by small bands of early postglacial foragers. The Star Carr site was clearly occupied on a seasonal basis, whereas Mount Sandel may have been occupied for a more extended portion of the year. Both sites are quite small and were probably occupied by a small number of families. Early Mesolithic sites, those dating before 7000 B.C., are generally small. Population density was probably quite low, and the conditions of life were not very different from those of the late Paleolithic when hunter-gatherers resettled northern Europe after the glaciers retreated.

A wide range of archaeological data suggest that substantial social and economic changes took place in Europe within the Mesolithic period. Many of those changes may have been related, either directly or indirectly, to population growth. While population densities may have been low during the early Mesolithic, the reliability of Mesolithic hunting, the presence of a larger hoofed-mammal biomass, and the increasing availability of plant foods almost guaranteed a population increase during Mesolithic times (Rowley-Conwy 1986: 24). The shift to larger settlements in the western part of the North European Plain at about 6000 B.C. probably resulted from that population increase (Newell 1973).

Mesolithic social groups occupied territories in which they hunted and gathered throughout the year. Subtle stylistic variations in stone tool manufacture have been used to define the individual territories of Mesolithic social groups in northern Europe. These stone tool studies suggest that early Mesolithic groups occupied territories of about 200 km (124 mi.) in diameter. During the later Mesolithic (ca. 7000–4000 B.C.), group territories were smaller, about 100 km (62 mi.) in diameter (Price 1981). These shrinking territories probably reflect the increasingly intensive and localized use of the landscape by larger numbers of Mesolithic foragers.

Late Mesolithic sites in southern Scandinavia and northern Germany also provide evidence for increasing settlement permanence. Many of the Danish kitchen midden sites, associated with the late Mesolithic culture known as the **Ertebølle** culture, appear to have been occupied throughout the year. Ertebølle sites were located along the coast, allowing foragers to make use of rich beds of marine shellfish. Other resources, such as mammals, wild birds, and fish, were probably obtained by organized collecting parties. Some western Baltic Ertebølle sites were clearly used for special purposes such as sealing and swan hunting (Whittle 1996: 196). The intensive use of shellfish, combined with hunting, fishing, and fowling, allowed these late Mesolithic foragers to occupy coastal sites on a year-round basis.

A LATE MESOLITHIC SITE: TYBRIND VIG IN DENMARK

Tybrind Vig is a Danish Mesolithic settlement located on the island of Fyn that was occupied between 5500 and 4000 B.C. (Andersen 1987). The site is unique because it is located underwater. It was initially discovered by amateur divers and had to be excavated by divers using tanks. As a result of rising sea levels in the late glacial and early postglacial periods, many Mesolithic sites in southern and southwestern Denmark are now submerged; the Tybrind area has sunk 2 to 3 m (6 to 10 ft.) since late Mesolithic times. The waterlogged conditions at Tybrind are ideal for the preservation of organic materials such as wood, and excavations there have expanded our knowledge of late Mesolithic technology and material culture.

In Mesolithic times, the Tybrind area formed a protected cove surrounded by reeds. Pollen analysis reveals that the surrounding area was covered by oak forest, with some lime, elder, and pine trees (Andersen 1987: 260). The main habitation area at Tybrind eroded away when the site was inundated, but excavations revealed the northwestern portion of the settlement, the beach, and the shallow area off the coast. Rows of pointed hazel stakes, probably the remains of fish traps, were found in this shallow area. In addition, the discovery of several leister prongs that were probably lost during fishing and of two dugout boats also points to the maritime orientation of the settlement. A burial of a young woman with an infant placed across her chest was also found; this burial is probably part of a larger Mesolithic cemetery. Chemical analyses of the young woman's bones indicate that her diet was composed primarily of marine foods such as fish, shellfish, and sea mammals. A large number of fish bones, primarily small cod, flatfish, and dogfish, were also recovered from the site, providing additional evidence for the important role of marine foods in the diet.

In addition to fish bones, the shells of oysters, clams, mussels, and periwinkles were also recovered. Red deer, wild pigs, and roe deer were commonly hunted, and seals and whales were hunted both at sea and along the coast. The remains of hazelnuts and acorns show that plant foods also played a role in the diet. Specialized and intensive fishing is reflected in the many bones of fish, including small cod, eel, and spurdog, and in the wealth of artifacts associated with fishing—nets, hooks, leisters, fish traps, and fish weirs (Andersen 1987: 266). Intensive fishing was supplemented by the more extensive and opportunistic use of a wide range of plant and animal resources. At Tybrind, and at many other late Mesolithic sites in northern Europe, the combination of specialization and diversification could have ensured an adequate and reliable food supply (Zvelebil 1986: 108).

The striking feature of the excavations at Tybrind Vig was the recovery of a wide range of artifacts made of organic materials, especially wood. These include the remains of several wooden dugout boats and a number of paddles (Figure 13.6). In addition, textiles made of twisted strings of lime and willow were recovered from Tybrind Vig. These

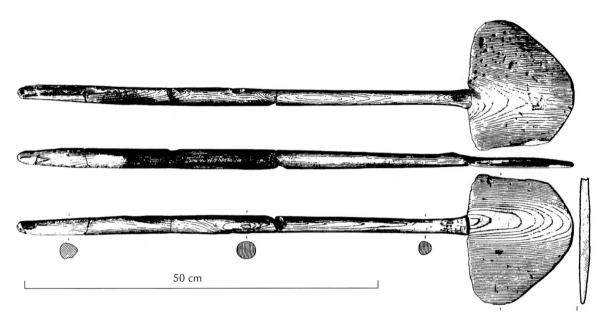

FIGURE 13.6   Wooden boat paddles recovered from the late Mesolithic site of Tybrind Vig, Fyn, Denmark.

are the oldest known textile remains from Europe (Andersen 2004: 143).

SOCIAL CHANGES IN THE LATER MESOLITHIC: THE EMERGENCE OF CULTURAL COMPLEXITY

Population growth and the increasing intensity of land use may have led to social changes in the later Mesolithic period. Cemeteries, as opposed to individual burials, become increasingly common in the later Mesolithic. Mesolithic cemeteries have provided evidence for individual differences in status and social roles (Clark and Neely 1987). At the seventh-millennium B.C. Deer Island (also known as Oleneostrouskii Megilnik) cemetery on Lake Onega in northern Russia, for example, some individuals were buried with necklaces of bear teeth, others with necklaces of moose teeth or deer incisors, and others with no grave goods at all (Zvelebil 2004). A group of male graves contained deposits of bone spear points, suggesting that those individuals may have had special responsibilities as hunters (Zvelebil 1986). In central Europe the presence of Mediterranean shells at Mesolithic sites

in Switzerland and southern Germany provides evidence for the existence of trade and exchange networks. These exchange networks may have mitigated the effects of occasional food shortages. In addition, some form of decision-making hierarchy may have emerged by the end of the Mesolithic (Bogucki 1988: 46–48). As population and settlement densities increased, more formalized leadership was necessary to coordinate both within-group activities and relationships between groups. The need for more formalized decision making may have led to some degree of social inequality.

CONCLUSION

The evidence for social differentiation, permanent or semipermanent settlements, and a combination of specialized and multipurpose technology has led some archaeologists to classify the late Mesolithic foragers of northern Europe as complex hunter-gatherers (Price 1985). Complex hunter-gatherers exhibit many features that are commonly associated with agricultural societies: permanent residences, specialized tool kits and storage facilities, the development of trade and exchange, and social elaboration (Zvelebil 1995). Thus, the Mesolithic was a period of significant social and economic change. Within a few thousand years, the highly mobile, small-scale hunting and gathering societies seen at sites like Star Carr had developed into affluent foragers with elaborate technologies, trade networks, and decision-making hierarchies. The Mesolithic period can no longer be seen as a great hiatus between the reindeer-hunting artists of the Upper Paleolithic and the farmers and herders of the Neolithic (early farming) period; the Mesolithic was an era of innovative human response to the changed and changing environmental conditions of early postglacial Europe.

KEY TERMS

Ertebølle   199

Kitchen middens   193

Leister prongs   193

Loess belt   195

Mesolithic   189

Mount Sandel   195

North European Plain   195

Palynology   190

Star Carr   196

Tybrind Vig   199

QUESTIONS FOR DISCUSSION

1. How did the Mesolithic inhabitants of Europe adapt their hunting and gathering practices to the changing world of the early postglacial period?

2. How does Mesolithic stone and bone technology differ from the technology of the European Paleolithic (Chapter 9)? Can you see any similarities?

3. Refer back to Chapter 1, Figure 1.11, the *Life* magazine illustration of daily life at Star Carr. After reading Chapter 13, do you think this illustration was an accurate reflection of early Mesolithic life? Why or why not?

FURTHER READING

Bogucki, Peter, and Pam J. Crabtree (eds)

2004   *Ancient Europe 8000 B.C.–A.D. 1000: Encyclopedia of the Barbarian World.* New York: Charles Scribner's Sons.

A comprehensive overview of European prehistory from the beginning of the Mesolithic to the end of the Viking Age. The encyclopedia includes entries on important Mesolithic sites in Europe.

14

POST-PLEISTOCENE ADAPTATIONS IN THE AMERICAS

The Development of the Archaic

The climatic changes associated with the end of the Pleistocene had profound effects on the North American environment. In addition to the disappearance of the Pleistocene megafauna, postglacial climatic changes led to increasing forestation in many parts of the eastern United States. In the west, increasing aridity led to the formation of deserts in areas such as the **Great Basin.** The Great Basin is the region of the American West that lies between the Sierra Nevada–Cascade Mountains and the Wasatch Range and includes nearly all of Nevada and parts of the surrounding states (Figure 14.1). In this chapter we will examine the ways native North Americans adapted to the changed environmental conditions in both the eastern woodlands and the Great Basin region of the American West.

As noted in Chapter 12, the term *Paleoindian* has been used to describe the late Pleistocene inhabitants of the Americas, whose tool kits often included distinctive fluted points. The term **Archaic** has been applied to the hunting and gathering cultures of the post-Pleistocene period throughout the Americas (Willey and Phillips 1958: 107). Archaeologists of past generations saw the distinction between Paleoindian and Archaic as one that reflected both differences in chronology and differences in adaptation. Paleoindians were viewed as hunters who relied extensively on large mammals, while the later Archaic period Native Americans were seen as broad-spectrum foragers who made greater use of plants, fish, and small mammals. The well-known late Pleistocene mammoth and bison kill sites from the southern Great Plains have undoubtedly contributed to the impression that hunting played a major role in Paleoindian subsistence. However, these kill sites are not typical of Paleoindian adaptations in either the Great Basin or the eastern

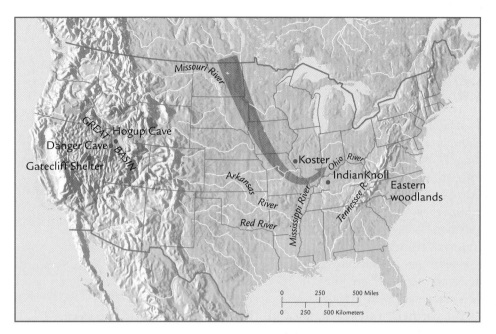

FIGURE 14.1   Locations of sites and geographical regions mentioned in this chapter. The arrow shows the well-defined river valley route to the east.

United States. In those regions, one cannot draw a simple dichotomy between late Pleistocene hunters and Holocene foragers. The changes in subsistence that took place between the end of the Pleistocene and the early Holocene are far more complex and reflect human adaptations to local changes in resource availability.

THE AMERICAN GREAT BASIN

In late Pleistocene times, the American Great Basin was a land filled with lakes. These shallow lakes and marshes and the flowing streams and springs that fed them would have been attractive habitats for human hunter-gatherers because they were rich in both plant and animal resources. In the drier areas, cool sagebrush steppe supported large herbivores, including animals now extinct in America, such as native wild horses, camels, and mammoths. The late Pleistocene lakes began to shrink in size around 13,700 years ago, but they rose briefly around 12,000 years ago. This change correlates

with the Younger Dryas event.[1] The lake levels started to drop again between 12,000 and 10,600 years ago as a result of increasing summer temperatures during the early Holocene. By 8200 years ago, however, the continuing postglacial warmth and decreasing precipitation had produced environmental conditions that are similar to those of today. Many of the lakes, marshes, and streams had disappeared, and desert scrub vegetation

---

[1] All dates used in Chapters 13 and 14 and in all subsequent chapters are corrected or recalibrated radiocarbon dates. The recalibration process is explained in the Archaeology in Practice section of this chapter.

replaced marshland and sagebrush steppe (Beck and Jones 1997).

THE PALEOINDIAN AND EARLY ARCHAIC BACKGROUND

The archaeological record of human settlement in the Great Basin during the terminal Pleistocene and early Holocene is based primarily on stone tools that have been recovered from surface sites. Few deeply stratified sites have been excavated, and plant and animal remains are rarely preserved. However, an increasing sample of radiocarbon dates from these early sites indicates that humans were present in the Great Basin by 13,200 years ago (Beck and Jones 1997: 196). The fluted and stemmed points (Figure 14.2) that have been recovered from these early sites are referred to as **Paleoarchaic,** a general term used for the human populations that lived in the Great Basin during the terminal Pleistocene and early Holocene. Sites containing these fluted and stemmed points date between 13,200 and 8200 years ago. The fluted points, which appear to be the earliest forms, are similar to Clovis points recovered from other parts of North America. All these tools could have been used as spear points or dart tips, although some of them may also have been used to cut and scrape animal carcasses (Beck and Jones 1997: 204). In short, the lithic evidence suggests that hunting played an important role in Great Basin subsistence during the terminal Pleistocene–early Holocene period.

Ground stone artifacts, including grinding stones and milling slabs, may have been used to process small seeds. While a small number of ground stone tools first appear in the Great Basin during the terminal Pleistocene period, the use of this technology increased dramatically after 8200 years ago (6250 B.C.). Therefore, the use of ground stone tools increased at a time when marshlands were drying out and the sagebrush steppe was contracting. The increased aridity would have decreased the availability of both large game and marsh resources such as waterfowl and fish. The deteriorating environmental conditions after 6250 B.C. may have led to the increased use of small seeds and other plant resources.

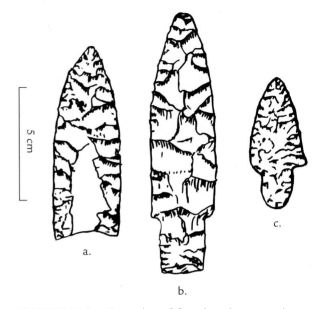

FIGURE 14.2 Examples of fluted and stemmed points from the terminal Pleistocene and early Holocene of the Great Basin: a. Fluted; b. Windust Square Stem/Cody; c. Lind Coulee. Source: After Beck and Jones 1997.

RECENT RESEARCH ON GREAT BASIN ADAPTATIONS

The variability and diversity that is seen in Great Basin subsistence practices throughout the Holocene continues to interest archaeologists working in the region today. In particular, models derived from ecological theory have been used to explain the increased use of small seeds and other plant foods in the Great Basin after 6250 B.C. (see, for example, O'Connell et al. 1982). Experimental research on the collection and processing of small seeds has shown that these plant resources yield far fewer calories per hour than does hunting large and small mammals (Simms 1987). If hunting large and small mammals produces higher food yields per hour, why and under what circumstances would hunter-gatherers bother to collect plant foods?

The problem that these hunter-gatherers faced is that the abundance of large and small game varied widely through both space and time in the Great Basin. When game animals were rare, hunter-gatherers were forced to rely on less productive plant resources. In addition, seeds may have been

ARCHAEOLOGY IN PRACTICE

The Recalibration of Radiocarbon Dating

As we saw in Chapter 9, most archaeological sites that are younger than about 40,000 years are dated using the radiocarbon method. Radiocarbon dating is based on the assumption that the proportion of radioactive carbon-14 in the atmosphere is constant through time. In fact, scientific research carried out within the past 40 years has shown that this assumption is not entirely true. The first inkling of the problem came from the study of Egyptian wooden artifacts. Many of these artifacts can be closely dated on the basis of historical records. However, when radiocarbon dates were run for Egyptian artifacts that were known to be between 4000 and 5000 years old, the carbon-14 dates were consistently about 500 years too young.

Beginning in the 1960s, a program of research using tree rings was developed to calibrate or correct radiocarbon dates. The correction was based on the use of tree rings from the bristlecone pine, a long-lived species of tree that is found in the White Mountains of southern California and Arizona. Individual tree rings are formed each spring as the tree grows. The oldest standing bristlecone pine is about 4900 years old, but the wood of older, dead trees was found lying in the forest. Unique patterns of narrow and wide tree rings allowed this older wood to be placed in the sequence (Figure 14.A, tree ring samples), and the tree ring sequence has been extended backward about 10,000 years. The deviations between radiocarbon years and calendrical years can be assessed by systematically radiocarbon dating tree rings of known age. The tree ring data have been used to create a calibration curve

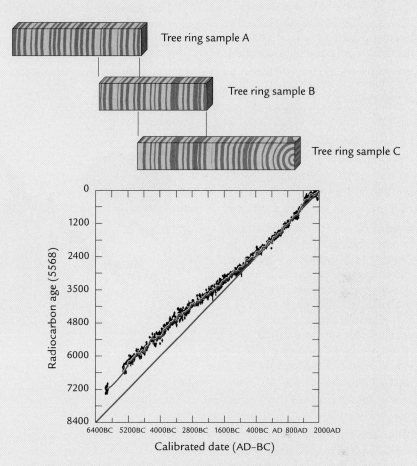

FIGURE 14.A The drawing at the top shows how fragments of ancient wood are placed in a chronological sequence. The pieces of wood are sequenced by matching signatures, distinctive patterns of wide and narrow rings that represent particular periods of time. The line graph shows the radiocarbon recalibration curve. Redrawn with permission of *Radiocarbon*.

that allows radiocarbon dates to be converted into calendar years (see Klein et al. 1982). The recalibration curve is depicted in the line graph in Figure 14.A.

Initially, it was assumed that the rate of formation of carbon-14 in the atmosphere had been relatively constant, so that the **recalibration of radiocarbon** age determinations would be a straightforward correlation.

Unfortunately, this is not precisely true. The formation of carbon-14 varies slightly from one year to the next. As a result, the recalibration curve is not smooth but instead has several kinks in it. For certain time spans, such as around the close of the Pleistocene, a given radiocarbon age may correspond to more than one possible corrected date. The probabilities of the various corrected dates can be statistically determined. A widely-used program for calibrating radiocarbon dates, CALIB, has been developed by Minze Stuiver and Paula Reimer (1993). It is available on the Internet. Figure 14.B, produced by the CALIB program, illustrates the probability of various corrections for a radiocarbon age determination of 9500 ± 100 B.P. (7550 ± 100 B.C.).

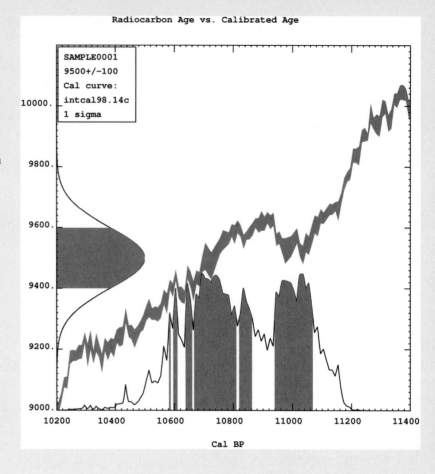

Radiocarbon Age vs. Calibrated Age

SAMPLE0001
9500+/-100
Cal curve:
intcal98.14c
1 sigma

Cal BP

FIGURE 14.B Recalibration of a radiocarbon age determination of 9500 ± 100 years B.P., showing how this determination corresponds to several possible recalibrated dates, with varying probabilities. This graphic was automatically generated by the recalibration software CALIB, developed by M. Stuiver and P. J. Reimer and available on the Internet.

collected and stored for winter use (Simms 1987: 79). What the ecological perspective reveals is that diet breadth is likely to have been variable throughout the Holocene in the Great Basin. Instead of focusing on long-term continuities in Great Basin subsistence practices, ecological models and recent archaeological research emphasize the "general level of subsistence variability" in Great Basin prehistory (Simms 1987: 90).

This variability is reflected in some recent Great Basin archaeological projects. For example, excavations at the **Gatecliff Shelter** in the Monitor Valley in Nevada revealed 10 m (33 ft.) of sediments and 16 cultural horizons. The Gatecliff rock shelter was initially occupied by human foragers about 4000 B.C. Throughout its history Gatecliff appears to have served as a short-term field camp, "a place where small groups of people stayed no more than a few days" (Thomas et al. 1983: 527). While Gatecliff functioned as a short-term field camp throughout its long history, the ways it was used changed through time. During the Middle Holocene (approximately 4000 to 3500 B.C.), the site was visited by small groups of hunters who made tools from cobbles of green chert that could be collected near the shelter. After 1600 B.C. the rock shelter was more intensively occupied; it appears to have been visited both by hunters and by gatherers who used large limestone slabs to process seeds. One of the final occupations of the site reveals a different pattern of activities. About A.D. 1350, the site was occupied briefly by a group of hunters who had killed approximately two dozen bighorn sheep nearby. At that time the Gatecliff shelter was used for the rapid field butchering of these animals so that the meat could be transported elsewhere for consumption. It is estimated that the hunters carried at least a ton of bighorn carcasses into the shelter and that they left bearing about 700 kg (1500 lb.) of meat (Thomas et al. 1983: 529).

EASTERN NORTH AMERICA: THE PALEOINDIAN BACKGROUND

Studies of Paleoindian lifeways most often focus on the Clovis and Folsom hunters of the American Great Plains (see Chapter 12). However, Clovis-type projectile points are commonly found east of the Mississippi, indicating that the eastern United States was also settled by Clovis foragers in the late Pleistocene. Mobile hunter-gatherer populations who traveled down the ice-free corridor from Alaska would have encountered the Missouri, Arkansas, Platte, and Red Rivers, all of which led to the Mississippi. From the Mississippi Valley, the Ohio, Cumberland, and Tennessee Rivers would have provided well-defined routes to the east (see Figure 14.1; Anderson 1996: 36). These river valleys would have been particularly attractive areas for early human settlement because they supported a wide variety of game animals and supplied raw materials for stone tool manufacture.

Two different environmental zones have been identified in eastern North America in late Pleistocene and early Holocene times. The peri-glacial regions in the north were dominated by a tundra vegetation, while a complex boreal forest extended across a broad region south of the tundra, covering much of the eastern and southeastern United States. The boreal forest was dominated by spruce but included such deciduous trees as black ash, oak, and elm (Meltzer and Smith 1986).

Subsistence practices are likely to have differed greatly between the two regions. Although plant and animal remains are generally poorly preserved at eastern Paleoindian sites, the available archaeological data suggest that the inhabitants of the tundra zone may have been specialized caribou hunters. Tool kits from sites in the tundra zone are dominated by projectile points, scrapers, bifacial knives, and drills, and most tools are heavily worn. In contrast, sites in the boreal forest zone appear to have been occupied by generalized foragers who used a wide range of plant and animal species. Forest zone tool kits are far less specialized and are dominated by simple flake tools. The more generalized adaptive strategy that was adopted by the inhabitants of the boreal forest zone continued into early Archaic times (Meltzer and Smith 1986: 13), while the specialized tundra zone adaptations appear to have disappeared at the end of the Pleistocene.

EARLY ARCHAIC SUBSISTENCE IN THE EASTERN WOODLANDS

Early Archaic sites in the forest zone have produced the remains of a range of small and large mammals, birds, fish, reptiles, invertebrates, and plants, including acorns, hickory nuts, and walnuts (Meltzer and Smith 1986: Table 1-3). The variety of plants and animals present at early Archaic sites suggests that these foragers were using resources of the forest, forest edge, and more open or disturbed habitats. These data suggest that the generalized use of a broad range of plant and animal resources has a great antiquity in the eastern United States.

While it has generally been assumed that the population of the northeastern United States was highly mobile and quite low in density in early Archaic times, it is important to bear in mind that the early postglacial environment of New England was considerably different from the environment of more recent times. In early Holocene times (ca. 10,000 to 5800 B.C.) former glacial lake basins may have provided wetland-dominated environments that were rich in both resource diversity and overall biomass (Nicholas 1988). These basins appear to have provided focal points for early human settlement; in the northeast, human settlements are most often found near glacial lake basins. These areas would have been characterized by lowered or fluctuating lakes, ponds, extensive wetlands, and streams and would have provided prehistoric hunter-gatherers with a diverse range of plant and animal resources. Glacial lake basins did not continue as focal points for human settlement in later prehistoric times, however. The warmer, drier conditions of the postglacial climatic optimum (6800

CASE STUDY

Great Basin Subsistence: Danger Cave and Hogup Cave

Pioneering excavations at a series of deeply stratified cave sites have provided information on human subsistence and settlement in the desert west (Aikens 1978). The arid conditions of the Holocene Great Basin have preserved organic materials such as basketry and plant remains in these caves. **Danger Cave** in western Utah (Jennings 1957) was one of the first caves to be excavated. This site revealed a deeply stratified sequence of occupations covering nearly the entire Holocene period. The cave appears to have been repeatedly occupied on a seasonal basis by small bands of mobile hunter-gatherers. Studies of **coprolites,** fossilized excrement, and other plant and animal materials indicate that the inhabitants of Danger Cave collected small seeds and other plant materials and hunted a wide range of small- and medium-sized mammals. The material culture was generally light and portable, including such items as baskets, milling stones, and small tools made of chipped stone. The inhabitants of Danger Cave have been seen as highly mobile foragers who made use of a broad range of plant and animal resources and whose lifeways changed very little from the early Holocene to historic times. The excavator of the cave, Jesse Jennings, emphasized the continuities in lifeways between the hunter-gatherers known from the archaeological record of Danger Cave and the Native American foraging populations

FIGURE 14.C   Duck decoys from excavations at Lovelock Cave in west central Nevada. The excavations at Lovelock Cave showed the importance of lacustrine resources in prehistoric subsistence in the Great Basin.

that continued to occupy the Great Basin in the twentieth century.

Similar information has been recovered from the excavation of **Hogup Cave** on the Great Salt Lake in northern Utah (Aikens 1970). Hogup Cave yielded over 4 m (13 ft.) of archaeological deposits spanning the past 9300 years. The earliest inhabitants (ca. 7350 B.C.) foraged along the edge of a lake, which became progressively

to 3700 B.C.) led to wetland shrinkage and shifts in vegetation.

Archaic hunters and gatherers may have burned some wooded areas, encouraging new plant growth, which in turn would have attracted game and maintained resource diversity (Nicholas 1988: 277). As Nicholas notes:

Controlled burning can be utilized in land clearing; in this it also provides an influx of nutrients into the soil. In hunting it can be used as part of an immediate return strategy to drive or concentrate game, or with longer-term goals of encouraging new browse that will attract deer that can later be exploited. Burning can also stimulate the growth of many different plants (e.g., berries) and improve

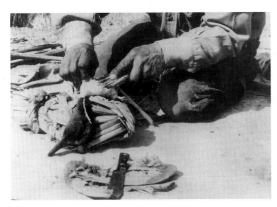

a.

b.

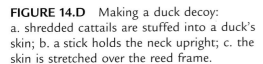

c.

FIGURE 14.D   Making a duck decoy:
a. shredded cattails are stuffed into a duck's
skin; b. a stick holds the neck upright; c. the
skin is stretched over the reed frame.

shallower through time. A nearby salt marsh
supported waterfowl and aquatic plants, which
were collected by the Hogup inhabitants. A duck
decoy recovered from Lovelock Cave (Figure
14.C) provides information on the way waterfowl
were hunted during the early Holocene. Similar
duck decoys were made by the Paiute peoples of
the Great Basin in the first half of the twentieth
century (Figure 14.D). In addition, the early inhabitants hunted bison, pronghorn, mule deer,
mountain sheep, hares, and small mammals
in the marshlands and the nearby uplands. A
rise in the level of the lake, which drowned the
spring-fed marsh sometime between 3700 and
2100 years ago, led to a decrease in the intensity
of occupation of the site. The history of the site
illustrates the important role that marshland
resources could play in Great Basin subsistence
practices in areas where the marshlands survived
after 8200 years ago.

the yield of the harvest. Finally, it creates and
maintains ecologically heterogeneous mosaics.
(1999: 35)

The use of fire in the northeastern United States
during the Archaic is clearly similar to its use in the
European Mesolithic.

MIDDLE HOLOCENE CHANGES IN SUBSISTENCE AND SETTLEMENT

As noted, a broad range of evidence suggests that
the Paleoindian and early Archaic inhabitants of the
forest zone in eastern North America had a generalized subsistence base. Detailed regional studies (Carr 1998) indicate continuities in technology,

CASE STUDY

Excavations at the Koster Site and the Emergence of Complex Hunter-Gatherers

Few sites have had a greater impact on archaeological understanding of Archaic settlement patterns and subsistence practices than the **Koster** site in southwestern Illinois. Excavations began at the Koster site in 1969 when the site became the Northwestern University archaeological field school. The site was chosen because it possessed a large and well-preserved Late Woodland (A.D. 550–1200) component and because it also might include an undisturbed record of the then poorly known Archaic. During the first season of excavation, it became clear that the site possessed a deeply stratified archaeological sequence extending as far back as the early Archaic period (ca. 8200 to 5800 B.C.). As a result of the discovery of the well-preserved Archaic levels at the site, the study of Archaic settlement patterns and subsistence practices became the focus of the excavations. By 1977 the research, which centered on the study of increasingly complex hunter-gatherer subsistence and settlement systems, had taken on a distinctly ecological orientation.

The Koster site (Figure 14.E) is made up of at least 23 stratigraphically distinct cultural layers situated on an alluvial fan (Hajic 1990: 68). This deeply stratified site provided evidence for increasing settlement permanence and for increasingly intensive use of a wide range of plant and animal resources. When the Koster site was initially occupied, around 7500 B.C., it served as a temporary campsite for seasonally mobile hunters and gatherers. Hearths, pits, and dense middens are present, but there is no evidence for substantial houses (Brown 1985: 215). These early Koster foragers hunted and collected a wide range of plant and animal foods, including deer, small mammals, fish, freshwater mussels, hickory nuts, and pecans. The early Archaic levels at the Koster site have also produced burials of domestic dogs. Dogs are the only animals that were domesticated in both the Old World and the Americas; domestic dogs are also commonly found in Mesolithic sites in Europe, including Star Carr and Mount Sandel (see Chapter 13).

The nature of the Koster settlement changed dramatically between 6400 and 5800 B.C. Substantial buildings appear for the first time, covering an area of 0.7 ha. (1.7 ac.). The buildings were approximately 7 by 4 m (23 by 13 ft.) in area, and their long walls were built of wooden posts set in trenches. The gaps between the posts were filled with clay and branches. The houses appear to have been occupied for a sizable portion of the year, at least from early spring through the fall. Environmental changes that took place between 6900 and 4800 B.C. in the Illinois River Valley would have increased the proportions of backswamps, which are home to waterfowl, fish, shellfish, wild seeds, and marshland roots and tubers. The changes would have greatly increased the natural productivity of this habitat (Brown 1985). Human foragers responded by shifting away from the wide-ranging and opportunistic foraging seen in the early Archaic. Instead, they

stone tool use, and settlement patterns between the Paleoindian and early Archaic periods in the eastern United States. While the data are limited, it is reasonable to see the early inhabitants of eastern North America as seasonally mobile foragers. The range of species exploited by eastern hunter-gatherers appears to have increased during Archaic times. In particular, the use of shallow water molluscs appears to have increased dramatically in many parts of the southeast and midwest (Smith 1986: 22). Climatic changes that took place during the Middle Holocene (5800 to 3800 B.C.) led to the expansion of shallow-water and shoal-area aquatic habitats along some midlatitude river systems.

FIGURE 14.E   Excavations at the Koster site showing the deeply stratified nature of the excavation.

concentrated on a smaller number of highly productive resources, including freshwater mussels, deer, and hickory nuts (Winters 1974).

Further changes in settlement and subsistence are seen during the late Archaic period at the Koster site. Between 4700 and 3500 B.C., the site appears to have been occupied on a year-round basis. The late Archaic houses were built of large wooden posts and had sunken earthen floors. Each dwelling had a floor area of approximately 12 to 15 sq. m (130 to 160 sq. ft.). The village, which covered an area of 2 ha. (5 ac.), may have housed up to 100 to 150 people (Fagan 2000: 392). This relatively large population needed substantial and reliable sources of food. The late Archaic inhabitants of the Koster site intensively fished the backwater lakes and swamps surrounding the site for shallow-water species, such as catfish, buffalo fish, and bass. They also hunted waterfowl during the spring and fall migrations, collected nuts, hunted deer and small game, and collected and processed many small seeds, including marsh elder. The site was abandoned about 3500 B.C. and was not reoccupied until about 800 years later.

These areas would have provided an easily accessible variety of aquatic plant and animal resources (Smith 1992: 102), especially freshwater molluscs. The increased use of shellfish in the diet has been described as "an opportunistic response to a localized, seasonally abundant, dependable, and easily collected resource" (Smith 1986: 24).

The increasingly intensive use of these riverine resources was accompanied by a shift in human settlement patterns. Floodplain settlements were more intensively occupied over a wide area from southern Illinois to northern Mississippi. Specific floodplain locations were occupied throughout the late spring to early winter growing season and were reoccupied on an annual basis. Deep shell mounds and midden mounds point to the repeated reoccupation of a limited range of locations after about 5400 B.C. The shell mounds were formed from large quantities of freshwater mollusc shells, while the midden mounds included a broader range of domestic rubbish, such as animal bones and plant remains. The increasing use of freshwater molluscs led to increasing sedentism and decreasing residential mobility. Following Binford's (1980) terminology, the later Archaic inhabitants of the Midwest and Southeast should be seen as collectors who occupied base camps for a substantial portion of the year. Similar changes in settlement patterns have been observed in the northeastern states during the later Archaic period (Raber et al. 1998: 127). The Archaic subsistence and settlement system of the Eastern Woodlands provides some striking parallels with the late Mesolithic settlement patterns and subsistence practices in northern Europe.

LATER ARCHAIC SETTLEMENT AND SUBSISTENCE IN THE EASTERN WOODLANDS

The Koster case study illustrates a number of important changes in settlement patterns and subsistence practices that are also seen at many other Archaic period sites in the eastern woodlands. There is evidence for population growth, increasing settlement permanence, and the exploitation of new plant and animal resources, such as fish, shellfish, and small seeds. Plant and aquatic foods clearly played more important roles in Archaic subsistence than they did during the Paleoindian period, and their increasing importance can be seen in Archaic tool kits; these include new tools, such as grinding stones and plant processing equipment (Custer 1985: 65).

In eastern North America, the seeds of such plants as goosefoot, sumpweed, and sunflower (Figure 14.3a, b, and c) were collected by humans and thereby introduced to the disturbed midden areas surrounding human settlements. The plants would have quickly established themselves in the disturbed habitats. Once humans recognized the value of those stands, they may have begun to eradicate competing weeds and even to plant the

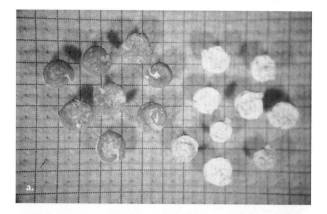

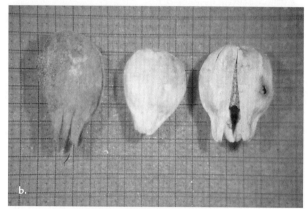

FIGURE 14.3 Early North American cultigens: a. goosefoot; b. sumpweed; and c. sunflower.

seeds of those species. The beginnings of deliberate planting, if continued over the long term, would have led to the establishment of domesticated species of goosefoot, sumpweed, and sunflowers that were different in appearance from their wild relatives. In eastern North America, domesticated varieties of these plants have been recovered from a number of archaeological sites dating to between 2500 and 1200 B.C. (Smith 1992), indicating that they had been domesticated by late Archaic times.

In addition to these native domesticates, a number of fragments of squashes and gourds have also been recovered from sites in eastern North America (Hart and Sidell 1996; Peterson and Sidell 1997). It is not clear whether these squashes and gourds were locally domesticated or whether they were introduced to eastern North America from Mesoamerica, where they were domesticated at a very early date (see Chapter 17).

In addition to incipient domestication, later Archaic foragers may have intensified the collection of highly productive animals and plants. The late American prehistorian Howard Winters (1974) has argued that later Archaic sites such as **Indian Knoll** in southwestern Kentucky had a narrow-spectrum, or harvesting, economy that focused on a small number of highly productive resources. At Indian Knoll those resources included deer, freshwater mussels, and nuts such as acorns and hickory. In Winters's view the Indian Knoll economy was characterized by the "intensive exploitation of a small number of plant and animal species" (Winters 1974: X).

These well-documented changes in subsistence during the Archaic period were accompanied by changes in social organization. Beginning between 5800 and 4800 B.C., there is evidence for long-distance trade in exotic items, such as marine seashells, galena, copper, and exotic flints. These prized materials may have formed part of a system of intergroup cooperation and exchange that included reciprocal social obligations (Brown 1985: 223). Cemeteries also appeared for the first time in eastern North America during the middle Archaic period. The presence of formal cemeteries and fixed burial places may reflect the increased identification of particular families or kin groups with particular places in the landscape. They may be a visible reflection of a social group's claim to the use of a particular territory. In addition, late Archaic graves in the midwest and southeast often include exotic and utilitarian grave goods, including copper, shells, beads, projectile points, and axe heads. For example, at the Indian Knoll site in southwestern Kentucky (Webb 1974), about 4% of the roughly 1000 graves excavated during the Great Depression contained exotic objects, such as copper from the Great Lakes and marine shells. These elaborate burials may reflect emerging differences in wealth and social status. In addition, the challenge of organizing the more intensive and highly scheduled subsistence systems needed to support higher population densities may have led to the emergence of some degree of hierarchy in decision making (Bogucki 1988; Green and Sassaman 1983). Lake sites such as Indian Knoll were part of complex socioeconomic systems that also included many smaller sites that were used for specialized purposes such as nut processing or stone tool production (see, for example, Levine 2004a).

Other important technological innovations also appear during the late Archaic period. As noted previously, copper from the Great Lakes appears as an exotic material in some Indian Knoll burials. Between 3000 and 1000 B.C., Native Americans in many parts of the Eastern Woodlands began to work native copper (Martin 1999), a very pure form of copper that does not require smelting to remove impurities (see Archaeology in Practice, Chapter 23). Native American metalsmiths in the Northeast obtained copper from both local and Great Lakes sources (Levine 1999). The copper was worked by hammering, a technique derived from stoneworking (Martin 1999: 216). Native Americans in the Eastern Woodlands developed one of the oldest metalworking traditions in the world (Levine 2004b).

CONCLUSION

Human populations adapted to the changing environments of postglacial North America in very different ways. In the Great Basin, variability in subsistence practices reflected the environmental variability that existed in that region, both spatially and temporally. Resources such as large and small game were not always available, and foragers often had to make use of small seeds and other plant resources that required significant processing time. Seeds may also have provided storable resources for the winter months. This variability continued until the twentieth century. As Simms (1987: 89) noted, "Subsistence strategies in the Great Basin, characterized by a generalized technology used by mobile hunter-gatherers, could be changing by the week, month, season, or year."

In the eastern United States, on the other hand, mid-Holocene climatic changes led to the creation of rich floodplain environments that included large quantities of freshwater molluscs. The abundance and dependability of those resources led to a decreasing diet breadth in the mid-Archaic as foragers chose to focus on highly productive resources, such as molluscs, deer, nuts, and seeds. The changes led to increasing sedentism and increasing cultural complexity.

KEY TERMS

Archaic 202	Indian Knoll 213
Coprolites 208	Koster 210
Danger Cave 208	Paleoarchaic 204
Gatecliff Shelter 206	Recalibration of
Great Basin 202	radiocarbon 205
Hogup Cave 208	

QUESTIONS FOR DISCUSSION

1. In what ways is the Archaic of eastern North America similar to the Mesolithic of temperate Europe? Can you identify any differences between the North American Archaic and the European Mesolithic?

2. Compare and contrast Archaic subsistence practices in the Eastern Woodlands with those in the Great Basin.

3. How did Archaic hunter-gatherers use fire to manipulate their environment?

FURTHER READING

Beck, Charlotte, and George T. Jones
  1997 The Terminal Pleistocene/Early Holocene Archaeology of the Great Basin. *Journal of World Prehistory* 11 (2): 161–236.
  A recent and comprehensive overview of early Great Basin prehistory with an extensive bibliography. Highly recommended for the advanced student.

Fagan, Brian M.
  2000 *Ancient North America: The Archaeology of a Continent,* 3rd ed. New York: Thames and Hudson.

Sassaman, Kenneth E., and David G. Anderson (eds)
  1996 *Archaeology of the Mid-Holocene Southeast.* Gainesville, FL: University of Florida Press.

15

THE ORIGINS OF AGRICULTURE

A Crucial Step

For more than 4 million years, more than 99% of human existence, our ancestors subsisted by hunting, scavenging, fishing, and gathering wild plants. These ancient adaptations were eminently successful. As we have seen in the past few chapters, hunter-gatherer populations were able to expand beyond their African homeland, spread across Europe and Asia, colonize Australia, and, ultimately, people both continents of the New World. In biological terms these foragers were most successful indeed; they created niches for themselves from the tropics to the Arctic.

There were real advantages to a foraging economy. Ethnographic data suggest that if wild game and plant resources were plentiful, the time and effort needed to obtain a livelihood would not have been excessive. Among the present-day !Kung San hunter-gatherers of the Kalihari Desert in southern Africa, for instance, about 25 hours of effort a week per adult are needed to obtain an adequate diet for the community (Lee 1968). Presumably, in the rich environments of the Pleistocene, plenty of extra time would have been available for leisure and social activities. The food supply was very likely adequate to ensure a substantial measure of security. The population in a region, however, could not exceed its natural **carrying capacity,** the maximum population size that an environment can support using a particular technology. Although foragers sometimes practiced activities such as burning to encourage wild plant growth and to provide browse for game, they did not directly control the populations of wild resources on which they depended. So long as those resources met their needs, there was no reason to do so.

CHANGING RELATIONSHIPS BETWEEN HUMANS AND THE ENVIRONMENT: CLIMATIC CHANGE AND POPULATION GROWTH

What, then, was the reason for the broad economic changes that occurred at the close of the Paleolithic? Fundamentally, the stimulus for technological and social change must have derived from an alteration of the relationship of those foraging societies to their natural resource base. The root cause for this new relationship may have been a change in the environment; alternatively, human populations may have gradually grown to exceed the carrying capacity of the environment.

Climatic change has frequently been cited as a prime mover behind cultural change. Clearly, humans must live within the framework of their natural environment. As other animals replace traditional game species, hunting societies must also change if they are to continue to exist. Changing plant communities may make traditional diets difficult but may also provide new opportunities for foragers.

Climatic change is not necessary, however, for an alteration in the relationship between a human society and the natural environment to occur. Population growth, for instance, either through natural increase or through the movement of new groups into an area, can eventually cause populations to approach or exceed the carrying capacity of the region (Binford 1968). People must respond to these difficult conditions by limiting population growth; by changing their technology to utilize their traditional resource base more intensively; by finding new, previously unutilized resources in the region; by seeking new territory; or, finally, by modifying their environment to increase its carrying capacity.

Chapters 13 and 14 discussed how European Mesolithic peoples and the Archaic peoples of eastern North America responded to the changing flora and fauna at the close of the Pleistocene. On both sides of the Atlantic, the postglacial era brought widespread forestation and, with the forest, a wealth of new game animals. Hunting and gathering populations modified their subsistence strategies and diversified their diets to take advantage of the changes in plant and animal species. At the same time, the richness and diversity of the forest resources permitted them to remain foragers.

Some peoples of the Near East, however, followed a different trajectory. Whatever the basic cause, the path followed by those peoples would ultimately lead them to replace wild plant gathering with cereal agriculture, and hunting with animal husbandry. A similar process occurred in the New World at a somewhat later date. The primacy of the Near East in the development of wheat and barley agriculture has long been accepted; why it developed has been a topic of intense debate among archaeologists for more than 60 years. The theoretical debate over the origins of agriculture will be discussed in this chapter; the following chapter will provide a fuller description of the evidence for early Near Eastern agriculture. Agricultural origins in the New World will be discussed in Chapter 17, as will other early centers of plant and animal domestication.

THE DIFFERENCES BETWEEN FARMING AND FORAGING SOCIETIES

Farming societies differ from foraging societies in many ways, and the social consequences of the introduction of agriculture will be discussed subsequently. The primary difference, however, is that while foragers depended on wild resources, farmers made use of plants and animals that had been domesticated. Foraging peoples may have manipulated their environment to provide improved conditions for plants or to attract game, but they did not directly control the plant and animal populations. When the early farmers domesticated plants and animals, they took control over the reproduction of these species. In doing so, they modified plant and animal populations to make them more suitable for human exploitation. Crops were planted in locations convenient for the farmer, and animal herds were confined or their movements were restricted. Under these conditions the plants and animals began to change, as a result of the selective pressures exerted by humans. In effect, the plants and animals were on their way to becoming new **species.** (A species is defined as an interbreeding population of plants or animals.) Domestication can be considered partial speciation under human control (Crabtree 1993). Some of the changes may have been selected consciously or unconsciously because they were advantageous for humans; other changes may have been more subtle adaptations to environments that had been heavily modified by human activities. Farmers and their domesticates became dependent on each other for their existence.

Anyone who has ever worked on a farm or known a farmer realizes that farming is hard work. Farmers generally spend more hours per week earning a living than do hunters and gatherers. In times of stress, such as severe drought or extreme flooding, farming may be more risky than foraging. When farmers experience a crop failure or loss of livestock, they may lose their livelihood. If a wild plant or animal is unavailable, foragers may be able to make use of other wild plant and animal resources. One major advantage that farming provides over hunting and gathering is that farming can produce a higher yield per hectare. Another advantage of farming is that it may provide more predictable access to resources (Marshall and Hildebrand 2002). In examining the theories that have been put forward to explain the origins of agriculture, we must ask why past human populations needed to increase food yields or to produce more predictable food yields. Changes in either the environment or human population numbers or both could force humans to take steps to increase yields.

THEORIES OF AGRICULTURAL ORIGINS: THE PIONEERING WORK OF V. GORDON CHILDE

The eminent prehistorian Vere Gordon Childe (1892–1957) was among the first to emphasize the pivotal role of the origin of agriculture in human history. Childe's primary interest had always been the rise of complex, urban societies in the Old World. He recognized, however, that ancient urban societies, such as Egypt and Sumer, depended on an economy based on agriculture and stock rearing. Childe knew that to understand the development of ancient civilizations, he must first approach the problem of their economic underpinning. Childe (1936) termed the initial appearance of farming and stock raising the Neolithic revolution. Childe saw a clear analogy between the prehistoric Neolithic revolution and the nineteenth-century industrial revolution. In both instances, changes in technology led to alterations in many other aspects of people's lives.

FIGURE 15.1   The primary Near Eastern domesticates: a. emmer wheat, *Triticum dicoccum* (wild form *T. dicoccoides*); b. einkorn wheat, *Triticum monococcum* (wild form *T. boeoticum*); c. barley, *Hordeum vulgaris* (wild form *H. spontaneum*); d. goats, *Capra hircus* (wild form *C. aegagrus*, the Bezoar goat); and e. sheep, *Ovis aries* (wild form *O. orientalis*, the Asiatic mouflon).

In the case of the Neolithic revolution, the adoption of farming technologies led to changes in village size, settlement permanence, land ownership and use, and many other aspects of social life.

To Childe, writing on the topic in 1929, the answer to where agriculture first developed seemed quite clear. Only in the Near East were the wild ancestors of the ancient domesticates to be found. These included the wild ancestors of **emmer** and **einkorn wheat, barley,** and goats and sheep (Figure 15.1). The reasons farming appeared when

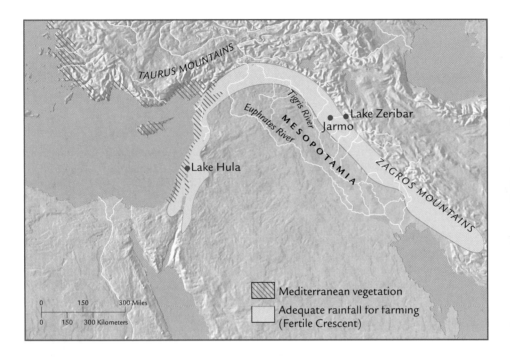

FIGURE 15.2 Map of the Near East showing the approximate location of the Mediterranean vegetation zone in the southern Levant. The shaded area marks the hilly flanks, where rainfall agriculture was possible. The locations of Jarmo and the Lake Zeribar and Lake Hula pollen cores are also shown. Source: After Braidwood 1975.

it did also seemed fairly straightforward. The prevailing view among geologists at that time was that the Pleistocene glaciations in Europe were accompanied by a southward shifting of the moisture-carrying winds, resulting in periods of markedly increased rainfall, termed **pluvials,** over the southern Mediterranean. As the Pleistocene drew to a close, the rain track moved northward to its present location, and the Near East became increasingly desiccated. Childe argued that the climatic changes at the end of the Pleistocene would have forced humans, animals, and plants together near the remaining sources of water. Childe's concept is known as the **oasis** or **propinquity theory** of domestication:

> Animals and men would be herded together round pools and wadis that were growing increasingly isolated by desert tracts, and such enforced juxtaposition might almost of itself promote that sort of symbiosis between man and beast that is expressed in the word "domestication." (Childe 1929: 42)

In this view, climatic change was the underlying cause of the Neolithic revolution.

A MODERN VIEW OF POST-PLEISTOCENE CLIMATIC CHANGES IN SOUTHWEST ASIA

Although the Near East was never covered with massive ice sheets during the height of the last glaciation, the climate of the Near East in the late Pleistocene was very different from the climate of the region today. Pollen cores, such as the core taken from former Lake Hula in northern Israel, have allowed archaeologists to trace the vegetational changes that occurred in the Near East at the end of the Ice Age. During the height of the last glaciation, about 18,000 years ago, the climate of the Near East was relatively cold and dry. Woodland was very limited, and **Mediterranean vegetation,** a mixed-oak–pistachio woodland, was probably restricted to a small number of refuge areas in northern Africa. About 14,000 to 15,000 years ago, the climate in the Near East became warmer and wetter, and the areas of Mediterranean vegetation expanded, especially in the southern Levant (modern Israel, the West Bank, Jordan, southern Lebanon, and southern Syria). Figure 15.2 shows the extent of the Mediterranean parkland in the Near East today in relationship to the sites mentioned in this chapter. The

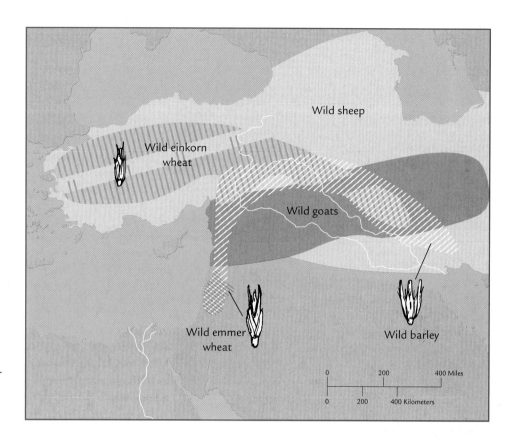

FIGURE 15.3 The distribution of wild wheats, barley, sheep, and goats in the modern Near East. Source: Plant distributions after D. Zohary 1969.

wild ancestors of wheat and barley were found within this Mediterranean forest zone, and these areas would have been attractive to human hunter-gatherers.

We now know that Childe's explanation for the origins of agriculture was too simple; the Near Eastern terminal Pleistocene desiccation was not nearly as marked as he supposed. In fact, the most recent evidence suggests that although there was a marked cold, dry period about 13,000 years ago in the Jordan Valley, corresponding to the Younger Dryas event, after 11,500 B.P. when cereal agriculture first appears in the Near East, the climate was becoming gradually moister (Baruch and Bottema 1991).

WHERE DID NEAR EASTERN AGRICULTURE ORIGINATE? ROBERT BRAIDWOOD'S HILLY FLANKS HYPOTHESIS

Childe had pointed out that the earliest farming must have appeared in an area where the natural progenitors of the ancient domesticates could all

be found together. His assumption was that the Neolithic revolution was a single, unified phenomenon during which both **plant domestication** and **animal domestication** were undertaken simultaneously. As did most scholars, Robert J. Braidwood, of the Oriental Institute in Chicago, accepted this assumption. Consequently, when he set out to discover the archaeological evidence for the first farmers, he decided to concentrate his efforts on that area of the Near East where wild wheat and barley and the wild progenitors of both sheep and goats were known (Braidwood and Howe 1960).

Modern representatives of these species were spread over broad areas of Anatolia, the Levant, and mountainous areas of Iraq and Iran (Figure 15.3). The species overlapped, however, in only a limited area: the low foothills of the Zagros-Taurus mountain arc that surrounds the Mesopotamian floodplain.

Braidwood termed this area the **hilly flanks** of the **Fertile Crescent.** The Fertile Crescent is the arc-shaped region including the Jordan Valley and the Tigris-Euphrates floodplain of Mesopotamia

ARCHAEOLOGY IN PRACTICE

How Do We Reconstruct the Near Eastern Climate at the Close of the Pleistocene?

Climate—temperature, rainfall, and seasonal variability—clearly was of great importance in shaping prehistoric societies. Childe hypothesized that climatic change was crucial in stimulating the Neolithic revolution. In previous chapters we have discussed how deep-sea cores and palynology have contributed to our understanding of ancient climates. Can we apply these methods to the Near East?

Numerous disciplines have had input into our understanding of ancient climates. Until recently, the most important evidence has come from geology. Fossil beaches, ancient beaches above the present shoreline, indicate periods of higher sea levels. Glacial **moraines**—deposits of soil and stone pushed along by a glacier and deposited at its margins—can indicate the greatest extent reached by mountain glaciers in the past. There is clear evidence of mountain glaciers in Anatolia and Iraqi Kurdistan during the late Pleistocene. Mountain glaciers imply extended periods of cold. On the other hand, **fluvial deposits**—sediments laid down

by rivers—dating to the last glacial are common within the Mediterranean lowlands. Such deposits in the lower reaches of streams can indicate periods of greater runoff, which may imply higher rainfall.

PLANTS AND ANIMALS AS ENVIRONMENTAL INDICATORS

Plant and animal remains provide another line of evidence for Near Eastern climate. The abundance of large woodland animals, most notably the fallow deer, *Dama mesopotamica*, at a number of late Pleistocene archaeological sites suggests that forests were extensive at that time. Small mammals such as rodents, however, are much more sensitive indicators of fine-scale environmental differences. In the Levant—the lands bordering the eastern Mediterranean—during the Kebaran period, there was a decrease in arboreal rodents and an increase in species favoring an open environment (Tchernov 1981). Although a few arid zone species appear, the large temperate zone mammals persist; there is no

evidence of the extreme desiccation Childe's hypothesis requires.

THE POLLEN EVIDENCE

By far the most important evidence, however, comes from a number of pollen cores scattered over the Near East, most notably from Lake Zeribar in the Zagros Mountains of western Iran (van Zeist 1969) and from the Hula Valley in northern Israel (Baruch and Bottema 1991). As might be expected, these two widely separated samples show a number of differences (Figure 15.A). In the Zeribar core there is very little arboreal (tree) pollen during the last glacial at 30,000 years ago. By about 11,500 years ago, however, arboreal pollen starts to increase gradually until about 6800 years ago, indicating an open woodland environment dominated by oaks and pistachios. By 6800 years ago, the present oak forest became established.

The Hula pollen shows a somewhat different picture. Prior to 18,000 years ago, trees must have been quite limited, but after that date, forests began gradually to expand,

where the earliest civilizations flourished (see Figure 15.2). The hilly flanks are the low grass-covered foothills of the Zagros, Taurus, and Lebanon-Amanus mountains that surround the Fertile Crescent. Today, this region receives sufficient winter rainfall—25 to 50 cm (10 to 20 in.) per year—to support agriculture without irrigation. The high mountains above would not be suitable for agriculture; the Mesopotamian floodplain, although very fertile, receives very little rainfall and required irrigation before it could support cereal

crops. The foothills, reasoned Braidwood, had to be the area of the first farming villages, and in the 1940s and 1950s he organized an expedition to search for them.

Braidwood recognized that to understand how farming originated, he must reach beyond the usual confines of an archaeological expedition. Farming was closely tied to the environment; many new data were needed so that the landscapes, climate, flora, and fauna of the region, both today and in earlier times, could be understood.

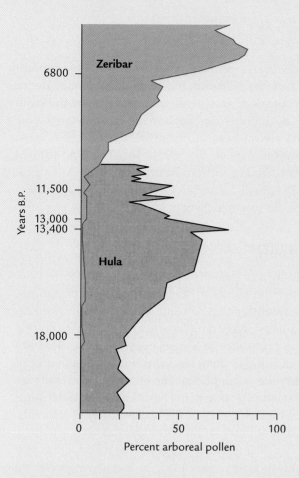

FIGURE 15.A Diagrams showing the proportions of arboreal (tree) pollen from Zeribar, Iran, and the Hula Valley, Israel. A high arboreal pollen proportion suggests widespread forests and relatively high rainfall. Note the marked contrast between the two cores at about 13,400 years ago and the dip in the Hula pollen at 13,000 years ago. Source: Data derived from van Zeist 1969 and Baruch and Bottema 1991.

suggesting a considerable increase in rainfall. At 13,400 years ago, however, and for about 1000 years, the forest contracted markedly, indicating a rapid drop in precipitation; following that period, the forest slowly began to expand once more.

These climatic changes do not approach the severe desiccation envisioned by Childe. Wild wheat and barley grew within the oak–pistachio woodlands. During relatively dry periods, however, such as that beginning at 13,000 years ago, these cereal resources would have been more limited, possibly providing an incentive for cereal collectors to experiment with agriculture.

Braidwood, therefore, included a range of natural scientists—geologists, geographers, botanists, and zoologists—in his expedition staff. These specialists gathered a wealth of new information. In addition to identifying and interpreting what was found in the archaeological sites, they gathered information on the local geology, soils, plants, and animals. Working in a frame of reference quite outside that of archaeology, they also had a great deal to offer in terms of new ideas about the possibilities of early farming.

Braidwood's investigations in Iraqi Kurdistan did produce some sites that seemed to qualify as among the earliest farming communities. Particularly noteworthy is **Jarmo,** with a radiocarbon age of about 7750 B.C. Preserved cereal grains included domesticated emmer and einkorn wheat and barley, and the animal bones indicated domesticated dogs, sheep, and goats—the full suite of Near Eastern domesticates. At the time of its discovery, Jarmo was the earliest known farming village. As will be seen in Chapter 16, we know

now that cereal agriculture began far earlier, about 11,500 years ago.

Braidwood's research failed to find evidence for the widespread desiccation that Childe's oasis model required. It had become clear that the climate of the Zagros foothills at the end of the Ice Age was not radically different from that of today. If the relatively well-watered hilly flanks were indeed the earliest agricultural hearth, models for the origin of agriculture based on environmental stress appeared to be untenable. The root cause for the Neolithic revolution had to be sought elsewhere. Numerous researchers, therefore, turned from models based on environmental change to models based on population growth.

DEMOGRAPHIC CHANGES AND AGRICULTURAL ORIGINS

Questions of population growth and its consequences interested social scientists from a variety of disciplines, including anthropology and archaeology, in the 1960s. Ethnographic studies of modern hunting and gathering peoples suggested that foraging peoples generally maintained population levels well below the carrying capacity of the land. However, specific historical circumstances, such as rising sea levels and decreasing seasonal mobility, might cause an imbalance between human population levels and the available wild plant and animal foods (see Binford 1968). Under those circumstances, human populations might be forced to adopt agriculture as a way of increasing food yields. The American archaeologist Nathan Cohen (1977) argued that this phenomenon was occurring on a worldwide basis during late Pleistocene and early Holocene times. He argued that human population levels had been rising slowly throughout the Pleistocene, and the late Pleistocene human populations had settled all the available regions of the globe. As populations continued to grow, humans faced a food crisis. People around the world began to make use of labor-intensive foods such as fish, shellfish, and wild seeds, and ultimately, people began to domesticate plants and animals as a way of providing more food for a growing population. Contrary to Cohen's hypothesis, however, the archaeological record indicates that population

growth is a primary *consequence* of the adoption of farming (Chapter 20); there is far less evidence for sustained worldwide population growth before the beginnings of agriculture. Since the demographic data are, at best, inconclusive, archaeologists have begun to explore the role of social factors, such as ritual feasting and production for exchange, as possible stimuli for initial agricultural experimentation (see, for example, Bender 1978).

CURRENT APPROACHES

During the past 30 years, while the theorists debated the merits of their alternative explanations, the interpretation of some older data has been reevaluated. New data have also continued to accrue. Many new sites have been excavated, and what has been found in them has led us to reevaluate some of our basic assumptions. The archaeological evidence now indicates that in the Near East plant domestication took place before the domestication of animals, and very likely in different areas as well.

Current evidence suggests that wheat and barley cultivation first took place in the region stretching from the Jordan River Valley northward into Syria around 9500 B.C. Only a few sites from this period have been excavated; these will be discussed in greater detail in Chapter 16. Domesticated animals do not appear until somewhat later, after 7500 B.C. We are left, therefore, with two questions where there had been one: (1) Why did the gatherers of wild cereals begin to cultivate these crops? and (2) Why did early cereal farmers take up animal husbandry?

CONCLUSION

To some degree thinking about the origin of cereal domestication has come full circle. Braidwood, like most other scholars, was misled in assuming that plant and animal domestication was a unified phenomenon. Instead, these processes seem to have occurred independently. In the Near East, plant domestication came first, and it occurred in an area where, unlike the hilly flanks in Iran and Iraq, there had been significant climatic fluctuations during the late Pleistocene and early Holocene. The cold, dry snap of 13,000 years ago (corresponding to the

Younger Dryas) could well have led to the contraction of the wild cereals on which people were dependent, leading them to experiment with agriculture in order to maintain their way of life. The returning moisture in the subsequent Neolithic then provided the conditions under which the new agriculturalists could flourish.

KEY TERMS

Animal domestication 219	Jarmo 221
Barley 217	Mediterranean vegetation 218
Carrying capacity 215	Moraines 220
Einkorn wheat 217	Oasis or propinquity theory 218
Emmer wheat 217	
Fertile Crescent 219	Plant domestication 219
Fluvial deposits 220	Pluvials 218
Hilly flanks 219	Species 216

QUESTIONS FOR DISCUSSION

1. What roles did climatic change, population growth, and social factors play in the beginnings of agriculture?

2. Why did agriculture develop in several different parts of the world in the early Holocene?

3. Was the agricultural revolution really revolutionary? Why or why not?

4. How has the early work of Childe, Braidwood, and Binford affected the ways archaeologists study the beginnings of farming?

FURTHER READING

McCorriston, Joy, and Frank Hole
    1991   The Ecology of Seasonal Stress and the Origins of Agriculture in the Near East. *American Anthropologist* 93 (1): 46–69.
    A summary of the botanical evidence for plant domestication in the Near East.

Richerson, Peter J., Robert Boyd, and Robert L. Bettinger
    2001   Was Agriculture Impossible during the Pleistocene but Mandatory during the Holocene? A Climate Change Hypothesis. *American Antiquity* 66 (3): 387–411.
    A contemporary approach to worldwide agricultural origins. For the advanced reader.

16

LAST FORAGERS AND FIRST FARMERS

The Origins of Agriculture in the Old World

As Childe recognized more than 60 years ago, the beginnings of agriculture and animal husbandry led to profound changes in many aspects of human society. Sedentary villages replaced mobile campsites, concepts of property and land ownership changed, and populations grew. Plant and animal domestication was a prerequisite for the emergence of complex urban societies (Childe 1936; Diamond 2002). In this chapter we will examine the archaeological record of the earliest villages and the beginning of farming in the ancient Near East. We will also explore the origins of plant and animal domestication in other parts of the Old World, including Africa, East Asia, and New Guinea.

LATE PLEISTOCENE HUNTER-GATHERERS IN SOUTHWEST ASIA

Before about 15,000 years ago, the population of the Near East appears to have been quite low. The southern Levant was populated by small, mobile hunter-gatherer bands who moved on a seasonal basis. Small campsites such as Ein Gev I near the Sea of Galilee (see Chapter 8) were used by hunter-gatherers as part of their annual rounds. The climatic amelioration that began between 14,000 and 15,000 years ago led to profound changes in human settlement and subsistence in the Near East. These changes are seen most clearly in the southern Levant, where sites of the **Natufian culture** (Bar-Yosef 1998; Bar-Yosef and Valla 1991; Henry 1989) first appeared about 15,000 years ago.

The first Natufian site to be excavated was **Shukbah** in northern Israel (Figure 16.1). Shukbah is located on the Wadi Natuf, a seasonal stream that gave its name to the culture. Shukbah was excavated by the British archaeologist Dorothy Garrod in the 1920s, and it was Garrod who provided the first systematic description of the Natufian culture

in the 1950s. Natufian sites have produced a wide variety of artifacts, including small lunate (half-moon-shaped) microliths; flint sickle blades, including some with a characteristic **sickle gloss** (polish left on flint from cutting grain stalks); bone sickle hafts; and stone mortars and pestles (Figure 16.2). Garrod saw the Natufians as a kind of Mesolithic with agriculture (Garrod 1957). She described the Natufians as Mesolithic because the many small microliths reminded her of the microlithic assemblages of Mesolithic Europe. However, the presence of sickle blades, sickle hafts, and grinding equipment at Natufian sites led Garrod to suggest that the Natufians may have been the first farmers in the Near East. Today, it is generally accepted that the Natufians were intensive collectors of wild grain.

Garrod's pioneering work on the Natufians ushered in several decades of intensive research on the late Pleistocene cultures of the Levant. One of the most important excavations was the site of **Mallaha/Eynan,** located in the northern Jordan Valley in Israel (Perrot 1966, 1968). Extensive excavations at the site during the 1950s and 1960s under the direction of

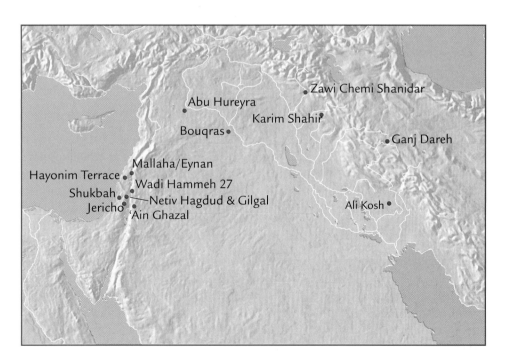

FIGURE 16.1 Map of the Near East showing the locations of the sites mentioned in this chapter.

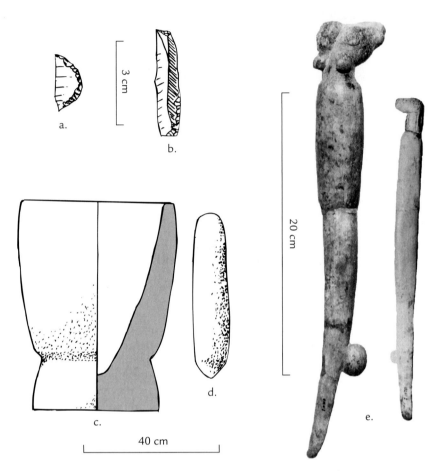

FIGURE 16.2   Typical artifacts recovered from Natufian sites include: a. small lunate microliths; b. flint sickle blades; c. and d. basalt mortars and pestles; and e. bone sickle hafts. Source: a. through d. after Perrot 1968; e. courtesy Israel Antiquities Authority.

Jean Perrot revealed a series of small, circular dwellings with stone foundations and a number of human burials (Figure 16.3). The stone foundations and burials suggested a degree of settlement permanence that is not typically associated with hunter-gatherers. The excavator of the site concluded that Mallaha was occupied by a sedentary population, but one that made its living by hunting and gathering rather than by agriculture. The Natufians, like the late Mesolithic Ertebølle peoples of northern Europe, were complex foragers whose use of storable resources such as wild cereals allowed them to occupy sites on a year-round or nearly year-round basis (Henry 1985).

In 1996 François Valla began a new program of excavation at Mallaha. The original excavations in-

dicated that Mallaha was occupied between about 14,500 and 12,000 B.P. Excavations at other Natufian sites in the Galilee and Mount Carmel areas indicated that many of these sites were abandoned during the final phase of the Natufian (ca. 12,500 to 12,000 B.P.). Mallaha is one of the few sites in the region with substantial evidence for late Natufian settlement. When Mallaha was finally abandoned, it served as a burial ground for a short period of time. Shortly after its abandonment, the earliest Neolithic settlements appear in the Jordan Valley.

Mallaha is one of a number of Natufian sites that have provided evidence for small, circular huts with stone foundations. Other sites with similar architectural features are **Hayonim Terrace** in northern Israel

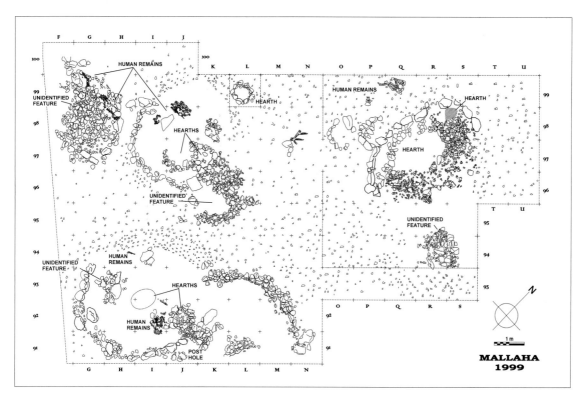

FIGURE 16.3 Plan of Mallaha/Eynan showing small, circular dwellings with stone foundations.

and **Wadi Hammeh 27** in northern Jordan. In fact, most of the Natufian sites with stone architecture are found in northern Israel and Jordan. Many of these sites are located on ecotones, the borders between different ecological zones, allowing the inhabitants to make use of the wild cereals and nuts from the Mediterranean zone as well as the resources of the drier steppe zone. Not all Natufian sites, however, include stone architecture. Smaller sites in southern and eastern Jordan and in the Jordan Valley appear to lack the architecture and human burials that are found at the larger sites such as Mallaha.

Several lines of zooarchaeological evidence suggest that the larger Natufian sites were occupied on a year-round, or nearly year-round, basis. The first is the high frequency of house mice and other species that are commensal with humans found at Natufian sites such as Mallaha (Tchernov 1984). Commensalism is a relationship between species in which one (the mice in the Natufian case) benefits, while the other (humans in this case) is

neither benefited nor harmed (Tchernov 1984: 91). Permanent human settlements would have provided food and shelter for these commensal species; therefore, high numbers of house mice may indicate that human habitations were occupied on a year-round basis. In addition, studies of seasonal increments on gazelle teeth indicate gazelles were being hunted at a number of different seasons at many, but not all, Natufian sites (Lieberman 1993). These data strongly suggest that these sites were occupied on a multiseasonal basis. The Natufian settlement pattern has been described as a radiating one. Large base camps such as Mallaha were occupied throughout most of the year, and smaller sites were occupied on a temporary basis for specific purposes, such as hunting or plant collecting. The smaller sites in the Jordan Valley that lack permanent architecture may well represent sites used for logistical purposes. Faunal evidence indicates that these sites were occupied on a seasonal basis (Lieberman 1993).

CASE STUDY

Karim Shahir and the Background to Agriculture in the Zagros

In the Zagros region of northern Iraq, excavations at the site of Karim Shahir revealed the lifeways of the preagricultural inhabitants of that region. An archaeological site need not be large, deeply stratified, or complex to be of major importance. **Karim Shahir,** a small site excavated in 1951 by Dr. Bruce Howe of the Braidwood team (Braidwood and Howe 1960: 52; Braidwood 1967: 104–108), lies on the top of a hill about a mile from Jarmo. The area of the settlement was about 60 by 70 m (200 by 230 ft.), but the actual archaeological deposit was very thin, nowhere deeper than 40 cm (16 in.) below the surface. About 500 sq. m (600 sq. yds.) of the site were excavated. There was no architecture, but the surface was covered with a sort of irregular pavement of stream pebbles. These stones were not found in their natural context and were clearly carried into the site. There were some rock-filled pits and traces of fire in the form of charcoal and many fire-cracked rocks. Karim

Shahir appeared to the excavators to represent a brief or seasonal encampment.

Mingled with the stones were some 30,000 artifacts and many animal bones. The chipped stone tool kit included, in addition to chipping debris and cores, many notched blades and flakes plus some microlithic bladelets. With the chipped tools, however, appeared representatives of a new technology: stone that had been pecked, or shaped by battering with a hammerstone to remove small fragments, and then ground and polished (Figure 16.A). The inventory included querns (grinding stones), pestles, and rubbing stones. Such pecked and ground stone artifacts are hallmarks of early farming villages in the Near East and elsewhere. In fact, the term *Neolithic* (*neo,* meaning "new," and *lithic,* meaning "stone"), or *New Stone Age,* originally referred to the appearance of these new pecked and ground stone implements. Now, however, the term is used to refer to early farming societies in the Old World (as in Childe's Neolithic revolution).

Decorative items at Karim Shahir included stone beads and pendants as well as marble bracelets and rings. These items seemed to be antecedent to similar artifacts found at Jarmo. There was no pottery, but of particular interest

The economic basis of the Natufian settlements has been subject to intensive research and debate. More than 35 years ago, the American archaeologist Kent Flannery (1969) argued that late Pleistocene hunters in the Near East began a broad-spectrum revolution in their subsistence practices and diet. This broad-spectrum revolution was seen as a shift away from intensive large mammal hunting and toward the use of a wider range of food resources, including small mammals, birds, amphibians, reptiles, fish, invertebrates, and, possibly, wild cereals. However, recent archaeological research does not support Flannery's original notion of a broad-spectrum revolution (Edwards 1989; Henry 1989).

Most Natufian faunal assemblages are dominated by the remains of gazelles (Byrd 1989), and some sites have provided evidence for communal hunting of entire gazelle herds, probably through the use of game drives or surrounds (Henry 1975; Legge and Rowley-Conwy 1987; Campana and Crabtree 1990). While many species of smaller vertebrates have been recovered from Natufian sites, gazelles clearly would have provided the bulk of meat in the diet. The faunal evidence suggests that the Natufians were specialized, intensive gazelle hunters, not broad-spectrum foragers.

It has been more difficult to determine the role of different plant foods in the Natufian diet; however,

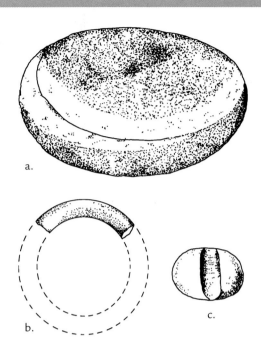

were two crudely shaped, little animal figurines of baked clay. Similar, better-made animal figurines were also found at Jarmo.

The animal species represented in the bone assemblage included many that were potential domesticates—sheep, goats, pigs, and cattle—although there is no indication that any of them actually were domesticated, nor were there any remains to indicate domesticated cereals. The combination of traits found at Karim Shahir, however, suggested to Braidwood and Howe that the site represented a critical juncture in the development of the region that would lead to the appearance of the Neolithic. "This combination of the old with at least some of the new hints, we believe, at a position for Karim Shahir on the threshold of the transition" (Braidwood and Howe 1960: 54).

FIGURE 16.A   Ground stone artifacts from Karim Shahir: a. quern; b. stone ring; c. possible shaft smoother. Source: Redrawn from Braidwood, Robert, 1967: *Prehistoric Men*, 7th ed. Glenview, IL: Scott, Foresman. Reproduced with the permission of the McGraw-Hill Companies.

the presence of flint sickle blades, sickle hafts, and mortars and pestles at many Natufian sites certainly suggests that plant foods such as wild cereals may have played an important role in the Natufian economy. In the Near East, wild cereal grains could have been harvested in the spring and stored for use throughout the year. Unfortunately, soil conditions in many parts of the southern Levant are not favorable to the preservation of plant remains. At sites such as Wadi Hammeh 27 in Jordan (Edwards 1991), where plant remains have been preserved, Natufian foragers appear to have collected many different plants from a wide range of habitats. At present there is no clear evidence to suggest that

the Natufians experimented with plant cultivation. However, that possibility cannot be ruled out on the basis of the meager botanical evidence available. In summary, the archaeological data suggest that the Natufians were intensive gazelle hunters who also made use of a wide range of other plant and animal foods, including wild cereals.

The Natufians of the southern Levant are the best known of a number of late Pleistocene hunter-gatherer populations who inhabited the Near East immediately before the beginnings of agriculture. The inhabitants of the earlier levels at **Abu Hureyra** in northern Syria seem to have had a similar way of life, relying on a combination of wild plant collection

FIGURE 16.4 Foundations of the small, oval dwelling structures at the early Neolithic site of Netiv Hagdud in the West Bank.

and seasonal hunting of gazelles (Moore 1979, 1991; Moore et al. 2000; Legge and Rowley-Conwy 1987). Recently, Gordon Hillman and Sarah Colledge of the University of London have identified cultivated rye from Abu Hureyra, dated to approximately 13,000 years ago. If these dates are correct, the Abu Hureyra rye may be the earliest cultivated cereal grain in the Near East (Pringle 1999). Hillman and his colleagues argue that the inhabitants of Abu Hureyra may have begun cultivating rye in response to a decline in the availability of wild plants during the Younger Dryas climatic event (Hillman et al. 2001). This process, however, appears to be independent of the somewhat later domestication of emmer wheat and barley in the southern Levant.

ARCHAEOLOGICAL EVIDENCE FOR EARLY PLANT DOMESTICATION IN THE NEAR EAST

Sites that have provided archaeological evidence for early agriculture extend in a band northward from the southern Jordan Valley into northern Syria (Bar-Yosef and Belfer-Cohen 1989). In general, these sites are located on alluvial fans near permanent sources of fresh water. Radiocarbon dates for these early farming villages range between 9750 and 8550 B.C. A cluster of early farming sites has been identified in the lower Jordan Valley near Jericho. Sites that have produced evidence of domesticated or cultivated plants include **Jericho** itself, **Gilgal** (Noy et al. 1980; Noy 1989), and **Netiv Hagdud** (Bar-Yosef

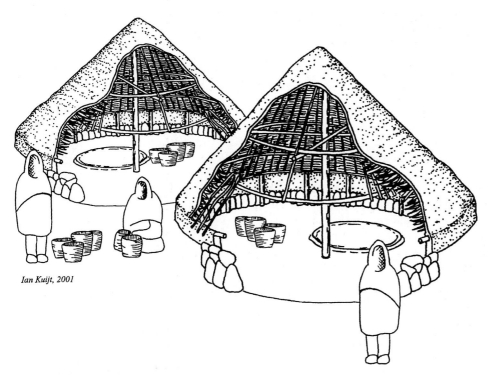

Ian Kuijt, 2001

FIGURE 16.5 Ian Kuijt's reconstruction of an early Neolithic dwelling.

et al. 1991). Small quantities of domesticated emmer wheat and barley were found at Jericho (Hopf 1969); Netiv Hagdud and Gilgal both yielded large quantities of seeds and nuts, particularly barley (Bar-Yosef and Kislev 1989; Noy 1989). While the barley grains from these sites are morphologically wild, the quantities of these grains suggest that they were cultivated (Zohary 1989). The ancient city of Jericho is a huge city mound, including extensive archaeological remains from many prehistoric and early historic periods (Kenyon 1957, 1981; Kenyon and Holland 1983). In addition to providing evidence for early cereal agriculture, the early Neolithic levels at Jericho have revealed an enigmatic stone tower. It is impossible to determine whether this tower was part of a larger structure, because only a small area of the early Neolithic settlement was excavated. The architectural remains recovered from the nearby early Neolithic site of Netiv Hagdud are probably more typical of early Neolithic settlements in the Middle East. Excavations at Netiv Hagdud revealed a series of small oval dwellings with stone foundations (Figure 16.4). A reconstruction of a typical

early Neolithic dwelling is shown in Figure 16.5. The structures recovered from Netiv Hagdud are not very different from those recovered from earlier Natufian hamlets in the Levant. The inhabitants of Netiv Hagdud cultivated barley and supplemented their diet by hunting gazelles, wild pigs, wild birds, and other wild mammals (Tchernov 1994).

The archaeological evidence clearly indicates that cereal cultivation was established at a number of sites in the West Bank, Israel, and Syria by 8500 B.C. The question of why people shifted from plant collection in the Natufian to cereal cultivation in the early Neolithic is difficult to answer. It is important to emphasize that while agriculture is more labor-intensive than hunting and gathering, it can provide a higher yield per hectare. Most explanations for the origins of agriculture in the Near East have focused on some combination of sedentism (Bar-Yosef and Belfer-Cohen 1989), population growth (Cohen 1977), climatic changes (Henry 1989), and social change (Bender 1978).

Clearly, one of the hallmarks of the Natufian culture in the Levant is the shift to sedentism. As

ARCHAEOLOGY IN PRACTICE

Archaeological Evidence for Plant Domestication

By examining the remains of plants recovered from archaeological sites, **archaeobotanists** can distinguish wild cereals from domestic grains. However, the study of early cereal husbandry depends on the recovery of very small and often fragile plant remains.

Plant remains are preserved by waterlogging and extreme aridity; they can also be preserved by charring. The technique of **flotation,** or water separation, is often used to recover organic remains from archaeological deposits. Flotation uses moving water to separate light organic materials, such as seeds and wood charcoal, from heavier archaeological soils, for example, the fill of a pit. The moving water holds the light materials in suspension so that they can be removed from the water with a fine-mesh sieve. A number of flotation machines have been designed to process large quantities of archaeological soils quickly (Figure 16.B). Where flotation machines and running water are not available, plant remains, along with

other small archaeological finds, can be recovered using wet sieving and very fine mesh screening (often 1-millimeter mesh).

How do domesticated cereals differ from wild grains, and how can archaeologists identify domesticated cereals in the archaeological record? Wild cereals such as wheat and barley have a brittle **rachis,** the axis of the plant to which the grains are attached (Figure 16.C). When the cereal grains ripen, the rachis shatters, allowing the wild plant to reseed itself. Domestic cereals, unlike their wild relatives, have a nonbrittle rachis. When the grains ripen, the axis of the plant does not shatter. These cereals are unable to reseed themselves and must be planted by humans.

How could the change from a brittle to a nonbrittle rachis take place?

FIGURE 16.B   Flotation machine in operation.

noted, the presence of substantial stone architecture, cemeteries, high frequencies of commensal species, and multiseasonal hunting at the larger Natufian sites suggests that those sites were occupied on a year-round or nearly year-round basis. This sedentism represents a fundamental change in the archaeological record of the Near East, because earlier Upper Paleolithic sites in the region provide clear evidence for seasonal mobility (Chapter 8). While the availability of a wide range of plant and animal resources in the immediate vicinity of these Natufian sites may have made sedentism possible, sedentism can have long-term consequences for human populations. Sedentary human populations

may deplete the wild plant and animal resources in the immediate vicinity of the site, leading to experiments with cultivation. Sedentism can lead to population growth if decreased mobility leads to a decrease in human birth spacing. Moreover, the availability of starchy foods made from cereals may have allowed for earlier weaning of infants, thereby reducing birth spacing and encouraging population growth. Population growth may have encouraged human attempts to extend the natural ranges of wild cereals through cultivation (Flannery 1969).

Sedentism was accompanied by a wide range of social and cultural changes during Natufian times.

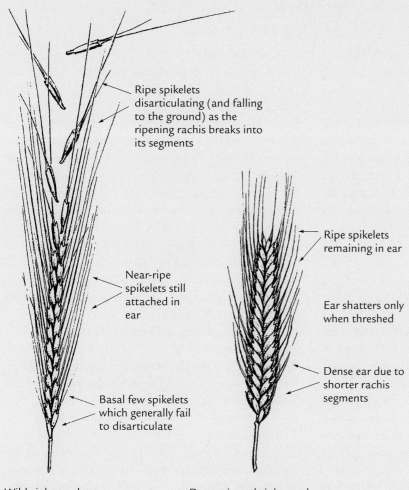

Ripe spikelets
disarticulating (and falling
to the ground) as the
ripening rachis breaks into
its segments

Near-ripe
spikelets still
attached in
ear

Basal few spikelets
which generally fail
to disarticulate

Ripe spikelets
remaining in ear

Ear shatters only
when threshed

Dense ear due to
shorter rachis
segments

Wild einkorn wheat   Domesticated einkorn wheat

FIGURE 16.C Changes in the structure of wild wheat as a result of domestication.

The genetic mutation that causes a nonbrittle rachis can occur naturally. In most circumstances, natural selection would work against this mutation, since these plants would be unable to reseed themselves. However, if humans are harvesting cereals using sickles, the cereals with the nonbrittle rachises are less likely to shatter when harvested. They would be more likely to be carried home in harvest baskets and therefore more likely to form part of the seed grain for next year's planting. Under early farming conditions, the shift from a brittle to a nonbrittle rachis could have taken place rapidly if early cultivators were using sickles to harvest the grains (see Hillman and Davies 1990). Since both sickle blades and sickle hafts have been found at many Natufian sites, the assumption that early farmers were harvesting with sickles seems a reasonable one.

Differences in the nature and quantity of grave goods that accompany Natufian burials may reflect some degree of social inequality (Wright 1978; Byrd and Monahan 1995). For example, some Natufian burials include elaborate headdresses and belts made of *Dentalium* shells. *Dentalium* shells from the Mediterranean and the Red Sea have been recovered from many inland Natufian sites, providing evidence for extensive trade networks. The need to increase production for trade and exchange may well have encouraged experiments with plant domestication (Bender 1978).

Finally, climatic change may have played a role in the transition to agriculture in the Near East. The later part of the Natufian period coincides with the Younger Dryas climatic event. Environmental evidence from both northern Europe and eastern North America indicates a return to nearly full glacial conditions about 13,000 years ago. In the Near East, the climate became both colder and drier about 13,000 years ago. These climatic changes would have reduced the range of Mediterranean vegetation, including wild cereals. Human populations may have attempted to increase the range of those cereals through cultivation. The return to warmer, wetter conditions at the beginning of the Holocene may have contributed to the success of those early farming ventures.

To answer the question of why human populations began to cultivate cereals in the Near East, we need more archaeological, and especially floral, data from late Natufian sites. The vast majority of the extensively excavated Natufian sites date to the earlier Natufian period, before the Younger Dryas climatic deterioration. While early experiments in plant cultivation may be difficult to detect in the archaeological record, excavations at late Natufian sites may allow us to determine the long-range effects of sedentism and social elaboration on human subsistence practices.

THE ARCHAEOLOGY OF ANIMAL DOMESTICATION

As a result of the pioneering work of Robert Braidwood and his colleagues, research into early animal domestication in the Near East intensified in the 1960s and 1970s. Many archaeologists claimed to have found evidence for early domesticated animals, but not all the claims have withstood the test of time. Today, archaeologists are more interested in studying the pattern and process of animal domestication than in simply identifying the earliest domestic sheep or goats.

The study of the domestication of sheep in the Near East shows how archaeological thinking about animal domestication has changed over the past 40 years. (See Crabtree 1993 for a detailed review of this evidence.) **Zawi Chemi Shanidar** (Solecki 1981), a small village site located in the Zagros region of northern Iraq, has been radiocarbon dated to 10,900 B.C. and is therefore contemporary with the late Natufian or very early Neolithic sites in the Levant. While Zawi Chemi may have been a sedentary village, there is no evidence that agriculture was practiced at the site. In 1964 the zooarchaeologist Dexter Perkins (1964) claimed that sheep bones recovered from Zawi Chemi were the remains of domesticated sheep. Although the Zawi Chemi sheep were morphologically indistinguishable from wild sheep, Perkins argued that the high numbers of juvenile sheep in the faunal assemblage meant that the bones must have come from domesticated livestock. Unfortunately, the sample of animal bones on which Perkins based his conclusions was relatively small.

Since the early 1960s, a number of sites in Syria and Anatolia have produced more convincing evidence for domesticated sheep at a considerably later date. Sheep bones from the late eighth-millennium B.C. levels at the early Neolithic village of **Bouqras** in Syria are smaller than the earlier sheep from that region. The high percentage of sheep in the Bouqras assemblage and the evidence for size decrease led the excavators to argue that the Bouqras sheep were domesticated (Akkermans et al. 1983). Unlike Zawi Chemi, Bouqras is one of a number of sites producing evidence for early domesticated sheep in the northern Levant during the late eighth and early seventh millennia B.C. By the later eighth millennium, there is a clear pattern of sheep domestication in the eastern Mediterranean (Crabtree 1993: 220–221).

The evidence for goat domestication reveals a similar patterning. Some of the earliest evidence for goat domestication comes from the early eighth-millennium levels at the site of **Ganj Dareh** in western Iran (Hesse 1984; see also Zeder and Hesse 2000). At that time there is evidence for an increased slaughter of 1- to 2-year-old male goats, animals that were most likely slaughtered for meat. There is also some evidence for changes in the form of the goat horn cores at that time. In addition, the excavators found footprints in some of the mud bricks at the site, suggesting that tamed goats were being kept near the brickyard. The nearest wild goat populations would have been located in the mountains well away from the site.

The evidence for goat domestication at Ganj Dareh does not stand in isolation. At the site of **Ali Kosh** in southwestern Iran, goats are the predominant species as early as the early eighth millennium B.C. By the eighth millennium B.C., there is clear evidence of goats with medially flatted horn cores (see Figure 16.D). Age profiles also indicate that a high proportion of young animals were slaughtered before they reached maturity.

There is also evidence to suggest that domestic goats first appeared in the southern Levant around 8000 B.C. At that time, there is a clear increase in the proportion of goats and a corresponding decrease in the numbers of gazelles in many faunal assemblages (Davis 1982). At Jericho changes in the shape of goat horn cores appear at that time (Clutton-Brock 1979),

ARCHAEOLOGY IN PRACTICE

What Is a Domestic Animal?

As noted in Chapter 15, modern archaeological research has shown that plant domestication preceded animal domestication in the Near East. While the earliest evidence for plant domestication in the Near East appears at about 9500 B.C., the earliest evidence of animal domestication, with the notable exception of the domestic dog, does not appear until more than a millennium later. Archaeologists want to determine why early agriculturalists in the Near East began to experiment with the domestication of animals. What is a domesticated animal, and how do we recognize animal domestication in the archaeological record?

Animal domestication is both a biological and a cultural process (Clutton-Brock 1981: 21). Domesticated animals reproduce under human cultural control, and the process of animal domestication leads to significant changes in an animal's biology. A number of morphological changes can be recognized in early domestic animals; the most obvious is a decrease in body size. Domestic animals are smaller than their wild counterparts (Figure 16.D). In addition, domestication can produce changes in the shape and size of horn cores,

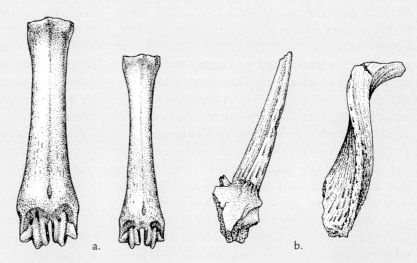

FIGURE 16.D Morphological changes that result from animal domestication include: a. size diminution; and b. changes in horn core form.

the bone that lies under the horn, in sheep and goats. Domestication will generally lead to an increase in the numbers of the newly domesticated species because domestication makes animals more accessible to humans (Hecker 1982: 219). It can often produce changes in the age and sex structure of an animal population, in part because only a small number of adult males may be needed for reproductive purposes. Finally, animal domestication may lead to the appearance

of an animal outside its natural range. Unfortunately, this criterion is often difficult to use because the late Pleistocene and early Holocene distributions of many wild species are still poorly known. Size decrease and changes in animal population structure can also result from causes other than animal domestication. Therefore, archaeologists often use several criteria when trying to identify animal domestication in the archaeological record.

and at the Neolithic site of **'Ain Ghazal** in Jordan, a majority of the goats appear to have been killed before reaching maturity. The 'Ain Ghazal goats also show evidence of arthritis, which may have resulted from unsuitable husbandry conditions (Köhler-Rollefson et al. 1988). What is not yet clear is whether goats were independently domesticated in the southern Levant or whether they were introduced to the Levant from the Zagros region.

Goats and sheep appear to have been domesticated by early farmers after the appearance of cereal cultivation in the Near East. It is possible that game depletion around early farming villages may have encouraged experiments with the domestication of sheep and goats. Domestic animals may also have served as "walking larders" (Clutton-Brock 1989) that could absorb agricultural surpluses and be slaughtered in times of food shortage. One animal, however, was domesticated considerably earlier, and that is the dog. Early domestic dogs appear at Natufian sites (Davis and Valla 1978) in the Near East; they also appear at both Mesolithic and late Upper Paleolithic sites in Europe. The reasons wolves were domesticated by hunting and gathering populations in both the Near East and Europe are unclear. They may have been used primarily as hunting and guard dogs, or they may have served as walking larders for hunting populations.

Pigs and cattle appear to have been domesticated somewhat later than goats and sheep in the Middle East. The ancestors of domestic cattle and pigs were widely distributed across Europe, Asia, and North Africa during the early Holocene, and it is possible that these animals may have been domesticated more than once. Domestic cattle and pig bones have been recovered from a number of sites in the Near East and the eastern Mediterranean dating to about 7000 B.C. DNA studies have identified three separate centers for cattle domestication: one in Eurasia, one in South Asia, and one in northeast Africa (see following). At present there is not enough evidence to determine whether cattle and pigs were domesticated only once or whether they were domesticated independently in several different parts of the Old World.

OTHER CENTERS OF PLANT AND ANIMAL DOMESTICATION IN THE OLD WORLD

Much of the archaeological research on early farming societies in the Old World has focused on the beginnings of cereal agriculture in the Near East. However, archaeological and biological researchers have identified a number of other important centers of early plant and animal domestication in the Old World.

The pattern of plant and animal domestication in Africa contrasts markedly with the Near Eastern evidence. Both zooarchaeological and DNA data indicate that cattle were domesticated independently in the eastern Sahara between 8000 and 10,000 years ago (Gauthier 1987; Bradley et al. 1998; Bradley 2001). Domestic sheep and goats were introduced to Africa from the Middle East. Plant domestication began much later, some time after 4000 B.P.

(Marshall and Hildebrand 2002). Although "studies of indigenous African agriculture have been much neglected" (Harlan 1992: 59), a wide variety of plants were domesticated throughout sub-Saharan Africa. Important indigenous African domesticates include sorghum, pearl millet, African rice (*Oryza glaberrima*), yams, and watermelon. While archaeological evidence for these early African domesticates remains limited, the distribution of these African crops and their wild ancestors does not reveal a single center of African plant domestication (Figure 16.6). Instead, "plants were domesticated throughout sub-Saharan Africa, from one side of the continent to the other" (Harlan 1992: 69).

At least two separate centers of plant domestication have been identified in East Asia. Traditionally, archaeologists thought that Asian rice (*Oryza sativa*) was domesticated in tropical or subtropical Southeast Asia (Crawford 1992: 24). However, recent archaeological research suggests that Asian rice was domesticated farther north along the banks of the Yangtze River in southern China. The earliest domestic rice grains known from this region date to about 8000 years ago. Recent research on rice phytoliths (silica bodies in plant tissues) from Diaotonghuan Cave along the Middle Yangtze River suggests that rice cultivation may have an even longer history in this part of China (Pringle 1999: 1449; Zhao 1998). However, domestic rice did not become a staple until about 7000 years ago. Today, domesticated Asian rice is a staple of diets throughout the world.

Common, or broomcorn, millet (*Panicum miliaceum*), a cereal grain that was widely used for food during prehistory, appears to have been domesticated in China. Remains of domesticated broomcorn millet have been identified from a number of Neolithic sites in the loess plateau region of North China. Loess is a fine-grained soil that was deposited by wind during the late Pleistocene. Light, fertile loess soils were attractive to early farmers in both northern Asia and central Europe (Chapter 18). Broomcorn millet requires less water than many other cereals, making it particularly suitable for the relatively dry loess plateau regions of North China. The earliest domesticated broomcorn millets date to 6300 B.C. (Underhill 1997). Thus plant domestication

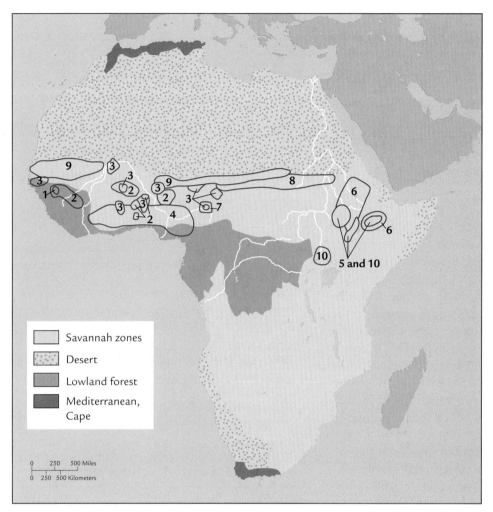

FIGURE 16.6 Areas of plant domestication in Africa. 1. Guinea millet; (after Harlan, 1971); 2. Fiono and black fonio; 3. African rice; 4. Yam (*Dioscorea cayenensis* complex); 5. Enset; 6. Tef; 7. Groundnuts (Kerstingiella and Vooandezeia); 8. Sorghum; 9. Bullrush/pearl millet; 10. Finger millet.

appears to have taken place at roughly the same time in eastern Asia and the Near East.

Highland New Guinea is another independent center of plant domestication in the Eastern Hemisphere. As early as the 1970s, Jack Golson (1977, 1989) suggested that farming had begun in highland New Guinea as early as 7000 years ago, based on his excavations at **Kuk,** which revealed early drainage ditches that appeared to be associated with plant cultivation. New excavations at Kuk, under the direction of T. P. Denham, have provided a detailed radiocarbon chronology for the beginnings of farming in the New Guinea highlands (Denham et al. 2003). Denham's multidisciplinary studies included

analyses of plant phytoliths, small silica structures formed in and around plant cells (See Archaeology in Practice, Chapter 17), and studies of starch residues on stone tools. The new data from Kuk indicate that some limited planting of bananas and digging of taro roots may have begun as early as 10,000 B.P. Evidence for widespread plant cultivation appears around 6500 B.P. Large mounds were constructed in order to plant bananas, sugarcane, and yams. Taro roots were grown in the wetter areas between the mounds. The data on early agriculture in New Guinea are important for two reasons. First, they indicate that banana cultivation developed independently in New Guinea several millennia before other domesticated plants were introduced from Southeast Asia. Second, although New Guinea is an important center for plant domestication, complex societies never developed in New Guinea. This evidence indicates that although domesticated foods provided the economic basis for complex societies in the Old World and the Americas, plant domestication alone is not sufficient to cause the development of stratified, urban societies.

CONCLUSION

The archaeological evidence from early Neolithic sites in the Near East indicates that farming villages based on a mixture of cereal agriculture and animal husbandry were widespread through the region by 7000 B.C. Although the Near East has been an important center for archaeological research on the origins of agriculture, archaeological and botanical studies indicate that the Near East was but one of a number of independent centers of plant domestication in the Old World. Additional research on early plant domestication in Africa and East Asia will shed light on the transition from foraging to farming in the Old World.

While the role of population growth in the origins of agriculture remains unclear, there is no question that one of the *consequences* of the establishment of farming villages was population increase. After examining the origins of farming villages in the New World (Chapter 17), we will examine the consequences of the agricultural revolution for human societies in both the Old World and the Americas (Chapter 18).

QUESTIONS FOR DISCUSSION

1. Why were plants domesticated before animals in the Middle East? Why is the pattern of domestication so different in Africa?

2. How did the beginnings of farming affect other aspects of society?

3. How have DNA studies contributed to our understanding of the pattern of plant and animal domestication in the Old World?

FURTHER READING

Bar-Yosef, O.
   1998   The Natufian Culture in the Levant: Threshold to the Origins of Agriculture. *Evolutionary Anthropology* 6 (5): 159–177.
   An up-to-date overview of the Natufian culture and its relationship to the beginnings of agriculture by one of the leading scholars in the field.

Bradley, Daniel G.
   2003   Genetic Hoofprints: The DNA Trail Leading Back to the Origin of Today's Cattle. *Natural History* 112 (1): 36–41.
   A popular account describing the use of DNA to trace the paths of cattle domestication.

Diamond, Jared
   2002   Evolution, Consequences and Future of Plant and Animal Domestication. *Nature* 418: 700–707.
   A highly readable review of some of the important questions regarding the origins and consequences of plant and animal domestication.

KEY TERMS

Abu Hureyra 229	Karim Shahir 228
'Ain Ghazal 235	Kuk 237
Ali Kosh 234	Mallaha/Eynan 225
Archaeobotanists 232	Natufian culture 225
Bouqras 234	Netiv Hagdud 230
Flotation 232	Rachis 232
Ganj Dareh 234	Shukbah 225
Gilgal 230	Sickle gloss 225
Hayonim Terrace 226	Wadi Hammeh 27 227
Jericho 230	Zawi Chemi Shanidar 234

17

AGRICULTURAL ORIGINS IN THE NEW WORLD

While Native American peoples have inhabited both North and South America since late Pleistocene times, contact between Native Americans and Europeans was limited to a small number of Viking settlements in Greenland and Newfoundland prior to 1492. Columbus's voyages and the voyages of discovery that followed them ushered in a period of intensified contact between the Old World and the Americas. Nowhere can this be seen more clearly than in the study of food.

It is almost impossible for Americans today to imagine a diet without potatoes, tomatoes, and corn (maize), but the medieval European diet was, in many respects, quite limited. While a variety of meats, including beef, pork, mutton, and poultry, would have been available, there was little variety in the plant portion of the diet. Cereals, such as wheat, barley, oats, and rye, would have been used for breads and gruel, but only a small number of vegetables— beans and peas, carrots, onions, and cabbages—would have been included in the medieval diet.

Potatoes, tomatoes, and corn were all domesticated in the New World by Native American peoples. Other plants that were domesticated in the Americas include chili peppers, squashes, gourds, pumpkins, avocados, and several kinds of beans (different kinds of beans were domesticated in the New World and the Old World).

In this chapter we will examine the archaeological evidence for the domestication of plants and animals in the New World. Particular emphasis will be placed on the domestication of maize, beans, and squash. These three plants, known as the New World triad, or "three sisters," played a central role in the farming economies throughout the Americas before the arrival of Columbus. The study of plant domestication in the Americas is important for several reasons. First, just as wheat and barley agriculture served as an economic foundation for the development of complex urban societies in the Near East, so maize agriculture was equally important for the development of the pre-Columbian civilizations of the Americas (see Part 4). Second, New World agriculture developed completely independently of Old World agriculture. Comparisons between the regions allow us to study similarities and differences in the transition to agriculture in different parts of the world. Finally, New World domesticates form an important part of modern diets throughout the world. Maize meal is a staple of West African cuisine; the tomato is basic to southern Italian cooking; and the potato forever changed Irish history. In studying the origin of these New World domesticates, the descendants of both New and Old World peoples learn more about their cultural heritage.

THE DOMESTICATION OF MAIZE

At the time Columbus arrived in the New World, domesticated maize (*Zea mays*), or what Americans call corn, was grown from eastern Canada to South America. The origin of maize is one of the most controversial issues in all of botany, one that has been debated for over a century. Some scholars argued that the wild ancestor of maize is a now extinct wild popcorn (Mangelsdorf 1974; see also Mangelsdorf 1986). Today, however, most scholars think that domesticated maize is descended from a wild grass known as **teosinte** (*Zea mexicana*), which is closely related to domestic maize. Some varieties of teosinte are found in the arid, highland regions of **Mesoamerica,** the geographical region that includes southern Mexico and the adjacent regions of Central America— Guatemala, El Salvador, Belize, and the western parts of Honduras, Nicaragua, and Costa Rica (Figure 17.1; see Chapter 24). It is in the highland regions of southern Mexico that the search for the early ancestors of modern maize has taken place.

EARLY STUDIES OF PLANT DOMESTICATION: THE TEHUACÁN VALLEY PROJECT

The **Tehuacán Valley project** was designed to study the origins of agriculture in Mesoamerica. The project was directed by Richard MacNeish who, like Childe and Braidwood in the Old World, was interested in studying the origins of plant cultivation be-

cause maize agriculture formed the economic basis of later complex societies such as the Maya and the Aztecs (Chapter 24). The Tehuacán Valley is located in the state of Puebla, Mexico (see Figure 17.1). During the course of the project, which was conducted between 1961 and 1965, 9 stratified sites were excavated, and an additional 18 were tested archaeologically (MacNeish 1991: xvii).

The Tehuacán Valley project was important both methodologically and theoretically. It was one of the first archaeological projects in Mesoamerica that was designed specifically to collect data on plant domestication. One reason that the Tehuacán Valley was chosen as a site for this project was that the dry caves of the Mexican highlands preserve organic materials such as seeds and bones quite well. During the excavation project, more than 40,000 plant remains and human feces containing plant remains were collected.

The Tehuacán Valley is located in an area of great ecological diversity within the Mexican highlands. The region includes humid river bottom areas, valley steppes, slopes, and an oak–pine forest in the higher elevations (MacNeish 1991: 112–113). A range of potentially domesticable plant species would have been available in the area. The region is subject to marked seasonal variations in rainfall. Most of the rain falls between May and November, and the winter dry season is harsh. However, at one oasis in the valley, the vegetation remains lush throughout the year, and animals are available even in the dry months.

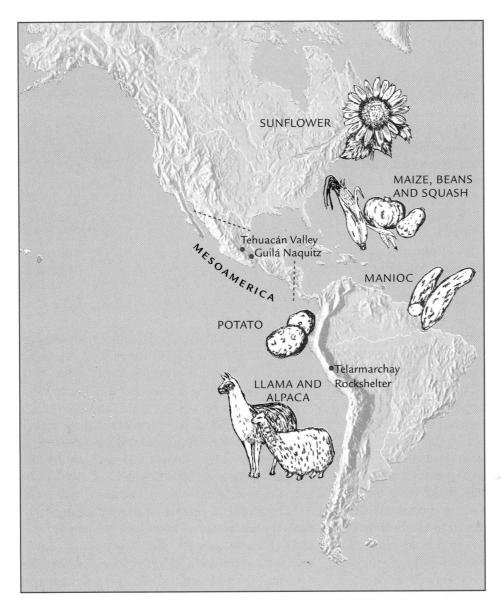

FIGURE 17.1   Map of the Americas showing the locations of sites mentioned in the text and the major early New World domesticates.

MacNeish (1967) and his collaborators defined four major pre-pottery phases as a result of the excavations in the Tehuacán Valley (see Hardy 1996 for an alternative viewpoint). MacNeish based the dates for the phases on 120 radiocarbon age determinations. These original dates were based on wood charcoal recovered from individual archaeological layers within the excavated sites. More recently, some of the actual plant remains recovered from the Tehuacán Valley project have been dated using the AMS radiocarbon method (see Archaeology in Practice, Chapter 9). These AMS dates have led to new interpretations of the process of plant domestication in Mesoamerica.

MacNeish and his collaborators argued that domesticated maize cobs appeared in the archaeological record during the Coxcatlán Phase, dated to between 5800 and 4000 B.C. However, the new AMS dates (Long et al. 1989) indicate that the earliest maize cobs from the Tehuacán Valley are only about 5300 years old. In other words maize first appeared in the Tehuacán Valley about 3350 B.C., not between 5800 and 4000 B.C. as MacNeish and his colleagues originally suggested. The AMS dates for beans are even more surprising. The earliest bean pod fragment from the Tehuacán Valley is only about 2300 years old (Smith 1994: 163). These new dates indicate that early farming began much later in the Tehuacán Valley than the original researchers thought (Fritz 1994).

The new dates have some interesting implications for our understanding of plant domestication in Mesoamerica. One possibility is that the Tehuacán Valley may not be an area in which the initial domestication of maize took place. It is important to note that the early maize from the Tehuacán Valley was fully domesticated; it had lost its ability to reproduce without human intervention. The beginnings of maize domestication certainly took place in areas where teosinte, the wild progenitor of maize, was available (Figure 17.2). The variety of teosinte that is most similar to maize grows along the central Balsas River drainage about 250 km (160 mi.) west of the Tehuacán Valley (Doebley 1990). The initial domestication of maize may have taken place in western Mexico, and the already domesticated maize may then have been adopted by hunter-gatherer populations in the Tehuacán Valley.

Between about 4000 and 3400 B.C., there is evidence for increasing settlement permanence in the Tehuacán Valley. Camps appear to have been occupied for longer periods, and three large sites yielded evidence for dwellings. These pit houses were about 5 to 6 m (16 to 20 ft.) long by 3 m (10 ft.) wide and about 1 m (3 ft.) deep. Poles were used to construct a tentlike roof frame, which was probably covered with a brush roof. These houses, which were located in the fertile river bottom areas, appear to have been occupied on a year-round basis. Annual schedules were adjusted to accommodate the planting of maize and other domesticated crops during the spring and

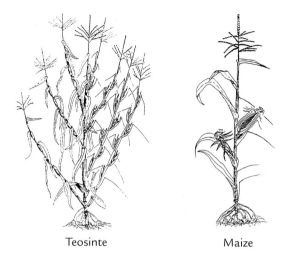

Teosinte   Maize

FIGURE 17.2 Domesticated maize compared with its wild ancestor, teosinte.

summer. Other subsistence activities, such as hunting and trapping, were concentrated in the nonagricultural seasons of the year (Flannery 1968).

If we assume that the Tehuacán Valley archaeological sequence reflects the initial domestication of maize and beans, then it appears that sedentism follows plant domestication in Mesoamerica. This pattern is in marked contrast to the Near Eastern pattern where sedentary populations clearly precede the beginnings of agriculture by more than 2000 years. The Near Eastern pattern appears to be more typical of the beginnings of farming in other parts of the world. In other areas of the world, such as eastern North America, where plants were domesticated independently, agriculture appears initially among increasingly sedentary hunters and gatherers who have access to an abundance of plant and animal resources (Gebauer and Price 1992a; Price and Gebauer 1995). If, on the other hand, maize was domesticated somewhere other than the Tehuacán Valley, then the initial farming populations may well have been semisedentary, affluent foragers (Gebauer and Price 1992b: 8). The central Balsas River drainage, where teosinte is found today, is a region that may well have supported semisedentary foragers. Only additional research on plant domestication in other areas of Mesoamerica, including the Balsas River drainage, can answer this question definitively.

GUILÁ NAQUITZ

While no studies of the size and scope of the Tehuacán Valley project have been undertaken in recent years, smaller archaeological projects have shed light on the beginnings of farming in Mesoamerica. Of particular importance is **Guilá Naquitz,** a cave site located in the Valley of Oaxaca in highland southern Mexico. The site itself is located about 6 km (4 mi.) northeast of the town of Mitla. It appears to be a small encampment, housing perhaps only three to five people. An interdisciplinary team, under the direction of Kent Flannery (1986), excavated the entire site to study the transition from foraging to farming in Oaxaca.

The site was initially occupied between 10,700 and 7600 B.C. The earliest levels at the site produced no domesticated plants. However, evidence for rinds of bottle gourds were found in archaeological layers dating between 8600 and 7600 B.C. Remains of domesticated squash also date to that period.

In the light of the newer, younger dates for domesticated maize and beans in the Tehuacán Valley, a program was initiated to restudy and redate the squash remains from Guilá Naquitz. The seeds of these early domesticates were dated directly using the AMS method of radiocarbon dating. Squash remains from Guilá Naquitz were dated to 10,000–8000 years ago, making them the earliest domesticated plants known from the Americas (Smith 1997). Maize from later levels at the site, representing intermittent visits to the site after the initial occupation, has recently been dated to 6250 B.P. (4300 B.C.). The maize is morphologically domesticated; it has a nonbrittle rachis, indicating that plants depended on humans for propagation and dispersal (Benz 2001). At present the Guilá Naquitz plant remains are the oldest domesticated corn cobs known from the New World (Piperno and Flannery 2001). Even earlier maize pollen, dated to about 5100 B.C., has been identified from the San Andrés region of the Gulf Coast of Mexico (Pope et al. 2001). Guilá Naquitz is located 400–500 km (248–310 mi.) east of the Balsas River Valley where the wild ancestors of maize grow today (Smith 2001). Wild maize is not native to the San Andrés region of the Gulf Coast either. The questions of when, how, and why maize was

initially domesticated in Mesoamerica can only be answered by further archaeological research.

Flannery's work at Guilá Naquitz has led to new models for the transition from foraging to farming in Mesoamerica. Flannery (1986: 515) suggests that early experimentation with agriculture would have been a logical extension of the preagricultural pattern of subsistence, which was based on the collection of a broad range of plant and animal resources. He notes that there is long-term stability in the plant and animal species used by the Guilá Naquitz foragers, but that this is coupled with a gradually increasing commitment to agriculture. Flannery suggests that foragers might have tried out new subsistence strategies, such as planting, during periods of abundance (wet years). Those strategies might have been expanded if they proved successful. A goal of the early agricultural strategies was risk reduction, evening out the variations between the good years and the bad years. Thus agriculture developed gradually as hunter-gatherers attempted to adapt to "the unpredictable availability of subsistence resources" (McClung de Tapia 1992: 161). This model is similar to Marshall and Hildebrand's (2002) model for the domestication of cattle in Africa, which suggests that cattle were initially domesticated as a way of providing more predictable access to subsistence resources.

The Guilá Naquitz data are even more important for what they do not show. In 1977 M. N. Cohen wrote *The Food Crisis in Prehistory*, in which he argued that:

> The nearly simultaneous adoption of agricultural economies throughout the world could only be accounted for by assuming that hunting and gathering populations had saturated the world approximately 10,000 years ago and had exhausted all possible (or palatable) strategies for increasing their food supply within the constraints of the hunting-gathering life-style. The only possible reaction to further growth in population, worldwide, was to begin artificial augmentation of the food supply [i.e., agriculture]. (Cohen 1977: 279)

In short, Cohen argued the origin of agriculture was the result of worldwide population growth that had reached a crisis level during the late Pleistocene or early Holocene. The Guilá Naquitz project, however, provides no evidence to support the notion that population growth or population pressure forced Mesoamerican foragers to adopt agriculture as a way of feeding a population that had exceeded the limits of the available food resources. Population levels appear to have been quite low throughout the occupation of the Guilá Naquitz site. Similarly, the Tehuacán Valley project provides no evidence to suggest that population pressure forced people in the Mexican highlands to begin to practice agriculture.

PLANT DOMESTICATION IN HIGHLAND SOUTH AMERICA

The South American highlands were another major center for the domestication of plants in the New World. A number of different early domesticates form part of the high-elevation agricultural complex. The best known of these plants, and the only one that spread widely outside this highland region, is the potato. The other plants that make up the highland complex are grown primarily at altitudes between 3000 and 3500 m (10,000 to 11,500 ft.) above sea level. They include quinoa and several tubers. Quinoa is a small-seeded, cereal-like plant that can be used to make bread and similar foods.

Few highland archaeological sites have produced evidence for early cultivated plants. Most of the evidence for the initial domestication of this highland complex of plants comes from sites at middle elevations (between 1500 and 3000 m, or 5000 to 10,000 ft., above sea level). Plant remains from these midelevation sites indicate that potatoes, quinoa, and possibly other high-altitude crops were domesticated by the fifth millennium B.C. (Pearsall 1992: 188).

Maize was a staple crop for the Inca and their predecessors. As noted, maize was initially domesticated in Mesoamerica. It has been difficult to trace the introduction of maize to South America since charred plant remains dating before about 4000 B.C. are rare. However, evidence from phytoliths (see Archaeology in Practice, this chapter) suggests that maize may have been introduced to South America prior to 5000 B.C.

ANIMAL DOMESTICATION IN THE AMERICAS

Domestic animals played a much smaller role in the economies of early farming villages in Mesoamerica than they did in the Old World. Domestic animals played an important role in the early farming economies of the Near East and other parts of the Old World. While the archaeological evidence from the Near East indicates that plant domestication preceded animal domestication in the eastern Mediterranean regions, by about 7000 B.C. farming communities from Greece to Pakistan were keeping domestic animals, including cattle, sheep, goats, and pigs. The situation is different in the Americas. Only two domestic animals have been recovered from pre-Columbian archaeological sites in Mesoamerica: the dog and the turkey. The dog is the only animal that was domesticated in both the Old World and the Americas. Domestic dogs first appear in the Tehuacán Valley during the Abejas period. They appear to have been used as a source of food and were probably not locally domesticated. As noted in Chapter 14, domestic dogs appear at a much earlier date in prehistoric North America. Domestic turkeys appear in Mesoamerica at approximately A.D. 275.

One reason domestic animals played a less important role in the pre-Columbian societies of Mesoamerica than they did in Eurasia is that there were simply fewer animal species in Mesoamerica that could be easily and successfully domesticated. Animals such as deer, which was one of the commonest large mammals in pre-Columbian Mesoamerica, are not easily domesticated. If deer are constrained in a pen or herded too closely together, they will not feed or breed readily (Clutton-Brock 1981: 15).

The situation is very different in highland South America. The indigenous population of South America had a number of small domesticated animals, including guinea pigs, muscovy ducks, and dogs. While we are familiar with guinea pigs as popular pets and laboratory animals, in pre-Columbian times Peruvians raised guinea pigs for meat and also used them in religious ceremonies (Clutton-Brock 1981: 152). In addition to these small domestic animals, two large mammals—the llama and the alpaca—were domesticated in the South American highlands. The llama (*Lama glama*) and the

FIGURE 17.3 The alpaca and the llama, two members of the camel family that were domesticated in highland South America in prehistoric times. The smaller alpaca was kept primarily for its wool. The larger llama was a multipurpose animal that was raised for both meat and transport.

alpaca (*Lama pacos*) are members of the camel family (Figure 17.3). The larger llama was a multipurpose animal used for meat and for bearing burdens, while the smaller alpaca was raised primarily for its fine wool. Both animals may have been domesticated from the guanaco (*Lama guanacoe*), a wild member of the camel family that today is distributed from the Andes highlands to the Patagonian plains. A smaller wild camelid, the vicuña (*Vicugna vicugna*), was widely hunted throughout prehistory.

Archaeological sites from the Peruvian Andes document the transition from the intensive hunting of wild camelids (members of the camel family) through the appearance of domesticated forms of those animals (Wheeler 1984). The domestication of these animals appears to have taken place in the **puna** zone, the highest area in the Andes that is fit for human habitation. The puna lies at an elevation between 3900 and 5000 m (13,000 to 16,000 ft.) above sea level. Although the environment is somewhat of a mosaic, the abundant grasslands would have supported sizable wild camelid populations in prehistory. The evidence from the **Telarmachay** rock shelter, a deeply stratified site located 170 km (105 mi.) northeast of Lima, Peru, at an elevation of 4420 m (14,500 ft.) above sea level, can be used to trace the development from hunting to camelid herding. The Telarmarchay evidence indicates that between 8200 and 6000 B.C., hunters in the puna hunted both wild camelids and deer. Between 6000 and 4800 B.C., hunters began to specialize in the hunting of guanacos and vicuña, and early domestic camelids first appear by 4800 to 4300 B.C. Fully domestic animals appear after 4300 B.C. The evidence indicates that camelid herding has a great antiquity in the Peruvian Andes. The cold, dry puna region is near the absolute limits for crop growth; the area experiences 330 nights of frost per year, and rainfall can be irregular. Grazing animals are the most reliable food resources in the region because they can convert the dry grasses of the puna into stored protein, which can be used for human consumption (Wheeler 1984: 397). In general, domesticated animals played a greater role in early farming economies in the Old World, while a rich variety of domestic plants formed the basis of early agricultural economies in the Americas. However, in areas such as the highland South American puna, where domestic and wild plant resources were limited, domestic animals came to play a central role in early food-producing economies.

OTHER CENTERS OF PLANT DOMESTICATION IN THE AMERICAS

As noted in Chapter 14, Archaic hunter-gatherers in eastern North America domesticated a number of plants, including sumpweed (*Iva annua*), sunflowers (*Helianthus annus*), and goosefoot (*Chenopodium berlandieri*), beginning as early as 2500 to 1200 B.C. (Smith 1992). However, an early domesticated sunflower seed, dated to about 2700 B.C., was recently recovered from the Mexican Gulf Coast (Pope et al. 2001), and it is possible that sunflowers were first domesticated in Mesoamerica rather than North America (Piperno 2001). The lowland tropical forest region of eastern South America is another center of early plant domestication in the New World. One of the most important early domesticates from the tropical forest regions is manioc (*Manihot esculenta*), a root crop whose edible, fleshy rootstocks yield a nutritious starch. Unfortunately, plant remains are often poorly preserved in the tropical lowland regions in South America, and

ARCHAEOLOGY IN PRACTICE

Phytolith Analysis

Phytoliths are microscopic particles of silica that are derived from the cells of plants. These plant remains, also known as plant opal or plant silica bodies, are formed from the silica that occurs in groundwater. They play an important role in the study of early agriculture in both the Americas and the Eastern Hemisphere because they are produced in large numbers, survive in ancient sediments even where charred seeds and other large plant remains do not, and have distinctive shapes that allow them to be identified by trained researchers (Piperno and Pearsall 1993: 9; Piperno 1988: xi). Many culturally and economically important domestic plants, such as bananas and squash, have distinctive phytoliths, and these remains have been used to trace the spread of these cultigens.

The extraction of phytoliths from soil samples is a multistage laboratory procedure conducted by specially trained botanists. The procedure begins with disaggregation, so that the phytoliths can be separated from the soil matrix. Carbonates, organic materials, and clays are removed from the soil sample, and then the phytoliths are extracted using chemical flotation. Chemical solutions of high specific gravity are added to the cleaned and disaggregated soil samples, so that the phytoliths will float to the top of the heavy liquid. The phytoliths can then be mounted and examined under a biological microscope at magnifications between 125× and 1000×.

While the process of extracting and identifying phytoliths is difficult, the study of phytoliths has made important contributions to our understanding of the origins and spread of domesticated plants. Phytoliths have played an especially significant role in the study of tropical domesticates, since seed remains are often poorly preserved in tropical environments. In the Old World, phytoliths have been used to study the domestication and spread of the banana (Vrydaghs et al. 2003), while in the Americas phytoliths

Longitudinal view

Polar view

FIGURE 17.A   Drawing of a banana (*Musa*) phytolith.

have been used to trace the spread of maize cultivation from Central America to South America (Pearsall 1992).

Bananas are one of the oldest cultivated tropical plants; today, they serve as a staple crop for millions of people. As we noted in Chapter 16, bananas (members of the genus *Musa*) were initially domesticated in New Guinea about 7000 years ago. Although bananas are staple crops in many parts of

the early history of manioc cultivation is not well known. Starch grains identified as manioc have been recovered from the Aguadulce Shelter in Panama, dating to between 7000 and 5000 years ago (Piperno et al. 2000). Pollen that appears to be domesticated manioc, dating to 4600 b.c., has been recovered from the Mexican Gulf Coast (Pope et al. 2001). These data suggest an even earlier date for the initial domestication of manioc in South America.

AGRICULTURAL HEARTHS: SIMILARITIES AND DIFFERENCES

The archaeological evidence from both the New World and the Old World indicates that plant and animal domestication took place in a number of different localities throughout the world during the early to middle Holocene period. What can the similarities and differences between the various centers of plant and animal domestication tell us about the process or processes by which foragers became farmers?

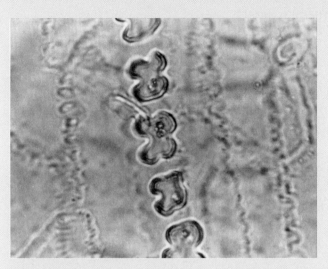

FIGURE 17.B Photograph of a maize leaf phytolith.
Courtesy of Dolores Piperno.

Africa, wild *Musa* is unknown from the African continent. Therefore, phytoliths of *Musa* (Figure 17.A) can be taken as evidence of banana cultivation. It has traditionally been assumed that bananas were introduced to Africa within the past 1500 years. However, recent analyses of phytoliths from the site of Nkang in Cameroon have indicated that bananas were cultivated there much earlier, between 2500 and 2000 years ago (Vrydaghs et al. 2003).

Maize was a staple crop throughout South America at the time of the Spanish conquest; it was a dietary staple for the Incas and their predecessors (Chapter 25). Phytolith studies can also be used to trace the spread of maize from Mesoamerica where it was first domesticated to South America (Figure 17.B). Phytoliths extracted from soil samples from central and northern South America, including the coastal site of Vegas in Ecuador, suggest that maize may have been introduced to South America between 7700 and 6000 years ago (Piperno 2001; Pearsall 1992: 191). Since maize is not native to Ecuador, these data suggest that maize was initially domesticated in highland southern Mexico at an even earlier date. Although the early dates for the introduction of maize to South America are not universally accepted (see, for example, Staller 2002, 2003), even those archaeologists who argue that maize was not introduced into South America until about 2200–1900 B.C. base their arguments on the presence of maize opal phytoliths recovered from the interiors of early pottery vessels from Ecuador.

An important similarity is that many of the early plant domesticates were starchy cereals and root crops: maize in Mesoamerica, wheat and barley in the Near East, rice in Southeast Asia, potatoes in highland South America, manioc in tropical South America, and sorghum in sub-Saharan Africa. Many hunter-gatherer populations may have had only limited access to starchy foods. Studies of exchanges between foraging and farming populations have shown that "a recurring theme is the exchange of wild protein obtained by hunting populations for domestic carbohydrates produced by farmers" (Bogucki 1988: 107). Early domesticated root and cereal crops would have provided easily storable sources of high-quality carbohydrates.

An important difference is seen in the timing of the beginnings of plant and animal domestication. While the initial domestication of wheat and barley in the Near East began at least 10,000 years ago, the earliest domesticated plants in North America do not appear until about 4500 years ago. Plant domestication appears to have begun in different places at various times throughout the early and middle Holocene. It is therefore very difficult to view the beginnings of farming as an adaptive response to the worldwide climatic changes that took place at the end of the Pleistocene. While the beginning of farming in the Near East does coincide with marked vegetational changes that occurred in that region during the final Pleistocene, this pattern is not seen in Mesoamerica. The Tehuacán Valley sequence indicates that foragers in Mesoamerica responded to the disappearance of large game animals at the end of the Pleistocene by shifting to the hunting of smaller game and the collection of a range of wild plant resources. Only later did Mesoamerican foragers begin to experiment with plant cultivation.

Similarly, the Mesoamerican data suggest that agriculture was not simply an adaptive response to worldwide population growth. While sedentism (and possibly population growth) clearly preceded the beginnings of farming in the Near East, the same cannot be said for Mesoamerica. In highland southern Mexico, the beginnings of plant domestication clearly preceded sedentary villages. Permanent villages do not appear until well after the beginnings of farming. Moreover, population levels in highland Mesoamerica were low throughout the period of initial plant cultivation.

CONCLUSION

With the exception of the domestication of the llama and alpaca in South America, domesticated animals were far less important than plant crops in the economies of the Americas. Maize, along with beans and squash, formed the basis of the Native American diet, and maize cultivation was crucial for the development of the New World complex societies.

Cereal agriculture, centered on maize, appears in Mesoamerica about 7000 years ago, several millennia after the beginning of agriculture in the Near East. The beginnings of agriculture in areas as diverse as tropical lowland South America, Southeast Asia, the ancient Near East, and highland southern Mexico cannot be explained by a single prime mover, such as climatic change or population growth. The environmental and cultural circumstances that led foragers to experiment with farming are probably unique to each region. Detailed archaeological records of early plant cultivation are available only from the Near East and Mesoamerica. Unfortunately, we cannot answer the question of why farming began until more archaeological data are recovered from areas of the world such as sub-Saharan Africa, Southeast Asia, and tropical lowland South America. It is only through the comparative study of agricultural origins in different areas of the world that archaeologists can understand the processes of plant and animal domestication.

KEY TERMS

Guilá Naquitz 243	Tehuacán Valley
Mesoamerica 240	project 240
Phytoliths 246	Telarmarchay 245
Puna 245	Teosinte 240

QUESTIONS FOR DISCUSSION

1. Compare the beginnings of farming in the Old World with the beginnings of agriculture in the Americas. What are the main similarities? What are the most important differences?

2. Why do you think that squashes were domesticated so early in highland southern Mexico?

3. How have phytolith studies and pollen analyses changed our understanding of the spread of maize agriculture throughout Central and South America?

FURTHER READING

Cowan, C. W., and P. J. Watson, eds.
  1992   *The Origins of Agriculture: An International Perspective.* Washington, DC: Smithsonian Institution Press. *This volume presents a series of essays on the origins of agriculture in various parts of the Old World and the Americas. The coverage of agricultural origins in the Americas is particularly strong. Several essays on agricultural origins in different regions of the Americas (including North America, Mesoamerica, and South America) are included.*

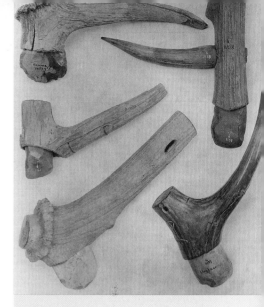

18

THE CONSEQUENCES OF THE AGRICULTURAL REVOLUTION

Archaeologists have always been interested in origins—the origins of stone tools, the origins of modern humans, and the origins of agriculture. However, the consequences of a biological or technological change are just as important as its origins. In the past 10,000 years, our world has changed from a planet inhabited by small populations of human hunters and gatherers to one peopled by agriculturalists and city dwellers. We live with the consequences of the agricultural revolution—including overpopulation and epidemic diseases—every day of our lives. In this chapter we will examine the consequences of the agricultural revolution for early farming populations in the Old World.

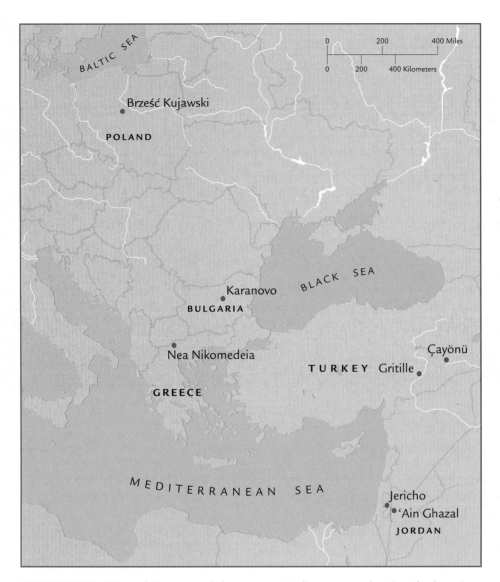

FIGURE 18.1 Map of Europe and the eastern Mediterranean showing the location of the sites mentioned in this chapter.

SEDENTISM AND POPULATION GROWTH

While archaeologists have debated the role that population growth played in encouraging the initial adoption of agriculture in the Near East and elsewhere, there is no question that adoption of agriculture *led to* significant population increases. Several factors underlie such population growth. First, farmers are generally less mobile than hunter-gatherers. Highly mobile hunter-gatherer populations often space the birth of their children as much as five years apart so that women do not have to carry more than one child at a time from place to place. Although farmers need not live in the same location all year around, they must stay in one location during the growing season to plant, tend, and harvest their crops. Activities that require greater mobility, such as hunting, are scheduled around the growing season. Since agriculture generally leads to decreased mobility, birth spacing may also decrease.

In addition, the economic role of children changes when foragers adopt agriculture. Small children are unable to participate in lengthy hunting or gathering expeditions because they do not have the stamina to walk great distances. Children may be economic assets, however, for farmers. Children can help in planting, weeding, and harvesting and can also help tend domestic animals—tasks that do not require great physical strength or stamina. Larger families may be advantageous to farmers, since additional children can mean more available labor at planting and harvesting time.

Finally, the availability of carbohydrates may encourage early weaning. Mobile hunter-gatherers may nurse children for as long as four to five years. One reason for this long period of nursing may be that many hunter-gatherer populations lack the starchy carbohydrates that often serve as early foods for babies. The cultivation of cereals and other starchy food would have allowed for earlier weaning. Since lactation can suppress ovulation and thereby limit a woman's fertility, earlier weaning may lead to closer birth spacing and population growth.

Studies of human skeletal populations (see Chapter 26) in the lower Illinois River region of the American Midwest have shown that the birthrate rose significantly during the period when maize agriculture was adopted and intensified. While a number of factors may have played a role in this increase, "the shift to a high starch diet . . . would have facilitated earlier weaning and decreased birth interval because of the availability of soft, easily digestible foods" (Larsen 1995: 198).

The archaeological record for early farming villages in the Near East also points to population growth and increased residential stability. While many of the earliest Neolithic sites in the southern Levant are small villages like Netiv Hagdud (Chapter 16) in the West Bank, the site of **Jericho** seems to represent a far more substantial settlement. Jericho, a deeply stratified tell (city-mound) site, is also located in the West Bank (Figure 18.1). The ancient city of Jericho rises to a height of 21 m (70 ft.) and covers an area of 4 ha (10 ac.). The tell is located at a permanent spring, 'Ain es Sultan, which has made it a focal point for human settlement since late Pleistocene times. The

FIGURE 18.2   Early Neolithic (PPNA) tower from the site of Jericho, West Bank.

early Neolithic levels of the site are deeply buried under many meters of occupation debris because the ancient city of Jericho was intensively occupied during biblical times. Therefore, only a small portion of the early Neolithic settlement of Jericho was excavated when Kathleen Kenyon (1957) carried out a major program of excavation at the site in the 1950s. Kenyon's excavations revealed an early Neolithic settlement surrounded by a city wall that was 2 m (6 ft.) thick and survived to a height of 4 m (13 ft.). A large stone tower (Figure 18.2) was built against the inside of the wall. The tower was at least 8.5 m (28 ft.) in height and 8 m (26 ft.) in diameter (Kuijt and Goring-Morris 2002: 373). The wall and tower date to the earliest part of the Neolithic of Palestine, often termed the **Pre-Pottery Neolithic A (PPNA);** they appear to have been constructed about 11,000 years ago. The PPNA is generally dated between 9750 and 8550 B.C. (Kuijt and Goring-Morris 2002: 366).

The tower and town wall were probably part of a much more extensive system of fortifications. Why

FIGURE 18.3   Plastered human skull from the PPNB levels at Jericho, West Bank.

would an early farming village need such sizable defenses? An obvious possibility is that they were designed to protect and control access to the 'Ain es Sultan spring. As Kenyon (1970: 39) notes, "Only in areas within reach of the waters of some permanent source such as that of the spring of 'Ain es Sultan at Jericho can the rich soil of the [Jordan] valley be made truly productive." In a broader sense, the fortifications may reflect changing relationships between people and the landscape. Mobile hunter-gatherers may exercise the rights to use a particular land area in a particular season, but they generally do not own land. When farmers establish permanent, year-round settlements, they may also claim ownership of the territory surrounding their settlement, including its natural resources. The Jericho walls may reflect this changing concept of land ownership.

The PPNA settlement at Jericho was replaced by a slightly later farming community that built rectangular mud-brick houses. This second phase of the pre-pottery or aceramic Neolithic in the southern Levant is often referred to as the **Pre-Pottery Neolithic B,** or **PPNB** and dates to between 8550

and 6300 B.C. One of the most striking features of the PPNB settlement at Jericho is the presence of a series of plastered human skulls whose eyes had been replaced by shells (Figure 18.3). The plastered features give the skulls a very naturalistic appearance, almost suggesting portraits. The special treatment of the human skull appears to be a feature of PPNB burial rites. Similar plastered skulls were recovered from the important PPNB site of 'Ain Ghazal in Jordan.

INCREASED DISEASE LOAD AND EARLY FARMING COMMUNITIES

The evidence that the beginning of farming may have been associated with poorer health and an increased disease load is not limited to 'Ain Ghazal.[1] Studies of human skeletons from early farming communities in North America, South America, and Europe reveal similar patterns. As Clark Larsen, an anthropologist who has studied biological changes associated with the beginnings of agriculture, notes:

> Reduced population mobility and increased aggregation provide conditions that promote the spread and maintenance of infections and parasitic diseases and the increase in pathogen load in humans. That is, closer, more crowded living conditions facilitate greater physical contact between members of a settlement, and permanent occupation can result in decreased sanitation and hygiene. (1995: 198)

In short, the establishment of sedentary farming communities may have produced larger but less healthy human communities.

POPULATION GROWTH AND THE EXPANSION OF AGRICULTURAL SETTLEMENTS

As noted, one of the consequences of the establishment of permanent agricultural villages was population growth. Early farming villages such as

---

[1]See Jared Diamond's *Guns, Germs, and Steel* (1997) for a popular account of the relationship between the beginnings of farming and the increased incidence of disease.

CASE STUDY

'Ain Ghazal, Jordan

'Ain Ghazal, located on the outskirts of the Jordanian capital of Amman, is one of the largest early farming settlements in the southern Levant. This early farming village was excavated over six seasons between 1982 and 1989 (Rollefson et al. 1992) and again in the early 1990s. The site covers 12 to 13 ha (30 to 32.5 ac.) and has yielded an unbroken sequence of early Neolithic occupation from 8400 to 5800 B.C. Only about 700 sq. m (840 sq. yd. or 0.5%) of the site could be excavated. While most of the excavated remains from 'Ain Ghazal date to the PPNB (8400 to 7500 B.C.), the site continued to be occupied throughout the sixth millennium.

The inhabitants of 'Ain Ghazal made their living by farming. Plant remains indicate that they grew wheat, barley, peas, lentils, and chickpeas. Goats were domesticated by 7500 B.C., and by approximately 7000 B.C. the inhabitants of 'Ain Ghazal raised goats, pigs, cattle, and possibly sheep.

The houses at 'Ain Ghazal were built with stone walls and lime plaster floors. During the Middle PPNB (8400 to 7500 B.C.), the rooms were generally 5 by 5 m (16 by 16 ft.) in floor area, with circular hearths built into the centers of the floors. More than 100 human burials were recovered during the 'Ain Ghazal excavations. During the PPNB period, most of the adolescents and adults were buried underneath the floors of the houses or under the courtyards. The heads were removed from the bodies some time after the initial burial. Burial underneath the floors of buildings is a continuation of a tradition that was originally established during the Natufian period at sites such as Mallaha/Eynan. In 1983 a cache of four skulls was found at 'Ain Ghazal, two of which had been plastered. The parallel to the plastered skulls from Jericho is striking and suggests that PPNB burial practices may have been quite standardized, at least throughout parts of the southern Levant. The meaning of these plastered skulls is far more difficult to reconstruct. Clearly, they reflect elaborate rituals surrounding death, but whether they reflect ancestor cults, clan rituals, or something entirely different is difficult to determine on the basis of the archaeological evidence alone.

While the majority of the adults and adolescents were buried under floors and courtyards, about one-third of the adolescent and adult burials were found in trash deposits with their skulls attached. The differences in burial practice may reflect some broader social differences, perhaps indicating the beginnings of real social inequality. Infants were also discarded in the trash. Infant mortality appears to have been high; about one-third of children died during infancy. In addition, many adolescent and adult teeth showed defects in the enamel, which can result from poor childhood health, inadequate nutrition, congenital or developmental abnormalities, or sustained stress (Rollefson et al. 1992: 463). This evidence indicates that life in an early farming village in the Near East may have been rather hard. One of the consequences of agriculture may well have been an increased disease load. With the establishment of permanent villages, early farmers could no longer simply pack up and walk away from their disease-ridden refuse. Moreover, the larger and denser populations in these villages may have facilitated the spread of infectious diseases.

'Ain Ghazal and Jericho were clearly larger than the hunter-gatherer settlements that preceded them in the Near East. One of the consequences of this population growth was the spread of agricultural settlements outside the southern Levant, where the transition to wheat and barley agriculture first took place. Agricultural settlements initially expanded into areas that were similar to the southern Levant in both climate and topography, such as Anatolia and Greece. The regions surrounding the Mediterranean all share a Mediterranean climate characterized by hot, dry summers and cooler, wetter winters. From the eastern Mediterranean, agricultural settlements then expanded into the Balkans and eventually into central Europe. These areas differ in both climate and vegetation from the southern Levant, and agricultural practices had to be adjusted accordingly. In this chapter we will trace the spread of agricultural technology from the southern Levant to Anatolia and Greece, and then to southeastern and central Europe.

EARLY FARMING VILLAGES IN TURKEY

As noted in Chapter 16, the earliest farming villages in the eastern Mediterranean are located in an arc that extends from the southern Jordan Valley northward into Syria. Early farming villages are also known from eastern Turkey, and the question of whether these villages represent a movement of early farming populations northward from the Levant or the adoption of agricultural technologies by indigenous foraging populations remains an open one. Until recently, little was known about the late Pleistocene settlement of eastern Anatolia. However, new research in the region has revealed a number of late Paleolithic sites that are broadly contemporary with the Natufian settlements in the southern Levant. In particular, the recently excavated site of Hallan Çemi in eastern Turkey (Rosenberg et al. 1998) revealed a small village that relied on the gathering of nuts and legumes, hunting, and possibly pig rearing during the late Pleistocene (see Chapter 16).

Some early farming villages in eastern Turkey appear to have close ties with PPNB populations of the southern Levant. The site of **Gritille** (Voigt 1985), located on the Euphrates River in southeastern Anatolia, is an early Neolithic settlement dated between 8100 and 6300 B.C. Gritille produced a chipped stone industry that shows broad similarities to the Levantine PPNB. The site also yielded a number of small clay figurines of humans and animals that are quite similar to figurines recovered from 'Ain Ghazal in Jordan. The Gritille economy, which was based on emmer wheat, barley, legumes, and domesticated animals, including sheep and goats, also shows

broad similarities to PPNB sites farther south. Gritille may be an example of the gradual movement of farming communities northward along the Euphrates (Voigt 1985: 21).

The data from **Çayönü**, an early farming village located northeast of Gritille in Turkey, present a somewhat different picture. The site, which was occupied between about 8700 and 7500 B.C., yielded the remains of early domesticated einkorn wheat. This cereal, whose wild ancestor is widely distributed in Anatolia, was originally thought to have been introduced to Çayönü from western Turkey (Van Zeist 1972). Recent microbiological studies, however, have shown the domesticated einkorn is most closely related to the wild einkorn found in southeastern Turkey (Heun et al. 1997). The domestication of einkorn appears to be completely independent of the domestication of emmer wheat and barley in the southern Levant. These data suggest that Anatolia may have been an independent center of plant domestication. Thus, the beginnings of farming in Turkey involved at least two processes. Indigenous hunting and gathering populations may have independently domesticated einkorn and pigs, while early farming populations may also have moved into Turkey from the south, bringing Levantine domesticates, including emmer and barley, with them.

EARLY FARMERS IN GREECE AND SOUTHEAST EUROPE

Greece is the region of Europe that is geographically closest to the Near East, and it is not surprising to find that Greece was home to the earliest farming communities in Europe. The Mediterranean climate of Greece, with its hot, dry summers and cooler, moister winters, also resembles the climate of the Levantine regions of the Near East. The earliest farming villages in Greece date to the early seventh millennium B.C. (Runnells 2004). At sites such as **Nea Nikomedeia** in Greek Macedonia (Rodden 1962, 1965), farmers inhabited small, single-roomed, square houses and raised wheat, barley, sheep, goats, cattle, and pigs.

The question of how farming was introduced to Europe has been a subject of intensive debate for at

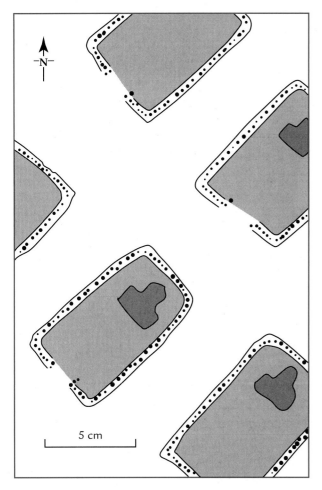

FIGURE 18.4 Plans of Neolithic mud-walled and wattled houses from Karanovo, Bulgaria.

Greece appears to have been very low (Runnells 2004); the number of early Neolithic sites is much higher, suggesting significant population increase during the early Neolithic period.

Similar early Neolithic sites are known from southern and central Bulgaria, beginning about 6200 B.C. (Budja 2004). At the site of **Karanovo** (Figure 18.4), small, square houses—about 7 by 7 m (23 by 23 ft.) in floor area—were framed with poles and plastered with mud. The earliest farming village at Karanovo would have contained about 60 of these small houses, sheltering about 300 people. By 6000 B.C. successful farming settlements had been established throughout Greece and the Balkans. However, farming settlements were not established in temperate Europe until considerably later.

EARLY FARMERS IN TEMPERATE EUROPE

The climate of temperate Europe, the area of Europe north of the Mediterranean zone, is characterized by cool, wet summers and cold winters. Systems of agriculture and animal husbandry that were developed in the Mediterranean regions of the Near East and Europe had to be adapted to the more rigorous climate of central and northern Europe. For example, Near Eastern cereals are planted in the fall and harvested in the late spring and early summer. In temperate Europe cereals are planted in either the fall or spring. Cereal crops grow throughout the spring and summer, and the harvest takes place in the late summer to early fall.

It was not until about 5700 B.C. that farming villages first appeared in central Europe. These early farming settlements are found in the valleys and tributaries of the Danube and Rhine Rivers in a region known as the **loess belt.** This region lay between the Scandinavian and Alpine ice sheets during the height of the last glaciation. The fine soils of this region were deposited by wind during the late Pleistocene. Since the loess belt is relatively dry and uniform in vegetation, it was not a particularly attractive area for settlement by Mesolithic hunter-gatherers (see Chapter 13). However, these light and easily tilled soils would have been ideal for early cultivators.

least 50 years (see Dennell 1992 for a recent review of the issue). Most archaeologists would argue that agriculture was introduced to Europe by immigrant farmers who brought domesticated emmer wheat, barley, sheep, and goats with them (but see Whittle 1996 for an alternative model). Several lines of evidence support this view. First, the wild ancestors of sheep, goats, emmer wheat, and barley were not generally available in southeast Europe, making local domestication impossible. Second, the earliest farming villages in Turkey, Syria, and the southern Levant are considerably earlier than the earliest agricultural settlements in southeast Europe (Whittle 1985: 54). Finally, the pre-Neolithic population of

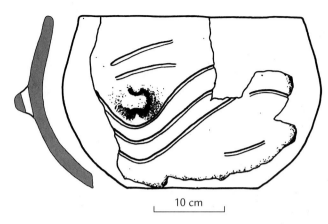

FIGURE 18.5   A Linearbandkeramik vessel from the site of Eitzum in Germany.

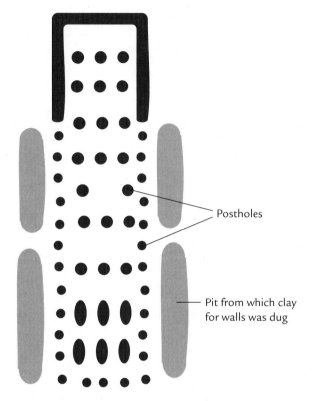

FIGURE 18.6   Idealized plan of an LBK house. Such a house can be up to 50 m (165 ft.) in length.

The earliest farming settlements in central Europe are part of the **Linearbandkeramik** or **LBK (Linear Pottery culture),** named for its distinctive pottery, which was decorated with curvilinear designs (Figure 18.5). Linear pottery settlements spread rapidly across the loess belt of central and western Europe between 5500 and 4900 B.C., at a rate of about 3.5 to 5 km (2 to 3 mi.) per year (Keeley and Golitko 2004: 260). The LBK houses are long, rectangular structures built of large posts (Figure 18.6). The walls would have been filled in with wickerwork and plastered with mud. The farming economy of the Linearbandkeramik culture was based on the cultivation of cereals, particularly emmer wheat, and on stock rearing. Agricultural plots were located in fertile riverine environments that could have produced sustained crop yields for many decades (Bogucki 1988: 82).

At a somewhat later date, farming settlements expanded into the North European Plain, a far more diverse environment, with a variety of soil types, as well as lakes, bogs, and streams. Pioneering agricultural villages were established in this area between 4800 and 4000 B.C. A well-documented example of an early farming village in the North European Plain is the site of **Brześć Kujawski** (Bogucki and Grygiel 1983, 1993; Bogucki 2004), located northwest of Warsaw in Poland (Figure 18.7). The settlement is composed of a series of trapezoidal longhouses whose narrow ends faced into the prevailing winds. The farmers at

Brześć Kujawski raised emmer wheat and may have supplemented their diets through plant collection. They also herded cattle, sheep, goats, and pigs, but domestic animals were supplemented by fishing, hunting, fowling, and shellfish collecting. Hunting was generally carried out in the winter when agricultural activities were less demanding. The Brześć Kujawski economy was highly diversified, especially when compared with the Linearbandkeramik economies, which were based primarily on cattle rearing and cereal cultivation. This difference reflects the greater environmental diversity of the North European Plain and, possibly, interaction with native Mesolithic populations.

The initial farming settlements in both the loess belt and North European Plain were most likely established by colonists who were not native to the area. The case for colonization is based on the marked differences in settlement patterns, subsistence systems, and material culture (e.g., pottery)

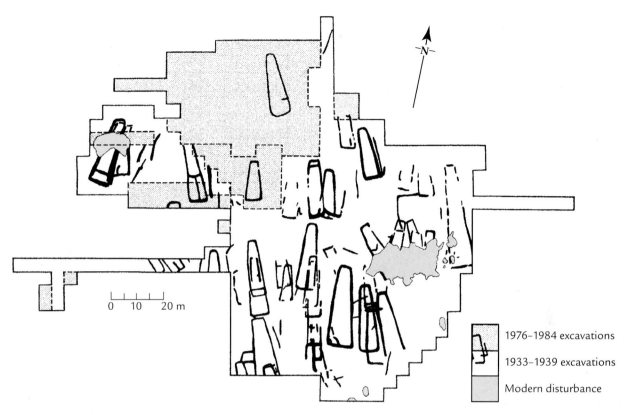

FIGURE 18.7   Plan of the early Neolithic settlement of Brześć Kujawski, Poland.

between the indigenous Mesolithic populations of central Europe (Chapter 13) and these early agriculturalists (Bogucki 1988: 50). While the homogeneous loess belt supported very limited Mesolithic settlement, the North European Plain supported a much larger indigenous hunter-gatherer population. Early farming populations must have come in regular contact with native hunter-gatherers in central Europe, although the nature of those contacts is not well understood. Did the Mesolithic hunter-gatherers provide the farmers with meat and labor in exchange for cereals (Bogucki 1988: 108), or were the contacts of a more hostile nature? New archaeological data suggest that some of the contacts may have been hostile. Between 6 and 19% of Linearbandkeramik individuals show pathologies indicting that they died violently. In addition, the Linearbandkeramik site of Vaihingen in Germany includes trash pits containing a number of robust (probably Mesolithic) skeletons with traumatic in-

juries (Keeley and Quick 2004: 111–112). Eventually, these foragers adopted agricultural technology, although the process was by no means a simple and straightforward one. Initially, foragers may have incorporated some domestic animals or crops into a hunting and gathering way of life. The increasing sedentism of many late Mesolithic populations in Europe may have facilitated the adoption of domestic plants and animals. By 3500 B.C. agriculture and stock raising had replaced hunting and gathering throughout most of temperate Europe.

The important lesson to be learned from the study of early farming communities in Europe is that the spread of agriculture was a complex process. The spread of agriculture outside the southern Levant involved several changes, including population growth and colonization, the adoption of agricultural practices by indigenous foraging communities, technological changes, and indigenous domestication of crops such as einkorn.

ON THE CUTTING EDGE

Identifying Migration in Neolithic Europe: The Role of Stable Isotope Studies

The role of human migration in establishing Neolithic communities in Europe north of the Alps has been a subject of debate for at least two decades. Since the economy of early Neolithic Central Europe is based on a package of distinctive architecture, artifact types, and nonnative plants and animals, including sheep, goats, barley, and emmer wheat, many archaeologists have argued that the Neolithic was introduced to central Europe as a result of population movement. In addition, some have argued that these immigrant farmers may have introduced Indo-European languages into central Europe as well (Renfrew 1987, 1989). Recently, some scholars have challenged the migration-based model for the introduction of agriculture. They argue that the beginnings of farming in central Europe resulted from indigenous Mesolithic hunters and gatherers adopting nonnative domestic plants and animals and aggregating into small farming settlements (see, for example, Whittle 1996). Others have argued that the beginning of European farming was a more complex process, involving both migration and the adoption of agriculture by native hunter-gatherer populations (Bogucki 1988, 1996). To evaluate these competing models, archaeologists need to develop techniques to identify population migrations in the archaeological record. Strontium isotope analyses of human skeletal remains offer a promising new approach to this problem.

Strontium is a relatively common element in the earth's crust. Strontium derived from local bedrock travels through the groundwater and is ingested by plants, animals, and humans. In humans, strontium makes its way into the inorganic portion of human bones and teeth, where it substitutes for calcium. Human permanent teeth are generally formed between ages 4 and 12 and undergo little change, so the strontium composition of human teeth reflects the environment in which a person grew up. Bone, on the other hand, is chemically renewed throughout an individual's lifetime, so the strontium composition of bone reflects the individual's later life. Since strontium isotopes vary locally, differences between the strontium isotope composition of an individual's teeth and that of the bones may indicate that he or she is a migrant (Price et al. 2002; Bentley et al. 2003).

Several different isotopes of strontium are found in the earth's crust; the isotope composition varies depending on the age and composition of the local bedrock. Variations in strontium composition in human skeletons and other biological materials are generally expressed as the strontium isotope ratio, which is the ratio of radioactive strontium-87 to nonradioactive strontium-86. The $^{87}Sr/^{86}Sr$ ratio generally varies between 0.700 and 0.750.

Alex Bentley and his colleagues have examined the strontium isotope ratios for human bones and teeth from several early Neolithic LBK cemeteries in southwestern Germany, including Flomborn, Schwetzingen, and Dillingen (Price et al. 2001; Bentley et al. 2002). Their research identified many possible nonlocals in these early Neolithic cemeteries. In addition, they noted that many of the nonlocals were females. Nonlocals, both male and female, were generally buried without shoe-last adzes, woodworking tools that are commonly found as grave goods in LBK burials. In addition, the strontium isotope ratios for the nonlocals were generally higher than those of the local population. While the lowland regions where these cemeteries are located are generally characterized by strontium isotope ratios of .708 to .710 (Bentley et al. 2003: 476), higher strontium ratios characterize the surrounding highland regions. Bentley and his colleagues (Bentley et al. 2002) have suggested that hunter-gatherer women from the highland regions may have married into these early farming communities. This is a far more complex pattern of interaction between hunter-gatherers and farmers than that envisioned by either the simple migration-based model of agricultural origins or the model based on the adoption of domestic plants and animals by native foraging communities.

FIGURE 18.8   Neolithic polished stone axes.

THE DEVELOPMENT OF NEW TECHNOLOGIES AND CRAFTS

The adoption of agriculture led to several important changes in technology and craft production. Among the most important were changes in the technology of stone tool manufacture. Before the beginnings of farming, stone tools were manufactured primarily by flaking. Although today archaeologists recognize that ground stone objects actually were first made much earlier, with the beginnings of the Neolithic we see the widespread use of stone tools that are shaped by grinding and polishing. The most important of these new tools were ground and polished stone axes (Figure 18.8).

The manufacture of these stone tools was a multi-stage process. A stone nodule was initially flaked into the approximate shape of an axe. The blank was then ground to shape by rubbing it against a gritty rock such as sandstone. The final polish was provided by rubbing the axe with a more finely grained stone, using sand as an abrasive (Bordaz 1970: 99). These tools were particularly useful for woodworking and for forest clearance because they were able to penetrate wood more deeply than a flaked stone axe. They were also more durable, and the edges of these ground and polished stone tools were also less likely to chip or break.

ARCHAEOLOGY IN PRACTICE

The Development of Pottery Technology

Pottery is made of clay, a fine-grained material that is plastic when wet but becomes hard and brittle when heated. Clay's plasticity when wet means that it can be pressed into almost any shape, from bowls and jugs to figurines and statues. As the clay dries, it loses its plasticity. When the clay is heated to a high temperature in either a bonfire or a kiln, it undergoes an irreversible chemical change, producing a hard and durable material. The physical properties of clay make it an ideal material for the construction of storage jars and other containers. The temperature at which pottery is fired greatly influences the nature of the finished product. Low-fired ceramics are generally soft and porous; highly fired ceramics tend to be very hard and impermeable.

Storage vessels would have been especially useful to early farmers. Farmers rely on a small number of staple crops, such as barley or maize, which are harvested once a year. The crops must be stored so that they can be used throughout the year as food. Additionally, a portion of the harvest must be stored to serve as seed for the following year's crop. Large pottery storage jars can protect stored crops from rodents and other pests. Pottery also served a variety of other purposes in past societies, as cooking pots and serving bowls and, of course, as dinnerware.

Even before the appearance of the first pottery vessels, there is evidence that early farmers were beginning to work with clay and to investigate its unique properties. For example, the pre-pottery levels at the site of 'Ain Ghazal in Jordan have produced a variety of human and animal figures made of both fired and unfired clay (Figure 18.A).

Pottery's hardness and durability mean that it can survive for millennia. It is therefore one of the most common classes of artifacts recovered from archaeological sites. Archaeologists examine several different criteria in order to analyze and classify pottery (Figure 18.B). The first criterion is the nature of the clay that is used to manufacture the pottery vessel. The clays used to make pottery can differ in structure, chemical composition, and impurities. In the manufacture of a pottery vessel, clays are usually combined with nonplastic materials known as **temper**. Temper counteracts shrinkage and reduces the risk of cracking as a clay vessel dries. A wide variety of nonclay materials can be used for temper, including sand, shell, and straw.

Pottery can be manufactured in a number of different ways. Pottery

FIGURE 18.A Animal figurines made of clay from the pre-pottery Neolithic levels at 'Ain Ghazal, near Amman, Jordan.

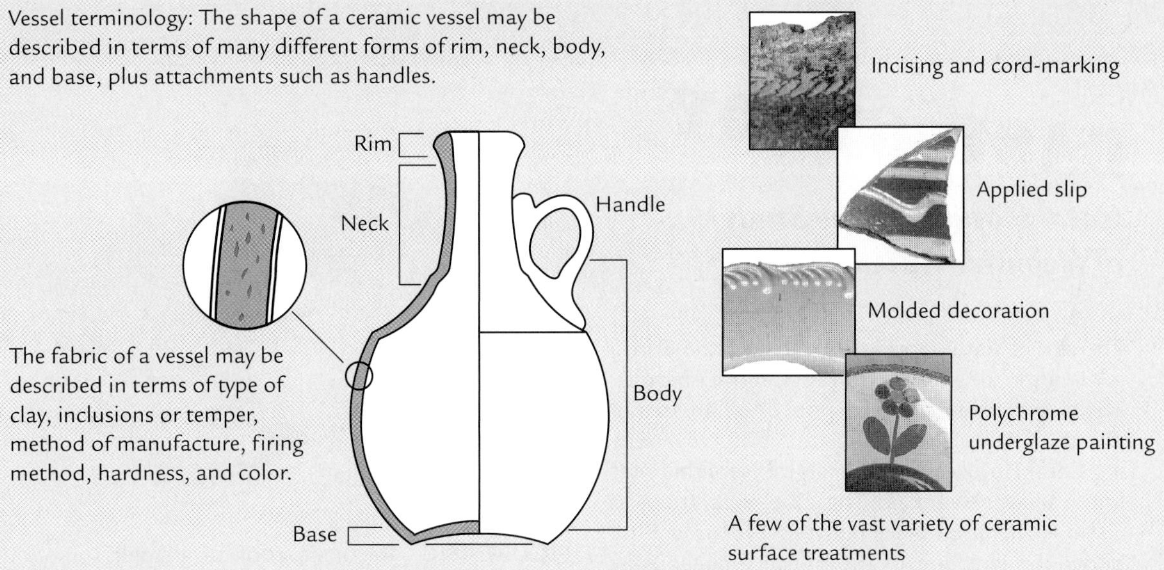

Vessel terminology: The shape of a ceramic vessel may be described in terms of many different forms of rim, neck, body, and base, plus attachments such as handles.

Rim

Neck

Handle

The fabric of a vessel may be described in terms of type of clay, inclusions or temper, method of manufacture, firing method, hardness, and color.

Body

Base

Incising and cord-marking

Applied slip

Molded decoration

Polychrome underglaze painting

A few of the vast variety of ceramic surface treatments

FIGURE 18.B Idealized pottery vessel showing the criteria that archaeologists use to classify pottery.

can be thrown on a potter's wheel, or a variety of different hand-building techniques can be used. The simplest technique is to form the vessel by hand from a lump of clay, much the way a first-grader makes a clay bowl. Vessels can also be hand-built from coils of clay that are pressed together or from large, flat slabs. In addition, pottery can be shaped in a mold.

Pottery vessels can be produced in an almost endless variety of forms—including bowls, cups, jars, plates, and pitchers. The base of the pot can be flat or rounded, the rim can be shaped in a number of different ways, and various handles or decorations can be attached. The outer and inner surfaces of the vessel may be either left plain or decorated. The possibilities for decoration

are almost limitless. Early pottery was frequently decorated with surface incisions; or fingertips, a shell, or a cord-wrapped paddle might have been used to press patterns into the wet clay surface. The clay surface may be **burnished,** rubbed with a small stone or other hard object after firing to make the surface shinier. Burnishing also closes the pores in the clay vessel, thus decreasing its porosity. Before firing, the vessel may be covered with a **slip,** a thin wash of clay and water, or painted with various earth pigments. Sometimes a combination of decorative techniques was used. Later pottery is frequently covered with a **glaze,** a material that melts during firing to produce a glasslike surface.

The multitude of combinations of pottery fabric, temper, firing

methods, surface decorations, and glazes make the pottery produced by any culture or period unique. Archaeologists use these characteristics to classify pottery, permitting them to trace the changes in pottery technology and style within an archaeological culture. Studies have shown that the shapes of pottery vessels, their forms of decoration, and even the ways they are manufactured change through time. Pottery, therefore, is a particularly useful indicator of relative chronology. The distribution of certain distinctive pottery types over wide geographical areas provides archaeologists with a clear indication that the sites containing the pottery were contemporaneous and that cultural contact existed among them.

CASE STUDY

Çatal Höyük and the Study of Neolithic Ritual Life

The site of **Çatal Höyük** is located in the Konya lowlands in the southern part of Central Anatolia. The Neolithic remains at the site cover an area of about 13 ha or 32 ac. (Mellaart 1975: 98), making Çatal Höyük one of the largest Neolithic sites in the ancient Near East. The initial excavations at Çatal Höyük took place between 1961 and 1963 under the direction of the British archaeologist James Mellaart (1967; 1975). Mellaart's excavations revealed a Neolithic settlement constructed of small (25 sq. m or 270 sq. ft.), square dwellings with flat roofs. The houses were built of sun-dried mud bricks and were entered through the roof by means of a ladder (Figure 18.C). Each house had its own walls, but the houses were built up against one another (Figure 18.D). The size of the site and the density of the housing indicate that Çatal Höyük was home to several thousand people. Mellaart excavated only about one-thirtieth of the mound at Çatal Höyük. A series of radiocarbon dates indicates that the site was occupied from about 7300 to 6200 B.C. (Cessford 2001).

The most striking feature of Mellaart's excavation was the evidence for ritual and religious life that he uncovered. The burial rituals at Çatal Höyük were unique. After death, the bodies were exposed to vultures and the elements. The defleshed bones were then wrapped in cloth, mats, or baskets and buried beneath the sleeping platforms in the houses. Nearly all the houses produced evidence for wall paintings, statues, plaster reliefs, or cattle crania and horns set into the walls. Many of the wall paintings seem to depict textile-like patterns, while others show hunting and burial scenes. The reliefs and carvings include images of animals (Figure 18.E), female figures, and even women giving birth to bulls. The elaborate imagery certainly reflects a well-developed set of religious beliefs and prac-

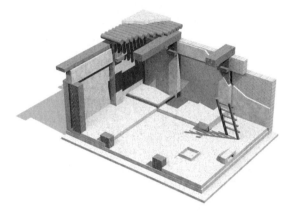

FIGURE 18.C   Reconstruction of a small, square dwelling from Çatal Hoyuk.

tices. Because many statues of women have been identified from Mellaart's excavations, the role of women in the ritual life of Çatal Höyük is particularly intriguing.

The role of women in Neolithic ritual is one of the questions that is being explored by a new program of excavations that began at Çatal Höyük in 1995. The new excavations are being conducted under the direction of Dr. Ian Hodder from Cambridge University and will continue for approximately 25 years. Dr. Hodder's team is using up-to-date methods of excavation, conservation, and interpretation to explore the site and its environment, to conserve the wall paintings and other artifacts, and to develop Çatal Höyük as a well-planned heritage site that will attract visitors from all over the world. The research team plans to study the environmental, economic, and social contexts of the wall paintings as well as their religious symbolism.

FIGURE 18.D Plan of Çatal Höyük (southeast quarter, Level VIB) showing houses built up against one another.

FIGURE 18.E Two leopards depicted in clay and plaster relief from the north wall of shrine VII.44 at Çatal Höyük.

An equally important technological innovation was the development of pottery. While the world's earliest pottery was manufactured by late Pleistocene hunter-gatherers in Japan, the widespread use of pottery containers is associated with early agricultural societies in both the Old World and the Americas. The earliest farmers in the Near East did not manufacture pottery, and, as noted, this period is often referred to as the aceramic or pre-pottery Neolithic. However, after 6250 B.C. pottery was widely manufactured throughout the Near East. Its spread through Europe coincided with the introduction and spread of agriculture throughout the continent. The Archaeology in Practice box describes how pottery is manufactured, how it is used, and why it is of particular interest to archaeologists studying ancient societies.

TRADE AND EXCHANGE IN EARLY FARMING COMMUNITIES

Many early archaeologists viewed Neolithic villages as isolated and self-sufficient, producing everything they needed to sustain life. Subsequent research, however, has shown that Neolithic communities almost always engaged in trade and exchange, including the long-distance distribution of a variety of functional and decorative items. For example, Mediterranean seashells are sometimes found as grave goods in early Neolithic cemeteries in central Europe (Bogucki 1988: 126). High-quality stone for the manufacture of stone tools was also exchanged throughout both Europe and the Near East. In particular, small quantities of obsidian (a volcanic glass that can be obtained from a limited number of sources in the eastern Mediterranean) are often recovered from early Neolithic sites in the Near East. One source of this obsidian is located in south central Turkey, near the important early Neolithic site of Çatal Höyük. As detailed in the Case Study box, the excavation of this important Neolithic site has also shed new light on the importance of ritual and religion in early farming societies.

The archaeological evidence from Çatal Höyük demonstrates that this Neolithic settlement was home to perhaps 10,000 people who were engaged in agriculture, animal keeping, hunting and gathering, trade, religious ritual, and a variety of craft activities. The site, however, is more of an overgrown village than a true town or city. The basic social units appear to be extended families grouped into clusters of four to five houses. There is no clear evidence for full-time craft specialists at Çatal Höyük. Craft activities, such as obsidian working, were carried out by individual households (Balter 1998).

As we shall see in Part 4, craft production, trade, and religion came to play increasingly important roles in later urban societies in the Old World and the Americas. The appearance of full-time craft specialists, who are not engaged in agriculture and other subsistence pursuits, is one of the hallmarks of truly urban societies.

CONCLUSION

While archaeologists have often focused on the origins of farming communities, the results of the adoption of agriculture are equally important. The consequences of the adoption of agriculture included increased disease load and poorer health, population growth, and the resulting expansion of agricultural communities outside the initial centers of plant and animal domestication. This expansion took place relatively rapidly. In approximately three millennia, Europe was transformed from a land of hunters and gatherers to a continent populated by farmers and stockkeepers.

KEY TERMS

'Ain Ghazal   253

Brześć Kujawski   256

Burnished   261

Çatal Höyük   262

Çayönü   254

Glaze   261

Gritille   254

Jericho   251

Karanovo   255

Linearbandkeramik or LBK (Linear Pottery Culture)   256

Loess belt   255

Nea Nikomedeia   254

Pre-Pottery Neolithic A (PPNA)   251

Pre-Pottery Neolithic B (PPNB)   252

Slip   261

Temper   260

QUESTIONS FOR DISCUSSION

1. Since agriculture appears to have led to higher incidence of disease, why did agriculture eventually replace hunting and gathering in the Near East and Europe?

2. What roles did ritual and religion play in early Neolithic societies?

3. What are the technological consequences of the agricultural revolution?

FURTHER READING

Bogucki, Peter, and Pam J. Crabtree
  2004   *Ancient Europe 8000 B.C.–A.D. 1000: Encyclopedia of the Barbarian World*. New York: Charles Scribner's Sons.
  This two-volume work surveys European prehistory from the Mesolithic through the Viking Period. Part 2 provides a detailed survey of the transition to agriculture in Europe, and Part 3 outlines the consequences of agriculture in Europe.

Kuijt, Ian, and A. Nigel Goring-Morris
  2002   Foraging, Farming, and Social Complexity in the Pre-Pottery Neolithic of the Southern Levant: A Review and Synthesis. *Journal of World Prehistory* 16 (4): 361–440.
  A comprehensive overview of the Pre-Pottery Neolithic, including evidence for settlement patterns, architecture and site structure, ritual, and economy.

PART 4

HOW AND WHY DID CITIES AND STATES DEVELOP?

Part 4 focuses on the development of complex societies in both the Eastern and Western Hemispheres. Complex societies are characterized by marked social, political, and economic inequality and by social and economic differentiation. In complex societies many people are engaged in activities other than food production, so the agricultural systems must be sufficiently productive to support nonfarm workers such as craftspeople, scribes, priests, and merchants. Chapter 19 reviews a number of the basic models for the evolution of complex societies, examining such factors as trade, irrigation, religion, and social change. Particular emphasis is placed on the origins and growth of cities and the formation of states. The chapter focuses on the emergence of complex societies in Mesopotamia, a region that was intensively studied by archaeologists throughout the twentieth century. Subsequent chapters outline the development of cities and states in other regions of the Old World, including the Indus Valley, Egypt, sub-Saharan Africa, and later prehistoric Europe.

We begin our study of the origins of New World urbanism and state formation in Mesoamerica (Chapter 24), where complex societies developed in several different geographical regions. Chapter 25 reviews the archaeological evidence for urbanism and state formation in Peru. At the time of the Spanish conquest in 1532, the Inca Empire was the largest empire in the Americas. We trace the roots of Inca imperialism beginning with the early farming societies that were established in the coastal regions of Peru by about 3000 B.C. We conclude our survey of complex societies in the Americas with an examination of the emergence

266

of social complexity in eastern North America and the American Southwest. (The origins of agriculture in the American Southwest will also be covered in Chapter 26.)

The concluding chapter explores the future of archaeological research, including the destruction of archaeological sites through looting, development, and warfare. We consider the role that the Native American Graves Protection and Repatriation Act (NAGPRA) will have on the future of archaeology in the United States.

TIMELINE

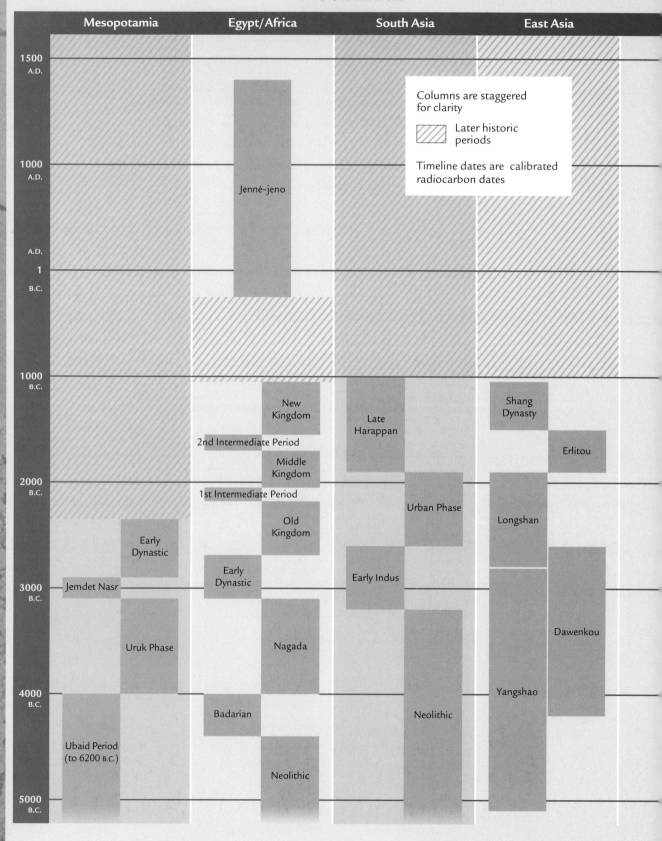

	Mesopotamia	Egypt/Africa	South Asia	East Asia

Columns are staggered for clarity

Later historic periods

Timeline dates are calibrated radiocarbon dates

1500 A.D.

1000 A.D.

A.D. 1
B.C.

1000 B.C.

2000 B.C.

3000 B.C.

4000 B.C.

5000 B.C.

Jenné-jeno

New Kingdom

2nd Intermediate Period

Middle Kingdom

1st Intermediate Period

Old Kingdom

Early Dynastic

Early Dynastic

Jemdet Nasr

Uruk Phase

Nagada

Badarian

Ubaid Period (to 6200 B.C.)

Neolithic

Late Harappan

Urban Phase

Early Indus

Neolithic

Shang Dynasty

Erlitou

Longshan

Dawenkou

Yangshao

Europe	Mesoamerica	Peru	North America
	(Maya region)		

Europe	Mesoamerica (Maya region)	Peru	North America	
		Late Horizon		1500 A.D.
	Postclassic Period	Late Intermediate Period	Mississippians	
				1000 A.D.
	Classic Period	Middle Horizon		
		Early Intermediate Period	Late Woodland	A.D.
			Middle Woodland	1
				B.C.
Iron Age — La Tène / Hallstatt	Preclassic Period	Early Horizon	Early Woodland	
				1000 B.C.
Bronze Age		Initial Period		
				2000 B.C.
	Archaic	Preceramic	Archaic	
				3000 B.C.
Neolithic	Archaic	Archaic		
				4000 B.C.
				5000 B.C.

19

THE DEVELOPMENT OF CITIES AND STATES

Mesopotamia and the Urban Revolution

In Chapter 18 we examined the effects of the beginnings of agriculture on population growth, health and disease, trade, technology, and the development of ritual life. One of the most important consequences of the beginnings of farming in both the Old World and the Americas was that it laid the foundation for the development of **complex societies** (McGuire 1983). Complex societies are characterized by marked social inequality. In the preceding chapters, we have studied societies that were relatively egalitarian. Most hunter-gatherer and simple agricultural societies are characterized by relatively small differences in social status, political power, and material wealth. It is important to emphasize, however, that no society is completely egalitarian. Differences exist, for example, between the roles of men and women and between the roles of children and adults. In complex societies certain individuals and groups of individuals have differential access to both material and social resources, and the differences in status and wealth between individuals are much greater in complex societies than they are in noncomplex societies. Complex societies, by definition, include both the haves and the have-nots. In addition, complex societies are heterogeneous. Many more social roles exist in complex societies. In simple societies most of the population is engaged in subsistence activities. A small number of other social roles may exist—priest, part-time flint knapper, expert hunter, and the like—but the variations are strictly limited. In more complex societies, substantial portions of the population are engaged in activities other than farming, fishing, and foraging. Complex societies often include specialist potters and metalworkers, full-time priests and priestesses, scribes, tax collectors, and merchants.

THE ORIGIN OF COMPLEX SOCIETIES: THE CONTRIBUTION OF V. GORDON CHILDE

The Australian prehistorian V. Gordon Childe was one of the first archaeologists to recognize the connection between the beginnings of farming and the development of complex societies. Childe recognized that the beginnings of farming, which he termed the Neolithic Revolution, were a necessary precondition for what he termed the Urban Revolution, the sweeping set of social, political, and economic changes that are often associated with the beginning of complex societies. The critical link is that agriculture, which produces a higher yield per hectare than hunting and gathering, can be used to produce a storable surplus of food. This food surplus can then be utilized to support a wide range of nonagricultural activities, including the production of crafts, religious activities, and trade. Increasingly intensified agricultural techniques, such as terracing or irrigation, may be required to support larger numbers of nonagricultural workers. Moreover, individuals or groups who are able to gain control of this agricultural surplus can clearly develop greater access to both material and social resources.

For V. Gordon Childe, the rise of **urbanism,** or the origin and growth of cities, was a critical feature of his Urban Revolution. Cities are more than mere dense concentrations of population. While cities are usually defined as concentrations of more than 5000 persons, the critical feature of cities is that they are home to large numbers of nonsubsistence workers. Farmers in the countryside must somehow supply these nonfarmers with food. Some administrative mechanism or other means must be developed to ensure that the nonfarmers in the city are fed (see, for example, Zeder 1991).

Archaeologists studying the emergence of complex societies have focused on the processes of urban growth. Most early archaeologists chose to excavate cities that yielded the remains of temples, palaces, and elaborate specialized crafts. Until relatively recently less attention was paid to the transformation of the countryside. It is clear, however, that "in the process of city-state formation, the countryside was created as a hinterland of city-states and as a fertile no-man's land to be contested by rival city-states"

(Yoffee 1995: 284). The character of the countryside changed with the beginnings of urbanism. Village farmers became producers and consumers in a more complex urban economy.

THE CHARACTERISTICS OF URBAN SOCIETIES

In 1950 Childe published a set of ten characteristics of the Urban Revolution that could be recognized in the archaeological record. More recently, Charles Redman (1978), an archaeologist who has studied the rise of complex societies in the Near East, reorganized the criteria into five primary and five secondary characteristics. The five primary characteristics are the basic changes to society that resulted from the Urban Revolution; the secondary characteristics are the effects of those social changes that can be seen in the archaeological record (Table 19.1). While several of Childe's criteria focus on the technological innovations that accompanied the urban revolution, it is important to note that not all the consequences of the urban revolution were necessarily positive. The class stratification that accompanied the rise of urbanism led to marked differences in social status, political power, and material wealth between a small elite class and the mass of commoners. Some feminist anthropologists have even suggested that the rise of the state led to increasing subjugation of women by men (see, for example, Gailey 1987).

When we examine the five primary characteristics in detail, we can see important links between them. For example, cities are usually the home of large numbers of full-time craft specialists. The surplus food that is produced in the countryside must be mobilized and concentrated to support these nonagricultural workers. If certain groups of individuals regularly have greater access to social and material resources, such as surplus food and craft products, this difference in access may lead over time to the formation of a class-stratified society.

The fifth characteristic identified by Childe and Redman is the appearance of a form of political organization known as the **state.** State societies have been defined in several different ways. State societies have permanent government institutions that

TABLE 19.1   Childe's Ten Characteristics of Urban Civilization, as Reorganized by Redman 1978

Primary Characteristics	
1. Increased size and density of cities	Larger population requiring broader social integration
2. Full-time specialization of labor	Institutionalized labor specialization, distribution, and exchange
3. Concentration of surplus, termed the *social surplus*	Institutional control of surplus food and craft products
4. Class-structured society	Privileged religious, military, and political leaders
5. State organization	Political membership based on place of residence rather than kinship affiliations; permanent government institutions

Secondary Characteristics	
1. Monumental public works	Temples, palaces, storehouses, and irrigation systems
2. Long-distance trade	Organized exchange beyond the confines of the city or region
3. Standardized, monumental artwork	Art for enjoyment and social identification
4. Writing	Facilitates organization and management
5. Arithmetic, geometry, and astronomy	Beginnings of exact science and engineering

Source: Based on Redman 1978: 218.

outlast individual rulers or leaders. In American society the institution of the presidency outlasts the term of office of any particular president. The institutions and machinery of the U.S. government—the IRS, the Bureau of the Census, the National Park Service, and the Department of State—remain in place regardless of who occupies the White House. In addition, states control particular territories and have the ability to defend those territories, if necessary, by military force. As complex societies develop, state institutions may take over many of the functions that kinship ties play in simpler societies. One of these important functions is defense and security; as a result, states usually monopolize military force, controlling the army and the police.

State institutions are clearly linked to other aspects of early urban societies. Government officials, such as soldiers, scribes, and bureaucrats, are often full-time specialists who must be supported by the surplus food produced in the countryside. Rulers and administrators clearly have increased access to social and material resources; they may develop into a distinct ruling class.

It is important to note that Childe saw the political, social, and economic changes associated with the Urban Revolution as truly revolutionary. He modeled his Urban Revolution on the Industrial Revolution of the nineteenth century, when changes in technology, such as the development of the steam engine, led to profound and rapid changes in almost every other aspect of nineteenth-century life. Today, we recognize that social change can be evolutionary as well as revolutionary. Childe's Urban Revolution may well have taken centuries or even millennia. Moreover, modern and ancient human societies are highly varied. While urban, state-level societies are certainly complex societies, some societies that exhibit social and economic inequality and some degree of heterogeneity lack cities and state institutions. An example of a nonstate, nonurban complex society would be Ireland at the time of St. Patrick, approximately 1500 years ago. Early Christian Ireland was certainly a class-stratified society. Wealthy chiefs, nobles, and landowners constituted the highest levels of society; at the bottom were poor farmers and even slaves. In between the social extremes were poets and men and women of arts, craftworkers in metal, and, of course, priests. The Ireland of St. Patrick's day, however, lacked cities (or even towns) and permanent governmental institutions. Irish chiefs governed more by their personal charisma and leadership abilities than by the machinery of government. Archaeologists have often used the term **chiefdom** to describe complex societies that lack urbanism and the institutions of the state.

CONTEMPORARY THEORETICAL APPROACHES TO THE STUDY OF COMPLEX SOCIETIES

A number of important changes have taken place in the study of the origins and development of complex societies since the 1970s. These changes mirror broader changes in archaeological theory. Many processual archaeologists of the 1960s and 1970s viewed complex societies as integrated decision-making systems that were well adapted to their environments, while postprocessual archaeologists have seen these societies as more heterogeneous and competitive (Stein 1999: 6). In general, the postprocessual movement (see Chapter 1) in archaeology has encouraged increased interest in issues of race, class, and gender (Delle et al. 2000); in studies of factions within complex societies (Brumfiel 1992); and in the role of individuals in the decision-making process. These new interests have altered the ways archaeologists define and study complex societies.

Archaeologists today are less inclined to see complex societies as hierarchical decision-making systems that benefit both the ruling classes and the governed. Different factions within an urban society may have different goals and values, and several different hierarchical structures may exist within a single complex society. For example, in the European Middle Ages, the Roman Catholic Church had a hierarchy of priests and bishops that was largely separate from the secular ruling families. Some archaeologists have used the term **heterarchy** (Crumley 1995) to describe these multiple competing hierarchies.

Along with this interest in heterarchy has come the realization that decisions are made by individuals, and not societies as a whole. Individual decisions, however, can have profound consequences for an entire society and even an entire region. The recognition of the importance of the individual in prehistory has led to an increased interest in the unique history of each complex society. Thirty years ago, archaeologists tried to identify broad patterns in the emergence of urban societies, and some archaeologists even hoped to develop a set of laws for human behavior, similar to the gas laws in physics. This effort has been largely unsuccessful. Today, archaeologists recognize that each complex society has a unique historical trajectory that results, in part, from the unique decisions made by individual actors who may be members of particular factions or classes. The differences between the rise of cities in Mesopotamia and the growth of urbanism in Mesoamerica (Chapter 24) are as enlightening as the similarities between the two regions.

Since archaeologists of the 1970s were interested in studying cross-cultural processes of urban growth and state formation, many archaeologists focused their attention on a small number of early urban societies—usually Mesopotamia, Egypt, the Indus Valley, China, Mesoamerica, and Peru—where social complexity allegedly developed independently. Less attention was paid to the formation of secondary states, those complex societies that arose later in time or in response to these so-called primary states. Today, most archaeologists recognize that the distinction between primary and secondary states is largely arbitrary. No complex societies anywhere on earth developed in a vacuum; trade and warfare are salient features of all complex societies. This interest in interaction between emerging complex societies has led archaeologists increasingly to adopt a regional or multiregional perspective (see, for example, Stein 1999) and to focus on the ways in which different polities interacted with one another.

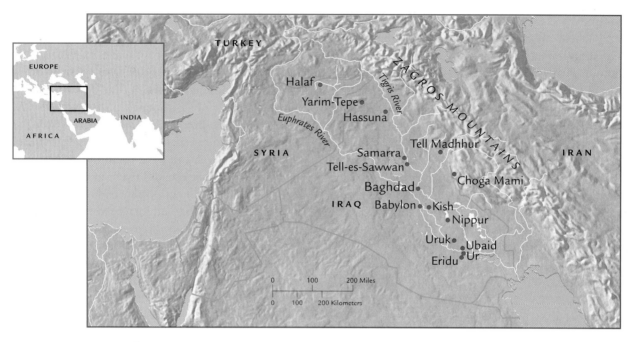

FIGURE 19.1 Map of Mesopotamia showing the sites discussed in this chapter.

Finally, the interest in history has led archaeologists to make use of a broader range of data in the study of urban origins and state formation. Archaeologists have moved beyond the study of basic archaeological data—artifacts, ecofacts, features, and sites—to the study of past landscapes. In addition, archaeologists have made increasing use of historical sources in their study of social complexity. For example, the deciphering of the Maya script (see Chapter 24) has radically altered our understanding of Classic Maya political organization and kingship. The integration of archaeological and historic sources can provide a more well-rounded picture of the ways ancient societies functioned and changed through time.

THE EVOLUTION OF COMPLEX SOCIETIES IN MESOPOTAMIA

We have chosen to begin our story in **Mesopotamia,** the alluvial lowland lying between the Tigris and Euphrates Rivers in what today is Iraq (Figure 19.1). Childe was particularly interested in Mesopotamia because that region is home to the world's oldest urban societies, beginning with the Sumerians some

5000 years ago. In Chapter 16 we saw that villages practicing mixed farming, including both cereal agriculture and livestock husbandry, were established in the Middle East by about 8000 B.C. (Aurenche et al. 2001).

What led these descendants of modest farming communities such as Jarmo to the radical changes in social organization that in a few thousand years would create the great urban societies of the ancient world? Scholars have advanced a number of hypotheses to account for the rise of complex societies, each of which may tell some portion of the story. It is clear, however, that the beginning of complex or urban society in Mesopotamia followed the movement of farmers from the rain-watered hilly flanks down onto the dry Tigris-Euphrates floodplain.

To the north and east of the Tigris River, the land rises up to form the foothills of the Zagros Mountains. This zone, the hilly flanks of the Fertile Crescent, was discussed in Chapters 15 and 16. At elevations of more than 350 m (1100 ft.), sufficient rain falls to permit crops to be grown without irrigation, and it was here that the earliest farming communities in the region were established. The eastern side of the

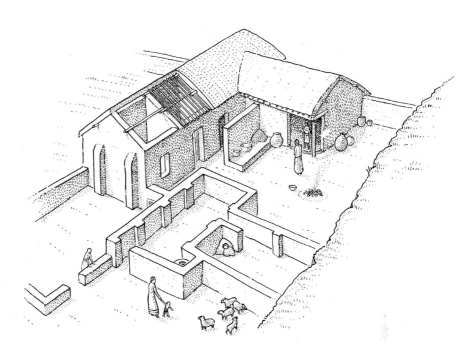

FIGURE 19.2 A typical Hassuna house.

Fertile Crescent, Mesopotamia, is, for the most part, a hot, dry, and barren plain; it could be made fertile only by long, concerted, and organized effort.

Mesopotamia (between rivers) is an ancient name. It refers, literally, to the alluvial lowland lying between the Tigris and Euphrates Rivers. These great rivers arise in the mountains of eastern Turkey and flow roughly parallel southeastward across the entirety of modern Iraq to join finally and empty into the Persian Gulf. In time the name Mesopotamia came to refer to the whole of the Tigris-Euphrates lowland, the setting of the earliest urban societies of the ancient world. The land between the rivers 150 km (93 mi.) or so north of Baghdad is a barren limestone plateau. To the south, however, the rivers have continuously deposited an annual load of silt, creating a vast, flat, potentially fertile plain, ideal for agriculture. Ideal, that is, provided the crops can be supplied with water. No rain falls in southern Mesopotamia during the summer, and temperatures frequently top 40° C (104° F). When the mountain snows melt in the spring, the rivers flood, sometimes dangerously. The floods arrive in May or June, however, too late to water the crops planted in the fall and already harvested in April. Control of the river waters was essential for agriculture to succeed in Mesopotamia.

THE SETTLING OF THE MESOPOTAMIAN LOWLANDS

Shortly after 7000 B.C., village farmers had begun to move into the lowlands of northern Mesopotamia. These settlers are known as the **Hassuna culture** (ca. 6900–6500 B.C.), after the type site of **Hassuna,** near Mosul in northwestern Iraq; the culture is better known, however, from the nearby site of **Yarim Tepe.** The Hassuna region, in the foothills of the Zagros Mountains, receives 300 to 400 ml (12 to 16 in.) of rain annually, so agriculture without irrigation was possible (Maisels 1993: 113). At Yarim Tepe the farmers raised einkorn, emmer, and bread wheats; spelt wheat; barley; lentils; and peas. They obtained most of their meat from domesticated animals, primarily cattle, but also sheep, goats, and pigs. Wild onager (a wild ass), deer, and gazelle were hunted (Maisels 1993: 124).

The Hassuna villages were small settlements with a few hundred inhabitants, differing little from earlier Neolithic farming communities. Still, the Hassuna settlements display, in rudimentary form, many of the features that would typify the archaeology of later Mesopotamian societies. The villagers lived in rectangular houses of several rooms, some with wooden doors, as shown by the pivot sockets in the stone doorsills. Several of the houses were grouped around a courtyard (Figure 19.2). A few circular structures of uncertain function also occur. Coarse pottery bins, probably for grain storage, were sunk into the floor, and some of the rooms contained bread ovens. The walls were built of clay slabs, plastered on both sides, with floors of tamped earth. On the exterior the walls were buttressed. Perhaps originally used to strengthen clay walls, increasingly complex buttressing and niche patterns would continue to become dominant architectural features of the Sumerian temple.

Pottery first appears in Mesopotamia around 7000 B.C. (Aurenche et al. 2001). From Hassuna times onward, pottery styles became increasingly standardized and geographically widespread. Pottery typology, therefore, has become one of the principal tools of the Mesopotamian archaeologist. Pottery styles are used to identify specific archaeological cultures and phases and to establish cultural and temporal relationships between archaeological sites and regions. Hassuna pottery includes well-made, well-fired bowls and straight-necked globular jugs decorated with incised herringbone designs and/or chevrons and triangles in black paint. At the site of Hassuna itself these wares are later joined by other pots, evidently imports, known as Samarra pottery— finely made jars and bowls, covered with a fine slip (a watery clay coating) and painted with basketry-like patterns and sometimes stylized animal figures (Figure 19.3).

It was the people of the **Samarran culture** who first became established in the Mesopotamian lowlands proper. The Samarran is best known from the site of **Tell-es-Sawwan,** on the banks of the Tigris about 100 km (62 mi.) northwest of Baghdad, near the type site of **Samarra.** The two earliest levels of Tell-es-Sawwan, first settled about 6300 B.C., resemble Hassuna, both in the pottery types found and in the form of the externally buttressed, multiroomed, rectangular dwellings. The houses are much larger, however, with up to 15 rooms. The next level, however, Level III (ca. 6100–5900 B.C.), is markedly different. Hassuna pottery is joined by typical Samarran wares. (Hassuna wares are eventually completely displaced by Samarra pottery in the upper levels of the site.) The architecture changed considerably, to become a group of separate, multiroomed dwellings, most having a T-shaped layout,

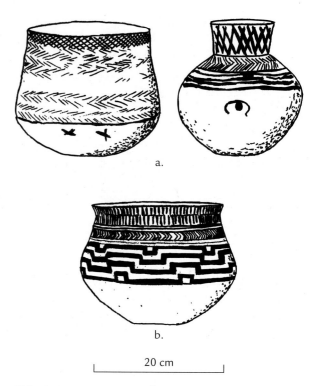

FIGURE 19.3 Pottery style: a. Hassuna and b. Samarra pottery. Source: After Childe (1957, Plates XIV and XVIa).

which reappears at many later Mesopotamian sites. The settlement faces the Tigris on one side and is enclosed on the other three sides by a mud-brick wall. Outside the wall a ditch 3 m (10 ft.) deep was cut into the rock. The presence of these clearly defensive structures implies that the people of Tell-es-Sawwan were threatened by outsiders, possibly raiders attracted to the village's growing wealth in grain and livestock.

The people of Tell-es-Sawwan grew wheats and barley and raised sheep, goats, and cattle. They hunted deer, gazelle, boar, and onager and took large fish from the river. The precipitation in the region would have been too low to permit agriculture based on rainfall, but the proximity of the river made farming possible:

Most probably agriculture was conducted on the basis of the seasonal flood of the river, spill pools were exploited, run-off checked in favourable spots by primitive damming—and generally the activities which we may visualize as the forerunners of full-fledged canal irrigation. (Helbaek 1965: 47)

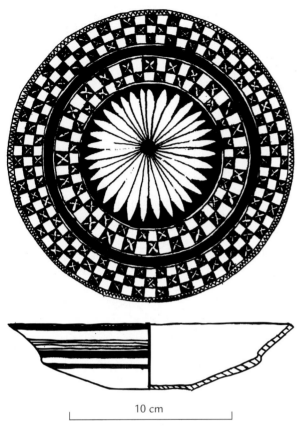

FIGURE 19.5 Figurine of woman with "coffee-bean eyes" from Choga Mami, similar to those found in the Ubaid period.

FIGURE 19.4 Interior and profile of a Halafian bowl. Source: After Childe (1957, Plate XVIa).

In the northern uplands, the Hassuna and Samarra cultures are succeeded by another group of people, the **Halafians** (6500–5500 B.C.), noted for their exceptionally attractive, finely made pottery, with complex red and black painted geometric patterns, sometimes combined with stylized animals (Figure 19.4). Halafian ceramics are found over a wide area, suggesting an extensive trade network. In the southern lowlands, though, the Samarran culture seems to lead directly to the culture generally recognized as the earliest manifestation of the later Mesopotamian urban societies: the **Ubaid** culture (ca. 6200–4000 B.C.). Evidence for this continuity can be seen in the mound of **Choga Mami,** where several transitional levels, with pottery forms of intermediate style, separate the lower Samarran and the upper Ubaid levels at the site. Equally important, the Samarran levels at Choga Mami have produced

a series of terracotta figures, mostly of women, that stylistically resemble the cult figurines of the Ubaid period (particularly in the feature of "coffee-bean eyes") (Figure 19.5). These figurines may represent the predecessors of the classic Mesopotamian goddesses (Maisels 1993: 149).

THE UBAID PERIOD

By about 6000 B.C., the southernmost extent of the Tigris-Euphrates floodplain had been settled by farmers. This early cultural phase is named after the small village site of Al Ubaid, where it was first described, but settlements belonging to the Ubaid phase have been found in the lowest levels of the tell sites of many Sumerian cities, notably Ur, Uruk, and Eridu (see Figure 19.1). Earlier generations of Mesopotamian archaeologists tended to concentrate on the monumental structures (primarily temples) in these city-mounds, but some newer excavations

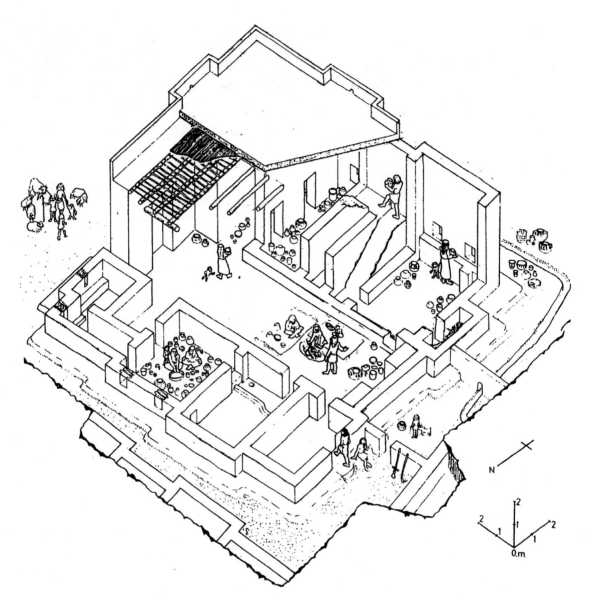

FIGURE 19.6 Reconstruction of a house at Tell Madhhur.

have provided more insight into the broader society.

An exceptionally well-preserved example of a late Ubaid dwelling has recently been excavated at **Tell Madhhur,** near the Diyala River north of Baghdad (Figure 19.6). The 14 by 14-m (46-ft. by 46-ft.) mud-brick structure was built around a T-shaped central hall, with rows of flanking rooms on either side. The structure had been burned, leaving many of its contents inside. These objects— including many pots, quantities of carbonized barley, mullers and grindstones for grinding flour, and clay

spindle whorls for making thread—attest to the domestic life of the period. Animal figurines were also found, along with thousands of clay sling bullets (Maisels 1993: 158). Maisels (1993) has argued that such a large, complex structure was not the dwelling of a single nuclear family, but, rather, housed an extended family group, including servants.

Eridu, near Al Ubaid, far to the south in Mesopotamia, was believed by the Sumerians to be the first city in the world, a belief that, for Mesopotamia at least, archaeology has not refuted. Eridu lies in an area of environmental extremes,

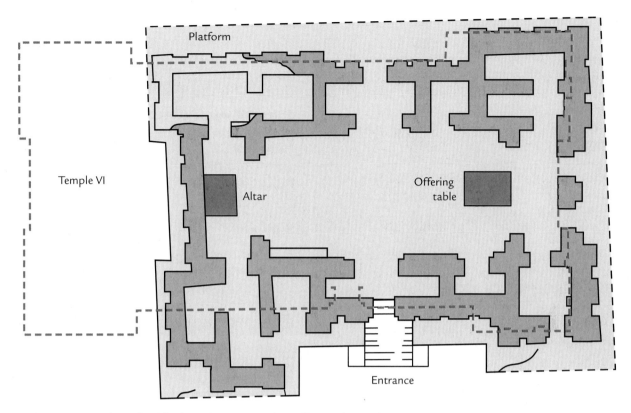

FIGURE 19.7   Plan of Eridu Temple VII. Temple VI lies underneath.

"a quagmire during the winter and a furnace during the summer" (Mallowan 1967: Part I, 7). Still, in ancient times nearby lakes would have provided the inhabitants with abundant fresh water (and plentiful fish for their diet). This mixed environment is reflected in the earliest houses, some of which are mud-brick structures while others seem to have been huts made from reeds plastered with clay. Even in modern times, the Arab inhabitants of the marshlands near the Persian Gulf built dwellings made from reeds.

Sun-dried mud brick, on the other hand, soon became the prevalent Mesopotamian building material. Stable enough in the dry Mesopotamian climate and an effective insulator against the searing heat, mud brick is still in use today in the remote villages of the region. In ancient times very little else was available. Other than potentially rich soil, the Mesopotamian plain offered practically nothing in the way of resources. Wood, for building or for firing brick, was nonexistent, and what was used had to be imported from far away. The same was true for building stone and metal ores. Still, by the

end of the Ubaid period, Eridu had grown to more than 8 ha (20 ac.) and may have had a population of 4000 to 5000. The inhabitants were buried in an adjacent cemetery, each interred with a cup and a plate (surely a food offering) within mud-brick coffins. Two individuals were buried with their pets—Saluki-like dogs (Mallowan 1967: Part I, 23).

During this transitional time, Eridu grew from a village to a sizable town. Although the growth of the residential and craft areas of Eridu has received relatively little attention, they must have expanded greatly to support the construction of the increasingly impressive temples (Lloyd 1984). Within the mound of Eridu, the excavators uncovered a long series of superimposed temples from the Ubaid phase, beginning with a simple chapel at the base. By 3500 B.C. the temple had become a monumental mud-brick structure, marked by altars and offering tables and characterized by externally buttressed walls and a tripartite layout—a large central hall flanked by two rows of smaller chambers (Figure 19.7). The tripartite plan of the temples appears to have its antecedents in the large domestic dwellings of the Ubaid period, such as the buildings discovered at Tell Madhhur.

Similar temple sequences, along with settlement growth, occurred at **Uruk** (biblical Erech), Ur, and other sites. The Ubaid culture spread throughout Mesopotamia, displacing the Halafian culture in the north. During the Ubaid phase, however, settlements remained near the rivers and natural water sources; irrigation systems were still relatively simple. Further expansion of settlements would depend on the development of far-reaching and elaborate systems for the distribution and control of the rivers' waters.

THE EMERGENCE OF CITIES

The changes that brought about the rise of **Sumer,** Mesopotamia's earliest urban society, took place in a span of about a millennium, beginning with the end of the Ubaid phase at 4000 B.C. This period is known as the **proto-literate period.** The first Sumerian dynasties would appear in 2900 B.C. The earlier portion of this timespan is known as the **Uruk phase** (4000 to 3100 B.C.); the succeeding **Jemdat Nasr period** (3100 to 2900 B.C.) was essentially similar, showing continued development from the Uruk phase.

During this time many of the technologies that were to make complex, urban societies possible first appeared. A light, ox-drawn plow seems to have been invented during the fourth millennium B.C., enabling the farmers to till the Mesopotamian silts on a much larger scale. The wheel came into use. Wheeled carts pulled by draft animals would have facilitated the long-distance transport of materials and commodities. The invention of the potter's wheel led to the mass production of pottery. The working of metals became increasingly important. Metals were used not only for utilitarian objects and weapons but also for the manufacture of luxury goods and jewelry, symbols of status and wealth. Metal objects (copper ore fragments, a copper ring and bead, and a lead bracelet) appear in Yarim Tepe as early as the Hassuna period (ca. 6500 B.C.), but metallurgy and metalworking, including the working of silver and gold, advanced greatly during the Uruk and Jemdat Nasr periods.

FIGURE 19.8   Typical cuneiform tablet.

Metal ores (along with precious and semiprecious stones, building stone, and wood) had to be imported from far away, implying the development of organized prospecting expeditions and trade networks.

The earliest written records appeared toward the end of the Uruk period. These consisted at first of pictorial representations impressed into clay with a stylus. The clay tablet was then dried to create a permanent record. Gradually, these pictures, or **pictographs,** evolved into **cuneiform** writing, made up of wedge-shaped symbols pressed into clay, each symbol representing a spoken syllable (Figure 19.8). The earliest tablets were accounting documents—records of transactions and lists of commodities, including land, grain, and livestock. Literature and poetry would come later. Another characteristic Mesopotamian artifact, the **cylinder seal**—a smooth stone cylinder carved with intricate scenes, often including humans and animals—became widespread in the Uruk period (Figure 19.9). These seals produced a unique mark of authorship or ownership when rolled over the wet clay of a tablet or the clay seal of a vessel. Thousands of such sealings have been found, attesting to a well-developed concept of property rights.

FIGURE 19.9 Clay impression produced from a typical cylinder seal.

During the Uruk phase, Eridu, Ur, and Uruk, along with Nippur and Kish (see Figure 19.1), expanded in size to become cities. Uruk was by far the largest settlement (Figure 19.10). By the end of the period, Uruk had grown to an area of about 100 ha (250 ac.); such a large settlement must have been supported by the produce of an extensive region of surrounding countryside, watered by an effective system of irrigation canals. To the east, in what is modern Iran, other cities also developed to become Elam, an ancient complex society about which much less is known, because their early writing has not yet been deciphered. Alongside the cities many other much smaller sites of the period have been found in southern Mesopotamia. They lay, for the most part, along the banks of now dry channels of the Euphrates that in Uruk times meandered through much of the Mesopotamian plain (Figure 19.11). (See Archaeology in Practice, this chapter, for a discussion of the use of remote sensing techniques in the reconstruction of ancient landscapes.) How the cities, towns, and villages of Uruk times were related to one another is still a matter of speculation. The larger cities may have been able to call upon the surrounding towns and villages for labor or agricultural produce, but the cities' political control does not seem to have extended beyond their immediate surroundings.

Each of the large cities was dominated by a temple of monumental proportions. A striking example is the so-called Eanna Precinct at Uruk, dating to 3100 B.C. Temple D at Uruk, with a great T-shaped central hall surrounded on all sides by many smaller chambers, measures 80 by 55 m (262 by 180 ft.) (Figure 19.12). Such a large structure implies that the temple priesthood could exercise control over a sizable force of laborers and craftspeople and that a sufficient agricultural surplus was available to support a nonfarming segment of the population. At a somewhat later time, when textual accounts became available, it is evident that the temples were receiving grain, livestock, and other agricultural commodities, as well as labor, from farmers who were essentially tenants of the temple. These goods were then used to provision workers and craftspeople and to reward favored individuals.

The early Sumerian cities were clearly religious centers, focused on a temple precinct. Surrounding the temples, however, was an increasing population of workers and craft specialists who had their homes and shops within the city. No longer full-time farmers, these people exchanged their wares and services to the temples and secular elites for their livelihood. The cities became production centers where the farmers from the surrounding

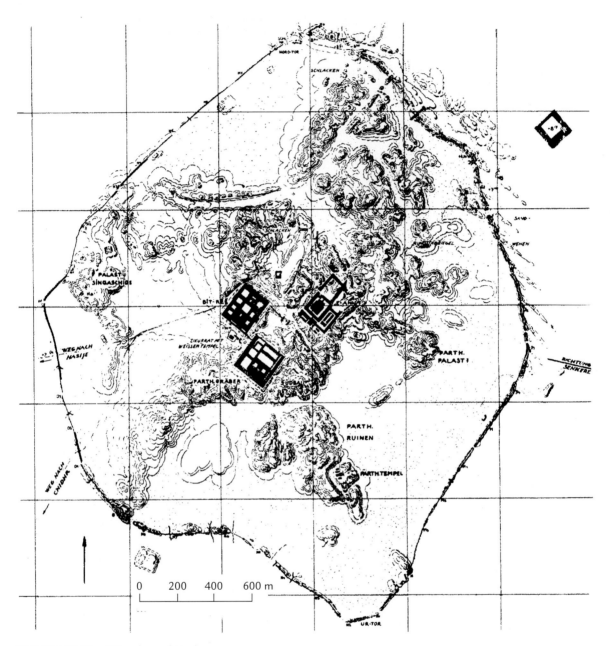

FIGURE 19.10   City plan of Uruk.

countryside could obtain everyday items, such as pottery, and, for those who could afford them, luxury goods brought by traders from far away. The typical Sumerian city is surrounded by a massive defensive wall; in times of stress (perhaps occasioned by a bad agricultural season), the nearby farmers may have moved into the cities for protec- tion from the raids of marauding nomads or the military adventures of other neighboring cities. It remains an open question whether the early cities grew because the inhabitants were drawn there by the opportunities the cities offered or because they were forced into the cities by the dangers of the countryside.

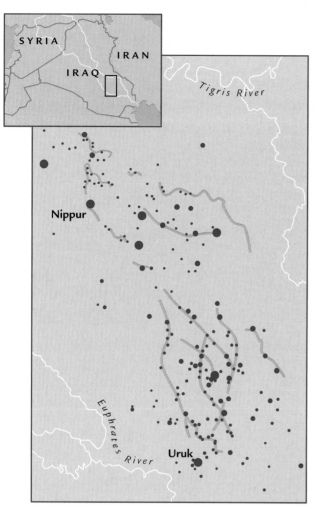

FIGURE 19.11 Early and Middle Uruk settlement patterns. Settlements cluster along water channels, shown as shaded lines. Source: Adapted from Adams 1981, Fig. 12.

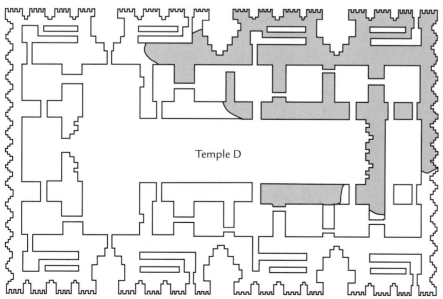

FIGURE 19.12 Temple D at Uruk (Warka).

ARCHAEOLOGY IN PRACTICE

Remote Sensing and Landscape Reconstruction in Archaeology

Robert McC. Adams (1981), in researching his classic study of the Mesopotamian flood plain, depended on aerial photography to trace the ancient water courses and landscape features. Aerial photography is one form of **remote sensing**, a series of nondestructive techniques for recovering geographical, geological, ecological, and archaeological data from a distance (El-Baz 1997).

The remote sensing techniques available to Adams at the time of his study were relatively limited compared to those available today. He worked with low-altitude aerial photographs that he physically taped together into mosaics so that watercourses could be traced. Adams had to employ much effort and ingenuity to correlate the site locations he identified on the ground with the features seen in the aerial photographs (Adams 1981: 28).

Today, many more remote sensing options are available. Conventional aerial photography is joined by widely available, high-resolution satellite imagery, in both visible and infrared portions of the spectrum. Computer correction and enhancement techniques can be used to fit images to exact geographic coordinates and to make subtle features visible. Infrared images can be processed to indicate subtle variations in surface temperature, which in turn can indicate natural features such as wooded areas or archaeological features such as roadways. A newer technology, thermal infrared multispectral scanning (TIMS), can now provide very high-resolution thermal images of the earth's surface that can reveal

FIGURE 19.A TIMS image of strikingly linear prehistoric roadways at Chaco Canyon, NM (see Chapter 26).

THE BEGINNING OF HISTORY

Uruk and Jemdat Nasr times are sometimes referred to as the proto-literate period. Later, the Sumerians would populate these times with a series of heroes and rulers they would call the kings before the flood. Indeed, the Sumerian cities of Shuruppak and Kish both contain deposits of flood silts overlying the Jemdat Nasr deposits. The Sumerian myth of the deluge (from which the biblical story of the Great Flood was derived) clearly recalls an actual event, a localized natural catastrophe, but one that encompassed much of the Sumerian world.

The succeeding period, the **Early Dynastic** (beginning ca. 2900 B.C.), brings the beginning of the historical record. A crucial historical document, the King List, records the names of the rulers of the cities of Sumer (Figure 19.13). The names of some of these kings also appear on inscriptions found in Early Dynastic sites; at Al Ubaid, for instance,

a foundation stone of a temple was inscribed with the name of Mesannipadda, first king of the first dynasty of Ur. Gilgamesh, the Sumerian epic hero, is based on an actual king of Uruk, where his name has been found in the Early Dynastic deposits.

The social world of Early Dynastic times was radically different from the simple, largely egalitarian society of the Neolithic. Full-time craft specialists, such as potters and metalworkers, depended on farmers for their sustenance. Specialist traders profited from the export of Mesopotamian produce and the import of raw materials and luxury goods. Elite groups developed, first among the priesthood and later as secular leaders, who could monopolize an increasing proportion of the wealth and power in the community. Many of the population were servants or tenants of the elites. Some less fortunate individuals were reduced to slavery.

small-scale archaeological features such as walls and ditches (Figure 19.A). Another airborne and satellite instrument coming into use is synthetic aperture radar (SAR), which, under proper conditions, can penetrate the surface and reveal buried features such as watercourses and roadways (Figure 19.B). Lidar, an airborne laser measuring instrument, can make profiles of subtle archaeological features.

All these forms of data can now be readily collated and correlated using geographical information system (GIS) software. Archaeological features identified on the ground can be geographically located within a few meters or less through the use of the global positioning system (GPS), a satellite system originally developed for the military.[1] These data can also be entered easily into a GIS database.

These techniques are a far cry from the methods used by Adams. The politics of the Middle East

FIGURE 19.B Synthetic Aperture Radar SAR image of Angkor Wat temple in Cambodia (12th century A.D.). The Kalipura Mound had not previously been recognized and was found to contain undiscovered temple remains. Courtesy: NASA/JPL-Caltech.

have prevented their full application in Mesopotamia, but there is much potential for the future.

[1]Aerial photography was also first developed by the military during World War I and was first used by archaeologists in the 1920s.

FIGURE 19.13 The King List, copied by the Assyrians from an earlier document.

WHAT LED TO THE RISE OF EARLY STATE SOCIETIES?

What forces led to the progressive concentration of power into the hands of certain individuals and groups and eventually to the political unification of much of Mesopotamia? Karl Wittfogel (1957) suggested that the most important factor was the power gained by those individuals and groups who could control the flow of water for irrigation and/or flood control. This idea has been called the hydraulic hypothesis. Survival on the Mesopotamian plain depended on access to water to irrigate the crops; settlements near the head of an irrigation canal could cut off or ration the water flowing to other settlements farther down the canal. Wittfogel

CASE STUDY

The Royal Cemetery of Ur

The excavations of the British archeologist Sir Leonard Woolley at **Ur** during the 1920s have provided us with some spectacular insights into early Sumerian society. By the end of the Early Dynastic period, individual differences in wealth and power had grown enormously. Woolley excavated in a portion of the mound of Ur adjacent to the temples that had served the city first as a rubbish heap, but later became a major burial area. Thousands of overlapping graves were dug into the rubbish, mostly the simple burials of common people but also the tombs and funeral pits of the elite and powerful.

FIGURE 19.C The golden helmet of Mes-kalam-dug.

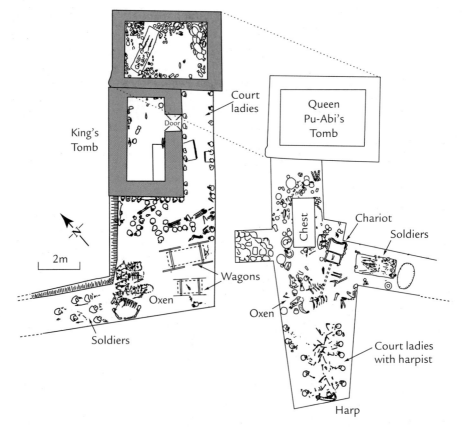

FIGURE 19.D Plan of the royal graves.

FIGURE 19.F Gold and silver vessels from the royal graves.

FIGURE 19.E Harp from the royal graves.

The common people of Early Dynastic Ur were buried in simple coffins, generally with only a cup of liquid pressed to their lips to take them into the next world. Some graves, however, were much richer in offerings than those of the common folk. One in particular stands out. The burial itself was that of a common person—a simple shaft dug into the ground, holding a wooden coffin. Surrounding the coffin, however, was a most remarkable array of offerings. At the head and foot of the coffin were copper-headed spears with golden hafts, stuck blade-down into the ground. Alongside the coffin were copper daggers, some mounted in gold; clay and alabaster vessels; and many copper and silver bowls. Within the coffin were even greater riches:

> The body lay in normal fashion on its right side; round the waist was a broad belt of silver, now decayed, from which hung a gold dagger...; between the hands was placed a bowl of heavy gold, a larger oval

gold bowl lay close by, and near the elbow a gold lamp in the form of a shell, while yet another gold bowl stood behind the head. (Woolley 1965: 58)

Axes of electrum (an alloy of gold and silver) were placed at either shoulder. A mass of golden jewelry—beads, bracelets, and earrings—also lay in the grave. Most striking, though, was the superbly worked golden helmet, still upon the head (Figure 19.C). We know the name of this individual, because three of the golden objects bear the same inscription: "Mes-kalam-dug. Hero of the Good Land" (Woolley 1965: 59).

Yet, for all its splendor, this burial was modest in comparison with the 16 interments Woolley describes as the royal graves. Unlike the simple coffin of Mes-kalam-dug, these personages were buried in stone tombs, sunk deep into the ground, and they did not go alone to their graves. In an elaborate burial ceremony, not only were great material riches interred with the dead but also an entire cadre of servants and soldiers who were sacrificed beside the tomb.

Of these burials the best known is that of Queen Pu-Abi. She was buried in a stone tomb at the base of a great ramped pit dug into the earth. An entire funeral procession followed her down the ramp into the pit. A chariot, inlaid with blue and white and decorated with gold, drawn by two asses, was driven into the pit (Figure 19.D). Following the chariot were ten women, in two rows, elaborately dressed with gold headdresses and beads. A harp-

ist accompanied them (Figure 19.E). A group of soldiers followed behind. All who went into the pit were sacrificed, animals and humans. The bodies of the asses lay beside those of their grooms; the driver of the chariot died within it. The corpse of the harpist lay atop the harp. The bodies of the ten women were found neatly arranged in rows. There is no sign of violence; the excavator concluded that they probably took poison. Although masses of stone, gold, and silver vessels and jewelry and many other wonderful objects accompanied the dead (Figure 19.F), it is the human cost that sets these graves apart. Clearly Queen Pu-Abi, or the elite group to which she belonged, commanded enormous power within the society of Ur, including the absolute power of life or death.

---

argued that the more distant settlements, therefore, could be coerced into a subservient relationship. This, he believed, laid the foundation for the hierarchical associations among communities that would eventually develop into state society.

This model is surely overly simplistic. Other factors could also have given some individuals or groups of individuals advantages over their neighbors. Because Mesopotamia was dependent on long-distance trade for many basic resources such as wood, stone, and metals and for luxury goods such as precious stones, traders were in a position to become increasingly wealthy and powerful. Cities that were located where they could control the trade routes had an advantage over others down the road. When certain individuals or groups, such as a temple priesthood or a local ruler, had amassed significantly greater wealth than their neighbors, they could afford to finance trading expeditions that would further enhance their status and wealth, extending their influence and control over increasingly larger territories.

The extension of the city-states' control over the surrounding countryside, as well as rivalries in pursuit of trade, led to competition, bickering, and eventually, warfare among the city-states, as evidenced by the thick defensive wall surrounding the cities. They came into conflict with other early urban societies, such as the neighboring Elamites to the east. The nomadic peoples of the deserts also found the wealth of the cities a tempting target for raiding. The need for defense led to the rise of military leaders. Mes-kalam-dug, whose burial is described in the Case Study, was probably such a leader. Powerful and effective military leaders could bring increasingly larger territories under their control by force of arms. The unification of a broad area of Mesopotamia would ultimately come with the conquests of Sargon of Akkad about 2350 B.C. Sargon was the ruler of the Semitic-speaking Akkadians to the north of Sumer. He was the first, by force of arms, to unite all of Mesopotamia politically, including the Sumerians and Elamites, under a single ruler.

Archaeological research conducted during the past 30 years has shown that single factors, such as irrigation or warfare, are not sufficient to explain the rise of the state. Instead, a number of conditions are necessary for state formation to occur. Johnson and Earle (1987: 270) have argued that two preconditions are necessary for state formation. The first is a high population with a need for a system of administrative integration. The second is the ability to mobilize

ON THE CUTTING EDGE

Archaeology and War in Iraq

The world was shocked, following the United States' 2003 invasion of Iraq, to hear that the Iraq Museum, the repository that held much of the archaeological heritage of ancient Mesopotamia, had been left unguarded and open to the depredations of groups of looters. Newspapers, magazines, and television displayed startling images of emptied display cases and corridors littered with the remains of smashed and scattered artifacts and records. It was feared that the entire contents of the museum had been ransacked. Ultimately, this proved not to be entirely true. The most spectacular of the museum's treasures, it turned out, had been put away elsewhere for safekeeping before the war. Some had indeed been hidden away since before the Iran-Iraq War in the 1980s. Still, the damage to the collection was enormous. While only a few dozen major pieces proved to be missing, thousands of other artifacts of great research value (including many cylinder seals) had been stolen. Some items have since been recovered; many, however, have surely left the country to enter the world's illicit antiquities market.

The international trade in Iraq's antiquities is by no means a new phenomenon. Poor Iraqi villagers have mined the thousands of sites that dot the Mesopotamian plain ever since Western visitors provided a market for exotic ancient objects. The Saddam Hussein regime's record for the protection of ancient sites was at best mixed. Ancient sites were guarded, but members of Saddam's government profited from the sale of antiquities. Saddam saw himself as the inheritor of the ancient glory of Mesopotamia. He built himself a palace overlooking the city of Babylon

FIGURE 19.G
U.S. serviceman tour the ancient city of Babylon. The brick architecture in the foreground is mostly the original, but the large structure in the background is Saddam Hussein's reconstruction. It was built upon the original footings, to the dismay of archaeologists. In imitation of Nebuchadnezzar, Saddam had his name imprinted on many of the bricks.
Credit line: U.S. Navy.

and undertook the reconstruction of the ancient city, a reconstruction that caused more harm than good (Figure 19.G).

Following the 2003 American invasion of Iraq, coalition troops were assigned to Babylon to protect the ancient city from looting and further damage. Their good intentions, however, quickly seem to have gone awry. Apparently lacking adequate guidance, military personnel seem to have bulldozed helicopter pads and parking lots into the precious temple ruins and filled sandbags with soil dug from the site. As of this writing, the damage is under investigation.

After the first Gulf War (1990–91), pillaging of the ancient tells and city sites increased enormously.

With the economy in a state of collapse as a result of international sanctions, poor Iraqis were desperate for a source of income, and the Antiquities Department could afford few guards to protect the sites. The corruption of Saddam's regime exacerbated the problem. Since the fall of Saddam in May of 2003, the massive looting and chaos have continued in Iraq, despite international efforts to stem the tide.

sufficient economic resources, through control of trade and/or agricultural surpluses, to support a ruling class and administrative institutions. The second condition is similar to Childe's social surplus.

One of the ways states differ from complex chiefdoms is that states possess complex systems of administrative integration and decision making. Decision-making organizations in state societies are internally specialized and hierarchically structured. Johnson (1973) has suggested that states typically have three-tiered decision-making hierarchies. These complex bureaucracies allow state governments to control populations that may number in the hundreds of thousands or millions, often including significant economic and ethnic diversity.

The growth of state society in Mesopotamia was surely not the result of a single cause. Once certain individuals and groups, however, had gained an advantage in power and wealth, they could invest those resources to further enhance their position. They could finance improvements in architecture, crafts, and technology, and they could promote trade expeditions and military forays. Once initiated, the process of state formation and expansion was a self-sustaining cycle. Like a boulder rolling down a mountainside, the process of urbanization and state formation rapidly gained momentum, changing the nature of human society forever.

Archaeological research conducted throughout the twentieth century has shed light on the urban revolution in southern Mesopotamia. However, much research remains to be done. In particular, Pollack (1999: 223) notes that most archaeological research in Mesopotamia has focused on the lives of the military, religious, and political elites. These higher ranking individuals are also featured in historic texts such as king lists. Much less is known about the day-to-day lives of common people, such as farmers and craft specialists. Since it was the efforts of the common people that made the temples and palaces of Mesopotamia possible, a deeper understanding of their lives should lead to a more balanced understanding of the urban revolution. Unfortunately, the political and military situation in Iraq has curtailed almost all archaeological research.

CONCLUSION

At about 7000 B.C., small farming communities were established in northern Mesopotamia, and within 1000 years farmers had settled the southernmost regions of the Mesopotamian lowlands. During the Ubaid period, some of these small farming communities developed into sizable villages with increasingly elaborate temples. In the following proto-literate period, true cities developed in Mesopotamia along with cuneiform writing and increasingly elaborate systems of long-distance trade. No single factor can explain the rise of cities in Mesopotamia. However, it is clear that the development of simple systems of irrigation for agriculture was a prerequisite for the rise of cities, since the surplus agricultural production was necessary to support craft specialization, long-distance trade, and the construction of monumental architecture such as temples. Ultimately, factors such as the need for defense and the organization of long-distance trade would lead to the concentration of power and wealth in the hands of an elite and the development of a multitiered administrative hierarchy, characteristics of the nascent Mesopotamian states.

KEY TERMS

Chiefdom 273	Proto-literate period 280
Choga Mami 277	Remote sensing 284
Complex societies 270	Samarra 276
Cuneiform 280	Samarran culture 276
Cylinder seal 280	State 271
Early Dynastic 284	Sumer 280
Eridu 278	Tell-es-Sawwan 276
Halafians 277	Tell Madhhur 278
Hassuna 275	Ubaid 277
Hassuna culture 275	Ur 286
Heterarchy 273	Urbanism 271
Jemdat Nasr period 280	Uruk 280
Mesopotamia 274	Uruk phase 280
Pictographs 280	Yarim Tepe 275

QUESTIONS FOR DISCUSSION

1. What can governments, archaeologists, and others do to reduce the illicit trade in looted Mesopotamian artifacts?

2. What factors do you think were most important in the beginnings of urbanism and the rise of complex societies in Mesopotamia?

3. How did the harsh environment of southern Mesopotamia affect the development of complex societies in the region?

FURTHER READING

Pollack, Susan
1999 *Ancient Mesopotamia.* Cambridge: Cambridge University Press.
A comprehensive overview of the rise of complex societies in Mesopotamia from about 5000 to 2100 B.C.

20

THE INDUS AGE: THE ORIGINS OF URBANISM IN SOUTH ASIA

The Indian subcontinent has a long literary and religious tradition. The oldest literature, the Rigveda, appears to have been compiled about 1500 to 1300 B.C. and was passed on orally for many generations. The Rigveda is made up of a series of hymns to gods such as Agni, the fire god, and Indra, the warrior charioteer. Later Vedic texts, probably composed between 1200 and 500 B.C., speak of ancient ruined mounds, of people who have gone away, and of finding pottery sherds in the wilderness along the banks of the Indus River. A scout who was sent on an excursion to the east by Alexander the Great in 326 B.C. described finding an area that included more than 1000 abandoned towns and villages that were deserted after the Indus River changed its course (Parpola 1994: 5).

Archaeological research since the 1920s has begun to shed light on the early urban society on the Indian subcontinent that existed long before the time of the Rigveda. The **Indus Valley, or Harappan, civilization** flourished in northwest India and Pakistan (Figure 20.1) during the third millennium B.C. The great cities of **Mohenjo-daro** and **Harappa** (which gave its name to the Harappan culture) were first investigated in the early 1920s, at a time when the whole Indian subcontinent was part of the British Empire. The excavation of these spectacular sites brought to light another great ancient society, to take its place alongside those in Mesopotamia and Egypt. The term **Indus Age** (Possehl 2002) has been used to describe the societies that existed in South Asia from the origins of farming about 9000 years ago to the beginnings of iron technology in the Vedic Period (about 1000 B.C.).

This chapter will begin with a brief overview of the environmental background of the Indus Valley region of Pakistan and India. This discussion will be followed by a consideration of the beginnings of farming in the Indus Valley area. The chapter will conclude with an extended discussion of the archaeology of the Indus Valley society, including the attempts to decipher its script, and the many elements of the Harappan culture reflected in later cultures and religions of the Indian peninsula.

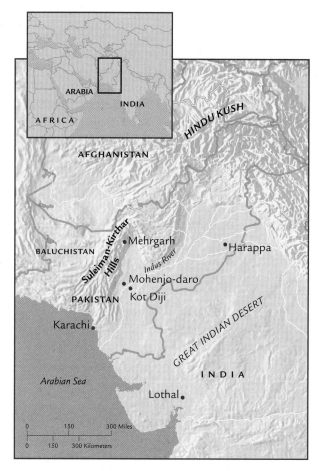

FIGURE 20.1 Map of the Indus Valley region showing the sites discussed in this chapter and the relation of the region to the larger Indian subcontinent.

THE GEOGRAPHY AND ECOLOGY OF THE INDUS VALLEY REGION

The Indian subcontinent includes the modern countries of India, Pakistan, and Bangladesh. This region is separated from the rest of Asia by a series of mountain chains: the Suleiman-Kirthar Hills in the west, the Hindu Kush in the northwest, and the Himalayas to the northeast. The Indus River and its four main tributaries are critical to our understanding of the ecology of the Indus Valley region. These five rivers arise in the Punjab, meaning "five waters," region of northern India. The Indus has twice the flow of the Nile because it receives waters from both the eastern Afghan mountains and the Himalayas (Fairservis 1971: 228). It carries a vast

quantity of alluvial soil and inundates a very wide floodplain. As a result, the Indus region is a very rich environment, but one that faces constant dangers of flooding.

Cereal agriculture in the Indus Valley region depends on the flooding of the river, and many Indus Valley archaeological sites are located along the active floodplain of the river and near the inundation lakes that form as a result of the flooding. The Indus Valley is flooded twice a year. Floods in April result from the melting of the snows in the Himalayas, while those in November and December result from summer monsoonal rains in the Punjab region. Cereals were grown in the Indus regions during the winter months; they were planted after the November–December floods and harvested before the spring flooding in April (Fairservis 1971: 229). The alluvial soils retain moisture quite well, even in the driest areas of Pakistan, facilitating wheat and barley cultivation.

THE BEGINNINGS OF FARMING IN THE INDUS REGION

At the end of the Ice Age, about 10,000 years ago, the Indian subcontinent, like much of the rest of Eurasia, was occupied by small bands of mobile hunter-gatherers. Until recently it had been assumed that farming had spread gradually from the hilly flanks regions of the Middle East into the Indian subcontinent. The earliest known farming villages dated only to the mid-fifth millennium B.C. (Meadow 1993: 295). However, recent archaeological research at the site of **Mehrgarh** in Pakistan (Jarrige and Meadow 1980; Jarrige et al. 1995) has shed new light on the origins of farming in the region.

Mehrgarh is located in the Kachi District of Baluchistan in Pakistan (see Figure 20.1). Although the site is bordered by high mountains to both the east and the west, it is located in an alluvial plain less than 200 m (660 ft.) above sea level. The rich alluvial soils and the perennial Bolan and Nari Rivers would have made this site an attractive area for early farmers. The site may have been initially occupied about 7000 B.C. and was not finally abandoned until the middle of the third millennium B.C.

Conservative dates for the aceramic Neolithic occupation range from 6300 to 5300 B.C. (Meadow 1993: 301).

The Bolan river cut a 12-m (39 ft.) deep section through the cultural deposits and alluvium, revealing the presence of 7 to 8 m (23 to 26 ft.) of aceramic Neolithic deposits. The earliest dwellings are simple, multiroomed buildings of mud brick. The spaces between these buildings were used for domestic purposes and for burials. The earliest inhabitants of Mehrgarh were cereal farmers who grew wheat and barley. There is no evidence to suggest that wheat was initially domesticated at Mehrgarh; wild wheat is not native to the Baluchistan region. It was probably introduced to the Mehrgarh region from the west. The evidence for barley is more problematic. Although wild barley is not native to the Mehrgarh region today, both wild and domesticated barley were recovered from the earliest levels of the Mehrgarh site. Whether this cereal was independently domesticated or introduced from farther west remains an open question. The faunal evidence, however, does suggest that this area may represent an independent center for animal domestication. In the earliest aceramic Neolithic levels, the faunal assemblages are dominated by the remains of wild game, such as gazelle, deer, and blackbuck. However, domestic goats also appear to have been kept by at least some of the early aceramic Neolithic inhabitants of the site. The numbers of domestic cattle, sheep, and goats increase throughout the aceramic Neolithic, and it is likely that cattle and sheep were domesticated from local wild stock at that time (Meadow 1993). The Mehrgarh cattle appear to be zebu (humped cattle), animals that are well adapted to the hot, dry climate of South Asia. These animals continued to play an important role in the Indus Valley economy throughout prehistory and into historic and recent times. The data from Mehrgarh can be used to make "a very strong case for the indigenous process of domestication within the Indian subcontinent" (Possehl 1990: 265). Unfortunately, this important archaeological site is currently threatened by tribal warfare (Ansari 2003).

THE EARLY INDUS PERIOD

The archaeological data from Mehrgarh indicate that village farming communities were established in the Indus Valley region by the midseventh millennium B.C. Archaeologists working in the Indus Valley, as in Mesopotamia, have been interested in how these small agricultural villages developed into a complex urban society. Recent archaeological research, beginning with the work at Mehrgarh, has shown that the complex Indus Valley urban society represents an essentially indigenous development (Parpola 1994). "There is continuity in the prehistoric sequence of northwestern India and Pakistan from the beginnings of the village farming community to the eclipse of the ancient cities of the Indus" (Possehl 1990: 267–268).

The evidence from the later phases of Mehrgarh and elsewhere in South Asia points both to agricultural intensification and to population growth during the ceramic Neolithic periods. Pottery vessels first appear around 5500 B.C. During the fourth millennium B.C. at Mehrgarh, irrigation canals replaced simpler irrigation systems based on stone or earthen dams. In addition, settlements expanded from the Baluchistan area into the marshes and jungles of the Indus Valley proper at that time. The areas around the riverbanks were probably originally heavily wooded, providing habitats for jungle animals such as tigers. Agricultural settlements based on cereal growing and stock rearing appear throughout the Indus plain during the later fourth and early third millennia B.C.

The period between 3200 and 2600 B.C. has been termed the **Early Indus, or Pre-Urban, period.** Settlements from this period show many continuities with early Neolithic communities; however, some changes begin to foreshadow the cultural transformations that mark the appearance of the mature urban Harappan period. During the Early Indus period, most settlement sites remain small, averaging only 5.4 ha (13.3 ac.) (Possehl 1990: 270). There is evidence for increasing trade during this period. An intensive caravan trade that linked the Indus Valley, the Iranian Plateau, and Central Asia peaked around 3000 B.C. (Parpola 1994: 17).

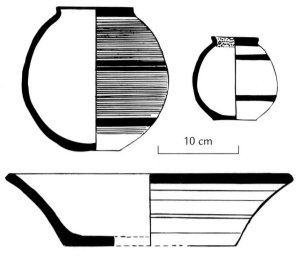

FIGURE 20.2   Kot Dijian pottery.

During the Early Indus period, distinctive local and regional styles of pottery were replaced by a widespread type of ceramics known as Kot Dijian ware. Kot Dijian wares include globular vessels with a wide, black band painted around the neck (Figure 20.2). The uniformity of this ceramic style over a wide area points to increased communications and trade between villages. Standardized brick sizes also appear at this time.

Kot Dijian pottery takes its name from the Early Indus site of **Kot Diji,** located near productive agricultural land along one of the ancient flood channels of the Indus near the Harappan city of Mohenjo-daro (see Case Study). The site of Kot Diji was excavated in the 1950s by the Pakistan Archaeological Service. Excavations revealed houses of stone and mud brick surrounded by a wall of limestone and mud brick. The function of this wall is unclear; it may have served to contain the floodwaters of the Indus. Alternatively, it may have served to keep people or livestock out. The Early Indus occupation at Kot Diji concludes with two huge conflagrations (Allchin and Allchin 1982: 145–146). Similar events have been recorded at the end of the Early Indus period at other Indus Valley sites. It is possible that these fires may represent some form of violent political conquest, since the subsequent layers at Kot Diji are predominantly Harappan in character (Allchin and Allchin 1982: 146), but the fires may also have resulted from more mundane causes.

THE EMERGENCE OF COMPLEX SOCIETIES IN THE INDUS VALLEY

Around 2600 B.C. the Indus Valley region underwent rapid social and cultural changes leading to the appearance of true urbanism in the Indus Valley. The period between 2600 and 2500 B.C. is seen as a period of transition between the Early Indus and the Mature Harappan phases in South Asia. One of the most important changes was in the nature and intensity of trade. The focus of long-distance trade shifted from the overland caravan trade with Central Asia and Iran to a more maritime orientation centering on the Persian Gulf, probably as a result of the adoption of water transport (Parpola 1994: 21–22). In recent years, a number of sites with clear links to the Indus Valley have been discovered on the Arabian peninsula.

In addition to the growth in the volume of trade, significant changes are evident in settlement patterns at that time. While Early Indus sites are generally small and show little differentiation in size, the beginning of the **Mature Harappan, or Urban, phase** (2550 to 1900 B.C.) is marked by the appearance of a small number of very large settlements (Possehl 1990: 271). The larger Indus sites include an acropolis, a high platform of mud brick surrounded by walls, that may have served as an administrative center, and a lower town that included workshops, markets, and living quarters. The upper portions of the towns should not be seen as citadels, however, as they are not designed as fortifications and are not meant to serve as places of refuge in times of war (Possehl 2002: 247). The large Indus sites also include extensive public sewage and drainage systems, designed to carry wastewater away from the settlements (Figure 20.3). These public sanitary systems would have required complex engineering and maintenance (Possehl 1990: 271). Evidence for intentional town planning can be seen at both the larger Indus cities and at the smaller towns. For example, at the Mature Harappan town of **Lothal,**

FIGURE 20.3 Street with drains, from Mohenjo-daro.

located on the coastal flats at the head of the Gulf of Cambay in northwest India, residential quarters are clearly separated from areas of craft production. The archaeological evidence from Lothal and elsewhere points to significant craft specialization in metallurgy, pottery manufacture, stoneworking, and other crafts, implying a degree of occupational differentiation that is not seen in the Early Indus period (Possehl 1990: 272). In addition, Lothal appears to have served as a gateway settlement (Figure 20.4) through which the Harappans gained access to raw materials from the Indian peninsula, including semiprecious stones, ivory, steatite, seashells, and possibly metals (Possehl and Raval 1989: 16).

Other important changes in material culture are apparent at this time. Perhaps the most important is the appearance of a system of writing (see the Archaeology in Practice box). Unlike the Sumerian writing system in Mesopotamia, whose gradual evolution has been traced by archaeologists, the Indus system appears at the beginning of the urban Harappan period without any obvious antecedents. The Harappan script appears to have been an indigenous development, although it may have some relationship with the proto-Elamite script that was used in Iran during the fourth and early third millennia B.C. The use of a standardized system of weights and measures, also adopted at the beginning of the Mature Harappan period, clearly reflects the increasing importance of trade and exchange in Harappan society.

Mature Indus Valley sites are found in a region that covers 1.25 million sq. km (483,000 sq. mi.), about four times the size of southern Mesopotamia. The use of a common script, a uniform system of weights and measures, and a common system of urban planning, as well as the similarities in a broad range of artifact types over such a vast area, are remarkable. These commonalities certainly indicate intensive communication and trade between the Indus Valley cities, towns, and villages, and they may also indicate some form of administrative or political integration within the Indus Valley region. However, the question of whether the whole Indus region was ever politically united is one that cannot be answered on the basis of present archaeological evidence.

FIGURE 20.4   The Harappan port site of Lothal in northwest India, showing the possible loading dock.

Archaeological data do suggest that the beginnings of the Mature, or Urban, phase saw increasing social stratification. The larger Harappan urban sites have provided evidence for houses of varying sizes, ranging from one-room tenements to great houses with several courtyards and several dozen rooms (Allchin and Allchin 1982: 177). The Urban period also is marked by the increased use of luxury goods, including metals, beads, and other items of personal adornment (Possehl 1990: 272). As noted, there is clear evidence for craft specialization and occupational differentiation, indicating that an increasing portion of the population was engaged in activities other than agriculture and animal husbandry. The ability to support a large number of nonfarm workers is a testament to the agricultural productivity of the Indus region.

A striking feature of the Indus Valley cities is the absence of large temples or other monumental architecture of a religious nature. In addition, Harappan cities have provided no clear evidence for palaces. These data suggest that Harappan society may have been organized in a way very differ-ent from that of Sumer or Egypt. It is even possible that the Harappans had no kings (Possehl 1996: 14). The nature of Indus Valley political organization remains largely unknown.

THE POST-URBAN PHASE AND THE HARAPPAN ECLIPSE

Beginning around 1900 B.C., the Indus Valley region underwent significant cultural and economic changes. Those changes mark the beginning of the **Late Harappan, or Post-Urban, phase** of the Harappan civilization (1900 to 1000 B.C.). The most striking of the changes was the abandonment of many of the larger cities, including Mohenjo-daro. At that time, a number of items of material culture disappeared, including stamp seals, certain types of pottery, and the Indus Valley script. Long-distance trade declined, except for trade in metals, and a reduced range of specialized crafts was produced. The uniformity of the Mature Indus material culture was replaced by a cultural mosaic (Possehl and Raval 1989: 25). This transformation can be seen clearly in

ARCHAEOLOGY IN PRACTICE

Deciphering the Indus Valley Script

One of the most enigmatic features of the Indus Valley civilization is its written language. As was noted, writing first appears in the twenty-sixth century B.C. at the beginning of the Mature Urban Harappan phase. The Harappan writing system cannot be derived directly from any other known script (Parpola 1994: 53). Moreover, no bilingual texts including inscriptions in Harappan and a second language are known.

The archaeologists and linguists who have attempted to decipher the Harappan writing system have faced a number of additional challenges and obstacles. Only about 4000 examples of Harappan writing are known, and most are found on stone stamp seals (Figure 20.A), on amulets, and on fragments of pottery. The stamp seals are made on square fragments of soapstone and usually include both an inscription and a picture. Most of the Harappan inscriptions are quite short, averaging only about five or six characters (Fairservis 1983: 58). The longest known inscription includes only 26 signs.

The first challenge faced by scholars attempting to decipher this script is the question of whether

FIGURE 20.A A Harappan stone stamp seal showing an inscription. The character to the right of the animal's horns may indicate the number 3.

FIGURE 20.B Impression of a stamp seal from Mohenjo-daro (M735), showing cramping of the final incised sign.

the characters are read from left to right (as English is) or from right to left (as Hebrew is). One way to determine this is to look for cramping at the end of inscriptions when inscriptions are squeezed to fit into limited spaces (Figure 20.B). A few Harappan inscriptions show cramping along the left margin, suggesting that the script was read from right to left.

A second question facing linguists is the nature of the writing

system itself. Does each character represent a single sound (an alphabetic system like our own), a syllable (a syllabic system), or a word (a logographic system)? The Indus script includes between 400 and 450 signs (Parpola 1994: 85). True logographic systems, such as modern Chinese, include thousands of characters. On the other hand, the Indus script includes far too many characters to represent a purely syllabic language. The Indus script

the changes in settlement and subsistence that mark the end of the Urban phase and the beginnings of the Post-Urban period. The number of sites in the Sind region of Pakistan (the area around Mohenjo-daro) was dramatically reduced, and many of the large urban sites disappeared forever. In the Punjab and northern India, however, archaeology has revealed a rich and varied Post-Urban settlement with

many permanent agricultural communities. The Harappan town of **Rojdi** on the Saurashtra peninsula in northwest India reveals continuity from the Mature Harappan to the Late Harappan period (Figure 20.5). Around 2500 B.C. Harappans from the Sind region of Pakistan moved into Saurashtra, probably to obtain access to raw materials. Towns such as Rojdi were supported by a rich and diverse appears to use some signs to represent words and others to represent syllables. Such systems are termed logosyllabic. Egyptian hieroglyphics and early Sumerian writing are other examples of ancient logosyllabic languages.

A more difficult and fundamental question is the problem of what language is represented by these characters. Is it a member of any known language family? Many scholars have hypothesized that the Harappan language is likely to have belonged to the Dravidian language family (Allchin and Allchin 1982: 213). Twenty-five Dravidian languages are spoken in South Asia today, primarily in southern and southeastern India. The most widespread of these, Tamil, is spoken by 37.7 million individuals. One argument favoring a Dravidian reading for the Harappan script is based on the number system. The Harappan numbers from 1 to 7 are indicated by a series of strokes; a different character is used to represent the number 8 (Figure 20.C). This appears to represent a system with a base of 8 (our numerical system has a base of 10). Linguistic research indicates that the original Dravidian number system probably also had a base of 8. Recently, some scholars have suggested that the Harappan script may be a written form of a language in the proto-Elamo-Dravidian family (Possehl 1996:

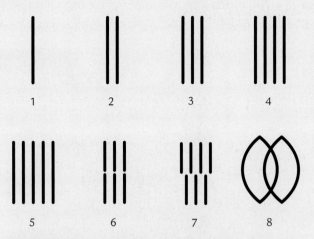

FIGURE 20.C Characters representing the numbers from 1 to 8 in the Harappan script.

165). This family would include both the proto-Elamite languages of Iran and the antecedents to the Dravidian languages of South Asia.

Once these basic questions have been answered, the process of decipherment of the language is almost like solving a crossword puzzle (Parpola 1994: 273). One clue is that many Indus Valley signs appear to be pictures of common objects. For example, one sign seems to resemble a fish. However, this sign appears too frequently in Harappan inscriptions to always mean "fish." Therefore, many hypothetical interpretations are based on the homophone principle: that words that sound alike but have different meanings are likely to be rep-

resented by the same character or characters. For example, in many Dravidian languages, the word for "fish," *min*, also means "star" (Parpola 1994: 181). Similar interpretations have been made of other signs (see, for example, Fairservis 1983).

Clearly, much work remains to be done before the Indus script can be deciphered. However, the results of this labor are likely to shed invaluable light on "Harappan polity, social organization, and ideology" (Fairservis 1983: 66). These aspects of ancient societies are often difficult to reconstruct on the basis of archaeological evidence alone.

agricultural economy, including both summer and winter crops.

While sites such as Rojdi provide clear evidence for continuity between the Mature Harappan and the Late Harappan periods, the evidence from Mohenjo-daro points to significant cultural changes at the end of the Mature Harappan phase. At Mohenjo-daro there is no evidence for a Late

Harappan occupation. In addition, excavations of the final Late Harappan layers at the site have revealed groups of hastily buried corpses or unburied corpses left in the streets, as well as buried hoards of jewelry and copper items. Mortimer Wheeler interpreted these hastily buried bodies and hoards as evidence for an invasion of the Indus Valley by Aryan speakers, people speaking Indo-European

FIGURE 20.5   Rojdi, a town in northwest India that shows continuity from the Mature Harappan to the Late Harappan period.

languages. His interpretation relied heavily on literary records. The earliest Indian literature, the Rigveda, which is written in Sanskrit, an ancient Indo-European language, describes victorious invaders attacking the walled cities of the aboriginal Indian peoples. Wheeler argued that decadent Harappan urbanism was replaced by the heroic barbarism of the early Aryans (Wheeler 1968: 136).

Today, few archaeologists would accept Wheeler's interpretation. The so-called massacre victims from Mohenjo-daro do not appear to have died of traumatic injuries (Kennedy 1982). Moreover, the uppermost levels of Mohenjo-daro provide no evidence for the kind of widespread destruction that could reasonably be associated with a major invasion or military defeat. In fact, by the end of the Mature Harappan period, parts of Mohenjo-daro may have become urban slums. The archaeological evidence points to economic and administrative decline, rather than military invasion.

In general, it has been difficult to identify Indo-European speakers on the basis of archaeological evidence such as pottery and metalwork. It has also been impossible to determine whether the introduction of Indo-European languages into the Indian

subcontinent took place at the end of the Mature Harappan period when sites such as Mohenjo-daro were abandoned. As noted previously, Harappan eclipse was not a uniform phenomenon across the Indus Valley region. Sites such as Harappa in the Punjab and Rojdi in Saurashtra continued to be occupied into the Late Harappan period. A variety of causes have been suggested for the abandonment of sites in the Sind region of southern Pakistan at the end of the Mature Harappan period. Natural causes for the abandonment of Indus Valley sites may have included flooding and changes in river courses. Overirrigation (which can lead to a buildup of salt in the soil), administrative failure, and the decline in long-distance trade may also have played a role in the abandonment of these sites.

THE LEGACY OF THE HARAPPAN CIVILIZATION

Although the Indus Valley civilization ended more than 3000 years ago, elements in Indus Valley culture may have influenced later societies of the Indian subcontinent. Early archaeologists working in South Asia noticed some remarkable similarities

CASE STUDY

Indus Valley Urbanism: Mohenjo-daro and Harappa

Much of our knowledge of the urban period in the Indus region has come as a result of intensive archaeological excavations at two of the largest Indus Valley cities: Mohenjo-daro and Harappa. A large number of archaeological excavations have been carried out at both sites, including extensive excavations by the British archaeologist Sir Mortimer Wheeler in the 1940s (Wheeler 1968). Excavation was resumed at Harappa in 1986 under the direction of the late George Dales, and the project continues under the direction of Richard Meadow of Harvard University and Jonathan M. Kenoyer of the University of Wisconsin. Excavations at Mohenjo-daro and Harappa have shed light on the nature of urban development in the Indus Valley and on the relationship between the cities and the Indus Valley civilization as a whole (Dales 1992: 1).

Harappa is located in the Punjab region of northern Pakistan, adjacent to a dry bed of the Ravi River (one of the five rivers of the Punjab). Stamp seals were discovered at Harappa in the late nineteenth and early twentieth centuries, and archaeological excavations began there in 1920 to 1921 under the direction of the Archaeological Service of India. The site covers an area of at least 150 ha, or 370 ac., (Kenoyer 1992: 33) and may have housed 40,000 people at its height (Parpola 1994: 6). The town included both an acropolis (Mound AB) and a lower town (Figure 20.D). Although the acropolis was termed a "citadel" by Wheeler (1968), the walls surrounding it were not constructed for military defense. As Kenoyer

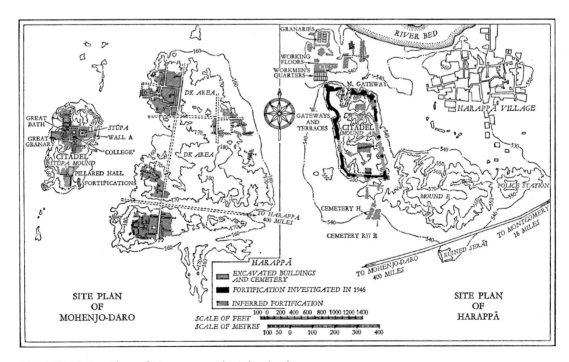

FIGURE 20.D   Plan of Harappa and Mohenjo-daro.

(1998: 56) notes, "The gates and walls of Harappa were never meant to withstand battle, but were more symbolic in nature and intended to control the trade and commerce which was the lifeblood of the city." Recent excavations have revealed the presence of an Early Indus period settlement and continued occupation into the Mature, or Urban, Indus period with no evidence of a break, or hiatus (Kenoyer 1992: 38). Excavations in the Mound E area indicate that the settlement was expanding in the late pre-urban period (Figure 20.E). During that period there is evidence for the laying out of large north–south streets and for the segregation of craft activities and residential areas (Kenoyer 1992: 57).

The beginning of the Urban Period occupation is marked by the use of baked brick, in addition to mud brick, for the construction of houses and other structures. There is evidence for extensive construction in the upper town (Mound AB) at this time; this is followed by significant efforts at urban renewal in the Mound E area. By the latest part of the Harappan period, there is evidence of urban congestion in many areas of the site, possibly resulting from

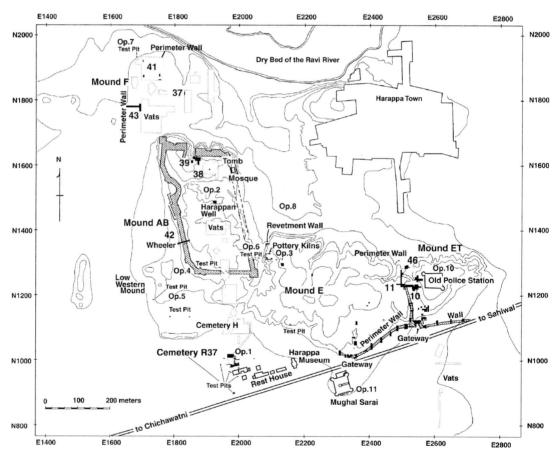

FIGURE 20.E   Map showing the extent of occupation at Harappa during different periods. Periods 1 and 2 are Early Indus, while period 3A corresponds to the early part of the Mature Harappan period.

FIGURE 20.F   The Great Bath at Mohenjo-daro.

overpopulation. For example, brick pavings and drains encroach on through streets, narrowing those thoroughfares. The final phases of occupation at Harappa have been heavily disturbed by brick robbing, and those periods have not been dated by radiocarbon. The available data, however, do not indicate urban decay, military invasions, or the abandonment of the site at the end of the Mature Harappan period (Kenoyer 1992: 56).

The other major Harappan urban center, Mohenjo-daro, is located approximately 670 km (416 mi.) southwest of Harappa in the Indus Valley. Excavations at Mohenjo-daro have revealed a quite similar urban layout (see Figure 20.D). The mounded upper town includes a number of public buildings, the most impressive of which is the Great Bath (Figure 20.F). The bath measures 12 by 7 by 3 m (39 by 23 by 10 ft.) deep and was supplied with water from a well in an adjacent room. Ritual bathing has played an important role in Indian religion throughout history, and it is likely that it also played a role in the rituals of the Indus cities. Evidence for other public buildings

in the upper town includes the foundations of a warehouse that Wheeler (1968: 43) interpreted as a granary and a large block of buildings that may be associated with administrators or priests (Allchin and Allchin 1982: 181–182).

The lower town at Mohenjo-daro may have been home to the Harappan upper classes. However, many of the wealthier houses had small rooms that could have served as dwellings for the lower classes, such as servants (Possehl 2002: 211). In its final phases, Mohenjo-daro included a variety of dwellings ranging from single-roomed tenements to houses with many rooms and courtyards. There is also evidence for substantial craft activity within the lower town, including shops, dyers' vats, and workshops for pottery manufacture, metalworking, and shell bead making. Several buildings in the lower town have been identified as temples, based on their large size or unusual plan (Allchin and Allchin 1982: 180). However, unlike Egypt and Mesopotamia, there is no evidence for a state religion marked by large temples and other public monuments in the Indus region (Possehl 2002: 6).

FIGURE 20.6   Stamp seal from Mohenjo-daro showing a male figure wearing a buffalo-horn headdress.

FIGURE 20.7
Female figurine from Mohenjo-daro.

between Indus Valley images and later Hindu gods. For example, a number of stamp seals (Figure 20.6) show a male figure sitting cross-legged in a low throne, often flanked by wild goats, and surrounded by other jungle creatures. The male figure wears a buffalo-horn headdress, and in some cases a plant sprouts in between the horns. All these features can be found in later descriptions of the Hindu god Siva. Similarly, many Indus Valley sites have produced numerous female figurines (Figure 20.7). These figures, which some scholars have interpreted as mother goddesses, may parallel the cult of Parvati, the spouse of Siva. The Parvati cult described in Indian literature continues to be practiced in India today (Allchin and Allchin 1982: 213–214). In addition to possible continuities in religious practice, the Indus Valley legacy can also be seen in areas of technology, craft production, and agricultural practice. For example, the terracotta model carts that have been recovered from Mohenjo-daro (Figure 20.8) are virtually identical to carts still in use in the upper Sind region of Pakistan today (Allchin 1982: 326).

CONCLUSION

At about 2600 B.C., the first true cities appear in the Indus Valley along with the Indus Valley script, increasing craft specialization, and significant social stratification. The factors that led to the development of Harappan urbanism are unclear, but the shift from overland to sea trade may have played a critical role.

Clearly, much remains to be learned about the ancient Harappans. The decipherment of the Indus Valley script will undoubtedly shed new light on Harappan trade practices, administrative patterns, and even religious ideology. However, even if the Indus script is never fully deciphered, ongoing excavations at Indus Valley sites such as Harappa will provide new insights into the nature of Indus Valley urbanism and the growth and development of Harappan society.

FIGURE 20.8   Terracotta model of a cart drawn by oxen, recovered from Mohenjo-daro.

KEY TERMS

Early Indus, or Pre-Urban, period   294

Harappa   292

Indus Age   292

Indus Valley, or Harappan, civilization   292

Kot Diji   295

Late Harappan, or Post-Urban, phase   297

Lothal   295

Mature Harappan, or Urban, phase   295

Mehrgarh   293

Mohenjo-daro   292

Rojdi   298

FURTHER READING

Kenoyer, Jonathan Mark
1998   *Ancient Cities of the Indus Valley Civilization.* Oxford: American Institute of Pakistan Studies. *A beautifully illustrated exhibition catalog with lots of useful background material on the Indus Valley.*

Possehl, Gregory
2002   *The Indus Civilization: A Contemporary Perspective.* Walnut Creek, CA: Altamira Press. *A readable and well-illustrated introduction to the emergence of complex societies in South Asia.*

QUESTIONS FOR DISCUSSION

1. How has our inability to decipher the Indus Valley script affected our understanding of Harappan social and political organization?

2. Do you think that the Indus Valley formed a single, politically unified state? What archaeological data can be used to support your position?

3. What role did trade play in the origin and growth of urbanism in South Asia?

21

THE RISE OF COMPLEX SOCIETIES IN EGYPT AND SUB-SAHARAN AFRICA

To the average person, the cities and states of ancient Mesopotamia are obscure at best, and those of the Indus Valley are practically unknown. Ancient Egypt, by contrast, is a familiar image in our common culture. We think immediately of the Egypt of the pharaohs, illustrated, perhaps, by the pyramids and sphinx floodlit against the night sky in Cairo's nightly sound-and-light show (Figure 21.1). We might recall the famous image of the British archaeologist Howard Carter crouched before the newly opened entrance to the tomb of the boy-king Tutankhamen, peering at the magnificent golden treasures within (Figure 21.2). The Egyptian world has been a familiar subject of literature and the arts from Shakespeare's *Antony and Cleopatra* through the adventure movies of today.

FIGURE 21.1   The popular image of Egypt: the floodlit pyramids and sphinx at Giza.

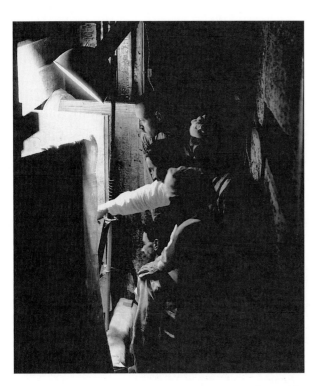

FIGURE 21.2 Howard Carter peering into the newly opened tomb of the boy-king Tutankhamen.

FIGURE 21.3 The Rosetta stone, the key to the decipherment of Egyptian hieroglyphics.

The Egyptians left behind in the pyramids monumental structures that were among the wonders of the ancient world and that have been the subject of fascination ever since. Scholars, too, were fortunate that with the discovery of the **Rosetta stone** in 1799, they soon found the key to the Egyptian hieroglyphic writing (Figure 21.3). The Rosetta stone is inscribed with the same text in Greek and two forms of Egyptian writing, a script and hieroglyphics. Starting with the premise that the language of the ancient Egyptians was related to Coptic, a language still spoken by their descendants, Jean François Champollion, in 1822, was able to decipher the meaning of the hieroglyphic writing. An enormous body of Egyptian writing has come down to us, engraved on tombs and monuments, and penned onto a multitude of papyrus (reed-paper) scrolls. Once this writing could be read, the politics, religious and moral beliefs, and daily life of the ancient Egyptians became a part of history.

This chapter, however, will deal primarily with the archaeology of Egypt before the earliest hieroglyphics began the recording of history and before the rise of the pharaohs. We will discuss what is known of the inhabitants of the Nile Valley, who would become the Egyptian people, and we will conclude with the formation and development of the earliest Egyptian kingdom. We will also explore the archaeology of Nubia, Egypt's southern rival, and examine the archaeological evidence for the rise of complex societies in Africa south of the Sahara.

ANCIENT EGYPT: THE GIFT OF THE NILE

The fifth-century B.C. Greek historian Herodotus wrote of Egypt as the gift of the Nile. Unlike the difficult-to-manage, unpredictable, and sometimes dangerous flooding of the Tigris-Euphrates plain or the Indus Valley, the flooding of the Nile was usually predictable, gentle, and well timed for the purposes of agriculture, arriving once each year around October. Unlike the irrigation waters from the Tigris and Euphrates, which each season brought with them a further deposit of salt to degrade the fertility of the soil, the annual layer of Nile silts continuously enriched the farmers' lands. Complex irrigation and drainage systems were unnecessary; the Nile's water needed only to be allowed to pool in the fields.

The early Egyptian farmers grew barley and emmer wheat and raised sheep, goats, cattle, and pigs, along with greyhoundlike dogs and donkeys. Sheep, goats, barley, and emmer wheat were introduced to Egypt from southwest Asia, but, as noted in Chapter 16, archaeological and DNA evidence indicates that cattle were independently domesticated in Africa. The archaeological evidence is sparse, but agriculture appears to have arrived late in Egypt as compared with southwest Asia. The earliest agricultural settlements known in the Nile Valley date to about 6100 B.C. (Wendorf and Schild 1980), about 3000 years later than the earliest agricultural villages in southwest Asia. In the past it was suggested that these domesticated plants and animals were introduced into the Nile Valley by an influx of migrant peoples from Asia. Today, that scenario is regarded as unlikely; the material cultures of the early farmers generally resemble those of the late Paleolithic inhabitants of the Nile Valley. Most likely, the indigenous hunter-foragers of the Nile Valley adopted farming and stock rearing, as did some of the Mesolithic peoples of northern Europe (Chapter 18). Why they chose to adopt agriculture is still unclear.

THE EGYPTIAN ENVIRONMENT

The Nile Valley today is a place of remarkable contrasts. Virtually no rain falls south of Cairo, but in all those areas of bottomland that are flooded by the Nile, the land is lush and green, covered with farmers' fields, orchards, and palm groves. Beyond

FIGURE 21.4   Desert and agricultural fields meet at Saqqara.

the Nile's silts, the desert begins. The transition is so abrupt that in places one can literally stand with one foot in farmland and the other on the barren desert sands (Figure 21.4). In the north (Lower Egypt), the Nile floodplain is flat and broad, spreading out to form the Nile delta. As one travels south (into Upper Egypt), the strip of fertile floodplain becomes more and more constricted, enclosed between high cliffs, above which lie the Sahara Desert to the west and the Arabian Desert to the east (Figure 21.5). The eastern cliffs are broken by a number of now dry tributary valleys that permit access to and from the world beyond the Nile. The unique semi-isolated and protected character of the Egyptian homeland has had profound effects on the nature of ancient Egyptian society.

The Egyptian environment in late Paleolithic times was quite different from today's. After the end of the Pleistocene, from about 11,000 to 5000 B.C., north Africa received considerably more rainfall than it does today. In Upper Egypt the now dry streambeds flowed with water. Trees grew on the hillsides and grasses grew in the valleys. The wildlife of the area resembled that of sub-Saharan Africa, including elephants, rhinoceroses, giraffes, wild cattle,

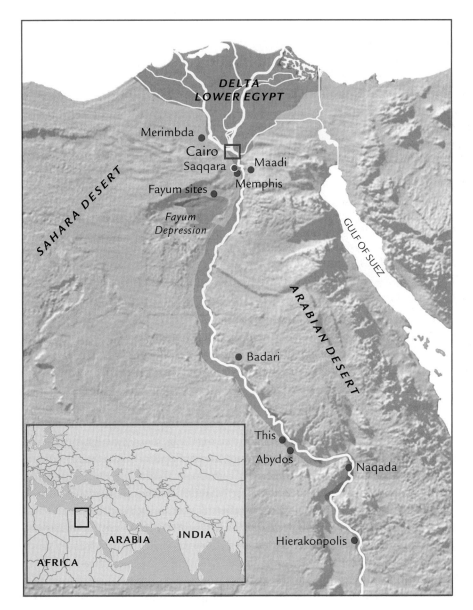

FIGURE 21.5 Map of the Nile Valley, showing the sites discussed in this chapter. The shaded area in the valley and across the delta indicates the region made fertile and green by the annual flooding of the Nile.

and antelopes. The streams, ponds, and rivers were filled with fish, along with crocodiles and hippopotamuses. This rich environment provided a land of plenty for the hunter-foragers living there, which explains why farming was relatively late in reaching the Nile Valley. It is more difficult to explain why agriculture was adopted when it was. Perhaps expanding populations, combined with a gradually drying climate, drove away the game, making stock raising and planting more attractive. By the time of the first Egyptian dynasties (about 3100 B.C.) the largest animals, such as elephants and giraffes, had disappeared. By 2000 B.C., the smaller game such as ibex, antelope, and gazelle were gone as well, survived only by the crocodiles and hippos in the river (Butzer 1958, cited in Trigger et al. 1983).

FIGURE 21.6   Basket found in the Neolithic settlement in the Fayum.

THE EARLIEST EGYPTIANS

Perhaps surprisingly, Egypt before the first pharaohs is not very well known to archaeologists. A number of factors have contributed to this state of affairs. First, the very richness of later Egyptian architecture and material culture, as opposed to the simple remains of the most ancient sites, attracted most of the attention of earlier generations of scholars. Second, unlike the floodplains of Mesopotamia and the Indus Valley, the Nile floodplain has remained rich and productive and today sustains one of the highest population densities in the world. Thus the most ancient sites may lie buried beneath settlements still occupied, and many others may have been destroyed by millennia of continuous plowing. Third, the Nile itself has conspired either to destroy or to hide the earliest archaeological sites, either scouring them away or burying them ever deeper under the river's annual deposit of silt.

Despite these problems, archaeologists have gathered some information about the earliest settlers on the Nile. Before the unification of Egypt under the earliest pharaohs, the settlers in the Nile delta (Lower Egypt) seem to have been culturally distinct from those living in the south (Upper Egypt). The evidence for these early settlements is better preserved and studied in the delta than in the Nile Valley to the south.

A few sites represent the Neolithic period in the north of Egypt. Some of the earliest known farmers in Egypt were found during excavations conducted in the 1930s in the **Fayum Depression,** an ancient lake bed west of the Nile in central Egypt (Caton-Thompson and Gardner 1934). The Fayum farmers, probably dating to about 5200 B.C., dug large numbers of straw-lined storage pits, in which were found quantities of well-preserved emmer wheat and barley. The Fayum Neolithic people harvested their crops with flint-edged sickles and hunted game with flint-tipped weapons. It is not certain whether they raised any domestic animals. They made pottery from clay tempered with straw, fine basketry (Figure 21.6), and linen cloth woven from flax.

EARLY SETTLEMENTS IN THE DELTA

The best evidence for an early settlement comes from **Merimbda,** in the western delta (see Baumgartel 1965). The artifacts at Merimbda, especially the pottery, resemble those found in the Fayum, and the grains cultivated at Merimbda were much like those of the Fayum, including barley and emmer wheat. Dating to between 4800 and 4400 B.C., Merimbda was a large site, covering an area of 600 by 400 m (2000 by 1300 ft.). Merimbda began as a scatter of temporary reed or matting shelters and eventually grew into a small village of oval or round mud-walled houses up to 6 m (20 ft.) in diameter, arranged along either side of a path or street. The Merimbda people were buried lying on their sides in simple graves without grave offerings, interspersed among the houses.

The settlement at **Maadi,** near Cairo, dates to around 3650 B.C. (Caneva et al. 1987: 106). The site stretches over an area 1300 m (4300 ft.) long by over 100 m wide (330 ft.), but different areas seem to have been occupied at different times. Like the people of Merimbda, the inhabitants of Maadi grew barley and emmer wheat, and they lived in houses made from mud and reed matting. They raised cattle, goats, sheep, and pigs and kept dogs as well.

The dead were buried in a cemetery adjoining the settlement, in small, simple pits without any grave goods. Despite the general resemblance to the earlier Neolithic sites, Maadi is quite distinctive. This is especially apparent in the pottery, which, tempered with sand, resembles neither that from Merimbda nor that from the Upper Egyptian sites.

The distinctive artifacts in these sites, especially the pottery, and the simple burials without grave offerings set the delta sites apart from those in Upper Egypt. The late Neolithic sites in the delta are now often distinguished as the **Maadi culture.** Influences from western Asia are apparent in all these sites. The plants cultivated and the animals herded were all initially domesticated in western Asia and presumably entered the Nile delta from the Levant. Some of the pottery forms from the Fayum and from Merimbda resemble Levantine types. A small portion of the pottery at Maadi seems to have been imported directly from the Levant. Some other pottery at Maadi was imported from Upper Egypt, clearly demonstrating that while the people of Maadi were distinctive, they did not live in isolation.

SETTLEMENTS AND CEMETERIES IN UPPER EGYPT

In Upper Egypt burials of the earliest farmers, dating to about 4400 to 4000 B.C.,[1] have been found along the middle portion of the Nile Valley, near the site of **Badari,** which gives its name to the **Badarian culture.** The limited settlement evidence suggests these people were probably mobile, perhaps living in simple tents or huts. They appear to have raised cattle, goats, and sheep; hunted; and fished. (Domesticated animals were buried in the cemeteries, in a manner similar to that of humans.) The Badarian settlement sites included storage pits, lined with basketry, containing emmer wheat and barley. Grinding stones and cooking pots show that the grain was prepared and eaten at the site (Baumgartel 1965: 8). Most of our knowledge of the Badarian, however, comes from the graves. Unlike those found in the delta, Badarian graves, well preserved by the extreme desert dryness, contain a wealth of grave goods. The dead were usually buried in oval pits covered with matting, lying on their sides with their knees drawn close to the body (Figure 21.7). Fragments of their clothing have been preserved, which included robes and skirts of skin and linen fabric. Belts, necklaces, bracelets, and anklets of beads were worn, made from shell, coral, copper, and turquoise, but mostly of steatite that had been glazed blue to look like turquoise. Many graves held bone and ivory combs, spoons, and ladles, often decorated with carvings of birds and animals. Graves also held slate palettes, used to grind green malachite, which was kept in ivory vases and used as a cosmetic (Figure 21.8). Pottery was the most common object in the graves; the most characteristic were hemispherical bowls, covered with a red slip, stroked with a comb to produce a rippled surface, and then polished smooth. These pots were fired in such a way as to produce a black band at the top, around the rim. Many of the burial practices and artifacts of the Badarians are clearly predecessors of the later dynastic Egyptians (Figure 21.9).

In the 1890s the British archaeologist Sir Flinders Petrie excavated two settlements and several large cemeteries at **Naqada** (also spelled Nagada), in Upper Egypt. Among them, the cemeteries contain about 3000 predynastic burials. Most of the graves belong to the time span following the Badarian and before the earliest Egyptian dynasty. Flinders Petrie was the first scientific archaeologist to excavate in Egypt. He was faced with the need to place these many burials (and the settlements associated with them) in some form

---

[1]Most of the archaeology of predynastic Egypt was conducted before the advent of radiocarbon age determinations. Date ranges for the predynastic periods given in this chapter are estimates based on a variety of methods.

FIGURE 21.7 Badarian burials as excavated by Sir Flinders Petrie in the 1890s.

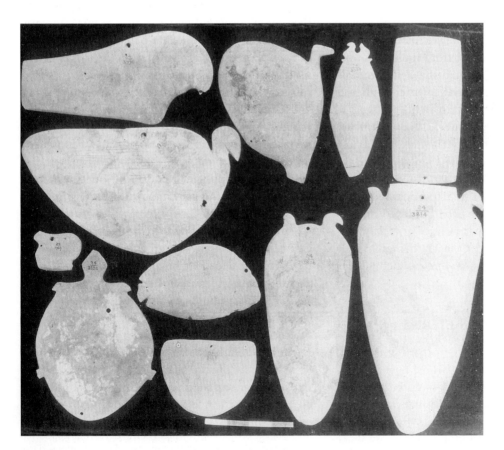

FIGURE 21.8 Typical slate pallets from the Badarian period.

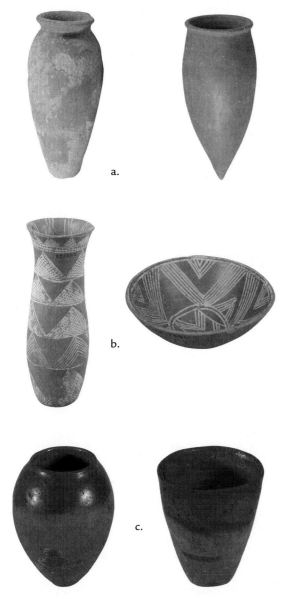

FIGURE 21.9 Characteristic Egyptian pottery of the predynastic period: a. Naqada II; b. Naqada I; c. Badarian.

and **Naqada III.** The Naqada sequence dates to circa 4000 to 3100 B.C. Since Petrie's time, a few absolute dates have been obtained to anchor the sequence, and modern computer methods have refined Petrie's conclusions, but the Naqada sequence has largely stood the test of time.

The Naqada sequence appears to represent a continued development of the preceding Badarian. Sites from the earlier Naqada I period are found only in Upper Egypt. There is little settlement evidence. Only a few simple circular hut foundations, made from stone fragments and mud, have been properly excavated. The huts themselves were probably made from wattle and daub, interwoven sticks packed with mud. Graves continue to be the major source of evidence for Naqada I material culture. They are much like those of the Badarian and contain similar objects. The black-topped pottery gradually gives way to a red pottery painted with white lines, sometimes with images of animals. A tradition of fine flint working appears, to be developed further in the Naqada II period. The Naqada I people also ground hard stone into a variety of objects, including basalt vases and circular mace heads. Their burial costume included beads, bone and ivory rings, armlets, hairpins and combs, as well as slate cosmetic palettes. One hair comb shows a figure of what appears to be the earliest known representation of the Egyptian god Seth (Baumgartel 1965: 17). In historic times Naqada would become the cult center for the god Seth (Trigger et al. 1983: 35).

Greater changes appear during the succeeding Naqada II-Gerzean period. Naqada II sites are much more widely distributed, from the southern border of the delta in the north to the border with Nubia in the south. Major population centers are found at Naqada and, farther south, at **Hierakonpolis.** At Naqada, Petrie found the remains of a rectangular dwelling made from mud brick and what appeared to be a defensive wall. A Naqada II period grave also contained a pottery model of a rectangular house. Excavations at Hierakonpolis have uncovered much more extensive settlement evidence (Hoffman 1982), including the mud-brick footing of a rectangular house that was unusually well-preserved because it had been burned. Its walls were likely made of wattle and daub. Adjacent

of chronological sequence. To do this Petrie devised a technique known as sequence dating, based on the sequential occurrence of pottery types in the grave assemblages (see the Archaeology in Practice box). He broke up the sequence into three succeeding phases, which he called Amratian, Gerzean, and Semainian, and which are now termed **Naqada I, Naqada II,**

ARCHAEOLOGY IN PRACTICE

Sequence Dating and Archaeological Seriation

When Sir Flinders Petrie excavated the thousands of artifact-laden burials at Naqada in the late nineteenth century, he was faced with a crucial analytical problem: How could this wide range of archaeological assemblages be ordered in time? No calendrical dates could be given to these prehistoric remains, and the absolute dating methods on which modern archaeologists rely would not be developed for many decades to come. Still, Petrie observed, "The main value of dates is to show the sequence of events... The order of events and the relation of one country to another is the main essential of history" (Petrie 1899: 295). Although Petrie was unable to assign actual dates to the Upper Egyptian prehistoric graves, he found he could logically order the various grave assemblages according to the types and forms of artifacts they contained. Petrie inferred that this order represented a temporal sequence.

Petrie termed his method **sequence dating**. An early version of Petrie's sequence dating procedure is illustrated in Figure 21.A. Each horizontal row represents some of the pottery types typical of the assemblages for seven successive chronological periods. With each successive period some pottery types disappear while other new types make their appearance. The vertical lines in the illustration indicate pottery types that persist from one period into the next. These links permitted Petrie to chain together the assemblages into a consistent temporal sequence. The pottery vessels on the far left, so-called wavy-handled jars, provide a second line of evidence. The style of the vessels changes gradually through time, shifting from

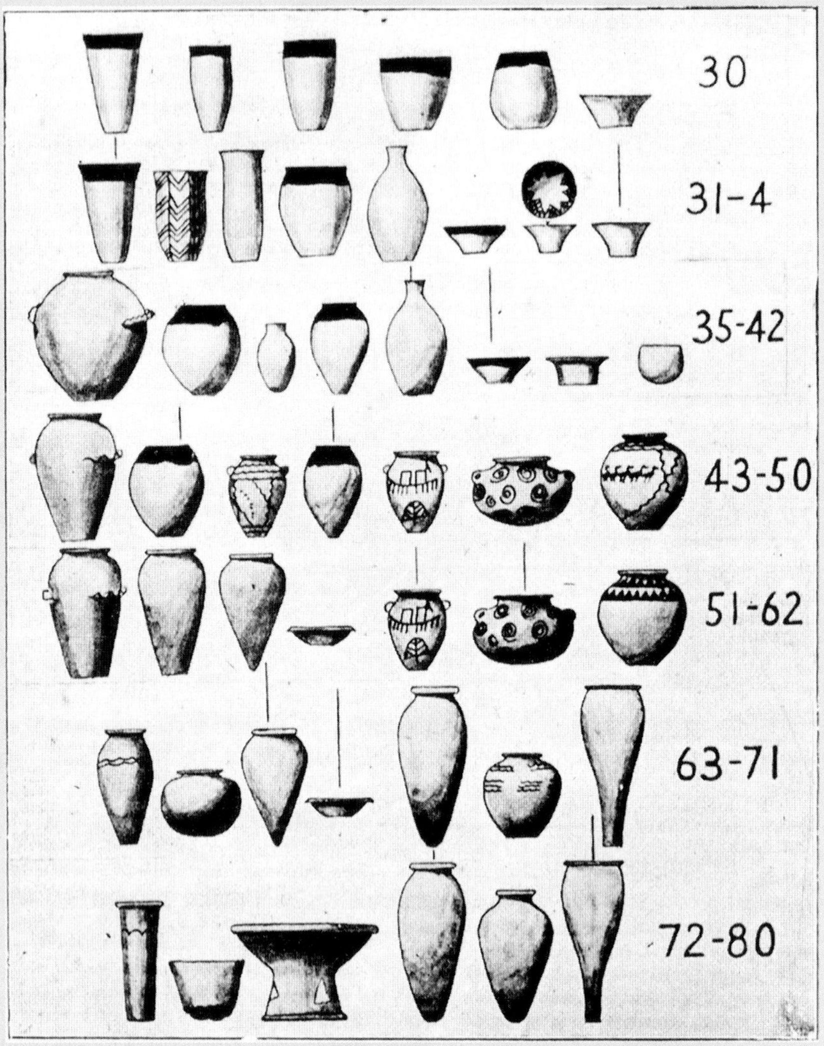

FIGURE 21.A Sir Flinders Petrie's original presentation of his method of sequence dating. The horizontal rows represent successive time periods. The vertical bars link pottery types that persist from one period to the next. The sequence of wavy-handled jars is shown on the left.

rounded forms in the early periods to straight-sided forms in the later periods, accompanied by the evolution of the functional wavy handles in the early forms into purely decorative elements in the latest forms. This degeneration of a functional element into a decorative element allowed Petrie to determine which way was up, that is, which end of the connected chain of periods was the most recent.

During subsequent research Petrie continued to alter and revise his criteria for the sequence dates assigned to the Egyptian prehistoric assemblages. Since his time, as more evidence has accumulated and has been analyzed, the specifics of the sequence dates have been found to be incorrect in various details. It has become clear that the actual time span represented by the sequence dates is not uniform; the more recent sequence dates represent progressively shorter periods of time.

Overall, however, the method remains valid. A modern statistical seriation study of a group of 60 Egyptian grave assemblages (Kendall 1969) reached conclusions very similar to those assigned according to the sequence dating method.

Since sequence dating relies on the appearance and disappearance of artifact types from one period to the next, it is sometimes referred to as occurrence seriation. Another form of seriation, frequency seriation, relies on changing *proportions* of various artifact types through successive time periods (see Trigger 1989: 200; Deetz 1967: 26–33). This method was first introduced in the early twentieth century as a means for chronologically ordering Native American pottery assemblages. It has since come into use worldwide.

Frequency seriations are often presented as a type of chart known as a battleship diagram. An example of such a diagram is shown in Figure 21.B. The horizontal rows in the chart represent the successive time periods. The width of the vertical bars represents the proportions of several artifact types (in this case, gravestones). When the rows representing the time periods are correctly ordered, the vertical bars indicate the gradual appearance of an artifact type, followed by its disappearance. This pattern looks like a battleship viewed from above.

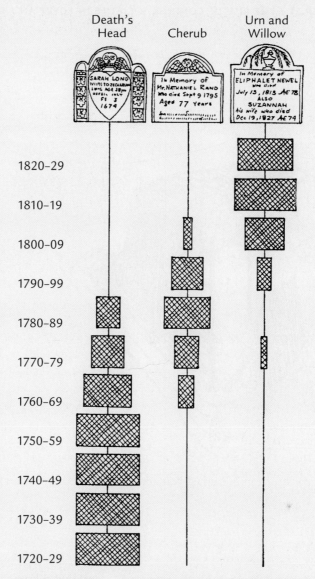

FIGURE 21.B   An example of frequency seriation, showing how the proportions of different gravestone styles in a New England cemetery varied consistently over time, forming practically perfect "battleship curves."

315

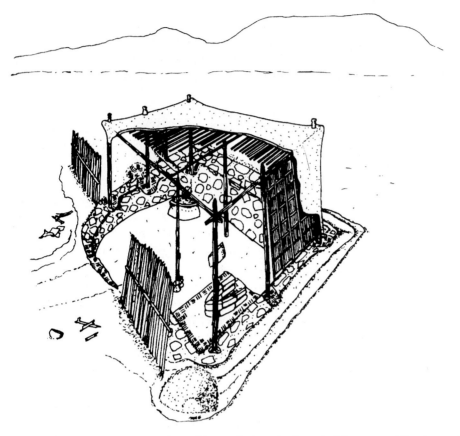

FIGURE 21.10   Reconstruction of burned Naqada II period house at Hierakonpolis.

to the house was a pottery kiln, probably the source of the fire that destroyed it (Figure 21.10). Surveys of the Hierakonpolis area indicate that the local population grew explosively around 3800 B.C., during the end of the Naqada I and beginning of the Naqada II periods. Settlements consisted of groups of rectangular houses enclosed within walled compounds. The region was gradually taking on an urban character (Hoffman et al. 1986: 181). Late in the period, the settlements become more concentrated. In addition to the more intensive residential development, an oval courtyard surrounded by wooden structures represents a possible temple complex.

Changes were occurring in the burial practices as well. In the Naqada II period, some graves were much larger and more elaborate than others, indicat-ing that differences in wealth and social status were appearing. A separate cemetery at Naqada included several very large rectangular tombs, lined with mud brick, with the body laid in a semiseparate niche at one side. One tomb of this type, now known to date to Naqada II times, was excavated at Hierakonpolis in 1898. This tomb (known as the Decorated Tomb) had a plastered wall on which were painted scenes, including humans, animals, and boats, in the same style found on Naqada II pottery (Figure 21.11).

These larger graves came to include more and more offerings of luxury goods, a practice that would remain a prominent feature of Egyptian culture. Specialized craft industries, including the manufac-ture of fine stone vessels, elaborate and ornate objects flaked from flint, and particularly pottery, grew up

FIGURE 21.11 Wall paintings from the Decorated Tomb.

in molds (See Archaeology in Practice, Chapter 23). Objects were made from silver and gold as well.

The wider trade networks within Egypt were complemented by increasing contacts with Mesopotamia. Mesopotamian traders may have been attracted by Egyptian gold, to be found in the desert east of the Nile. Suggestively, the ancient name for Naqada is *Nubt*, which means "gold." Imports of Mesopotamian pottery vessels and cylinder seals have been found in Naqada II burials. Some Mesopotamian art motifs appear briefly as well. In the Decorated Tomb mentioned previously, for instance, one of the paintings features a person holding apart two lions (see Figure 21.11), a distinctly Mesopotamian theme associated with the Sumerian *Epic of Gilgamesh*. This tomb is usually considered that of a local king or chieftain. Just what role contact with Mesopotamia may have played in instigating the development of the Egyptian state is an open question. It is interesting to observe, however, that the earliest palace architecture known, dating to the First Dynasty (ca. 3100 B.C.), displays elaborately niched and buttressed brick walls that are clearly derived from Mesopotamian palace prototypes.

EGYPTIAN KINGDOMS AND THE UNIFICATION OF EGYPT

The following Naqada III period is sometimes called the **Proto-dynastic period.** During this time the populations of the Naqada and Hierakonpolis regions gradually moved into the towns, which ultimately acquired walls. The earliest hieroglyphic writing appears shortly before 3100 B.C., near the end of Proto-dynastic times. Very little is known of Proto-dynastic social structure and of the political events leading up to the unification of Egypt. Small kingdoms probably grew up with their capitals at Naqada and Hierakonpolis. Those centers surely competed with one another, perhaps for access to trade networks or mineral resources. Hierakonpolis eventually grew more powerful and became dominant. The ancient conflict between those kingdoms appears to be reflected in Egyptian mythology. Just as Seth was the patron god of Naqada, the falcon-headed god Horus was the patron deity of Hierakonpolis. According to

largely to furnish the tombs. Much of the economy, it seems, was fueled by the demand for luxury goods that were continually removed from circulation by the wealthy and prominent members of society who took those goods with them when they died.

Some types of pottery, notably red wares, began to be mass-produced in a limited number of centers and distributed throughout all of Egypt. While a few copper artifacts have been found in Badarian and Naqada I sites, copper becomes much more common in the Naqada II period. Ornaments and weapons were made from both hammered copper and copper cast

FIGURE 21.12   The Narmer palette.

the legend, Horus avenges the murder of his father Osiris by Osiris's brother Seth. Horus kills Seth, after which he becomes the ruler of all Egypt.

The unification of all Egypt under a single king is symbolized by the elaborate carving on a large slate palette found at Hierakonpolis (Figure 21.12). The palette is a descendant of the functional cosmetic palettes found in graves since Badarian times, but elaborated into a ritual object. On one side of the palette is a representation of the king smiting an enemy with a mace while wearing the conical crown symbolic of Upper Egypt. On the other side, the king (this time wearing the red crown of Lower Egypt) and his retinue view a group of decapitated enemies. Early hieroglyphic symbols identified with his name, **Narmer,** appear at the top of the palette. Narmer, whose reign precedes the earliest dynasties in the historic Egyptian lists of kings, is

often regarded as the unifier of Egypt. Other earlier kings, however, may have held widespread domination. The symbol for a slightly earlier king known only as Scorpion has been found carved on a mace head at Hierakonpolis, wearing the crown of Lower Egypt, suggesting his control over Lower as well as Upper Egypt. Practically nothing is known of how the kingdoms of Upper and Lower Egypt came to be unified, but the carvings on the Narmer palette surely point to violence.

With Narmer, the seat of power moved northward to **Abydos,** north of Naqada. Narmer and his successors of the First Dynasty were buried at Abydos, which was probably their homeland. Abydos was located within a probable third predynastic kingdom with its center at This, just north of Abydos, but archaeologists know little of that region's early history.

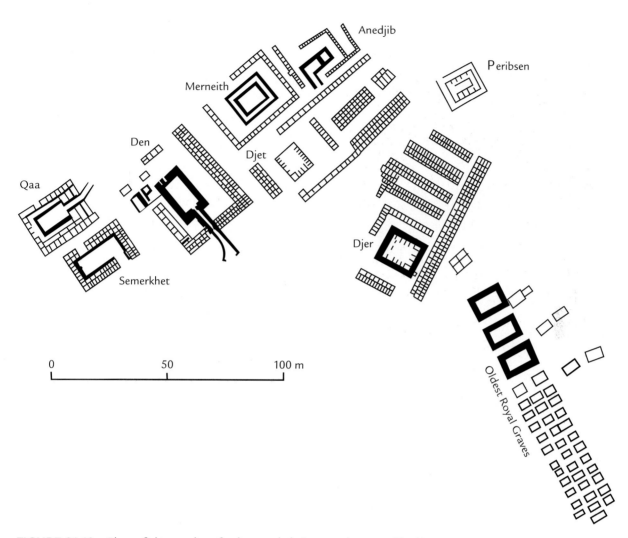

FIGURE 21.13 Plan of the tombs of rulers and their attendants at Abydos.

THE RISE OF THE PHARAOHS

At Abydos we see the beginning of the elaboration of royal burials, which would reach its peak with the pyramids of the Old Kingdom. The increasing size and complexity of the royal tombs reflect the steadily growing power of the pharaohs. The Abydos tombs consist of underground, rectangular brick chambers, roofed over and covered with a mound of sand. These large tombs were surrounded by multiple rows of small graves, joined into a common structure (Figure 21.13). Accompanying inscriptions indicate that these were the graves of the royal harem, servants, and various artisans. Very

probably these people were sacrificed to serve their king in the afterlife (Trigger et al. 1983: 52). (See On the Cutting Edge, this chapter.)

Traditionally, the founder of the First Dynasty was **Menes,** who may have been Narmer or an immediate successor. Menes was said to have founded the city of **Memphis,** near modern Cairo, which was to become ancient Egypt's first capital. Nearby, at **Saqqara,** a new cemetery was founded. Important officials were buried there, in large tombs with an aboveground superstructure known as **mastabas** (Figure 21.14). These flat-topped, rectangular tombs, sometimes including internal rooms, were the predecessors of

FIGURE 21.14   A mastaba tomb, with a pyramid in the background.

the pyramids. The earliest pyramid, the step-pyramid built by Djoser at Saqqara in the Third Dynasty, is essentially several successively smaller mastabas stacked one upon the other (Figure 21.15).

Pyramid building reached its peak during the Old Kingdom with the construction of the Great Pyramid of Cheops at Giza, near Cairo. (The Old Kingdom, ca. 2980 to 2475 B.C., includes the fourth through the sixth dynasties of pharaohs.) The immense size of the pyramids and the enormous expenditure of labor commanded to construct them demonstrate the monopoly of power held by the pharaohs, who early on took on the role of god-king. The tombs also reflect the increasing centralization of Egyptian government, with the growth of a powerful nobility and the establishment of an extensive bureaucracy to serve their administrative needs. Hieroglyphic writing developed during the Early Dynastic period to provide the necessary record keeping, just as cuneiform writing had evolved in Mesopotamia.

These powerful, wealthy elites provided the impetus for thriving arts and craft industries, including

the highest levels of artistry in woodwork, metalwork, stone carving, and painting. Egypt would remain primarily a society of small agricultural villages throughout its history. Nevertheless, the Egyptians, protected from the outside world within the Nile Valley, formed a strongly unified society. Egyptian religious beliefs and legends legitimated the power of the pharaohs. The pharaohs and Egyptian nobility extracted much from the common people in taxes and labor. In turn Egypt grew into a self-contained, self-conscious, and unified state that remained remarkably stable for millennia.

THE FORMATION OF THE EGYPTIAN STATE

How can the growth and unification of the Egyptian state be explained? As we saw in Chapter 19, a number of causes may have led society to urbanization and state formation in Mesopotamia. Mesopotamian society was characterized by an economy based on an elaborate system of irrigation agriculture and dependent on raw materials obtained through long-distance trade. Certain favored groups may have gained an advantage because they could monopolize control over those vital resources. The need for protection from hostile neighbors may also have driven villagers into fortified cities, where they could seek the protection of increasingly powerful military leaders.

It is difficult to see similar forces at work in Egypt. The dependable, widespread flooding of the Nile required little in the way of engineering to ensure that the crops were watered. There was little opportunity for any particular group of people to monopolize or control the river's flow. Long-distance trade did bring in some luxury goods, as well as lumber from the Levant, but Egypt was relatively rich in stone and metals and was far less dependent on the outside world for raw materials than was Mesopotamia. Much of the unique character of ancient Egyptian society, in fact, derives from its isolation from its neighbors. The influence of Mesopotamia during the Predynastic period did not last long; trade with Mesopotamia had practically disappeared before the start of the Old Kingdom.

FIGURE 21.15 The step-pyramid of Djoser at Saqqara, essentially a series of mastaba tombs piled one upon the other.

Secure within the Nile Valley, the Egyptian people had no powerful, warlike neighbors to threaten them.

In this relatively benign environment, it is very difficult to perceive any single driving force behind the rise of the Egyptian state. There were surely local rivalries and strife, and individuals or groups may have seized the advantage when the opportunity arose. Barry Kemp (1989: 32) has envisioned the growth of the Egyptian state as analogous to playing a game of Monopoly. In the inevitable competition among more or less equal individuals or groups, the luck of the draw will permit some groups to gain an advantage. Once they are ahead, they can use their added resources to consolidate more and more power and wealth:

> Thus the game inexorably follows a trajectory towards a critical point where one player has accumulated sufficient assets to outweigh the threats posed by the other players and so becomes unstoppable. It becomes only a matter of time before he wins by monopolizing the assets of all. (Kemp 1989: 32)

In this way the leaders of small agricultural communities may have ultimately extended their influence to become kings of a unified Egypt.

NUBIA: EGYPT'S NEIGHBOR TO THE SOUTH

Ancient Egypt extended along the Nile Valley as far south as Aswan. South of Aswan, above the first cataract of the Nile, was Nubia (Figure 21.16). Throughout its history, Egypt contended with Nubia in one way or another, sometimes peacefully as a trading partner and frequently as its military conqueror. The relative powers of Nubia and Egypt waxed and waned through the centuries. For the most part, though, Lower Nubia, which extended from the first to the second Nile cataract, was dominated by Egypt, while Upper Nubia, extended farther south into Sudan to the sixth cataract, remained fiercely independent.

Nubian culture, although strongly influenced by that of Egypt, was nevertheless completely distinct and had prehistoric roots as deep as those of

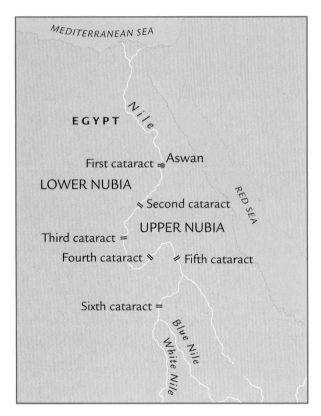

FIGURE 21.16   Map of Nubia.

Egypt. By 9000 years ago, Nubia had been settled by hunter-gatherer-fishers who also produced well-made pottery, among the earliest known. As the climate became markedly drier after 4500 B.C, Neolithic farmers, known as the **Khartoum Neolithic**, established themselves along the banks of the Nile. In Lower Nubia, by 3500 B.C., they had grown into a distinctive culture, the "**A-Group**," who traded extensively with Egypt beginning with the rise of the First Dynasty about 3100 B.C.

As is the case in early Egypt, most of the archaeological research in Nubia has centered on the excavation of cemeteries. Marked differences in the size and richness of A-Group graves indicate that their society was highly stratified, with some of the graves possibly belonging to local chiefs. An especially large and richly furnished cemetery from the end of the period suggests that A-Group society may have been moving toward the formation of a unified state under a single ruler (O'Connor 1993: 21).

In 2900 B.C. the Egyptians invaded Lower Nubia, completely displacing the Nubian population and driving them southward. Lower Nubia was populated by Egyptians for the next 6000 years. It was to remain Egyptian in character even after the return of the Nubian population. Upper Nubia, on the other hand, while frequently raided by Egyptians, remained independent. Ultimately, Upper Nubia became a kingdom, known to the Egyptians as Kush, that was sufficiently powerful to regain control of Lower Nubia for about 100 years before the whole of Nubia was reconquered by the Egyptians about 1550 B.C. Around 900 B.C., when Egypt was once again weakened, Nubian pharaohs conquered and ruled all of Egypt as the Egyptian 25th Dynasty.

COMPLEX SOCIETIES IN PRECOLONIAL SUB-SAHARAN AFRICA

Prior to the 1970s, archaeologists who were interested in the beginnings of urbanism and state formation focused most of their attention on regions such as Egypt, Mesopotamia, and Mesoamerica (see Chapter 24). These regions were seen as areas of primary state formation and were therefore presumably less influenced by the societies surrounding them. Archaeologists attempted to develop theories of urbanism and state formation based on studies of Egypt, the Indus Valley, Mesopotamia, China, Mesoamerica, and Peru (see, for example, Service 1975 and Adams 1966). Little attention was paid to the development of so-called secondary state formation in other regions of the world. Traditionally, secondary states were seen as those complex societies that developed after the first states and cities in a particular geographical region. Today, archaeologists recognize that this approach is both limited and limiting. First, we know that none of the so-called primary states developed in a vacuum. Contact with other regions through trade, warfare, and other means is a feature of all complex societies, including both primary and secondary states. The long-standing rivalry between Egypt and Nubia is a classic example of ongoing cultural contact. Second, the rich archaeological and historical records for many secondary states make them of great interest to archaeologists and other social scientists who are interested in the origins of social complexity.

ON THE CUTTING EDGE   *Human Sacrifice in Egypt*

New investigations at Abydos are demonstrating that, in one respect at least, First Dynasty Egypt resembled its near contemporary in Mesopotamia, Sumer. A team led by David O'Connor of New York University and William Kelly of Yale have recently found new evidence for human sacrifice associated with the earliest First Dynasty ruler, King Aha. Aha may have been Narmer's son. Excavations carried out between 2001 and 2003 uncovered Aha's mortuary compound (ca. 2950 B.C.) (Figure 21.C). Surrounding the enclosure were six subordinate graves, containing the bodies of servants, craftsmen, and officials who had served the king during his lifetime. They were evidently all sacrificed so that they could serve him in the afterlife. Although the graves had been robbed, they were originally richly furnished with grave goods. It is clear that all the deaths occurred in a short span of time, since the entire mortuary complex, including all the graves, was covered over with a single, continuous flooring; in effect, the entire complex was ritually buried. The burial complex of Aha's son, Djer, was also examined. Here,

FIGURE 21.C   Aha's mortuary compound. Courtesy: David O'Connor.

too, the subordinate graves were all constructed and buried simultaneously.

A few clues, such as a sketchy pictorial representation, had suggested many years ago that the kings' retinues might have been sacrificed, but the new excavations at Abydos have offered the first proof. Although very different in detail, human sacrifices are also seen at the Royal Cemetery at Ur (Chapter 19). As at Ur, the Abydos graves attest to the rapid expansion of the power of the king. Only First Dynasty kings were accompanied by human sacrifices. In later dynasties the towns of the pharaohs would be surrounded by the tombs of the Egyptian elite.

The broader interest in urban origins has led archaeologists to examine the archaeological record of urbanism in precolonial sub-Saharan Africa. Archaeological research conducted since the 1970s has shed new light on the complex urban societies that developed in sub-Saharan Africa beginning in the first millennium B.C.

Farming forms the economic basis for complex societies, since it allows for the production of a storable surplus that can be used to support craft specialists and others not engaged in food production. As noted in Chapter 16, cattle were independently domesti-

cated in Africa just south of the Sahara beginning about 10,000 years ago (Marshall and Hildebrand 2002). Plant domestication did not begin until about six millennia later. Beginning about 4000 years ago, a variety of different plants, including grains and tubers such as rice and yams, were domesticated in a wide range of locations across Africa just south of the Sahara. For example, pearl millet appears to have been domesticated by semisedentary herders in the savannas of West Africa.

The West African savannas are also home to one of sub-Saharan Africa's earliest urban societies. Until

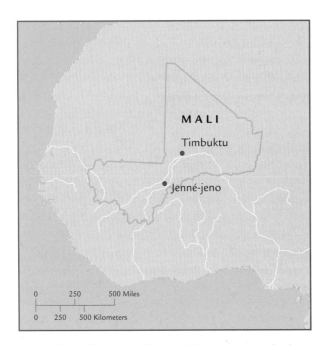

FIGURE 21.17   Map of West Africa showing the location of Jenné-jeno.

the late 1970s, almost all that we knew about these cities came from historical sources (Figure 21.17). They are described in Arabic texts primarily written between the tenth and seventeenth centuries A.D. by Islamic traders. The nature of these textual sources affected historians' view of precolonial cities in the savanna zone of West Africa. As Connah (2001: 115) notes, most historians argued that "cities and states in this zone developed as a result of external stimulus, in the form of long-distance trade. In addition, this view usually emphasized the role of Islam in these developments." Archaeological research, conducted under the direction of Roderick McIntosh and Susan Keech McIntosh of Rice University, has shown that urbanism had a much longer history in the savanna region of western Africa (McIntosh and McIntosh 1980; McIntosh 1995).

Since the late 1970s, McIntosh and McIntosh have developed a program of excavation and regional survey designed to examine urban origins in the Inland Niger Delta of Mali. Excavations at the site of **Jenné-jeno** reveal an urban center that was established about

250 B.C. and underwent rapid growth (Figure 21.18). The site reached its maximum extent by about 800 A.D. when it covered 33 ha (73 ac.). The site is made up of a series of closely spaced compounds containing mud huts. At its height, Jenné-jeno may have been home to about 6400 people. When the other mounds within a 5 km (3 mi.) radius are included, the Jenné-jeno region may have been home to about 22,000 people (S. McIntosh 1999: 73, Table 5.2).

The subsistence economy of Jenné-jeno remained largely unchanged throughout its occupation. While rice cultivation and the herding of cattle and smaller livestock played an important role in the farming economy, hunting, fishing, and the collection of wild cereals were also important subsistence practices. Although there is no clear evidence for subsistence intensification at Jenné-jeno, specialization in fishing and farming may have been established soon after the region was colonized (S. McIntosh 1999: 74).

The evidence for trade at Jenné-jeno strongly challenges the idea that the site was established as a long-distance trading center. In the early phases of occupation, most trade goods, including iron and stone, were obtained from a 50 km (30 mi.) radius around the site. Copper appears around A.D. 500, and gold, whose nearest source is 600 km (372 mi.) away, is present by 900. However, North African brass, glass, and spindle whorls do not appear until after A.D. 1000. Jenné-jeno began to decline shortly after the initial North African contacts and was abandoned by 1400. In short, the archaeological data indicate that urbanism developed at Jenné-jeno as a result of internal social, political, and economic changes, rather than external stimulus through the trans-Saharan trade.

The archaeological data from Jenné-jeno reveal a different kind of complex society than is known from Egypt, Sumer, or the Indus Valley. While Jenné-jeno had a dense population, evidence for urban planning (a substantial city wall was erected around A.D. 900), and craft specialists, there is no evidence for the kind of social and economic stratification that is so clearly present in Egypt and Sumer. The Inland Niger Delta also lacks monumental public architecture such as the Egyptian pyramids, the Sumerian temples, or even the Great Bath at Mohenjo-daro.

FIGURE 21.18 Excavations at Jenné-jeno.
Courtesy of Roderick McIntosh.

While the nature of the social and political organization of Jenné-jeno remains unknown, it is possible that "political action and coordination [was] achieved through assemblies, councils, and other forms of horizontally arrayed structures" (S. McIntosh 1999: 77), quite unlike the more hierachically organized Egyptians and Sumerians. Jenné-jeno may have been more heterarchical than hierarchical. As such, it may help archaeologists rethink the basic characteristics of complex societies on a worldwide basis.

CONCLUSION

Throughout its long history, Egyptian culture has been shaped by the Nile. The Nile's reliable annual floods and deposits of rich silts provided early Egyptian farmers with a secure and highly productive environment for growing their crops. Along its length the Nile provided a ready route for communication and trade. In Upper Egypt the steep sides of the Nile Valley provided a protective barrier from the outside world, except along certain well-defined routes. Limited trade contacts with Mesopotamia may have provided some impetus, but from the earliest times the peoples of the Nile Valley developed a culture that was uniquely Egyptian.

While hieroglyphic writing has provided us with a rich record of dynastic Egypt, the Egypt of predynastic times is far less well-known. The erosion and silt deposition of the Nile has either destroyed or hidden from view many of the earliest sites. Despite a century of archaeology, the social structure and political character of the presumed predynastic kingdoms remain obscure. It seems clear, from evidence such as the Narmer palette, that the political unification of Egypt was achieved through warfare and conquest. In the absence of written documents, and with the archaeological evidence still limited, it is very difficult to discern what factors (such as access to needed resources or trade routes) may have led to conflicts among the early kingdoms or provided certain polities with the wherewithal to dominate the others.

Both cereal agriculture and urbanism developed later in sub-Saharan Africa than they did in Egypt. However, recent archaeological research on urban origins in the Inland Niger Delta in Mali has revealed a very different form of cultural complexity that developed in that region beginning in the late first millennium B.C. While the inhabitants of Jenné-jeno and the surrounding area had a dense population and evidence for craft specialization and large-scale urban planning, they lacked the hierarchical political and economic structures that are typical of Egypt and Sumer.

KEY TERMS

QUESTIONS FOR DISCUSSION

1. How does the development of complex societies in Egypt compare to Sumer? What are the main differences between the two regions?

2. How did the geography of Egypt affect the emergence of cities and states in the Nile Valley?

3. Why did urbanism develop in the Inland Niger Delta in the first millennium B.C.?

FURTHER READING

Brewer, Douglas J., and Emily Teeter
   1999   *Egypt and the Egyptians.* Cambridge: Cambridge University Press.
   A comprehensive introduction to Egypt at the time of the pharaohs, written for a general audience.

Connah, Graham
   2001   *African Civilizations: An Archaeological Perspective,* 2nd ed. Cambridge: Cambridge University Press.
   A survey of the development of urbanism and state formation in seven regions of precolonial sub-Saharan Africa. Recommended for the serious student.

O'Connor, David
   1993   *Ancient Nubia: Egypt's Rival in Africa.* Philadelphia: The University Museum.
   This book was written in conjunction with an exhibit on Nubia that appeared at the University Museum in Philadelphia. The text is authoritative and well-illustrated.

22

EARLY CITIES AND STATES IN CHINA

A group of Chinese farmers digging a well made one of the most spectacular archaeological discoveries of the twentieth century. In 1974 the farmers were digging near the burial mound of Qin Shihuangdi, a Chinese monarch who died in 210 B.C. and is known from historical sources as the first emperor of China. The farmers discovered the first of more than 7000 life-size terracotta warriors designed to guard Emperor Qin's tomb (Figure 22.1). Each terracotta figure is unique; each warrior's face, armor, and weaponry are distinctive and individual. These impressive figurines must have been produced by an army of specialist craftsmen. Today, the site of this discovery is a world heritage site, one of a series of archaeological sites that are considered by UNESCO to be of outstanding value to humanity.

FIGURE 22.1 Ceramic tomb warriors from Xian.

The story of Emperor Qin Shihuangdi is equally impressive. At age 13 he became king of one of seven Chinese states that existed at that time. Shortly thereafter, he embarked on a program of military conquest, creating the first Chinese empire. At about the same time, the construction of his mausoleum began. While the tomb itself has never been excavated archaeologically, historical accounts indicate that the tomb took 36 years and the labor of 700,000 individuals to complete (Hoh 2001). At the time of Qin's death in 210 B.C., cities and states had existed in China for well over a millennium. In this chapter we will examine the origins of complex societies in China. We will begin with the establishment of farming villages along the Yellow River in China and then trace the roots of social, economic, and political inequality in the later Neolithic and Early Bronze Age cultures of northern China. We will end with the establishment of urbanism and state formation in the second millennium B.C.

THE YELLOW RIVER (HUANG HE) VALLEY

Modern China is an enormous country, covering over 3.7 million square miles of territory. The climate and vegetation range from subarctic taiga (coniferous forests) in Manchuria to tropical jungles in the south (Chang 1986: 1). As noted in Chapter 16, China was home to two separate centers of plant domestication during the early Holocene. Rice was domesticated in south China and the adjacent areas of Southeast Asia, while broomcorn and foxtail millet were domesticated farther north (Crawford 1992). Although Neolithic villages are known from a number of different regions within China, this chapter will concentrate on the Huang He or Yellow River Valley of northern China. This region was home to China's earliest cities and states. Many archaeological excavations and surveys have been conducted in this region, especially since the Chinese government began allowing collaborative projects between Chinese and non-Chinese scholars in the 1990s (Underhill 2002: 21).

The Yellow River Valley (Figure 22.2) lies primarily in the temperate region of northern China, an area that is characterized by warm summers, colder winters, and an average annual rainfall of between 400 and 800 mm (approximately 16 to 32 in.). The area includes the Loess Plateau in the west and alluvial plains, the North China Plain, further east, as well as the Shandong peninsula along the coast (Chang 1986: 1). The central and eastern portions of the Yellow River Valley have produced evidence for some of the earliest Neolithic villages in China.

THE NEOLITHIC IN THE YELLOW RIVER VALLEY

While late Pleistocene and early Holocene hunters and gatherers in China may have collected wild millets, "there is a gap of about 3000 to 4000 years before there is direct archaeological evidence for domesticated millet in northern China" (Underhill 1997: 120). Early Neolithic villages with clear evidence for domesticated crops appear in the Central Yellow River Valley around 6000 B.C. Broomcorn millet (*Panicum miliaceum*) appears more commonly on western sites, while foxtail millet (*Setaria italica*) is more common in the east. These sites do not represent the initial phases of experimentation with cultivation; they are established farming villages with houses, kilns, storage pits, and burials (Underhill

THE NEOLITHIC IN THE YELLOW RIVER VALLEY

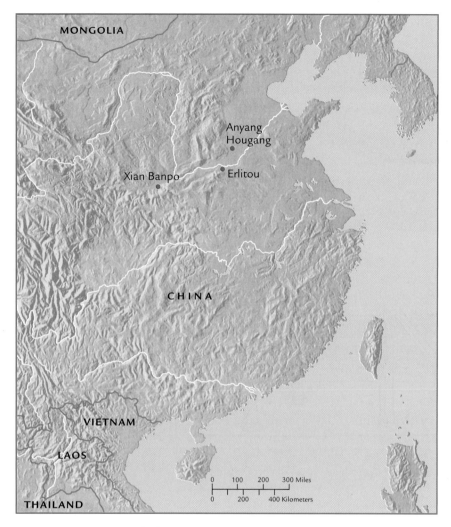

FIGURE 22.2   Map of China showing the locations of sites mentioned in this chapter.

1997: 120). Domesticated animals, including dogs, pigs, sheep, cattle, and chickens, have been reported from a number of these early Neolithic sites.

While a number of local early Neolithic cultures have been described for the Central Yellow River Valley, the cultures of the later Neolithic show a greater degree of homogeneity. The **Yangshao period** (ca. 5100–2800 B.C.) is marked by the widespread use of red pottery painted with black designs, including many images of plants, animals, and fish (Figure 22.3). Polished axes and knives, which may have functioned as sickles, are also common at Yangshao period sites. Yangshao farmers cultivated millets using a swidden or slash-and-burn method of cultivation. Stone axes were used to clear a field of trees, and then fire was used to burn off the remaining brush. Ethnographic data from Taiwan indicate that these fields can be used for millet cultivation for up to 20 years (Fogg 1983: 100). Pigs were the most common domestic animal at Yangshao period sites, and dogs and chickens were also regularly recovered from later Neolithic contexts. Silkworms may have been raised as well. Chinese silks were one of the most valuable trade

FIGURE 22.3 Yangshao painted basin with a fish design.

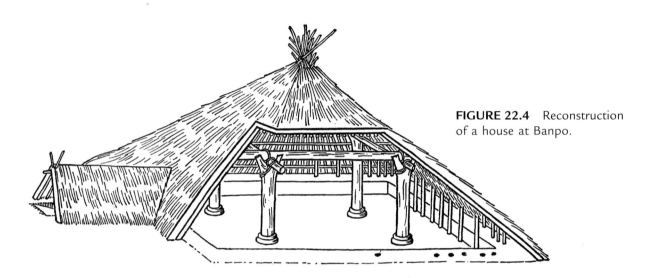

FIGURE 22.4 Reconstruction of a house at Banpo.

goods in later European and Asian history. In the Middle Ages, they were traded as far west as Viking Sweden (Wicker 2004: 540). The presence of a portion of a cocoon suggests that the production of silk may have begun as early as Neolithic times. In addition, some evidence for cattle and water buffalo and a few possible sheep and goat bones have also been reported from later Neolithic sites in northern China. In seventeenth-century China, farm animals, including silkworms, served as important sources of manure for farmers (Dazhong and Pimentel 1996), but it is not clear how far back in prehistory this pattern of manuring can be traced. Manuring maintains soil fertility by replacing nutrients such as nitrogen that are depleted through cereal cultivation.

The best known of the Yangshao period sites is undoubtedly the site of **Banpo** (formerly Pan p'o) in Xian. The site, which covered about 50,000 sq. m (a little more than 12 ac.), is located in a river terrace overlooking a tributary of the Wei River. The houses, which range in shape from round to square and oblong, were generally between 3 and 5 m (10–16 ft.) in diameter (Figure 22.4). Some had semisubterranean foundations. The foundations were constructed of wattle and daub, and wooden posts supported their upper portions. The houses were clustered in the center of the site, surrounded by a ditch. The site also included six pottery kilns. A cemetery with 130 adult burials was excavated, but children were generally buried in pottery vessels between the houses (Chang 1986: 116).

In the eastern portion of the Yellow River Valley, the **Dawenkou** culture (ca. 4300–2600 B.C.) is broadly contemporary with the Yangshao. This culture was first identified in the 1950s (Chang 1986: 157) and is characterized by red pottery and distinctive flat

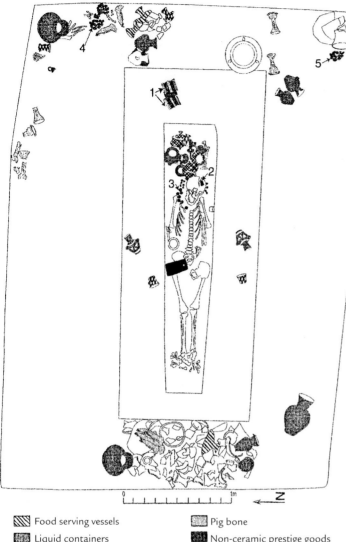

FIGURE 22.5 Grave M10, Dawenkou site.

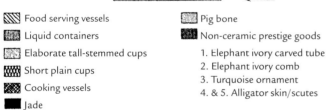

▨ Food serving vessels	▨ Pig bone
▨ Liquid containers	▨ Non-ceramic prestige goods
▨ Elaborate tall-stemmed cups	1. Elephant ivory carved tube
▨ Short plain cups	2. Elephant ivory comb
▨ Cooking vessels	3. Turquoise ornament
▉ Jade	4. & 5. Alligator skin/scutes

polished stone axes, some of which are perforated. Dawenkou sites provide abundant evidence for the cultivation of millets, and there is also some limited evidence for rice cultivation in the eastern Yellow River Valley during this period (Underhill 1997: 131).

Burials from the late Dawenkou period (around 2600 B.C.) reveal evidence for mortuary competition between different families and lineages through both offerings to the deceased and ritual feasting. At this time a minority of graves contained large quantities of pottery vessels. The richest male graves included numerous vessels, such as thin-walled stemmed cups, that may have been used to store and serve alcoholic beverages, while the wealthiest female graves contained many food vessels (Figure 22.5). A number of these pottery vessels were made specifically for ritual purposes, probably by specialist potters. Powerful families and lineages may have used funerary offerings and feasting as a way of manifesting their economic power and their ability to generate and control agricultural surpluses. As Underhill (2002: 246) notes, "Feasts would also have provided opportunities for hosting groups to acquire commitments for labor projects such as aid in farming, repairing houses, or defense. If they invested this additional labor at least partially in agriculture, they could provide a means to continue their position of economic power over time." Thus, there may have been a direct relationship between control of surplus agricultural products, feasting and funerary rituals, and the emergence of economic stratification. Craft specialization in mortuary pottery vessels may have been a consequence of this competition for agricultural surpluses.

THE LATE NEOLITHIC LONGSHAN CULTURE

The **Longshan culture** (2800/2600–1900 B.C.) appears over a wide area of northern China in the early third millennium B.C. as a result of increasing interactions between different geographical regions (Chang 1986: 242). Typical Longshan artifacts include black or gray pottery that is manufactured on a wheel and fired at a high temperature, highly polished thin black ritual vessels, mammal scapulae (shoulder blades) that are burned to produce cracks, and jade axes decorated with animal masks. In later historic times, the pattern of cracks in burned animal scapulae was used in divination, as a way to foretell the future and to make decisions. In the early Longshan period in Shandong, potters produced an eggshell-thin, tall cup with a stemmed base (Figure 22.6). These cups were labor intensive to manufacture and designed to hold fermented beverages (Underhill 2002: 248). The quality and quantity of these items indicate that a very rich ritual life had developed in China by the third millennium B.C.

The appearance of these eggshell-thin vessels also points to changes in social and economic status

FIGURE 22.6   Black egg-shell thin cup.

that emerged during the late Neolithic period. These fine stemmed vessels appear in a minority of graves. They are extremely fragile and were probably designed to be used only in mortuary rituals (Underhill 2002: 192). Since these vessels were both laborious to produce and designed to hold prestigious fermented beverages, they can be reasonably interpreted as status symbols. In addition, large-scale food offerings appear to be restricted to a small number of burials. Underhill (2002: 197) has suggested that the archaeological evidence points to the emergence of an elite social and ritual identity at this time, marking the beginnings of what was to become a class-stratified society by early historic times.

One of the most extensively excavated Longshan settlement sites is the site of **Hougang** near **Anyang** in Henan Province. The site covers an area of 400 by 250 m (437 by 273 yd.) and is enclosed by a wall made of stamped earth. The wall surrounds several dozen round houses, averaging 3.6 to 5 m (about 12 by 16 ft.) in diameter. The floors of the Hougang houses are covered with lime plaster, and the walls are made of wattle and daub or clay slabs. Burials of infants, either in pits or in urns, are ritual sacrifices associated with house construction activities. The infants were buried under wooden posts, house foundations, and even in the walls of the houses (Chang 1986: 269–270). A contemporary Longshan site has produced evidence for six adult human skulls interred within a house foundation. The skulls show signs of blows and appear to have been scalped after death. This is the earliest evidence for warfare, or interpersonal violence, in Chinese prehistory (Chang 1986: 270). Chang (1986: 288) suggests that this evidence of interpersonal violence is characteristic of societies that feature marked political and economic differentiation.

The Longshan period has also produced some early evidence for copper working (see Archaeology in Practice, Chapter 23). The metal items are mostly trinkets and small tools (Chang 1986: 287), but they do point to the beginnings of development of metallurgy, a technology that will play an increasingly important role in the early complex societies of the Chinese Bronze Age.

THE EARLY BRONZE AGE IN NORTH CHINA: THE ERLITOU PERIOD

The Chinese Early Bronze Age is the period where history and prehistory converge. The **Erlitou period** (ca. 1900–1500 B.C.) is named for the site of Erlitou in Henan Province. Excavations, which began at the site in the late 1950s, have revealed a complex, stratified site covering an area of about 1.5 by 2.5 km, or 1 by 1.5 mi. (Chang 1986: 309). The most impressive structures that archaeologists have uncovered to date are two rectangular palaces with stamped-earth foundations. The better preserved of the two sits on a foundation measuring 58 by 73 m (190 by 240 ft.). The foundation supported a hall surrounded by a corridor and entered by a gated veranda on the south (Figure 22.7). A number of smaller houses were also uncovered as well, pointing to substantial economic inequality in the Erlitou period. In 1978 archaeologists recognized a rammed-earth wall underlying the remains of the second palace. The remains of two earlier palaces, which may be about a century earlier in date, have been uncovered beneath

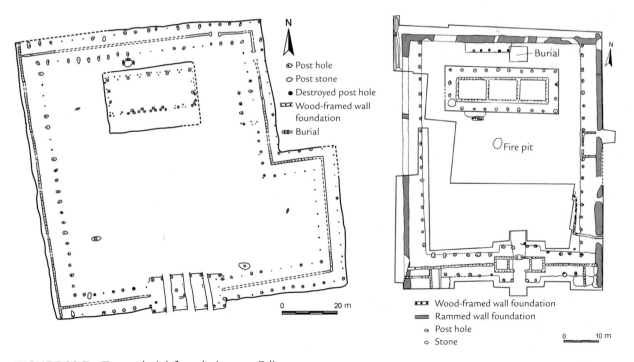

FIGURE 22.7 Two palatial foundations at Erlitou.

CASE STUDY

Excavations at Anyang

The discovery of the ruins of Yin, near Anyang in Henan Province, illustrates the interplay of history and archaeology in the study of early complex societies in China. In the late nineteenth century, a number of oracle bones with early Chinese inscriptions came to the attention of Chinese historians. The oracle bones describe divinations that were conducted on behalf of Shang kings who ruled from the capital city of Yin (Chang 1986: 317). The bones were traced to a village outside the city of Anyang, and excavations began at the site in 1928, under the direction of the Chinese historian Dong Zuobin (Yang 1999: 21). The Anyang excavations uncovered Shang temples, palaces, oracle bones, and a series of Shang royal mausoleums. The initial campaign of excavations was interrupted in 1937 by the events leading up to World War II, but excavations continue at the ruins of Yin to this day.

One of the most important discoveries made during the initial excavation was the excavation of 11 Shang royal tombs, including one that was unfinished, at the site of Xibeigang in Anyang. The excavation of the royal mausoleums was a massive logistical operation. During the 1934 and 1935 seasons, the excavators hired 500 workers per day to take part in the excavations (Yang 1999: 32). More than 1000 smaller graves have also been found in the cemetery (Chang 1986: 326). The best known of the royal tombs, Tomb 1001, is cruciform in plan, with four earthen ramps leading into the burial pit. The burial pit contained a wooden chamber, but the main burial was looted in antiquity. The royal tomb was surrounded by a series of human sacrifices; in many cases the heads of these victims were detached from their bodies (Chang 1986: 331). Grave goods included in this royal tomb included objects made of jade, shell, and bone, as well as pottery and ceramic vessels and stone sculptures. In describing the rich, late Shang tombs from Anyang, Underhill (2002: 209) notes that "as offerings to the deceased, bronze vessels symbolize privileged individual conspicuous consumption of food and drink in the afterlife."

Although all original 11 royal tombs that were excavated during the 1928–37 excavation seasons were robbed in antiquity, in 1976 Chinese archaeologists discovered an intact royal burial of Fu Hao, who appears to have been a royal consort. The tomb includes a number of very large bronze cooking and serving vessels. They may have been used for feasting during her lifetime, or they may symbolize her ability to provide large quantities of food for others (Underhill 2002: 215). The tomb clearly reflects her power and wealth.

While the royal burials are among the most spectacular finds from the ruins at Yin, a wide range of other structures and features have been uncovered as well. Excavations of Anyang have also revealed the foundations of palaces, as well as more humble dwellings that must have been inhabited by the lower classes. Workshops for the production of bronze artifacts, carved bone, and pottery vessels are also widely distributed around the Shang capital at Anyang. Shang society was clearly a class-stratified one where the agricultural surplus was mobilized to support craft specialists, monumental palace architecture, and the construction of the spectacular royal mausoleums. The human sacrifices reflect the power of the Shang ruling elite.

the second palace. A number of richly furnished tombs have been excavated in the courtyard of one of the earlier palaces. Over 3000 sq. m (0.75 ac.) have been excavated in and around the early palace structures since 2001.

The artifacts recovered from the Erlitou site were equally intriguing. In addition to utilitarian pottery vessels that must have been used for everyday culinary tasks, a variety of pots and cups were recovered that appear to have been used for serving and drinking alcoholic beverages. These vessels are identical in shape to later bronze vessels that were used for the same purposes. Other finds include long jade knives and axes and scapulae that appear to have been used in divination. While most utilitarian objects were made of stone and bone, a small number of copper tools and bronze tools were recovered from the site. In particular, bronze artifacts have been recovered from the tombs located in the courtyard of one of the early palaces at Erlitou. An early smelting workshop, where copper was separated from its impurities, has also been recovered from the Erlitou site.

What is most interesting about the Erlitou Period is that Erlitou and contemporary sites are located in central and western Henan and southwestern Shanxi, a region that was home to the earliest historically known Chinese dynasty, the Xia. The **Xia Dynasty** is the earliest of three Chinese Bronze Age dynasties that are described in historical sources from the later second and early first millennia B.C. These sources include inscriptions on oracle bones, bronze vessels, silk fabrics, and bamboo and wooden tablets. While no inscriptions have been recovered from Erlitou and contemporary sites, today many archaeologists equate the Erlitou culture and the Xia Dynasty (Chang 1986: 316; Underhill 2002: 25).

Cast bronze vessels first appear during the Erlitou period (Underhill 2002: 25). These objects must have been made by highly skilled craft specialists. Like the ceramic vessels described previously, these bronze cups appear to be associated with wine drinking. The evidence for palatial architecture and for tombs furnished with pottery and bronze vessels used for wine drinking point to significant social changes in the Chinese Early Bronze Age. In addition, the Erlitou site has produced evidence

for possible human sacrifice; one individual was apparently buried alive with his hands tied over his head. These data have led Chang (1986: 314) to suggest that "a powerful and wealthy elite that was decidedly a higher level than the chiefly aristocracy of the Lung-shan [Longshan] Culture sites" had developed by Erlitou times.

THE SHANG DYNASTY: THE APPEARANCE OF CITIES AND STATES IN BRONZE AGE CHINA

The emergence of a high degree of social stratification during the Erlitou period laid the basis for the appearance of complex societies, including urbanism and state formation, during the **Shang Dynasty** (ca. 1600–1046 B.C., also known as the Yin Dynasty). While the Erlitou period is known to us primarily through archaeological research, both historical records and archaeological research can shed light on the emergence of complex societies during the Shang Dynasty (Keightley 1983; Chang 1980).

While the excavations at Anyang clearly indicate that a complex state-level society had developed in China by late Shang Dynasty times, the excavations at Anyang are important for several other reasons as well. Anyang was the first site that allowed early Chinese written history to be directly linked to archaeological remains. The excavations were conducted with scientific precision and meticulous organization, setting a high standard for all subsequent Chinese excavation projects. As Chang (1986: 318) notes, "The importance of the Anyang excavations in the history of archaeology in China cannot be exaggerated."

THEORIES TO EXPLAIN THE RISE OF COMPLEX SOCIETIES IN CHINA

While complex, state-level societies had developed in China by the Shang Dynasty period, the roots of these developments can be traced back to the later Neolithic period. Underhill (2002) has argued that control over food surpluses may have been the key to the emergence of these complex societies. Underhill notes that many Chinese late Neolithic tombs contain food vessels that were designed to hold food

ARCHAEOLOGY IN PRACTICE

Remote Sensing Closer to Earth: Nondestructive Archaeology

FIGURE 22.A Using a computerized resistivity meter to search for buried archaeological features. The electrodes pushed into the soil are the base of the frame.

FIGURE 22.B Ground-penetrating radar equipment mounted on a mobile cart (SmartCart, manufactured by Sensors & Software, Inc.). SmartCart photograph courtesy of Sensors & Software, Inc.

Aerial and satellite photography and radar were described in Archaeology in Practice, Chapter 19. Archaeologists today are making increasing use of a number of other forms of remote sensing that are applied on the ground. These techniques and instruments can measure and map spatial variations in the geophysical properties of the soil that can reflect human-made features, such as buried walls, ditches, or graves. These data help guide the placement of conventional archaeological excavations and can frequently recover valuable data, such as the outline of a structure's buried foundation, without any destructive digging at all.

Although there are many variants, the most frequently used techniques today include soil resistivity surveying, magnetometry, and ground-penetrating radar.

Resistivity surveying involves measuring the resistance of the soil to the flow of electrical current. Soil resistivity reflects the physical properties of the soil—most importantly, the soil's moisture content. Soil moisture tends to be higher in disturbed soils (such as in ditches, pits, or graves). Since water is highly conductive of electricity, moist soils have a low electrical resistance. Conversely, buried stone

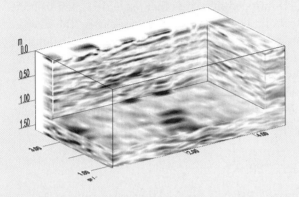

FIGURE 22.C Three-dimensional computer display of a 4 by 3 m subsample block derived from a GPR survey of the Han Dynasty tomb mound at Xian, shown on top. Dark blocks represent individual tombs, while the dark horizontal bands are construction layers.

walls tend to have high electrical resistance. Resistivity surveys are usually conducted by taking measurements across carefully spaced electrodes inserted into the soil at regular intervals within a grid laid out over the archaeological site (Figure 22.A). These measurements are then plotted to show the variations in the readings over the site, which may reveal distinctive areas, known as anomalies, that may indicate archaeological features. Modern resistivity-measuring instruments are quite sophisticated; the readings are recorded automatically within the instrument and are downloaded directly into computer-mapping and analysis software.

A magnetometry survey is carried out in much the same manner as a resistivity survey. A precision magnetometer measures subtle distortions of the Earth's magnetic field resulting from variations in the magnetic properties of the soil and bedrock of a site. Buried iron

objects create distinctive magnetic anomalies, but iron-containing soils and rocks, burned clay (such as beneath a hearth), and fired bricks can also be detected. In practice, resistivity and magnetometry surveys are often carried out in tandem, as the two methods provide complementary data about a site.

Ground-penetrating radar (GPR) can provide a wealth of data about the subsurface character of a site. The GPR instrument consists of a special small radar antenna, usually pulled or rolled over the site, that directs its beam vertically downward into the earth (Figure 22.B). Modern GPR equipment is frequently directly linked to a computer display that can present a subsurface profile of the site as the survey is conducted. The radar beam is partially reflected back into the antenna at depths where the character of the soil or rock changes abruptly, so the profiles produced reflect the site's stratigraphy. Buried

walls, pits and ditches, and voids also show clearly. A series of radar profiles can be combined by sophisticated software to provide both two-dimensional maps and three-dimensional computer models of subsurface features. Figure 22.C shows a GPR survey of a Han Dynasty tomb at Xian.

and fermented beverages. She argues that powerful Neolithic families and lineages may have been able to control food surpluses. They used these surpluses to finance lavish funerary displays and to host ritual feasts. Powerful families were able to use these feasts to secure labor which, in turn, could be used to finance progressively more elaborate feasts and funerals. Specialized crafts, such as pottery and bronze manufacture, developed in order to produce vessels that could be used to prepare and serve food for funerals and feasts. Thus, in China, craft specialization appears to be a consequence of control of food surpluses. Viewed in Childe's (Chapter 19) terms, the critical issue in the late Chinese Neolithic and early Bronze Age may have been the control of the social surplus, which could then be used to sponsor progressively more elaborate funerals and feasts.

Underhill's arguments are based on detailed analyses of pottery and bronze vessels that were deposited in later Neolithic and early Bronze Age tombs. Many Chinese tombs have been excavated at Anyang and elsewhere; however, many more remain to be excavated. As noted in the introduction to this chapter, the actual burial mound of Emperor Qin has not yet been excavated. One problem facing archaeologists is that tombs are very expensive and laborious to excavate. For example, each of the royal tombs at Anyang required 7000 work days to excavate (Chang 1986: 327). In order to guide the excavation of tombs and other large buried features, archaeologists have developed a number of remote sensing techniques that allow them to "see" below the surface of the ground prior to excavation. Some of these techniques are described in the Archaeology in Practice box in this chapter.

CONCLUSION

Exciting new finds are discovered in China almost every year. For example, in 2001 archaeologists working at the Yin ruins in Anyang discovered the intact tomb of a high-ranking military officer of the Shang Dynasty. New finds will continue to clarify our understanding of early Chinese society and culture. However, the excavations that have been conducted over the past 80 years have revealed a clear pattern of social change beginning in the later Neolithic.

While the earliest stages of plant domestication in northern China remain poorly known, farming villages were well-established in the Yellow River Valley by 5000 B.C. By later Neolithic time, burials reveal clear evidence for economic and social differentiation. The richest burials contain many ceramic food vessels, including prestige items such as eggshell-thin ceramic cups that were designed to hold alcoholic beverages. Palaces appear by the Erlitou period, indicating that power lineages or families had gained political and economic control over the lower classes. By late Shang times, the evidence for human sacrifice in the royal tombs indicates that the rulers had the power of life and death over their subjects.

KEY TERMS

Anyang   332
Banpo   330
Dawenkou   330
Erlitou period   333
Hougang   332

Longshan culture   332
Shang (or Yin)
   Dynasty   335
Xia Dynasty   335
Yangshao period   329

QUESTIONS FOR DISCUSSION

1. Why do you think that increasing interaction between different regions developed during the late Neolithic Longshan period? What role might this interaction have played in the development of complex societies?

2. How do the late Shang Dynasty tombs at Anyang compare to the royal tombs at Ur in Mesopotamia?

3. How can remote sensing techniques be used to guide excavation projects?

FURTHER READING

Underhill, Anne P.
   2002   *Craft Production and Social Change in Northern China.* New York: Plenum.
   An innovative study of the rise of complex societies in northern China that examines the role that control over food surpluses may have played in this process. It is one of the few up-to-date summaries of the archaeological evidence for later Neolithic and Bronze Age China written in English.

23

LATER PREHISTORIC EUROPE

A Different Pattern of Cultural Complexity

Stonehenge, perhaps the world's most famous prehistoric monument, has fascinated scholars for centuries (Figure 23.1). In 1620 Inigo Jones, King James I's architect, interpreted Stonehenge as a provincial Roman temple, while eighteenth-century antiquaries saw it as a sanctuary of the Druids, or Celtic priests. Even today, neo-Druids gather at Stonehenge on June 21 to observe the summer solstice. Archaeological research in and around Stonehenge, in its final form, has shown that this impressive monument is far older than the Romans or even the Druidic priests. Stonehenge was built by the prehistoric inhabitants of Britain nearly 4000 years ago, a full 2000 years before the Roman conquest of Britain. What kind of society could have organized the building of such a large and impressive stone structure?

Stonehenge was not built by people who lived in cities. Until the middle of the first millennium B.C., all the inhabitants of temperate Europe (Europe north of the Alps) lived in small agricultural villages, hamlets, and isolated farmsteads. Beginning about 4000 B.C., however, the inhabitants of temperate Europe began to develop many characteristics of complex societies, including widespread trade networks, craft specialization (especially in the production of metal artifacts), agricultural intensification, and elaborate social hierarchies. This chapter will trace the development of complex societies in later prehistoric Europe, beginning about 6000 years ago.

FIGURE 23.1 Stonehenge today.

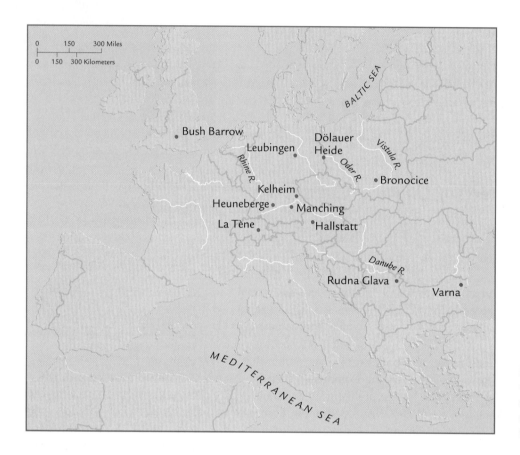

FIGURE 23.2 Map of temperate Europe showing locations of sites mentioned in this chapter.

CHANGES IN SETTLEMENT AND SUBSISTENCE IN THE LATER NEOLITHIC OF TEMPERATE EUROPE

As we saw in Chapter 18, farming communities were established throughout temperate Europe by about 4000 B.C., and by about 3000 B.C. farmers had replaced hunter-gatherers throughout the region. Mixed farming villages, whose economy was based on cultivating cereals and herding domestic animals, extended from the Balkans to Scandinavia and from Ireland to the Ukraine. At that time several important changes took place in subsistence technology and settlement that set the stage for the development of more complex societies in temperate Europe. One of the most important was the introduction of wheeled carts and the consequent use of oxen as draft animals. The introduction of wheeled carts allowed farmers to spread out across the landscape. In central Europe villages and farms were no longer concentrated in the river valleys.

Farming settlements spread into the upland areas between the watersheds; as a consequence, settlements became more dispersed, and the landscape filled up with small farming villages.

A second important technological innovation was the introduction of the scratch plow, or ard, which allowed farmers to till larger plots of land than could be planted using a simple digging stick or hoe. In addition, plowing would have maintained soil fertility by aerating and incorporating new organic materials into the soil (Bogucki 1988: 176). Traces of plow marks can be seen when old land surfaces are preserved, for example, under mounds of earth. The ard, like carts, would have been pulled by oxen. The use of animal power is one of the most important technological innovations in later Neolithic Europe.

During the early Neolithic period in Europe, farming settlements were uniformly small villages and hamlets. By the fourth millennium B.C., larger

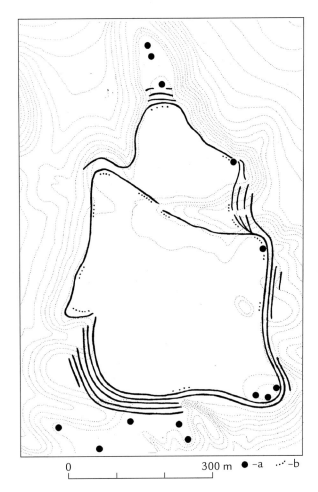

FIGURE 23.3 Complex earthworks surrounding the Neolithic site of Dölauer-Heide in central Germany. a = barrows   b = palisade traces

excavators of Bronocice, hypothesize that the site was the seat of authority for a small polity, a sort of regional capital. Alternatively, these sites may have served as periodic gathering places for large groups of people for feasting or other ritual purposes (Whittle 1996: 223).

The fortified nature of these larger sites raises the possibility that they may have played some role in warfare or raiding. Neolithic warfare most likely served to resolve conflicts, maintain buffer zones between neighboring groups, and capture resources, for example, through cattle raiding (Bogucki 1988: 207). In those situations the larger fortified sites may well have served as refuge places for both people and livestock.

Whether the larger sites such as Bronocice served as refuge places during raiding or whether they served as seats of authority and ritual gathering places, their presence indicates that the later Neolithic inhabitants of central Europe had some form of political organization that was larger than the individual family or village. The nature of this political leadership, however, is very difficult to determine; later Neolithic burials provide little evidence for sizable differences in status and wealth. Did this leadership take the form of clan elders, community leaders, or even war leaders? Whatever form this incipient leadership took, the emergence of political organization beyond the level of the family clearly represents one of the first steps toward the development of more complex societies in later prehistoric temperate Europe.

A second, related change is seen in the patterns of trade and exchange during the later Neolithic. Long-distance trade in exotic items such as Mediterranean shells existed throughout the Neolithic in Europe. However, during the late Neolithic, regional trade networks developed for commodities such as flint and salt. A large number of later Neolithic flint mines are known from both the British Isles and continental Europe, and the miners appear to have used antler picks to extract the flint from the earth. Commodities such as flint and salt may have been exchanged as part of a process of alliance formation in the later Neolithic.

sites appear for the first time in central and western Europe. Well-excavated examples from central Europe include the hilltop sites of **Bronocice** in Poland and **Dölauer-Heide** in Germany (Figure 23.2). At Dölauer-Heide a complex series of ditches and earthen banks encloses an area of 25 ha (about 62 ac.) (Figure 23.3). The site of Bronocice (Milisauskas and Kruk 1993) is even larger, covering an area of more than 50 ha (125 ac.). The site is located on high ground overlooking the floodplain of the Nidzica River, a tributary of the Vistula. At Bronocice a series of smaller earthworks was constructed over a long period of time. A number of functions have been suggested for these large fortified sites. Milisauskas and Kruk (1993: 86), the

ARCHAEOLOGY IN PRACTICE

Analysis of Metal Artifacts

Metal artifacts have been recovered from a wide variety of contexts in Europe, Mesopotamia, Egypt, the Indus Valley, China, western Mexico, and Peru. These objects are of particular interest to archaeologists who study complex societies, since manufacture of metal objects is a complex, multistage process that may have involved either full-time or part-time craft specialists. Historically, the study of ancient metal artifacts has played a central role in later European prehistory because changes in the style of bronze artifacts have been used to subdivide the European Bronze Age into distinctive chronological phases (Champion et al. 1984: 198). The study of metal artifacts recovered from archaeological sites is termed **archaeometallurgy.** Laboratory studies of metal artifacts can reveal both the ways in which these objects were manufactured and the chemical composition of the metals used

(see, for example, Hamilton 1996; Vandkilde 1996). In addition, archaeometallurgists often design experiments that attempt to reproduce ancient techniques used to extract and smelt ores and to manufacture metal objects.

The production of copper and bronze items involved several different processes, beginning with mining. Most copper ores contain impurities, so copper has to be smelted, or heated to a sufficiently high temperature to separate the copper from its impurities. Once the copper is separated from its impurities, copper and bronze artifacts are generally produced by casting. The copper is heated to its melting point, about 1100° C. The molten copper is then poured into a single or multipart mold. Once the copper object has been cast, it can be further shaped by annealing, or reheating, and hammering the metal. Annealing and cold-hammering can

be used to strengthen the cutting edge of a tool, such as a dagger.

Metallography, the microscopic examination of the structure of metals, can reveal the ways in which a metal object was manufactured. In order to prepare a sample, a small piece of metal is taken from an artifact. The metal sample is mounted in a resin, polished with a series of progressively finer grits, and sometimes etched. When the sample is examined under a high-power microscope, the microstructure of the metal is revealed. For example, structures known as annealing twins indicate that the metal was worked by annealing (Figure 23.A).

Compositional analyses are also important in the study of metal objects. Techniques such a proton-activated X ray fluorescence (PIXE) can reveal the elemental composition of the metal. This is particularly important in distinguishing copper from its alloys, such as tin

THE BEGINNINGS OF METALLURGY IN EUROPE

Small numbers of copper objects are found at Neolithic sites throughout the Near East and Europe. At some early Neolithic sites in Turkey, native copper (naturally occurring metallic copper) was hammered to shape as early as the seventh millennium B.C. However, the smelting of copper (the removal of impurities from copper ore) and the casting of copper objects require more sophisticated technologies (see Archaeology in Practice box above). Copper can be separated from oxide and carbonate ores at temperatures of 700° to 800° C (1300° to 1500° F), while sulfide ores are more difficult to reduce and require higher temperatures. Melting and casting

copper requires temperatures of approximately 1100° C (2000° F). It is important to note, however, that the development of metallurgy did not take place in isolation. Some forms of pottery from southeast Europe were regularly heated to temperatures of 700° C (1300° F). In technological terms pottery technology seems to have paved the way for early metallurgy in Europe (Renfrew 1972: 175). By the fifth millennium B.C., the smelting and casting of copper had developed in southeast Europe. Molds, crucibles, and copper slag provide evidence for the development of a copper technology. In addition, sites such as **Rudna Glava** (Jovanovic 1980) provide evidence for the mining of copper ores. Rudna Glava is located in northeast Serbia, far from contemporary bronze. For example, X ray fluorescence analyses conducted on the surface of the Iceman's axe showed that it was 99.7% copper and not bronze as originally thought (Spindler 1994: 90). In the 1960s and 1970s, archaeologists had hoped to use trace elements within the metals to identify metal sources. However, this has not proved practicable, in part because broken metal objects from different regions can be melted and recast together.

Iron ores were common throughout Europe, and iron was also mined and smelted. The slags recovered from smelting sites throughout Europe suggest that iron was smelted at temperatures of about 1100 to 1200° C (Geselowitz 2004). However, iron, unlike copper and bronze, was not cast. Technologies for casting iron were not developed in the West until the Industrial Revolution. Instead, iron was worked by forging or heating and hammering the solid metal. A few hammers, tongs, and anvils have been recovered from early Iron Age sites in Europe, documenting the forging process.

FIGURE 23.A Metallograph of a Bronze Age object from Armenia showing annealing twins. Credit line: Laura A. Tedesco.

In the early Iron Age, iron was usually smelted in a shaft furnace. The Kelheim site discussed in this chapter has produced substantial evidence for iron working, including many tons of slag. As an outgrowth of the Kelheim excavations (Wells 1993), the SMELT project was designed to reconstruct a replica of an Iron Age shaft furnace. The furnace was fired for a period of eight days, using three tons of charcoal and producing hundreds of pounds of iron bloom—raw metallic iron. The remains of the experimental furnaces have been excavated using standard archaeological techniques so that they can be compared to the furnaces that have been recovered from Iron Age sites.

settlement sites. At Rudna Glava miners followed veins of copper ores up to 20 m (65 ft.) into the ground. Alternating heating and cooling were used to break up the ore and to facilitate quarrying.

Copper is an attractive, but relatively soft, metal. Copper tools do not provide a technological advantage over stone implements. Therefore, early copper items are more likely to have served as objects of prestige and display than as functional tools. Copper and gold ornaments are often found in burials from the later Neolithic in southeast Europe. One of the best-known sites is the fifth-millennium B.C. **Varna** cemetery on the Black Sea coast in Bulgaria (Bailey 2004). Of the 281 graves known from the Varna cemetery, 82 included copper objects and 61 included items of gold. The 3000 gold ornaments recovered from the Varna cemetery represent the oldest gold metallurgy known anywhere in the world. The copper items recovered from the Varna graves include needles, axes, and other tools, although few appear to have been used. Some of the graves at Varna are very richly furnished, while others contain only small numbers of grave goods. The adult male buried in Grave 43, for example, was accompanied by over 990 gold objects weighing more than 1.5 kg, or about 3.3 lbs. (Whittle 1996: 97). Striking variations in grave wealth are uncommon in the late Neolithic, but they become more common in the subsequent Bronze Age.

The use of copper was widespread in Europe during the fourth and third millennia B.C. For

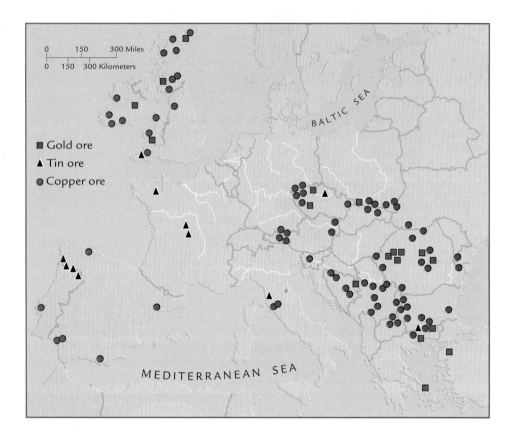

FIGURE 23.4 Map showing copper, tin, and gold sources in Europe.

example, the Ice Man (see Chapter 1) carried a copper axe as part of his equipment. Some archaeologists use the term **Copper Age** (or **Chalcolithic**) to describe the European late Neolithic societies of the fourth and third millennia B.C.

THE BEGINNINGS OF THE BRONZE AGE IN TEMPERATE EUROPE

Metal technology was revolutionized in the third millennium B.C. with the development of bronze. Bronze was most commonly made by alloying copper with tin (about 10 percent tin was used), although copper-arsenic alloys were also produced. When compared with pure copper, bronze is a harder metal, and it is easier to cast. The addition of tin can lower the melting point of copper by 200° C, or 392° F (Pearce 2004: 8). Bronze could be used to make tools that were technologically superior to stone tools. It was during the **Bronze Age,** beginning in the later third millennium B.C., that

metal replaced stone for most tools and weapons. In addition, the evidence for the extraction and working of metals becomes far more widespread in temperate Europe. The technology of bronze metalworking developed rapidly and distinctively in Europe, and it is likely bronze was manufactured by individuals who were at least part-time specialists.

The widespread use of metals had two important social consequences. First, it provided new opportunities for the accumulation of wealth. Unlike earlier stone tools, metal objects could be melted down and reused. Second, the widespread use of metals required the development of trade networks to guarantee regular supplies of raw materials. Unlike flint, which is widely distributed throughout Europe, deposits of copper and tin are highly localized. Areas such as southern Scandinavia and northern Germany were entirely lacking in raw materials (Figure 23.4); however, traces of molds and crucibles indicate that bronze was being cast in

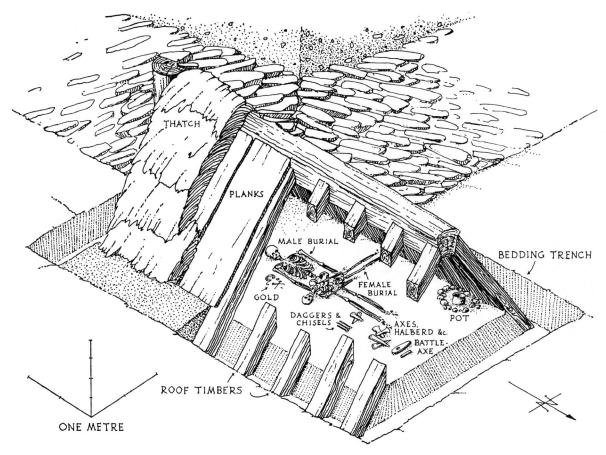

FIGURE 23.5 Diagram of the Leubingen burial, showing the burial chamber and the location of grave goods.

those regions. Scandinavian and northern German metalworking was dependent on the regular, long-distance trade networks in metals. The foundations for that trade may have been established through the development of regional trade networks in the later Neolithic.

The control of the trade in metals may have provided new opportunities for the accumulation of wealth. It is in the early Bronze Age, beginning about 2300 B.C., that we see real evidence for increasing differences in social status and material wealth in temperate Europe. They are reflected in variations in the wealth placed in burials and in the amounts of energy that are devoted to burial rituals. The differences are seen most clearly in areas that are near major ore sources or along important trade routes. One such area is in east central Europe, including parts of Austria, eastern Germany, and the Czech and Slovak

Republics. Tin was available in the Bohemian Ore Mountains, along the border between the Czech Republic and eastern Germany, while copper could be obtained from the Hartz Mountains, the Alps, and the central part of the Slovak Republic.

This region has produced a small number of very rich graves that contrast sharply with typical burial practices. Most individuals were buried in pits with pottery vessels as the only grave goods. However, the **Leubingen burial** in eastern Germany included a far richer assemblage of grave goods (Figure 23.5). The body of an elderly man was placed in an oak chamber and covered with a mound of stones, which, in turn, was covered with an earthen mound. A second body, possibly female and probably immature, was placed across his hips. Included among the grave goods were gold jewelry, pottery, a whetstone, a pick, a halberd, three

FIGURE 23.6 Gold plate and belt buckle recovered from the early Bronze Age Bush Barrow in southern Britain.

formed part of a helmet, a gold clothing plate and belt hook, and a bronze axe. In addition, the grave goods included bone zigzag mountings that originally decorated the wooden shaft of a stone mace head. These items may well symbolize authority, suggesting that the person who was interred in Bush Barrow wielded some degree of political power. Traditionally, early Bronze Age societies in temperate Europe have been viewed as **chiefdoms,** or societies that are ruled by a chief or leader but that lack a permanent government or bureaucracy (see Chapter 19). Political authority lies in the power and person of the chief.

By the end of the early Bronze Age, temperate Europe had developed many of the characteristics seen in complex societies of the ancient Near and Middle East: craft specialization, regular patterns of long-distance trade and exchange, social differentiation, and the development of political organizations that were larger than the individual family or village. Bronze Age Europe differed, however, in one important respect from the ancient societies of Egypt, Mesopotamia, and the Indus Valley. Bronze Age Europe lacked towns and cities. It was not until the middle of the first millennium B.C., over 1000 years later, that towns and cities began to develop in Europe north of the Alps.

EUROPE'S FIRST TOWNS: LATE HALLSTATT TOWNS AND TRADE

Europe's towns first developed during the **Iron Age** (ca. 800 to 1 B.C.), a period in which iron gradually replaced bronze in the manufacture of tools and weapons. The European Iron Age is generally divided into two phases, an earlier period known as the **Hallstatt** (800 to 480 B.C.) and a later period known as the **La Tène** (ca. 480 to 1 B.C.) (Malin-Boyce 2004a). In prehistoric Europe, iron tools were wrought or forged, unlike bronze, which was cast. The production of wrought iron was a complex process, and early iron tools were often either too brittle or too soft. Iron, however, had one major advantage over bronze. Iron ores were ubiquitous across temperate Europe, while copper and tin sources were relatively rare. As we shall see, iron production increased throughout the Iron Age in Europe, and by the late first millennium B.C. some temperate

daggers, two flanged axes, three chisels, and additional gold objects. The contrast between this rich burial and the typical early Bronze Age burial is far greater than the contrast between the richest and the poorest Neolithic burials, suggesting increasing social and economic inequality.

Rich early Bronze Age burials are not limited to east central Europe. In the area around Stonehenge (Mallone 2004) in southern Britain, a group of very rich burials is contemporary with the final phase of construction of the monument around 2000 B.C. The Stonehenge region not only is rich in agricultural and pasture land but also is near an important source of tin located in Cornwall, southwestern Britain. The elaborate early Bronze Age burials in the Stonehenge area were placed under tumuli, or earthen mounds. One of the most spectacular is **Bush Barrow,** which yielded a diverse assemblage of metal objects (Figure 23.6), including copper and bronze daggers, bronze rivets that may have

European communities were exporting iron, including finished iron objects, to the Romans.

Trade seems to have played a major role in the formation of Europe's first towns, which appear in west central Europe between about 600 and 480 B.C., during the later part of the Hallstatt period (Wells 1980). In the seventh and sixth centuries B.C., Greek merchants from the eastern Mediterranean established a number of trading colonies in the western Mediterranean (Boardman 1980; Wells 2004a). The Greek merchants needed to obtain raw materials and agricultural products for the rapidly increasing Greek populations. One of those colonies was Massilia (modern Marseille), located at the mouth of the Rhône River on a hill north of the old harbor.

At about 600 B.C., towns appear for the first time in eastern France and southern Germany. The best known of these early towns is the **Heuneberg** (Arnold 2004; Kimmig 1975), a site that overlooks the Danube in southern Germany and is surrounded by rich burials. Archaeological evidence indicates that pottery manufacturing, bronze working, and ironworking took place at the Heuneberg. The site housed several thousand people at its peak. In addition, a number of artifacts and features point to close contacts with the Mediterranean world. These include amphorae, which were used to transport wine, and Greek pottery, as well as part of the town wall itself. The wall was built of sun-dried bricks set on a limestone foundation, a technique that was common in the Mediterranean areas but previously unknown in temperate Europe.

The burial mounds that surround the Heuneberg also include Mediterranean imports. These Iron Age burials were often placed in wagons within wooden chambers and included imported objects such as bronze and pottery vessels, which reflected close ties with the Mediterranean world. The character of the individuals who are buried in these so-called princes' graves has been a subject of debate. Are they members of the traditional elite classes who were able to gain control over long-distance trade (Champion et al, 1984: 287), or do they represent a new class of wealthy entrepreneurs who were able to organize and profit from trade with the Mediterranean (Wells 1984)? Regardless of who controlled the trade with the Mediterranean, it is clear that the initial development of towns in central Europe is closely related to the establishment of trade relationships with the Mediterranean world. Although we have no record of the types of goods that were exported from central Europe, it is likely that agricultural produce, animal products, and forest products such as timber and furs were exported from the Heuneberg region.

The reliance of the late Hallstatt towns such as the Heuneberg on trade with the Mediterranean is underscored by their rapid collapse in the early fifth century B.C. In the late sixth century B.C., the Greek colonists at Massilia developed trade relationships with the inhabitants of the Po Valley in northern Italy, trade with central Europe decreased dramatically, and by about 450 B.C., sites such as the Heuneberg were abandoned.

THE OPPIDA AND THE ORIGINS OF URBANISM IN TEMPERATE EUROPE

Around 480 to 475 B.C., a new style of decorated metalwork appeared in temperate Europe. The style is known as La Tène, after the type site in Switzerland. The art included anthropomorphic and zoomorphic figures as well as stylized floral motifs borrowed from Greek and Etruscan art (Figure 23.7). This style of decoration was associated with people whom

FIGURE 23.7 Early La Tène art: a fifth-century B.C. gold necklace from Rodenbach.

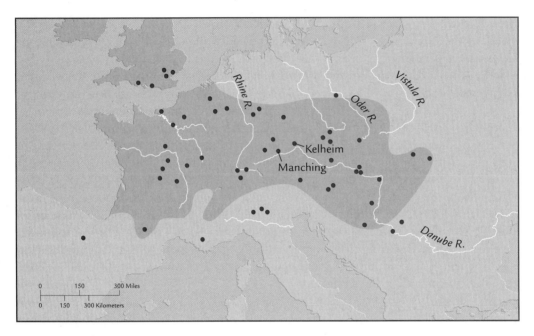

FIGURE 23.8 Map of temperate Europe, showing the distribution of the oppida (after Cunliffe 1979: 64).

the Greek and Roman authors called Celts (Malin-Boyce 2004b). The Celts occupied a large part of central Europe, from the Atlantic to the Black Sea, in the last few centuries B.C. Greek and Roman accounts of the Celts can be used in conjunction with archaeology to provide information about the ways of life of these late Iron Age peoples.

During the early La Tène period, there is no archaeological evidence for towns and cities in Europe north of the Mediterranean. However, both archaeological and historical records indicate that Celtic populations were expanding rapidly throughout the fourth and third centuries B.C. Historical sources indicate that Celtic societies were chiefdoms. La Tène societies lacked a permanent bureaucracy and many formal institutions of government; instead, these societies were held together by bonds of **clientship.** Patron–client relationships are long-term relationships established between unequals. The patron, who is usually a wealthy, high-status individual, may provide the client with seed grain, livestock, or other necessities. In return the client may be required to labor on the patron's farm or to pay the patron in food as a form of rent. The

client owes allegiance and loyalty to the patron, especially in times of war. Historical sources, such as Julius Caesar's account of the Gallic wars, indicate that clientship was a central organizing principle of late La Tène society.

About 200 B.C., large, fortified sites appear across much of central and western Europe. These sites, which are termed **oppida,** are permanently occupied, urban sites that appear to have served a variety of different functions (Collis 2004). The oppida, like the earlier commercial towns of the late Hallstatt period, served as centers of craft production and trade. However, unlike their late Hallstatt predecessors, the oppida appear to have served a number of other political functions. They served as refuge places for people and livestock in times of war, and they may have served as residences of the landed nobility or patron classes (Bintliff 1984: note 67). As can be seen in Figure 23.8, the oppida are quite regularly distributed across the European landscape, suggesting that they may also have served as regional political capitals.

As the archaeological evidence from Manching and Kelheim shows, the oppida represent Europe's

CASE STUDY

Manching and Kelheim

One of the best-known oppida is the site of **Manching** in southern Germany (Malin-Boyce 2004c). Excavations, conducted at the site since the 1950s, have yielded a wealth of information on late Iron Age life in central Europe. Manching is located at the conjunction of the Danube and Paar Rivers, and its fortifications enclose an area of 380 ha (940 ac.) (Figure 23.B). About 200 ha (500 ac.) at the center of the site were densely occupied by a planned community with wide streets and rectangular timber buildings. A variety of craft activities took place at Manching, including pottery making, woodworking, iron manufacture, and the production of glass jewelry. Different crafts appear to have been practiced in different parts of the site, another indication of urban planning. The large size of the oppida and the degree of urban planning seen at sites such as Manching distinguish the oppida from the earlier late Hallstatt towns.

Since the late 1980s, excavations have also taken place at the oppidum at **Kelheim** in Bavaria, southern Germany, under the direction of Peter

Wells of the University of Minnesota (Wells 1987, 1993; 2004b). The oppidum at Kelheim is located about 30 km (19 mi.) from Manching, at the confluence of the Danube and the Altmühl Rivers. Kelheim is one of the largest oppida in Europe; its fortification walls enclose about 600 ha (1500 ac.) of land (Figure 23.C). Kelheim appears to have been the site of intensive iron production at about 100 B.C. The hilltop portion of the site is pockmarked with pits that were used to obtain iron ore. Excavations were focused on an area of settlement along the Altmühl River. In addition to pottery, animal bones, and a range of iron objects, the excavations yielded enormous quantities of iron ore and slag, a by-product of iron manufacture. At Kelheim, it is estimated that 75,000 tons of iron ore were used to produce 25,000 tons of iron. The scale of iron production is unmatched in later European prehistory. In addition, it was during the late Iron Age that iron became commonly used for a wide range of specialized tools and weapons, including many specialized agricultural tools that continued to be used in Europe until the mechanization of farming in the late nineteenth and early twentieth centuries. Sites such as Kelheim supplied the raw materials for the production of those specialized iron tools.

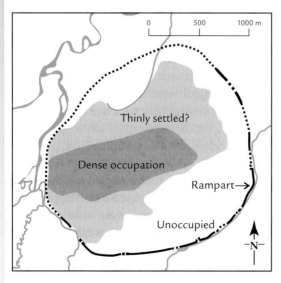

FIGURE 23.B   Plan of the oppidum at Manching.

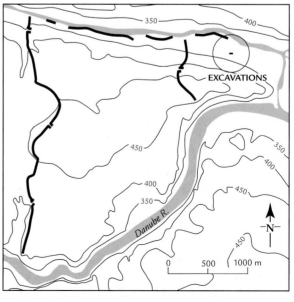

FIGURE 23.C   Map of the oppidum at Kelheim, showing locations of the excavations and of the site's defenses.

first cities. Most of the oppida, however, fell out of use with the Roman conquest of much of western and central Europe in the first century B.C. The Romans established their own towns and cities in western Europe; sites such as Paris, London, York, and Cologne were initially established by the Romans. However, even the Roman cities were relatively short-lived. For example, long-term excavations at the city of York in England have shown that the town was largely depopulated in the fifth and sixth centuries A.D. It was not until the early Middle Ages that cities were successfully established in most of temperate Europe. It is these successful early medieval towns that are the predecessors of the towns and cities of modern Europe.

CONCLUSION

When compared with Mesopotamia, Egypt, and the Indus Valley, later prehistoric Europe represents a different kind of complex society. By the later Neolithic period, European agriculture had intensified dramatically through the use of the cart and the plow. In addition, regional trade networks and the beginnings of political leadership had developed by about 3000 B.C. Excavations of early Bronze Age cemeteries have shown that by 2000 B.C. European societies were characterized by real differences in social status, political power, and material wealth. Regular long-distance trade in metals was established throughout temperate Europe during the early Bronze Age, and the rapid development of European metallurgy suggests that metal objects were made by craft specialists. Thus, it is clear that by 2000 B.C. Europe had developed many of the characteristics that we traditionally associate with complex societies.

Urbanism, however, was a relatively late development in prehistoric Europe. The first towns did not develop until the middle of the first millennium B.C., and the first cities did not develop until the last two centuries B.C. When urban sites did appear in Europe, they were clearly related to intensive trade and commerce. The Hallstatt towns owed their existence to trade with the Greek colonies in the west, while many of the oppida were involved in commercial production of commodities such as iron.

KEY TERMS

Archaeometallurgy 342	Heuneberg 347
Bronocice 341	Iron Age 346
Bronze Age 344	Kelheim 349
Bush Barrow 346	La Tène 346
Chiefdoms 346	Leubingen burial 345
Clientship 348	Manching 349
Copper Age (Chalcolithic) 344	Oppida 348
Dölauer-Heide 341	Rudna Glava 342
Hallstatt 346	Varna 343

QUESTIONS FOR DISCUSSION

1. How did the introduction of the plow and the cart affect prehistoric European societies?

2. Why did urbanism develop so late in European prehistory?

3. Should prehistoric Europe be considered a complex society? Why or why not?

4. How does the distinctive European archaeological record contribute to our understanding of the origins and development of complex societies?

FURTHER READING

Bogucki, Peter, ed.
1993 *Case Studies in European Prehistory.* Boca Raton, FL: CRC Press.
Several case studies in this volume focus on later Neolithic, Bronze Age, and Iron Age sites in temperate Europe. The case studies not only present new data on recent excavation projects but also focus on the ways archaeological research projects develop over time. By reading these case studies, students can begin to understand both the intellectual and the personal sides of archaeological research.

Bogucki, Peter, and Pam J. Crabtree, eds.
2004 *Ancient Europe 8000 B.C.–A.D. 1000: Encyclopedia of the Barbarian World.* New York: Charles Scribner's Sons.
This two-volume work surveys European prehistory from the Mesolithic through the Viking Period. Part 4 covers the later Neolithic, Part 5 covers the European Iron Age, and Part 6 covers the Iron Age.

Cunliffe, B., ed.
1998 *Prehistoric Europe: An Illustrated History.* Oxford and New York: Oxford University Press.
This textbook provides an overview of European prehistory from the Paleolithic through the Roman period. The individual chapters are written by specialists.

24

COMPLEX SOCIETIES IN MESOAMERICA

In 1519 the Spanish conquistador Cortez and his followers were the first Westerners to lay eyes on the Aztec capital **Tenochtitlán** in the Valley of Mexico. This native American city, home to perhaps 200,000 people, was centered on an island within Lake Texcoco in central Mexico (Figure 24.1). To European eyes, Tenochtitlán would

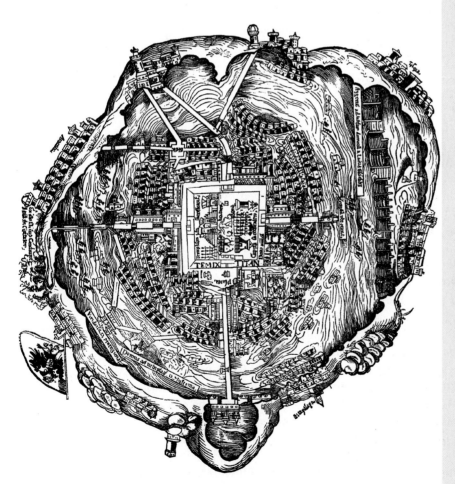

FIGURE 24.1   Sixteenth-century Spanish view of the Aztec capital of Tenochtitlán.

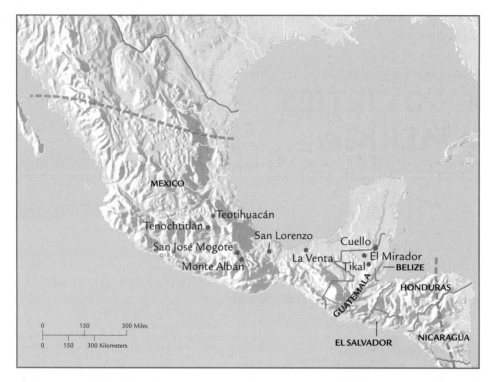

FIGURE 24.2 Map of Mesoamerica, showing the geographical limits of the region and the major sites discussed in the chapter.

have teemed with people; the Aztec capital was far larger than most of the contemporary cities of Europe. The center of the city was reached by three causeways from the mainland and was dominated by a great pyramid topped by twin temples dedicated to the Aztec gods of war and rain. Nearby, an enormous rack of skulls provided mute testimony to the thousands of human sacrifices that were regularly performed for the Aztec gods. The temples and plazas of the central precinct were surrounded by the palaces of the Aztec emperors, including the palace of the emperor Moctezuma II, who would lose his kingdom to Cortez and his followers. Tenochtitlán was not just a political and military capital; it was also a center of commerce and craft activity. The Aztec capital was home to specialist potters, feather workers, and metalworkers, as well as the farmers whose surplus agricultural products supported the craftsworkers and merchants (Willey 1966: 156–159). The bustling market at Tlateloclo was visited by between 20,000 and 50,000 people each day (Nichols 2004: 272). The Aztecs, however, were only the latest in a long series of complex, urban societies that had developed in Mexico and the adjacent regions of Central America during pre-Columbian times. In this chapter we will trace the development of those societies in the region that archaeologists call **Mesoamerica.**

    Mesoamerica is a cultural, linguistic, and geographical term that describes the region extending from western Honduras, Nicaragua, and northwest Costa Rica in the south to Mexico, excluding the northern deserts (Figure 24.2). It therefore includes most of Mexico, Guatemala, Belize, El Salvador, western Honduras, western Nicaragua, and the northwestern portion of Costa Rica. The region exhibits marked variations in climate, geography, and soils, ranging from the cool, temperate highlands of central Mexico to the rain forests of the Petén region of northern Guatemala. This varied region was home to some of the most highly developed complex societies in the Americas. In tracing the development of complex societies in various parts of Mesoamerica, we will examine how the urban, state-level societies that were encountered by Cortez developed from the simple agricultural villages that arose in this region during the earlier Holocene. The earliest complex societies appear during the **Formative (or Preclassic) period** in Mesoamerica (approximately 2000 B.C. to A.D. 250). It is during this period that we see the appearance of the earliest monumental architecture and sculpture in Mesoamerica and the beginnings of urbanism in the region.

OLMEC BEGINNINGS

The study of the development of complex societies in Mesoamerica usually begins along Mexico's southern Gulf coast (see Figure 24.2). The Gulf coast was home to people known to archaeologists as the **Olmecs,** although we do not know what they called themselves. The name Olmecs, which means "rubber people," comes from the word *Olmeca*, used by the Aztecs to refer to the people who lived in the Gulf coast region at the time of the Spanish conquest. However, there is no clear evidence for continuity between the Olmecs of the Formative period and the Olmeca of Aztec times. The Olmecs of the Formative period have fascinated scholars since the early twentieth century because they created Mesoamerica's earliest monumental art. In particular, they carved enormous human heads weighing up to 25 tons from basalt blocks (Figure 24.3). The Olmecs also created the earliest monumental architecture in Mesoamerica.

Olmec sites are located in a rich, low-lying area along Mexico's southern Gulf coast, an area traversed by three major rivers and their tributaries. Abundant water for maize agriculture is provided by two rainy seasons—the first extending from June to November, the second from January to February. Periodic flooding enriches the soil along the riverbanks (Soustelle 1985: 23). Farming villages were established in the Gulf coast region as early as 2250 B.C. (Rust and

FIGURE 24.3   A carved Olmec head, San Lorenzo, Monument 1.

Sharer 1988). In addition to its agricultural potential, the southern Gulf coast was home to many species of wild game, including deer, tapirs, monkeys, pheasants, and iguanas, and its lakes and rivers provided early farmers with fish and shellfish. In short, the Olmec region was rich in subsistence resources and could have provided the food surplus necessary to support nonagricultural labor and trade.

Excavations at Olmec sites have focused largely, though not exclusively, on sites that have produced monumental stone sculpture. The largest of these sites, which have been termed ceremonial centers, have yielded monumental stone sculpture and public architecture, as well as evidence for status differences between elites and commoners. The earliest of these centers is the site of **San Lorenzo,** which sits atop a large (1000 by 500 m, or 3300 by 1650 ft.) plateau overlooking the Rio Coatzacoalcos. Excavations at San Lorenzo revealed the presence of Olmec-style ceramics at the site as early as 1150 B.C. (3100 B.P.). In addition, excavations in the 1960s revealed 35 carved stone monuments (2 had been recovered earlier). Recent excavations at the site, under the direction of Ann Cyphers, have shown that many of the monumental stone heads stood on prepared floors and that one of the tabletop altars at the site had been located within a walled enclosure (Grove 1997: 70). Cyphers has also identified many additional stone monuments, bringing the total to well over 80 (Grove 1997: 71). Workshop areas for the manufacture and recycling of stone monuments have also been identified.

What kind of a society produced these enormous heads and other stone sculptures? The limited evidence available suggests that Olmec society was a nonegalitarian one, populated by both elites and commoners. Items such as greenstone jewelry and polished iron mirrors, whose raw materials were obtained through long-distance trade, have been identified as possible markers of elite status. In addition, the recent excavations at San Lorenzo have revealed marked differences in house construction that may reflect differences in status and wealth. The larger houses (presumably the elite residences) are built on top of large clay platforms, while the humbler houses of the commoners are simple wattle-and-daub structures with earthen floors.

San Lorenzo appears to have played an active role in riverine trade. Three raised causeways that run inland from the river have been interpreted as wharves or docks associated with this trade. It is not clear whether rivers or overland routes were used to transport the large stone blocks used to manufacture the monumental heads to the Olmec center at **La Venta,** because geological uplifting has changed the course of several rivers in the Olmec region. Geological changes may have also been responsible for the decline of San Lorenzo at about 800 B.C. by changing the course of the rivers on which San Lorenzo's trade depended.

The site of La Venta emerged as a leading ceremonial center between about 900 and 400 B.C. Although the site may have been established as early as San Lorenzo, evidence for the earliest phases of occupation is limited (see Grove 1997 for a review of the chronological issues surrounding Olmec sites). La Venta is located on a small swamp island in the Tabasco region of Mexico. Because petroleum was discovered in the La Venta region in the first half of the twentieth century, many parts of this important Olmec site were destroyed when an oil pipeline was cut through it. Archaeological excavations conducted at La Venta since the early 1940s have revealed evidence for monumental public architecture, including a low, rectangular earthen mound 32 m (105 ft.) high and measuring 70 by 120 m (230 by 390 ft.) at the base; several other mound complexes; a carefully laid out plaza; and mosaic pavements of serpentine blocks (Figure 24.4).

By 600 to 400 B.C., La Venta had developed as a true city (Lesure 2004: 86). The settlement covered more than 200 ha (500 ac.). The layout of the central core of the city was carefully planned and included a range of administrative and ceremonial buildings, as well as a number of carved heads. High-status burials included jade objects and other valuable items. The elite residents of La Venta were "able to command significant amounts of local labor and linked to other Mesoamerican groups by exchange networks through which flowed large amounts of exotic materials" (Lesure 2004: 86–87).

The large Olmec centers such as San Lorenzo and La Venta stood at the apex of a settlement system that also included about a dozen smaller

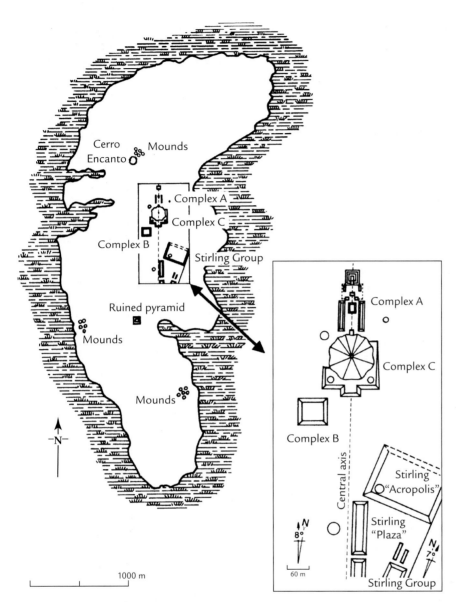

FIGURE 24.4   Plan of the main architectural monuments at the Olmec center of La Venta. The architectural complex, known as the Stirling Group, is named after Matthew Stirling, who excavated at La Venta in the 1940s.

centers with just a few stone monuments and large numbers of agricultural villages and hamlets that must have supported those centers. While the large Olmec centers have yielded evidence for craft production and monumental public construction, there is no evidence to suggest that the Olmec region was politically unified under a single ruler or king. The early appearance of monumental art and architecture in the southern Gulf coast region led some scholars to see the Olmecs as a kind of "mother culture" for later complex societies throughout the Mesoamerican region. The true picture is probably far more complex. As we shall show in this chapter, complex societies began to develop during the Formative period in a number of different geographical regions of Mesoamerica.

These areas were all engaged in trade and contact with one another, just as contacts existed between the early complex societies of the Old World. One important region with which the Olmec traded was the Oaxaca Valley, home to one of Mesoamerica's earliest urban centers.

EARLY URBANISM IN OAXACA

The Oaxaca Valley lies in the center of Mexico's southern highland region, a mountainous zone located south of the Olmec heartland (see Figure 24.2). The three-armed Oaxaca Valley (Figure 24.5) contains 1500 sq. km (580 sq. mi.) of arable land, the largest expanse of farmland in the southern highlands (Blanton et al. 1993).

Farming communities were established in the Oaxaca Valley by 1500 B.C. The villagers raised maize, avocados, beans, and squash, and most communities included fewer than 10 wattle-and-daub houses. One larger village, **San José Mogote,** has been discovered. This village covered 7 ha (17 ac.), more than two times the size of any other contemporary settlement. This site also included some evidence for nonresidential, public construction in the form of an open area that was set off from the residential portion of the site by a double line of posts. Although this feature contained no structures, it was aligned slightly (8°) west of true north, like much of the later public architecture in the Oaxaca Valley (Blanton et al. 1993: 56–57). This open area soon fell out of use and was replaced by a series of rectangular structures with altarlike platforms running along the southern interior wall. These structures were also oriented 8° west of true north and appear to have been centers of ritual activity, constructed by a society that was largely egalitarian. Neither the houses nor the burials provide evidence for marked differences in social status and material wealth. However, the presence of the ritual structures does reflect some degree of incipient leadership, since labor and resources would have had to be mobilized to construct and maintain the buildings.

After 1150 B.C. there is evidence for significant social, economic, and demographic change in the Oaxaca Valley. The town of San José Mogote expanded to 70 ha (173 ac.), while the remainder of villages in that arm of the Oaxaca Valley were no

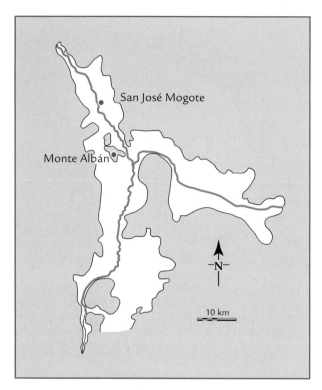

FIGURE 24.5 Map of the Oaxaca Valley region, showing locations of sites mentioned in the chapter.

larger than 2 ha (5 ac.). At San José Mogote, there is evidence for the production of magnetite mirrors, prestige items that were traded as far away as the Gulf coast. Both burials and houses began to reflect significant social and economic differences. For example, at San José Mogote some individuals were buried without grave goods, while others were interred with such items as finely crafted ceramic vessels, jade earspools, shell ornaments, and items made of magnetite (Blanton et al. 1993: 61). San José Mogote may have been the seat of a chiefdom that controlled part of the Oaxaca Valley. In many ways, the level of social and political development seen at San José Mogote parallels the kinds of societies that developed at the same time in the Olmec area.

The political and social landscape of the Oaxaca Valley changed with the founding of a new regional capital at **Monte Albán** at about 500 B.C. Monte Albán is strategically located on a hilltop in the very center of the Oaxaca Valley (see Figure 24.5). Although Monte Albán lacks water sources and is surrounded

FIGURE 24.6   View of the Oaxaca Valley from Monte Albán, showing its strategic location in relation to the surrounding countryside.

by marginal agricultural land, its hilltop location provides views of the Oaxaca Valley in all directions (Figure 24.6). Unlike San José Mogote, which had developed as a head town for a portion of the Oaxaca Valley, Monte Albán developed as a political and military capital for the entire Oaxaca Valley. Residential housing in Monte Albán was located in three distinct neighborhoods, but the central Main Plaza lacked residential settlement even in the earliest phases. Carved stone sculptures from the Main Plaza appear to depict opposing military leaders who had been brought back to Monte Albán to be tortured and killed.

The site grew rapidly to an estimated population of 5000 inhabitants in less than 200 years. Population also grew in the rural areas surrounding Monte Albán, leading to an increase in the settlement of the hilly piedmont regions surrounding the capital. By 200 B.C. the population of Monte Albán had risen to about 17,000 people, and the piedmont regions surrounding the capital had become even more densely occupied. Archaeological evidence also suggests that administrative activity, one of the characteristics of a

state level of political organization, expanded during the later first millennium B.C. Much of the population growth that took place outside the Monte Albán region was centered at secondary administrative centers rather than rural villages. The secondary centers had larger populations than the small, rural villages and included public architecture, such as platforms, mound groups, and possibly ball courts. Ball courts are found throughout many parts of prehistoric Mesoamerica. The ball games were ritualized contests between two teams that involved the use of a small, hard rubber ball.

The costs of the construction and maintenance of Monte Albán and the secondary administrative centers as well as the support of an expanding non-agricultural population must have been financed through the production of a substantial agricultural surplus. This would have placed a significant burden on the rural farming population, especially those living in the agriculturally risky piedmont regions. The first evidence for irrigation in the piedmont regions appears shortly after 500 B.C., indicating that farmers may have shifted toward the production of two or three crops per year (Blanton et al. 1993: 74). This agricultural intensification is accompanied by an intensification in the production of crafts such as pottery.

After about 200 B.C., the rulers of Monte Albán appear to have focused their energy on external conquests rather than internal administration. A possible military outpost has been identified approximately 100 km (62 mi.) northeast of Monte Albán. In the capital itself, a distinctive structure (Structure J) was added to the southern part of the Main Plaza. Its carved slabs depict conquests of places outside the valley itself.

Within the Oaxaca Valley, the population of Monte Albán, and especially that of the surrounding piedmont region, appears to have declined. Agricultural settlements shifted to the richer alluvial areas and away from the more risky piedmont zones. Monte Albán, however, remained the largest urban center within the Oaxaca Valley. Public construction, possibly financed through external conquest, continued and expanded within the capital. Construction of large, defensive walls around Monte Albán was completed, and the process of leveling the entire Main Plaza, an area the size of six football fields, was begun.

Monte Albán's imperial expansion was relatively short-lived. After A.D. 300 Monte Albán's military conquests decreased dramatically, and it may have lost many of its former territories and tributaries as a result of the expansion of the urban state of **Teotihuacán,** centered in the Valley of Mexico. (The archaeological history of Teotihuacán is described in detail below.) The complex interrelationship between Oaxaca and Teotihuacán illustrates that no single region in Mesoamerica may be studied in isolation. As in the Old World, early complex societies interacted with one another in a number of different ways, some peaceable and some hostile.

The loss of Monte Albán's empire was accompanied by an internal reorganization, marked by the rapid expansion of many of the secondary administrative centers within the valley. The formation and expansion of new secondary and smaller tertiary centers fostered continued agricultural expansion within the Oaxaca Valley. After A.D. 500 much of

the population growth centered on Monte Albán and its immediate vicinity. The capital's population approached 25,000 during the middle of the first millennium A.D. The Main Plaza was surrounded by public buildings, including temples, mounds, and the residence of the rulers of the city. Craft production was centered in Monte Albán and other major centers, and it appears to have been tightly controlled by the ruling elite.

Monte Albán was unable to maintain tight political and economic control over the Oaxaca Valley in the later part of the first millennium A.D. At that time Monte Albán's population was dramatically reduced to about 4000 people, and it appears to have been just one of several competing urban centers in the Oaxaca Valley. The collapse of Monte Albán is mirrored by the collapse of a number of complex urban societies in Mesoamerica in the later first millennium A.D. The possible causes for these urban collapses will be discussed in greater detail as follows.

TEOTIHUACÁN AND THE VALLEY OF MEXICO

The development of urbanism and state formation in the Oaxaca Valley is paralleled in many ways by developments in the Valley of Mexico. Located in the central highlands of Mexico, the Valley of Mexico covers a 120- by 70-km (75- by 43-mi.) area that lies more than 2000 m (6600 ft.) above sea level. Portions of the valley bottom were covered by a series of marshy, interconnected lakes that provided fish, waterfowl, and other resources. The lakeshore plains provided valuable agricultural lands, and during the later pre-Columbian periods intensive methods were developed to cultivate many of the low-lying, marshy areas as well.

The Valley of Mexico is one of the most intensively studied archaeological regions in the world. Systematic archaeological surveys have been conducted over 5000 of its approximately 7000 sq. km, or 2700 sq. mi. (Blanton et al. 1993: 106). In addition, detailed archaeological survey and excavation, much of it under the direction of Rene Millon (Millon 1981; Millon et al. 1973), has been conducted within the city of Teotihuacán itself. These data allow archaeologists to study

FIGURE 24.7   View of Teotihuacán looking south, showing the Pyramid of the Moon, the Pyramid of the Sun, and the Avenue of the Dead.

the rise and fall of Teotihuacán in relation to changes in human settlement throughout the Valley of Mexico.

While the presence of small, permanent villages occupied by pottery-making farmers can be traced back to 1400 B.C., this section will focus primarily on the development of the city and state of Teotihuacán. The Teotihuacán region (see Figure 24.2), in the northern part of the Valley of Mexico, was an attractive area for human settlement for two reasons. First, it was located at the head of a series of springs that could have been used for irrigation. Second, and more important, Teotihuacán was located near important deposits of obsidian, or volcanic glass, an excellent raw material for the manufacture of stone tools, and one that was traded throughout Mesoamerica. The earliest settlement of Teotihuacán, dating to about 200 B.C., is a series of villages, one of which may have specialized in obsidian manufacture. By the end of the first century B.C., settlement extended over 8 sq. km (3 sq. mi.), suggesting a population of at least 20,000 individuals (Blanton et al. 1993: 122). At the end of the first millennium B.C., Teotihuacán was one of two major urban centers in the Valley of Mexico. The other was Cuicuilco, located in the

southern end of the valley. However, a series of volcanic eruptions in the first millennium A.D. eventually buried Cuicuilco, and Teotihuacán emerged as the dominant political center in the Valley of Mexico in the first century A.D.

During the first century A.D., the population of Teotihuacán grew to an estimated 80,000 persons spread over an area of approximately 20 sq. km (8 sq. mi.). This phenomenal growth rate was undoubtedly a result of immigration from the countryside as well as local population growth. During the first two centuries A.D., Teotihuacán was laid out along a precise grid aligned 15.5° east of true north (Figure 24.7). The main north–south street, now known as the Avenue of the Dead, is intersected by a major east–west street, dividing the city into quadrants (Millon 1967). In the early first millennium A.D., approximately 20 temple complexes lined the Avenue of the Dead. This investment in public architecture is dwarfed, however, by the construction of the Pyramid of the Sun, a stone-faced structure 70 m (230 ft.) high, with a total construction volume of 1 million cu. m of fill. Construction of the smaller Pyramid of the Moon (see Figure 24.7) was also initiated at that time, as was the construction of the Ciudadela, a group of four platforms enclosing a plaza that could have held 100,000 people. The Ciudadela is located at the intersection of the main north–south and east–west streets; its geographical position certainly reflects its political and/or religious importance. In addition to these civic and religious structures, residences of the ruling elite and nobility were also located along the Avenue of the Dead. The Great Compound, which served as the city's major marketplace, was constructed at a somewhat later date. Elaborate sewage and water systems were established by A.D. 200–350 (Manzanilla 2004: 124).

By A.D. 200 Teotihuacán had clearly established itself as the center of religious, political, and economic activity in the Valley of Mexico. Most of the valley's specialized craft activities were centered at Teotihuacán, and there is evidence for increasing specialization in both obsidian manufacture and pottery production. Secondary administrative centers were only about 5% of the size of Teotihuacán and contained limited public architecture (Blanton et al. 1993: 129). During the mid-first millennium A.D., Teotihuacán and the area immediately around the city continued to grow, drawing population from other parts of the Teotihuacán valley. The city itself reached a population of 125,000, and the area within 30 km (19 mi.) of the capital housed an additional 65,000 people (Blanton et al. 1993: 129, 134). These demographic trends parallel those seen in Sumer (southern Mesopotamia) during the Early Dynastic period (third millennium B.C.) when the earlier widespread rural settlement was progressively replaced by a smaller number of large urban centers such as Uruk (Adams and Nissen 1972: 12).

What was urban life like in Teotihuacán, and why were residents attracted to the city and its immediate hinterland? The residents of Teotihuacán lived in multifamily compounds housing 60 to 100 persons and surrounded by high walls. Most of the city's obsidian production was carried out within the residential compounds, and it is estimated that perhaps 25% of Teotihuacán's population was engaged in craft activities. Approximately 600 workshops have been identified in the city. Groups of residential compounds were oriented around temple complexes; these larger units appear to represent

barrios, or neighborhoods. In some cases specialized occupations or crafts were centered within the barrios. Ceramic evidence indicates that one barrio was occupied by people from Oaxaca whose descendants lived in Teotihuacán for generations, although the role that they played in the day-to-day life of Teotihuacán is unclear. Perhaps they functioned as traders or diplomats.

At the height of its power in the middle of the first century A.D., the Teotihuacán state controlled all the Valley of Mexico; it also controlled some centers outside the valley and had widespread contacts throughout Mesoamerica. At A.D. 500 Teotihuacán was one of the largest cities in the world. As is the case for many complex societies, Teotihuacán's success was not to last. Its foreign influence was weakening by A.D. 600, and the city itself appears to have declined rapidly at about A.D. 750. The population was reduced to about 30,000, and there is evidence for widespread destruction of buildings (and sometimes people), especially along the Avenue of the Dead. Fires were set deliberately to destroy the city center and its civic and religious buildings. It is not clear whether this destruction was carried out by a foreign military power or whether it represents an internal revolt against the political establishment. It is interesting to note, however, that the subsequent residents of Teotihuacán avoided reusing the civic and religious architecture in the city center, suggesting that the victors "wanted to dissociate themselves from these buildings and their political and religious symbols" (Blanton et al. 1993: 135). It is also important to emphasize that the destruction of Teotihuacán's center is nearly contemporaneous with the fall of Monte Albán, which suggests that the period around A.D. 750 was one of major political turmoil in Mesoamerica generally. It is possible to compare this situation in a very general way to the decline of the Western Roman Empire in the fifth century A.D. Unified Roman political authority in areas such as Britain, Gaul, and Spain was replaced by a series of smaller barbarian kingdoms, and many symbols of Roman political authority, such as the major urban centers, declined dramatically at that time.

As we shall see, the later first millennium A.D. was also a period of dramatic change in Mesoamerica's

FIGURE 24.8   Topographic map of the Maya area, showing the major sites and landforms.

eastern lowlands. However, we must begin by examining the rise of what was perhaps Mesoamerica's greatest urban society, that of the Classic Maya of the eastern lowlands.

THE BEGINNINGS OF THE CLASSIC MAYA

The ancient Maya inhabited a unique and environmentally diverse region in the southeastern part of Mesoamerica (Figure 24.8). Most sites are located in the lowland areas of the Petén-Yucatán peninsula, areas that today include Belize as well as northern Guatemala, northwestern Honduras, and southern Mexico. The peninsula is, in fact, a limestone shelf that extends outward into the Gulf of Mexico and the Caribbean Sea. Unlike the relatively arid regions of Oaxaca and the Valley of Mexico, the southern

portion of the Petén-Yucatán peninsula may receive as much as 250 cm (100 in.) of rainfall per year. Rainfall decreases as one moves northward, and the northern portions of the Yucatán may receive as little as 50 cm (20 in.) of rainfall per year. Most of the rain falls during the season from May to October. The vegetation of the peninsula closely mirrors the rainfall patterns. The southern lowlands are covered by a monsoon forest dominated by huge mahogany trees; in a few areas of extremely high rainfall, a true rain forest exists. (Unlike the trees in a true rain forest, the trees in a monsoonal forest lose their leaves during the dry season.) Much of the rain forest and monsoon forest has been deforested in the past few decades, especially in Mexico. The vegetation changes to low, thorny jungle as one moves into the drier northern lowlands, and the most northerly areas of the Yucatán are covered with arid scrub vegetation.

FIGURE 24.9   Reconstruction of the Late Preclassic architecture at El Mirador in Guatemala.

Additional Maya sites have been identified in the highland regions to the south of the Petén-Yucatán peninsula. The highland areas lie above 305 m (1000 ft.) in elevation and are dominated by volcanic peaks, some as high as 4000 m (13,000 ft.). Vegetation varies with altitude; grasses and pines are found in the higher elevations, while oaks trees are found at lower elevations with adequate moisture.

As in other areas of the world, the beginning of farming was critical to the development of complex societies. Early farming villages appear in Chiapas, Mexico, and the adjacent areas of Guatemala by about 2000 B.C. (Clark and Blake 1994). However, early farming villages do not appear in the Maya lowland regions until nearly a millennium later. These early farming villages were undoubtedly based on a method of shifting cultivation known as swidden or slash and burn. In the slash-and-burn method, the vegetation is cleared from an area of forest and burned. The field is used for only a few seasons and then abandoned, allowing the natural vegetation to regrow and the soil's fertility to be restored. The initial appearance of pottery-using farmers marks the beginning of the **Preclassic** (or Formative) **period** (ca. 2000 B.C.) in the Maya area. The Preclassic period continues to A.D. 250, when

dated inscriptions first appear in the lowland Maya areas. During earlier phases of the Preclassic, the Maya areas were populated by small agricultural villages. One of the earliest known villages in the Maya lowland areas is the site of **Cuello** in Belize (Hammond 1991; Hammond et al. 1995). The initial occupation at Cuello dates to 1200 B.C. A long-term program of excavation at the site, which began in 1975 and concluded in 1993, has revealed a long sequence of mud- and plaster-floored houses and their associated yards from the Middle Preclassic period (1200 to 400 B.C.). The Cuello excavations have also revealed 180 burials. Those earlier than 900 B.C. contain no grave goods; after 900 B.C. pottery vessels were included in graves.

In the Late Preclassic (400 B.C. to A.D. 250) Maya society changed from a simple, village agricultural society to an emerging complex society. During that period monumental architecture—pyramids, platform mounds, and temples—appeared at a number of sites, indicating that certain individuals or groups of individuals had control over the large amounts of human labor needed to construct those monuments. One example is the Late Preclassic site of **El Mirador** (Figure 24.9), in the swampy northeast Petén about 360 km (225 mi.) north of Guatemala

City (Matheny 1986, 1987). The site includes two areas of monumental architecture that are connected by a causeway. The east group includes a 70-m (230-ft.) high pyramid and its associated platforms, while the west group includes the 55-m (180-ft.) high Tigre pyramid, which has an estimated volume of 380,000 cu. m (Coe 1993: 67) and faces the rising sun. Causeways extend outward from this Preclassic urban center, and it is likely that El Mirador controlled trade with the Yucatán to the north and with the Maya highlands and the Pacific coast to the south.

In addition, Late Preclassic tombs from the site of **Tikal** in Guatemala reflect increasing social, political, and economic inequality. One of the most intriguing is Tomb 85. The burial was placed in front of what was then the central temple on Tikal's acropolis and enclosed in a vaulted tomb. The body was bundled in textiles and buried in a seated position. The skull and thighbones had been removed from the body. The reason the skull and femurs are missing is not clear. Was the deceased a victim of battle whose body had been mutilated and subsequently recovered by relatives (Coe 1993: 64), or were the bones removed by grieving family members and retained as keepsakes (Culbert 1993: 49)?

Whatever the reason for this unusual burial, it is clear that this was the final resting place of a high-ranking man. His skull had been replaced by a greenstone mask (Figure 24.10), and he was accompanied by 26 finely made ceramic vessels, 4 of which had been manufactured in the Guatemalan highlands, 320 km (200 mi.) away. The burial dates to the early first century A.D., and its contents and position show that distinct social and economic inequalities had developed by the Late Preclassic period.

One question that has plagued archaeologists for years is the problem of how swidden farming could have provided a sufficient agricultural surplus to support the urban centers, such as Tikal and El Mirador, that were clearly well established by Late Preclassic times. More intensive agriculture systems must have played a role in supporting those cities, and the systems are likely to have been established by Late Preclassic times. Agricultural yields could have been increased in several ways. In the lowland areas, however, the most likely means was the use of raised fields. In

FIGURE 24.10 Greenstone mask from Tomb 85, Tikal.

swampy areas, such as those that surrounded El Mirador, canals were used to drain the fields after the rainy season or to raise the fields above the water level.

THE CLASSIC MAYA

The beginning of the **Classic period** (ca. A.D. 250 to 930) is marked by the appearance of dated monuments in the southern lowlands. These dated monuments have been crucial to the chronology and interpretation of Classic Maya archaeology. The Maya used two different calendar systems: the Calendar Round and the Long Count (Coe 1999a). The Calendar Round was also used by many other Mesoamerican peoples. It was made up of two cycles—a 260-day cycle that combined 20 named days with the numbers from 1 to 13 and a 365-day cycle that included 18 named months of 20 days with 5 unlucky days at the end of the cycle. A specific combination of named days would occur

ARCHAEOLOGY IN PRACTICE

Archaeology and History: The Evidence from the Maya Inscriptions

The Maya differ from most other complex societies in the New World because they used an elaborate and well-developed writing system. Most inscriptions are preserved on stelae (upright carved stone slabs) and on architectural monuments, but some inscriptions have also been recovered from pottery vessels. The Maya also produced books written on bark paper, but only four of them have survived to modern times. Many were burned by early Spanish clerics who considered them the products of heathenism and therefore deserving of destruction. What remains today is only a small fraction of the once rich literary record of the Maya.

One of the most important developments in Maya archaeology in the past 20 years has been the gradual decipherment of the Maya writing system (Coe 1999b). As recently as 40 years ago, about all that could be identified from Maya inscriptions were their dates. Two discoveries were of primary importance for the decipherment of the ancient Maya script. The first was the realization that the inscriptions detailed actual political histories (Proskouriakoff 1960); the inscriptions were not simply abstract religious and astronomical texts. The second realization was that the Maya language was logo-syllabic, rather than alphabetic (see the Archaeology in Practice box in Chapter 20). That is, some glyphs represent a single idea, while others represent a syllable, a consonant–vowel combination. For example, the Maya word *balam*, meaning "jaguar," may be written in two different ways: as a picture of a jaguar (Figure 24.A) or by using the glyphs for the *ba, la,* and *ma* (the final *a* is silent). The decipherment process has been aided by the fact that

languages closely related to ancient Maya are still spoken in many parts of Mesoamerica today. As a result of painstaking epigraphic (epigraphy is the study of inscriptions) research, most of the Maya syllabary has been reconstructed, and it is estimated that about 85 percent of the known inscriptions can be read with some degree of certainty.

How has the decipherment of the Maya writing system changed our view of the Maya, and how does the information revealed in the texts differ from the kinds of data that have been recovered through archaeological excavation and survey? The inscriptions focus on the highest levels of Maya society. They record important events, such as births, marriages, and deaths, in the lives of the ruling families of the Maya urban centers. The decipherment of the glyphs has allowed archaeologists to reconstruct king lists and the dynastic history of the main urban centers (see, for example, Schele and Freidel 1990). The ruling families of the Maya cities "had been intricately connected through marriages

and alliances and had continually jockeyed for position in relation to one another and for control and influence over lesser sites" (Culbert 1985: 44).

While the inscriptions detail the Machiavellian intrigues of the Maya ruling classes, the lives of the Maya lower classes can be explored only through archaeology. In addition to providing information about day-to-day life, archaeology has shed light on urban settlement patterns, Maya subsistence and diet, population dynamics, and craft activities—subjects that are not addressed in the inscriptions. The synthesis of archaeological and historical data has allowed archaeologists to paint a richer and more well-rounded picture of ancient Maya society. The decipherment of the texts has allowed scientists to envision the individual actors who peopled the highest levels of Maya society; archaeological data have allowed scholars to understand the socioeconomic context in which those individuals' actions took place.

Logographic

Balam / Jaguar

Phonetic

ba-la-ma

FIGURE 24.A The Maya glyphs for the word *balam*, meaning "jaguar."

FIGURE 24.11 Temple 1, part of the central plaza at Tikal.

only once every 52 years. The Long Count was a day-by-day count that started in 3114 B.C. (long before the Maya). Maya-dated monuments also bear written inscriptions, and the recent decipherment of the Maya script has opened a new chapter in Mesoamerican archaeology (see the Archaeology in Practice box).

The Classic period is conventionally divided into an Early Classic (ca. A.D. 250 to 600) and a Late Classic period (ca. A.D. 600 to 830). Influence from and contact with Teotihuacán is seen clearly in the Early Classic but not in the Late Classic period, owing to the collapse of the Teotihuacán state in the late mid-first millennium A.D. A Terminal Classic period (A.D. 830 to 930) has recently been defined. During this final phase, many of the Maya cities of the southern lowlands appear to collapse dramatically.

TIKAL

Major archaeological projects involving both excavation and archaeological surveys have been conducted at a number of Maya urban centers. One of the most well studied is the important Maya city of Tikal in Guatemala. Tikal was the subject of a long-term archaeological research project (1956 to 1971) under the direction of William Coe (1988) of the University of Pennsylvania; Guatemalan archaeologists have conducted more than 10 years of research since the end of the University of Pennsylvania project.

One of the most important tasks undertaken by the Tikal project was the preparation of a map of the structures identified within a 16-sq. km (6-sq. mi.) region centered on Tikal's Great Plaza (Figure 24.11). (The late Preclassic burial, Tomb 85, discussed previously is located in the acropolis on the north end of the Great Plaza.) Later surveys mapped an additional 20 sq. km (8 sq. mi.) beyond the central map. These surveys have revealed that Tikal was a densely populated urban center during Classic times. During Late Classic times, it is estimated that Tikal housed 62,000 people (Culbert et al. 1991).

While archaeologists have debated the nature of ancient Maya political organization, it is clear from both archaeological and historical evidence that the Maya lowlands were never politically unified. The inscriptions clearly demonstrate that competition between the Maya urban centers was a fact of Maya political life. During the Late Classic period, it is likely that four or five major Maya urban centers, including Tikal, controlled the surrounding minor towns and cities to form a small number of competing states (Marcus 1993). Competition between these major urban centers, expressed in intensive monument-building programs during the Late Classic, may have played a role in the collapse of the Classic Maya in the southern lowlands.

THE COLLAPSE OF THE CLASSIC MAYA

The collapse of the Classic Maya (Culbert 1973, 1988) is an issue that has intrigued scholars for decades. After about A.D. 750, the political landscape of the southern lowlands was changing; the large states of the earlier Late Classic period appear to have fragmented into a series of smaller polities. The political instability in the southern lowlands at that time mirrored the situation in the Valley of Mexico and the Oaxaca Valley. In the southern lowlands, however, the political changes are mirrored by dramatic demographic shifts. By the Terminal Classic period, the population of the southern lowland Maya sites had declined by at least two-thirds from its eighth-century peak (Culbert 1993: 118). By the end of the Terminal Classic (ca. A.D. 930), only small, remnant populations remained in the southern Maya lowlands. What factors could have led to the political and demographic collapse of this vibrant, complex society?

One critical factor in the collapse may have been an increasing instability in the relationship between a growing population and the available agricultural resources. Agricultural products were needed both to feed that population and to provide the surplus that supported the growing elite class and its increasing desire for monumental public construction. Population growth may have been a two-edged sword for the Classic Maya. During the Late Preclassic and Early Classic periods, a growing population would have provided more labor for agricultural activities and public construction. By the end of the Late Preclassic period, however, Maya lowland populations had reached the maximum levels that could be supported by slash-and-burn agriculture (Culbert 1988). Increasingly intensive methods of farming had to be used to support the growing population. While intensive agricultural methods may have increased yields in the short term, in the long term they may have led to the loss of soil fertility and to soil erosion. Long-term environmental degradation, when combined with short-term risk factors such as crop diseases, variations in precipitation, and even human disease epidemics, may have led to the demographic collapse that occurred in the southern lowlands in the Terminal Classic period.

It is important to emphasize that the Maya did not disappear at the end of the Terminal Classic period. While the urban sites in the southern lowland area were depopulated and never reoccupied, a number of Maya urban centers were established in the northern Yucatán during the **Postclassic period** (A.D. 930 to 1519). People speaking languages related to ancient Maya continue to inhabit the northern lowlands, the Yucatán, and many areas of highland Guatemala and southern Mexico. Today more than 4 million people still speak some form of Maya language.

THE POSTCLASSIC PERIOD IN MESOAMERICA AND THE RISE OF THE AZTEC EMPIRE

The reconstruction of the political, economic, and demographic history of Mesoamerica in the Postclassic period (ca. A.D. 900 to 1500) is a complex process involving the use of archaeological data from survey and excavation as well as historical sources such as the accounts of the

Spanish conquistadors. While a detailed history of Mesoamerica during the Postclassic period is beyond the scope of this text, we will conclude this chapter where we began, with an account of the rise of the Aztec Empire, the greatest empire in pre-Columbian Mesoamerica.

The Aztec rise to power was as dramatic as its fall at the hands of the Spaniards. The Aztecs, or Mexica, were a small group of people who entered the Valley of Mexico from the north in the fourteenth century and established their capital at Tenochtitlán, which was then an undesirable, insect-ridden swamp. The Mexica were "despised by their neighbors as backward northern barbarians" (Conrad and Demarest 1984: 11). The Mexica made their living by exploiting Lake Texcoco's resources, by selling themselves as mercenaries, and by establishing a market in Tenochtitlán. "Through cunning and generally shabby behavior, they eventually established themselves and their island city . . . as a force to be reckoned with" (Blanton et al. 1993: 148).

THE ARCHAEOLOGY OF AZTEC DAILY LIFE

While historical accounts have focused on the politics of Aztec imperialism, an increasing body of archaeological research can provide information on day-to-day life in the Aztec Empire. A series of site surveys conducted since the 1960s indicates that the Valley of Mexico was densely populated in Aztec times. The region was home to between 800,000 and 1.25 million people in the sixteenth century (Nichols 2004: 265). The city-state was the basic political unit in the Valley of Mexico throughout the Postclassic period (Nichols 2004: 272). These city-states, which were in existence by 1200 A.D., were incorporated into the Aztec empire as semiautonomous administrative units. Aztec city-states included markets, plazas, temples, residences, and full-time craft specialists manufacturing obsidian tools, pottery, and textiles.

The city-states were supported by intensive agricultural systems. Hillsides were terraced, irrigation was used to supplement rainfall, and **chinampas** or floating gardens were established

in low-lying swampy areas. The chinampa fields were surrounded by drainage canals. The soil that was removed to dig the canals was used to raise the field above the water level. The maintenance of these systems required substantial effort, but these fields could produce up to seven crops a year if they were continuously cultivated (Nichols 2004: 274). Farming surpluses produced by these intensive agricultural systems supported both the Aztec city-states and Aztec imperial expansion.

THE END OF THE AZTEC EMPIRE

The Aztec conquest of much of central and southern Mexico was both a military and a commercial juggernaut. The Mexica combined guile and military prowess with intensive trading activity in the conquered provinces. The initial successful conquest of the nearby provinces fueled attempts to conquer areas that were progressively farther from Tenochtitlán. At the time of the Spanish conquest, the Mexica found themselves fighting farther and farther from home. The Aztec policy, however, continued to be one of expansion rather than consolidation (Conrad and Demarest 1984: 185). They had created an empire that they could no longer successfully administer. It is at that point that Cortez and his band of followers arrived on the scene. The political impact of the Spanish conquest of Mexico was dwarfed by the demographic impact of the diseases that the Europeans introduced. Native Mesoamerican peoples lacked immunities to Old World diseases such as measles, mumps, and smallpox. These imported diseases decimated the population of Mesoamerica in a way that European military activities never could.

CONCLUSION

During the first millennium B.C. and the first millennium A.D., complex, urban societies developed in a number of different regions in Mesoamerica, including the Oaxaca Valley, the Valley of Mexico, and the Maya lowlands. These developments cannot be examined in isolation. The societies interacted with each other through trade, warfare, and other forms of cultural contact. While the Maya were never politically unified, the Aztecs used military and commercial prowess to assemble an enormous empire in the two centuries before the Spanish conquest of Mexico. The New World states shared many characteristics with the complex societies of the Old World, including long-distance trade in luxury items, a class-stratified society, and the concentration of military power in the hands of the ruling classes. The recent decipherment of the Maya script has shed new light on the political dynamics of one of these complex societies.

KEY TERMS

Chinampas 367	Olmecs 353
Classic period 363	Postclassic period 366
Cuello 362	Preclassic period 362
El Mirador 362	San José Magote 356
Formative (or Preclassic) period 353	San Lorenzo 354
La Venta 354	Tenochtitlán 351
Mesoamerica 352	Teotihuacán 358
Monte Albán 356	Tikal 363

QUESTIONS FOR DISCUSSION

1. How has the decipherment of the Maya script affected our understanding of Classic Maya society?

2. How did contact between the various geographical regions of Mesoamerica affect the development of complex societies there?

3. Compare the development of cities, states, and empires in Mesoamerica with the development of complex urban societies in Mesopotamia. What are the most important similarities? What are the significant differences?

FURTHER READING

Blanton, Richard E., Stephen A. Kowalewski, Gary M. Feinman, and Laura M. Finsten
1993   *Ancient Mesoamerica: A Comparison of Change in Three Regions,* 2nd ed. Cambridge: Cambridge University Press.
This useful volume compares the development of complex societies in three different regions of Mesoamerica—the Valley of Mexico, Oaxaca, and the Mayan area. This book is highly recommended for the more advanced reader.

Coe, Michael
1999   *The Maya,* 6th ed. New York: Thames and Hudson.
This standard introduction to Maya archaeology is now in its sixth edition. Although it has been substantially revised, this book is beginning to show its age. Note, however, that the illustrations are beautiful.

Culbert, T. Patrick
1993   *Maya Civilization.* Washington, DC: Smithsonian Books.
Culbert is one of the foremost experts on the question of the collapse of the Classic Maya in the southern lowlands. He has written a well-illustrated and readable introduction to Mayan civilization, which is strongly recommended.

Hendon, Julia A., and Rosemary A. Joyce, eds.
2004   *Mesoamerican Archaeology: Theory and Practice.* Oxford: Blackwell.
An up-to-date and clearly written survey of new developments in Mesoamerican archaeology written for students by a number of the leading authorities in the field. Highly recommended.

Marcus, Joyce, and Kent V. Flannery
1996   *Zapotec Civilization: How Urbanism Evolved in Mexico's Oaxaca Valley.* New York: Thames and Hudson.
An up-to-date and readable account of the development of urbanism in Oaxaca.

Smith, Michael A.
2004   *The Aztecs,* 2nd ed. Malden, MA: Blackwell.
An authoritative treatment of the Aztecs by a leading scholar.

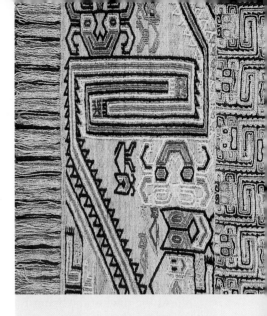

25

CITIES, STATES, AND EMPIRES IN THE ANDES

As noted in the previous chapter, Western diseases introduced by the Spanish conquistadors had a devastating impact on the native populations of Mesoamerica. Old World diseases such as smallpox had an equally disastrous effect on the native inhabitants of South America. (See Diamond (1997) for a readable account of the effect of these diseases on native New World populations.) American history books tell us that Francisco Pizarro and a small band of 260 mercenaries conquered Peru for the Spanish crown in 1532. The Spaniards tricked the **Inca** emperor, held him for ransom, and subsequently killed him and marched into the Inca capital city of **Cuzco** (Figure 25.1). What high school history books do not tell

FIGURE 25.1 Santo Domingo Church, built by the Spaniards on the foundations and against the curved stone walls of the Inca temple of Coricancha. After the conquest, the Spaniards sought to supplant Inca culture and religion. They often built churches on the top of Inca temples.

369

us is that six years before the Spanish conquest, the population of highland South America had been decimated by an epidemic of smallpox, a disease to which the native South Americans had no natural immunity. This epidemic spread southward from Mesoamerica, where the Spaniards had already conquered Mexico. The disease not only killed large numbers of people in South America but also threw the Inca empire into political turmoil. These circumstances made it possible for Pizarro's small band of mercenaries to conquer the great Inca Empire.

At the time of the Spanish conquest, the Inca Empire stretched from southern Colombia and Ecuador in the north to northern Chile and highland Argentina in the south (Figure 25.2). The Inca domain extended over 4000 km (2400 mi.) of Andean territory; it included coastal deserts and high mountains and reached eastward to the borders of the rain forest. The Inca Empire, the largest empire of the prehistoric New World, was, however, only the last in a long series of states and empires that developed in Peru and the adjacent areas of South America during pre-Columbian times. In this chapter we will examine the development of cities and states in highland South America, beginning with the small agricultural villages that developed in highland and lowland South America more than 5000 years ago.

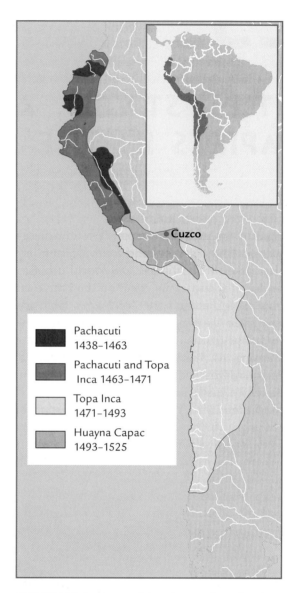

Pachacuti
1438–1463

Pachacuti and Topa
Inca 1463–1471

Topa Inca
1471–1493

Huayna Capac
1493–1525

Cuzco

FIGURE 25.2 Map of South America, showing modern political boundaries and the extent of the Inca Empire at its height.

ENVIRONMENTAL BACKGROUND

It is impossible to understand the development of complex societies in the Andes without understanding the varied environments of Peru and the surrounding countries of highland South America.

Environmental extremes played a crucial role in shaping farming practices in this region. The coast of Peru is one of the world's driest deserts. In most areas no appreciable rain falls throughout the year. The coastal areas, however, are covered with a thick fog for approximately six to eight months of the year. In the areas of dense winter fogs, some grasses and bushes can survive on trapped and condensed moisture, producing **lomas** (fog meadows), which can support animals such as foxes, lizards, birds, and snails (Lanning 1967: 10). The coastal waters are home to a rich variety of marine life, including both small and large fishes, water birds, and shellfish. The dry coastal desert is transected by approximately 40 rivers, which run from east to west (Figure 25.3). The rivers are fed by summer (December to March) rains in the highlands, but the smallest will run dry during the winter. Agriculture is possible in the coastal desert areas only through the use of irrigation.

The Andes mountains form the backbone of South America. The Andes are divided into several parallel chains of mountains by a series of rivers that run north-south. The river valleys were suitable for agriculture, and some of the lower slopes also could be farmed with the help of terracing and irrigation. Additional farmland was located in the **altiplano,** the high flatland surrounding Lake Titicaca, which straddles the border between Peru and Bolivia. High plateaus, called **puna,** were occupied up to elevations of 5000 m (16,000 ft.). These areas were used primarily for grazing livestock—herds of llamas and alpacas that provided meat, wool, and transportation for Andean farmers (Figure 25.4).

HERDING, FARMING, AND FISHING: THE ECONOMIC BACKGROUND TO THE EMERGENCE OF COMPLEX SOCIETIES IN PERU

In Chapter 17, we noted that the highlands of Peru were one of a number of centers for plant domestication in the New World. Crops such as the potato and the grain quinoa were initially cultivated in the Andean highlands. Early herders and farmers in the highlands made use of the verticality of the highland environment by using different elevations for different purposes. Plant cultivation took place at lower elevations in the valley bottoms, while the high plateaus, or puna, were used primarily for grazing llamas and alpacas. The diverse

FIGURE 25.3 Map showing major landforms and the sites mentioned in this chapter.

FIGURE 25.4 A Moche stirrup-spout bottle, showing a llama carrying jars in its saddlebags. Llamas were used for transportation, for food, and for fibers throughout much of Peruvian prehistory.

geography of the Andean region, however, led to radically different subsistence systems in different parts of Peru.

In the coastal areas, the rich marine life may have supported sedentary foraging communities even before the beginnings of farming in the region (Moseley 1975b). The transition to sedentism can be seen at the site of **Paloma,** located approximately 4 km (2.5 mi.) from the sea behind San Bartolo Bay in Peru. The site was occupied between 4500 and 3000 B.C. Although Paloma was initially occupied by mobile hunter-gatherers, the inhabitants eventually became sedentary, occupying small circular houses. Studies of the faunal remains recovered from the site indicate that Paloma's residents consumed a diet that was dominated by small fish, such as sardines and anchovies. Remains of small quantities of cultivated plants have also been found in the trash middens at Paloma. Squash, beans, and gourds were undoubtedly cultivated in the local streambeds after their annual flooding. The site itself is located in the lomas, or fog meadows, rather than along the coast. The lomas areas would have provided wood for cooking and heating. The location of this site within the lomas region indicates that while the sea provided the vast majority of the foodstuffs consumed at Paloma, plant materials played a critical role in the economy because of their importance for fuel and for fiber for fishing line and netting.

After 3000 B.C., plants and plant cultivation came to play an even more central role in lowland subsistence in Peru, although fishing, hunting, and gathering remained the primary sources of food (Moseley 2001: 107). Cultivated food plants included beans, squash, fruits, and peppers; however, the industrial cultigen cotton played an important role in the economy. Cotton could be used for fishing nets and lines, as well as for textiles. Cultivated gourds could also be used for containers and as floats for fishing lines and nets. The period between 3000 B.C. and 1800 B.C. is known as the **Preceramic period.** The term preceramic indicates that this period antedates the introduction of pottery to the Peruvian lowlands; pottery was introduced to the coastal regions about 1800 B.C.

During the Preceramic period, public ceremonial architecture appears for the first time in the coastal regions of Peru. Between 3000 and 2500 B.C., large, raised platform mounds were constructed at a number of sites along the central Peruvian coast. These large platforms would have been used for religious or ceremonial purposes. The raised structures were constructed by filling in and burying earlier ground-level buildings with rubble. The rubble was placed into large, open reed containers, and the fill and container were placed inside the building to be filled. This technique allowed for the work to be divided into repetitive tasks, so that the large amounts of labor required could be coordinated (Moseley 2001: 118). By maintaining a standardized unit of fill, the builders could more easily estimate the amounts of fill necessary to bury the buildings and raise the platforms (Pineda 1988: 79). The construction of these large mounds indicates that certain individuals or groups controlled large quantities of labor, evidence that social differentiation was already present in Peru during the late Preceramic period. Moreover, these civic or ceremonial monuments "were built by, and were meant to be seen and used by, a social group larger than a few families" (Stanish 2001: 45). As such, they are similar to the large sites, such as Bronocice in Poland, that first appear in the later European Neolithic (Chapter 23). However, unlike the European sites, the Peruvian sites do not appear to be centers for regional polities (Stanish 2001: 48).

The site of **Río Seco** is typical of the coastal Preceramic sites. The site covers 11.8 ha (29.2 ac.) and includes two major platform mounds that were built by in-filling rooms. The mounds measure 10 to 15 m (33 to 49 ft.) in diameter and stand 3 m (10 ft.) in height. Río Seco also includes the remains of a large number of small dwellings that were probably covered with thatch or mats. Although the residential architecture provides only limited evidence for social differentiation, hierarchical chains of command must have been necessary to mobilize the local labor needed for monumental construction. The appearance of monumental architecture and a degree of institutional hierarchy marks the appearance of complex societies in Peru.

INITIAL PERIOD

The beginning of the **Initial period** (1800 to 900 B.C.) is marked by the appearance of pottery, which could

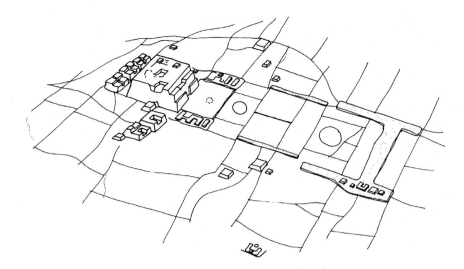

FIGURE 25.5 Plan of Sechín Alto, lower Casma River Valley, showing the main platform mound and associated plazas.

be used to store, cook, and brew agricultural produce. During the Initial period, farming came to play a more central role in the Peruvian economy. While Preceramic farmers had focused on cotton and gourds, which were used primarily for nonfood purposes, during the Initial period domesticated food plants become increasingly important in the diet. Maize, which was initially domesticated in Mesoamerica, is found only rarely at coastal Preceramic sites and played only a minor role in the diet at the sites where it is found. Maize is far more common at lowland Initial period sites, along with other cultivated plants, including squash, peppers, lima and kidney beans, peanuts, avocados, and guavas (Pineda 1988: 82). The mastery of irrigation techniques made farming possible in the coastal desert areas. Populations moved inland from the coast to areas along the river valleys that could be easily irrigated.

The population growth that resulted from the spread of irrigation agriculture is reflected in the construction of larger ceremonial architectural complexes located farther from the Pacific coast. The largest and most impressive of these is the site of **Sechín Alto** (Figure 25.5), located in the lower Casma River Valley. Work was begun on this ceremonial complex by 1400 B.C. The central structure, a stone-faced platform mound, stands 40 m (131 ft.) high and measures 250 by 300 m (820 by 980 ft.) at its base. Five large plazas lie in front of the main platform, covering an area of 400 by 1400 m (1300 by 4600 ft.). Studies based on aerial photographs suggest that the whole Sechín Alto complex covers

an area of 300 to 400 ha (740 to 990 ac.) of the valley plain (Pineda 1988: 87). At about 1400 B.C., Sechín Alto was the "largest settlement in the Western Hemisphere" (Stanish 2001: 49). Clearly, a significant agricultural surplus must have been mobilized to support the labor needed to construct this massive complex.

How was this surplus mobilized? Initial period burials provide relatively little evidence for personal wealth or hereditary rule. Decision making and governance appear to have been vested in offices such as the priesthood, rather than in individuals (Moseley 1992: 140). Monumental construction centered on the building of large platform mounds and temples. The priesthood may have been particularly important in integrating early farming communities in Peru. If the priesthood used its religious power to gain control over the labor force, it would have been able to reaffirm and increase that power by constructing ever larger and more grandiose public monuments (Pineda 1988: 94).

THE EARLY HORIZON AND THE CHAVÍN CULT

The **Early Horizon** (approximately 900 to 200 B.C.) is traditionally defined as the period when artistic influences from the site of **Chavín de Huántar** in the Peruvian highlands spread across much of central and northern Peru. The site includes both residential areas housing an estimated 2000 to 3000 individuals (Burger 1984: 247) and a complex of

FIGURE 25.6 The New Temple (part of the Castillo) at Chavín de Huántar, Peru.

monumental stone buildings known as the Castillo. The Castillo was formed out of two U-shaped structures known as the Old and New Temples (Figure 25.6). The most striking feature of Chavín de Huántar is its monumental stone sculpture, which features both a unique style and a distinctive iconography. The caiman, a South American relative of the alligator, is the most important animal represented in these sculptures. A humanlike figure known as the Staff God carried a staff in each hand and had projecting canine teeth and claws (Figure 25.7).

While monumental stone sculpture is uncommon outside the Chavín de Huántar area, similar designs and iconography are found on pottery and textiles from other parts of Peru. The spread of this art and iconography over large areas of northern and central Peru appears to represent the expansion of a regional religious cult (Burger 1988). The expansion of the Chavín cult can be compared to the spread of early Christianity across the late Roman Empire in the first few centuries A.D. What is even more important than the spread of the Chavín

cult itself is that the diffusion of this religious cult was accompanied by the spread of a number of important technological changes in textiles and metallurgy. These changes include such innovations as the use of camelid (llama and alpaca) hair in cotton textiles, textile painting, and the use of the heddle loom in place of finger weaving in textile production. Innovations in metallurgy that appear at this time include soldering, which allowed workers to create large, three-dimensional pieces, and the production of gold–silver alloys (Burger 1988: 129–130). These technological innovations laid the foundations for later developments in craft production.

In addition, the spread of this cult and these technologies may have linked across a wide geographical area ethnically distinct communities that previously had little communication with one another. Archaeologically, this communication can be seen in an increase in long-distance trade. For example, nearly all the obsidian recovered from Chavín de Huántar came from the site of Quispisisa, 750 km (470 mi.) to the south (Burger 1988: 132). The increasing use of llamas as pack animals may have played a critical role in this expanded trade. While llamas were initially domesticated in the southern highlands of Peru by the third millennium B.C., they were not widely used in northern Peru until the Early Horizon. Llamas may have played a critical role as pack animals in transporting raw materials and exotic goods over long distances (Miller and Burger 1995).

THE EARLY INTERMEDIATE PERIOD

The Chavín cult was a relatively short-lived phenomenon. The period that followed the Chavín, or Early Horizon, is termed the **Early Intermediate period** (ca. 200 B.C. to A.D. 600). This period sees the abandonment of many ceremonial centers associated with the Chavín cult. New construction ceases at the site of Chavín de Huántar itself. The unity of the Early Horizon is followed by a period of diversity when various regions of Andean South America develop in very different ways. In some regions there is evidence for the emergence of states, while in others no such central authority exists. Moreover, the emergence of complex societies in Peru is not a linear process in which progressively larger kingdoms and states develop, culminating in the emergence of the Inca empire. In some periods we see a limited number of powerful states, while in others, including the Early Intermediate period, we see a larger number of smaller polities. In the following sections, we will examine two very different cultures of the Early Intermediate period: the Nasca culture of the southern Peruvian coast and the Moche, or Mochica, culture of the northern coastal region.

THE NASCA OF THE SOUTHERN COAST

The southern coastal region, centered on the Nazca and Ica River Valleys, is well known for its artistry in ceramics and textiles. One of the finest collections of textiles comes from the **Paracas** necropolis, or cemetery. This site, which was excavated by Julio C. Tello in 1929, is made up of a cache of 429 mummies, which were wrapped in cloth and piled in an

FIGURE 25.7   An example of Chavín art: the Raimondi stone from Chavín de Huántar, showing the Staff God. Drawing courtesy of John H. Rowe.

ARCHAEOLOGY IN PRACTICE

The Preservation of Organic Materials

Organic materials can be broadly defined as the remains of living things—plants and animals. Organic materials were often used by ancient societies, not only as foods, but also for a range of craft and construction activities. Ancient peoples regularly made use of wood, animal skins, sinew, horn, antler, and bone. Matting, cordage, and textiles were made from a variety of plant and animal fibers, including reeds, flax, cotton, wool, and hair.

Bone is one of the most durable of all organic materials because it is composed of both mineral and organic matter. Animal bones survive poorly in acid soils (pH of 6 or less), which rapidly dissolve the mineral component of bone. Once the mineral component of bone is destroyed, the organic component is then broken down by bacteria. In neutral or alkaline soils, the mineral component of bone can survive unchanged for thousands of years, even though the organic component may be quickly destroyed by bacteria (Rackham 1994: 19). As a result, animal bones are among the most common finds in many archaeological sites.

Other organic materials, including skins, hides, and plant and animal fibers, decay rapidly in most environments. Biological agents of decay, such as bacteria, fungi, and insects, can destroy buried textiles, hides, and matting in a matter of months or years. Organic materials such as textiles can survive only in burial contexts that inhibit the action of bacteria, insects, and fungi. Waterlogging and extreme desiccation can inhibit the action of these biological agents of destruction.

FIGURE 25.A   Restored loom excavated in the Chancay Valley in Peru.

Waterlogging provides an anaerobic environment (an environment lacking in oxygen), which inhibits bacterial action. As we saw in Chapter 13, waterlogged Mesolithic sites in Europe have yielded remains of wooden canoes, paddles, and other organic artifacts that are rarely preserved archaeologically.

Extreme desert conditions will also inhibit the activity of bacteria, fungi, and insects. Such dry conditions exist in Egypt in the Old World and along the Peruvian coastal desert in the Americas. The extreme dryness of the Peruvian coast has resulted in the preservation of a unique series of textiles made of cotton and camelid (llama and alpaca) hair. These unusual preservation conditions have allowed archaeologists to study both the technology of weaving (Figure 25.A) and the design motifs on the textiles themselves.

FIGURE 25.8   Detail of the Hoover mantle from the Paracas necropolis.

abandoned house on the Paracas peninsula. In addition to the cloth, the mummies were accompanied by food, ceramic vessels, and other grave goods, such as beautifully embroidered headbands, mantles (Figure 25.8), loincloths, turbans, ponchos, tunics, and skirts (Paul 1990). The burials from the Paracas necropolis are dated to the late part of the Early Horizon and the early part of the Early Intermediate period; radiocarbon dates range from 300 B.C. to A.D.

200 (Silverman 1991: 351). The dry, desert conditions that exist on the Peruvian coast allowed these finely made textiles to be preserved from antiquity (see the Archaeology in Practice box).

The embroidered designs on the Paracas textiles show remarkable similarities to the images painted on later Nasca pottery. The art, technology, and iconography of the Paracas culture clearly had an influence on the subsequent Nasca culture, but the

FIGURE 25.9 A richly decorated Nasca ceramic vessel.

nature of the relationship between the two cultures remains unclear (Silverman 1991: 351). Part of the problem is that the pottery that was found in association with the Paracas textiles is generally unpainted (Paul 1991: 25).

The **Nasca** culture, known for its beautiful ceramics and textiles, developed on the south coast of Peru during the Early Intermediate period. The most important Nasca center, **Cahuachi,** was once seen as the capital city of the Nasca polity. The site covers an area of 150 ha (390 ac.) and includes more than 40 mounds. Recent research at Cahuachi, however, has shown that the center was a ceremonial, not a major urban, center (Silverman 1993). Excavations at the site have yielded little evidence for defensive works, permanent residences, and day-to-day activities (Silverman 1993: 300). The mounds at the site appear to be temple mounds,

rather than elite residences. Cahuachi appears to have served as a center of pilgrimage and ritual. It never developed into a true city with a substantial residential population engaged in nonsubsistence activities.

Nasca artisans are world-famous for their ceramics (Figure 25.9) and their textiles, a fact that has led to the extensive looting of many Nasca sites (see Chapter 27). The Nasca textiles include large quantities of alpaca hair, indicating that extensive trade relationships were maintained with the highland regions of the Andes (Conklin and Moseley 1988: 155). While Nasca sites share common styles of pottery, textiles, and other aspects of material culture, the Nasca do not appear to represent an early state society. Although the Nasca were clearly a complex society, with differences in access to social status, political power, and material wealth, the evidence for the centralization of political power in the Nasca region is limited. Instead, the Nasca appear to be a segmentary society (a society based on lineages and descent groups), "but with a universally accepted cult center at Cahuachi" (Silverman 2002: 166).

THE MOCHICA STATE ON THE NORTH COAST

At a superficial level, the **Mochica, or Moche,** culture of the north coast of Peru shows some similarities to the Nasca of the south coast. The Mochica were skilled craftworkers in both pottery and metals. Moche metal production built on the innovations that appeared during the Early Horizon. The Mochica made use of silver and copper in addition to gold, and they alloyed metals and occasionally cast copper (Donnan 1978). Moche potters used molds to produce high-quality ceramics, such as their portrait vessels, which are realistically painted to represent distinctive individuals (Figure 25.10).

While the Moche and the Nasca both produced high-quality ceramics and other crafts, the degrees of urbanism and political integration in the two regions were very different indeed. Unlike the Nasca ceremonial center of Cahuachi, the Moche capital at **Cerro Blanco** in the Moche Valley appears to have been a political capital and urban center. The capital

FIGURE 25.10 A Mochica portrait vessel.

There is abundant evidence for social differentiation in the Moche capital and elsewhere along the northern Peruvian coast during the Early Intermediate period. Elite residences were constructed of adobe, while those of the lower classes were built of cane with stone foundations. Elite burials contained large quantities of sumptuary goods. Among the most impressive are the rich burials recently recovered from the **Sípan** pyramid complex in the Lambayeque Valley. These burials were accompanied by prodigious quantities of metal, presentation goblets, and distinctive uniforms and headdresses.

Finally, there is greater evidence for centralization of authority in the Moche region than there is in the Nasca areas to the south. Administrative centers, modeled on the Huaca del Sol and Huaca de la Luna but smaller in size, were established in many north coast valleys. The Moche state also possessed a road system and a warrior-based elite (Stanish 2001: 55), which allowed them to control the northern Peruvian coast both militarily and politically. At the apex of its power in the sixth century A.D., the Moche state controlled one-third of the Peruvian coast (Shimada 1994: 35). As Moseley (2001: 196) notes, Moche "represents a remarkable achievement in statecraft, ranging from taxation and labor organization to art and ideology. For the first time, the largest of coastal populations were united together by shared notions of the nature of rule and governance."

THE MIDDLE HORIZON

The **Middle Horizon** (A.D. 600 to 1000) saw the rise of two powerful states in South America—**Tiwanaku** in the southern highlands and **Wari,** whose capital was located in the Ayacucho Valley in central Peru. These states developed at a time of profound environmental stress in the Andean areas. There is environmental evidence for a series of severe El Niño events in the sixth century A.D., which caused flooding along the normally dry coast and drought in the Andean highlands. (El Niño events are caused by a warming of the waters of the South Pacific. They can cause storms and flooding all along the Pacific coast and unusual weather patterns throughout the world. A recent event took

was dominated by two major structures, the Huaca del Sol (Pyramid of the Sun) and the smaller Huaca de la Luna (Pyramid of the Moon). As can be seen in Figure 25.11, the Huaca del Sol is a multilevel platform built of adobe bricks. Around A.D. 500 it would have been surrounded by elite residences, workshops, and extensive cemeteries for the nobility. The Huaca del Sol appears to have served as a palace and mausoleum for Moche leaders. The Huaca de la Luna, on the other hand, lacks domestic rubbish and was decorated with murals. It appears to have served as a ritual center. Archaeological finds from the Moche area indicate that the Moche capital was a center of specialized craft production for both ceramic and metal objects. By A.D. 500 the Moche capital had developed into a "functionally complex and differentiated settlement with a substantial resident population" (Shimada 1994: 97).

FIGURE 25.11   The Huaca del Sol at the Moche capital of Cerro Blanco. Only a small part of the original platform structure survives. The Spanish diverted the Moche River to undercut the mound and loot its contents. The remaining portion of the Huaca del Sol measures 340 by 160 m (1100 by 525 ft.) and stands 40 m (130 ft.) high.

place in 1997.) As will be shown, both the Wari and the Tiwanaku state appear to have been involved in innovations in agricultural technology that may be related, at least in part, to the climatic instability of the mid-first millennium A.D.

The city of Wari is located on the eastern edge of the Ayacucho Valley, at an elevation of approximately 3000 m (9800 ft.) above sea level. The most intensively occupied core of the city covers an area of about 300 ha (740 ac.). The architectural remains at Wari are poorly preserved and difficult to interpret because of looting and plowing by modern farmers; virtually the entire area is dry-farmed today. The available archaeological evidence from survey and excavation indicates that the city was divided into a series of building compounds divided by walled enclosures (Isbell 1988: 168). The buildings within the enclosures were two to three stories high; within the compounds rooms were organized around courtyards, or patios. The population of Wari is estimated to have been between 16,000 and 35,000 during the Middle Horizon (Moseley 2001: 231). Wari was a large city in which a range of administrative, ceremonial, and craft activities were carried out (Isbell 1988: 173).

At the height of its power during the Middle Horizon, the Wari state appears to have exercised political control over a large area of the Peruvian highlands, and its influence extended to many areas of the Peruvian coast. The ability of the Wari state to expand beyond the Ayacucho region was based on an important administrative innovation—the development of a system of labor taxation (Isbell 1988). The state required its subjects to perform agricultural labor on state lands; in return, the Wari administrators provided the laborers with food and drink. At least three Wari provincial administrative centers have been identified by archaeologists. These centers often include barrackslike accommodations for temporary agricultural workers, storage areas for produce, and communal kitchens for the preparation of meals for the agricultural workers.

Recent excavations at **Cerro Baul,** a mesa-top Wari citadel, have uncovered a large-scale *chicha* brewery. *Chicha* is an alcoholic beverage brewed from maize. The large, 40-to-60 l (10 to 15 gal.) ceramic vats could have produced thousands of liters of *chicha* each day. The excavator, Ryan Patrick Williams, suggests that the Wari elite may have

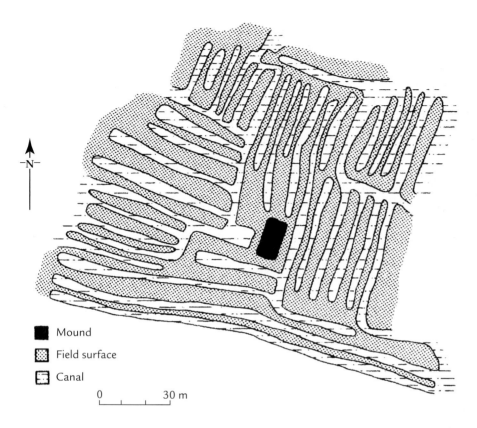

Mound

Field surface

Canal

0   30 m

FIGURE 25.12 Plan of the Tiwanaku raised field system. The house mound in the center, which dates to approximately A.D. 800 to 1000, was occupied on a seasonal basis by field guardians.

hosted large drinking festivals to reward faithful subordinates from all parts of the Wari empire. The use of feasting to reward loyalty by the Wari elite parallels its use by powerful families in the Chinese late Neolithic (see Chapter 22).

A second Wari innovation can be seen in the area of agricultural technology (Moseley 1992). During the Early Intermediate period, farming in the highlands took place at the higher elevations, where rainfall alone was adequate to support the cultivation of potatoes and other highland crops. Irrigation farming was limited to the coastal valleys and the river valley areas within the uplands. The Wari introduced terracing and irrigation agriculture to the steep mountain slopes of the highlands. The water for irrigation was drawn from elevated streams and springs, water sources that were less affected by variations in rainfall. This new agricultural technology would have been particularly important in the drought conditions that existed during the Middle Horizon.

A second, smaller state developed in the southern Andes during the Middle Horizon. Its capital city of Tiwanaku is located 15 km (9 mi.) south of Lake Titicaca in Bolivia. The Tiwanaku state flourished between A.D. 400 and 1000. Its heartland was the flatland surrounding Lake Titicaca, but llama caravans provided links with distant regions in the southern highlands. Recent archaeological research has shown that the Tiwanaku state was directly involved in reclaiming for agricultural use the flat, marshy areas that surround Lake Titicaca (Kolata 1991).

Tiwanaku agriculture in the Lake Titicaca region was based on a system of raised fields. The raised fields were "large elevated planting platforms ranging from 5 to 20 m in width and up to 200 m in length" (Kolata 1991: 101) and were surrounded by canals (Figure 25.12). The canals supported aquatic plants, which were used as fertilizer for the raised fields, and also protected the fields from killer frosts, a serious problem at high elevations. The construction of the Tiwanaku raised field system depended on the creation of a regional system of canals, aqueducts, and groundwater regulation and would have required the mobilization of a substantial labor force. Like the Wari system of irrigated terraces, the raised field system of the Titicaca basin was a highly productive agricultural system that would have required large amounts of coordinated labor for its construction and maintenance.

Stanish (2001: 55) has pointed out several important similarities between the Tiwanaku and the Wari states. Both have "palaces, planned urban capitals, high populations, evidence of socioeconomic classes, site-size hierarchies, expansionist policies, agricultural intensification, economic specialization, and colonial enclaves." The two states, however, appear to have developed largely independently. There is little archaeological evidence for contact between these two early states.

THE LATE INTERMEDIATE PERIOD

The **Late Intermediate period** (A.D. 1000 to 1476) begins with the collapse of the Wari and Tiwanaku states and ends with the rapid expansion of the Inca Empire in the century before the Spanish conquest of Peru. The archaeology of the Late Intermediate period is best known from the north coast of Peru as a result of intensive archaeological excavation in the Moche Valley. During the Late Intermediate period, the Moche Valley was dominated by the city of **Chan Chan,** the capital of **Chimor, or the Chimú state.** Chimor was the most powerful state of the Late Intermediate period; at its height the Chimú state controlled two-thirds of the Peruvian coast.

The central core of Chan Chan (Moseley 1975a; Moseley and Day 1982) covers an area of 6 sq. km (2.3 sq. mi.) and may have housed between 25,000 and 30,000 people at its height (Parsons and Hastings 1988: 193). The most striking feature of the central core is a series of compounds termed *ciudadellas* (little cities) that appear to have been built by successive Chimú rulers (Figure 25.13). The *ciudadellas* "combined the functions of royal entombment, elite residence, centralized storage, and closely administered redistribution" (Parsons and Hastings 1988: 193). They included a number of U-shaped rooms, which appear to control access

to storage facilities. Similar U-shaped structures appear to serve administrative functions in areas conquered by the Chimú state. Oral histories recorded by the Spanish conquistadors indicate that Chimor fell to the Incas in about A.D. 1470.

THE LATE HORIZON

In the study of the dramatic rise to power of the Incas in Peru, archaeological evidence is supplemented by written accounts of the Spanish conquistadors. Much of the information in the Spanish chronicles is based on interviews with native oral historians. Thus, both historical data and archaeological evidence can be used to study the rise of the Inca Empire.

The **Late Horizon** (A.D. 1476 to 1532) refers to the period of Inca imperial expansion, ending with the Spanish conquest of Peru in 1532. The beginning date of 1476 refers specifically to the Incas' conquest of the Ica Valley in the southern coastal region, since the basic chronology for Peruvian archaeology was based on early research in the Ica Valley. However, Inca political expansion had begun well before the conquest of the Ica Valley. As noted in the previous section, Chan Chan and Chimor fell to the Incas about 1470, and ethnohistorical sources suggest that Inca imperial expansion began in 1438 under the Inca ruler Pachakuti. In the late fourteenth and early fifteenth centuries, the Inca were one of a number of small kingdoms and chiefdoms competing for power in the southern highlands of Peru. The ethnic Incas probably numbered no more than 40,000 individuals (Moseley 2001: 9). Within a century the Inca had transformed themselves into the rulers of the largest empire in the pre-Columbian Americas. What factors made this dramatic change of fortunes possible?

A social institution that clearly played a role in the rapid expansion of the Inca state is the system of **split inheritance,** a system that can be traced back to the Chimú state (Moseley 1975a). Under the split inheritance system, a newly crowned Inca ruler inherited the title to the throne, including the rights to govern, wage war, and impose taxes. He did not inherit, however, the material possessions of the previous emperor. They were entrusted to a corporate group made up of other male heirs of the previous ruler who perpetuated the cult of the previous emperor. The new

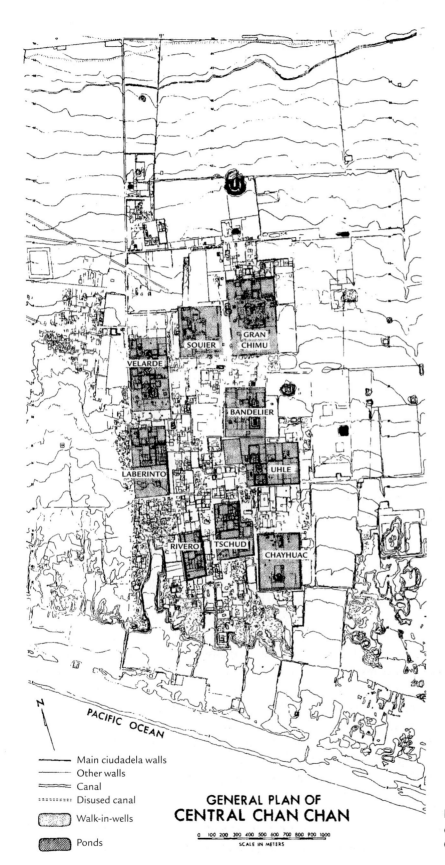

N

PACIFIC OCEAN

——— Main ciudadela walls
——— Other walls
≈≈≈≈ Canal
······ Disused canal
Walk-in-wells
Ponds

**GENERAL PLAN OF
CENTRAL CHAN CHAN**

0 100 200 300 400 500 600 700 800 900 1000
SCALE IN METERS

FIGURE 25.13 Plan of the central part of the city of Chan Chan, showing the *ciudadellas*.

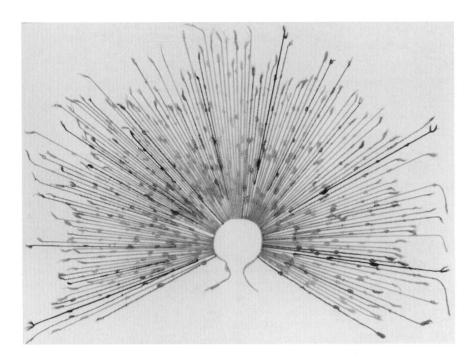

FIGURE 25.14   A *quipu*, a record-keeping device based on knotted strings that was used by the Inca.

emperor was forced to acquire new possessions—that is, territories that could be taxed to sustain a royal lifestyle, reward his supporters, and provide his male kinship group with the ability to perpetuate his cult after his death (Conrad and Demarest 1984: 118). The split inheritance system provided an ideological basis for rapid imperial expansion.

The expansion of the Inca Empire was also facilitated by a number of social institutions that had been developed by pre-Inca states in the Andean area. Foremost among those was the institution of the labor tax, or *mit'a*. The labor tax was levied on all able-bodied males and could include military service, construction of irrigation systems and terracing for agriculture, and road construction. The Inca Empire was connected by more than 23,000 km (14,000 mi.) of roads (Hyslop 1984: 222), which were built using the labor tax system. The Inca state also imposed agricultural taxes on men and women. Agricultural lands were divided into thirds: one-third supported the gods and religious shrines, one-third supported the Inca state, and the final third supported the local community. Produce raised on the state lands was used to provide food and drink for the many workers who toiled on behalf of the state. In addition, textile taxation was a part of Inca statecraft. Men and women were required to produce cloth and cordage from raw wool, cotton, and fiber. The finished textiles, which were collected by the government, were often used as rewards for government service.

Record keeping was critical to the administration of the Inca state. While the Inca differ from the Maya and many of the complex societies of the Old World because they lacked written records, the Inca did develop an elaborate system of record keeping based on knotted strings, known as the *quipu* (Figure 25.14). The *quipu* was based on the decimal system; knots of different sizes, locations, sequences, and colors were used to indicate quantities (Morris 1988: 250). A simplified version of the *quipu* is still in use in the Peruvian highlands.

CONCLUSION

In the space of 100 years, the Inca built an empire that extended from the tropics to northern Chile and Argentina. The Incas' success in building and administering this vast empire was based on a tradition of statecraft that has deep roots in Peruvian prehistory. For example, the ability to mobilize large quantities of labor for monumental construction can be traced back to the Late Preceramic and Initial periods. Systems of labor and agricultural taxation also appear to have developed in pre-Inca times. In short, "much of [the Incas'] spectacular but short-lived empire was based upon institutions that they shared with their competitors and precursors" (Conrad and Demarest 1984: 86).

KEY TERMS

Altiplano 371	Late Intermediate
Cahuachi 378	period 382
Cerro Baul 380	Lomas 371
Cerro Blanco 378	Middle Horizon 379
Chan Chan 382	Mochica, or Moche 378
Chavín	Nasca 378
de Huántar 373	Paloma 372
Chimor, or the Chimú	Paracas 375
state 382	Preceramic period 372
Cuzco 369	Puna 371
Early Horizon 373	Río Seco 372
Early Intermediate	Sechín Alto 373
period 375	Sípan 379
Inca 369	Split inheritance 382
Initial period 372	Tiwanaku 379
Late Horizon 382	Wari 379

QUESTIONS FOR DISCUSSION

1. How did the Inca make use of techniques of statecraft developed by pre-Inca societies in the Andes?

2. What are the similarities and differences between the development of cities and states in Peru and the rise of complex societies in Mesoamerica?

3. How did the Inca develop the largest empire in the Americas without writing?

FURTHER READING

Malpass, Michael A.,
1996 *Daily Life in the Inca Empire.* Westport, CT: Greenwood Press.
Malpass's book is one in a series of volumes on daily life in ancient societies. It provides a very accessible introduction to day-to-day life in the Inca Empire based on both archaeological and historical sources. The beginning chapter includes a brief summary of the pre-Inca prehistory of Andean South America. The final chapter on the destruction of archaeological sites by looters and pothunters is highly recommended.

Moseley, Michael E.,
2001 *The Incas and Their Ancestors: The Archaeology of Peru,* revised ed. New York: Thames and Hudson.
Moseley's book is a very readable and well-illustrated introduction to the archaeology of Andean South America. He begins with the Inca empire and then provides a detailed survey of the pre-Inca prehistory of Peru.

Stanish, Charles
2001 The Origins of State Societies in South America. *Annual Review of Anthropology* 30: 41–64.
A recent review article that examines the archaeological evidence for state formation in the Andes. Stanish argues that states first developed in the Andes in the first millennium A.D.

26

MIDDLE-RANGE AND COMPLEX SOCIETIES IN NORTH AMERICA

At the time of initial European contact in the sixteenth and seventeenth centuries, North America was a mosaic of different cultures, languages, and ways of life. Native American peoples made a living by various combinations of hunting, gathering, fishing, and farming. For example, the Shoshoni and other native peoples of the Great Basin were mobile hunter-gatherers, moving seasonally to make use of a range of different plant and animal resources. The Natchez of the southern Gulf Coast region, on the other hand, were sedentary farmers who raised maize, beans, and squash, and supplemented their diet by hunting deer and smaller animals. The diversity of Native American cultures is so great that no single introductory textbook can begin to cover them all (but see Fagan 2000 for an introduction to North American archaeology).

In this chapter we focus on the development of complex societies in eastern North America, specifically the U.S. Midwest and Southeast, between 1000 B.C. and A.D. 1500. The complex societies that developed in eastern North America differed fundamentally from the cities, states, and empires that developed in pre-Columbian Peru and Mesoamerica. Native North Americans never built cities the size of Teotihuacán or Tenochtitlán; their polities were chiefdoms rather than states or empires. However, Native American societies in the Southeast and Midwest were characterized by significant social, political, and economic inequality. The later prehistoric inhabitants of these areas built monumental mound complexes and engaged in long-distance trade and exchange of exotic items. In many ways the development of complex societies in North America parallels the process of cultural evolution seen in later prehistoric Europe (see Chapter 23). In both regions, archaeologists have documented the emergence of chiefdom-level societies that were characterized by significant differences in social status, political power, and material wealth. In tracing the development of cultural complexity in eastern

North America, we will begin in the Early Woodland period at about 1000 B.C., a time when pottery first appeared in parts of the Midwest.

We conclude this chapter with an overview of the archaeology of farming societies in the American Southwest. The sedentary agricultural societies that developed in the Southwest in the first and second millennia A.D. produced large-scale irrigation systems, monumental architectural complexes, and specialized crafts and trade. These societies lacked the hierarchical social and political organization that characterized the chiefdom societies of the Midwest and Southeast. However, they are classic examples of middle-range or tribal societies, sedentary societies that rely on an agricultural base but that are not complex, urban societies.

THE EARLY WOODLAND PERIOD AND THE BEGINNING OF CULTURAL COMPLEXITY IN THE MIDWEST

As we saw in Chapter 14, by the Late Archaic period in the riverine areas of the Midwest and Southeast, Native Americans had domesticated a number of indigenous plants, including sunflowers, marsh elder, goosefoot, and gourds (Smith 1994). The cultivation of these plants began as early as 2500 B.C. They were part of a broad-based diet that also included aquatic resources such as fish, shellfish, and waterfowl, and terrestrial foods, including wild mammals, wild turkeys, and wild plants.

The beginning of the Woodland period, approximately 1000 B.C., is marked by the appearance of pottery in the Eastern Woodlands. As it did in many other parts of the world, pottery served a variety of functions for early agriculturalists. Pottery certainly would have been useful for storing and cooking crop plants, especially since the early North American domesticates may have served as storable food reserves for the winter and early spring (Smith 1994: 197). In addition, pottery may have played an important role in the processing of wild plants such as hickory, whose nuts are crushed and boiled during processing (Taladay et al. 1984).

During the first millennium B.C., cultivated plants came to play an even more important role in the economies of the Southeast and Midwest. In addition to the four indigenous domesticates, three other plants

appear to have been cultivated at this time: knotweed (*Polygonum erectum*), little barley (*Hordeum pusillum*), and maygrass (*Phalaris caroliniana*). The starchy seeds of these three plants have a high carbohydrate content and would have been valuable additions to the Early Woodland diet.

Also during the first millennium B.C., some of the earliest evidence for the emergence of complex societies appears in the Eastern Woodlands. As we have noted before, complexity is sometimes defined by inequality of access to material and human resources (McGuire 1983). In the American Midwest during the **Early Woodland period** (approximately 1000 to 200 B.C.), we see two clear indicators of increasing social and economic complexity—a growing trade in exotic, luxury items, and increasingly elaborate burial rituals. These characteristics are seen most clearly in the **Adena** cultural complex that is known from Ohio and the surrounding areas (Figure 26.1).

The Adena cultural complex is best known for its elaborate burial mounds, which are found in eastern Indiana, southern and central Ohio, northern Kentucky, and western Pennsylvania and West Virginia. Important individuals were buried in rectangular log tombs; then the tombs were covered with earth. After the first burial was completed, other individuals were buried in or around the mounds. The largest Adena mounds were enormous. For example, the Grave Creek mound in

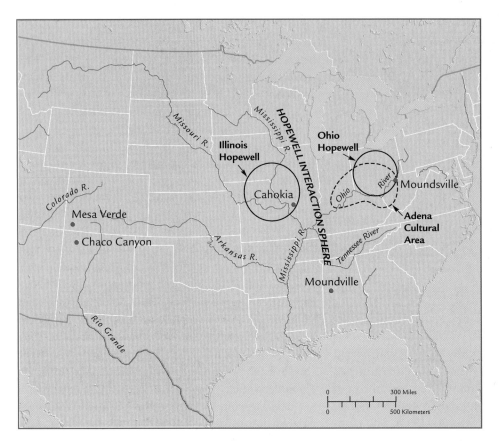

FIGURE 26.1   Map of the eastern United States, showing the location of the sites mentioned in this chapter.

Moundsville, West Virginia, originally stood 20 m (66 ft.) high and contained nearly 70,000 cu. m (92,000 cu. yds.) of earth fill (Fagan 2000: 412). The construction of these mounds would have involved large quantities of human labor, especially since the work would have been done by hand using shovels and baskets. The coordination of the labor needed to construct these huge mounds would have required some degree of leadership, and that, in turn, may indicate the beginnings of social and political inequality.

Local and interregional trade also increased during the Early Woodland period. The archaeological evidence for this increased trade comes primarily from exotic materials that are found interred with Adena Complex and other Early Woodland burials. The exotic goods are often nonutilitarian items that may have served as indicators of wealth, status, or prestige. These grave goods include crescents made from North Carolina mica, carved pipes made from Ohio pipestone (Figure 26.2), and bracelets and finger rings made from copper from the region around Lake Superior. The appearance of the exotic items of exchange in Adena burials may reflect the emergence of a prestige goods economy, in which exotic and valuable items were exchanged among an emerging elite group, possibly leaders of lineages or other kinship groups. The exotic pipestone, copper, and mica objects found in Adena graves may have played the same role that early copper items played in the emerging complex societies of later prehistoric Europe (see Chapter 23). They were, in effect, status symbols of an emerging elite.

While the exchange of these exotic items may have been carried out by group leaders, the maintenance of the exchange networks may have benefited the society as a whole. It has been argued that these exchange relationships served to maintain alliances with social groups in other areas. In times

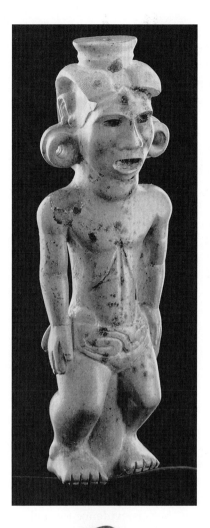

FIGURE 26.2 A carved stone pipe recovered from an Adena mound, Ohio (height: about 20 cm, or 8 in.).

of stress, such as droughts, floods, or crop failures, lineage leaders may have been able to call on their allies in unaffected areas for subsistence resources. In this way, exchange of ceremonial items became a form of subsistence insurance (Brose 1979).

COMPLEX SOCIETIES OF THE MIDDLE WOODLAND PERIOD: THE HOPEWELL INTERACTION SPHERE

The trend toward increasingly elaborate burial practices and long-distance trade in exotic items and raw materials continues during the **Middle Woodland period** (approximately 200 B.C. to A.D. 400). At that time a widespread network of trade and exchange, known as the **Hopewell Interaction Sphere,** developed throughout the entire Midwest and Southeast. The network was centered on the Ohio River Valley. As Kelly (1979: 1) notes, "In the Midwest the Hopewell interaction sphere has been conceptualized as a model growing out of an early widespread network of long-distance trade in ceremonial goods." It is clear that this exchange network was well established by Early Woodland times, and its antecedents may date back to the Late Archaic period.

Although the Hopewell Interaction Sphere was centered in Ohio, it extended from the Great Lakes to the Gulf Coast and from the Appalachian Mountains to the Mississippi Valley and westward along the Missouri River. Many local groups within this region exchanged exotic raw materials, distinctive finished products, and ideas about mortuary rituals. The exotic raw materials included obsidian, most of which was obtained from a source in Yellowstone National Park (Hatch et al. 1990); seashells from the east coast of Florida; and silver and native copper from the Great Lakes region. Finished objects that were traded included small pottery jars and pipes (Figure 26.3).

Much of what we know of Hopewellian archaeology comes from the excavation of elaborate

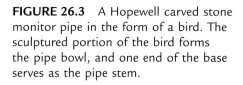

FIGURE 26.3 A Hopewell carved stone monitor pipe in the form of a bird. The sculptured portion of the bird forms the pipe bowl, and one end of the base serves as the pipe stem.

FIGURE 26.4   Copper falcon from the Hopewell mound group in Ohio.

burial mounds, especially those in the Ohio and Illinois Valleys. While the majority of Hopewellian individuals appear to have been cremated, elite individuals were placed into log-lined tombs and often accompanied by rich grave offerings (Figure 26.4). Those offerings included copper ear spools, freshwater pearls, copper breastplates, and large quantities of exotic raw materials, such as western obsidian and mica from the southern Appalachians.

The elaborate Hopewellian burials clearly reflect some degree of social differentiation, but the nature of Middle Woodland society has long been a subject of debate among archaeologists. Do the Hopewell societies represent early chiefdoms with a centralized hierarchy of leaders who are set apart from the remainder of the population (Earle 1987), or are the Hopewell societies in Illinois and Ohio simply lineage-based societies whose leaders used exotic trade goods in accordance with their roles as kin-group leaders? This question is not easy to answer, and a case can be made for each point of view.

Chiefdom societies are characterized by a class of leaders whose decision-making authority sets them apart from the rest of the population. This decision-making hierarchy may be reflected in a hierarchy of settlement types, including both small rural sites and larger regional centers. Those who would see the Hopewellian societies as early chiefdoms argue that there is evidence for a clear hierarchy of settlement sites in the Illinois Valley during the Middle Woodland period. The small sites include farmsteads and hamlets, which were occupied by people engaged in horticulture, plant collection, hunting, and fishing. The larger sites, which are associated with floodplain mounds and contain large quantities of exotic materials, are interpreted as regional transaction centers where elite individuals engaged in the trade and redistribution of prestige goods (Streuver and Houart 1972).

While the settlement pattern data can be used to make a case for Hopewellian chiefdoms, the data from the burials are somewhat more equivocal. Mature adult males are most likely to be buried in elaborate tombs with exotic grave goods. This has led some scholars to suggest that Hopewellian status was not inherited; instead, the elaborate burials reflect an individual's accomplishments during his or her lifetime (Braun 1979). The burial data suggest that there may not have been an established ruling elite during Middle Woodland times. Instead, status and decision-making authority were more volatile and dependent on the personal accomplishment of individual lineage leaders.

The network of trade and exchange that made up the Hopewell Interaction Sphere collapsed around A.D. 400. The end is marked by a curtailment in trade and mortuary ceremonialism (Tainter 1988: 15). The reasons for the collapse are unclear, and simple monocausal explanations such as climatic changes are not supported by the available archaeological evidence. Perhaps the costs of participation in the exchange system simply came to outweigh the benefits (cf. Tainter 1988). If the main benefit of the interaction sphere was the creation of alliances to mitigate against food shortages, then it is possible that people developed alternative ways of alleviating food shortfalls, such as increased food storage. What appears to have happened, however, is the disappearance of the highest levels of Middle Woodland society (Peregrine 1992: 99), creating a Late Woodland society that was both less complex and more egalitarian.

THE LATE WOODLAND PERIOD AND THE ADOPTION OF MAIZE AGRICULTURE

The adoption of maize agriculture was one of the most profound subsistence changes in all of North American prehistory. As noted in Chapter 17, maize was initially domesticated in Mesoamerica and must have been introduced to eastern North America from the outside. It is not clear, however, whether maize reached the eastern United States directly from Mesoamerica by way of the American Southwest or whether it was introduced to Florida from South America via the Antilles. Both studies of seed remains from archaeological sites and studies of human bone biochemistry (see the Archaeology in Practice box) indicate that maize first appeared in the Eastern Woodlands during the **Late Woodland period** (ca. A.D. 400 to 800), but that its role in the diet was initially quite variable. Human skeletal analyses indicate that maize made up between 0 and 55% of the diet during the later part of the Late Woodland period. This variability may well be expected when people are beginning to experiment with a new resource. However, during the subsequent Mississippian period (ca. A.D. 800 to 1500), maize con-

sistently made up between 40 and 55% of the diet (van der Merwe and Vogel 1978; Buikstra 1984: 226).

Why did the horticulturalists-fishers-hunters of the American Midwest and Southeast adopt maize agriculture? While maize cultivation certainly provided a storable, high-carbohydrate resource that may have alleviated seasonal shortages in food, the introduction of maize was a mixed blessing. Studies of human skeletons from the lower Illinois Valley (Cook 1984) indicate that childhood health worsened at the time that maize agriculture was introduced. These data have led Cook (1979) to suggest that the adoption of maize agriculture may have been a response to population growth, which would have placed increasing stress on the other available food resources. In other words the adoption of maize agriculture may be seen as a form of subsistence intensification as a response to demographic stress.

THE EMERGENCE OF MISSISSIPPIAN SOCIETIES

The widespread adoption of maize agriculture provides the economic backdrop for our understanding of the emergence of complex, chiefdom-level societies in the Eastern Woodlands. However, it would be an oversimplification to argue that the adoption of maize cultivation *caused* the emergence of chiefdom societies in the Eastern Woodlands. As we shall see, the widespread adoption of maize, which began about A.D. 800, was accompanied by other social, political, and economic changes that reflect the emergence of more complex societies.

These complex societies are described by the general term **Mississippian.** Mississippian societies are chiefdom-level societies that initially developed in the several parts of the Eastern Woodlands of the United States between about A.D. 750 and 1050 (Smith 1992). The question of how and why these chiefdoms emerged in eastern North America at that time is a complex one. As Bruce Smith (1992: 1–2) of the Smithsonian Institution has noted, "It is . . . far from clear to what degree this broadly similar process of cultural transformation was due to developmental interaction between river valley societies in transition, as opposed to their independent response to similar developmental constraints

ARCHAEOLOGY IN PRACTICE

The Analysis of Human Burials

As we have seen in this chapter, Adena, Hopewell, and Mississippian sites from the eastern United States have produced large numbers of human burials. Burial mounds have been of particular interest to archaeologists who study the emergence of complex societies because the construction of elaborate burial mounds can provide information about the mobilization of labor within those societies. In addition, the quantity and quality of grave goods included with individual burials can shed light on increasing social differentiation. However, the human skeletons interred in the mounds and cemeteries are themselves important sources of information about human diets and about the incidence of disease in ancient human populations.

The analysis of human skeletons generally begins with the determination of the sex and age of each individual. The pelvis is the most reliable criterion for distinguishing males from females. The female pelvis is specially adapted so that a baby can pass through the birth canal during the process of childbirth. One difference between male and female pelvises is the wider angle of the sciatic notch in the female pelvis (Figure 26.A).

Teeth are among the most valuable indicators of the age at death of a individual. In humans, as in other mammals, the milk, or deciduous, teeth erupt in a set sequence, and they are gradually replaced by the permanent teeth. While there is always some degree of individual variation, dental eruption can be used to provide quite accurate estimates of age at death for subadult individuals. For example, dentists commonly talk about the eruption of 6-year and 12-year molars. The general sequence of dental eruption

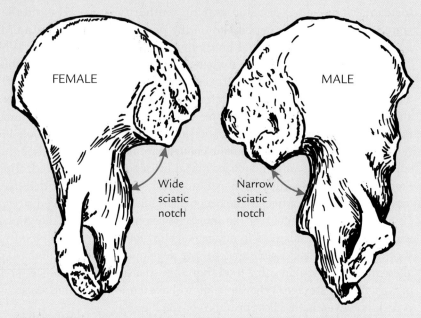

FIGURE 26.A Male and female pelvises, showing the wider sciatic notch in the female pelvis.

is shown in Figure 26.B For mature adults, the degree of dental wear can give a more general indication of age.

Once the sex and age of each archaeological skeleton have been determined, a number of techniques can be used to study diet, health status, and disease in ancient human populations. Biochemical analyses have been particularly useful in the study of prehistoric diets. Among the most important techniques are those involving stable carbon isotopes (Ambrose 1987), nonradioactive forms of carbon that vary only in their atomic weight. There are two stable isotopes of carbon: a lighter and more common ^{12}C and a heavier ^{13}C. Plants obtain carbon from the atmosphere during the process of photosynthesis. Most native North American plants metabolize carbon in a way that discriminates against the heavier ^{13}C.

Maize and other tropical grasses, however, metabolize carbon in a different way, one that does not discriminate against the heavier isotope. As a result, when Native Americans shifted from a diet of native North American plants to one that was high in maize, the amount of ^{13}C in the skeletons (indicated by rising delta ^{13}C values) increased substantially (Figure 26.C). Stable isotope analysis has been a useful tool for determining when various Native American populations incorporated maize into their diets.

Studies of skeletal collections can also reveal information about the health status of prehistoric populations. However, it is often difficult to identify specific diseases or dietary deficiencies from bones alone (Larsen and Harn 1994: 223). For example, anemia (low red blood cell counts) can lead to some very specific changes in the bones of the skull.

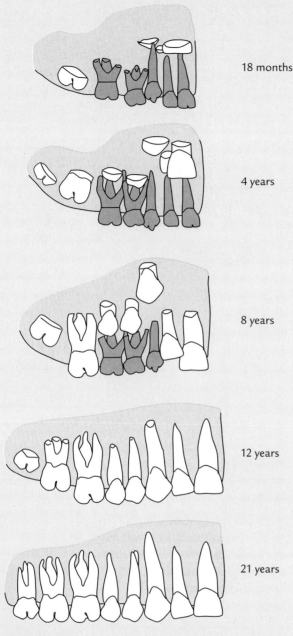

18 months

4 years

8 years

12 years

21 years

FIGURE 26.B General sequence of human dental eruption.

thropologists assess childhood nutrition by comparing height and age. In general, well-nourished children tend to be taller than poorly nourished children. Skeletal populations are somewhat different because juvenile skeletons represent only those children who failed to thrive. Cemetery samples, therefore, may include more evidence for nutritional stress than would be found in the population as a whole. Nevertheless, archaeologists often compare dental age and bone length for juvenile skeletons as a way of looking at nutritional stress in prehistoric populations.

Archaeologists can use evidence of arrested growth as an indicator of the health status of prehistoric populations. Lines of arrested growth, known as Harris lines (Figure 26.D), form on the long bones when bone growth is interrupted as a result of malnutrition or disease (Goodman and Clark 1981). Similarly, defects can form in the enamel surfaces of the milk and permanent teeth when growth is disrupted. These enamel defects are often subject to caries. It should be emphasized that both Harris lines and tooth enamel defects are general indicators of stress that can result from malnutrition and/or infectious disease.

In addition to the osteological evidence for patterns of bone growth and development, archaeologists look for a number of bone pathologies that can provide evidence for disease. As mentioned, anemia can cause changes to the bones of the skull, including thickening of the cranial vault and perforation of the roof of the orbit (termed *cribra orbitalia*). Bone infections, which can result from traumatic injury or from the spread of infection from the soft tissues of the body, can also provide a general indication of the health status of earlier human populations (Larsen and Harn 1994: 227). Changing frequencies

However, anemia can result both from inadequate diet and from infectious diseases that cause food to be absorbed poorly by the body. The relationship between diet, disease, and skeletal biology is therefore quite complicated. As a result, most osteologists use a variety of measures to assess the health status of past populations. These measures can be grouped into two main classes: (1) indicators of skeletal growth and development and (2) evidence of pathology or disease of the skeleton.

Archaeologists can examine the pattern of growth and development in human skeletons in a number of ways. In living populations, an-

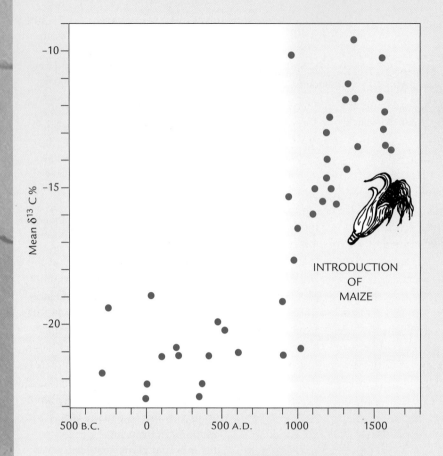

FIGURE 26.C The shift to a diet based on maize farming is revealed by the changing delta ^{13}C values from human bone collagen samples drawn from human skeletal materials of the Woodland and Mississippian periods in eastern North America.

INTRODUCTION
OF
MAIZE

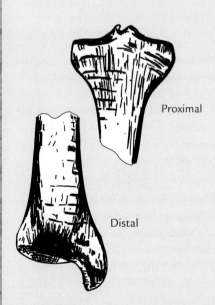

FIGURE 26.D Drawing based on radiographs of a proximal and a distal tibia from a pre-Roman site in Britain, showing lines of arrested growth known as Harris lines.

of dental pathologies such as caries and antemortem tooth loss may reflect changes in diet. The shift to sticky, high-carbohydrate foods such as maize can lead to a higher incidence of tooth decay and premature tooth loss.

Despite the important information about health, diet, and disease that can be gained from the analysis of human skeletal collections, important ethical issues surround the excavation and analysis of these human remains. For years, many Native American peoples have objected to the excavation, analysis, and curation of Indian skeletal remains. Recent federal legislation, the Native American Graves Protection and Repatriation Act (NAGPRA), has required museums and other cultural institutions to return human skeletal remains and grave goods to the appropriate Native American tribes. Many prehistoric skeletons have been reburied, and more are likely to be reburied in the near future. This important issue will be treated in greater detail in Chapter 27.

and opportunities." What is clear, however, is that this process is not the result of influences from outside the Eastern Woodlands; chiefdom-level societies developed independently in the eastern United States during the late first millennium A.D.

A number of scholars have suggested that the development of a prestige goods economy based on the production and exchange of luxury items manufactured from valuable, imported materials may have played a crucial role in the emergence of Mississippian chiefdoms (Peregrine 1992; Brown et al. 1992). Prestige goods were needed to arrange marriages and to form alliances. The production and control of these prestige goods would have conferred both status and power to successful lineage leaders. Agricultural surpluses could have been mobilized to finance the manufacture of these prestige goods and the obtaining of exotic raw materials used to produce them. The maize-based agricultural societies of the Mississippian period were capable of generating greater surpluses than the earlier horticultural economies of the Eastern Woodlands.

The process of political and economic transformation initially involved competition between lineage leaders within a local area. When particular lineage leaders became successful, they may have reached out beyond the local area to form alliances with more distant lineage leaders. These distant alliances may have afforded successful leaders access to rare and exotic items that were unavailable locally. This, in turn, may have led to a process of political consolidation in which the successful leaders developed new political structures and alliances to control trade and to control manufacture and transport of prestige goods.

MISSISSIPPIAN SETTLEMENT AND SOCIAL ORGANIZATION

Mississippian sites are concentrated in the meander-belt zone of river valleys in the eastern United States. The meander belt includes the river floodplains with their oxbow lakes, seasonally flooded low areas, and the surrounding natural levees. These areas contain a variety of soil types and support a wide range of plants and animals. The Mississippians made use of fish; hunted waterfowl and terrestrial game; col-

lected nuts, fruits, berries, and seed-bearing plants; and grew maize and other crops (Smith 1978: 483). These environments were particularly attractive to Mississippian farmers because periodic floods would have maintained the fertility of the soil, making the meander belt a naturally subsidized environment.

Mississippian sites are generally characterized by a two-tiered settlement hierarchy. Small agricultural villages and hamlets make up the bottom tier; larger administrative centers, which include platform mounds, make up the top tier of the settlement system. The large sites served as administrative centers for the Mississippian chiefdoms, and the mounds served as platforms for important buildings. Studies of the distribution of these administrative centers indicate that most Mississippian chiefdoms controlled territories that were no more than 30 km (19 mi.) in diameter (Hally 1993). The individual territories were separated by lightly used buffer zones that were at least 10 km (6 mi.) in diameter. The buffer zones may have served as military buffer zones and as reserves for wild plant foods (Hally 1993: 162).

MISSISSIPPIAN COLLAPSE?

Cahokia's power and influence appear to have declined after about A.D. 1250, and the site had been long abandoned as a major administrative center by the time of European contact at about 1700. In the Southeast, however, many powerful Mississippian chiefdoms survived until the time of the initial European contact in the sixteenth century. The history of the entire Mississippian period (ca. A.D. 800 to 1500) is characterized by the rise and fall of local and regional chiefdoms throughout the Midwest and Southeast.

What factors could have led to the failure of individual Mississippian chiefdoms? Recent archaeological and environmental research on Mississippian chiefdoms in the Savannah River valley (the Savannah River forms the border between Georgia and South Carolina) suggests that both political and environmental factors may have played a role in the success or failure of particular chiefdoms (Anderson et al. 1995). Archaeological researchers in this region have identified 14 mound centers and over 500 small sites in the Savannah River Basin

CASE STUDY

Cahokia and Moundville

The largest of the Mississippian administrative centers is the site of **Cahokia** near East St. Louis in Illinois (Fowler 1975; Pauketat and Emerson 1997; Emerson 1997). This important site is located in a region known as the American Bottoms, near the point where the Illinois and Missouri Rivers join the Mississippi. The size and importance of Cahokia cannot be overestimated; the Cahokia site includes more than 100 earthen mounds that cover an area of 14 sq. km (5 sq. mi.). Most of these mounds supported temples, council houses, and elite residences (Pauketat 1994: 5). The largest of these mounds, Monks Mound, rises to a height of 30 m (100 ft.) and covers an area of 6 ha (15 ac.) (Figure 26.E). Monks Mound, whose name derives from a brief Trappist settlement on the site, was built in stages between A.D. 900 and 1200. This 600,000-cubic meter (785,000 cu. yd.) mound is the largest pyramid in North America north of Mexico; only the Pyramid of the Sun at Teotihuacán and the Great Pyramid at Cholula in Mexico are larger (Fowler 1975: 93). It is estimated that Monks Mound would have taken about 370,000 workdays to build (Fagan 2000: 454). Even though the work was carried out over several centuries, the construction of this mound is a visible testament to the Mississippian chiefs' abilities to mobilize labor for public construction. "The scale of Monks Mound . . . is expressive of the overriding power of the chief and of the importance of the central hierarchy" (Dalan 1997: 100).

What kind of society was responsible for this monumental public construction? While most Mississippian societies were simple chiefdoms that controlled small territories, Cahokia and the site of **Moundville** in west central Alabama with its 29 platform mounds were most likely centers of more complex chiefdoms. Complex chiefdoms are characterized by two or more tiers of political hierarchy. In the American Bottoms area surrounding Cahokia, there are several smaller centers that include at least one mound. These mounds may have been centers of small polities who owed their allegiance to the paramount chief of Cahokia.

How did a complex chiefdom develop at Cahokia? Pauketat (1994) has argued that the consolidation of regional chiefly authority was the result of the political actions of a small group of high-ranking individuals over a brief period around A.D. 1050. Critical to this process were the expansion of long-distance trade and

FIGURE 26.E   Monks Mound, Cahokia, Illinois. Monks Mound rises to a height of 30 m (100 ft.) and covers 6 ha (15 ac.).

FIGURE 26.F One of the platform mounds at Moundville, Alabama.

the production of luxury items. The expansion of long-distance trade is seen in the increasing density of exotic chert around Cahokia at about A.D. 1050. This material was transformed into a variety of symbols and tools, including projectile points, under the patronage of Cahokia chiefs. Significant changes in settlement patterns and building techniques are also apparent at about 1050 A.D. Buildings with wall-trench foundations replaced older post-built constructions. Small clusters of houses surrounded by courtyards were replaced by large plazas. These changes in settlement layout may mirror the transition in social organization from a kinship-based system to one based on patron–client relations (Pauketat 1994). The emergence of patron–client relations and the expansion of long-distance exchange are part of a regional political transformation. Local Cahokia elites also worked to alleviate factional disputes, dethroned local leaders, and created a divine chiefship. All these factors led to the development of a complex chiefdom centered at Cahokia.

The symbols of divine chieftaincy appear about a generation later, around 1100 A.D. Ritual was used to reinforce the status differences between the chiefs and the commoners. The symbols include giant houses, compounds, and rotundas, as well as the construction of the first ritual Post-Circle Monument, which was used by the Cahokia elite to contact the gods (Pauketat 1994: 184–5). This monumental construction transformed Cahokia "from a political capital to a sacred center and cemetery" (Pauketat and Emerson 1997b: 278). Although the political consolidation of Cahokia took place quickly, the symbols of divine chieftaincy remained in place for more than a century.

While Cahokia clearly represents an important ceremonial site that served as the administrative center for a complex Mississippian chiefdom, the question of whether Cahokia can truly be considered urban is a far more difficult one to answer. The site is undoubtedly large, and it apparently housed a sizable population. It is estimated that about 800 ha (2000 ac.) of the site were covered with dwellings. The number of people housed in those dwellings has been a matter of debate. Estimates have ranged from a low of 10,000 to a high of 43,000. While Cahokia was clearly home to craft specialists, including the makers of stone axes and shell beads, it is not clear that Cahokia housed the markets and other nonagricultural activities that are traditionally found in cities. Whether Cahokia represents a city or simply a large and heavily populated administrative and ceremonial center remains an open question.

The history of Moundville (Figure 26.F), the center of a complex chiefdom in west-central Alabama, shows some striking parallels with Cahokia. Moundville is located on the Black Warrior River. The site was initially mapped in the late nineteenth century, and large-scale excavations were carried out by the Alabama Museum of Natural History, using Civilian Conservation Corps labor, between 1930 and 1941. A number of smaller excavations were carried out in the second half of the twentieth century. However, new studies conducted during the past 15 years have refined Moundville's chronology and led to new interpretations of its history (Knight and Steponaitis 1998a).

The central portion of Moundville covers 75 ha (18.5 ac.) and includes at least 29 mounds arranged around a central plaza (Knight and Steponaitis 1998b: 3). The site was surrounded by a palisade on three sides and the river on the fourth.

The new chronological data indicate that Moundville was probably not occupied before about 1050 A.D. At that time important changes in subsistence and settlement patterns are apparent. Maize came to play a greater role in subsistence, and small truncated mounds, which probably served as residences for an emerging elite class, were built for the first time (Knight and Steponaitis 1998b: 12).

By about 1250, Moundville was the center of a complex chiefdom that controlled a 40-km swath of the Black Warrior River Valley. Between 1200 and 1250 A.D., the construction of most of the major mounds at Moundville began, and the palisade around the site was erected for the first time. The plaza area was leveled, and the major mounds were laid out around it. At this time Moundville was home to just under 1000 people (Knight and Steponaitis 1998b: 14–15).

The later history of Moundville parallels Cahokia. After 1300 A.D., a number of rich burials were interred at Moundville. The richest graves contained such exotic items as beads made from marine shells and copper ear spools. Moundville's population had declined dramatically, so that by 1300 A.D. Moundville was home to a small population of high-ranking families (Steponaitis 1998: 39). Moundville had become a regional center for mortuary rituals (Knight and Steponaitis 1998b: 19). Like Cahokia, Moundville served first as a political center for an emerging complex chiefdom and later as a ritual and religious center.

that date between A.D. 1000 and 1600. Their research indicates that the lower portion of the Savannah Basin was depopulated in the mid-fifteenth century, probably as a result of an extended period of drought. Even though favorable rainfall conditions returned in the late fifteenth century, the region was not repopulated, because the Savannah River Mississippian populations were sandwiched between two powerful complex chiefdoms—the Ocute of central Georgia and the Cofitachequi of central South Carolina—who were competing with one another for control of the region. The Savannah River area came to form a buffer zone between those two expanding polities. It is likely that similar constellations of causes are responsible for the rise and fall of chiefdoms throughout the Mississippian period.

MIDDLE-RANGE SOCIETIES

In Chapter 16 we noted that not all early agricultural societies developed urbanism, class stratification, and complex political institutions. Middle-range or tribal societies are sedentary societies that are small-scale and nonhierarchical (Gregg 1991: xvii). Most tribal societies rely on agriculture for their subsistence. While tribal societies are known from many parts of the world, they have been less intensively studied by archaeologists than either complex, urban societies or mobile hunter-gatherer bands. The farming societies of the southwestern United States are some of the best known of all prehistoric tribal societies. In this brief review of the archaeology of the American Southwest, we begin with establishment of farming communities in the region.

THE ORIGINS OF AGRICULTURE IN THE NORTH AMERICAN BORDERLANDS

The Desert Borderlands region includes the American Southwest and major portions of northern Mexico. The region lies between the Great Plains to the east and the Rocky Mountains to the West. The northern part of the Borderlands region abuts the Great Basin (see Chapter 14), while the southern part borders on more humid regions in Mexico. The Borderlands region contains both deserts, including the Sonoran and Chichuahuan Deserts, and mountain ranges (Minnis 1992: 125). Like Europe in the Old World, the Desert Borderlands region does not appear to be a primary center for plant domestication, although it is possible that some native plants, including agave (century plant), may have been cultivated. Instead, the major cultigens—maize, squash, and beans—were introduced to the Borderlands region from Mesoamerica.

The archaeological evidence from a number of cave and open-air sites suggests that domesticated maize, beans, and squash were first introduced to the Borderlands region during the Late Archaic period (ca. 2000–1000 B.C.). Many direct AMS radiocarbon dates on early domesticated maize remains from the Borderlands cluster around 1000 B.C., and both beans and squash appear to have been introduced at about the same time (Minnis 1992: 128 and Table 7.3). Today, archaeologists estimate that maize was first introduced to northern Mexico and the American Southwest around 1400 B.C. (Roney and Hard 2002a: 131).

Both the way that farming was introduced to the Borderlands and the speed with which farming was adopted by Native American foragers has become a subject of debate in recent years (Roney and Hard 2002a). The traditional model posits that Archaic hunters and gatherers in the Borderlands region incorporated a small amount of plant cultivation into a mobile foraging lifestyle. These Archaic forager-farmers made use of small, scattered plots in fertile, well-watered locations. They camped near their fields during the planting and harvesting seasons but moved more frequently during the rest of the year. Minnis (1992) suggests that the adoption of small-scale cultivation would have provided a more diverse subsistence base without disrupting the foraging way of life. The traditional model suggests that the pattern of hunting, gathering, and casual agriculture persisted for centuries and that permanent agricultural villages were not established in the Borderlands regions until the early first millennium A.D.

This traditional model has been challenged on several grounds. First, archaeologists working in some parts of the Borderlands have suggested that the adoption of farming may have led to fundamental changes in Late Archaic lifeways. Excavations at a series of hilltop villages in northwestern Chihuahua (Roney and Hard 2002b) indicate that the largest of these villages may have housed a population of about 200 people at around 1240 B.C. The site appears to have been occupied for about 200 years. While the inhabitants of these sites did collect wild plants, domestic maize and amaranth appear to have played a major role in the economy. These data suggest that the adoption of agriculture led to settlement permanence in some parts of the Borderlands regions.

Second, the gradualist model suggests that agriculture was adopted by indigenous foragers in the Borderlands region and that migration played no role in the spread of farming to the American Southwest and northern Mexico. Archaeological and linguistic data from Northern Mexico suggest that maize farming may have been spread throughout the Borderlands region by speakers of Uto-Aztecan languages (a language family that includes many Native North American languages). These migrants moved into what were essentially empty desert regions of the Borderlands after the end of the hot, dry Middle Holocene climatic phase (Carpenter et al. 2002).

The new archaeological data suggest that the introduction of maize agriculture into the Borderlands regions was a far more complex process than the traditional model suggested. It is likely that, as in Europe, both migration and the adoption of agriculture by native peoples played a role in the beginning of farming in the American Southwest. What the archaeological record does clearly show is that many farming villages were established throughout the Borderlands region in the first millennium A.D. Between 200 and 800 A.D., farming villages were established from northern Mexico to southern Utah and Colorado. The appearance of these permanent settlements marks the end of the Archaic period (see Chapter 14) in the American Southwest. As we have seen in the Middle East and Europe, a number of important technological changes accompanied the beginnings of village life in the Borderlands. These changes include the appearance of houses and the manufacture of pottery.

The first houses to appear in the Borderlands region are pithouses, which are usually round or oval in shape. They are excavated about 0.5 m (about 20 in.) into the soil, so that earth forms the lower part of the house walls; the walls were sometimes lined with upright slabs of rock. These houses are generally 4.5 to 5 m in diameter, or 14.5 to 16.5 ft. (Cordell 1997: 233). The superstructures are variable and can include both logs and frameworks of poles covered with mud. The sizes of the pithouse settlements in the Borderlands varied greatly. The smallest villages had only 3 or 4 houses, while the largest had more than 100.

A second major technological change is the appearance of pottery. In the American Southwest, pottery was handmade, generally using a coiling technique. The pottery was painted with a variety of materials, including both organic (plant) materials and minerals such as hematite or iron oxide (Cordell 1997: 232). In the Borderlands pottery was used both for storage and for cooking. Differences in the form and decoration of pottery vessels have

also been used to define a number of different cultural traditions in the Southwest. A complete overview of all of southwestern prehistory is beyond the scope of this text, but see Cordell (1997) for a detailed review of the culture history of the American Southwest.

The period between A.D. 800 and 1000 appears to have been an era of agricultural expansion and intensification throughout the Borderlands region. Water is the limiting factor for agriculture in southern Arizona, and during this period, a network of canals and ditches was constructed to irrigate agricultural fields. These systems would have required the coordination of labor among agricultural villages. In other areas farming was concentrated on well-watered alluvial fans. In Chaco Canyon in northwestern New Mexico, a series of strategies, including dams, canals, ditches, and headgates, was developed to use runoff water for irrigation (Cordell 1997: 287).

FARMS, VILLAGES, AND "TOWNS" IN THE AMERICAN SOUTHWEST

By A.D. 1000 the intensive agricultural systems in the American Southwest supported a diverse range of settlement systems. These have been described as dispersed, aggregated, and integrated settlements (Cordell 1997: 305). Dispersed settlements are small agricultural villages that were permanently occupied for relatively short periods. Aggregated systems are associated with large dwellings, known as **pueblos,** which served as year-round residences for large numbers of people. They also included architectural features such as kivas (a chamber constructed for ceremonial purposes) "or special ceremonial rooms that served to integrate large numbers of people" (Cordell 1997: 305). Unlike the earlier pithouses, these pueblos were multiroomed surface-level structures with walls made of adobe or stone. **Mesa Verde** in Colorado is a classic example of an aggregated settlement of the eleventh and twelfth century A.D. (Figure 26.5).

Integrated settlement systems have two important attributes: 1) they have hierarchies of

FIGURE 26.5   The pueblo at Mesa Verde.

permanent settlements of different sizes, and 2) these settlements are integrated through the production and exchange of materials, pooled labor, and a shared religious tradition (Cordell 1997: 305). The best-known example of an integrated system was centered at **Chaco Canyon** in New Mexico (Figure 26.6). At its height, this system encompassed 65,000 sq. km (about 25,000 sq. mi.) of the San Juan River Basin and the neighboring highlands in the Four Corners region of the American Southwest. This integrated settlement system included 14 large multistoried great houses built between A.D. 900 and 1150. The great houses had an average of 216 rooms (Cordell 1997: 312). Small houses were single-storied and had an average of only about 16 rooms. An elaborate road system connected Chaco Canyon and a series of outlying settlements that

were spread throughout the Four Corners region (see Archaeology in Practice, Chapter 19). The roads have been seen either as part of a complex economic system that may have been used to organize labor and trade or as part of a religious and symbolic system that served to integrate the region (Cordell 1997: 326). The level of regional integration seen at Chaco Canyon shares some characteristics with the complex societies that are the focus of Part 4 of this text. Unfortunately, however, the Chaco system was relatively short-lived. At about A.D. 1130 new construction ceased in Chaco Canyon and at some outlying settlements. Many communities in the San Juan Basin appear to have been abandoned at this time, and the system of regional integration either disappeared or was radically reorganized (Roney 1996: 157). One factor that may have played a role

FIGURE 26.6 A view of Pueblo Bonito, one of the great houses at Chaco Canyon.

in this abandonment was the major drought that began in A.D. 1130 and continued through A.D. 1180. The drought was characterized by below normal spring and summer rainfall and may have led to radical changes in settlement distribution in the San Juan Basin.

CONCLUSION

While complex societies developed in many parts of the Eastern Woodlands in the first and second millennia A.D., not all Native American agricultural societies developed hierarchical social structures and complex political organizations. The pueblo-dwellers of the American Southwest were sedentary agriculturalists who were organized along more egalitarian lines. The southwestern farmers, however, were capable of constructing monumental architecture, building substantial irrigation systems, and organizing elaborate trade networks. The rich archaeological record from the American Southwest provides a particularly

well-documented example of the ways in which middle-range societies are organized.

The development of chiefdom societies in the Eastern Woodlands during the Mississippian period was the culmination of a long process of cultural change whose roots can be traced back to the Late Archaic and Early Woodland periods. In many ways, the process parallels the development of complex chiefdoms in later prehistoric Europe. In both areas there is a clear correlation between the emergence of nonegalitarian societies and increasing long-distance and regional trade. Agricultural intensification—the introduction of the cart and the plow in Europe and the adoption of maize agriculture in the Eastern Woodlands—allowed progressively larger agricultural surpluses to be mobilized by emerging elites. These surpluses could be used to finance trade in exotic luxury items and to support monumental construction.

The emergence of complex societies in North America and Europe also parallels the early phases of the emergence of state-level societies in areas such as Mesoamerica, Mesopotamia, and Egypt. We will never know whether or not state-level societies would have developed independently in either North America or Europe. Contact with imperial societies—the Romans in Europe and the English and Spanish colonists in North America—forever changed the history of these two regions. In North America in particular, the introduction of epidemic diseases to which American Indians had no immunities led to a decimation of the Native American population in the Southeast in the first two centuries after European contact.

KEY TERMS

Adena   387

Cahokia   396

Chaco Canyon   401

Early Woodland
period   387

Hopewell Interaction
Sphere   389

Late Woodland
period   391

Mesa Verde   400

Middle Woodland
period   389

Mississippian   391

Moundville   396

Pueblos   400

QUESTIONS FOR DISCUSSION

1. Why did chiefdoms arise in the American Midwest and Southeast beginning about A.D. 800?

2. Can you identify any similarities between the Mississippian societies of eastern North America and the late Iron Age societies of temperate Europe (Chapter 23)?

3. How do the Mississippian chiefdoms differ from the contemporary states and empires of Latin America? Can you identify any similarities between the Mississippian chiefdoms and the Aztec and Inca Empires?

FURTHER READING

Pauketat, T.R.
1994   *The Ascent of Chiefs: Cahokia and Mississippian Politics in Native North America.* Tuscaloosa, AL: University of Alabama Press.
An innovative study of the rise of Cahokia, based on new archaeological research. Well-illustrated and highly recommended.

Smith, Bruce D., ed.
1992   *The Mississippian Emergence.* Washington and London: Smithsonian Institution Press.
This volume presents a number of important case studies of the emergence of Mississippian chiefdoms in various parts of the Southeast and Midwest. The concluding chapter argues that the development of a prestige goods economy may have been a critical factor in the emergence of those societies.

27

THE FUTURE OF ARCHAEOLOGY

In this book we have shown how archaeology can be used to trace the development of human societies, beginning with our earliest stone tool-making ancestors and continuing to the present day. We have examined the evolution of human behavior, the appearance of modern humans and their colonization of the globe, the beginnings of agriculture, and the development of cities and states. In addition, the Archaeology in Practice boxes have explored some of the techniques used by archaeologists in the study of the past, and On the Cutting Edge boxes have examined some of the theories and issues that are the subject of current archaeological debate. In our review of over 2.5 million years of human prehistory, it is clear that many important archaeological questions remain unanswered. For example, the discovery of the Monte Verde site in Chile has documented a pre-Clovis occupation of the Americas, but we still do not know when and how the first people reached the New World. Our ability to answer these questions depends on the preservation of our archaeological heritage. In this chapter we will examine the effects of looting, development, and warfare on the archaeological record. We will also consider the effects of the **Native American Graves Protection and Repatriation Act (NAGPRA)** on the future of archaeology in the United States, and the broader relationship between archaeology and nationalism in today's world.

FIGURE 27.1 Aerial photograph of the Nasca site of Cahuachi in Peru, showing the massive looting that has taken place at the site. The many holes at lower left are looters' pits.

THE DESTRUCTION OF ARCHAEOLOGICAL SITES

The greatest threat to archaeology's future is the continued destruction of archaeological sites by looting, development, and warfare. For every site that is excavated by an archaeologist, many others are damaged, looted, or destroyed by other human activities. As the earth's population continues to increase, the potential for damage to archaeological resources increases dramatically.

The sweeping destruction of lives and property that is the result of warfare can also damage and destroy archaeological sites, and the precious collections and records of past research may be lost as well. The massive looting of the Iraqi Museum in 2003 made worldwide headlines. Many such losses followed the ravages of the Second World War; the disappearance of the Zhoukoudian *Homo erectus* fossils is a striking example. Many important Mesopotamian archaeological sites may have been damaged by bombing during the Persian Gulf War, by the recent war in Iraq, and, as discussed in Chapter 19, by postwar looting and even by misguided attempts to protect ancient sites.

As the world's population grows, many former agricultural lands have been converted to residential and commercial use. The construction of housing developments, industrial parks, and shopping malls has led to the discovery of archaeological sites, but too often, also to their destruction. One of the greatest dangers to archaeological sites, however, is looting—the theft of artifacts from archaeological sites. When looters steal an object from an archaeological site, its context is destroyed and its associations are lost. Without context and association, artifacts have little value for the study of the past. While looting continues in almost every country on earth, nowhere has the effect of looting been more devastating than in Peru (see Malpass 1996: chap. 8). As Helaine Silverman (1993: xii), the excavator of the important Nasca ceremonial center of Cahuachi (see Chapter 25), has noted, "Much of what we could have known [about the Nasca capital of Cahuachi] is lost to archaeologists because of the destruction wrought by massive illicit excavations at the site over the past century." Figure 27.1 is a photograph of Cahuachi showing the massive looting that has taken place at this important Peruvian site.

Although the destruction that has taken place at Cahuachi is a graphic demonstration of the damage that looters can do to archaeological sites, looting is not just a Peruvian problem. In the United States, archaeological sites located on private land have very limited protection. Archaeological sites on state and federal lands are protected by state and federal antiquities laws. One such law is the **Archaeological Resources Protection Act (ARPA),** which protects archaeological sites on federal properties such as national parks and national forests. Many states have enacted laws to protect burials found on private lands. For the most part, however, landowners are free to damage or destroy sites on their property without regard for the important historical information that might be lost through those actions.

Despite the laws that are designed to protect our nation's archaeological heritage, every year federal authorities arrest looters who are engaged in stealing part of our nation's past. Two flagrant examples have been described in detail in the *SAA Bulletin*, a publication of the Society for American Archaeology. In Oregon three individuals were convicted of looting the Lava River cave site, a Native American site in the Deschutes National Forest, in 1989. Two of the defendants were fined $1000, and the third was required to perform 100 hours of community service. In looting this prehistoric site, the perpetrators stole artifacts and destroyed both their archaeological context and important environmental information. Since each archaeological site is unique, the looters damaged an irreplaceable part of the American past.

An even more flagrant violator of American antiquities laws was recently convicted of looting a site in the Southwest. A man from Utah was sentenced to 6½ years in federal prison and ordered to pay $5510 in reparations for using a helicopter to loot an Anasazi site in the Canyonlands National Park. The looter's unrepentant attitude, his prior conviction for an ARPA violation, and his desecration of several Native American graves, including the grave of a small child wrapped in a ceremonial blanket, led to the stiff sentence and fine.

The preservation of our nation's past, however, depends on more than just the vigorous enforcement of laws against looting. It requires public education. Americans must recognize that the removal of any piece of cultural property from federal lands is both immoral and illegal. When entering our national parks and forests, tourists must be advised to take only photographs and leave only footprints. Only through greater public awareness can this country's rich archaeological heritage be preserved for future generations.

In the Utah case just described, a looter received a stiff fine and a lengthy jail sentence for excavating and looting Native American burials in a national park. As we shall see in the following section, national laws regarding the excavation and display of American Indian skeletal materials have changed significantly in the past 15 years, and those changes have important implications for archaeologists working in the United States.

THE NATIVE AMERICAN GRAVES PROTECTION AND REPATRIATION ACT

Through much of the nineteenth and twentieth centuries, archaeologists excavated and collected the material remains of Native Americans. A multitude of Native American sites, including burial mounds and cemeteries, have been excavated, and both the artifacts and human remains within them have been transferred to university collections and museums. Large-scale federal development and survey projects during the Great Depression, continuing through the 1970s, greatly swelled the numbers of sites excavated and resulted in large collections of Native American objects as well as human remains held in museums. The actual number is not known, but in the early 1990s more than 100,000 Native American whole or partial skeletons may have been held in museum storage across the United States.

For most archaeologists the intent of such investigations was surely the advancement of knowledge about early humans in the Americas. Unfortunately, few excavators took into consideration the fact that the people whose remains they were studying had living descendants. Native Americans observed that the remains of those they regarded as their ancestors were not accorded the level of respect given to European burials. Over the years many Native Americans have come to be distrustful of archaeology and the motivations of some archaeologists. Some Native Americans see in archaeology an effort to dispossess them of their traditional cultural history. In the past Native Americans have sometimes fallen victim to the misrepresentation of archaeological findings to denigrate the cultural achievements of Native Americans and thus to justify their displacement from their lands by Europeans.

In 1990 more than 20 years of activism resulted in Congress's passing the Native American Graves Protection and Repatriation Act (NAGPRA), which requires that Native American human remains, ceremonial objects, and objects of cultural patrimony be returned to the Native American tribes. The law applies to all such remains or objects on Indian lands, under federal control, or held by institutions receiving federal funds. NAGPRA also requires that the appropriate Native American groups be consulted before excavations that will remove cultural objects from federal lands are permitted.

A few archaeologists have expressed their concern that the new federal laws will stifle future archaeological research in the United States (see On the Cutting Edge box, this chapter). The authors of this text believe that this need not be true. In the short term, the process of identifying and classifying the vast holdings of Native American artifacts and human remains now in museums for their return to the appropriate tribes has in itself stimulated much new research. Before the passage of NAGPRA, only about 30% of the Native American skeletons in museum collections now subject to that law had been studied by bioarchaeologists. Today, that figure approaches 100% (Rose et al. 1996). In the long run, many Native American groups are becoming interested in establishing museums of their own and in participating in and conducting their own archaeological research on their ancient past. It is incumbent on the existing scholarly community to incorporate these new members into the fabric of American archaeological research. Prehistoric archaeological research will continue and will be better informed through the participation and insights of the prehistoric peoples' physical and cultural descendants. As Ferguson (1996: 74) notes: "Archaeologists and Native Americans are moving beyond the contentious rhetoric of the 1970s and 1980s. Together, they are forging new partnerships to change archaeology so it is more acceptable and relevant to the descendants of the people who produced the archaeological record many archaeologists study."

ARCHAEOLOGY AND NATIONALISM

Native Americans' desire to retain control over their cultural heritage parallels similar trends around the world. Many nations, notably in eastern Europe, the Middle East, and Africa, have moved toward developing their own culture histories and archaeology. Locally and nationally sponsored archaeological research, educational programs, and museums can do much to bolster peoples' awareness of their cultural history. The results of archaeological research can expand the time depth of local histories and serve to support and enrich peoples' concept of cultural, ethnic, or national identity. Clearly, there are both positive and negative sides to archaeology's power in this respect. On one hand, the open-minded sharing of archaeological knowledge and insights among locally oriented scholars and the scholarly community, and the public at large, can go far toward promoting interethnic and intercultural understanding. On the other hand, as Native Americans have found to their detriment, the findings of archaeology can be cited, or distorted, to support a one-sided political or social agenda.

Perhaps the most flagrant example of the distortion of archaeological interpretations to

FIGURE 27.2 Textbook used in German schools during the World War II period. The picture shows a Linear Pottery village and the title, as translated, reads "Five Thousand Years Germany" (emphasis added). (After Jörg Lechler.)

support a political agenda is the use of archaeology by the Nazis during World War II (Figure 27.2) (see also Arnold 1990, 1992). Under the Nazis archaeology became entirely ethnocentric, focusing on the German peoples and attempts to identify them from prehistoric and early historic sites. Journal titles were changed to reflect German archaeology's nationalistic bias. For example, in 1934 the *Zeitschrift für Vorgeschichte (Journal of Prehistory)* became the *Zeitschrift für Deutsche Vorgeschichte (Journal of German Prehistory)*. Most distressingly,

prehistoric data were distorted to justify Germany's claims to Czech and Polish lands.

A less well-known example is the history of interpretation of Great Zimbabwe, a complex of stone ruins located near the modern town of Masvingo in Zimbabwe (Figure 27.3). In the late nineteenth and early twentieth centuries, British colonists were reluctant to accept that these impressive ruins had been constructed by black Africans. The ruins were seen as the work of northerly (i.e., nonblack) peoples and variously identified as the lost palace of the Queen of Sheba and a Phoenician colony. Although detailed archaeological work carried out in the 1920s had shown that the ruins had been constructed by Africans during the Middle Ages, the myth that Great Zimbabwe had been constructed by whites was maintained until quite recently for political reasons. In 1965 Southern Rhodesia (now called Zimbabwe) declared its independence from the British Empire and established a white supremacist government under Ian Smith that lasted until 1980. Whites, who made up less than 10 % of Rhodesia's population, needed to denigrate native Africans' achievements to justify their claim to the region. The whites were concerned that the ruins would become a symbol of African achievement and heritage for blacks who were struggling for majority rule. As a result the Ian Smith government issued a secret memorandum forbidding any official publication from stating that the Great Zimbabwe ruins were the product of African craftsmanship and engineering (Trigger 1989: 134; see also Phillipson 1993). Since independence, of course, Great Zimbabwe has become an important symbol of the Africans' cultural heritage and has given its name to the independent state of Zimbabwe.

Archaeological research at Great Zimbabwe (Vogel 1994) has shown that this impressive urban center was built by the ancestors of the Shona people (Connah 2001: 235). The monumental stone architecture was part of a dense urban complex that included mud huts and probably housed a population of about 10,000 people between the thirteenth and fifteenth centuries A.D. The wealth of the population was based on cattle keeping

FIGURE 27.3   Monumental stone ruins at the site of Great Zimbabwe. Recent archaeological research indicates that the most elaborate stone buildings were built between the thirteenth and fifteenth centuries A.D. The site served as a center of political authority and trade.

combined with long-distance trade in gold, copper, and ivory. Great Zimbabwe was one of a number of urban societies that developed in sub-Saharan Africa in the first and second millennia (see Chapter 21).

The postcolonial, post–cold war world is fraught with ethnic rivalries in such areas as the Middle East, the former Yugoslavia, Northern Ireland, and southern Africa. The challenge for archaeology is clear. Archaeology must be used as an instrument for the appreciation of both cultural diversity and our common human heritage, not as a tool of political and cultural domination. As Kohl notes:

> Ethical standards for accepting or rejecting nationalist uses of archaeology may vary in specific cases, but they should ideally satisfy the following three criteria: (a) the construction of one group's national past should not be made at the expense of others'; (b) all cultural traditions should be recognized as worthy of study and respect; and (c) the construc-

tion of a national past should not be made at the expense of abandoning the universal anthropological perspective of our common humanity and shared past and future. (1998: 243)

SOME FINAL THOUGHTS ON THE FUTURE OF ARCHAEOLOGY

Preserving the past for the future is not an easy task. As we have tried to show in this textbook, archaeological research is both painstaking and expensive. Archaeological excavation is supported by both public funds and private benefaction. For this support to continue, archaeological research must benefit the public at large. Archaeologists cannot simply report their research to small groups of like-minded colleagues at scholarly conferences. The results of archaeological research must be presented to a variety of audiences, including the entire archaeological community, students, and the general public. Advances in communications such

ON THE CUTTING EDGE *The Kennewick Controversy*

In July 1996 two college students, spectators at the annual hydroplane race near the city of Kennewick, Washington, made an unexpected discovery. Walking along the muddy banks of the Columbia River, they came across a human skull in the shallow water. Spread along the shore, a broad scatter of bones lay in the litter.

No one at the time could know that this discovery would spark a firestorm of controversy and a deep philosophical and legal clash among government agencies, academic anthropologists, and Native Americans. Kennewick Man, as the skeleton came to be called by anthropologists, or the Ancient One, as he was called by Native Americans, became the focal point for profoundly opposing worldviews. Seen by anthropologists as a precious source of new information about America's past but as a revered and sacrosanct ancestor by Native Americans, the Kennewick bones were soon to become embroiled in a legal battle that has yet to be fully resolved.

The students reported the find to the police, and the Benton County coroner called upon James Chatters, an anthropologist at Central Washington University, to investigate the skeleton. Little suspecting what was to come, Chatters, who served as a consultant for the coroner's office and regularly assisted them when human remains were found, visited the site. He observed that the bones, scattered over more than 30 m (98 ft.) of beach, appeared to be eroding from the 2 m bank that bordered the river. No grave or other bones could be seen there. The site was located on federal land; Chatters requested and was issued a permit from the Army Corps of Engineers,

the responsible federal agency, and he made numerous additional trips to the site to collect as much bone as he could find and to study the site's geology. After numerous trips he eventually collected most of the bones of a human body from the beach. He brought the bones to his lab where he began a preliminary study of the skeleton.

Chatters proceeded to document the find. The bones were photographed and measured, following the usual procedures. The nearly complete Kennewick skeleton proved to be the remains of a male between 5' 9" and 5' 10" in height. The teeth, skull, and pelvis suggested that he was between 40 and 55 years of age at the time he died. Chatters initially thought this individual was a Caucasian, rather than Native American, based on the shape of his skull and his body proportions. Numerous nineteenth- and twentieth-century artifacts had been recovered near the bones, so at first it seemed that the skeleton might have been that of an early European settler.

The man had clearly suffered numerous injuries during his lifetime, including blows to the head, arm, and chest. Most striking, however, was an open wound in the man's pelvis. Although partially healed over, Chatters observed through the remaining opening that a stone projectile point was deeply embedded in the wound, although it was not possible to see what sort of point it was. However, CAT scans of the pelvis showed that the projectile point was a Cascade point, an ancient type that was in use between about 4500 and 9000 years ago.

Now doubting the historic dating for the skeleton, Chatters made

a casting of the skull. He also sent a fragment of bone to a radiocarbon dating laboratory. That age determination suggested the Kennewick skeleton was between 8340 and 9200 years old. Chatters arranged to bring the skeleton to the Smithsonian Institution for study.

Before the transfer could be made, however, five local Native American tribes claimed the skeleton, asserting that according to law it must be turned over to them so that it might be reburied according to their customs. Almost immediately, the Army Corps of Engineers seized the Kennewick skeleton and ordered an end to all further studies. The Corps determined that the bones must be Native American, and as such fell under the provisions of NAGPRA. The skeleton was to be returned (repatriated) to the local Native American tribes.

The five tribes claimed the Kennewick skeleton. For example, the Umatilla's traditional hunting, fishing, and plant-gathering grounds included the place where the Kennewick skeleton was found. The Umatilla and the other four tribes who also claimed the skeleton share oral traditions that they assert go back 10,000 years (Minthorn 1996). They also share religious beliefs that dictate that human remains should be reburied as soon as possible. As the local tribes stated in a later court document:

> When a body goes into the ground, it is meant to stay there until the end of time. When remains are disturbed and remain above the ground, their spirits are at unrest. . . . To put

these spirits at ease, the remains must be returned to the ground as soon as possible. (Joint Tribal Amici Memorandum quoted in the opinion of the U.S. District Court for the State of Washington, 2002)

The Corps of Engineers' decision to repatriate the Kennewick skeleton provoked a quick reaction. Many anthropologists were concerned about the effect that NAGPRA might have on the study of early North American prehistory. In October 1996 a group of eight prominent anthropologists and archaeologists filed suit against the Corps to prevent the repatriation of the bones. They argued that the Army Corps did not have sufficient evidence to show that the Kennewick man was affiliated with any of the five Native American tribes who claimed him. Furthermore, they claimed that additional studies were needed to determine whether Kennewick Man was, in fact, Native American and therefore subject to the provisions of NAGPRA. The scientists petitioned the court to allow DNA tests, and analysis and measurement of the bones and teeth of the Kennewick skeleton. The critical legal question raised by the Kennewick controversy was whether NAGPRA's provisions could be stretched back to early prehistory.

The court's decision, reached in 1997, neither granted the bones to the Native Americans nor to the scientists for study. Further study was needed to determine whether these remains met the criteria to be included under NAGPRA. The responsibility for this decision was passed to the Department

of the Interior. In early 1999 a team of physical anthropologists, archaeologists, curators, and conservators headed by Dr. Francis P. McManamon of the National Park Service conducted an initial detailed examination of the Kennewick human remains (McManamon 1999). Prior to these examinations, the interdisciplinary team consulted with tribal representatives and with the plaintiffs in the lawsuit. The initial studies conducted by the interdisciplinary team were nondestructive; no skeletal material was destroyed during this process. The team inventoried the human remains, measured the bones and teeth, and recorded other data that may provide evidence for the health and way of life of the individual in question. In addition, the team analyzed the soil sediments and projectile point associated with the Kennewick skeleton. These analyses were intended to help determine whether the Kennewick remains are subject to NAGPRA.

The research was made more difficult by the decision of the Corps of Engineers in April 1998 to deeply bury the Kennewick site, an action taken despite bills pending in Congress intended to prevent it. The Corps claimed this was done to control the erosion of the riverbanks; nevertheless, the tons of rock and dirt dumped on the discovery site made it inaccessible along with any additional archaeological evidence it might have contained.

In January 2000 the Department of the Interior released the results of their studies. Following a detailed series of metrical and statistical comparisons (Powell and Rose 1999), the researchers concluded that the Kennewick skeleton did

not closely resemble any modern population, including both modern Native Americans and Europeans. The most closely related human groups were certain Polynesian islanders and the Ainu, a native Japanese group with South Asian affinities.

On the other hand, the radiocarbon dating of the skeleton has indicated that the Kennewick bones are more than 9000 years old, and the Kennewick skeleton bears a resemblance to several other previously known skeletons of similar antiquity from the Great Basin and from the Eastern Woodlands. Nine thousand years may well have been sufficient time for a population similar to Kennewick to evolve and change, and possibly to be ancestral to modern Native Americans. However, only a detailed study of human remains from the region, spanning the 9000 years of change (data that are not currently available), could conclusively demonstrate such a direct biological relationship (Powell and Rose 1999).

The great antiquity of the Kennewick remains makes it clear that they do not derive from any modern, non-American group.

On the basis of this evidence, but relying primarily on the undoubted great antiquity of the bones, in September 2000 the Secretary of the Interior determined that the Kennewick skeleton was Native American, as NAGPRA was interpreted by the Department of the Interior. The skeleton was to be given to the five tribes, and no further studies were to be allowed. For the immediate future the remains were to be kept locked away at the Burke Museum in Seattle.

This was, however, by no means the end of the story. The original group of scientists immediately challenged the Secretary of the Interior's decision. The wrangling that was to follow had far less to do with science or with Native American beliefs than it did with the legal interpretation of Congress's intent in formulating NAGPRA. The case was returned to the same Washington district court that had vacated the Corps of Engineers' original decision. In a strongly worded opinion, the court vacated the Secretary of the Interior's determination to repatriate as well. The court ruled that the Department of the Interior had misinterpreted the intent of NAGPRA and that the simple facts of the bones' antiquity and their discovery within the United States was not sufficient for NAGPRA to apply. A cultural connection between the remains and a present-day Native American group was also required, and no such connection could be demonstrated.

Once again, the issue was appealed to a higher court. On February 4, 2004, the Ninth Circuit Court of Appeals upheld the district court, also ruling that as no cultural connection could be demonstrated NAGPRA did not apply, that the tribes claim to the bones was denied, and that the skeleton was to be made available for study. As of this writing, it seems likely that this decision will not be further appealed either by the tribes or the federal government.

The Kennewick case has been extensively and often vociferously debated on television, in the popular press, in scientific journals, and on the Internet. Several books have been published on the topic, with widely opposed points of view. Every administrative or legal decision has been met immediately with deeply felt dissents from those with the opposing point of view. Some scientists have feared that their ability to continue their research about the past would be threatened by an overbroad application of NAGPRA. Native Americans have felt that their rights and religious beliefs have been treated with disdain. NAGPRA was created and administered by Congress in the context of a legal system in which Native Americans are a small minority. Although the final legal decision appears to favor making the skeleton available for scientific study, the issues raised by the Kennewick affair are bound to be argued for many years to come.

as the Internet and the World Wide Web will make the dissemination of archaeological information easier. Communication is critical to archaeology's future, for the preservation of the past depends on public education.

KEY TERMS

Archaeological Resources
    Protection Act
    (ARPA)   406
Native American
    Graves Protection
    and Repatriation Act
    (NAGPRA)   404

QUESTIONS FOR DISCUSSION

1. What could have been done to protect the Iraqi Museum during the recent war in Iraq?

2. What can ordinary citizens do to protect archaeological sites and artifacts in their own country?

FURTHER READING

Arnold, Bettina
    1992   Germany's Nazi Past: How Hitler's Archaeologists Distorted European Prehistory to Justify Racist and Territorial Goals. *Archaeology,* July/August, pp. 30–37.
    This article provides a detailed study of how European prehistory was distorted to fit the political goals of the Third Reich.

Malpass, Michael A.
    1996   *Daily Life in the Inca Empire.* Westport, CT: Greenwood Press.
    This popular introduction to the Inca Empire includes an excellent final chapter that addresses the problem of looting at Peruvian sites and the need to preserve our archaeological heritage.

BIBLIOGRAPHY

CHAPTER 1

Bates, D. G., and F. Plog
1990 *Cultural Anthropology,* 3rd ed. New York: McGraw-Hill.

Binford, L. R.
1962 Archaeology as Anthropology. *American Antiquity* 28: 217–225.

Brain, C. K.
1967 Hottentot Food Remains and Their Bearing on the Interpretation of Fossil Bone Assemblages. *Scientific Papers of the Namibian Desert Research Station* 32: 1–11.
1981 *The Hunters or the Hunted? An Introduction to African Cave Taphonomy.* Chicago: University of Chicago Press.

Chippendale, Chris
2004 *Stonehenge Complete,* 3rd ed. New York: Thames and Hudson.

Daniel, Glyn
1959 The Idea of Man's Antiquity. *Scientific American,* November, pp. 7–11.
1967 *The Origins and Growth of Archaeology.* Harmondsworth, England: Penguin.

Daniel, Glyn, and Colin Renfrew
1988 *The Idea of Prehistory.* Edinburgh: Edinburgh University Press.

Dickson, James H., Klaus Oeggle, and Linda L. Handley
2003 The Iceman Reconsidered. *Scientific American* 288 (5): 70–79.

Eiseley, Loren
1958 *Darwin's Century: Evolution and the Men Who Discovered It.* Garden City, NY: Doubleday.

Gilchrist, Roberta
1994 *Gender and Medieval Culture: The Archaeology of Religious Women.* London: Routledge.

Grayson, D. K.
1983 *The Establishment of Human Antiquity.* New York: Academic Press.

Hodder, I., and James Hudson
2003 *Reading the Past: Current Approaches to Interpretation in Archaeology,* 3rd ed. Cambridge: Cambridge University Press.

Orser, Charles E., Jr.
1990 Archaeological Approaches to New World Plantation Slavery. In *Archaeological Method and Theory,* vol. 2, edited by M. B. Schiffer, pp. 111–154. Tucson, AZ: University of Arizona Press.

Steward, Julian
1955 *Theory of Culture Change: The Methodology of Multilinear Evolution.* Urbana, IL: University of Illinois Press.

Trigger, Bruce G.
1989 *A History of Archaeological Thought.* Cambridge: Cambridge University Press.

Tringham, Ruth
1991 Households with Faces: The Challenge of Gender in Prehistoric Architectural Remains. In *Engendering Archaeology: Women and Prehistory,* edited by J. R. Gero and M. W. Conkey, pp. 93–131. Oxford: Blackwell.

Watson, P. J., LeBlanc, S. A., and C. L. Redman
1971 *Explanation in Archaeology: An Explicitly Scientific Approach.* New York: Columbia University Press.
1984 *Archaeological Explanation: The Scientific Method in Archaeology.* New York: Columbia University Press.

West, S. E.
1985 *West Stow: The Anglo-Saxon Village.* East Anglian Archaeology, Report No. 24. Ipswich, England: Suffolk County Planning Department.

Willey, G. R., and J. A. Sabloff
1980 *A History of American Archaeology.* 2nd ed. London: Thames and Hudson.

CHAPTER 2

Aitken, M. J.
1990 *Science-Based Dating in Archaeology.* London and New York: Longman.

Ardrey, R.
1961 *African Genesis.* New York: Atheneum.

Asfaw, B., White, T., Lovejoy, O., Latimer, B., Simpson, S., and G. Suwa
1999 *Australopithecus garhi:* A New Species of Early Hominid from Ethiopia. *Science* 284: 629–635.

Brain, C. K.
1981 *The Hunters or the Hunted? An Introduction to African Cave Taphonomy.* Chicago and London: University of Chicago Press.

Brunet, M., Guy, F., Mackaye, H. T., Likius, A., Ahounta, D., Beauvilain, A., Blondel, C., Bocherens, H., Boisserie, J.-R., De Bonis, L., Coppens, Y., Dejax, J., Denys, C., Duringer, P., Eisenmann, V., Fanone, G., Fronty, P., Geraads, D., Lehmann, T., Lihoueau, F., Louchart, A., Mahamat, A., Merceron, G., Mouchelin, G., Otero, O., Camponanes, P. P., Ponce de Leon, M., Rage, J.-C., Sapanet, M., Schuster, M., Sudre, J., Tassy, P., Valentin, X., Vignaud, P., Viriot, L., Zazzo, A., and C. Zolilkofer
2002 A New Hominid from the Upper Miocene of Chad. Central Africa. *Nature* 418: 145–151.

Butler, Robert F.
1992 *Paleomagnetism: Magnetic Domains to Geologic Terrains.* Boston: Blackwell Scientific Publications.

Cooke, H. B. S.
1966 Pleistocene Mammal Faunas of Africa, with Particular Reference to Southern Africa. In *African Ecology and Human Evolution,* edited by F. C. Howell and F. Boulière, pp. 65–116. Chicago: Aldine.
1978 Pliocene-Pleistocene Suidae from Hadar, Ethiopia. *Kirtlandia* 29: 1–63.
1983 Horses, Elephants and Pigs as Clues in the African Later Cainozoic. In *Late Cainozoic Palaeoclimates of the Southern Hemisphere,* edited by J. C. Vogel, pp. 473–482. Rotterdam: A. A. Balkema.
1985 Plio-Pleistocene Suidae in Relation to African Hominid Deposits. In *L'Environment des Hominidés au Plio-Pléistocene,* edited by M. Michel Beden et al., pp. 101–117. Paris: Masson.

Dart, R. A.
1929 A Note on the Taung Skull. *South African Journal of Science* 26: 648–658.
1953 The Predatory Transition from Ape to Man. *International Anthropological Linguistics Review* 1: 201–218.

Deino, Alan L., Renne, Paul R., and Carl L. Swisher III
1998 ^{40}AR/^{39}AR Dating in Paleoanthropology and Archeology. *Evolutionary Anthropology* 6 (2): 63–75.

Delson, Eric
1988 Chronology of South African Australopith Site Units. In *Evolutionary History of the "Robust" Australopithecines*, edited by F. Grine, pp. 317–324. New York: Aldine.

Delson, Eric, Tattersall, Ian, Van Couvering, John A., and Alison S. Brooks, eds.
2002 *Encyclopedia of Human Evolution and Prehistory*, 2nd ed. New York: Garland.

Feibel, C. S., Brown, F. H., and I. Mc-Dougall
1989 Stratigraphic Context of Fossil Hominids from the Omo Group Deposits: Northern Turkana Basin, Kenya and Ethiopia. *American Journal of Physical Anthropology* 78: 595–622.

Grine, F. E.
1988 Evolutionary History of the "Robust" Australopithecines: A Summary and Historical Perspective. In *Evolutionary History of the "Robust" Australopithecines*, edited by F. E. Grine, pp. 509–519. New York: Aldine de Gruyter.
1993 Australopithecine Taxonomy and Phylogeny: Historical Background and Recent Interpretation. In *The Human Evolution Source Book*, edited by R. L. Ciochon and J. G. Fleagle, pp. 198–210. Englewood Cliffs, NJ: Prentice Hall.

Haile-Selassie, Yohannes
2001 Late Miocene Hominids from the Middle Awash, Ethiopia. *Nature* 412: 178–181.

Haile-Selassie, Yohannes, Suwa, Gen, and Tim. D. White
2004 Late Miocene Teeth from Middle Awash Ethiopia, and Early Hominind Dental Evolution. *Science* 303: 1506–1508.

Harris, J. M., and T. D. White
1979 Evolution of the Plio-Pleistocene African Suidae. *Transactions of the American Philosophical Society* 69 (2): 1–128.

Hay, R. L., and M. D. Leakey
1982 The Fossil Footprints of Laetoli. *Scientific American* 246 (2): 50–57.

Ilani, G.
1975 Hyenas in Israel. *Israel—Land and Nature*. October 1975: 10–18.

Johanson, D. C., and T. D. White
1979 A Systematic Assessment of Early African Hominids. *Science* 202: 321–330.

Johanson, Donald, and Maitland Edey
1981 *Lucy: The Beginnings of Humankind*. New York: Simon and Schuster.

Keyser, A. W.
2000 The Drimolen Skull: The Most Complete Australopithecine Cranium and Mandible to Date. *South African Journal of Science* 96: 189–193.

Klein, Richard G.
1999 *The Human Career: Human Biological and Cultural Origins*, 2nd ed. Chicago: University of Chicago Press.

Leakey, M. G., Feibel, C. S., McDougall, I., and A. Walker
1995 New Four-Million-Year-Old Hominid Species from Kanapoi and Allea Bay, Kenya. *Nature* 376: 565–571.

MacDougall, J. D.
1976 Fission-Track Dating. *Scientific American* 235 (6):114–122.

Senut, B., Pickford, M., Gommery, D., Mein, P., Cheboi, K., and Y. Coppens
2001 First Hominid from the Miocene (Lukeino Formation, Kenya). *C. R. Acad. Sci. Paris, Earth and Planetary Sciences* 332: 137–144.

Skelton, R. R., McHenry, H. M., and G. M. Drawhorn
1986 Phylogenetic Analysis of Early Hominids. *Current Anthropology* 27: 21–35.

Walker, A. C., Leakey, R. E. F., Harris, J. M., and F. H. Brown
1986 2.5 Myr *Australopithecus boisei* from West of Lake Turkana, Kenya. *Nature* 322: 517–522.

White, T. D., and J. M. Harris
1977 Suid Evolution and Correlation of African Hominid Localities. *Science* 198: 13–22.

White, T. D., Suwa, G., and B. Asfaw
1994 *Australopithecus ramidus*, a New Species of Early Hominid from Aramis, Ethiopia. *Nature* 372: 306–312.
1995 *Australopithecus ramidus*, a New Species of Early Hominid from Aramis, Ethiopia. Corrigendum. *Nature* 375: 88.

Wolpoff, M. H., Senut, B., Pickford, M., and J. Hawks
2002 Palaeoanthropology— *Sahelanthropus or 'Sahelpithecus'?* *Nature* 419: 581–582.

Wong, Kate
2003 An Ancestor to Call Our Own. *Scientific American* 288 (1): 54–63.

CHAPTER 3

Asfaw, B., White, T., Lovejoy, O., Latimer, B., Simpson, S., and G. Suwa
1999 *Australopithecus garhi*: A New Species of Early Hominid from Ethiopia. *Science* 284: 629–635.

Backwell, L. R., and F. d'Errico
2001 Evidence of Termite Foraging by Swartkrans Early Hominids. *Proceedings of the National Academy of Sciences* 98 (4): 1358–1363.

Binford, L. R.
1981 *Bones, Ancient Men and Modern Myths*. New York: Academic Press.
1985 Human Ancestors: Changing Views of Their Behavior. *Journal of Anthropological Archaeology* 1: 5–31.

Blumenschine, R. J.
1986 *Early Hominid Scavenging Opportunities*. Oxford: British Archaeological Reports, International Series 283.
1987 Characteristics of an Early Hominid Scavenging Niche. *Current Anthropology* 28 (4): 383–407.
1995 Percussion Marks, Tooth Marks, and Experimental Determinations of the Timing of Hominid and Carnivore Access to Long Bones at FLK *Zinjanthropus*, Olduvai Gorge, Tanzania. *Journal of Human Evolution* 29: 21–51.

Blumenschine, R. J., and J. A. Cavallo
1992 Scavenging and Human Evolution. *Scientific American* 267 (4): 90–96.

Blumenschine, R. J., and M. M. Selvaggio
1988 Percussion Marks on Bone Surfaces as a New Diagnostic of Hominid Behavior. *Nature* 333: 763–765.

Blumenschine, Robert J., Peters, Charles R., Masao, Fidelis T., Clarke, Ronald J., Deino, Alan L., Hay, Richard L.,

Swisher, Carl C., Stanistreet, Ian G., Ashley, Gail M., McHenry, Lindsay J., Sikes, Nancy E., van der Meuve, N., Kolaas, J., Tactikos, Joanne C., Cushing, Amy E., Deocampo, Daniel M., Njau, Jackson K., and Janis I. Ebert
2003 Late Pliocene *Homo* and Hominid Land Use from Western Olduvai Gorge, Tanzania. *Science* 299: 1217–1221.

Boesch, C., and H. Boesch-Achermann
2000 *The Chimpanzees of the Taï Forest.* Oxford: Oxford University Press.

Bunn, H. T.
1982 *Meat-eating and Human Evolution: Studies on the Diet and Subsistence Patterns of Plio-Pleistocene Hominids in East Africa.* Ph.D. Dissertation. Dept. of Anthropology, Univ. of California, Berkeley.
1983 Evidence on the Diet and Subsistence Patterns of Plio-Pleistocene Hominids at Koobi Fora, Kenya, and Olduvai Gorge, Tanzania. In *Animals and Archaeology: I. Hunters and Their Prey,* edited by J. Clutton-Brock and C. Grigson, British Archaeological Reports International Series 163.
1991 A Taphonomic Perspective on the Archaeology of Human Origins. *Annual Review of Anthropology* 20: 433–467.
2001 Hunting, Power Scavenging, and Butchering by Hadza Foragers and by Plio-Pleistocene *Homo.* In *Meat-eating and Human Evolution,* edited by Craig B. Stanford and Henry T. Bunn, pp. 199–218. Oxford: Oxford University Press.

Bunn, H. T., and E. M. Kroll
1986 Systematic Butchery by Plio-Pleistocene Hominids at Olduvai Gorge, Tanzania. *Current Anthropology* 27: 431–452.

d'Errico, F., and L. R. Backwell
2003 Possible Evidence of Bone Tool Shaping by Swartkrans Early Hominids. *Journal of Archaeological Science* 30: 1559–1576.

Domínguez-Rodrigo, Manuel
2002 Hunting and Scavenging by Early Humans: The State of the Debate. *Journal of World Prehistory* 16 (1): 1–54.

Isaac, G. L.
1978 The Food-sharing Behavior of Protohuman Hominids. *Scientific American* 238 (4): 90–106.

1983 Bones in Contention: Competing Explanations for the Juxtaposition of Early Pleistocene Artifacts and Faunal Remains. In *Animals and Archaeology: I. Hunters and Their Prey,* edited by J. Clutton-Brock and C. Grigson, pp. 3–19. Oxford: British Archaeological Reports, International Series 163.

Keeley, L., and N. Toth
1981 Microwear Polishes on Early Stone Tools from Koobi Fora, Kenya. *Nature* 293: 464–465.

Kroll, E., and G. Issac
1984 Configurations of Artifacts and Bones at Early Pleistocene Sites in East Africa. In *Intrasite Spatial Analysis in Archaeology,* edited by H. J. Hietala, pp. 4–31, Cambridge: Cambridge University Press.

Leakey, M. D.
1971 *Olduvai Gorge,* vol. 3. London: Cambridge University Press.

Milton, K.
1999 A Hypothesis to Explain the Role of Meat-Eating in Human Evolution. *Evolutionary Anthropology* 8: 11–21.

Oakley, K. P.
1950 *Man the Tool Maker.* Chicago: University of Chicago Press.

Plummer, T., Bishop, L. C., Ditchfield, P., and J. Hicks
1999 Research on Late Pliocene Oldowan Sites at Kanjera South, Kenya. *Journal of Human Evolution* 36: 151–170.

Potts, R.
1984 Home Bases and Early Hominids, *American Scientist* 72: 338–347.
1988 *Early Hominid Activities at Olduvai.* New York: Aldine de Gruyter.

Potts, R., and P. Shipman
1981 Cutmarks Made by Stone Tools on Bones From Olduvai Gorge, Tanzania. *Nature* 291: 577–580.

Roche, H., Delagnes, A., Brugal, J.-P., Feibel, C., Kibunjia, M., Mourre, V., and P.-J. Texier
1999 Early Hominid Stone Tool Production and Technical Skill 2.34 Myr Ago in West Turkana, Kenya. *Nature* 399: 57–60.

Rose, Lisa, and Fiona Marshall
1996 Meat Eating, Hominid Sociality, and Home Bases Revisited. *Current Anthropology* 37 (2): 307–338.

Selvaggio, M. M.
1998 Evidence for a Three-Stage Sequence of Hominid and Carnivore Involvement with Long Bones at FLK *Zinjanthropus,* Olduvai Gorge, Tanzania. *Journal of Archaeological Science* 25: 191–202.

Semaw, S.
2000 The World's Oldest Stone Artifacts from Gona, Ethiopia: Their Implications for Understanding Stone Technology and Patterns of Human Evolution Between 2.6–1.5 Million Years Ago. *Journal of Archaeological Science* 27: 1197–1214.

Semaw, S., Rogers, M. J., Quade, J., Renne, P. R., Butler, R. F., Dominguez-Rodrigo, M., Stout, D., Hart, W. S., Pickering, T., and S. W. Simpson
2003 2.6-Million-Year-Old Stone Tools and Associated Bones from OGS-6 and OGS-7, Gona, Afar, Ethiopia. *Journal of Human Evolution* 45: 169–177.

Shipman, P.
1986 Scavenging or Hunting in Early Hominids: Theoretical Framework and Tests. *American Anthropologist* 88: 27–43.

Toth, Nicholas
1985 The Oldowan Reassessed: A Close Look at Early Stone Age Artifacts. *Journal of Archaeological Science* 12: 101–120.
1987 The First Technology. *Scientific American* 256 (4): 112–121.

CHAPTER 4

Aiello, L. C., and J. C. K. Wells
2002 Energetics and the Evolution of the Genus *Homo. Annual Review of Anthropology* 31: 323–338.

Asfaw, Berhane, Beyenne, Yonas, Suwa, Gen, Walter, Robert C., White, Tim D., Woldegabriel, Giday, and Tesfaye Yemane
1992 The Earliest Acheulian from Konso-Gardula. *Nature* 360: 732–735.

Bar-Yosef, Ofer
1994 The Lower Paleolithic of the Near East. *Journal of World Prehistory* 8: 211–265.

Bar-Yosef, O., and A. Belfer-Cohen
2001 From Africa to Eurasia—Early Dispersals. *Quaternary International* 75: 19–28.

Bar-Yosef, O., and N. Goren-Inbar
1993 *The Lithic Assemblages of*

'Ubeidiya: A Lower Paleolithic Site in the Jordan Valley. Jerusalem: Qedem 34.

Brain, C. K., and A. Sillen
1988 Evidence from the Swartkrans Cave for the Earliest Use of Fire. *Nature* 336: 464–466.

Clark, J. Desmond
1994 The Acheulian Industrial Complex in Africa and Elsewhere. In *Integrative Paths to the Past: Paleoanthropological Advances in Honor of F. Clark Howell*, edited by R. S. Corruccini and R. L. Crochon, pp. 451–469. Englewood Cliffs, NJ: Prentice Hall.

Dennell, Robin
2003 Dispersal and Colonisation, Long and Short Chronologies: How Continuous Is the Early Pleistocene Record for Hominids Outside East Africa? *Journal of Human Evolution* 45: 421–440.

Gabunia, L., and A Vekua
1995 A Plio-Pleistocene Hominid from Dmanisi, East Georgia, Caucasus. *Nature* 373: 509–512.

Gabunia, L., Antón, S., Lordkipanidze, D., Vekua, A., Justus, A., and C. C. Swisher III
2001 Dmanisi and Dispersal. *Evolutionary Anthropology* 10: 158–170.

Gabunia, L., Vekua, A., Lordkipanidze, D., Swisher, C., Ferring, R., Justus, A., Nioradze, M., Tvalchrelidze, M., Antón, S. C., Bosinski, G., Jöris, O., de Lumley, M., Majsuradze, G., and Mouskhelishvili, A.
2000 Earliest Pleistocene Hominid Cranial Remains from Dmanisi, Republic of Georgia: Taxonomy, Geological Setting. *Science* 288: 1019–1025.

Goren-Inbar, N., Lister, A., Werker, E., and M. Chech
1994 A Butchered Elephant Skull and Associated Artifacts from the Acheulian Site of Gesher Benot Ya'aqov, Israel. *Paléorient* 20 (1): 99–112.

Goren-Inbar, Naama, Alperson, Nira, Kislev, Mordechai E., Simchoni, Orit, Melamed, Yoel, Ben-Nun, Adi, and Ella Werker
2004 Evidence for Hominin Control of Fire at Gesher Benot Ya-aqov. *Science* 304: 725–727.

Gowlett, A. J., Harris, J. W. K., Walton, D., and B. A. Wood.
1981 Early Archaeological Sites, Hominid Remains and Traces of Fire from Chesowanja, Kenya. *Nature* 294: 125–9.

Klein, R. J.
1999 *The Human Career: Human Biological and Cultural Origins*, 2nd ed. Chicago: University of Chicago Press.

McPherron, S. P.
2000 Handaxes as a Measure of Mental Capabilities of Early Hominids. *Journal of Archaeological Science* 27: 655–663.

Rightmire, G. Philip
1990 *The Evolution of Homo Erectus: Comparative Anatomical Studies of an Extinct Human Species*. Cambridge: Cambridge University Press.

Sillen, A., and C. K. Brain
1990 Old Flame: Burned Bones Provide Evidence of an Early Human Use of Fire. *Natural History* 4: 6–10.

Toth, Nicholas
1987 The First Technology. *Scientific American* 256 (4): 112–121.

Toth, Nicholas, Clark, Desmond, and Giancarlo Ligabue
1992 The Last Stone Ax Makers. *Scientific American*, 267 (1): 88–93.

Vekua, A., Lordkipanidze, D., Rightmire, G. P., Agusti, J., Ferring, R., Maisuradze, G., Mouskhelishuil, A., Nioradze, M., Ponce de Leon, M., Tappen, M., Tvalchredidze, M., and C. Zolilkofer
2002 A New Skull of Early *Homo* from Dmanisi. *Science* 297: 85–89.

Verosub, K. L., Goren-Inbar, N., Feibel, C., and I. Saragusti
1998 Location of the Matuyama/Brunhes Boundary in the Gesher Benot Ya'aqov Archaeological Site, Israel. *Journal of Human Evolution* 34: A22. Walker, Alan, and Richard Leakey, eds.
1993 *The Nariokotome Skeleton: Homo Erectus*. Cambridge: Harvard University Press.

Wong, Kate
2003 Stranger in a New Land. *Scientific American* 289 (5): 74–83.

Wynn, Thomas
1995 Handaxe Enigmas. *World Archaeology* 27 (1): 10–24.

CHAPTER 5

Antón, S. C.
2003 Natural History of *Homo erectus*. *American Journal of Physical Anthropology* 122: 126–170.

Bermúdez de Castro, J. M., Arsuaga, J. L., Carbonell, E., Rosas, A., Martínez, I., and M. Mosquera
1997 A Hominid from the Lower Pleistocene of Atapuerca, Spain: Possible Ancestor to Neandertals and Modern Humans. *Science* 276: 1392–1395.

Bermúdez de Castro, J. M., Martinón-Torres, M., Carbonell, E., Sarmiento, S., Rosas, A., van der Made, J., and M. Lozano
2004 The Atapuerca Sites and Their Contribution to the Knowledge of Human Evolution in Europe. *Evolutionary Anthropology* 13: 25–41.

Binford, Lewis R.
1981 *Bones, Ancient Men and Modern Myths*. New York: Academic Press.
1987 Were There Elephant Hunters at Torralba? In *The Evolution of Human Hunting*, edited by M. H. Nitecki and D. V. Nitecki, pp. 47–183. New York and London: Plenum Press.

Binford, Lewis R., and Nancy M. Stone
1986 Zhoukoudian: A Closer Look. *Current Anthropology* 27 (5): 453–475.

Carbonell, Eudald, and Xosé Pedro Rodriguez
1994 Early Middle Pleistocene Deposits and Artefacts in the Gran Dolina site (TD4) of the "Sierra de Atapuerca" (Burgos, Spain). *Journal of Human Evolution* 26: 291–311.

Carbonell, E., Bermúdez de Castro, J. M., Arsuaga, J. L., Diez, J. C., Rosas, A., Cuenca-Bescós, G., Sala, R., Mosquera, M., and X. P. Rodriguez
1995 Lower Pleistocene Hominids and Artifacts from Atapuerca-TD6 (Spain). *Science* 269: 826–830.

Carbonell, E., Esteban, M., Nájera, A. M., Mosquera, M., Rodriguez, X. P., Ollé, A., Sala, R., and J. M. Vergès
1999 The Pleistocene Site of Gran Dolina, Sierra de Atapuerca: A History of the Archaeological Excavations. *Journal of Human Evolution* 37: 313–324.

Dennell, R.
2003 Dispersal and Colonisation, Long and Short Chronologies: How Continuous Is the Early Pleistocene Record for Hominids Outside East Africa? *Journal of Human Evolution* 45: 421–440.

Freeman, Leslie G.
1994 Torralba and Ambrona: A Review of Discoveries. In *Integrative Paths to the Past: Paleoanthropological Advances in Honor of F. Clark Howell*, edited by R. S. Corruccini, pp. 597–637. Englewood Cliffs, NJ: Prentice Hall.

Gamble, Clive
1994 Time for Boxgrove Man. *Nature* 369: 275–276.
1999 *The Paleolithic Societies of Europe.* Cambridge: Cambridge University Press.

Grün, R., Huang, P.-H., Wu, X., Stringer, C. B., Thorne, A. G., and M. McCulloch
1997 ESR Analysis of Teeth from the Paleoanthropological Site of Zhoukoudian, China. *Journal of Human Evolution* 32: 83–91.

Larick, Roy, and Russel L. Ciochon
1996 The African Emergence and Early Asian Dispersals of the Genus *Homo. American Scientist* 84 (6): 538–551.

Lumley, H. de
1969 A Paleolithic Camp at Nice. *Scientific American* 220: 42–50.

Parés, Josep M., and Alfredo Pérez-Gonzales
1995 Paleomagnetic Age for Hominid Fossils at Atapuerca Archaeological Site, Spain. *Science* 269: 830–832.

Rightmire, G. B.
1998 Human Evolution in the Middle Pleistocene: The Role of *Homo heidelbergensis. Evolutionary Anthropology* 6: 218–227.

Roebroeks, Wil
2001 Hominid Behaviour and the Earliest Occupation of Europe: An Exploration. *Journal of Human Evolution* 41: 437–461.

Schick, Kathy D.
1994 The Movius Line Reconsidered: Perspectives on the Earlier Paleolithic of Eastern Asia. In *Integrative Paths to the Past: Paleoanthropological Advances in Honor of F. Clark Howell.* edited by R. S. Corruccini and R. L. Crochon. Englewood Cliffs, NJ: Prentice Hall, pp. 569–596.

Sémah, F., Salecki, H., and C. Falguères
2000 Did Early Man Reach Java During the Late Pliocene? *Journal of Archaeological Science* 27: 763–769.

Shapiro, Harry L.
1974 *Peking Man: The Discovery, Disappearance and Mystery of a Priceless Scientific Treasure.* New York: Simon and Schuster.

Swisher, C. C., III, Curtis, G. H., Jacob, T., Getty, A. G., Suprijo, A. Widiasmoro
1994 Age of the Earliest Known Hominids in Java, Indonesia. *Science* 263: 1118–1121.

Tattersall, Ian
1997 Out of Africa Again . . . and Again? *Scientific American* 276 (4): 60–67.

Thieme, H.
1997 Lower Paleolithic Hunting Spears from Germany. *Nature* 385: 807–10.

Toth, N., and K. Schick
1993 Early Stone Industries and Inferences Regarding Language and Cognition. In *Tools, Language and Cognition in Human Evolution,* edited by K. R. Gibson and T. Ingold, pp. 346–362. Cambridge: Cambridge University Press.

Villa, Paola
1983 *Terra Amata and the Middle Pleistocene Archaeological Record of Southern France.* Berkeley, CA: University of California Press.
1990 Torralba and Aridos: Elephant Exploitation in Middle Pleistocene Spain. *Journal of Human Evolution* 19: 299–309.
1994 Europe: Lower and Middle Pleistocene Archaeology. In *History of Humanity: Volume 1, Prehistory and the Beginnings of Civilization,* pp. 44–61. Routledge and UNESCO.

Weiner, S., Xu, Q., Goldberg, P., Liu, J., and O. Bar-Yosef
1998 Evidence for the Use of Fire at Zhoukoudian, China. *Science* 281: 251–53.

Wu, Rukang, and Lin Shenlong
1983 Peking Man. *Scientific American* 248 (6): 86–94.

Yamei, H., Potts, R., Baoyin, Y., Zhengtang, G., Deino, A., Wei, W., Clark, J., Guangmao, X., and H. Weiwen
2000 Mid-Pleistocene Acheulian-like Stone Technology of the Bose Basin. *Science* 287: 1622–1626.

CHAPTER 6

Bar-Yosef, O., Vandermeersh, B., Arensburg, B., Belfer-Cohen, A., Goldberg, P., Laville, H., Meignen, L., Rak, Y., Speth, J. D., Tchernov, E., Tillier, A. M., and S. Weiner
1992 The Excavations in Kebara Cave, Mt. Carmel. *Current Anthropology* 33 (5): 497–550.

Binford, Lewis R.
1984 *Faunal Remains from the Klasies River Mouth.* New York: Academic Press.

Binford, Lewis, and Sally Binford
1966 A Preliminary Analysis of Functional Variability in the Mousterian of Levallois Facies. *American Anthropologist* 68 (2): 238–295.

Bordes, F.
1968 *The Old Stone Age.* New York: McGraw-Hill.
1972 *A Tale of Two Caves.* New York: Harper and Row.
1984 *Leçons sur le Paléolithique II: Le Paléolithique en Europe.* Paris: Éditions du CNRS, Cahiers du Quaternaire 7.

Chase, P. G.
1986 *The Hunters of Combe Grenal: Approaches to Middle Paleolithic Subsistence in Europe.* Oxford: British Archaeological Reports International Series 286.
1988 Scavenging and Hunting in the Middle Paleolithic: The Evidence from Europe. In *Upper Pleistocene Prehistory of Western Eurasia,* edited by H. L. Dibble and A. Montet-White, pp. 226–232. Philadelphia: University Museum, University of Pennsylvania.

Dibble, H. L., and N. Roland
1992 On Assemblage Variability in the Middle Paleolithic of Western Europe: History, Perspectives, and a New Synthesis. In *The Middle Paleolithic: Adaptation, Behavior, and Variability,* edited by H. L. Dibble and P. Mellars, pp. 1–28. Philadelphia: University Museum.

Gargett, R.
1989 Grave Shortcomings: The Evidence for Neanderthal Burial. *Current Anthropology* 30: 157–190.

Klein, R. G.
1976 The Mammalian Fauna of the Klasies River Mouth Sites, Southern Cape Province, South Africa. *South African Archaeological Bulletin* 31: 75–98.

Leroi-Gourhan, Arlette
1975 The Flowers Found with Shanidar IV, a Neanderthal Burial in Iraq. *Science* 190: 562–564.

McBrearty, S., and A. S. Brooks
2000 The Revolution That Wasn't: Interpreting the Origin of Modern Human Behavior. *Journal of Human Evolution* 39: 453–563.

Mellars, P.
1996 *The Neanderthal Legacy: An Archaeological Perspective from Western Europe.* Princeton, NJ: Princeton University Press.

Scott, K.
1980 Two Hunting Episodes of Middle Paleolithic Age at La Cotte de Sainte-Brelade, Jersey (Channel Islands). *World Archaeology* 12: 137–152.

Solecki, Ralph S.
1971 *Shanidar—The First Flower People.* New York: Knopf.

Stiner, M. C.
1994 *Honor Among Thieves: A Zooarchaeological Study of Neanderthal Ecology*. Princeton, NJ: Princeton University Press.

Stringer, Christopher, and Clive Gamble
1993 *In Search of the Neanderthals*. New York: Thames and Hudson.

Trinkaus, Erik
1983 *The Shanidar Neanderthals*. New York: Academic Press.

Trinkaus, Erik, and Pat Shipman
1992 *The Neandertals: Of Skeletons, Scientists, and Scandal*. New York: Vintage Books.

White, T. D., Asfaw, B., DeGusta, D., Gilbert, H., Richards, G. D., Suwa, G., and F. C. Howell
2003 Pleistocene *Homo sapiens* from Middle Awash, Ethiopia. *Nature* 423: 742–747.

Wong, Kate
2000 Who Were the Neandertals? *Scientific American* 282 (4): 98–107.

CHAPTER 7

Bar-Yosef, Ofer
2002 The Upper Paleolithic Revolution. *Annual Review of Anthropology* 31: 363–393.

Brooks, Alison S., Helgren, David M., Cramer, Jon S., Franklin, Alan, Hornyak, William, Keating, Jody M., Klein, Richard G., Rink, William J., Schwarcz, Henry, Leith Smith, J. N., Stewart, Kathlyn, Todd, Nancy E., Verniers, Jacques, and John E. Yellen
1995 Dating and Context of Three Middle Stone Age Sites with Bone Points in the Upper Semliki Valley, Zaire, *Science* 268: 548–553.

Cann, R., Stoneking, M., and A. Wilson
1987 Mitochondrial DNA and human evolution. *Nature* 325: 31–36.

Clark, J. D., Beyene, Y., Wolde Gabriel, G., Hart, W. K., Renne, P. R., Gilbert, H., Defleur, A., Suwa, G., Katch, S., Ludwig, K. R., Boisserie, J.-R., Asfaw, B., and T. D. White
2003 Stratigraphic, Chronological and Behavioural Contexts of Pleistocene *Homo sapiens* from Middle Awash, Ethiopia. *Nature* 423: 747–752.

Conard, Nicholas J., and Michael Bolus
2003 Radiocarbon Dating the Appearance of Modern Humans and Timing of Cultural Innovations in Europe: New Results and New Challenges. *Journal of Human Evolution* 44: 331–371.

Dorit, R.L., Akashi, H., and W. Gilbert
1995 Absence of Polymorphism at the ZFY Locus on the Human Y Chromosome. *Science* 268: 1183.

Garrod, D. A. E., and D. M. A. Bate
1937 *The Stone Age of Mount Carmel*, vol. 1. Oxford: Clarendon Press.

Golavanova, L. V., Hoffecker, John F., Kharitonov, V. M., and G. P. Romanova
1999 Mezmaiskaya Cave: A Neanderthal Occupation in the Northern Caucasus. *Current Anthropology* 40: 77–86.

Grayson, Donald K., and Françoise Delpech
2003 Ungulates and the Middle-to-Upper Paleolithic Transition at Grotte XVI (Dordogne, France). *Journal of Archaeological Science* 30: 1633–1648.

Henry-Gambier, D.
2002a Les Fossiles de Cro-Magnon (Les Eyzies-de-Tayac, Dordogne): Nouvelles Données sur leur Position Chronologiques et leur Attribution Culturelle. *Bulletin de la Société d'Anthropologie de Paris*, n. s., 14: 89–112.
2002b Les Fossiles de Cro-Magnon (Les Eyzies-de-Tayac, Dordogne): Nouvelles Données sur leur Position Chronologiques et leur Attribution Culturelle. *Paléo* 14: 201–204.

Hoffecker, John F.
1999 Neanderthals and Modern Humans in Eastern Europe. *Evolutionary Anthropology* 7 (4): 129–141.

Howells, W. W.
1976 Explaining Modern Man: Evolutionists versus Migrationists. *Journal of Human Evolution* 5: 477–495.

Hrdlicka, A.
1927 The Neanderthal Phase of Man. *Journal of the Royal Anthropological Institute* 67: 249–269.

Kaufman, Daniel
2002 Re-evaluating Subsistence Skills of Levantine Middle and Upper Paleolithic Hunters: A Comparison of the Faunal Assemblages. *Oxford Journal of Archaeology* 21 (3): 217–229.

Klein, Richard G.
1979 The Mammalian Fauna of the Klasies River Mouth Sites, Southern Cape Province, South Africa. *South African Archaeological Bulletin* 31: 75–98.

1995 Anatomy, Behavior, and Modern Human Origins. *Journal of World Prehistory* 9: 167–198.
1999 *The Human Career: Human Biological and Cultural Origins*, 2nd ed. Chicago: University of Chicago Press.

Krings, M., Stone, A., Schmitz, R. W., Krainitski, H., Stoneking, M., and S. Pääbo
1997 Neanderthal DNA Sequences and the Origin of Modern Humans. *Cell* 90: 19–30.

Lévêque, F., Backer, M., and M. Guilbaud
1993 *Context of a Late Neanderthal*. Madison, WI: Prehistory Press, Monographs in World Prehistory 16.

Lieberman, D. E., and John J. Shea
1994 Behavioral Differences between Archaic and Modern Humans in the Levantine Mousterian. *American Anthropologist* 96 (2): 300–332.

McBrearty, Sally, and Alison S. Brooks
2000 The Revolution That Wasn't: A New Interpretation of the Origin of Modern Human Behavior. *Journal of Human Evolution* 39: 453–563.

Mithen, Steven
1996 *The Prehistory of the Mind: The Cognitive Origins of Art and Science*. New York: Thames and Hudson.

Ovchinnikov, I. V., Götherström, A., Romanova, G. P., Kharitonov, V. M., Lidens. K., and W. Goodwin
2000 Molecular Analysis of Neanderthal DNA from the Northern Caucasus. *Nature* 404: 490–493.

Pettitt, P. B.
1999 Disappearing from the World: An Archaeological Perspective on Neanderthal Extinction. *Oxford Journal of Archaeology* 18 (3): 217–240.

Pfeiffer, John
1985 *The Creative Explosion: An Inquiry into the Origins of Art and Religion*. Ithaca, NY: Cornell University Press.

Rightmire, G., and H. Deacon
1991 Comparative Studies of Late Pleistocene Human Remains from Klasies River Mouth, South Africa. *Journal of Human Evolution* 20: 131–156.

Schwarcz, H. P.
1994 Chronology of Modern Humans in the Levant. In *Late Quaternary Chronology and Paleoclimates in the Eastern Mediterranean*, edited by O. Bar-Yosef and R. S. Kra, pp. 21–31. Tucson, AZ: Radiocarbon.

Shea, John
1993 Lithic Use-Wear Evidence
for Hunting by Neanderthals and
Early Modern Humans from the
Levantine Mousterian. In *Hunting
and Animal Exploitation in the Later
Paleolithic and Mesolithic of Eurasia*,
edited by G. L. Peterkin, H. M.
Bricker, and P. Mellars, pp. 189–197.
Washington, DC: Archaeological
Papers of the American Anthro-
pological Association, 4.
2003 Neanderthals, Competition,
and the Origin of Modern Human
Behavior in the Levant. *Evolutionary
Anthropology* 12: 173–187.

Smith, F. H., Trinkaus, E., Pettitt, P. B.,
Karavanić, I., and M. Paunović
1999 Direct Radiocarbon Dates
for Vindija G. and Velika Pecina
Late Pleistocene Hominid Remains.
*Proceedings of the National Academy of
Sciences* 96 (22): 12281–12286.

Stringer, C., and P. Andrews
1989 Genetic and Fossil Evidence
for the Origin of Modern Humans.
Science 239: 1263–1268.

Tchernov, E.
1981 The Biostratigraphy in the
Middle East. In *Préhistoire du Levant*, edited by J. Cauvin and P.
Sanlaville, pp. 69–97. Paris: CNRS.
1989 The Middle Paleolithic Mammalian Sequence and Its Bearing on
the Origin of *Homo sapiens* in the
Southern Levant. In *Investigations in
South Levantine Prehistory*, edited by
O. Bar-Yosef and B. Vandermeersch,
pp. 25–42. Oxford: BAR International
Series 497.
1992 Biochronology, Paleoecology,
and Dispersal Events of Hominids
in the Southern Levant. In *The
Evolution and Dispersal of Modern
Humans in Asia*, edited by T. Aka-
zawa, K. Aoki, and T. Kimura, pp.
149–188. Tokyo: Hokusen-sha.

Tishkoff, S. A., Dietzsch, E., Speed, W.,
Pakstis, A. J., Kidd, J. R., Cheung,
K., Bonné-Tamir, B., Santachiara-
Benerecetti, A. S., Moral, P., Krings,
M., Pääbo, S., Watson, E., Risch, N.,
Jenkins, T., and K.K. Kidd
1996 Global Patterns of Linkage
Disequilibrium at the CD4 Locus
and Modern Human Origins. *Science*
271: 1380–1387.

Trinkaus, E., and C. Duarte
2000 The Hybrid Child from Portugal, pp. 102–103 in Who Were the
Neanderthals, by Kate Wong, *Scientific American* 282 (4): 98–107.

UniSci
1999 Neanderthals, Modern Humans, Coexisted, Likely Cohabited.
Daily University Science News, Oct.
26, 1999. http://unisci.com/sto-
ries/19994/102699.htm

Vandermeersch, Bernard
1981 *Les Hommes Fossiles de Qafzeh
(Israël)*. Paris: CNRS.

White, T. D., Asfaw, B., DeGusta, D.,
Gilbert, H., Richards, G. D., Suwa,
G., and F. C. Howell
2003 Pleistocene *Homo sapiens* from
Middle Awash, Ethiopia. *Nature* 423:
742–747.

Wolpoff, M.H.
1989 Multiregional Evolution: The
Fossil Alternative to Eden. In *The
Human Revolution: Behavioural and
Biological Perspectives on the Origins
of Modern Humans*, vol. 1, edited
by P. Mellars and C. Stinger, pp.
62–108. Edinburgh: Edinburgh University Press.

Yellen, John E., Brooks, Alison S.,
Cornelissn, Els, Mehlman, Michael J.,
and Kathlyn Stewart
1995 A Middle Stone Age Worked
Bone Industry from Katanda, Upper
Semliki Valley, Zaire. *Science*, 268:
553–556.

CHAPTER 8

Bar-Yosef, O.
2000 The Middle and Early Upper
Paleolithic in Southwest Asia and
Neighboring Regions. In *The Geography of Neanderthals and Modern Humans
in Europe and the Greater Mediterranean*,
edited by Ofer Bar-Yosef and David
Pilbeam, pp. 107–156. Cambridge:
Peabody Museum of Archaeology
and Ethnology, Harvard University,
Peabody Museum Bulletin Number 8.
2002 The Upper Paleolithic Revolution. *Annual Review of Anthropology*
31: 363–393.

Belfer-Cohen, Anna, and A. Nigel
Goring Morris
2003 Current Issues in Levantine
Upper Paleolithic Research. In *More
than Meets the Eye: Studies on Upper
Paleolithic Diversity in the Near East*,
edited by A. Nigel Goring-Morris
and Anna Belfer-Cohen, pp. 1–12.
Oxford: Oxbow Books.

Binford, L. R.
1980 Willow Smoke and Dogs' Tails:
Hunter-Gatherer Settlement Systems
and Archaeological Site Formation.
American Antiquity 45 (1): 4–20.

Brewer, Douglas T.
1992 Zooarchaeology: Method,
Theory, and Goals. In *Archaeological
Method and Theory*, vol. 4, edited by
M.B. Schiffer, pp. 195–244. Tucson,
AZ: University of Arizona Press.

Gilead, I.
1991 The Upper Paleolithic Period
in the Levant. *Journal of World Prehistory* 5 (2): 105–154.

Goring-Morris, A. Nigel, and Anna
Belfer-Cohen
2003 *More than Meets the Eye: Studies
on Upper Paleolithic Diversity in the
Near East*. Oxford: Oxbow Books.

Grayson, D.K.
1984 *Quantitative Zooarchaeology*. New
York: Academic Press.

Klein, Richard G.
1979 Stone Age Exploitation of
Animals in Southern Africa. *American Scientist* 67: 151–160.
1999 *The Human Career: Human Biological and Cultural Origins*. Chicago:
University of Chicago Press.

Kuhn, Steven L., Stiner, Mary C., Reese,
David S., and Erskin Gulec
2001 Ornaments of the Earliest
Upper Paleolithic: New Insights
from the Levant. *Proceedings of the
National Academy of Sciences* 98:
7641–7646.

Lee, R. B.
1968 What Hunters Do for a Living,
or, How to Make Out on Scarce
Resources. In *Man The Hunter*, edited by R. B. Lee and I. Devore, pp.
30–48. Chicago: Aldine.
1979 *The !Kung San: Men, Women
and Work in a Foraging Society*. Cambridge: Cambridge University Press.

Lieberman, D. E.
1993 Variability in Hunter-Gatherer
Seasonal Mobility in the Southern
Levant: From the Mousterian to the
Natufian. In *Hunting and Animal
Exploitation in the Late Pleistocene
Old World*, edited by G. Peterkin,
H. Bricker, and P. Mellars, pp.
207–219. Washington, DC: Archaeo-
logical Papers of the American An-
thropological Association.
1994 The Biological Basis for Seasonal
Increments in Dental Cementum and
Their Application to Archaeological
Research. *Journal of Archaeological
Science* 21: 525–539.

Lieberman, D. E., and John J. Shea
1994. Behavioral Differences between Archaic and Modern Humans

in the Levantine Mousterian. *American Anthropologist* 96(2): 300–332.

Lyman, R. Lee
1994 *Vertebrate Taphonomy.* Cambridge: Cambridge University Press.

Marks, Anthony E.
1993 The Early Upper Paleolithic: The View from the Levant. In *Before Lascaux: The Complete Record of the Early Upper Paleolithic,* edited by Heidi Knecht, Anne Pike-Tay, and Randall White, pp. 6–21. Boca Raton, FL: CRC Press.

Marks, A. E., and C. R. Ferring
1988 The Early Upper Paleolithic in the Levant. In *The Early Upper Paleolithic, Evidence from Europe and the Near East,* edited by J. F. Hoffecker and C. A. Wolf, pp. 43–72. Oxford: British Archaeological Reports, International Series 437.

Marks, A. E., and D. Kaufmann
1983 Boker Tachtit: The Artifacts. In *Prehistory and Paleoenvironments in the Central Negev, Israel,* vol. 3, edited by A. E. Marks, pp. 69–125. Dallas, TX: Southern Methodist University Press.

Marshall, F., and T. Pilgrim
1993 NISP vs. MNI in Quantification of Body-Part Representation. *American Antiquity* 58 (2): 261–269.

Monks, G.
1981 Seasonality Studies. In *Advances in Archaeological Method and Theory,* vol. 4, edited by M. B. Schiffer, pp. 177–240. New York: Academic Press.

Mortenson, P.
1972 Seasonal Camps and Early Villages in the Zagros. In *Man, Settlement and Urbanism,* edited by P. J. Ucko, R. Tringham, and G. W. Dimbleby, pp. 293–297. London: Duckworth.

Olami, Y.
1984 *Prehistoric Carmel.* Jerusalem and Haifa: Israel Exploration Society and M. Stekelis Museum of Prehistory.

Olszewski, D. I., and H. L. Dibble
1994 The Zagros Aurignacian. *Current Anthropology* 35 (1): 68–75.

Phillipson, David W.
1993 *African Archaeology,* 2nd ed. Cambridge: Cambridge University Press.

Rabinovich, Rivka
2003 The Levantine Upper Paleolithic Faunal Record. In *More than Meets the Eye: Studies on Upper Paleo-*

lithic Diversity in the Near East, edited by A. Nigel Goring-Morris and Anna Belfer-Cohen, pp. 33–48. Oxford: Oxbow Books.

Reitz, E. J., and E. S. Wing
1999 *Zooarchaeology.* Cambridge: Cambridge University Press.

Ronen, A.
1975 The Palaeolithic Archaeology and Chronology of Israel. In *Problems in Prehistory: North Africa and the Levant,* edited by A. E. Marks, pp. 229–248. Dallas, TX: SMU Press.

Schrire, C., ed.
1984 *Past and Present in Hunter-Gatherer Studies.* Orlando, FL: Academic Press.

CHAPTER 9

Andersen, B. G., and H. W. Borns
1994. *The Ice Age World.* Oslo: Scandinavian University Press.

Audouze, Françoise, and James Enloe
1991 Subsistence Strategies and Economy in the Magdalenian of the Paris Basin. In *The Late Glacial in North-West Europe: Human Adaptation and Environmental Change at the End of the Pleistocene,* edited by N. Barton, J. Roberts, and D. A. Roe, pp. 63–71. London: CBA Research Report No. 77.

Bokelman, Klaus
1991 Some Thoughts on Humans and Reindeer in the Ahrensburgian Tunnel Valley in Schlesweg-Holstein, Germany. In *The Late Glacial in North-West Europe: Human Adaptation and Environmental Change at the End of the Pleistocene,* edited by N. Barton, J. Roberts, and D. A. Roe, pp. 72–81. London: CBA Research Report No. 77.

Bordes, F.
1968 *The Old Stone Age.* New York: McGraw-Hill.
1984 *Leçons sur le Paléolithique II: Le Paléolithique en Europe.* Paris: Êditions du CNRS, Cahiers du Quaternaire 7.

Boyle, K. V.
1990 *Upper Palaeolithic Faunas from South-West France.* Oxford: British Archaeological Reports, International Series 557.

Davidson, I.
1974 Radiocarbon Dates for the Spanish Solutrean. *Antiquity* 48: 63–65.

Dawson, Alastair G.
1992 *Ice Age Earth: Late Quaternary Geology and Climate.* London and New York: Routledge.

Enloe, J., and F. David
1989 Le Remontage des Os par Individus: Le Partage du Renne chez les Magdaléniens de Pincevent (La Grande Paroise, Seine-et-Marne). *Bulletin de la Société Préhistorique Française* 86 (9): 275–281.

Enloe, J., David, F., and T. S. Hare
1994 Patterns of Faunal Processing at Section 27 of Pincevent: The Use of Spatial Analysis and Ethnoarchaeological Data in the Interpretation of Archaeological Site Structure. *Journal of Anthropological Archaeology* 13: 104–124.

Fischer, A.
1991 Pioneers in Deglaciated Landscapes: The Expansion and Adaptation of Late Paleolithic Societies in Southern Scandinavia. In *The Late Glacial in North-West Europe: Human Adaptation and Environmental Change at the End of the Pleistocene,* edited by N. Barton, J. Roberts, and D. A. Roe, pp. 100–121. London: CBA Research Report No. 77.

Freeman, L. G., Gonzáles Echegaray, J., Klein, R. G., and W. T. Crowe
1988 Dimensions of Research at El Juyo. In *Upper Pleistocene Prehistory of Western Eurasia,* edited by H. L. Dibble and A. Montet-White, pp. 3–39. Philadelphia: University Museum Monograph 54.

Gamble, Clive
1986 *The Palaeolithic Settlement of Europe.* Cambridge: Cambridge University Press.
1999 *The Palaeolithic Societies of Europe.* Cambridge: Cambridge University Press.

Hedges, R. E. M., and J. A. J. Gowlett
1986 Radiocarbon Dating by Accelerator Mass Spectrometry. *Scientific American* 254 (1): 100–107.

Hockett, Bryan Scott, and N. F. Bicho
2000 The Rabbits of Picareiro Cave: Small Mammal Hunting During the Late Upper Palaeolithic in the Portuguese Estremadura. *Journal of Archaeological Science* 27: 715–723.

Hoffecker, John F.
1999 Neanderthals and Modern Humans in Eastern Europe. *Evolutionary Anthropology* 7 (4): 129–141.

Klein, Richard G.
1973 *Ice-Age Hunters of the Ukraine*. Chicago: University of Chicago Press.

Leroi-Gourhan, André, and M. Brézillon
1972 *Fouilles de Pincevent: Essai d'analyse Ethnographique d'un Habitat Magdalénian*. Paris: Éditions du CNRS.

Renfrew, Colin
1973 *Before Civilization: The Radiocarbon Revolution and Prehistoric Europe*. Cambridge: Cambridge University Press.

Stordeur-Yedid, D.
1979 *Les aiguilles à chas au paléolithique*. Paris: *Gallia Préhistoire*, Supplement 13.

Strauss, Lawrence G., and Geoffrey A. Clark
1986 *La Riera Cave: Stone Age Hunter-Gatherer Adaptations in Northern Spain*. Tempe, AZ: Arizona State University Anthropological Research Papers, No. 36.

White, Randall
1985 *Upper Paleolithic Land Use in the Périgord*. Oxford: British Archaeological Reports, International Series 253.
2003 *Prehistoric Art: The Symbolic Journey of Humankind*. New York: Abrams.

CHAPTER 10

Bahn, Paul G., and Jean Vertut
1988 *Images of the Ice Age*. London: Windward.
1997 *Journey through the Ice Age*. Berkeley and Los Angeles: University of California Press.

Beaune, A. de, and Randall White
1993 Ice Age Lamps. *Scientific American* 266 (3): 108–113.

Breuil, Henri
1952 *Four Hundred Centuries of Cave Art*. Montignac: Centre d'Études et de Documentation Prehistoriques.

Casey, S.
1995 Examining Seasonality in Upper Paleolithic Art: Methodology and Research Implications. In *Before Farming*, edited by D. V. Campana. Philadelphia: MASCA Research Papers in Science and Archaeology, Vol. 12 Supplement.

Chase, P., and H. L. Dibble
1987 Middle Paleolithic Symbolism: A Review of Current Evidence and Interpretations. *Journal of Anthropological Archaeology* 6: 263–296.

Chauvet, Jean-Marie, Deschamps, E. B., and C. Hillaire
1996 *Dawn of Art: The Chauvet Cave: The Oldest Known Paintings in the World*. New York: Abrams.

Clottes, Jean
1996 Thematic Changes in Upper Paleolithic Art: A View from Grotte Chauvet. *Antiquity* 70: 276–288.

Clottes, Jean, and Jean Courtin
1996 *The Cave Beneath the Seas: Paleolithic Images at Cosquer*, translated by Marilyn Garner. New York: Abrams.

Conkey, Margaret
1980 The Identification of Prehistoric Hunter-Gatherer Aggregation Sites: The Case of Altamira. *Current Anthropology* 21: 609–630.

Deacon, Janette
1999 South African Rock Art. *Evolutionary Anthropology* 8 (2): 48–64.

Henshilwood, C., d'Errico, F., Vanhaeren, M., van Niekirk, K., and Z. Jacobs
2004 Middle Stone Age Shell Beads from South Africa. *Science* 304: 404.

Howard, Ken
1996 Artful Dating. *Scientific American* 274 (6): 24.

Leroi-Gourhan, André
1967 *Treasures of Prehistoric Art*. New York: Abrams.
1968 The Evolution of Paleolithic Art. *Scientific American* 218 (2): 58–70.

Leroi-Gourhan, Arlette
1982 The Archaeology of Lascaux Cave. *Scientific American* 246 (6): 104–112.

Marshack, Alexander
1972 *The Roots of Civilization*. London: Weidenfeld and Nicolson.

Martin, Yves
1993 Analyse des pigments. In *L'art Pariétal Paléolithique*, edited by the Groupe de Réflexion sur L'art Pariétal Paléolithique, pp. 261–4. Paris: Éditions du CTHS.

Pfeiffer, John
1983 *The Creative Explosion*. New York: Harper and Row.

Rice, P. C.
1981 Prehistoric Venuses: Symbols of Motherhood or Womanhood? *Journal of Anthropological Research* 37: 402–414.

Soffer, O., Adovasio, J. M., and D. C. Hyland
2000 The "Venus" Figurines. *Current Anthropology* 41: 511–537.

Ucko, Peter J., and Andrée Rosenfeld
1967 *Palaeolithic Cave Art*. New York: McGraw-Hill.

Valladas, H., Clottes, J., and J.-M. Geneste
2004 Chauvet, la Grotte Ornée la Mieux Datée du Monde. *Pour la Science* 42: 82–87.

Wendt, W. E.
1976 *Art Mobilier* from the Apollo 11 Cave, South West Africa: Africa's Oldest Dated Works of Art. *South African Archaeological Bulletin* 31: 5–11.

White, Randall
1986 *Dark Caves, Bright Visions: Life in Ice Age Europe*. New York: Norton.
2003 *Prehistoric Art: The Symbolic Journey of Humankind*. New York: Abrams.

Yellen, J. E., Brooks, A. S., Cornelissen, E., Mehlman, M. J., and K. Stewart
1995 A Middle Stone Age Worked Bone Industry from Katanda, Upper Semliki Valley, Zaire. *Science* 268: 553–556.

CHAPTER 11

Allen, H.
1979 Left Out in the Cold: Why Tasmanians Stopped Eating Fish. *The Artefact* 4: 1–10.

Allen, J.
1989 When Did Humans First Colonize Australia? *Search* 20 (5): 149–154.

Allen, J., Gasden, C., and J. P. White
1989 Human Pleistocene Adaptations in the Tropical Island Pacific: Recent Evidence from New Ireland, a Greater Australia Outlier. *Antiquity* 63: 548–561.

Binford, L. R.
1980 Willow Smoke and Dogs' Tails: Hunter–Gatherer Settlement Systems and Archaeological Site Formation. *American Antiquity* 45 (1): 4–20.

Birdsell, J. B.
1977 The Recalibration of a Paradigm for the First Peopling of Australia. In *Sunda and Sahul: Prehistoric Studies in Southeast Asia, Melanesia and Australia*, edited by J. Allen, J. Golson, and R. Jones, pp. 113–167. London: Academic Press.

Bowdler, S.
1977 The Coastal Colonisation of Australia. In *Sunda and Sahul: Prehistoric Studies in Southeast Asia, Melanesia and Australia*, edited by J. Allen, J. Golson, and R. Jones, pp. 205–246. London: Academic Press.

Bowler, J., Jones, R., Allen, H., and A. Thorne
1970 Pleistocene Human Remains from Australia: A Living Site and Human Cremation from Lake Mungo, Western New South Wales. *World Archaeology* 2: 39–60.

Bowler, J., and A. Thorne
1976 Human Remains from Lake Mungo: Discovery and Excavation of Lake Mungo III. In *The Origin of the Australians*, edited by R.L. Kirk and A.G. Thorne, pp. 127–138. Canberra, Australia: Australian Institute of Aboriginal Studies.

Bowler, J., Thorne, A., and N. Polach
1972 Pleistocene Man in Australia: Age and Significance of the Mungo Skeleton. *Nature* 240: 48–50.

Cosgrove, R.
1989 Thirty Thousand Years of Human Colonization in Tasmania: New Pleistocene Dates. *Science* 243: 1706–1708.

Dincauze, Dina
2000 *Environmental Archaeology: Principles and Practice.* Cambridge: Cambridge University Press.

Dortch, C.
1979 Devil's Lair: An Example of Prolonged Cave Use in Southwestern Australia. *World Archaeology* 10: 258–279.

Flood, J.
1990 *The Archaeology of the Dreamtime: The Story of Prehistoric Australia and Its People,* revised ed. New Haven, CT: Yale University Press.

Gillespie, Richard, and Richard G. Roberts
2000 On the Reliability of Age Estimates for Human Remains from Lake Mungo. *Journal of Human Evolution* 38: 727–732.

Golson, J., and P. J. Hughes
1977 Ditches Before Time. *Hemisphere* 21 (2): 13–21.

Groube, L., Chappell, J., Muke, J., and D. Price
1986 A 40,000 Year-Old Human Occupation Site at Huon Peninsula, Papua New Guinea. *Nature* 324: 453–455.

Henrich, Joseph
2004 Demography and Cultural Evolution: How Adaptive Cultural Processes Can Produce Maladaptive Losses—The Tasmanian Case. *American Antiquity* 69 (2): 197–214.

Horton, D. R.
1981 Water and Woodland: The Peopling of Australia. *Australian Institute of Aboriginal Studies Newsletter* 16: 21–27.
1991 *Recovering the Tracks: The Story of Australian Archaeology.* Canberra, Australia: Aboriginal Studies Press.

Irwin, Geoffrey
1992 *The Prehistoric Exploration and Colonisation of the Pacific.* Cambridge: Cambridge University Press.

Jones, Rhys
1977 The Tasmanian Paradox. In *Stone Tools as Cultural Markers: Change, Evolution and Complexity,* edited by V. S. Wright, pp. 189–204. Canberra, Australia: Australian Institute of Aboriginal Studies.
1978 Why Did the Tasmanians Stop Eating Fish? In *Explorations of Ethno-Archaeology,* edited by R. A. Gould, pp. 11–47. Albuquerque, NM: University of New Mexico Press.
1995 Tasmanian Archaeology: Establishing the Sequences. *Annual Review of Anthropology* 24: 423–446.

Lourandos, Harry
1997 *Continent of Hunter-Gatherers: New Perspectives in Australian Prehistory.* Cambridge: Cambridge University Press.

Mulvaney, John, and Johan Kammnga
1999 *Prehistory of Australia.* Washington, DC: Smithsonian Institution Press.

O'Connell, James F., and Jim Allen
1998 When Did Humans First Arrive in Greater Australia and Why Is It Important to Know? *Evolutionary Anthropology* 6 (4): 132–146.

Pearce, R. H., and M. Barbetti
1981 A 38,000-Year-Old Site in Upper Swan, Western Australia. *Archaeology in Oceania* 16 (3): 173–178.

Thorne, A., Grün, R., Mortimer, G., Spooner, N. A., McCulloch, M., Taylor, L., and D. Curnoe
1999 Australia's Oldest Human Remains: Age of the Lake Mungo 3 Skeleton. *Journal of Human Evolution* 36: 591–612.

Van Andel, T. H.
1989 Late Quaternary Sea-Level Changes and Archaeology. *Antiquity* 63: 733–745.

White, J. Peter, and James F. O'Connell
1982 *A Prehistory of Australia, New Guinea and Sahul.* New York: Academic Press.

CHAPTER 12

Bever, Michael R.
2001 An Overview of Alaskan Late Pleistocene Archaeology: Historical Themes and Current Perspectives. *Journal of World Prehistory* 15 (2): 125–191.

Colinvaux, P. A., and F. H. West
1984 The Beringian Ecosystem. *Quarterly Review of Archaeology* 5 (3): 10–16.

Dillehay, Tom D.
1989 *Monte Verde: A Late Pleistocene Settlement in Chile. Volume I: Palaeoenvironment and Site Context.* Washington, DC and London: Smithsonian Institution Press.
1997 *Monte Verde: A Late Pleistocene Settlement in Chile. Volume II: The Archaeological Context.* Washington, DC and London: Smithsonian Institution Press.
2000 *The Settlement of the Americas: A New Prehistory.* New York: Basic Books.

Dincauze, D.
1984 An Archaeo-Logical Evaluation of the Case for Pre-Clovis Occupations. In *Advances in World Archaeology,* vol. 3, edited by F. Wendorf and A. Close, pp. 275–323. New York: Academic Press.

Fagan, B. M.
1995 *Ancient North America: The Archaeology of a Continent,* 2nd ed. London: Thames and Hudson.

Fiedel, S. J.
1992 *Prehistory of the Americas,* 2nd ed. Cambridge: Cambridge University Press.

Fiedel, Stuart, and Gary Haynes
2004 A Premature Burial: Comments on Grayson and Meltzer's "Requiem for Overkill." *Journal of Archaeological Science* 31: 121–131.

Frison, G. C.
1978 *Prehistoric Hunters of the High Plains.* New York: Academic Press.

Goebel, Ted
1999 Pleistocene Human Colonization of Siberia and Peopling of the Americas: An Ecological Approach. *Evolutionary Anthropology* 8: 208–227.

Graham, R. W., Haynes, C. V., Johnson, D. L., and M. Kay
1981 Kimmswick: A Clovis-Mastodon Association in Eastern Missouri. *Science* 213: 1115–1117.

Grayson, D. K.
1991 Late Pleistocene Mammalian Extinctions in North America: Taxonomy, Chronology, and Explanations. *Journal of World Prehistory* 5 (3): 193–231.

Grayson, Donald K., and David J. Meltzer
2002 Clovis Hunting and Large Mammal Extinction: A Critical Review of the Evidence. *Journal of World Prehistory* 16 (4): 313–359.
2003 A Requiem for North American Overkill. *Journal of Archaeological Science* 30: 585–593.

Guthrie, R. Dale
1984 Mosaics, Allelochemics and Nutrients: An Ecological Theory of Late Pleistocene Megafaunal Extinctions. In *Quaternary Extinctions: A Prehistoric Revolution*, edited by P. S. Martin and R. G. Klein, pp. 259–298. Tucson, AZ: University of Arizona Press.
1990 *Frozen Fauna of the Mammoth Steppe: The Story of Blue Babe.* Chicago: University of Chicago Press.

Haven, S.
1856 *Archaeology of the United States.* Washington, DC: Smithsonian Contributions to Knowledge, No. 8 (2).

Haynes, C. V.
1987 Clovis Origins Update. *The Kiva* 52 (2): 83–93.
1991 Geoarchaeological and Paleohydrological Evidence for a Clovis-age Drought in North America and Its Bearing on Extinction. *Quaternary Research* 35: 435–450.
1992 Contributions of Radiocarbon Dating to the Geochronology of the Peopling of the New World. In *Radiocarbon after Four Decades: An Interdisciplinary Perspective*, edited by R. E. Taylor, A. Long, and R. S. Kra, pp. 355–374. New York: Springer-Verlag.

Haynes, Gary
2002 The Catastrophic Extinction of North American Mammoths and Mastodons. *World Archaeology* 33 (3): 391–416.

Hoffecker, John F., Powers, W. Roger, and Ted Goebel
1993 The Colonization of Beringia and the Peopling of the New World. *Science* 259: 46–53.

Hoffecker, John, and Scott A. Elias
2003 Environment and Archeology in Beringia. *Evolutionary Anthropology* 12: 34–49.

Hopkins, D., Matthews, J., Schweger, C., and S. Young, eds.
1982 *Paleoecology of Beringia.* New York: Academic Press.

Jennings, J. D.
1989 *Prehistory of North America*, 3rd ed. Mountain View, CA: Mayfield.

Keefer, D. K., deFrance, S. D., Moseley, M. E., Richardson, J. B., Satterlee, D. R., and A. Day-Lewis
1998 Early Maritime Economy and El Niño Events at Quebrada Tacahuey, Peru. *Science* 281: 1833–1835.

Kutzbach, J. E., and Thompson Webb III
1991 Late Quaternary Climatic and Vegetational Change in Eastern North America: Concepts, Models, and Data. In *Quaternary Landscapes*, edited by L. C. K. Shane and E. J. Cushing, pp. 175–217. Minneapolis, MN: University of Minnesota Press.

Kuzmin, Y. V.
1994 Prehistoric Colonization of Northeastern Siberia and Migration to America: Radiocarbon Evidence. *Radiocarbon* 36: 367–376.

Lynch, T. F.
1990 Glacial-age Man in South America? A Critical Review. *American Antiquity* 55 (1): 12–36.

Martin, P. S.
1984 Prehistoric Overkill: The Global Model. In *Quaternary Extinctions: A Prehistoric Revolution*, edited by P. S. Martin and R. G. Klein, pp. 354–403. Tucson, AZ: University of Arizona Press.

Meltzer. D. J.
1993 *Search for the First Americans.* Washington, DC: Smithsonian Books.

Meltzer, D. J., Grayson, D. K., Ardila, G., Barker, A.W., Dincauze, D. F., Haynes, C. V., Mena, F., Nuñez, L., and D. J. Stanford
1997 On the Pleistocene Antiquity of Monte Verde, Southern Chile. *American Antiquity* 62 (4): 659–663.

Nelson, D. E., Morlan, R. E., Vogel, J. S., Southon, J. R., and C. R. Harrington
1986 New Dates on Northern Yukon Artifacts: Holocene Not Upper Pleistocene. *Science* 232: 749–751.

Pielou, E. C.
1992 *After the Ice Age: The Return of Life to Glaciated North America.* Chicago and London: University of Chicago Press.

Powers, W. R., and J. F. Hoffecker
1989 Late Pleistocene Settlement in the Nenana Valley, Central Alaska. *American Antiquity* 54 (2): 263–297.

Sandweiss, D. H., McInnis, H., Burger, R. L., Cano, A., Ojeda, B., Paredes, R., Sandweiss, M., and M. D. Glasscock
1998 Quebrada Jaguay: Early South American Maritime Adaptations. *Science* 281: 1830–1832.

Turner, C. G., II
1989 Teeth and Prehistory in Asia. *Scientific American* 260: 88–96.
1994 Relating Eurasian and Native American Populations Through Dental Morphology. In *Method and Theory for Investigating the Peopling of the Americas*, edited by R. Bonnichsen and D. G. Steele, pp. 131–140. Corvallis, OR: Center for the Study of the First Americans.

CHAPTER 13

Andersen, S. H.
1987 Tybrind Vig: A Submerged Ertebølle Settlement in Denmark. In *European Wetlands in Prehistory*, edited by J. M. Coles and A. J. Lawson, pp. 253–280. Oxford: Clarendon Press.
2004 Trbrind Vig. In *Ancient Europe 8000 B.C.–A.D. 1000: Encyclopedia of the Barbarian World*, edited by Peter Bogucki and Pam J. Crabtree, pp. 141–143. New York: Charles Scribner's Sons.

Binford, Lewis R.
1980 Willow Smoke and Dog's Tails: Hunter-Gatherer Settlement Systems and Archaeological Site Formation. *American Antiquity* 45 (1): 4–20.

Bogucki, P. I.
1988 *Forest Farmers and Stockherders: Early Agriculture and Its Consequences in North-Central Europe.* Cambridge: Cambridge University Press.
1995 Prelude to Agriculture in North-Central Europe. In *Before Farming: Hunter-Gatherer Society and Subsistence*, edited by D. V. Campana, pp. 105–116. Philadelphia: MASCA Research Papers in Science and Archaeology, supplement to Volume 12.

Bogucki, Peter, and Pam J. Crabtree, eds.
2004 *Ancient Europe 8000 B.C.–A.D. 1000: Encyclopedia of the Barbarian*

World. New York: Charles Scribner's Sons.

Clark, G. A., and M. Neely
1987 Social Differentiation in European Mesolithic Burial Data. In *Mesolithic Northwest Europe: Recent Trends,* edited by P. Rowley-Conwy, M. Zvelebil, and H. P. Blankholm, pp. 121–130. Sheffield, England: University of Sheffield.

Clark, J. G. D.
1954 *Excavations at Star Carr.* Cambridge: Cambridge University Press.
1972 *Star Carr: A Case Study in Bioarchaeology.* Addison-Wesley Module in Anthropology, 10.

Clarke, D.
1976 Mesolithic Europe: The Economic Basis. In *Problems in Economic and Social Archaeology,* edited by G. de G. Sieveking, I. H. Longworth, and K. E. Wilson, pp. 449–481. London: Duckworth.

Conkey, M. W.
1980 The Identification of Prehistoric Hunter-Gatherer Aggregation Sites: The Case of Altamira. *Current Anthropology* 21: 609–630.

Delacourt, P. A., Delacourt, H. R., Ison, C. R., Sharp, W. E., and K. J. Gremillion
1998 Prehistoric Human Use of Fire, The Eastern Agricultural Complex, and Appalachian Oak-Chestnut Forests: Paleoecology of Cliff Palace Pond, Kentucky. *American Antiquity* 63 (2): 263–278.

Dimbleby, G. W.
1985 *The Palynology of Archaeological Sites.* New York: Academic.

Legge, A. J., and P. Rowley-Conwy
1989 *Star Carr Revisited.* London: Birbeck College.

Mellars, P.
1975 Ungulate Populations, Economic Patterns, and the Mesolithic Landscape. In *The Effect of Man on the Landscape, the Highland Zone,* edited by J. G. Evans, S. Limbrey, and M. Cleere, pp. 49–63. The Council for British Archaeology, Report 11. London: Council for British Archaeology.
1976 Fire Ecology, Animal Populations and Man: A Study of Some Ecological Relationships in Prehistory. *Proceedings of the Prehistoric Society* 42: 15-45.
2004 Star Carr. In *Ancient Europe 8000 B.C.–A.D. 1000: Encyclopedia of the Barbarian World,* edited by

Peter Bogucki and Pam J. Crabtree, pp. 153–156. New York: Charles Scribner's Sons.

Moore, P. D., Webb, J. A., and M. E. Collinson
1991 *Pollen Analysis,* 2nd ed. Oxford: Blackwell Scientific Publications.

Newell, R. R.
1973 The Post-Glacial Adaptations of the Indigenous Population of the North-West European Plain. In *The Mesolithic in Europe,* edited by S. K. Koslowski, pp. 399–440. Warsaw: University of Warsaw Press.

Pearsall, D. M.
1989 *Paleoethnobotany: A Handbook of Procedures.* New York: Academic Press.

Perry, David
1997 *The Paleoethnobotany of Hunter-Gatherers: Analysis of Botanical Remains from Mesolithic Sites in the Province of Groningen, the Netherlands.* Unpublished Ph.D. Dissertation, New York University.

Price, T. D.
1981 Regional Approaches to Human Adaptation in the Mesolithic of the North European Plain. In *Mesolithicum in Europa,* edited by B. Gramsch, pp. 217–234. Potsdam, Germany: Museum für Ur- und Frühgeschichte, Veröffentlichtungen 14–15.
1985 Affluent Foragers of Mesolithic Southern Scandinavia. In *Prehistoric Hunter-Gatherers: The Emergence of Cultural Complexity,* edited by T. D. Price and J. A. Brown, pp. 341–360. Orlando, FL: Academic Press.
1987 The Mesolithic of Western Europe. *Journal of World Prehistory* 1 (3): 225–305.

Rowley-Conwy, P.
1986 Between Cave Painters and Crop Planters: Aspects of the Temperate European Mesolithic. In *Hunters in Transition,* edited by M. Zvelebil, pp. 17–32. Cambridge: Cambridge University Press.

Simmons, I. G., Turner, J., and J. B. Innes
1989 An Application of Fine-Resolution Pollen Analysis to Later Mesolithic Peats of an English Upland. In *The Mesolithic in Britain,* edited by C. Bonsall, pp. 206–217. Edinburgh: John Donald.

Welinder, S.
1989 Mesolithic Forest Clearance in Scandinavia. In *The Mesolithic in*

Europe, edited by C. Bonsall, pp. 362–366. Edinburgh: John Donald.

Whittle, Alasdair
1996 *Europe in the Neolithic: The Creation of New Worlds.* Cambridge: Cambridge University Press.

Woodman, P. C.
1981 A Mesolithic Camp in Ireland. *Scientific American* 245: 120–128.
1985 *Excavations at Mount Sandel 1973–77,* Northern Ireland Archaeological Monographs No. 2. Belfast, UK: Her Majesty's Stationery Office.
2004 Mount Sandel. In *Ancient Europe 8000 B.C.–A.D. 1000: Encyclopedia of the Barbarian World,* edited by Peter Bogucki and Pam J. Crabtree, pp. 151–153. New York: Charles Scribner's Sons.

Zvelebil, M.
1986 Postglacial Foraging in the Forests of Europe. *Scientific American* 254 (5): 104–115.
1989 Economic Intensification and Postglacial Hunter-Gatherers in North Temperate Europe. In *The Mesolithic in Europe,* edited by C. Bonsall, pp. 80–88. Edinburgh: John Donald.
1994 Plant Use in the Mesolithic and the Implications for the Transition to Farming. *Proceedings of Prehistoric Society* 60: 95–134.
1995 Hunting, Gathering or Husbandry? Management of Food Resources by the Late Mesolithic Communities of Temperate Europe. In *Before Farming,* edited by D. V. Campana. Philadelphia: MASCA Publications in Archaeology and Science.
2004 Oleneostrovskii Mogilnik. In *Ancient Europe 8000 B.C.–A.D. 1000: Encyclopedia of the Barbarian World,* edited by Peter Bogucki and Pam J. Crabtree, pp. 192–198. New York: Charles Scribner's Sons.

CHAPTER 14

Aikens, C. Melvin
1970 *Hogup Cave.* Salt Lake City, UT: University of Utah Anthropological Paper 93.
1978 Archaeology of the Great Basin. *Annual Review of Anthropology* 7: 71–87.

Anderson, D. G.
1996 Models of Paleoindian and Early Archaic Settlement in the Lower Southeast. In *The Paleoindian*

and Early Archaic Southeast, edited by D. G. Anderson and K. E. Sassaman, pp. 29–45. Tuscaloosa, AL: University of Alabama Press.

Beck, Charlotte, and George T. Jones
1997 The Terminal Pleistocene/Early Holocene Archaeology of the Great Basin. *Journal of World Prehistory* 11 (2): 161–236.

Bogucki, P. I.
1988 *Forest Farmers and Stockherders: Early Agriculture and Its Consequences in North-Central Europe.* Cambridge: Cambridge University Press.

Brown, James A.
1985 Long-Term Trends to Sedentism and the Emergence of Complexity in the American Midwest. In *Prehistoric Hunter-Gatherers: The Emergence of Cultural Complexity*, edited by J. A. Brown and T. D. Price, pp. 201–231. Orlando, FL: Academic Press.

Carr, Kurt W.
1998 The Early Archaic Period in Pennsylvania. *Pennsylvania Archaeologist* 68: 42–69.

Custer, J. F.
1985 *Delaware Prehistoric Archaeology: An Ecological Approach.* Newark, DE: University of Delaware Press.

Dansie, A. J., Davis, J. O., and T. W. Stafford, Jr.
1988 The Wizard's Beach Recession: Farmdalian (25,500 yr B.P.) Vertebrate Fossils Co-Occur with Early Holocene Artifacts. In Willig, J. A., Aikens, C. M., and Fagan, J. L., eds., *Early Human Occupation in Far Western North America: The Clovis-Archaic Interface. Nevada State Museum Anthropological Papers* 21, Carson City, pp. 153–200.

Fagan, Brian M.
2000 *Ancient North America*, 3rd ed. New York: Thames and Hudson.

Green, S. W., and K. E. Sassaman
1983 The Political Economy of Resource Management: A General Model and Application to Foraging Societies in the Carolina Piedmont. In *Ecological Models in Economic Prehistory*, edited by G. Bronitsky, pp. 261–290. Tempe, AZ: Arizona State University Anthropological Research Paper 29.

Hart, John P., and Nancy Asch Sidell
1997 Additional Evidence for Early Cucurbit Use in the Northern Eastern Woodlands East of the Allegheny Front. *American Antiquity* 62: 523–537.

Hajic, E. R.
1990 *Koster Site Archeology I: Stratigraphy and Landscape Evaluation.* Kampsville, IL: Center for American Archeology Research Series, vol. 8.

Jennings, J. D.
1957 *Danger Cave.* Salt Lake City, UT: University of Utah Anthropological Paper 27.

Klein, J., Lerman, J. C., Damon, P. E., and E. K. Ralph
1982 Calibration of Radiocarbon Dates: Tables Based on the Consensus Data of the Workshop on Calibrating the Radiocarbon Time Scale. *Radiocarbon* 24 (2): 103–150.

Levine, Mary Ann
1999 Native Copper in the Northeast: An Overview of Potential Sources Available to Indigenous People. In *The Archaeological Northeast*, edited by M. A. Levine, K. E. Sassaman, and M. S. Nassaney, pp. 183–199. Westport, CT: Bergin and Garvey.
2004a The Clauson Site: Late Archaic Settlement and Subsistence in the Uplands of Central New York. *Archaeology of Eastern North America* 32: 161–181.
2004b Overcoming Disciplinary Solitude: The Archaeology and Geology of Native Copper in Eastern North America. *Geoarchaeology* 19 (8).

Martin, Susan L.
1999 *Wonderful Power: The Story of Ancient Copper Working in the Lake Superior Basin.* Detroit, MI: Wayne State University Press.

Meltzer, D. J., and B. D. Smith
1986 Paleoindian and Early Archaic Subsistence Strategies in Eastern North America. In *Foraging, Collecting, and Harvesting: Archaic Period Subsistence and Settlement in the Eastern Woodlands*, edited by S. W. Neusius, pp. 3–31. Southern Illinois University Center for Archaeological Investigations Occasional Paper No. 6.

Nicholas, G. P.
1988 Ecological Leveling: The Archaeology and Environmental Dynamics of Early Postglacial Land Use. In *Holocene Human Ecology in Eastern North America*, edited by G. P. Nicholas, pp. 257–296. New York: Plenum.
1999 A Light but Lasting Footprint: Human Influences on the North-

eastern Landscape. In *The Archaeological Northeast*, edited by M. A. Levine, K. E. Sassaman, and M. S. Nassaney, pp. 25–38. Westport, CT: Bergin and Garvey.

O'Connell, J. F., Jones, K. T., and S. R. Simms
1982 Some Thoughts on Prehistoric Archaeology in the Great Basin. In *Man and Environment in the Great Basin*, edited by D. B. Madsen and J. F. O'Connell, pp. 227–240. Washington, DC: Society for American Archaeology, SAA Papers No. 2.

Peterson, James B., and Nancy Asch Sidell
1996 Mid-Holocene Evidence of *Cucurbita* sp. from Central Maine. *American Antiquity* 61: 685–698.

Raber, Paul A., Miller, Patricia E., and Sarah M. Neusius
1998 The Archaic Period in Pennsylvania: Current Models and Future Directions. In *The Archaic Period in Pennsylvania: Hunter-Gatherers of the Early and Middle Holocene Period*, edited by Paul A. Raber, Patricia E. Miller, and Sarah M. Neusius, pp. 121–137.

Sassaman, Kenneth E., and David G. Anderson, eds.
1996 *Archaeology of the Mid–Holocene Southeast.* Gainesville, FL: University of Florida Press.

Simms, Steven R.
1987 *Behavioral Ecology and Hunter-Gatherer Foraging: An Example from the Great Basin.* Oxford: British Archaeological Reports, International Series 381.

Smith, B. D.
1986 The Archaeology of the Southeastern United States: From Dalton to de Soto, 10,500–500 B.P. In *Advances in World Archaeology*, vol. 5, edited by F. Wendorf and A. E. Close, pp. 1–92. Orlando, FL: Academic Press.
1992 Prehistoric Plant Husbandry in Eastern North America. In *The Origins of Agriculture: An International Perspective*, edited by C. W. Cowan and P. J. Watson, pp. 101–119. Washington, DC: Smithsonian Institution Press.

Struever, S., and F. A. Holton
1979 *Koster: Americans in Search of Their Prehistoric Past.* Garden City, NY: Anchor/Doubleday.

Stuiver, M., and P. J. Reimer
1993 Extended ^{14}C Data Base and Revised CALIB 3.0 ^{14}C Age

Calibration Program. *Radiocarbon* 35: 215–230.

Thomas, D. H., Davis, J. O., Grayson, D. K., Melhorn, W. N., Thomas, Trudy, and D. T. Trexler
1983 *The Archaeology of Monitor Valley 2. Gatecliff Shelter*. New York: Anthropological Papers of the American Museum of Natural History, vol. 59 (1).

Webb, W. S.
1974 *Indian Knoll*. Knoxville, TN: University of Tennessee Press.

Wheat, Margaret M.
1967 *Survival Arts of the Primitive Paiutes*. Reno, NV: University of Nevada Press.

Willig, J. A.
1988 Paleo-Archaic Adaptations and Lakeside Settlement Patterns in the Northern Alkali Basin, Oregon. In Willig, J. A., Aikens, C. M., and Fagan J. L., eds., Early Human Occupation in Far Western North America: The Clovis-Archaic Interface. *Nevada State Museum Anthropological Papers* 21, Carson City, NV pp. 417–482.

Willey, G. R., and P. Phillips
1958 *Method and Theory in American Archaeology*. Chicago: University of Chicago Press.

Winters, Howard D.
1974 Introduction to the New Ed. In *Indian Knoll*, by William S. Webb, pp. v–xxvii. Knoxville, TN: University of Tennessee Press.

CHAPTER 15

Baruch, U., and S. Bottema
1991 Palynological Evidence for Climatic Changes in the Levant ca. 17,000–9,000 B.P. In *The Natufian Culture in the Levant*, edited by O. Bar-Yosef and F. R. Valla, pp. 11–20. Ann Arbor, MI: International Monographs in Prehistory.

Bender, Barbara
1978 Gatherer-Hunter to Farmer: A Social Perspective. *World Archaeology* 10: 204–222.

Binford, L. R.
1968 Post-Pleistocene Adaptations. In *New Perspectives in Archaeology*, edited by S. R. Binford and L. R. Binford, pp. 313–341. Chicago: Aldine.

Braidwood, R. J.
1975 *Prehistoric Men*, 8th ed. Glenview, IL.: Scott, Foresman and Co.

Braidwood, R. J., Howe, B., et al.
1960 *Prehistoric Investigations in Iraqi Kurdistan*. Chicago: University of Chicago Press.

Childe, V. G.
1929 *The Most Ancient East: The Oriental Prelude to European Prehistory*. New York: Alfred A. Knopf.
1936 *Man Makes Himself*. London: Watts.

Cohen, M.
1977 *The Food Crisis in Prehistory*. New Haven, CT: Yale University Press.

Crabtree, Pam J.
1993 Early Animal Domestication in the Near East and Europe. In *Archaeological Method and Theory*, vol. 5, edited by M. B. Schiffer. pp. 201–245. Tucson, AZ: University of Arizona Press.

Henry, Donald O.
1989 *From Foraging to Agriculture: The Levant at the End of the Ice Age*. Philadelphia: University of Pennsylvania Press.

Lee, R. B.
1968 What Hunters Do for a Living, or, How to Make Out on Scarce Resources. In *Man the Hunter*, edited by R. B. Lee and I. DeVore. pp. 30–48. Chicago: Aldine.

Marshall, F., and E. Hildebrand
2002 Cattle Before Crops: The Beginnings of Food Production in Africa. *Journal of World Prehistory* 16 (2): 99–143.

McCorriston, Joy, and Frank Hole
1991 The Ecology of Seasonal Stress and the Origins of Agriculture in the Near East. *American Anthropologist* 93 (1): 46–69.

Richerson, Peter J., Boyd, Robert, and Robert L. Bettinger
2001 Was Agriculture Impossible during the Pleistocene but Mandatory during the Holocene? A Climate Change Hypothesis. *American Antiquity* 66 (3): 387–411.

Tchernov, E.
1981 The Biostratigraphy of the Middle East. In *Colloques Internationaux du C.N.R.S. No. 598—Préhistoire du Levant*, pp. 67–97. Ed.s du C.N.R.S., Paris.

van Zeist, W.
1969 Reflections on Prehistoric Environments in the Near East. In *The Domestication and Exploitation of Plants and Animals*, edited by P. J. Ucko and G. W. Dimbleby, pp. 35–46. London: Aldine.

Zohary, D.
1969 The Progenitors of Wheat and Barley in Relation to Domestication and Agricultural Dispersal in the Old World. In *The Domestication and Exploitation of Plants and Animals*, edited by P. J. Ucko and G. W. Dimbleby, pp. 47–66. London: Aldine.

CHAPTER 16

Akkermans, P. A., et al.
1983 Bouqras Revisited: Preliminary Report on a Project in Eastern Syria. *Proceedings of the Prehistoric Society* 49: 335–372.

Bar-Yosef, O.
1998 The Natufian Culture in the Levant: Threshold to the Origins of Agriculture. *Evolutionary Anthropology* 6 (5): 159–177.

Bar-Yosef, O., and A. Belfer-Cohen
1989 The Origins of Sedentism and Farming Communities in the Levant. *Journal of World Prehistory* 3: 447–498.

Bar-Yosef, O., and M. E. Kislev
1989 Early Farming Communities in the Jordan Valley. In *Foraging and Farming: The Evolution of Plant Exploitation*, edited by D. R. Harris and G. C. Hillman, pp. 632–642. London: Unwin and Hyman.

Bar-Yosef, O., Gopher, A., Tchernov, E., and M. E. Kislev
1991 Netiv Hagdud: An Early Neolithic Village Site in the Jordan Valley. *Journal of Field Archaeology* 18: 405–424.

Bar-Yosef, O., and F. R. Valla, eds.
1991 *The Natufian Culture in the Levant*. Ann Arbor, MI: International Monographs in Prehistory.

Bender, B.
1978 Gatherer-Hunter to Farmer: A Social Perspective. *World Archaeology* 10: 204–222.

Bradley, Daniel G.
2003 Genetic Hoofprints. The DNA Trail Leading Back to the Origin of Today's Cattle. *Natural History* 112 (1): 36–41.

Bradley, D. G., Loftus, R. T., Cunningham, P., and D. E. MacHugh
1998 Genetics and Domestic Cattle Origins. *Evolutionary Anthropology* 6 (3): 79–86.

Braidwood, R. J., Howe, B., et al.
1960 *Prehistoric Investigations in Iraqi Kurdistan*. Chicago: University of Chicago Press.

Byrd, B. F.
1989 The Natufian: Settlement Variability and Economic Adaptations in the Levant at the End of the Pleistocene. *Journal of World Prehistory* 3 (2): 159–197.

Byrd, B. F., and C. M. Monahan
1995 Death, Mortuary Ritual, and Natufian Social Structure. *Journal of Anthropological Archaeology* 14: 251–287.

Campana, D. V., and P. J. Crabtree
1990 Communal Hunting in the Natufian of the Southern Levant: Social and Economic Implications. *Journal of Mediterranean Archaeology* 3: 223–243.

Childe, V. G.
1936 *Man Makes Himself*. London: Tavistock.

Clutton-Brock, J.
1979 The Mammalian Remains from Jericho Tell. *Proceedings of the Prehistoric Society* 45: 135–157.

Clutton-Brock, J., ed.
1989 *The Walking Larder: Patterns of Domestication, Pastoralism, and Predation*. London: Unwin Hyman.

Cohen, M.
1977 *The Food Crisis in Prehistory*. New Haven, CT: Yale University Press.

Crabtree, P. J.
1993 Early Animal Domestication in the Middle East and Europe. In *Archaeological Method and Theory*, vol. 5, edited by M. B. Schiffer, pp. 201–245.

Crawford, G. W.
1992 Prehistoric Plant Domestication in East Asia. In *The Origins of Agriculture: An International Perspective*, edited by C. W. Cowan and P. J. Watson, pp. 7–38. Washington, DC: Smithsonian Institution Press.

Davis, S. J. M.
1982 Climatic Change and the Advent of Domestication: The Succession of Ruminant Artiodactyls in the Late Pleistocene-Holocene in the Israel region. *Paléorient* 8: 5–15.

Davis, S. J. M., and F. Valla
1978 Evidence for Domestication of the Dog 12,000 Years Ago in the Natufian of Israel. *Nature* 276: 608–610.

Denham, T. P., Haberle, S., Lentfer, C., Fullagar, R., Field, J., Therin, M., Porch, N., and T. Winsborough
2003 Origins of Agriculture at Kuk Swamp in the Highlands of New Guinea. *Science* 301: 189–193.

Diamond, Jared
2002 Evolution, Consequences and Future of Plant and Animal Domestication. *Nature* 418: 700–707.

Edwards, P. C.
1989 Revising the Broad Spectrum Revolution and Its Role in Southeast Asian Food Production. *Antiquity* 63: 225–246.

Flannery, K. V.
1969 Origins and Ecological Effects of Early Domestication in Iran and the Near East. In *The Domestication and Exploitation of Plants and Animals*, edited by P. J. Ucko and G. W. Dimbleby, pp. 73–100. London: Duckworth.

Garrod, D.
1958 The Natufian Culture: The Life and Economy of a Mesolithic People in the Near East. *Proceedings of the British Academy* 43: 211–227.

Golson, J.
1977 No Room at the Top: Agricultural Intensification in the New Guinea Highlands. In *Sunda and Sahul: Prehistoric Studies in South-East Asia, Melanesia and Australia*, edited by J. Allen, J. Golson, and R. Jones, pp. 601–638. London: Academic Press.
1989 The Origins and Development of New Guinea Agriculture. In *Foraging and Farming: The Evolution of Plant Domestication*, edited by D. R. Harris and G. C. Hillman, pp. 678–687. London: Unwin Hyman.

Harlan, J. R.
1992 Indigenous African Agriculture. In *The Origins of Agriculture: An International Perspective*, edited by C. W. Cowan and P. J. Watson, pp. 59–70. Washington, DC: Smithsonian Institution Press.

Hecker, H. M.
1982 Domestication Revisited: Its Implications for Faunal Analysis. *Journal of Field Archaeology* 9: 217–236.

Henry, D.
1975 Fauna in Near Eastern Archaeological Deposits. In *Problems in Prehistory: North Africa and the Levant*, edited by F. Wendorf, pp. 379–385. Dallas, TX: Southern Methodist University Press.
1985 Preagricultural Sedentism: The Natufian Example. In *Prehistoric Hunter-Gatherers: The Emergence of Cultural Complexity*, edited by T. D. Price and J. A. Brown, pp. 365–383. Orlando, FL: Academic Press.

1989 *From Foraging to Agriculture: The Levant at the End of the Ice Age*. Philadelphia: University of Pennsylvania Press.

Hesse, B.
1984 These Are Our Goats: The Origins of Herding in West Central Iran. In *Animals and Archaeology: 3. Early Herders and Their Flocks*, edited by J. Clutton-Brock and C. Grigson, pp. 243–264. Oxford: British Archaeological Reports, International Series 202.

Hillman, G. C., and M. S. Davies
1990 Measured Domestication Rates in Wild Wheats and Barley under Primitive Conditions, and Their Archaeological Implications. *Journal of World Prehistory* 4: 157–222.

Hillman, G., Hedges, R., Moore, A., Colledge, S., and P. Pettit
2001 New Evidence of Lateglacial Cereal Cultivation on the Euphrates. *The Holocene* 11 (4): 383–393.

Hopf, M.
1983 Jericho Plant Remains. In *Excavations at Jericho V*, edited by K. M. Kenyon and T. A. Holland, pp. 576–621. London: British School of Archaeology in Jerusalem.

Kenyon, K. M.
1957 *Digging Up Jericho*. London: Ernest Benn.
1981 *Excavations at Jericho*, vol. 3. London: British School of Archaeology in Jerusalem.

Kenyon, K. M., and T. A. Holland
1983 *Excavations at Jericho*, vol. 5. London: British School of Archaeology in Jerusalem.

Köhler-Rollefson, I., Gillespie, W., and M. Metzger
1988 The Fauna from Neolithic 'Ain Ghazal. In *The Prehistory of Jordan: The State of Research in 1986*, edited by A. N. Garrard and N. H. Gebel, pp. 423–430. Oxford: British Archaeological Reports, International Series 396 (i).

Kuijt, Ian, and Nigel Goring-Morris
2002 Foraging, Farming, and Social Complexity in the Pre-Pottery Neolithic of the Southern Levant: A Review and Synthesis. *Journal of World Prehistory* 16 (4): 363–440.

Legge, A. J., and P. Rowley-Conwy
1987 Gazelle Killing in Stone Age Syria. *Scientific American 238* (8): 88–95.

Lieberman, D. E.
1993 The Rise and Fall of Seasonal Mobility Among Hunter-Gatherers:

The Case of the Southern Levant. *Current Anthropology* 34 (5): 599–631.

Marshall, F., and E. Hildebrand
2002 Cattle Before Crops: The Beginnings of Food Production in Africa. *Journal of World Prehistory* 16 (2): 99–143.

Moore, A. M. T.
1979 A Pre-Neolithic Farming Village on the Euphrates. *Scientific American* 241 (2): 62–70.
1991 Abu Hureyra 1 and the Antecedents of Agriculture on the Middle Euphrates. In *The Natufian Culture in the Levant*, edited by O. Bar-Yosef and F. R. Valla, pp. 277–294. Ann Arbor, MI: International Monographs in Prehistory.

Moore, A. M. T., Hillman, G. C., and A. J. Legge
2000 *Village on the Euphrates: From Foraging to Farming at Abu Hureyra*. New York: Oxford University Press.

Noy, T.
1989 Gilgal I. A Pre-Pottery Neolithic Site, Israel. The 1985–1987 Seasons. *Paléorient* 15(1): 15–22.

Noy, T., Schuldenrein, J., and E. Tchernov
1980 Gilgal, A Pre-Pottery Neolithic A Site on the Lower Jordan Valley. *Israel Exploration Journal* 30: 63–82.

Perkins, D., Jr.
1964 Prehistoric Fauna from Shanidar, Iraq. *Science* 144: 1565–1566.

Perrot, J.
1966 Le gisement Natoufien de Mallaha (Eynan), Israël. *L'Anthropologie* 70: 437–483.

Pringle, H.
1999 The Slow Birth of Agriculture. *Science* 282: 1446–1450.

Solecki, R. S.
1981 *An Early Village Site at Zawi Chemi Shanidar*. Biblioteca Mesopotamica 13. Malibu, CA: Undena Publications.

Tchernov, E.
1984 Commensal Animals and Human Sedentism in the Middle East. In *Animals and Archaeology: 3. Early Herders and Their Flocks*, edited by J. Clutton-Brock and C. Grigson, pp. 91–115. Oxford: British Archaeological Reports, International Series 202.
1994 *An Early Neolithic Village in the Jordan Valley. Part II: The Fauna of Netiv Hagdud*. American School of Prehistoric Research Bulletin 44. Cambridge: Peabody Museum of Archaeology and Ethnology, Harvard University.

Underhill, Anne P.
1997 Current Issues in Chinese Neolithic Archaeology. *Journal of World Prehistory* 11 (2): 103–160.

Wright, G. A.
1978 Social Differentiation in the Early Natufian. In *Social Archaeology: Beyond Subsistence and Dating*, edited by C. L. Redman, M.J. Berman, E. V. Curtin, W. J. Langhorne, N. M. Versaggi, and J. C. Wanser, pp. 201–233. New York: Academic Press.

Zhao, Zhijun
1998 The Middle Yangtze Region in China Is One Place Where Rice Was Domesticated: Phytolith Evidence from the Diatonghuan Cave, Northern Jiangxi. *Antiquity* 72 (278): 885–897.

Zohary, D.
1989 Domestication of Southwest Asian Neolithic Crop Assemblage of Cereals, Pulses, and Flax: The Evidence from Living Plants. In *Foraging and Farming, the Evolution of Plant Exploitation*, edited by D. R. Harris and G. C. Hillman, pp. 358–373. London: Unwin Hyman.

CHAPTER 17

Benz, Bruce F.
2001 Archaeological Evidence for Teosinte Domestication from Guilá Naquitz, Oaxaca. *Proceedings of the National Academy of Sciences* 98 (4): 2104–2106.

Bogucki, P. I.
1988 *Forest Farmers and Stockherders: Early Agriculture and Its Consequences in North-Central Europe*. Cambridge: Cambridge University Press.

Clutton-Brock, J.
1981 *Domesticated Animals from Early Times*. Austin, TX: University of Texas Press.

Cohen, M. N.
1977 *The Food Crisis in Prehistory: Overpopulation and the Origins of Agriculture*. New Haven, CT: Yale University Press.

Cowan, C. W., and P. J. Watson, eds.
1992 *The Origins of Agriculture: An International Perspective*. Washington, DC: Smithsonian Institution Press.

Doebley, John
1990 Molecular Evidence and the Evolution of Maize. In *New Perspectives on the Origin and Evolution of New World Domesticated Plants*, edited by P. K. Bretting, pp. 6–28. *Economic Botany* 44 (supplement).

Flannery, K. V.
1968 Archaeological Systems Theory and Early Mesoamerica. In *Anthropological Archaeology in the Americas*, edited by B. Meggers, pp. 67–87. Washington, DC: Anthropological Society of Washington.

Fritz, G. J.
1994 Are the First American Farmers Getting Younger? *Current Anthropology* 35 (3): 305–309.

Gebauer, A. B., and T. D. Price, eds.
1992a *Transitions to Agriculture in Prehistory*. Madison, WI: Prehistory Press, Monographs in World Prehistory No. 4.
1992b Foragers to Farmers: An Introduction. In *Transitions to Agriculture in Prehistory*, edited by A. B. Gebauer and T. D. Price, pp. 1–10. Madison, WI: Prehistory Press, Monographs in World Prehistory No. 4.

Hardy, Karen
1996 The Preceramic Sequence from the Tehuacán Valley: A Reevaluation. *Current Anthropology* 37 (4): 700–716.

Long, Austin, Benz, Bruce F., Donahue, J., Jull, A., and L. Toolin
1989 First Direct AMS Dates on Early Maize from Tehuacán, Mexico. *Radiocarbon* 31: 1035–1040.

MacNeish, R. S.
1967 A Summary of the Subsistence. In *The Prehistory of the Tehuacán Valley, vol. 1: Environment and Subsistence*, edited by D. Byers, pp. 290–309. Austin, TX: University of Texas Press.
1991 *The Origin of Agriculture and Settled Life*. Norman, OK: University of Oklahoma Press.

Mangelsdorf, P. C.
1974 *Corn: Its Origin, Evolution and Improvement*. Cambridge: Harvard University Press.
1986 The Origin of Corn. *Scientific American* 254 (2): 72–79.

Marshall, F., and E. Hildebrand
2002 Cattle Before Crops: The Beginnings of Food Production in Africa. *Journal of World Prehistory* 16 (2): 99–143.

McClung de Tapia, Emily
1992 The Origins of Agriculture in Mesoamerica and Central America. In *The Origins of Agriculture: An International Perspective*, edited by C. W. Cowan and P. J. Watson, pp. 143–171. Washington, DC: Smithsonian Institution Press.

Pearsall, D. M.
1992 The Origins of Plant Cultivation in South America. In *The Origins of Agriculture: An International Perspective*, edited by C. W. Cowan and P. J. Watson, pp. 173–205. Washington, DC: Smithsonian Institution Press.

Piperno, D. M.
1988 *Phytolith Analysis: An Archaeological and Geological Perspective*. San Diego, CA: Academic.
2001 On Maize and the Sunflower. *Science* 292: 2260–2261.

Piperno, D. R., and D. M. Pearsall
1993 The Nature and Status of Phytolith Analysis. In *Current Research in Phytolith Analysis: Applications in Archaeology and Paleoecology*, edited by D. M. Pearsall and D. R. Piperno, pp. 9–18. MASCA Research Papers in Science and Archaeology, 10. Philadelphia: University Museum.

Piperno, D. R., and K. V. Flannery
2001 The Earliest Archaeological Maize (*Zea mays* L.) from Highland Mexico: New Accelerator Mass Spectrometry Dates and Their Implications. *Proceedings of the National Academy of Sciences* 98 (4): 2102–2103.

Piperno, D. R., Ranere, A. J., Holst, I., and P. Hansell
2000 Starch Grains Reveal Early Root Crop Horticulture in the Panamanian Tropical Forest. *Nature* 2000: 894–897.

Pope, Kevin O., Pohl, Mary D., Jones, John G., Lentz, David L., von Nagy, Christopher, Vega, Francisco J., and Irvy R. Quitmyer
2001 Origin and Environmental Setting of Ancient Agriculture in the Lowlands of Mesoamerica. *Science* 292: 1370–1373.

Price, T. D., and A. B. Gebauer
1995 *Last Hunters–First Farmers: New Perspectives on the Prehistoric Transition to Agriculture*. Santa Fe, NM: School of American Research.

Smith, B. D.
1992 Prehistoric Plant Husbandry in Eastern North America. In *The Origins of Agriculture: An International Perspective*, edited by C. W. Cowan and P. J. Watson, pp. 101–119. Washington, DC: Smithsonian Institution Press.
1994 *The Emergence of Agriculture*. New York: Scientific American Library.
1997 The Initial Domestication of *Cucurbita pepo* in the Americas 10,000 years ago. *Science* 276: 932–934.
2001 Documenting Plant Domestication: The Consilience of Biological and Archaeological Approaches. *Proceedings of the National Academy of Sciences* 98 (4): 1324–1326.

Staller, J. E.
2002 A Multidisciplinary Approach to Understanding the Initial Introduction of Maize into Coastal Ecuador. *Journal of Archaeological Science* 29: 33–50.
2003 An Examination of the Paleobotanical and Chronological Evidence for an Early Introduction of Maize (*Zea mays* L.) into South America: A Response to Pearsall. *Journal of Archaeological Science* 30 (3): 373–380.

Vrydaghs, L., Swennen, R. R., Mbida, C., Doutrelepont, H., De Langhe, E., and P. De Maret
2003 The Banana Phytolith as a Direct Marker of Early Agriculture: A Review of the Evidence. In *Phytolith and Starch Research in the Australian-Pacific-Asian Regions: The State of the Art*, edited by D. M. Hart and L. A. Wallis, pp. 177–185. Terra Australis 19. Canberra, Australia: Pandanus Books.

Wheeler, Jane C.
1984 On the Origin and Early Development of Camelid Pastoralism in the Andes. In *Animals and Archaeology: 3. Early Herders and Their Flocks*, edited by J. Clutton-Brock and C. Grigson, pp. 395–410. Oxford: British Archaeological Reports, International Series 202.

CHAPTER 18

Balter, M.
1998 Why Settle Down? The Mystery of Communities. *Science* 282: 1442–1445.

Bentley, R. A., Price, T. D., Lünning, J., Gronenborn, D., Wahl, J., and P. B. Fullagar
2002 Prehistoric Migration in Europe: Strontium Isotope Analysis of Early Neolithic Skeletons. *Current Anthropology* 43 (5): 799–804.

Bentley, R. A., Krause, R., Price, T. D., and B. Kaufmann
2003 Human Mobility at the Early Neolithic Settlement of Vaihingen, Germany: Evidence from Strontium Isotope Analysis. *Archaeometry* 45 (3): 471–486.

Bogucki, P. I.
1988 *Forest Farmers and Stockherders: Early Agriculture and Its Consequences in North-Central Europe*. Cambridge: Cambridge University Press.
1996 The Spread of Early Farming in Europe. *American Scientist* 84: 242–253.
2004 Brześć Kujawski. In *Ancient Europe 8000 B.C.–A.D. 1000: Encyclopedia of the Barbarian World*, edited by Peter Bogucki and Pam J. Crabtree, pp. 378–382. New York: Charles Scribner's Sons.

Bogucki, Peter, and Pam J. Crabtree, eds.
2004 *Ancient Europe 8000 B.C.–A.D. 1000: Encyclopedia of the Barbarian World*. New York: Charles Scribner's Sons.

Bogucki, P. I., and R. Grygiel
1983 Early Farmers on the North European Plain. *Scientific American* 248 (4): 104–112.
1993 Neolithic Sites in the Polish Lowlands: Research at Brześć Kujawski, 1933 to 1984. In *Case Studies in European Prehistory*, edited by P. I. Bogucki, pp. 147–180. Boca Raton, FL: CRC Press.

Bordaz, J.
1970 *Tools of the Old and New Stone Age*. Garden City, NY: Natural History Press.

Budja, M.
2004 Transition to Farming in the Balkans. In *Ancient Europe 8000 B.C–A.D. 1000: Encyclopedia of the Barbarian World*, edited by Peter Bogucki and Pam J. Crabtree, pp. 233–242. New York: Charles Scribner's Sons.

Cessford, C.
2001 A New Dating Sequence for Çatalhöyük. *Antiquity* 75 (290): 717–725.

Dennell, R. W.
1992 The Origins of Crop Agriculture in Europe. In *The Origins of Agriculture: An International Perspective*, edited by C. W. Cowan and P. J. Watson, pp. 71–100.

Washington, DC: Smithsonian Institution Press.

Diamond, Jared
1997 *Guns, Germs, and Steel: The Fates of Human Societies*. New York: Norton.

Keeley, L. H., and M. Golitko
2004 First Farmers of Central Europe. In *Ancient Europe 8000 B.C.–A.D. 1000: Encyclopedia of the Barbarian World*, edited by Peter Bogucki and Pam J. Crabtree, pp. 259–266. New York: Charles Scribner's Sons.

Keeley, L. H., and R. S. Quick
2004 Warfare and Conquest. In *Ancient Europe 8000 B.C.–A.D. 1000: Encyclopedia of the Barbarian World*, edited by Peter Bogucki and Pam J. Crabtree, pp. 110–118. New York: Charles Scribner's Sons.

Kenyon, Kathleen
1957 *Digging Up Jericho*. London: E. Benn.
1970 *Archaeology in the Holy Land*, 3rd ed. New York: Praeger.

Kuijt, Ian, and Nigel Goring-Morris
2002 Foraging, Farming, and Social Complexity in the Pre-Pottery Neolithic of the Southern Levant: A Review and Synthesis. *Journal of World Prehistory* 16 (4): 361–440.

Larsen, C. S.
1995 Biological Changes in Human Populations with Agriculture. *Annual Review of Anthropology* 24: 185–213.

Larsen, C. S., Heun, M., Schäfer-Pregl, R., Klawan, D., Castagna, R., Accerbi, M., Borghi, B., and F. Salamini
1997 Site of Einkorn Wheat Identified by DNA Fingerprinting. *Science* 278: 1312–1314.

Mellaart, James
1967 *Çatal Hüyük: A Neolithic Town in Anatolia*. London: Thames & Hudson.
1975 *The Neolithic of the Near East*. New York: Charles Scribner's Sons.

Price, T. D., Bentley, R. A., Gronenborn, D., Lünning, J., and J. Wahl
2001 Human Migration in the Linearbandkeramik of Central Europe. *Antiquity* 75: 593–603.

Price, T. D., Burton, J. H., and R. A. Bentley
2002 The Characterization of Biologically Available Strontium Isotope Ratios for the Study of Prehistoric Migration. *Archaeometry* 44 (1): 117–135.

Renfrew, Colin
1987 *Archaeology and Language*: The Puzzle of Indo-European Origins. London: Cape.
1989 The Origins of Indo–European Languages. *Scientific American* 261 (4): 106–114.

Rodden, R. J.
1962 Excavations at the Early Neolithic Site of Nea Nikomedeia, Greek Macedonia. *Proceedings of the Prehistoric Society* 28: 267–288.
1965 An Early Neolithic Village in Greece. *Scientific American* 212 (4): 82–92.

Rollefson, G. O., Simmons, A. H., and Z. Kafafi
1992 Neolithic Cultures at 'Ain Ghazal, Jordan. *Journal of Field Archaeology* 19 (4): 443–470.

Rosenberg, M., Nesbitt, R., Redding, R. W., and B. L. Peasnall
1998 Hallan Çemi, Pig Husbandry, and Post-Pleistocene Adaptations along the Taurus-Zagros Arc (Turkey). *Paléorient* 24 (1): 25–41.

Runnels, Curtis
2004 First Farmers of Europe. In *Ancient Europe 8000 B.C.–A.D. 1000: Encyclopedia of the Barbarian World*, edited by Peter Bogucki and Pam J. Crabtree, pp. 218–226. New York: Charles Scribner's Sons.

Van Zeist, W.
1972 Paleobotanical Results of the 1970 Season at Çayönü, Turkey. *Helinium* 12: 3–19.

Voigt, M. M.
1985 Village on the Euphrates: Excavations at Neolithic Gritille in Turkey. *Exped.* 27 (1): 10–24.

Whittle, Alasdair
1985 *Neolithic Europe: A Survey*. Cambridge: Cambridge University Press.
1996 *Europe in the Neolithic: The Creation of New Worlds*. Cambridge: Cambridge University Press.

CHAPTER 19

Adams, Robert McC.
1981 *Heartland of Cities: Surveys of Ancient Settlement and Land Use on the Central Floodplain of the Euphrates*. Chicago: University of Chicago Press.

Adams, Robert McC., and Hans J. Nissen
1972 *The Uruk Countryside: The Natural Setting of Urban Societies*. Chicago: University of Chicago Press.

Aurenche, O., Galet, P., Régagnon-Caroline, R., and J. Évin
2001 Proto-Neolithic and Neolithic Cultures in the Middle East—The Birth of Agriculture, Livestock Raising, and Ceramics: A Calibrated ^{14}C Chronology 12,500–5500 cal B.C. *Radiocarbon* 43: 1191–1202.

Brumfiel, Elizabeth
1992 Distinguished Lecture in Archaeology: Breaking and Entering the Ecosystem—Gender, Class, and Faction Steal the Show. *American Anthropologist* 94: 551–567.

Childe, V. Gordon
1957 *New Light on the Most Ancient East*. New York: Grove Press.

Crawford, Harriet
1991 *Sumer and the Sumerians*. Cambridge: Cambridge University Press.

Crumley, Carole L.
1995 Heterarchy and the Analysis of Complex Societies. In *Heterarchy and the Analysis of Complex Societies*, edited by Robert M. Erenreich, Carole L. Crumley, and Janet E. Levy, pp. 1–6. Archaeological Papers of the American Anthropological Association, no. 6. Washington, DC: American Anthropological Association.

Delle, James A., Mrozowski, Stephen A., and Robert Paynter
2000 *Lines That Divide: Historical Archaeologies of Race, Class, and Gender*. Knoxville, TN: University of Tennessee Press.

El-Baz, Farouk
1997 Space Age Archaeology. *Scientific American* 277 (2): 60–65.

Gailey, Christine Ward
1987 *Kinship to Kingship: Gender Hierarchy and State Formation in the Tongan Islands*. Austin, TX: University of Texas Press.

Helbaek, Hans
1965 Early Hassunan Vegetable Food at Tell as-Sawwan near Samarra. *Sumer* 20: 45–48.

Johnson, Allen W., and Timothy Earle
1987 *The Evolution of Human Societies: From Foraging Group to Agrarian State*. Stanford, CA: Stanford University Press.

Johnson, Gregory A.
1973 *Local Exchange and Early State Development in Southwestern Iran*. Anthropological Papers No. 51, Ann Arbor, MI: Museum of Anthropology, University of Michigan.

Lloyd, Seton
1984 *The Archaeology of Mesopotamia, from the Old Stone Age to the Persian Conquest*. London: Thames and Hudson.
Maisels, Charles Keith
1993 *The Near East: Archaeology in the 'Cradle of Civilization.'* London and New York: Routledge.
Mallowan, M. E. L.
1967 The Development of Cities from Al-'Ubaid to the End of Uruk 5, Parts I and II. In *The Cambridge Ancient History*, Cambridge: Cambridge University Press.
1968 The Early Dynastic Period in Mesopotamia. In *The Cambridge Ancient History*, Cambridge: Cambridge University Press.
McGuire, R. H.
1983 Breaking Down Cultural Complexity: Inequality and Heterogeneity. In *Advances in Archaeological Method and Theory*, vol. 6, edited by M. B. Schiffer, pp. 91–142. New York: Academic Press.
Pollack, Susan
1999 *Ancient Mesopotamia*. Cambridge: Cambridge University Press.
Redman, Charles L.
1978 *The Rise of Civilization from Early Farmers to Urban Society in the Ancient Near East*. San Francisco: W. H. Freeman and Company.
Stein, Gil J.
1999 *Rethinking World Systems: Diasporas, Colonies, and Interaction in Uruk Mesopotamia*. Tucson, AZ: University of Arizona Press.
Wittfogel, Karl A.
1957 *Oriental Despotism: A Comparative Study of Total Power*. New Haven, CT: Yale University Press.
Woolley, Sir Leonard
1965 *Excavations at Ur*. New York: Thomas Y. Crowell Company.
Yoffee, Norman
1995 Political Economy of Early Mesopotamian States. *Annual Review of Anthropology* 24: 281–311.
Zeder, M. A.
1991 *Feeding Cities: Specialized Animal Economy in the Ancient Near East*. Washington DC: Smithsonian Institution Press.

CHAPTER 20

Allchin, F. R.
1982 The Legacy of the Indus Civilization. In *Harappan Civilization:*
A Contemporary Perspective, edited by G. L. Possehl, pp. 325–333. Warminster, UK: Aris and Phillips.
Allchin, B., and R. Allchin
1982 *The Rise of Civilization in India and Pakistan*. Cambridge: Cambridge University Press.
Ansari, Massound
2003 Letter from Baluchistan: The Guns of Mehrgarh. *Archaeology* 56 (2).
Dales, George F.
1992 Project Director's Introduction. In *Harappa Excavations 1986–1990: A Multidisciplinary Approach to Third Millennium Urbanism*, edited by R. H. Meadow, pp. 1–4. Madison, WI: Prehistory Press, Monographs in World Archaeology No. 3.
Fairservis, Walter A.
1971 *The Roots of Ancient India: The Archaeology of Early Indian Civilization*. New York: Macmillan.
1983 The Script of the Indus Valley Civilization. *Scientific American* 248 (3): 58–66.
Jarrige, C., Jarrige, J.-F., Meadow, R. H., and G. Quiveron
1995 *Mehrgarh: Field Reports 1974–1985 from Neolithic Times to the Indus Civilization*. Karachi, Pakistan: Government of Sindh, Pakistan, Department of Culture and Tourism.
Jarrige, J.-F. and R. H. Meadow
1980 The antecedents of civilization in the Indus Valley. *Scientific American* 243 (2): 122–133.
Kenoyer, Jonathan Mark
1992 Urban Process in the Indus Tradition: A Preliminary Model from Harappa. In *Harappa Excavations 1986–1990: A Multidisciplinary Approach to Third Millennium Urbanism*, edited by R. H. Meadow, pp. 29–60. Madison, WI: Prehistory Press, Monographs in World Archaeology No. 3.
1998 *Ancient Cities of the Indus Valley Civilization*. Oxford: American Institute of Pakistan Studies.
Meadow, R. H.
1993 Animal Domestication in the Middle East: A Revised View from the Eastern Margin. In *Harappan Civilization: A Recent Perspective*, 2nd ed., edited by G. L. Possehl, pp. 295–320. New Delhi: American Institute of Indian Studies.
Parpola, Asko
1994 *Deciphering the Indus Script*. Cambridge: Cambridge University Press.
Possehl, G. L.
1990 Revolution in the Urban Revolution: The Emergence of Indus
Urbanization. *Annual Review of Anthropology* 19: 261–282.
1996 *Indus Age: The Writing System*. Philadelphia: University of Pennsylvania Press.
2002 *The Indus Civilization: A Contemporary Perspective*. Walnut Creek, CA: Altamira Press.
Possehl, G. L., and M. H. Raval
1989 *The Harappan Civilization and Rojdi*. Leiden, The Netherlands, and New York: E. J. Brill.
Wheeler, R. E. M.
1968 *The Indus Civilization*, 3rd ed. Cambridge: Cambridge University Press.

CHAPTER 21

Adams, Barbara
1988 *Predynastic Egypt*. Aylesbury, England: Shire Egyptology.
Adams, R. M.
1966 *The Evolution of Urban Society: Early Mesopotamia and Prehispanic Mexico*. Chicago: Aldine.
Bard, Kathryn A.
1994 The Egyptian Predynastic: A Review of the Evidence. *Journal of Field Archaeology* 21: 265–288.
Baumgartel, E. J.
1965 Predynastic Egypt, in *The Cambridge Ancient History*, vol. 1, Chapter IX. Cambridge: Cambridge University Press.
Brewer, Douglas J., and Emily Teeter
1999 *Egypt and the Egyptians*. Cambridge: Cambridge University Press.
Butzer, K. W.
1958 *Quaternary Stratigraphy and Climate in the Near East*. Bonn, Germany: F. Dummlers Verlag.
Caneva, I., Frangipane, M., and A. Palmieri
1987 Predynastic Egypt: New Data from Maadi. *African Archaeological Review* 5: 105–114.
Caton-Thompson, G., and E. W. Gardner
1934 *The Desert Fayum*. London: The Royal Anthropological Institute of Great Britain and Ireland.
Connah, Graham
2001 *African Civilizations: An Archaeological Perspective*, 2nd ed. Cambridge: Cambridge University Press.
Deetz, James
1967 *Invitation to Archaeology*. Garden City, NY: The Natural History Press.
Hoffman, M. A.
1982 *The Predynastic of Hierakonpolis. An Interim Report*. Cairo: Egyptian Studies Association Publication No. 1.

Hoffman, M. A., Hamroush, H. A., and R. A. Allen
1986 A Model of Urban Development for the Hierakonpolis Region from Predynastic through Old Kingdom Times. *Journal of the American Research Center in Egypt* 23: 175–187.

Kemp, Barry J.
1989 *Ancient Egypt: Anatomy of a Civilization*. London: Routledge.

Kendall, David G.
1969 Some problems and methods in statistical archaeology. *World Archaeology* 1: 68–76.

Marshall, Fiona, and Elisabeth Hildebrand
2002 Cattle Before Crops: The Beginnings of Food Production in Africa. *Journal of World Prehistory* 16 (2): 99–143.

McIntosh, S. K.
1999 Modeling Political Organization in Large-Scale Settlement Clusters: A Case Study from the Inland Niger Delta. In *Beyond Chiefdoms: Pathways to Complexity in Africa*, edited by S. K. McIntosh, pp. 66–79. Cambridge: Cambridge University Press.

McIntosh, S. K., ed.
1995 *Excavations at Jenné-Jeno, Hambarketolo, and Kaniana (Inland Niger Delta, Mali), the 1981 Season*. University of California Publications in Anthropology, volume 20. Berkeley, CA: University of California Press.

McIntosh, S. K., and R. J. McIntosh
1980 *Prehistoric Investigations in the Region of Jenne, Mali: A Study in the Development of Urbanism in the Sahel*, Parts 1 and 2. Cambridge Monographs in African Archaeology 2. British Archaeological Reports International Series 89. Oxford: British Archaeological Reports.

O'Connor, David
1993 *Ancient Nubia: Egypt's Rival in Africa*. Philadelphia: The University Museum.

Petrie, W. M. Flinders
1899 Sequences in Prehistoric Remains. *Journal of the Anthropological Institute of Great Britain and Ireland.*, vol. XXIX (New Series vol. II): 295–301.

Service, Elman R.
1975 *Origins of the State and Civilization: The Process of Cultural Evolution*. New York: Norton.

CHAPTER 22

Chang, Kwang-chih
1980 *Shang Civilization*. New Haven: Yale University Press.
1986 *The Archaeology of Ancient China*, 4th ed. New Haven: Yale University Press.

Crawford, G. W.
1992 Prehistoric Plant Domestication in East Asia. In *The Origins of Agriculture: An International Perspective*, edited by C. W. Cowan and P. J. Watson, pp. 7–38. Washington, DC: Smithsonian Institution Press.

Dazhong, Wen, and David Pimentel
1996 Seventeenth-Century Organic Agriculture in China. In *Case Studies in Human Ecology*, edited by Daniel G. Bates and Susan H. Lees, pp. 311–325. New York: Plenum.

Fogg, Wayne H.
1983 Swidden Cultivation of Foxtail Millet by Taiwan Aborigines: A Cultural Analogue of the Domestication of *Setaria italica* in China. In *The Origins of Chinese Civilization*, edited by David N. Keightley, pp. 95–115. Berkeley and Los Angeles: University of California Press.

Hoh, Erling
2001 China Great Enigma. What's Inside the Unexcavated Tomb of Emperor Qin Shihuangdi? *Archaeology* 54 (5): 34–37.

Keightley, David N.
1983 The Late Shang State: When, Where, and What? In *The Origins of Chinese Civilization*, edited by David N. Keightley, pp. 523–564. Berkeley and Los Angeles: University of California Press.

Underhill, Anne P.
1997 Current Issues in Chinese Neolithic Archaeology. *Journal of World Prehistory* 11 (2): 103–160.

2002 *Craft Production and Social Change in Northern China*. New York: Plenum.

Wicker, Nancy
2004 Pre-Viking and Viking Age Sweden. In *Ancient Europe: 8000 B.C.–A.D. 1000: Encyclopedia of the Barbarian World*, edited by Peter Bogucki and Pam J. Crabtree, pp. 537–541. New York: Charles Scribner's Sons.

Yang, Xiaoneng, ed.
1999 *The Golden Age of Chinese Archaeology: Celebrated Discoveries from the People's Republic of China*. New Haven, CT: Yale University Press.

CHAPTER 23

Arnold, Bettina
2004 The Heuneberg. In *Ancient Europe 8000 B.C.–A.D. 1000: Encyclopedia of the Barbarian World*, edited by Peter Bogucki and Pam J. Crabtree, vol. 2, pp. 249–252. New York: Charles Scribner's Sons.

Bailey, Douglass
2004 Varna. In *Ancient Europe 8000 B.C.–A.D. 1000: Encyclopedia of the Barbarian World*, edited by Peter Bogucki and Pam J. Crabtree, vol. 1, pp. 341–344. New York: Charles Scribner's Sons.

Bintliff, J.
1984 Iron Age Europe, in the Context of Social Evolution from the Bronze Age through to Historic Times. In *European Social Evolution*, edited by John Bintliff, pp. 157–225. Bradford, England: University of Bradford.

Boardman, J.
1980 *The Greeks Overseas: Their Early Colonies and Trade*, 3rd ed. London: Thames and Hudson.

Bogucki, P. I.
1988 *Forest Farmers and Stockherders: Early Agriculture and its Consequences in North-Central Europe*. Cambridge: Cambridge University Press.

Bogucki, Peter, ed.
1993 *Case Studies in European Prehistory*. Boca Raton, FL: CRC Press.

Bogucki, Peter, and Pam J. Crabtree, eds.
2004 *Ancient Europe 8000 B.C.–A.D. 1000: Encyclopedia of the Barbarian World*. New York: Charles Scribner's Sons.

Champion, T., Gamble, C., Shennan S., and A. Whittle
1984 *Prehistoric Europe*. Orlando, FL: Academic Press.

Collis, John
2004 Oppida. In *Ancient Europe 8000 B.C.–A.D. 1000: Encyclopedia of the Barbarian World*, edited by Peter Bogucki and Pam J. Crabtree, vol. 2, pp. 154–157. New York: Charles Scribner's Sons.

Cunliffe, B., ed.
1998 *Prehistoric Europe: An Illustrated History*. Oxford and New York: Oxford University Press.

Hamilton, Elizabeth
1996 *Technology and Social Science in Belgic Gaul: Copper Working at the Titelberg, Luxembourg, 125 B.C.–A.D. 300*. MASCA Papers in Science and Archaeology 13. Philadelphia: The University Museum.

Kimmig, W.
1975 Early Celts on the Upper Danube: The Excavations at the Heuneberg. In *Recent Archaeological Excavations in Europe*, edited by R. Bruce-Mitford, pp. 32–64. London: Routledge Kegan Paul.

Jovanovic, B.
1980 The Origins of Copper Mining in Europe. *Scientific American* 242 (5): 152–167.

Malin-Boyce, Susan
2004a Hallstatt and La Tène. In *Ancient Europe 8000 B.C.–A.D. 1000: Encyclopedia of the Barbarian World*, edited by Peter Bogucki and Pam J. Crabtree, vol. 2, pp. 144–148. New York: Charles Scribner's Sons.
2004b Celts. In *Ancient Europe 8000 B.C.–A.D. 1000: Encyclopedia of the Barbarian World*, edited by Peter Bogucki and Pam J. Crabtree, vol. 2, pp. 140–143. New York: Charles Scribner's Sons.
2004c Manching. In *Ancient Europe 8000 B.C.–A.D. 1000: Encyclopedia of the Barbarian World*, edited by Peter Bogucki and Pam J. Crabtree, vol. 2, pp. 158–159. New York: Charles Scribner's Sons.

Mallone, Caroline
2004 Stonehenge. In *Ancient Europe 8000 B.C.–A.D. 1000: Encyclopedia of the Barbarian World*, edited by Peter Bogucki and Pam J. Crabtree, vol. 2, pp. 61–67. New York: Charles Scribner's Sons.

Milisauskas, S., and J. Kruk
1993 Archaeological Investigations on Neolithic and Bronze Age Sites in Southeastern Poland. In *Case Studies in European Prehistory*, edited by Peter Bogucki, pp. 63–94. Boca Raton, FL: CRC Press.

Pearce, Mark
2004 The Significance of Bronze. In *Ancient Europe 8000 B.C.–A.D. 1000: Encyclopedia of the Barbarian World*, edited by Peter Bogucki and Pam J. Crabtree, vol. 2, pp. 6–11. New York: Charles Scribner's Sons.

Renfrew, Colin
1972 *Before Civilization: The Radiocarbon Revolution and Prehistoric Europe*. Cambridge: Cambridge University Press.

Spindler, Konrad
1994 *The Man in the Ice*. New York: Crown.

Vandkilde, H.
1996 *From Stone to Bronze: The Metalwork of the Late Neolithic and Earliest Bronze Age in Denmark*. Aarhus: Jutland Archaeological Society.

Wells, Peter S.
1980 *Culture Contact and Culture Change: Early Iron Age Central Europe and the Mediterranean World*. Cambridge: Cambridge University Press.
1984 *Farms, Villages, and Cities: Commerce and Urban Origins in Late Prehistoric Europe*. Ithaca, NY: Cornell University Press.
1987 Industry, Commerce, and Temperate Europe's First Cities: Preliminary Report on 1987 Excavations at Kelheim, Bavaria. *Journal of Field Archaeology* 14: 399–412.
1993 *Settlement, Economy, and Cultural Change at the End of the European Iron Age: Excavations at Kelheim in Bavaria, 1987–1991*. Ann Arbor, MI: International Monographs in Prehistory, Archaeological Series No. 6.
2004a Greek Colonies in the West. In *Ancient Europe 8000 B.C.–A.D. 1000: Encyclopedia of the Barbarian World*, edited by Peter Bogucki and Pam J. Crabtree, vol. 2, pp. 198–204. New York: Charles Scribner's Sons.
2004b Kelheim. In *Ancient Europe 8000 B.C.–A.D. 1000: Encyclopedia of the Barbarian World*, edited by Peter Bogucki and Pam J. Crabtree, vol. 2, pp. 247–249. New York: Charles Scribner's Sons.

Whittle, A.
1996 *Europe in the Neolithic: The Creation of New Worlds*. Cambridge: Cambridge University Press.

CHAPTER 24

Adams, R. McC., and H. J. Nissen
1972 *The Uruk Countryside: The Natural Setting of Urban Societies*. Chicago: University of Chicago Press.

Blanton, Richard E., Kowalewski, Stephen A., Feinman, Gary M., and Laura M. Finsten
1993 *Ancient Mesoamerica: A Comparison of Change in Three Regions*. 2nd ed. Cambridge: Cambridge University Press.

Coe, Michael D.
1999a *The Maya*, 6th ed. New York: Thames and Hudson.
1999b *Breaking the Maya Code*, revised ed. New York: Thames and Hudson.

Conrad, G. W., and A. A. Demarest
1984 *Religion and Empire: The Dynamics of Aztec and Inca Expansionism*. Cambridge: Cambridge University Press.

Culbert, T. Patrick
1985 The Maya Enter History. *Natural History* 85 (4): 42–49.
1988 The Collapse of Classic Maya Civilization. In *The Collapse of Ancient States and Civilizations*, edited by N. Yoffee and G. Cowgill, pp. 69–101. Tucson, AZ: University of Arizona Press.
1993 *Maya Civilization*. Washington, DC: Smithsonian Books.

Culbert, T.P., Kosakowsky, L. J., Fry, R. E., and W. A. Haviland
1991 The Population of Tikal Guatemala. *Precolumbian Population History in the Maya Lowlands*, edited by T. P. Culbert and D. S. Rice, pp. 103–121. Albuquerque, NM: University of New Mexico Press.

Grove, David C.
1997 Olmec Archaeology: A Half Century of Research and Its Accomplishments. *Journal of World Prehistory* 11: 51–101.

Hammond, Norman
1991 *Cuello: An Early Maya Community in Belize*. Cambridge: Cambridge University Press.

Hammond, Norma, Clarke, Amanda, and Sara Donaghey
1995 The Long Goodbye: Middle Preclassic Maya Archaeology at Cuello, Belize. *Latin American*

Antiquity 6 (2): 120–128.

Hendon, Julia A., and Rosemary A. Joyce, eds.
2004 *Mesoamerican Archaeology: Theory and Practice*. Oxford: Blackwell.

Lesure, Richard G.
2004 Shared Art Styles and Long-Distance Contact in Early Mesoamerica. In *Mesoamerican Archaeology: Theory and Practice*, edited by Julia A. Hendon and Rosemary A. Joyce, pp. 73–96. Oxford: Blackwell.

Manzanilla, Linda
2004 In *Mesoamerican Archaeology: Theory and Practice*, edited by Julia A. Hendon and Rosemary A. Joyce, pp. 124–127. Oxford: Blackwell.

Marcus, Joyce
1993 Ancient Maya Political Organization. In *Lowland Maya Civilization in the Eighth Century A.D.*, edited by J. A. Sabloff and J.S. Henderson, pp. 111–171. Washington, DC: Dumbarton Oaks.

Marcus, Joyce, and Kent V. Flannery
1996 *Zapotec Civilization: How Urbanism Evolved in Mexico's Oaxaca Valley*. New York: Thames and Hudson.

Matheny, Ray T.
1986 Investigations at El Mirador, Peten, Guatemala. *National Geographic Research Reports* 2 (3): 332–353.
1987 El Mirador: An Early Maya Metropolis Uncovered. *National Geographic* September: 317–339.

Millon, Rene
1981 Teotihuacan: City, State, and Civilization. In *Supplement to the Handbook of Middle American Indians, Volume 1, Archaeology*, edited by J.A. Sabloff, pp. 198–243. Austin, TX: University of Texas Press.
1967 Teotihuacan. *Scientific American* 216 (6): 38–48.

Millon, Rene, Drewitt, B., and G. Cowgill
1973 *Urbanization at Teotihuacan, Mexico, Volume 1: The Teotihuacan Map*. Austin, TX: University of Texas Press.

Nichols, Deborah L.
2004 The Rural and Urban Landscapes of the Aztec State. In *Mesoamerican Archaeology: Theory and Practice*, edited by Julia A. Hendon and Rosemary A. Joyce, pp. 265–295. Oxford: Blackwell.

Proskouriakoff, T.
1960 Historical Implications of a Pattern of Dates at Piedras Negras, Guatemala. *American Antiquity* 25: 454–475.

Rust, W. F., and Sharer, R. J.
1988 Olmec Settlement Data from La Venta, Tabasco, Mexico. *Science* 242: 102–4.

Schele, Linda, and David Freidel
1990 *A Forest of Kings: The Untold Story of the Ancient Maya*. New York: William Morrow and Co.

Smith, Michael A.
2004 *The Aztecs*, 2nd ed. Malden, MA: Blackwell.

Soustelle, Jacques
1985 *The Olmecs: The Oldest Civilization in Mexico*. Translated by Helen R. Lane. Norman, OK: University of Oklahoma Press.

Willey, Gordon
1966 *An Introduction to American Archaeology, Volume 1: North and Middle America*. Englewood Cliffs, NJ: Prentice-Hall.

CHAPTER 25

Burger, Richard L.
1984 *The Prehistoric Occupation of Chavín de Huántar, Peru*. Berkeley, CA: University of California Press.
1988 Unity and Heterogeneity within the Chavín Horizon. In *Peruvian Prehistory*, edited by Richard W. Keatinge, pp. 99–144. Cambridge: Cambridge University Press.

Conklin, W. J., and M. E. Moseley
1988 The Patterns of Art and Power in the Early Intermediate Period. In *Peruvian Prehistory*, edited by Richard W. Keatinge, pp. 145–163. Cambridge: Cambridge University Press.

Conrad, G. W., and A. A. Demarest
1984 *Religion and Empire: The Dynamics of Aztec and Inca Expansionism*. Cambridge: Cambridge University Press.

Diamond, Jared
1997 *Guns, Germs, and Steel: The Fates of Human Societies*. New York: Norton.

Donnan, C. B.
1978 *Moche Art of Peru: Pre-Columbian Symbolic Communication*. Los Angeles: UCLA Museum of Culture History.

Hyslop, John
1984 *The Inka Road System*. Orlando, FL: Academic Press.

Isbell, William H.
1988 City and State in Middle Horizon Huari. In *Peruvian Prehistory*, edited by Richard W. Keatinge, pp. 164–189. Cambridge: Cambridge University Press.

Keatinge, Richard W., ed.
1988 *Peruvian Prehistory*. Cambridge: Cambridge University Press.

Kolata, Alan
1991 The Technology and Organization of Agricultural Production in the Tiwanaku State. *Latin American Antiquity* 2 (2): 99–125.

Lanning, E.P.
1967 *Peru Before the Incas*. Englewood Cliffs, NJ: Prentice Hall.

Malpass, Michael A.
1996 *Daily Life in the Inca Empire*. Westport, CT: Greenwood Press.

Miller, G. R., and R. L Burger
1995 Our Father the Cayman, Our Dinner the Llama: Animal Utilization at Chavín de Huántar, Peru. *American Antiquity* 60 (3): 421–458.

Morris, Craig
1988 Progress and Prospect in the Archaeology of the Inca. In *Peruvian Prehistory*, edited by Richard W. Keatinge, pp. 233–256. Cambridge: Cambridge University Press.

Moseley, Michael E.
1975a *The Maritime Foundations of Andean Civilization*. Menlo Park, CA: Cummings.
1975b Chan Chan: Andean Alternative to the Preindustrial City. *Science* 187: 219–225.
1992 *The Incas and Their Ancestors: The Archaeology of Peru*. New York: Thames and Hudson.
2001 *The Incas and Their Ancestors: The Archaeology of Peru*, revised ed. New York: Thames and Hudson.

Moseley, Michael E., and K. C. Day, eds.
1982 *Chan Chan: Andean Desert City*. Albuquerque, NM: University of New Mexico Press.

Parsons, J. R., and C. M. Hastings
1988 The Late Intermediate Period. In *Peruvian Prehistory*, edited by Richard W. Keatinge, pp. 190–229. Cambridge: Cambridge University Press.

Paul, Anne
1990 *Paracas Ritual Attire: Symbols of Authority in Ancient Peru*. Norman, OK: University of Oklahoma Press.

Pineda, Rosa Fung
1988 The Late Preceramic and Initial Period. In *Peruvian Prehistory*, edited by Richard W. Keatinge, pp. 67–96.

Cambridge: Cambridge University Press.

Rackham, James
1994 *Animal Bones*. Berkeley and Los Angeles: University of California Press/British Museum.

Shimada, Izumi
1994 *Pampa Grande and the Mochica Culture*. Austin, TX: University of Texas Press.

Silverman, Helaine
1991 The Paracas Problem: Archaeological Perspectives. In *Paracas Art and Architecture: Object and Context in South Coastal Peru*, edited by Anne Paul, pp. 349–415. Iowa City, IA: University of Iowa Press.
1993 *Cahuachi in the Ancient Nasca World*. Iowa City, IA: University of Iowa Press.
2002 *Ancient Nasca Settlement and Society*. Iowa City, IA: University of Iowa Press.

Stanish, Charles
2001 The Origins of State Societies in South America. *Annual Review of Anthropology* 30: 41–64.

CHAPTER 26

Ambrose, S. H.
1987 Chemical and Isotopic Techniques of Diet Reconstruction in Eastern North America. In *Emergent Horticultural Economies of the Eastern Woodlands*, edited by William F. Keegan, pp. 87–107. Carbondale, IL: Southern Illinois University Center for Archaeological Investigations, Occasional Paper No. 7.

Anderson, D. G., Stahle, D. W., and M. K. Cleaveland
1995 Paleoclimate and Potential Food Reserves of Mississippian Societies: A Case Study from the Savannah River Valley. *American Antiquity* 60 (2): 258–286.

Braun, D. P.
1979 Illinois Hopewell Burial Practices and Social Organization: A Reexamination of the Klunk-Gibson Mound Group. In *Hopewell Archaeology: The Chillicothe Conference*, edited by D. S. Brose and N. Greber, pp. 66–79. Kent, OH: Kent State University Press.

Brown, J. A., Kerber, R. A., and H. D. Winters
1992 Trade and the Evolution of Exchange Relations at the Beginning

of the Mississippian Period. In *The Mississippian Emergence*, edited by B. D. Smith, pp. 251–280. Washington, DC: Smithsonian Institution Press.

Brose, D. S.
1979 A Speculative Model on the Role of Exchange in the Prehistory of the Eastern Woodlands. In *Hopewell Archaeology: The Chillicothe Conference*, edited by D. S. Brose and N. Greber, pp. 3–8. Kent, OH: Kent State University Press.

Buikstra, J. E.
1984 The Lower Illinois River Region: A Prehistoric Context for the Study of Ancient Diet and Health. In *Paleopathology at the Origins of Agriculture*, edited by M. N. Cohen and G. J. Armelagos, pp. 215–234. Orlando, FL: Academic Press.

Carpenter, John P., Sanchez, Guadalupe, and Maria Elisa Villalpando
2002 Of Maize and Migration: Mode and Tempo in the Diffusion of *Zea mays* in Northwest Mexico and the American Southwest. In *Traditions, Transitions, and Technologies: Themes in Southwestern Archaeology, Proceedings of the 2000 Southwest Symposium*, edited by Sarah H. Schlanger, pp. 245–256. Boulder, CO: University of Colorado Press.

Cook, D. C.
1979 Subsistence Base and Health in Prehistoric Illinois Valley. *Medical Anthropology* 3: 109–124.
1984 Subsistence and Health in the Lower Illinois Valley: Osteological Evidence. In *Paleopathology at the Origins of Agriculture*, edited by M. N. Cohen and G. J. Armelagos, pp. 235–269. Orlando, FL: Academic Press.

Cordell, Linda
1997 *Archaeology of the Southwest*, 2nd ed. San Diego, CA: Academic Press.

Dalan, Rinita
1994 The Construction of Mississippian Cahokia. In *Cahokia: Domination and Ideology in the Mississippian World*, edited by T. B. Pauketat and T. E. Emerson, pp. 89–102. Lincoln, NE, and London: University of Nebraska Press.

Earle, T. K.
1987 Chiefdoms in Archaeological and Ethnohistorical Perspective. *Annual Review of Anthropology* 16: 279–308.

Emerson, T. E.
1997 *Cahokia and the Archaeology of*

Power. Tuscaloosa, AL, and London: University of Alabama Press.

Fagan, Brian M.
2000 *Ancient North America: The Archaeology of a Continent*, 3rd ed. London: Thames and Hudson.

Fowler, M.L.
1975 A Pre-Columbian Urban Center on the Mississippi. *Scientific American* 233 (2): 92–101.

Goodman, Alan H., and George A. Clark
1981 Harris Lines as Indicators of Stress in Prehistoric Illinois Populations. In *Biocultural Adaptation: Comprehensive Approaches to Skeletal Analysis*, edited by Debra L. Martin and M. Pamela Bumstead, pp. 35–43. Amherst, MA: Department of Anthropology, University of Massachusetts at Amherst, Research Report No. 20.

Gregg, Susan A., ed.
1991 *Between Bands and States*. Carbondale, IL: Center for Archaeological Investigations, Southern Illinois University, Occasional Paper No. 9.

Hally, D. J.
1993 The Territorial Size of Mississippian Chiefdoms. In *Archaeology of Eastern North America: Papers in Honor of Stephen Williams*, edited by J. B. Stoltman, pp. 143–168. Jackson, MS: Mississippi Department of Archives and History, Archaeological Report No. 25.

Hatch, J. W., Michels, J. W., Stevenson, C. M., Scheetz, B. F., and R. A. Geidel
1990 Hopewell Obsidian Studies: Behavioral Implications of Recent Sourcing and Dating Research. *American Antiquity* 55 (3): 461–479.

Kelly, A. R.
1979 Hopewellian Studies in American Archaeology: Hopewell After Twenty Years. In *Hopewell Archaeology: The Chillicothe Conference*, edited by D. S. Brose and N. Greber, pp. 1–2. Kent, OH: Kent State University Press.

Knight, Vernon James, Jr., and Vincas P. Steponaitis, eds.
1998a *Archaeology of the Moundville Chiefdom*. Washington, DC: Smithsonian Institution Press.
1998b A New History of Moundville. In *Archaeology of the Moundville Chiefdom*, edited by Vernon James Knight, Jr., and Vincas P. Steponaitis,

pp. 1–25. Washington, DC: Smithsonian Institution Press.

Larsen, C. S., and D. E. Harn
1994 Health in Transition: Disease and Nutrition in the Georgia Bight. In *Paleonutrition: The Diet and Health of Prehistoric Americans*, edited by K. Sobolik, pp. 222–234. Carbondale, IL: Southern Illinois University Center for Archaeological Investigations, Occasional Paper No. 22.

McGuire, R.
1983 Breaking Down Cultural Complexity: Inequality and Heterogeneity. In *Advances in Archaeological Method and Theory*, vol. 6, edited by M. B. Schiffer, pp. 215–258. Orlando, FL: Academic Press.

Milner, G. R.
1986 Mississippian Period Population Density in a Segment of the Central Mississippi River Valley. *American Antiquity* 51 (2): 227–238.

Minnis, Paul E.
1992 Early Plant Cultivation in the Desert Borderlands of the American West. In *The Origins of Agriculture: An International Perspective*, edited by C. W. Cowan and P. J. Watson, pp. 121–141. Washington, DC: Smithsonian Institution Press.

Pauketat, T. R.
1994 *The Ascent of Chiefs: Cahokia and Mississippian Politics in Native North America*. Tuscaloosa, AL: University of Alabama Press.

Pauketat, T. R., and T. E. Emerson, eds.
1997a *Cahokia: Domination and Ideology in the Mississippian World*. Lincoln, NE, and London: University of Nebraska Press.

Pauketat, Timothy R., and Thomas E. Emerson
1997b Conclusion: Cahokia and the Four Winds. In *Cahokia: Domination and Ideology in the Mississippian World*, edited by Timothy R. Pauketat and Thomas E. Emerson, pp. 269–278. Lincoln, NE: University of Nebraska Press.

Peregrine, P.N.
1992 *Mississippian Evolution: A World-System Perspective*. Madison, WI: Prehistory Press, Monographs in World Archaeology, No. 9.

Roney, John R.
1996 The Pueblo III Period in the Eastern San Juan Basin and Acoma-Laguna Areas. In *The Prehistoric Pueblo World, A.D. 1150–1350*, edited

by Michael A. Adler, pp. 145–169. Tucson, AZ: University of Arizona Press.

Roney, John R., and Robert J. Hand
2002a Transitions to Agriculture: An Introduction. In *Traditions, Transitions, and Technologies: Themes in Southwestern Archaeology, Proceedings of the 2000 Southwest Symposium*, edited by Sarah H. Schlanger, pp. 129–136. Boulder, CO: University of Colorado Press.
2002b Early Agriculture in Northwestern Chihuahua. In *Traditions, Transitions, and Technologies: Themes in Southwestern Archaeology, Proceedings of the 2000 Southwest Symposium*, edited by Sarah H. Schlanger, pp. 160–177. Boulder, CO: University of Colorado Press.

Smith, Bruce D.
1978 Variation in Mississippian Settlement Patterns. In *Mississippian Settlement Patterns*, edited by B. D. Smith, pp. 479–503. New York: Academic Press.
1992 Introduction: Research on the Origins of Mississippian Chiefdoms in Eastern North America. In *The Mississippian Emergence*, edited by B. D. Smith, pp. 1–8. Washington, DC: Smithsonian Institution Press.
1992 *The Mississippian Emergence*. Washington, DC, and London: Smithsonian Institution Press.
1994 *The Emergence of Agriculture*. New York: Scientific American Library.

Steponaitis, Vincas P.
1998 Population Trends at Moundville. In *Archaeology of the Moundville Chiefdom*, edited by Vernon James Knight, Jr., and Vincas P. Steponaitis, pp. 26–43. Washington, DC: Smithsonian Institution Press.

Streuver, S., and G. L. Houart
1972 An Analysis of the Hopewell Interaction Sphere. In *Social Change and Interaction*, edited by E. Wilmsen, pp. 47–79. Ann Arbor, MI: University of Michigan, Museum of Anthropology, Anthropological Papers No. 46.

Tainter, Joseph A.
1988 *The Collapse of Complex Societies*. Cambridge: Cambridge University Press.

Taladay, L., Keller, D. R., and P. J. Munson
1984 Hickory Nuts, Walnuts, Butternuts, and Hazelnuts: Ob-

servations and Experiments Relevant to Their Exploitation in Eastern North America. In *Experiments and Observations on Aboriginal Wild Plant Food Utilization in Eastern North America*, edited by P. J. Munson, pp. 338–359. Indianapolis, IN: Indiana Historical Society Prehistoric Research Series, vol. 6, No. 2.

van der Merwe, N. J., and J. C. Vogel
1978 ^{13}C Content of Human Collagen as a Measure of Prehistoric Diet in Woodland North America. *Nature* 276: 815–816.

CHAPTER 27

Arnold, Bettina
1990 The Past as Propaganda: Totalitarian Archaeology in Nazi Germany. *Antiquity* 64 (244): 464–478.
1992 Germany's Nazi Past: How Hitler's Archaeologists Distorted European Prehistory to Justify Racist and Territorial Goals. *Archaeology*, July/August, pp. 30–37.

Confederated Tribes of the Umatilla Indian Reservation
2004 Ancient One/Kennewick Man. http://www.umatilla.nsn.us/ancient.html

Connah, Graham
2001 *African Civilizations: An Archaeological Perspective*, 2nd ed. Cambridge: Cambridge University Press.

Ferguson, T. J.
1996 Native Americans and the Practice of Archaeology. *Annual Review of Anthropology* 25: 63–79.

Joint Tribal Amici Memorandum
2002 Joint Tribal Amici Memorandum quoted in the opinion of the U.S. District Court for the State of Washington, 2002.

Kohl, Philip L.
1998 Nationalism and Archaeology: On the Constructions of Nations and the Reconstructions of the Remote Past. *Annual Review of Anthropology* 27: 223–246.

Malpass, Michael A.
1996 *Daily Life in the Inca Empire*. Westport, CT: Greenwood Press.

McManamon, Francis P.
1999 K-man Undergoes Complete Physical. *Anthropology Newsletter* 40 (8): 3, 22.
2000 *Determination That the*

Kennewick Human Skeletal Remains Are "Native American" for the Purposes of the Native American Graves Protection and Repatriation Act (NAGPRA). Memorandum, January 11, 2000, Archeology and Ethnography Program, National Park Service, Department of the Interior.

Phillipson, David W.
1993 *African Archaeology*, 2nd ed. Cambridge: Cambridge University Press.

Powell, Joseph F., and Jerome C. Rose
1999 *Report on the Osteological Assessment of the "Kennewick Man" Skeleton (CENWW.97.Kennewick)*. Archeology and Ethnography Program, National Park Service, Department of the Interior.

Rose, J. C., Green, T. J., and V. D. Green
1996 NAGPRA Is Forever: Osteology and the Repatriation of Skeletons. *Annual Review of Anthropology* 25: 81–103.

SAA Bulletin Website
1996 ARPA Violator Draws Record Sentence. *SAA Bulletin* 14 (1). http://www.anth.ucsb.edu/SAABulletin/14.1/SAA 15.html
1996 Lava River Cave Looters Convicted. *SAA Bulletin* 14 (1). http://www.anth.ucsb.edu/SAABulletin/14.1/SAA 16.html

Silverman, Helaine
1993 *Cahuachi in the Ancient Nasca World*. Iowa City, IA: University of Iowa Press.

Slayman, Andrew L.
1997 A Battle Over Bones. *Archaeology* 50 (1): 16–20, 22–23.

Trigger, Bruce G.
1989 *A History of Archaeological Thought*. Cambridge: Cambridge University Press.

Vogel, Joseph O.
1994 *Great Zimbabwe: The Iron Age in South Central Africa*. New York: Garland.

CREDITS

LINE ART CREDITS

Chapter 1
Figure 1.3. Jones, Inigo, 1655. *The Most Notable Antiquity of Great Britain, vulgarly called Stonehenge, Restored.* **Figure 1.4.** Frere, John, 1800. Account of Flint Weapons discovered at Hoxne in Suffolk. *Archaeologia* XIII, pp. 204–205. **Figure 1.8.** Courtesy of Prof. S. Milisauskas (*European Prehistory*, 1978) and Dr. P. Bogucki. **Figure 1.11.** ©1956 Time Inc. Reproduced by Permission.

Chapter 2
Figure 2.11. Reproduced courtesy of Prof. F. Grine. **Figure 2.D.** After Aitken, M. J., 1990: *Science-Based Dating in Archaeology.* London and New York: Longman, and Butler, Robert F., 1992: *Paleomagnetism: Magnetic Domains to Geologic Terrains.* Boston: Blackwell Scientific Publications. **Figure 2.E.** Reproduced with permission of Masson. **Figure 2.F.** After Brain, C. K., 1981: *The Hunters or the Hunted? An Introduction of African Cave Taphonomy.*, p. 220. Chicago: University of Chicago Press.

Chapter 3
Figure 3.2. After Leakey, M., 1971: *Olduvai Gorge, Vol. 3.* Cambridge: Cambridge University Press. **Figure 3.3.** Redrawn from Leakey, M., 1971: *Olduvai Gorge, Vol. 3,* **Figure 9.** Cambridge: Cambridge University Press. **Figure 3.4.** After Isaac, G. L., 1983: Bones In Contention: Competing Explanations for the Juxtaposition of Early Pleistocene Artifacts and Faunal Remains. In *Animals in Archaeology: I. Hunters and Their Prey*, edited by J. Clutton-Brock and C. Grigson, p. 14. Oxford: British Archaeological Reports, International Series 163. **Figure 3.C.** Redrawn from Leakey, M., 1971: *Olduvai Gorge, Vol. 3,* Figure 7. Cambridge: Cambridge University Press. Reprinted with permission of Cambridge University Press.

Chapter 4
Figure 4.3 a and b. Redrawn from Bordes, F., 1984: *Leçons sur Paléolithique, Volume 3,* Figures 114 and 115. **Figure 4.3c.** Copyright 1966 by the Israel Academy of Sciences and Humanities. All rights reserved. **Figure 4.A.** Skertchley, S. B. J., 1879: On the Manufacture of Gun Flints. *Memoir of the Geological Society of England and Wales.*

Chapter 5
Figure 5.8. Redrawn from Bordes, F., 1984: *Leçons sur Paléolithique, Volume 3,* Figure 167. **Figure 5.10.** Redrawn from Bordes, F., 1984: *Leçons sur Paléolithique, Volume 3,* Figures 16 and 30. Paris: CNRS Editions. **Figure 5.A.** Courtesy of Prof. Philip Rightmire. **Figure 5.13.** Reproduced with permission of Academic Press, Ltd. From Villa, P. 1990: Torralba and Aridos: Elephant Exploitation in Middle Pleistocene Spain. *Journal of Human Evolution* 19, p. 300, Figure 1. Copyright 1990.

Chapter 6
Figure 6.4. After Bordes, F., 1972: *A Tale of Two Caves,* Figure 31. New York: Harper and Row. **Figure 6.5.** Redrawn from Phillipson, D. W., 1992, *African Archaeology,* 2nd ed., Figure 4.2. Reproduced with permission of Cambridge University Press. **Figure 6.B.** From *In Search of the Neanderthals* by Christopher Stringer and Clive Gamble, published by Thames and Hudson, Inc., New York.

Chapter 7
Figure 7.3. After Clark, J. D., 1970: *The Prehistory of Africa,* Figure 50. **Figure 7.4.** Reprinted with permission from Yellen, J. E., *et al.*, 1995: A Middle Stone Age Worked Bone Industry from Katanda, Upper Semliki Valley, Zaire, Figure 1, p. 555. *Science* 268, 28 April 1995. Copyright 1995 American Association for the Advancement of Science.

Chapter 8
Figure 8.2. Reproduced with the permission of Prof. Anthony Marks, Southern Methodist University. **Figure 8.5.** Redrawn from Phillipson, D. W., 1992, *African Archaeology,* 2nd ed., Figure 4.1. Reproduced with permission of Cambridge University Press. **Figure 8.7.** Reproduced with permission of Professor R. G. Klein.

Chapter 9
Figure 9.2. Redrawn from Bordes, F., 1984: *Leçons sur Paléolithique, Volume 2,* Figures 141, 147, 122, 131, and 153. Paris: CNRS Editions. **Figure 9.7.** Klein, R. G., 1973. *Ice Age Hunters of the Ukraine,* Figure 24. Copyright 1973. The University of Chicago. **Figure 9.8.** Andersen, B. G. and H. W. Borns: *The Ice Age World.* Figure 2–53. 1994. Scandinavian University Press, Oslo, Norway.

Chapter 11
Figure 11.A. Redrawn from Flood, J., 1990: *The Archaeology of the Dreamtime,* revised edition. New Haven, CT: Yale University Press. Copyright 1983 Josephine Flood. **Figure 11.2a.** Lourandos, Henry, 1997: *Continent of Hunter-Gatherers: New Perspectives in Australian Prehistory,* p. 288, Figure 8.4 a-d. **Figure 11.2b.** Reproduced with permission from Johan Kamminga.

Chapter 12
Figure 12.2. Reproduced by permission of the Society for American Archaeology from *American Antiquity* 54 (2): 263–297. **Figure 12.3.** Reproduced by permission of the Society for American Archaeology from *American Antiquity* 54 (2): 263–297. **Figure 12.4.** After Dawson, Alastair G., 1992: *Ice Age Earth: Late Quaternary Geology and Climate,* Figures 5.6, 5.7, and 5.8. London and New York: Routledge. **Figure 12.5.** With permission of the Denver Museum of Nature and Science, the copyright owner. **Figure 12.8.** Redrawn with permission of Prof. Tom Dillehay, University of Kentucky. **Figure 12.A.** Redrawn from Kutzback, J. E., and Thompson Webb III. Late Quaternary Vegetation Changes in Eastern North America: Concepts, Models and Data. In *Quaternary Landscapes,* edited by L. C. K. Shane and E. J. Cushing (University of Minnesota Press, 1991), Figure 6. Reproduced with permission of the University of Minnesota Press.

Chapter 13
Figure 13.1. After Bogucki, P. I., 1988: *Forest Farmers and Stockherders: Early Agriculture and Its Consequences in North-Central Europe,* Figure 2.4. Reproduced with permission of Cambridge University Press. **Figure 13.2a-c.** Reproduced courtesy of Patricia J. Wynne. **Figure 13.2d.** Redrawn from a photograph in Clark, J. G. D., 1952: *Prehistoric Europe: The Economic*

439

Basis, Plate 1a. Stanford, CA: Stanford University Press. **Figure 13.3.** Reproduced courtesy of S. H. Andersen. **Figure 13.5.** Crown copyright is reproduced with the permission of the Controller of Her Majesty's Stationery Office. **Figure 13.7.** Reproduced courtesy of S. H. Andersen. **Figure 13.A.** Reproduced courtesy of the *New Phytologist*. **Figure 13.B.** Andersen, B. G. and H. W. Borns: *The Ice Age World*. Figure 2-88. 1994. Scandinavian University Press, Oslo, Norway.

Chapter 14
Figure 14.2. Redrawn after Beck, Charlotte, and R. T. Jones, 1997: The Terminal Pleistocene/Early Holocene Archaeology of the Great Basin. *Journal of World Prehistory* 11 (2): 186, Figure 3, published by Plenum Publishing. **Figure 14.A.** Reproduced courtesy of *Radiocarbon*. **Figure 14.B.** Reproduced courtesy of M. Stuiver and P. J. Reimer.

Chapter 16
Figure 16.2 a-d. "Préhistoire Palestinienne," J. Perrot in *Supplément au Dictionaire de la Bible*, Vol. VIII, col. 375–376, Letouzey et Ane, Paris, 1968. **Figure 16.3.** Reproduced couresty of François Valla. **Figure 16.4.** Redrawn from Braidwood, R., 1967: *Prehistoric Men*, 7th ed. Glenview, IL: Scott, Foresman. Reproduced with permission of the McGraw-Hill Companies. **Figure 16.B.** Reproduced courtesy of Gordon Hillman. **Figure 16.C.** The Natural History Museum, London. **Figure 16.6.** Courtesy Dr. Ian Kuijt. **Figure 16.7.** Redrawn after Marshall, F. And E. Hildebrand, 2002: Cattle Before Crops: The Beginnings of Food Production in Africa. *Journal of World Prehistory* 16 (2): 99–143, Figure 3.

Chapter 17
Figure 17.2. Reproduced courtesy of Prof. J. Doebley, Department of Genetics, University of Wisconsin. **Figure 17.3.** The Natural History Museum, London. **Figure 17.A.** From Vyrdaghs, L., Swennen, R., Mbida, C., Doutrelepont H., De Langhe, E., and P. De Maret, 2003: The Banana Phytolith as a Direct Marker of Early Agriculture: A Review of the Evidence. In *Phytolith and Starch Research in the Australian-Pacific-Asian Regions: The State of the Art*, edited by D. M. Hart and L. A. Wallis, pp. 177–185. Terra Australia 19. Canberra: Panandus Books. This image originally appeared in Mbida Mindzie, C., et al., 2001: First Archaeological Evidence of Banana cultivation in Central Africa During the Third

Millennium Before Present. *Vegetation History and Archaeobotany* 10 (1): 1–6. Reproduced with the kind permission of Springer-Verlag and Luc Vyrdaghs.

Chapter 18
Figure 18.4. After Piggott, S., 1965: *Ancient Europe*, Figure 14. Reproduced with permission of the estate of Prof. S. Piggott. **Figure 18.5.** After Bogucki, P. I., 1988: *Forest Farmers and Stockherders: Early Agriculture and Its Consequences in North-Central Europe*, Figure 4.4. Reproduced with permission of Cambridge University Press. **Figure 18.6.** Bogucki, P. I., 1988: *Forest Farmers and Stockherders: Early Agriculture and Its Consequences in North-Central Europe*, Figure 4.6. Reproduced with permission of Cambridge University Press. **Figure 18.7.** Reprinted with permission from Bogucki, P. I. and R. Grygiel, 1993: Neolithic Sites in the Polish Lowlands: Research at Brześć Kujawski, 1933 to 1984. In *Case Studies in European Prehistory*, edited by P. I. Bogucki, p. 155. Boca Raton, FL: CRC Press. Copyright Lewis Publishers, an imprint of CRC Press. **Figure 18.C.** Redrawn after *The Neolithic of the Near East* by James Mellaart, published by Thames and Hudson, Ltd., London. **Figure 18.D.** From *The Neolithic of the Near East* by James Mellaart, published by Thames and Hudson, Ltd., London. **Figure 18.E.** From *The Neolithic of the Near East* by James Mellaart, published by Thames and Hudson, Ltd., London.

Chapter 19
Figure 19.2. From C. Redman, 1978: *The Rise of Civilization*, Figure 6.5. Reproduced courtesy of Prof. Charles Redman. **Figure 19.3.** Redrawn after V. C. Childe, 1937: *New Light on the Most Ancient East*, Plates XIV and XVIb. **Figure 19.4.** Redrawn after V. C. Childe, 1937: *New Light on the Most Ancient East*, Plate XVIa. **Figure 19.6.** Courtesy of Michael Roaf. **Figure 19.7.** Redrawn after *The Archaeology of Mesopotamia* by Seton Lloyd, published by Thames and Hudson, Ltd., London. **Figure 19.10.** Reprinted from Strommenger, Eva, 1967: Gefässe aus Uruk von der Neubabylonischen Zeit bis zu den Sasaniden, Mit einem Beitrag über die Inschriften von Rudolf Macuch. Berlin: Gerb. Mann. Ausgrabungen der Deutschen Forschungsgemeinschaft in Uruk-Warka, Bd. 7. Reproduced with permission of the German Archaeological Institute, Berlin. **Figure 19.11.** Adapted from Adams, Robert McC., 1981: *Heartland of Cities*. Chicago. IL: University of Chicago Press. © 1981 by the University of Chicago. All rights reserved. **Figure 19.12.** After

C. Redman, 1978: *The Rise of Civilization*, Figure 8.3. Reproduced courtesy of Prof. Charles Redman. **Figure 19.D.** Redrawn after Wooley, L., 1965: *Excavations at Ur*. Figure 4.

Chapter 20
Figure 20.2. Redrawn after Allchin, Bridget and Raymond Allchin, 1982: *The Rise of Civilization in India and Pakistan*, Figure 6.23. Cambridge: Cambridge University Press. Reproduced with the permission of Cambridge University Press. **Figure 20.D.** Wheeler, Sir Mortimer, 1968: *The Indus Civilization*, Figure 5. Cambridge: Cambridge University Press. Reproduced with the permission of Cambridge University Press. Figure 20.E. © Harappa Archaeological Research Project.

Chapter 21
Figure 21.A. Petrie, W. M. Flinders, 1899: Sequences in Prehistoric Remains, *Journal of the Anthropological Institute of Great Britain and Ireland*, vol. XXIX, (New Series Vol. II): 295–301, Figure 1. **Figure 21.B.** From *In Small Things Forgotten* by James Deetz. © 1977 by James Deetz. Used with permission of Doubleday, a division of Random House, Inc. **Figure 21.10.** Hoffman, Michael A., 1980: Rectangular Amratian House from Hierakonpolis and Its Significance for Predynastic Research. *Journal of Near Eastern Studies* 39: Figure 11, p. 31. Chicago, IL: University of Chicago Press. © The University of Chicago. **Figure 21.13.** Redrawn from Trigger, Bruce G., Barry J. Kemp, D. O'Connor, and A. B. Lloyd, 1983: *Ancient Egypt: A Social History*, Figure 1.5. Cambridge: Cambridge University Press. Reprinted with permission of Cambridge University Press.

Chapter 22
Figure 22.4. Reproduced from *The Prehistory of China* by Judith Treistman, Figure 2, p. 45. Garden City, NY: Natural History Press. This image was reproduced with the permission of the American Museum of Natural History and Doubleday, a division of Random House. **Figure 22.5.** Underhill, Anne P., 2002: *Craft Production and Social Change in Northern China*, Figure 5.16, p. 109. New York: Kluwer Academic/Plenum, with kind permission of Springer Science and Business Media. **Figure 22.7.** Reproduced courtesy of Prof. Yun K. Lee. **Figure 22.D.** Reproduced with permission of Geophysical Survey Systems, Inc.

Chapter 23

Figure 23.2 After Bogucki, P. I., 1988: *Forest Farmers and Stockherders: Early Agriculture and Its Consequences in North-Central Europe*, Figure 6.2. Reproduced with permission of Cambridge University Press. **Figure 23.4.** After Champion, T. Gamble., C., Shennan, S., and A. Whittle, *Prehistoric Europe*, 1984, p. 166, by permission of the publisher Academic Press. **Figure 23.5.** After Piggott, S., 1965: *Ancient Europe*, p. 127. Reproduced with permission of the estate of Prof. S. Piggott. **Figure 23.8.** Data source: Cunliffe, B., 1979: *The Celtic World*, p. 64. New York: McGraw-Hill. **Figure 23.B.** Reprinted from Champion, T. Gamble., C., Shennan, S., and A. Whittle, *Prehistoric Europe*, 1984, p. 166, by permission of the publisher Academic Press. **Figure 23.C.** Reprinted from *Journal of Field Archaeology* with the permission of the Trustees of Boston University. All rights reserved.

Chapter 24

Figure 24.1. From Hernando Cortéz, *Praeclara Ferdínandi Cortesii de Nova maris Hyspania narratío* [Nuremberg], 1524. **Figure 24.4.** From *The Olmecs* by Jacques Soustelle, translated by Helen R. Lane, copyright 1984 by Doubleday and Co., Inc, a division of Random House, Inc. **Figure 24.5.** Adapted from Blanton, Richard E., Kowalewski, Stephen A., Feinman, Gary M., and Laura M. Finsten, 1993: *Ancient Mesoamerica: A Comparison of Change in Three Regions*, 2nd ed. Cambridge: Cambridge University Press. Reproduced with permission of Cambridge University Press. **Figure 24.A.** By Permission of University of Pennsylvania Museum Publications, John Harris and Steven Stearns, *Understanding Maya Inscriptions: A Heiroglyphic Handbook*, 2nd ed. (Philadelphia, University Museum Publications, 1997).

Chapter 25

Figure 25.4. From *Pampa Grande and the Mochica Culture* by Izumi Shimada, Copyright 1994. By permission of the University of Texas Press. **Figure 25.5.** From Keatinge, Richard W., ed., 1988: *Peruvian Prehistory*, Figure 3.4. Cambridge: Cambridge University Press. Reproduced with the permission of Cambridge University Press. **Figure 25.7.** Reproduced courtesy of Prof. John Rowe. **Figure 25.12.** Reproduced courtesy of Prof. Alan L. Kolata, University

of Chicago. **Figure 25.13.** Reproduced courtesy of Prof. Michael Moseley, University of Florida.

Chapter 26

Figure 26.A. Reproduced courtesy of Prof. D. R. Brothwell. **Figure 26.B.** Reproduced courtesy of Prof. D. R. Brothwell. **Figure 26.C.** Adaptation based on Smith, Bruce D., 1989, Origins of Agriculture in Eastern North America. *Science* 246: 1570 and Ambrose, F., 1987, Chemical and Isotopic Techniques Of Diet Reconstruction in Eastern North America, edited by W. F. Keegan, pp. 87–107. Carbondale, IL: Southern Illinois University Center for Archaeological Investigations, Occasional Paper No. 7. **Figure 26.D.** Reproduced courtesy of Prof. D. R. Brothwell.

TEXT PERMISSIONS

Chapter 14. Quote from G. Nicholas. Reproduced with permission of Mary Ann Levine and G. Nicholas.

Chapter 26. Quote from C. S. Larsen. With permission, from *Annual Review of Anthropology*, vol. 24, ©1995 www.AnnualReviews.org.

Chapter 27. Quote from P. Kohl. With permission, from *Annual Review of Anthropology*, vol. 27, ©1998 www.AnnualReviews.org.

PHOTO CREDITS

Chapter 1

Figure 1.1: Hinterleitner/Gamma. **Figure 1.2:** South Tyrol Museum of Archaeology, Bozen Italy, www.ice-man.it, photo by Marco Samadelli. **Figure 1.5:** Courtesy of the U.S. General Services Administration and John Milner & Associates, Inc. **Figure 1.6:** Pam Crabtree. **Figure 1.7:** Pam Crabtree. **Figure 1.9:** ©2000, Trustees of Princeton University. **Figure 1.10:** Peabody Museum, Harvard University. **Figure 1.12:** South Tyrol Museum of Archaeology, Bozen Italy, www.iceman.it, photo by Marco Samadelli. **Figure 1.13:** South Tyrol Museum of Archaeology, Bozen Italy, www.iceman.it, photo by Marco Samadelli. **Figure 1.B:** Pam Crabtree/Douglas Campana.

Chapter 2

Figure 2.2: Donald Johnson/Institute of Human Origins. **Figure 2.3:** Transvaal Museum. **Figure 2.5:** Des Bartlett/Photo Researchers. **Figure 2.6:** Cleveland

Museum of Natural History. **Figure 2.7:** John Reader/Science Photo Library/Photo Researchers. **Figure 2.8:** Professor Tim White. **Figure 2.10:** #634004 — Alan Walker/National Geographic Image Collection. **Figure 2.12:** David L. Brill. **Figure 2.C:** Courtesy Shari A. Kelley.

Chapter 3

Figure 3.1: #NGM 1963/08 304-5 — Jane Goodall/National Geographic Image Collection. **Figure 3.5:** David L. Brill. **Figure 3.6:** DR. R. Potts, Human Origins Program, Smithsonian Institution.

Chapter 4

Figure 4.2: National Museums of Kenya. **Figure 4.B:** Giancarlo Ligabue, Centro Studi Ricerche Ligabue, Venice. **Figure 4.D:** Kathy Schick/Stone Age Institute. **Figure 4.5:** Photo by Douglas Campana. Reproduced courtesy of Professor O. Bar-Yosef, Anthropology Department, Harvard University. **Figure 4.6:** Naama Goren-Inbar.

Chapter 5

Figure 5.2: American Museum of Natural History, Department of Library Services, Neg # 319781. Photo by Alex J. Rota. **Figure 5.3:** Courtesy of Professor Susan Antón. **Figure 5.6:** American Museum of Natural History, Department of Library Services, Neg # 335795. **Figure 5.7 top:** American Museum of Natural History, Department of Library Services, Neg # 315447. Photo by Charles H. Coles. **Figure 5.7 bottom:** American Museum of Natural History. **Figure 5.9:** Javier Trueba/Madrid Scientific Films. **Figure 5.12:** Courtesy of Professor F. Clark Howell.

Chapter 6

Figure 6.2: Philippe PLAILLY/EURELIOS. **Figure 6.3:** Pam Crabtree. **Figure 6.C:** Courtesy of Ofer Bar-Yosef, Harvard University.

Chapter 7

Figure 7.2: John Reader/Science Photo Library/Photo Researchers. **Figure 7.A:** The Natural History Museum, London. **Figure 7.5:** Instituto Português de Arqueologia.

Chapter 8

Figure 8.3b: Daniel E. Lieberman, Department of anthropology, Harvard University. **Figure 8.A left:** By permission of Guillermo L. Mengoni. **Figure 8.A right:** By permission of Alan Outram. **Figure 8.4:** Photo by Douglas Campana. Reproduced courtesy of Professor O. Bar-Yosef, Anthropology Department,

Harvard University. **Figure 8.B:** Irven DeVore/Anthro-Photo. **Figure 8.C:** John Eastcott/Yva Momatiuk/Woodfin Camp & Associates.

Chapter 9

Figure 9.4: Centre National de la Recherche Scientifique. **Figure 9.5:** Pam Crabtree. **Figure 9.6:** Olga Soffer, University of Illinois at Urbana-Champaign.

Chapter 10

Figure 10.2: Jean Vertut, Courtesy of Yvonne Vertut, Paris. **Figure 10.3:** Professor Randall White, Center for the Study of Human Origins, Anthropology Department, New York University. **Figure 10.4:** Erich Lessing/Art Resource, NY. **Figure 10.5:** Musée de l'Homme, Photo by J. Oster. **Figure 10.6a:** Photo courtesy of the French Ministry of Culture and Communication, Regional Direction for Cultural Affairs, Rhône-Alpes, Regional Department of Archaeology. Photo by Jean Clottes. **Figure 10.6b:** Photo courtesy of the French Ministry of Culture and Communication, Regional Direction for Cultural Affairs, Rhone-Alpes, Regional Department of Archaeology. Photo by Jean Clottes. **Figure 10.7:** Jean Vertut, Courtesy of Yvonne Vertut, Paris. **Figure 10.8:** Réunion des Musées Nationaux/Art Resource, NY. **Figure 10.A:** Pam Crabtree. **Figure 10.9:** Professor Randall White, Center for the Study of Human Origins, Anthropology Department, New York University. **Figure 10.10:** Art Resource, NY. **Figure 10.11:** Jean Vertut, Courtesy of Yvonne Vertut, Paris. **Figure 10.12:** Dr. David W. Phillipson, Cambridge, U.K.

Chapter 11

Figure 11.B: WL Gowther Library State, Library of Tasmania, Abott Album.

Chapter 12

Figure 12.B: Courtesy of Vance Haynes.

Chapter 13

Figure 13.4: Courtesy of Dr. David Perry. **Figure 13.C:** Courtesy of Dr. Peter Rowley-Conwy.

Chapter 14

Figure 14.C: National Museum of the American Indian, Smithsonian Institution. Photo by David Heald [T134512D & T134513]. **Figure 14. Da:** Special Collections Department, University of Nevada, Reno Library, Margaret M. Wheat Collection P89-32/81. **Figure 14.Db:** Special Collections Department, University of

Nevada, Reno Library, Margaret M. Wheat Collection P89-32/82. **Figure 14.Dc:** Special Collections Department, University of Nevada, Reno Library, Margaret M. Wheat Collection P89-32/84. **Figure 14.E:** Courtesy of Stuart Streuver and Felicia Holton. **Figure 14.3:** Dr. Kristen Gremillion, Ohio State University.

Chapter 16

Figure 16.2e: Courtesy of Israel Antiquities Authority. **Figure 16.5:** Figure 3.14 from Bar-Yosef and Avi Gopher, eds., *An Early Neolithic Village in the Jordan Valley, Part I: The Archaeology of the Netiv Hagdud,* American School of Prehistoric Research, Bulletin 43. Copyright 1997 by the President and Fellows of Harvard College. **Figure 16.B:** Courtesy of Professor Gil Stein.

Chapter 17

Figure 17.B: Courtesy Dr. Dolores Piperno.

Chapter 18

Figure 18.2: Ancient Art and Architecture Collection Ltd./Bridgeman Art Library. **Figure 18.3:** Ashmolean Museum, Oxford, U.K./Bridgeman Art Library. **Figure 18.8:** American Museum of Natural History, Photo by H. Millou, Neg #39604. **Figure 18.A:** Dr. Denise Schmandt-Besserat, University of Texas at Austin. **Figure 18.E:** From *The Neolithic of the Near East* by James Mellaart, published by Thames and Hudson Ltd., London.

Chapter 19

Figure 19.5: Joan Oates, Cambridge, U.K. **Figure 19.8:** University of Pennsylvania Museum, Philadelphia, Neg #S4-143183. **Figure 19.9:** University of Pennsylvania Museum, Philadelphia, Neg # G8-8645. **Figure 19.A:** Tom Sever, Nasa. **Figure 19.B:** NASA/JPL-Caltech. **Figure 19.13:** The Oriental Institute of the University of Chicago. **Figure 19.C:** The Trustees of the British Museum. **Figure 19.E:** The Trustees of the British Museum. **Figure 19.F top:** University of Pennsylvania Museum, Philadelphia, Neg. # G8-8344. **Figure 19.F bottom:** University of Pennsylvania Museum, Philadelphia, Neg. # B170725. **Figure 19.G:** U.S. Navy.

Chapter 20

Figure 20.3: Dr. Richard Meadow. **Figure 20.4:** Pam Crabtree. **Figure 20.A:** Archaeological Museum, New Delhi, Delhi, India/Scala/Art Resource, NY. **Figure 20.B:** Courtesy AsKo Parpola. **Figure 20.5:** Pam

Crabtree. Reproduced courtesy of the Rojdi excavations, directed by Prof. Gregory Possehl, University of Pennsylvania, and funded by the National Science Foundation. **Figure 20.F:** Borromeo/Art Resource, NY. **Figure 20.6:** Borromeo/Art Resource, NY. **Figure 20.7:** Karachi Museum/Borromeo/ Art Resource, NY. **Figure 20.8:** From *The Rise and Fall of Civilization in India and Pakistan,* courtesy of Bridget and Raymond Allchin.

Chapter 21

Figure 21.1: Douglas Campana. **Figure 21.2:** The Griffith Institute, Oxford, U.K. **Figure 21.3:** Art Resource, NY. **Figure 21.4:** Douglas Campana. **Figure 21.6:** British Museum. **Figure 21.7:** Petrie Museum of Egyptian Archaeology, University College London. **Figure 21.8:** Petrie Museum of Egyptian Archaeology, University College London. **Figure 21.9a:** Petrie Museum of Egyptian Archaeology, University College London, #UC66135. **Figure 21.9a:** Petrie Museum of Egyptian Archaeology, University College London, #UC36240. **Figure 21.9b:** Petrie Museum of Egyptian Archaeology, University College London, #UC15313. **Figure 21.9b:** Petrie Museum of Egyptian Archaeology, University College London, #UC15291+1. **Figure 21.9c:** Petrie Museum of Egyptian Archaeology, University College London, #UC25779. **Figure 21.9c:** Petrie Museum of Egyptian Archaeology, University College London, #UC25780. **Figure 21.11:** Petrie Museum of Egyptian Archaeology, University College London. **Figure 21.12:** Hirmer Fotoarchiv. **Figure 21.14:** Laurie Flentye. **Figure 21.15:** Douglas Campana. **Figure 21.C:** Courtesy Professor David O'Connor. **Figure 21.18:** Courtesy Professor Roderick McIntosh.

Chapter 22

Figure 22.1: Tricia Timmermans/Photo-J Inc. **Figure 22.3:** Asian Art & Archaeology, Inc./CORBIS. **Figure 22.5:** Ann Underhill/ Kluner Academic. **Figure 22.6:** Asian Art & Archaeology, Inc./CORBIS. **Figure 22.A:** Douglas Campana. **Figure 22.B:** Courtesy of Sensors & Software, Inc. **Figure 22.C:** Courtesy of GSSI, Inc.

Chapter 23

Figure 23.1: L.H. Jawitz. **Figure 23.A:** Dr. Laura A. Tedesco. **Figure 23.6:** Wiltshire Heritage Museum, Devizes, U.K. **Figure 23.7:** Historisches Museum der Pfalz, Speyer, Germany, Photo, Kurt Diehl.

Chapter 24

Figure 24.3: Robert Frerck/Odyssey Chicago. **Figure 24.6:** SEF/Art Resource, NY. **Figure 24.7:** Robert Frerck/Odyssey Chicago. **Figure 24.9:** #NGM 1987-09 322-4 — Terry Rutledge/National Geographic Image Collection. **Figure 24.10:** University of Pennsylvania Museum, Philadelphia, Neg #62-4-972. **Figure 24.11:** University of Pennsylvania Museum, Philadelphia, Photo by William Coe. Neg #62-4-1094.

Chapter 25

Figure 25.1: AnthroArcheArt.com. **Figure 25.6:** Richard Burger/Yale University. **Figure 25.A:** American Museum of Natural History, Neg #329715. **Figure 25.8:** Hoover Presidential Library-Museum, West Branch, Iowa. **Figure 25.9:** Professor Donald Proulx/University of Massachusetts. **Figure 25.10:** The Art Institute of Chicago. **Figure 25.11:** Servico Aerofotografico Nacional, Lima, Peru. **Figure 25.14:** American Museum of Natural History, Neg #325190.

Chapter 26

Figure 26.2: Ohio Historical Society. **Figure 26.3:** Ohio Historical Society. **Figure 26.4:** National Park Service, U.S. Department of The Interior. **Figure 26.E:** Art Grossman/Cahokia Mounds Museum Society. **Figure 26.F:** Douglas Campana. **Figure 26.5:** AnthroArcheArt.com. **Figure 26.6:** U.S. National Park Service, U.S. Department of the Interior.

Chapter 27

Figure 27.1: Helaine Silverman, University of Illinois at Urbana-Champaign. **Figure 27.2:** Photo courtesy of Professor Bettina Arnold, University of Wisconsin, Milwaukee, based on *5000 Jahre Deutschland: Germanischen Leben in 7000 Bildern* by Jeorg Lechler, 1937, Leipzig: Curt Kabitzsch Verlag. **Figure 27.3:** Dr. David W. Phillipson, Cambridge, U.K.

GLOSSARY

Absolute dating Dating methods that provide dates in calendar years, usually expressed as years before present (B.P.). By convention, *present* is defined as A.D. 1950, about the time when radiometric dating methods first came into use.

Abu Hureyra A large early Neolithic site near the Euphrates River in Syria. The lowest levels resemble the roughly contemporary Natufian culture. Like the Natufian people, these early preagricultural inhabitants of Abu Hureyra hunted gazelle and gathered wild barley and other plants for sustenance.

Abydos City about 300 miles south of Cairo, occupied from Predynastic times throughout Egyptian history. Its cemetery is especially noteworthy as the burial place of Narmer and the Kings of the First Dynasty.

Acheulian industry A stone tool industry characterized by bifacially worked core tools, primarily handaxes and cleavers. The Acheulian industry first appeared in Africa about 1.6 million years ago and lasted until about 200,000 years ago (and in some areas as late as 100,000 years ago).

Adena The cultural complex, dating to the Early Woodland period, centered in southern Ohio. Adena sites include large and elaborate burial mounds. The burials often include exotic items such as pipes made of Ohio pipestone.

A-Group A distinctive lower Nubian culture, established around 3500 B.C., that began to trade intensively with Egypt around 3100 B.C.

Ahmarian tradition The term used to refer to early upper Paleolithic assemblages in the Levant that are dominated by blades and bladelets.

'Ain Ghazal One of the largest early farming settlements in the southern Levant, located near Amman, Jordan. The site covers 12–13 ha (30–32.5 ac.) and has yielded an unbroken sequence of early Neolithic occupation from 8400 to 5800 B.C.

Ali Kosh An early Neolithic site located in the Deh Luran Plain in western Iran that has provided evidence for early goat domestication.

Altamira Cave A cave site in northern Spain where some of the first examples of Paleolithic parietal art were discovered by a local nobleman, de Sautuola. The Altamira images date to the Magdalenian period, ca. 15,500 years ago.

Altiplano The high flatlands in the areas surrounding Lake Titicaca on the Peruvian–Bolivian border.

AMS (accelerator mass spectrometry) A method of radiocarbon dating that uses an electrostatic accelerator and a mass spectrometer to measure the amount of radiocarbon (^{14}C) that remains in a sample of organic material. The technique allows small samples of organic materials to be dated using the radiocarbon method.

Animal domestication The process through which animal reproduction comes under human control. Humans isolate a portion of a wild animal population by restricting its movement or breeding practices. Over time, the portion of the population under human control begins to differ morphologically from the wild population.

Anthropology The study of the biology, evolution, and culture of human beings, both in the past and in the present. In the United States, anthropology includes four subfields: **cultural anthropology**—the study of modern human cultures, both of specific cultures and of the character of human cultures in general; **physical anthropology**—the study of the biology and evolution of human beings and their close primate relatives; **anthropological linguistics**—the study of the nature, development, and social functions of language; and **anthropological archaeology**—the study of the material remains of cultures and peoples in the past.

Anyang The site of the Yin ruins in the Henan province of China. The Yin ruins are a series of complexes, including royal tombs, palaces, houses, and workshops that date to the late part of the Shang Dynasty.

Apollo 11 Cave A site in southern Namibia that has produced painted images of animals dated to 28,000 years ago.

Archaeobotanists Scientists who study plant remains recovered from archaeological sites.

Archaeological culture A widespread and regularly occurring association of artifact types and features, usually assumed to belong to a specific human group.

Archaeology The study of the material remains of past human behavior.

Archaeometallurgy The study of ancient metals recovered from archaeological sites. Analyses usually include studies of the artifact's composition and the methods used in its manufacture.

445

Archaic   The term used to apply to the post-Pleistocene hunting and gathering cultures of the Americas.

Ardipithecus kadabba   A species of early hominin discovered in the Middle Awash region of Ethiopia and dated to between 5.2 and 5.8 million years ago. The canine teeth of this species are smaller than those seen in apes.

Ardipithecus ramidus   Early hominin fossils, dated to about 4.4 million years ago, which were discovered at Aramis in Ethiopia during the 1990s.

Aridos   An Acheulian site near Madrid, Spain, where bones and stone tools indicate that an elephant was butchered.

ARPA   The Archaeological Resources Protection Act, which protects archaeological sites on federal properties such as national parks and national forests.

Artifact   Any object made, modified, or utilized by humans.

Assemblage   A group of artifacts found together within a specific feature or layer, which appears to have been deposited together.

Aterian   A stone tools industry that replaced the Mousterian in North Africa, perhaps as early as 70,000 years ago. Aterian stone tools have distinctive tangs to facilitate hafting onto wooden shafts.

Aurignacian   Industry (ca. 40,000–28,000 B.P.) that is characterized by the presence of nosed and carinated end scrapers made on thick flakes and blades, large blades with continuous retouch, strangulated blades, and bone points, including those with split bases.

Australian Core Tool and Scraper Tradition   The stone tool industry that was brought to Australia by the first aboriginal colonists. The tradition includes cores that are shaped like horses' hooves and thick scrapers that could be used for a variety of tasks.

Australian Small Tool Tradition   About 5000 years ago, the Australian Small Tool Tradition spread across the Australian continent. Typical tools include microliths and small, finely flaked stone points.

Australopith   A general term used to describe the non-*Homo* members of the hominins, such as *Australopithecus, Paranthropus,* and *Ardipithecus.*

Australopithecus afarensis   A small-brained, fully bipedal hominin found at a number of East African sites extending from Hadar in Ethiopia to Laetoli in Tanzania. *A. afarensis* dates from about 3.8 to 3.0 million years ago.

Australopithecus africanus   A lightly built hominin found in South Africa, dating to between 3 and 2 million years ago. Although *A. africanus* probably evolved from *A. afarensis,* it is not yet clear whether *A. africanus* is ancestral to early members of the genus *Homo.*

Australopithecus anamensis   A recently discovered bipedal hominin dated to between about 4.2 and 3.9 million years ago. Although *A. anamensis* shows many similarities to *A. afarensis,* the shape of the jaws of *A. anamensis* is more like that of modern apes.

Australopithecus garhi   A new species of hominin discovered in the Middle Awash region of Ethiopia and dated to about 2.5 million years ago. The hominin fossils were found near butchered animal bones, and it is possible that *A. garhi* was an early stone tool user.

Badari   Site on the middle portion of the Nile Valley, dating to about 4400–4000 B.C. Numerous burials with elaborate grave goods were found there.

Badarian culture   The archaeological culture, belonging to the earliest farmers in Upper Egypt, associated with the burials found at Badari.

Banpo   A Yangshao period village overlooking a tributary of the Wei River in Henan. The site has yielded evidence for houses, domestic plants and animals, and distinctive red painted pottery.

Barley   *Hordeum vulgaris*—alongside emmer wheat, the most important of the ancient grain crops in the Near East.

Base camps   Areas occupied by a human group for some time, in which a variety of domestic activities took place, such as the preparation, distribution, and consumption of food and the manufacture and use of artifacts such as stone tools. Later base camps commonly show indications of some form of shelter and the use of fire in hearths.

Batons (or *batons de commandement*)   Enigmatic objects of mobiliary art, usually made of reindeer antler and pierced at one end. The function of these items remains unknown.

Bering Land Bridge   A land bridge that connected northeast Asia and Alaska, across what today is the Bering Sea, during late Pleistocene times. Humans moved from Asia to the Americas by way of this land bridge.

Beringia   The term applied to the land mass that extended from the Verkhoyansk Mountain Range in eastern Siberia to the maximum limit of the Laurentide (North American) Ice Sheet, west of the Mackenzie River in the Canadian Yukon, during the late Pleistocene.

Biface   A tool made by removing flakes from both sides of a stone core. Acheulian handaxes and cleavers are usually bifaces.

Bifacial flaking   The removal of flakes alternately from both sides of a stone core (or larger flake) to form an artifact worked on both sides.

Bipedal   Walking upright on two legs.

Bipolar percussion   A stone-working technique, characteristic of Zhoukoudian, in which the piece to be worked is placed upon a stone anvil and then struck with a hammerstone. The resulting flakes have bulbs of percussion on both ends.

Blackwater Draw   The type site for the Clovis Complex, near Clovis, New Mexico. In 1932 Clovis points and other stone tools were found in association with the remains of mammoth.

Blade   A long, narrow stone flake with parallel sides. Blades are generally at least twice as long as they are wide.

Blade core   A core from which blades are struck. Blade cores are generally prismatic (faceted) in shape, and blades are struck off in sequence all around the core.

Boker Tachtit   A site located in the Negev Desert in southern Israel dated to between 45,000 and 38,000 years ago. The site shows a technological transition from tools produced from Levallois cores to tools produced from single platform blade cores.

Border Cave   A site in the Natal region of South Africa that has produced the remains of anatomically modern humans.

Borers   Stone tools retouched to create an extended projection used for drilling holes in materials such as wood and bone.

Boucher de Perthes, Jacques (1788–1868)   French customs agent of aristocratic birth whose discoveries of ancient stone tools, along with the bones of extinct animals in the Somme Valley, north of Paris, provided key evidence for the antiquity of humans.

Bouqras   An early Neolithic site in Syria that has provided evidence for early domesticated sheep.

Breccia   A hard limestone concretion formed from percolating cave water in which ancient artifacts and fossils are frequently embedded.

Bronocice   A large, later Neolithic site in Poland that appears to have been occupied over a considerable period of time. Small parts of this hilltop site were fortified, although it is unclear whether the site served as a place of refuge, as the seat of a small polity, or as a site of ritual feasting.

Bronze Age   The European Bronze Age dated between 2300 B.C. and 800 B.C. During the Early Bronze Age, bronze began to replace stone as a raw material for tools and weapons. Bronze Age societies in Europe are characterized by the appearance of significant differences in status, power, and wealth between individuals.

Brześć Kujawski   A well-documented example of an early farming village in the North European Plain. The settlement, dated to 4500–4000 B.C., is located northwest of Warsaw in Poland and is composed of a series of trapezoidal long houses.

Burins   Stone tools with a chisel-shaped facet, used for engraving and sometimes cutting apart material such as bone and antler.

Burnished   The terms used to describe a clay surface that is rubbed with a small stone or other hard object after firing in order to make the surface shinier and less porous.

Bush Barrow   An Early Bronze Age burial under a tumulus, or earthen mound. The site is located near Stonehenge in southern Britain, and it produced a range of metal items including bronze and copper daggers and gold clothing ornaments.

Butchery marks   The marks left on animal bones during the processes of skinning, carcass disarticulation, and meat removal.

Butchery sites   Sites where meat is removed from the bones of one or more animals. The animal may have been either hunted or scavenged. These sites are marked by the bones of one or more animals plus cutting, chopping, and cleaving tools used to disarticulate the carcass and to remove meat from the bones.

Cahokia   A Mississippian mounded site that is located near the confluence of the Mississippi, Missouri, and Illinois Rivers. The site includes 120 earthen mounds that cover an area of 13 sq. km (5 sq. mi). Cahokia, which reached the height of its power between 1050 and 1250 A.D., appears to have been the administrative center of a complex Mississippian chiefdom.

Cahuachi   The most important Nasca center during the Early Intermediate period, which covers an area of 150 ha (370 ac.) and includes more than 40 mounds. Recent research at Cahuachi has shown that this center was a ceremonial center and not a major urban center.

Carrying capacity   The maximum population size that an environment can support using a particular technology.

Çatal Höyük   A large Neolithic site located in the southern part of Central Anatolia. The site was occupied between about 7300 and 6200 B.C. and may have been home to several thousand people.

Catastrophism   The idea that the succession of layers seen in the Earth's crust was the result of a series of catastrophes (such as universal floods) that wiped out many of the plant and animal species in existence, which were then replaced by new species.

Çayönü   An early farming village located in eastern Turkey. The site, which was occupied between about 8700 and 7500 B.C., yielded the remains of early domesticated einkorn wheat, a cereal that appears to have been domesticated independently in Anatolia.

Cerro Baul   A mesa-top Wari citadel with evidence for large-scale brewing of *chicha*, an alcoholic beverage made from maize. Wari elite may have hosted festivals and provided *chicha* to reward their subordinates.

Cerro Blanco   The Moche capital in the Moche Valley, which was dominated by two major structures, the Huaca del Sol (pyramid of the sun), which served as a palace and mausoleum for Moche leaders, and the smaller Huaca de la Luna (pyramid of the moon), which served as a ritual center. During the Early Intermediate period, the Moche capital was a center of craft production and housed a substantial population.

Chaco Canyon   The location of an integrated system of great houses and smaller settlements that existed in the San Juan River Valley between 900 and 1150 A.D.

Chan Chan   A site located in the Moche River Valley along the north coast of Peru. This vast site served as the political and administrative capital of the Chimú state during the Late Intermediate period.

Châtelperronian   A European stone tool industry that shows both Middle Paleolithic and Upper Paleolithic features. The industry includes Levallois flakes, Mousterian-like scrapers, and backed knives made on blades. This industry was associated with the Saint Césaire Neanderthal.

Chavín de Huántar   A site in the north-central Peruvian highlands whose monumental sculpture reveals a distinctive style and iconography that spread throughout many parts of Peru during the Early Horizon.

Chesowanja   An open site located in the Rift Valley of Kenya dated to 1.4–1.0 million years ago. The stone industry is Oldowan, including choppers and flakes. Areas of burned clay suggest that fire may have been in use. A *Paranthropus boisei* skull was found in the same formation.

Chiefdom   A complex society that lacks the institutions of the state. Chiefdoms are ruled by a chief or leader but lack a permanent government or bureaucracy.

Chimor or the Chimú state   The most powerful state of the Late Intermediate period. At its height the Chimú state controlled two-thirds of the Peruvian coastal desert.

Chinampas   Fields surrounded by canals, also known as floating gardens. This highly productive system of agriculture was used by the Aztecs.

Choga Mami   Site exhibiting several transitional levels between the Samarran culture and the beginnings of the Ubaid period.

Chopper   Pebble tool with only a few flakes removed from one side.

Chopping tool   Pebble tool with flakes removed alternately from two sides. The ridge between the two opposing sets of flakes forms a sharp edge.

Clactonian   A stone tool industry, named after Clacton-on-Sea in southern England, dominated by flakes and without handaxes. The Clactonian appears to be a separate industry from the Acheulian.

Classic period   The period (ca. 250–930 A.D.) that coincides with the florescence of Classic lowland Maya culture. The beginning is marked by the appearance of dated monuments in the southern lowlands. The Classic period ends with the collapse of many Maya urban centers in the southern lowlands.

Cleavers   Bifacially worked tools similar to handaxes, but with a flat, hoelike edge rather than a point.

Clientship   Patron–client relations are social relationships that are established between people of unequal status and wealth. The patron provides certain material goods to the clients, while the client provides labor and loyalty to the patron. Clientship was a fundamental organizing principle of late Iron Age society in Europe.

Clovis   Sites identified by the presence of distinctive, fluted spear points, known as Clovis points. In the American southwest, Clovis sites often produce the remains of mammoth and date between 11,200 and 10,900 years ago. Sites of the Clovis complex are widespread across North and Central America.

Colby   A Clovis Complex site in Wyoming where stacks of mammoth bones were recovered. It has been suggested that the bone stacks represent some form of meat storage.

Collectors   Logistically organized hunter-gatherers. Rather than moving their camps on a periodic or seasonal basis, they obtain particular resources through specially organized task groups.

Combe-Grenal   A Middle Paleolithic cave site along the Dordogne River in southwestern France illustrating the interstratification on layers containing Typical Mousterian, Denticulate Mousterian, and Quina-type Mousterian industries.

Comparative collection   A collection of well-documented modern animal skeletons that can be used to identify fragmented archaeological animal bones.

Complex societies   Societies characterized by inequality in access to resources and a wide variety of social roles.

Composite tools   Tools made of more than one material. Examples include a stone spearpoint attached to a wooden spear and small flint microliths used as barbs for wooden arrows.

Conchoidal fracture   Flint fractures along a cone, or portion of a cone, radiating from the point of impact. Concentric ripple marks usually form so that the surface resembles a sea shell.

Conjoined artifacts   Artifacts that can be fitted back together.

Copper Age (or Chalcolithic)   A term sometimes used to describe the Late Neolithic copper-using culture of Europe during the fourth and third millennia B.C.

Coprolites   Remains of fossilized excrement. The study of these remains can shed light on prehistoric diet, as many coprolites include small seeds, small bones, and other food remains.

Core   A stone from which flakes are detached. Either the core itself or the flakes removed may be used as tools.

Core tool   A tool shaped by removing a series of flakes from a stone core.

Covering laws   General laws that describe and explain a broad range of phenomena, similar to the basic laws of chemistry and physics.

Cranial capacity   The volume of the braincase in milliliters, reflecting the size of the brain.

Cro-Magnon   A cave site in the Dordogne region of southwestern France that has produced the remains of anatomically modern humans.

Cuello   A Preclassic farming village in Belize, where excavations have revealed a long sequence of mud-and-plaster floored houses and their associated yards from the Middle Preclassic period (1200–400 B.C.).

Cultural ecology   The study of the interrelationships between humans and their environment. The environment is defined broadly to include the physical environment, the plants and animals that make up the biological environment, and the social environment, which includes other social groups.

Culture   The system of shared ideas, beliefs, and practices of a group of people that permits them to relate to each other and to give meaning to their everyday lives. Archaeologists generally include the tangible products of these practices—artifacts—within their definition of culture.

Culture history   The chronicle of the successive cultures within a region, and the description of the character and relationships of those cultures.

Cuneiform   Writing, made up of wedge-shaped symbols pressed into clay, each symbol representing a spoken syllable.

Cuzco   The capital of the Inca Empire, located in the southern highlands of Peru.

Cylinder seal   A smooth stone cylinder carved with intricate scenes, often including humans and animals that produced a unique mark of authorship or ownership when rolled over the wet clay of a tablet or the clay seal of a vessel.

Danger Cave   A deeply stratified cave site in western Utah that appears to have been occupied by small, highly mobile bands of hunter-gatherers who subsisted on a broad range of plant and animal resources.

Dar-es-Soltan   A site in Morocco that contained the remains of robust but modern-looking humans associated with an Aterian stone tool industry.

Darwin, Charles (1809–1882)   One of the key figures in the development of our modern understanding of biological evolution, Darwin proposed that new plant and animal species arise as a consequence of natural selection—as organisms are confronted by new circumstances, only individuals that are well-adapted to their environments survive to reproduce. He published his theory in *On the Origin of Species* (1859).

Dawenkou culture   In the eastern portion of the Yellow River Valley, this culture (ca. 4300–2600 B.C.) is broadly contemporary with the Yangshao. Late Dawenkou cemeteries provide evidence for funerary offerings and ritual feasting.

Debitage   Small waste flakes and chips produced during the manufacture of stone tools.

Denali Complex   A stone tool tradition based on microblades produced from small, wedge-shaped cores, which first appears in Alaska about 10,700 years ago. It appears to be closely related to the microblade industries that are seen in Japan, China, and eastern Siberia between 10,000 and 15,000 years ago and may indicate the movement of a second wave of colonists into Alaska.

Denticulates Flake tools with a series of sawlike teeth retouched onto its edges.

Devil's Lair A site in western Australia that may date to as early as 33,000 years ago.

Diffusion The spread of cultural traits, such as technologies, practices, and artistic styles, from one culture to another.

Direct historical analogy The interpretation of archaeological artifacts or features by comparing them to similar artifacts or features in use today, in which a direct historical relationship is known to exist between the archaeological remains and the present-day culture.

Discoids Oldowan stone tools made by removing flakes from flattened pebbles.

DK An early hominin archaeological site found in 1962 in Lower Bed I of Olduvai Gorge by Mary Leakey. DK dates to greater than 1.75 million years ago. It contains an enigmatic and controversial circle of stones which has variously been interpreted as the remains of a shelter and as the result of natural phenomena.

Dmanisi A site in the Caucasus of Georgia, dated to about 1.7 million years ago. Three skulls and a mandible of *Homo ergaster/erectus* have been found at the site. The stone industry consists of flakes and choppers and is lacking in handaxes.

Dölauer-Heide A late Neolithic fortified site in Germany where a complex series of ditches and banks enclose an area of 25 ha (62 ac.).

Drimolen A site in South Africa that has produced the remains of *Paranthropus robustus,* including the most complete skull found to date.

Early Dynastic period The beginning (ca. 2900 to 2350 B.C.) of the historical record in Mesopotamia. This period includes the reigns of the first kings whose names are known from documentary evidence, the "King List."

Early Horizon The period (approximately 900–200 B.C.) traditionally defined as the time when artistic influences from the site of Chavín de Huántar in the Peruvian highlands spread across much of central and northern Peru.

Early Indus or Pre-Urban period The period in South Asia dated between 3200 and 2600 B.C., marked by an increasing intensity of trade, especially the long-distance caravan trade that linked the Indus Valley with Central Asia and Iran. This period is marked by population growth and an increasing concentration of settlements in the Indus Valley.

Early Intermediate period A period (ca. 200 B.C.–600 A.D.) of regional diversity in Peru that begins with the abandonment of many ceremonial centers associated with the Chavín cult.

Early Woodland period The period (approximately 1000–200 B.C.) in the Eastern Woodlands characterized by increasing social and economic complexity seen in a growing trade in exotic, luxury items and increasingly elaborate burial rituals.

Ecofacts Those natural remains that, while not made or manufactured by humans, become incorporated into archaeological deposits and can provide information about past environments and/or human behavior.

Ehringsdorf A site located near Weimar in Germany that is dated to about 230,000 years ago and yielded the human fossils that show many of the characteristics of later Neanderthals, including heavy brow ridges.

Ein Gev I A Kebaran hunters' campsite overlooking the Sea of Galilee. The site appears to have been used on a seasonal basis and was undoubtedly part of a broader circulating settlement pattern.

Einkorn wheat *Triticum monococcum*—an ancient cereal of somewhat lesser importance than emmer and barley. Einkorn was widespread in Anatolia.

Electron spin resonance (ESR) dating An absolute dating method related to thermoluminescence (TL) dating, based upon the electronic measurement of energy trapped in the mineral crystals of a sample. The method is suitable for dating sites of the Lower Paleolithic period and later.

El Mirador A major Preclassic Maya urban center located in northeastern Guatemala. The site has yielded evidence of two monumental architectural complexes and may have controlled long-distance trade in the region.

Emiran The Emiran or Initial Upper Paleolithic industry dates from about 47,000 to 38,000 years ago. It is marked by a gradual shift from a Levallois technology to one based on blades struck from prismatic blade cores. This transition is seen clearly at the site of Boker Tachtit in southern Israel.

Emmer wheat *Triticum dicoccum*—one of the principal ancient cereal crops.

Engis Cave A cave site in Belgium where the skull of a Neanderthal child was discovered in 1830. This was the first Neanderthal fossil to be discovered, although its importance was not recognized at the time.

Eridu City near Al Ubaid in southern Mesopotamia, believed by the Sumerians to be the first city in the world. Eridu is, in fact, one of the earliest urban centers of the region. It includes some of the earliest known temples to Sumerian religion.

Erlitou period The earliest part of the Bronze Age in China (ca. 1900–1500 B.C.). The period takes its name from the site of Erlitou, where a series of early palaces have been uncovered. Most archaeologists believe that the Erlitou period remains represent the material culture of the Xia Dynasty, China's earliest dynasty.

Ertebølle A late Mesolithic (ca. 5500–4000 B.C.) culture of Denmark characterized by a heavy reliance on shellfishing, plus hunting, fishing, and fowling. Ertebølle sites appear to have been occupied on a year-round or near year-round basis.

Ethnoarchaeology The study of the behavior of modern peoples and of the material remains of that behavior. This subfield of archaeology has developed since 1970.

Ethnography The recording and study of the culture, including social relationships and lifeways, of a specific group of people.

Étiolles A Magdalenian site located in the Paris basin where huge flint nodules were used to manufacture stone tools. Careful excavation and recording allowed the process of stone tool manufacure to be recorded.

Eustacy or eustatic sea level changes Variations in world sea levels that result from the growth and melting of glaciers. When large quantities of the earth's water are trapped in glacial ice, worldwide sea levels will fall, as they did many times during the Pleistocene.

Faunal assemblage The group of associated animal bones found together at an archaeological or paleontological site. In East Africa, a distinctive group of animal species, particularly the various species of pigs, is characteristic of a particular period of time, and the faunal assemblages have been used effectively to chronologically correlate the East African early hominin sites.

Fayum Depression An ancient lake bed west of the Nile in central Egypt where the earliest known farmers in Egypt were found.

Features The immovable products of human activities that are affixed to or embedded in the landscape, such as buildings, earthworks, pits, ditches, burials, hearths, and post holes.

Feldhofer The site in the Neander Tal, a valley near Düsseldorf, Germany, where a Neanderthal skeleton was discovered in 1856.

Fertile Crescent The arc-shaped region including the Jordan Valley and the Tigris-Euphrates floodplain of Mesopotamia where the earliest civilizations flourished.

Fission-track dating An absolute dating method that relies upon the counting of the visible trails left behind in mineral crystals by the fission products of uranium-238.

Flint nodules Rounded lumps of flint (a very fine-grained form of silica) originally deposited by silica-containing groundwater into hollows in limestone bedrock. Erosion commonly leaves deposits of flint nodules in the beds of streams, where they form a convenient source of flint for toolmaking.

Flint Run A Clovis quarry site in northern Virginia that was exploited for high-quality jasper.

FLK An early hominin archaeological site in Lower Bed I of Olduvai Gorge dating to about 1.75 million years ago. FLK is the site where the *Zinjanthropus* fossil was found by Mary Leakey in 1959. FLK is one of the most intensively studied of the early Olduvai archaeological sites, and it has figured prominently in the debate concerning hunting versus scavenging by early hominins.

Flotation technique A technique (also known as water separation) that uses rapidly moving water to hold light organic remains in suspension so that they can be separated from archaeological soils.

Fluvial deposits Sediments laid down by rivers.

Folsom A complex named after the type site in Folsom, New Mexico, where fluted points were found in association with the remains of an extinct form of bison. Folsom hunters used fluted points to hunt bison on the High Plains between 10,900 and 10,200 years ago.

Food-sharing hypothesis Hypothesis proposed by Glynn Isaac to account for the function of the early hominin sites at Olduvai Gorge and Koobi Fora. According to the food-sharing hypothesis, sites such as FLK served as home bases, to which hunter-scavengers (presumably males) brought meat and to which other group members (presumably females) brought gathered plant foods and small game. At the home base, these foods were shared and redistributed among the group. The food-sharing hypothesis makes the organization of early hominin groups seem very much like that of later humans.

Foragers Hunter-gatherers who move their campsites on a periodic or seasonal basis to make use of different patches of food resources.

Forbes' Quarry, Gibraltar A Neanderthal skull was discovered at this site in 1848 during military construction.

Formative period The period (approximately 2000 B.C.–250 A.D.) during which the earliest complex societies in Mesoamerica appear. During this period we see the appearance of the earliest monumental architecture and sculpture in Mesoamerica and the beginnings of urbanism in the region. The beginning of the period is marked by the appearance of pottery-using agriculturalists in Mesoamerica.

Frere, John (1740–1807)   English scholar who was one of the first to suspect the antiquity of human beings. He discovered flint tools buried deep below the surface, in the company of the bones of unknown animals, at Hoxne, Suffolk, in eastern England, and concluded that the flint tools must have been made in the very remote past.

Ganj Dareh   An early Neolithic site in western Iran that has provided evidence for the world's earliest domesticated goats.

Gatecliff Shelter   A site located in the Monitor Valley in Nevada. Excavations at the site revealed 10 m (33 ft.) of sediments and 16 cultural horizons. From 4000 B.C. onward, the shelter appears to have been occupied periodically as a short-term camp by small groups of hunter-gatherers.

Geomagnetic reversals   Abrupt interchanges of the Earth's North and South magnetic poles, reflected in the magnetization of the Earth's rocks, and useful for estimating the possible ages of geological deposits.

Gesher Benot Ya'aqov   An Acheulian site in the Jordan Valley of Israel roughly about 780,000 years ago. The site includes well-preserved organic remains (wood, seeds, fruits, and bark). An elephant skull at the site may have been manipulated with the help of a log that was found beneath it. In addition, the site has yielded evidence of early hearths.

Gilgal   An early Neolithic site located in the Jordan Valley north of Jericho that has provided evidence for very early cultivated barley.

Glacials   Episodes of worldwide cold temperatures during which much of the earth's water was trapped in large ice masses (glaciers) that covered large parts of northern Eurasia and North America.

Glaze   A material that melts during firing to produce a glasslike surface on pottery.

Gran Dolina   Cave site in the Atapuerca mountain range in northern Spain, containing long sequence strata with stone artifacts and numerous human fossils. The lower layers contain pebble tools and flakes and fossils of *Homo antecessor*. The site dates to greater than 780,000 years ago.

Gravettian   Industry (ca. 28,000–22,000 B.P.) characterized by the presence of gravette points, microgravette bladelets, tanged points, and burins made on truncations.

Great Basin   The region of the American West that lies between the Sierra Nevada-Cascade Mountains and the Wasatch Range and includes nearly all of Nevada and parts of the surrounding states.

Great Rift Valley   The great valley system of East Africa, extending from Mozambique in the south to the Red Sea in the north, that includes most of the early hominin sites of East Africa. The Great Rift Valley was formed by the movement of the geological rift that separates the continental African plate from the Somali plate to the east.

Gritille   An early Neolithic settlement dated between 8100 and 6300 B.C., located on the Euphrates River in southeastern Anatolia. The artifacts from the site show many similarities to the Levantine PPNB.

Grotte Chauvet   This painted cave site located in Vallon-Pont-d'Arc (Ardèche) in southern France and discovered in 1994 revealed an unusual range of Ice Age images. In addition to painted pictures of horses, bovids, and other common animals, the Grotte Chauvet included depictions of woolly rhinos and carnivores such as cave bears and felines. The images date to approximately 30,000 years ago.

Grotte Cosquer   A recently discovered painted cave near Marseilles whose entrance lies 37 m (120 ft.) under water. The images in the cave were painted between 19,000 and 27,000 years ago.

Guilá Naquitz   A small camp site located in the Valley of Oaxaca in southern Mexico. The site yielded the remains of early domesticated squash and gourds, as well as evidence for a pattern of seasonal use of a range of wild plant and animal resources.

Hadar   Site located in the Afar Triangle, Ethiopia, that has produced an extensive series of fossils of *Australopithecus afarensis*.

Halafians   Members of the culture that succeeded the Hassuna and Samarra cultures in the northern uplands, noted for their finely made pottery, with complex red and black painted geometric patterns, sometimes combined with stylized animals.

Half-life   The time required for one-half of a radioactive element to decay.

Hallstatt period   The first half of the European Iron Age (ca. 800–480 B.C.). During the later part of the Hallstatt period, commercial towns such as the Heuneberg were established in west-central Europe. These towns appear to have been engaged in extensive trade relations with the Greek colony of Massilia (Marseille).

Hammerstone A stone used as a striker to remove flakes from a stone core

Handaxe A large stone tool, usually bifacially worked and ovoid in shape, with a flattened cross-section. Handaxes are characteristic of the Acheulian industry, but they are found in later industries as well.

Harappa One of the largest urban centers of the Indus Valley civilization, located in the Punjab region of northern Pakistan. The site includes both a citadel and a lower town, and the city may have housed 40,000 inhabitants at its height.

Hassuna Type site, near Mosul in northwestern Iraq, of the Hassuna culture.

Hassuna culture Village farmers of about 6900–6500 B.C. who grew their crops at a sufficient altitude that rainfall agriculture was possible.

Hayonim Terrace A Natufian site in northern Israel that has provided evidence for small circular structures with stone foundations.

Herto Bouri A location in the Middle Awash region of Ethiopia that has yielded the remains of three hominins who appear to be directly ancestral to anatomically modern *Homo sapiens*. These fossils were associated with a stone industry that is transitional between the Acheulian and the Middle Stone Age.

Heterarchy Complex societies that are characterized by a series of separate, sometimes competing, hierarchies.

Heuneberg One of the early trading towns of the late Hallstatt period, the Heuneberg is located near the Danube in southern Germany. The site appears to have been engaged in trade with the Greek colony of Marseille.

Hierakonpolis The site in Upper Egypt of one of the most ancient cities in Egypt. Hierakonpolis was probably the capital of one of the kingdoms that preceded the unification of Egypt. The famous Narmer Palette was found there. Hierakonpolis continued as an important center throughout Egyptian history.

Hilly Flanks The low grass-covered foothills of the Zagros, Taurus, and Lebanon-Amanus mountains that surround the fertile crescent, an area that today receives sufficient winter rainfall to support agriculture without irrigation.

Hogup Cave A cave site located on the Great Salt Lake in northern Utah. The site yielded more than 4 m (13 ft.) of archaeological deposits spanning the last 9300 years.

Holocene The Holocene or Recent epoch begins with the end of the Pleistocene about 10,300 radiocarbon years ago. The beginning of the Holocene is marked by a worldwide rise in temperatures signaling the end of the Pleistocene glaciations.

Hominin A member of the tribe *Hominini* that includes modern humans and other members of the genus *Homo*, as well as closely related forms such as *Australopithecus*, *Paranthropus*, and *Ardipithecus*.

Homo antecessor A name given to the early hominin fossils from Gran Dolina in Spain. These hominins may be ancestral to both the Neanderthals and anatomically modern humans.

Homo erectus The successor to *Homo habilis*, *Homo erectus* includes a variable group of fossils with brain sizes generally greater than *H. habilis* but less than that of modern humans. *Homo erectus* generally had a low, sloping forehead with a thick bar of bone over the eyes and a forward-projecting face.

Homo erectus pekinensis Originally called "Sinanthropus pekinensis." The variety of *Homo erectus* found in China at Zhoukoudian.

Homo ergaster Some scholars reserve the term *Homo erectus* for the Asian fossil humans. They classify African specimens such as Nariokotome III as *Homo ergaster*.

Homo habilis The earliest members of the genus *Homo*. *Homo habilis* was first found at Olduvai Gorge. The best known of the Koobi Fora finds, ER-1470, is now classified by some scholars to a second genus, *Homo rudolfensis*. *H. habilis* has been identified at Omo and at Sterkfontein in South Africa as well and dates from 1.7 to 2.4 million years ago.

Homo heidelbergensis A form of early human, named after the mandible found at Mauer, near Heidelberg, which is intermediate in some respects between *Homo erectus* and early *Homo sapiens*.

Hopewell Interaction Sphere A widespread trade and exchange network, dating to the Middle Woodland period, marked by the exchange of exotic raw materials, distinctive finished items, and ideas across a broad region of the American Midwest and Southeast.

Hougang One of the best known Longshan sites. The site has provided evidence for houses surrounded by a stamped-earth wall. In fact, burials appear to be associated with construction activities at Hougang.

Howieson's Poort A Middle Stone Age industry, dating to about 70,000 years ago, characterized by the presence of microliths.

Hutton, James (1726–1797) Scottish geologist who contended that the Earth underwent a continuous cycle of mountain uplift, erosion, and the deposition of sediments to form new layers of rock. Hutton introduced the doctrine of uniformitarianism.

Hypothesis   A tentative explanation to account for an observed set of facts or events. A hypothesis is provisional and unproved, and its acceptance depends on the gathering of further evidence. A hypothesis often suggests specific consequences, so that it can be tested by an attempt to observe those consequences.

Inca   The term that refers to a small ethnic group from southern Peru. The Incas built and ruled the Inca Empire, which became the largest pre-Columbian empire in the Americas.

Independent invention   The independent development of a new trait or technology within a region without the influence of an outside source.

Indian Knoll   A Late Archaic (ca. 3100 B.C.) site in southwestern Kentucky that yielded the remains of more than 1000 burials. Many of the grave goods were utilitarian items such as axes, woodworking tools, and nutcracking stones, but some burials also included exotic materials such as copper and marine shells.

Indirect percussion   A method of producing stone tools in which the hammerstone never makes direct contact with the flint core. The hammerstone strikes an intermediate object, such as a punch, which is in contact with the stone core.

Indus Age   A term used to describe the societies of western South Asia from the beginning of agriculture about 9000 years ago to the beginning of the Iron Age (about 1000 B.C.).

Indus Valley or Harappan civilization   The earliest urban, literate society in the Indian subcontinent. Throughout the third millennium B.C., Indus Valley cities, towns, and villages were spread across Pakistan and northern India. These sites shared a common written language and material culture, but it is not clear whether they were politically unified.

Initial period   The period (1800–900 B.C.) whose beginning is marked by the appearance of pottery. During the Initial period, farming came to play a more central role in the Peruvian economy.

Interglacials   Warmer periods that alternated with the glacials when temperatures were often as high or higher than they are today.

Iron Age   The European age that begins with the replacement of bronze by iron in the manufacture of tools and weapons (ca. 800 B.C.) and ends with the Roman conquest of much of western Europe in the first century B.C. It is during the Iron Age that the first towns and cities appear in temperate Europe.

Isernia La Pineta   Site in central Italy containing stone tools and animal bones, dated by K-Ar to greater than 730,000 years ago, although faunal evidence suggests that the age of this site may be considerably younger.

Isostacy or glacio-isostatic sea level changes   Sea level changes that result from the weight of the glaciers on the earth's crust and from the release of that weight as a result of glacial melting.

Isotopes   Forms of a chemical element, distinguished by differences in atomic weight.

Jarmo   A prehistoric site, dated to about 7750 B.C. and located in Iraqi Kurdistan, that provided evidence for early domesticated wheat, barley, sheep, and goats, as well as domesticated dogs.

Jebel Irhoud   A skull from Morocco whose features are transitional between *Homo erectus* and modern humans.

Jemdat Nasr period   Period (3100–2900 B.C.) just preceding the Early Dynastic period, showing continued development from the Uruk phase.

Jenné-jeno   An urban center in the Inland Niger Delta of Mali that was established around 250 B.C. and reached its maximum extent in the ninth century A.D. The site was abandoned around A.D. 1400.

Jericho   A deeply stratified tell (city-mound) site located in the West Bank. The earliest Neolithic (PPNA) levels at Jericho have revealed an enigmatic stone tower and evidence for early cultivated wheat and barley.

Kabwe (Broken Hill)   A human skull discovered in Zambia that may be an ancestor of modern humans. This robust skull dates to perhaps 200,000 years ago and was formerly known as Rhodesian Man.

Karim Shahir   A late Pleistocene site in northern Iraq that appears to have been occupied by mobile hunter-gatherers but that shares some features, such as pecked and ground stone tools, with later early Neolithic sites in the region.

Karanovo   An early farming village in central Bulgaria. At Karanovo, small, square houses were framed with poles and plastered with mud.

Katanda   A site in the Congo, dated to approximately 90,000 years ago, that has produced Middle Stone Age artifacts and a number of finely worked bone points, many with barbs along one or both edges.

Kebara   A site in northern Israel that has yielded the remains of a nearly complete Neanderthal skeleton, as well as extensive evidence for hearths, faunal remains, and Middle Paleolithic stone tools.

Kebaran Complex   The term used to describe the later Upper Paleolithic industries in the Levant, dated between about 19,000 and 14,000 years ago. Microliths typically form a major part of Kebaran stone tool assemblages.

Kelheim   A large (approximately 600 ha, or 1500 ac.) Iron Age oppidum located in Bavaria in southern Germany. Recent excavations at the site have shown that large quantities of iron were being produced at Kelheim during the late La Tène period.

Khartoum Neolithic   The earliest farmers in Nubia. Farming communities were established along the banks of the Nile beginning around 4500 B.C.

Kill sites   Archaeological sites where an animal or animals were hunted and killed. These sites are usually marked by the bones of one or more animals plus weapons such as spear points.

Kimmswick   A site near St. Louis, Missouri, where Clovis artifacts were found to be associated with the skeleton of a mastodon.

Kitchen middens   Late Mesolithic shell mounds found in Denmark and North Germany that contain the remains of oysters, mussels, and cockles, as well as the bones of wild mammals, birds, and fish.

Klasies River Mouth   A site in South Africa, where Middle Stone Age tools appear before 120,000 years ago, associated with the remains of early anatomically modern humans.

Konso-Gardula   Dated to about 1.6 million years ago, Konso-Gardula in Ethiopia is one of the very earliest Acheulian sites. A *Homo erectus* mandible was found at the site.

Koobi Fora   Locality in Kenya that has produced many early hominin fossils, including fossils of *Paranthropus boisei* and *Homo erectus,* as well as some of the best preserved specimens of *Homo rudolfensis.*

Kostenki I   An Upper Paleolithic site on the Don River in eastern Ukraine that has yielded evidence for a large complex of habitation features, including storage pits, sleeping pits, work areas, and central hearths.

Koster   A deeply stratified site in southwestern Illinois that has provided a wealth of information on Archaic subsistence practices and settlement patterns in the American Midwest. The data reflect a shift toward increasing settlement permanence and increasingly intensive use of aquatic resources.

Kot Diji   An Indus Valley site that was occupied during the Early and Mature Harappan periods. The site is located near the major urban center of Mohenjo Daro. Kot Diji gave its name to a style of Early Harappan pottery that was widely distributed throughout the Indus Valley.

Kromdraai   Site in South Africa that has yielded fossils of *Paranthropus robustus.*

Kuk   A site in the highlands of New Guinea where charcoal associated with fire-cracked rocks has been dated to about 30,000 years ago. This site has also produced evidence for the domestication of bananas about 6500 years ago.

La Chapelle-aux-Saints   A site in central France where a relatively complete Neanderthal skeleton was discovered in 1908. The Old Man of La Chapelle suffered from severe arthritis.

La Cotte de Sainte-Brelade   A site on the Isle of Jersey in the Channel Islands where the bones of numerous woolly rhinos and mammoths have been found beneath a cliff. The site has been interpreted as the remains of a hunting drive.

Laetoli   Site in Tanzania that has produced fossils of *Australopithecus afarensis*. It is best known for the trail of footprints of an erect-walking hominin discovered there.

La Ferrassie   A site in the Dordogne region of southwestern France that yielded seven Neanderthal burials. The site has sometimes been interpreted as a family cemetery.

Lake Mungo   An archaeological locality in the Willandra Lakes region of New South Wales, Australia, that yielded human burials, stone tools, and hearths that were approximately 25–30,000 years old.

Lantian   An area in central China where *Homo erectus* fossils have been found.

Lapedo Child   A skeleton from Portugal of a four-year-old child dated to 24,000 years ago. The skeleton shows morphological features of both modern humans and Neanderthals. Some anthropologists have interpreted the child as a hybrid.

La Riera   A Solutrean, Magdalenian, and later site from northern Spain that reveals changes in Upper Paleolithic subsistence through time. The data suggest that marine and estuarine resources played an increasingly important role in the diet.

Lascaux Cave   A cave site located in the Dordogne region of southwest France, which was discovered in 1940. The extensive series of painted images, including horses, bison, deer, wild cattle, and an enigmatic human figure holding a bird-headed staff, have been the subject of detailed scientific investigations in recent years. Radiocarbon dating of the lamp wicks indicate that the cave was painted about 17,000 years ago.

Late Harappan or Post-Urban period   A period (ca. 1900 to 1000 B.C.) of major cultural change in northern India and Pakistan. The beginning of the Late Harappan period is marked by the abandonment of a number of towns and cities (e.g., Mohenjo-daro), the disappearance of the Indus Valley script, a reduction in long-distance trade, and the development of regional styles of pottery and metalwork.

Late Horizon   The period (1476–1532 A.D.) when the Inca empire expanded rapidly. It ends with the Spanish conquest of Peru in 1532.

Late Intermediate period   The period (1000–1476 A.D.) that begins with the collapse of the Huari and Tiwanaku states and ends with the rapid expansion of the Inca Empire in the century before the Spanish conquest of Peru.

La Tène period   The later part of the European Iron Age, approximately 480 B.C. to 1 B.C. The period is named after the type site in Switzerland where numbers of decorated metal artifacts were recovered in the nineteenth century. La Tène art style is associated with people whom the Greeks and Romans called Celts.

Late Stone Age   The term used to describe the late Pleistocene stone tool industries of sub-Saharan Africa. These industries are broadly contemporary with the Upper Paleolithic Cultures of Europe and the Near East.

Late Woodland period   The period (400–800 A.D.) during which the initial adoption of maize agriculture in the Eastern Woodlands took place. In comparison with the Middle Woodland societies that preceded them and the Mississippian chiefdoms that followed, Late Woodland societies in the Midwest and Southeast were relatively egalitarian.

La Venta   The site in southern Mexico that emerged as a leading Olmec ceremonial center between about 900 and 400 B.C.

Lehner   A Clovis kill site in extreme southwestern Arizona dated by radiocarbon to about 10,900 years ago. At the site numerous mammoths, as well as horses, bison, and tapirs, appear to have been killed and butchered on the spot.

Lehringen   An early Middle Paleolithic site in Germany that has produced the remains of a wooden spear found beneath the skeleton of an elephant.

Leister prongs   Parts of spears that are armed with prongs and used to catch fish. Mesolithic leister prongs were often made of bone or antler and barbed along the inside edges.

Le Moustier   A site in the Dordogne region of southwestern France that gave its name to the Mousterian stone tool industry. The cave site has yielded Neanderthal

skeletal remains in addition to a wide range of Middle Paleolithic stone tools.

Leubingen burial   A burial site in eastern Germany that includes two individuals who were interred in an oak chamber under a mound of stone and earth. The grave goods included a diverse array of gold and bronze objects, while most other Early Bronze Age burials include only pottery vessels.

Levallois index   The Levallois index is a measure of the proportion of Middle Paleolithic stone tools made using the Levallois technique.

Levalloiso-Mousterian   The term used to describe the Middle Paleolithic stone tool industry in the Near East. These assemblages generally include large numbers of Levallois flakes and points.

Levallois technique   A technique by which a stone core is specially shaped so that flakes of a predetermined shape and size could be struck from it.

Levantine Aurignacian   The term used to describe Early Upper Paleolithic sites that have produced relatively few blades and bladelets and greater numbers of flakes, end scrapers, and burins. Similar assemblages have been identified from Upper Paleolithic sites in Iran and Iraq; these are termed Zagros Aurignacian.

Linearbandkeramik or LBK (Linear Pottery Culture)   This culture is named for its distinctive ceramics that were decorated with curvilinear designs. LBK settlements spread rapidly across the Loess belt of central and western Europe between 5700 and 4900 B.C. The LBK houses are long, rectangular structures built of large posts.

Lithic industry   A set of artifacts, primarily tools, made from stone.

Lithic reduction sequences   Sequences of steps used to produce a stone tool. Using refitting techniques archaeologists can describe the steps used to produce a finished stone tool from an unmodified flint nodule. The ways in which a tool was resharpened and reused can also be determined.

Living floors   Ground surfaces upon which an assemblage of artifacts and (frequently) food remains is found. It implies a relatively undisturbed site, including the remains from a brief, well-defined period of occupation.

Loess belt   The area of central Europe that lay between the Scandinavian ice sheet and the Alpine ice sheet during the height of the last glaciation. This area was covered by fine, airborne sediments known as loess. This region was home to the earliest farming villages in central and western Europe.

Lomas   Areas of vegetation in the coastal regions of Peru that are supported by condensation from fog rather than by rainfall.

Longshan Culture   Sites of the late Neolithic Longshan Culture (2800/2600–1900 B.C.) appear over a wide area of northern China in the early third millennium B.C. Many Longshan graves include eggshell pottery cups that were designed to hold fermented beverages.

Lothal   A Mature Harappan town in northwestern India that has provided evidence for intentional urban planning, craft specialization, and trade in semiprecious stones, steatite, ivory, and sea shells.

Lyell, Charles (1797–1875)   English geologist whose extremely influential textbook, *Principles of Geology* (1830–33), revived and expanded the uniformitarian principles introduced by James Hutton. Lyell's work helped stimulate the young Charles Darwin in the development of his theory of the origin of species by natural selection.

Maadi   A site near Cairo, dating to around 3650 B.C. The people of Maadi lived in houses made from mud and reed matting and were buried in a cemetery adjoining the settlement in simple pits without any grave goods.

Maadi culture   The term frequently used for the late Neolithic sites of the Egyptian Delta.

Magdalenian   The term used to describe late Upper Paleolithic sites in western Europe, about 18,000–11,000 years ago. Magdalenian sites are characterized by the presence of bone and antler harpoons.

Makapansgat   Site in South Africa that has yielded many fossils of *Australopithecus africanus.*

Mallaha/Eynan   The site that is known as Mallaha (Arabic) and Eynan (Hebrew) is located in the northern Jordan Valley in Israel. Excavations during the 1950s and 1960s revealed the stone foundations of small, circular huts that appear to have been occupied by hunter-gatherer populations on a permanent basis.

Manching   An oppidum site located in southern Germany at the confluence of the Danube and the Paar Rivers. The site covers an area of 380 ha (939 ac.) and is surrounded by a fortification wall. Long-term excavations at the site have revealed a planned street layout and evidence for extensive craft production.

Mastabas   Flat-topped, rectangular tombs, sometimes including internal rooms, that were the predecessors of the pyramids.

Material culture   The tangible products of human behaviors. In archaeology, material culture refers to the artifacts, features, and sites left behind by earlier peoples.

Mature Indus or Urban period   The period (2500–1900 B.C.) in the Indian subcontinent characterized by the appearance of large urban sites, the intensification of trade and craft specialization, increasing social stratification, and the appearance of the Indus Valley script.

Mauer   The mandible found at Mauer, near Heidelberg, Germany, with features suggestive of both *Homo erectus* and an early form of *Homo sapiens.* It is sometimes given a separate name, *Homo heidelbergensis.*

Mediterranean vegetation   The mixed oak–pistachio parkland that historically covered many of the less arid parts of the Middle East. The Mediterranean vegetation zone expanded around 14,000 B.P. as a result of the warmer, wetter climatic conditions that prevailed during the late glacial period.

Mehrgarh   A site in the Baluchistan region of Pakistan that was occupied from about 7000 B.C. through the end of the Early Indus period (mid-third millennium B.C.). During the aceramic Neolithic (6300–5300 B.C.) occupation of the site, the farmers at Mehrgarh appear to have domesticated zebu cattle and probably also sheep from local wild animals.

Memphis   Ancient Egypt's first capital, said to have been founded by Menes. It was located near modern Cairo.

Menes   The traditional founder of the Egyptian First Dynasty, who may have been Narmer or an immediate successor.

Merimbda   An early settlement site in the western Delta dating to between 4800 and 4400 B.C. Originally a few temporary reed or matting shelters, it grew into a small village of oval or round mud-walled houses. The dead were buried without grave offerings among the houses.

Mesa Verde   A classic example of an aggregated pueblo settlement built in the eleventh and twelfth centuries A.D.

Mesoamerica   The geographic region that includes southern Mexico and the adjacent regions of Central America, including Guatemala, El Salvador, Belize, and the western portions of Honduras, Nicaragua, and Costa Rica. The area lies between 10° and 22° north latitude and includes both cool tropical highlands and warm tropical lowlands (along the Yucatan and the Gulf of Mexico). This region was the home of some of the earliest complex societies in the Americas.

Mesolithic   The time in Europe (ca. 9500–approximately 4000 B.C.) is the time between the end of the

Pleistocene Ice Age and the beginnings of farming. It is the period of postglacial foraging in Europe.

Mesopotamia   The alluvial lowland lying between the Tigris and Euphrates Rivers where the ancient urban societies, beginning with Sumer, arose.

Mezhirich   A late Upper Paleolithic site near the Dneiper River in Ukraine that has yielded evidence for several small dwellings constructed of mammoth bone. The site is dated to about 15,000 B.P.

Mezmaiskaya Cave   A cave in Georgia (Caucasus) that has yielded the remains of a 29,000-year-old Neanderthal infant. Recent studies have shown that the infant's mtDNA is outside the range of modern human variation but is quite similar to that of the Feldhofer Neanderthal from Germany.

Microlith   A very small tool, often hafted or used as a barb for an arrowhead.

Middle Horizon   The period (600–1000 A.D.) marked by the rise of two powerful states in South America—Tiwanaku in the southern highlands and Wari, whose capital was located in the Ayacucho Valley in central Peru.

Middle Paleolithic   The term used to describe the stone tool industries of Europe, the Middle East, and North Africa that date between about 200,000 and 40,000 years ago. They generally include a wider range of tool forms than the earlier Lower Paleolithic industries and often include large numbers of tools made using the Levallois technique.

Middle-range theories   Hypotheses and theories of a limited nature intended to explain specific archaeological phenomena.

Middle Stone Age   The term used to describe the African stone tool industries that are roughly contemporary with the Middle Paleolithic industries of Europe and the Near East. Middle Stone Age industries often include large numbers of parallel-sided flakes or blades, often produced using the Levallois technique.

Middle Woodland period   The period (approximately 200 B.C.–400 A.D.) during which a widespread network of trade and exchange, known as the Hopewell Interaction Sphere, developed in the Eastern Woodlands.

Migration   The physical movement of a people from one geographical area to another.

Mississippian   The term used to describe the chiefdom-level societies that developed in the Midwest and Southeast United States between 800–1500 A.D. Mississippian settlements are concentrated in the meander-belt zones of eastern rivers.

Mitochondrial DNA (mtDNA)   DNA (or units of heredity) that are enclosed mitochondria of the cell and are inherited from the mother only.

MNI (minimum number of individuals)   A method for estimating the relative proportions of different species in a faunal assemblage. It is based on an estimation of the number of animals needed to account for all the bones in the assemblage.

Mobiliary art   Portable objects made of stone, bone, antler, and ivory, including such items as decorated spear throwers, incised plaques, and female figurines.

Mochica, or Moche   The state that arose in the north coastal region of Peru during the Early Intermediate period.

Mode 1   A general term for core and flake industries such as the Oldowan.

Mohenjo-daro   One of the large Indus Valley urban centers. The site is located in the Indus Valley in southern Pakistan. It included both a citadel or upper town with a ritual bath and other administrative buildings and a lower town with residences, shops, and craft activities.

Mojokerto   Site in Java at which *Homo erectus* fossils have been found and recently redated to 1.8 million years old.

Monte Albán   The urban capital of the state that developed in the Valley of Oaxaca between about 500 B.C. and 750 A.D.

Monte Verde   A site in south-central Chile that provides evidence for human occupation of the region at about 12,500 B.P. The site has yielded evidence for stone tools and organic remains, including wood, bone, and skin.

Moraine   A deposit of soil and stone pushed along by a glacier and deposited at its margins.

Moundville   A large Mississippian center located in west-central Alabama. The site, which was extensively excavated from 1930 to 1941, includes at least 29 mounds arranged around a central plaza.

Mount Sandel   An early Mesolithic (ca. 8000 B.C.) site in Northern Ireland that has produced evidence for small, circular dwellings and a diversified economy based on hunting and fishing.

Mousterian   A term used to describe the Middle Paleolithic (200,000 to 40,000 years ago) industries of Europe, North Africa, and the Middle East. These industries are named for the type site of Le Moustier in southwestern France.

Movius Line   The line of demarcation between those parts of the Old World with handaxes (Africa, western Europe, the Near East, and India) and those areas with Oldowan-like or "chopper/chopping tool" industries without handaxes (eastern Europe, China, Southeast Asia, and Indonesia). This distinction was first proposed by Hallam Movius in the 1940s.

Mugharet es Skhul   A cave site in the Mount Carmel region of northern Israel that has produced the remains of 10 human individuals associated with a Levalloiso-Mousterian industry. The human fossils appear to be early anatomically modern people.

Mugharet et Tabun   A cave site in the Mount Carmel region of northern Israel that has yielded the skeleton of a woman, in addition to a Levalloiso-Mousterian stone tool assemblage.

Multiregional hypothesis   The multiregional hypothesis proposes that modern human populations in Africa, Asia, and Europe are descended from earlier *(Homo erectus)* populations in each area. Sufficient gene flow would have occurred between these groups to maintain *Homo sapiens* as a single, variable population.

Murray Springs site   The Clovis Complex site located in extreme southeastern Arizona. It includes a mammoth kill, a bison kill, and a hunters' camp. The site has also produced environmental evidence for a Clovis-period drought that ended about 10,900 years ago.

NAGPRA   The Native American Graves Protection and Repatriation Act, which requires that Native American human remains, ceremonial objects, and objects of cultural patrimony be returned to the Native American tribes.

Naqada   A settlement with several adjacent large cemeteries (containing about 3000 predynastic graves) excavated by the British archaeologist Sir Flinders Petrie in the 1890s. Most of these graves belong to the time span following the Badarian and before the earliest Egyptian dynasty.

Naqada I (Amratian)   The period, found only in Upper Egypt, dating from approximately 4000 to 3500 B.C. The Nagada I period is much like the preceding Badarian. Most of the evidence comes from cemeteries; few settlements have been found.

Naqada II (Gerzean)   The period dating to approximately 3500 to 3200 B.C. Naqada II is more widespread than Naqada I, appearing as far north as the Delta and as far south as Nubia. Substantial settlements appear, and some of the burials become much more elaborate, indicating the beginning of a hierarchical society.

Naqada III (Semainian)   The period, sometimes called the proto-dynastic period, dating to approximately 3200 to 3100 B.C., just preceding the unification of Egypt. Small kingdoms probably grew up with their capitals at Naqada and Hierakonpolis. These towns gradually became increasingly populated. A ruling elite developed, and hieroglyphic writing appeared toward the end of the period.

Nariokotome III   A very nearly complete skeleton of a young *Homo ergaster*—"Turkana Boy"—dating to about 1.5 million years ago, found near Lake Turkana, Kenya.

Narmer   A ruler whose reign precedes the earliest dynasties in the historic Egyptian lists of kings, who is often regarded as the unifier of Egypt. Narmer is often identified with Menes. Narmer's name appears on the palette found at Hierakonpolis showing a ruler wearing the double crowns of Upper and Lower Egypt, the first to do so.

Nasca   The culture centered on the Nazca and Ica Valleys of Peru's south coast during the Early Intermediate period. Although the Nasca appear to have been a nonurban, nonstate society, they constructed a large ceremonial center at Cahuachi and are well known for their craftsmanship in pottery and textiles.

Natufian culture   The Natufian culture extended over much of the southern Levant between 15,000 and 12,000 years ago. The Natufians were complex foragers who relied on a combination of intensive gazelle hunting and plant collection. Typical Natufian artifacts include small lunate microliths, flint sickle blades, sickle hafts, and stone mortars and pestles.

Neanderthals   Archaic form of *Homo sapiens* found in Europe and the Middle East between about 200,000 and 40,000 years ago. The Neanderthals are characterized by massive brow ridges, sloping foreheads, long, low skulls, and the absence of a chin.

Nea Nikomedeia   Site in Greek Macedonia dating to about 7000 B.C. and one of the earliest farming villages in all of Europe. At Nea Nikomedeia farmers inhabited small, single-roomed, square houses and raised wheat, barley, sheep, goats, cattle, and pigs.

Nelson Bay Cave   A Late Stone Age (19,000–12,000 years ago) site in South Africa that has yielded evidence for late Pleistocene hunting, fowling, and fishing practices.

Nenana Complex   A hunters' toolkit, found in the earliest Alaskan sites and dated to between 12,000 and 11,000 years ago. It included small, bifacially worked projectile points, retouched blades, scrapers, wedges, and planes.

Netiv Hagdud   An early Neolithic site located in the lower Jordan Valley north of Jericho that has provided evidence for small, oval houses and early cultivated barley.

New Archaeology   The view, advocated by such workers as L. Binford, P. J. Watson, S. LeBlanc, and C. Redman, that archaeology should focus on processes of culture change rather than the compilation of culture histories and that archaeologists should attempt to develop archaeological and cultural laws, similar to those of the natural sciences, through the formulation and testing of hypotheses.

Ngaloba   A skull from Tanzania that shows a mix of modern human and archaic (*Homo erectus*-like) features. It was found associated with a Middle Stone Age stone tool assemblage.

NISP (number of identified specimens per taxon)   A method for calculating the relative portions of various animals in a faunal collection. It is based on the total number of bones identified for each species.

North European Plain   The North European Plain stretches from northern France, across northern Germany, southern Scandinavia, Poland, and eastward into Russia. These areas were either covered by the Scandinavian ice sheet or by the outwash gravels and sands in front of it. This region is characterized by a great diversity of soil types.

Notches.   Stone flakes tool with a notch retouched into one edge, possibly for woodworking.

Oasis/propinquity theory   The oasis theory argues that a widespread desiccation at the end of the Pleistocene led to the concentration of humans, plants, and animals in well-watered oases where humans learned to domesticate these other species. This theory was first proposed by V. Gordon Childe.

Oldowan   The very early stone industry, first described by Mary Leakey, originally found in the archaeological sites in Bed I at Olduvai Gorge but since found elsewhere in Africa. The characteristic artifacts of the Oldowan are flakes and choppers and chopping tools made from pebbles. Other artifact forms also present include cores, polyhedrons, scrapers, spheroids, and discoids.

Olduvai Gorge   Locality in Tanzania that includes numerous fossil and archaeological sites and that has produced many early hominin fossils. *Paranthropus boisei* and *Homo habilis* were first identified at Olduvai Gorge, and *Homo erectus* has also been found there.

Olmecs   The people who inhabited the southern Gulf coast of Mexico during the Formative period. Their centers include monumental architecture and sculpture (huge stone heads). While the Olmecs were traditionally considered Mesoamerica's "mother culture," they now appear to be just one of a number of early complex societies that appear in Mesoamerica during the Formative period.

Omo   Site in southern Ethiopia, investigated by F. C. Howell and Y. Coppens, that includes, in addition to a number of early hominin fossils, a broad range of animal fossil assemblages in a particularly well-dated context. These animal bone data have been very useful in chronologically correlating the fossil hominin sites in eastern Africa.

Omo 2   A skull from Ethiopia, dating to about 130,000 years ago, whose face looks quite modern, but the rear portion of the skull resembles earlier *Homo erectus* fossils.

Omo Kibish   An anatomically modern skull and limb bones from Ethiopia dating to about 100,000 years ago.

Open-area excavation   A large excavation designed to reveal the spatial relationships between artifacts, ecofacts, and features.

Oppida   Urban sites that appear in temperate Europe in the last two centuries B.C. They are generally large, fortified sites and appear to have served a variety of functions—as political capitals, centers of craft production, places of refuge, and possibly residences of a landed elite.

Orrorin tugenensis   Also known as the "millennium man," this early hominin fossil dates to about 6 million years ago, shortly after the divergence of the human and the chimp lines. It was discovered in the Tugen Hills region of Kenya.

Osteodontokeratic   A technology based on bone, teeth, and horn that Raymond Dart ascribed to the Australopiths, in the absence of any clear evidence for the use of stone tools by these hominins.

Out-of-Africa model   This model proposes that all modern populations descended from an anatomically modern human ancestor that evolved in Africa between 100,000 and 200,000 years ago.

Oxygen-isotope stage   One of a series of alternating warm and cold climatic periods defined by the relative proportions of ^{18}O and ^{16}O in deep sea cores.

Paleoeconomy   The archaeological study of the means by which a prehistoric people gained their livelihood, that is, by hunting, gathering, fishing, farming, and so on.

Paleoindian   A general term that is applied to the Late Pleistocene big-game hunting cultures of

North America. Originally applied to the Clovis and Folsom cultures, it has recently been argued that the Nenana Complex should also be included within the Paleoindian tradition.

Paleolithic The Paleolithic or Old Stone Age begins with the appearance of the earliest stone tools about 2.6 million years ago and ends with the end of the Ice Age about 11,500 calendar years ago.

Paloma The site approximately 4 km (2.5 mi.) from the sea behind San Bartolo Bay in Peru, occupied between 4500 and 3000 B.C. Although it was initially occupied by mobile hunter-gatherers, the inhabitants of the site eventually became sedentary, occupying small, circular houses.

Palynological analysis Analysis of fossil plant pollen recovered from archaeological and geological sediments.

Paracas The site of the necropolis or cemetery that was excavated by Julio C. Tello in 1929. The site includes a cache of 429 mummies that were wrapped in cloth and accompanied by pottery and other grave goods. The burials date to the late Initial period and the early part of the early Intermediate period. The designs on the Paracas textiles appear to have influenced later Nasca ceramics.

Paranthropus aethiopicus A fossil hominin found at West Turkana, dating to about 2.5 million years ago, that combines primitive features with features similar to the robust Australopiths. Known as the "black skull," this fossil indicates that the evolutionary line of robust hominins is very ancient.

Paranthropus boisei A massively built hominin found in East Africa, even more robust than *P. robustus*. *P. boisei* dates from 2 to 1 million years ago, continuing in existence even after the appearance of *Homo erectus* (see Chapter 5).

Paranthropus robustus A heavily built hominin with large rear teeth and found in South Africa, appearing somewhat later in time than *A. africanus*, from 2 to 1.5 million years ago. *P. robustus* appears to have diverged significantly from the human ancestral line.

Parietal art The art that appears on the walls and ceilings of caves, including both cave painting and low-relief carving. The images painted and carved in cave walls include naturalistic animal figures and enigmatic signs. Human figures are comparatively rare and stylized.

Pech de L'Azé A deeply stratified cave site in southwestern France that illustrates the apparently random interstratification of different types of Mousterian industries, such as Typical Mousterian and Denticulate Mousterian.

Pengelly, William (1812–1894) English schoolteacher with a deep interest in natural history. Pengelly reinvestigated Kent's Cavern and later excavated Brixham Cave, near Windmill Hill, Torquay, in southwest England, under the close observation of a committee of prominent scientists. His discovery of flint tools together with the bones of ancient animals was a turning point in the acceptance of the antiquity of humans.

Percussion marks Marks on animal bones produced when a bone is struck with a hammerstone in order to fracture it for marrow removal.

Phytoliths Microscopic particles of silica that are derived from the cells of plants. Their distinctive shapes allow them to be identified by archaeological researchers.

Picareiro Cave A late Paleolithic cave site in Portugal (11,800–12,300 B.P.) that has produced large numbers of rabbit bones, indicating that small mammals played an increasingly important role in late Upper Paleolithic diets.

Pictographs Pictorial representations impressed into clay with a stylus, preceding the development of cuneiform writing.

Pietersburg A Middle Stone Age industry of southern Africa that is characterized by the production of parallel-sided flake-blades from prepared cores.

Pincevent A late Magdalenian hunters' encampment in the Paris basin of France. The site was occupied by reindeer hunters for a short period in the autumn.

"Pithecanthropus erectus" The name originally given by Eugene Dubois to the fossils he found in Java, now classified as *Homo erectus*.

Planes of cleavage Planes along which rocks or minerals split easily.

Plant domestication The process through which plant reproduction comes under human control. Plant domestication involves more than simply creating optimal conditions for the growth of plants through watering and weeding. It entails the planting and harvesting of crops, and often the storage of seeds for use in future years. Plant domestication can lead to changes in plant morphology, including changes in seed size.

Pleistocene A geological epoch beginning about 1.8 million years ago and ending about 11,400 years ago. The Pleistocene is characterized by a series of climatic oscillations. The Pleistocene is generally divided into the early Pleistocene (1.8 million to 780,000 years ago), the middle Pleistocene (780,000 to 130,000 years ago) and the late Pleistocene (130,000 to 11,400 years ago).

Pluvial   A period marked by abundant rain.

Polyhedrons   Oldowan stone tools, consisting of pebbles that have been flaked in several directions to form intersecting edges.

Postclassic period   The period (930–1519 A.D.) that begins with the collapse of the Classic Maya in the southern lowlands and ends with the Spanish conquest of Mexico in 1519.

Postprocessual movement   The postprocessual movement is unified by its critique of processual archaeology of the 1960s and 1970s. Postprocessual archaeologists make use of models developed in the social sciences and the humanities to study social and cultural change in the archaeological record.

Potassium-argon dating method   An absolute dating method, generally applied to volcanic rocks, that relies upon the determination of the relative proportion of potassium-40 to argon-40, the product of its radioactive decomposition.

Preceramic period   The period refers to Peruvian prehistory before the introduction of pottery. Pottery was introduced to Peru about 1800 B.C. During the later Preceramic (ca. 3000–1800 B.C.), domesticated cotton played an increasingly important role in the economies of the coastal regions of Peru.

Preclassic period   An alternative name for the Formative period that is most commonly used in the Maya areas of Mesoamerica.

Prehistoric Overkill Hypothesis   The hypothesis suggesting that humans may have played a major role in the extinction of many large mammal species during the late Pleistocene.

Prehistory   The reconstruction of the human events that occurred before the advent of writing.

Pre-Pottery Neolithic A (PPNA)   The earliest part of the Neolithic in the southern Levant. Dated between about 9750 and 8550 B.C., the PPNA is characterized by the presence of early domestic cereals (wheat and barley). PPNA houses generally have circular stone foundations.

Pre-Pottery Neolithic B (PPNB)   The later part (ca. 8550–6300 B.C.) of the aceramic Neolithic in the southern Levant. PPNB sites are generally characterized by rectangular houses, and many PPNB sites have economies based on cereal agriculture and animal husbandry.

Pressure flaking   A method of stone knapping by which pressure is applied to the edge of a stone tool, usually with a flaker made of wood or bone, in order to detach a small, flat flake. Pressure flaking was used to shape the Solutrean laurel leaf points.

Primate   The mammalian order to which humans and the other hominins belong, and which also includes the prosimians, the Old and New World monkeys, and the great and lesser apes.

Principle of superposition of strata   A principle derived from geology, which states that if the strata in a geological deposit are piled as layers from bottom to top, the oldest must be at the bottom.

Processual approach   An archaeological approach that focuses on the processes of culture change. The variables that influence culture change are studied using scientific methods that include the formulation and testing of specific archaeological hypotheses.

Proto-dynastic period   The term sometimes used to describe the Naqada III period in Egypt.

Proto-literate period   Period including Uruk and Jemdat Nasr times during which the very earliest writing appears in Mesopotamia.

Pueblos   Year-round residences for large numbers of people that were constructed in the American Southwest in the early second millennium A.D. They are generally multiroomed, surface-level structures with walls made of stone or adobe.

Puna   The highest environmental zone in the Andes that is suitable for human habitation. The puna lies at between 3900 and 5000 m (13,000 to 16,000 ft.) elevation, and its rich grasslands would have supported abundant camelid (llama and alpaca) populations in prehistory.

Punch technique   A method of indirect percussion used to strike a large number of long, narrow blades from a prismatic core. The hammerstone strikes a punch, a tapered piece of bone, wood, or antler, which is placed near the edge of a blade core. The resultant force detaches a long, slender blade. By moving the punch around the core, it is possible to detach many blades from a single piece of flint.

Puritjarrn rockshelter   A rockshelter near Alice Springs in the dry central portion of Australia that appears to have been occupied about 22,000 years ago. The site provides evidence for the Pleistocene occupation of at least some of the arid regions of the Australian continent.

Qafzeh   A cave site in northern Israel that has produced the remains of anatomically modern humans associated with a Levalloiso-Mousterian stone tool industry.

Quebrada Jaguay and **Quebrada Tacahuay**   Two late Pleistocene sites located along the south coast of Peru. The sites were occupied between about 11,000 and 10,000 years ago and provide evidence for extensive use of marine resources.

Rachis   The axis of a cereal plant to which the individual grains are attached.

Radiocarbon dating   A method for dating organic materials (e.g., charcoal, bone, shell, and wood) based on the decay of a radioactive isotope of carbon, ^{14}C.

Radiocarbon recalibration   The process of correcting radiocarbon age determinations to reflect slight changes in the quantities of atmospheric carbon-14 through time.

Refitting   The process of piecing together the matching portions of artifacts, particularly lithics, bones, and pottery. Matches of refitted artifacts between features or between layers provide information about activity areas, site formation processes, and the degree of integrity of a site.

Relative dating   Dating methods that do not provide dates in calendar years but that can be used to determine whether two sites are the same age or whether one site is older or younger than another.

Remote sensing   A series of nondestructive techniques for recovering geographical, geological, ecological, and archaeological data from a distance.

Retouch   Removal of a series of small flakes from one or more edges of a stone tool.

Río Seco   A site typical of the larger late Preceramic sites along the Peruvian coast. The site covers 11.8 ha (29 ac.) and includes two major platform mounds that were built by in-filling rooms.

Rojdi   A Harappan town located on the Saurashtra peninsula in northwest India. The site was occupied continuously from the Mature Harappan to the late Harappan period.

Rosetta Stone   The key to the Egyptian hieroglyphic writing, discovered in 1799. The Rosetta Stone is inscribed with the same text in Greek and two forms of Egyptian writing, a script and hieroglyphics.

Rudna Glava   A late Neolithic copper mining site located in northeastern Serbia (formerly Yugoslavia). At Rudna Glava miners followed seams of copper ore up to 20 m (66 ft.) below ground and used rapid heating and cooling to extract the copper ores from the surrounding rocks.

Sahul   The geographical region that includes New Guinea, Australia, and Tasmania. At the height of the last glaciation, these three areas would have been joined to form a single large continent. This region is also referred to as Greater Australia.

Saint Césaire   A site in western France where the remains of a Neanderthal, dated to about 36,000 years ago, was found in association with Châtelperronian tools.

Samarra   Type site of the Samarran Culture, about 100 km (62 mi.) northwest of Baghdad.

Samarran Culture   First people to become established in the Mesopotamian lowlands proper. The distinctive Samarran pottery is painted with basketry-like patterns and sometimes stylized animal figures.

Sangiran   Site in Java at which *Homo erectus* fossils have been found and recently redated to 1.6 to 1.0 million years old.

Sangoan   A Middle Stone Age industry of central and west Africa characterized by the presence of large core scrapers and bifacially worked core tools. It may represent an adaptation to forested environments.

San Jose Mogote   A Formative village in the Oaxaca Valley that has yielded early evidence for public architecture and social inequality.

San Lorenzo   The earliest of the large Olmec centers, overlooking the Rio Coatzacoalcos. Excavations at San Lorenzo revealed the presence of Olmec-style ceramics at the site as early as 1150 B.C., as well as numerous large stone carved heads.

Saqqara   Cemetery near Memphis where important officials were buried in mastaba tombs, the predecessors of the pyramids. The earliest pyramid, the Third Dynasty step-pyramid of Djoser, essentially several successively smaller mastabas stacked one upon the other, is at Saqqara.

Scrapers   Stone tools shaped to include an edge prepared so that the implement would be suitable for scraping activities (although these artifacts may not have functioned in this way).

Sechín Alto   A site located in the Lower Casma River Valley. It is the largest and most impressive of a number of Initial period ceremonial centers that were constructed along the Peruvian coast.

Sequence dating   The relative dating technique devised by Sir Flinders Petrie to order the artifact assemblages from prehistoric Egyptian graves into a chronological sequence. The technique is based on the observation of gradual changes through time of stylistic traits on artifacts, as well as the appearance and disappearance of artifact types from one assemblage to the next.

Shang (or Yin) Dynasty   The Shang or Yin Dynasty (1600–1046 B.C.) is the second Chinese dynasty known to scholars from historical sources. Extensive archaeological excavations at Anyang have revealed the tombs and palaces of the later Shang rulers.

Shanidar   A cave site in northern Iraq that produced the remains of nine Neanderthal individuals, including five that appear to have been intentionally buried.

Shukbah   A Natufian site located in the Wadi Natuf that was excavated by Dorothy Garrod in the 1920s. The site location gave its name to the Natufian culture.

Sickle gloss   The sheen that appears on flint sickles when they are used to harvest plants such as grains and reeds. The gloss results from the contact between the flint sickle and tiny silica bodies within the stems of plants.

Sípan   The site of a recently discovered Sípan pyramid complex in the Lambayeque Valley, which has yielded a number of rich burials accompanied by prodigious quantities of metal, presentation goblets, and distinctive uniforms and headdresses. The burials date to the early Intermediate period and are associated with the Moche culture.

Site   An area where artifacts and features indicate that human activity has taken place. A site may range from a few artifacts scattered on the ground to an entire ancient city.

Slip   A thin wash of clay and water that is applied to a pottery vessel before it is fired.

Solutrean period   The period in western European prehistory that corresponds to the coldest phases of the late glacial period, about 22,000–18,000 B.P. Solutrean assemblages are characterized by the presence of finely flaked points shaped like laurel leaves.

Species   An interbreeding population of plants or animals.

Spheroids   Oldowan stone tools consisting of a core from which numerous flakes have been removed from the entire surface, forming a roughly spherical shape.

Split inheritance   A social institution among the Incas that played a role in the rapid expansion of the Inca state. The system of split inheritance meant that while one son of the dead emperor inherited his title, ability to make war, and authority to tax, the dead emperor's other male kin inherited his property.

Star Carr   Star Carr is an early Mesolithic hunter's camp located in North Yorkshire in England. Recent reanalysis of the fauna from this site indicates that it was occupied during the summer months.

State   A territorially based political unit with an institutionalized government.

Stellmoor   A late Pleistocene (Younger Dryas period) site in northern Germany that provides evidence for the use of bows and arrows by late glacial hunters in northern Europe. These weapons were used to kill reindeer that had been driven into a lake.

Stone cache hypothesis   Hypothesis proposed by Richard Potts as an alternative explanation for the function of the early hominin sites at Olduvai Gorge and Koobi Fora. According to this hypothesis, sites such as FLK were simply places where caches of stone tools were stored. Animals were taken to these places and quickly butchered; then the site was abandoned before competing carnivores were attracted to the spot.

Strata   Distinct layers within an archaeological deposit formed through either cultural or natural processes. Strata can be distinguished by their color, texture, or the materials included within them.

Stratigraphic analysis   The recording and analysis of the layers within an archeological site, by which the sequence of events that led to the formation of the site is worked out.

Stratigraphic control   The use of stratigraphic analysis to determine whether artifacts and features found in separated areas of a site are contemporary.

Stratigraphic cross-section   A carefully excavated and carefully recorded vertical profile of an archaeological excavation, intended to delineate the sequence of layers and features in the site.

Striking platform   The point near the edge of a stone core that is struck to remove a flake.

Sumer   The first of the ancient urban societies of Mesopotamia.

Tabular chert   A fine-grained deposit of silica (suitable for making into stone tools) that is deposited between the layers of limestone bedrock. Tabular chert usually must be obtained by digging or quarrying.

Taphonomy   The study of the processes by which bones and artifacts finally become incorporated into a site and of the factors that modify the composition of these assemblages.

Tehuacán Valley project   An archaeological project, conducted between 1961 and 1965 in Puebla, Mexico, designed to study the domestication of maize and other plants in the highlands of southern Mexico. More than 40,000 plant remains were recovered from sites that range in date from the late Pleistocene to the era of the Spanish conquest of Mexico.

Telarmarchay The Telarmarchay rockshelter, a deeply stratified site located 170 km (105 mi.) northeast of Lima, that provided evidence for the transition from the intensive hunting of wild camelids to their domestication at about 4300 B.C.

Tell-es-Sawwan Well-known site of the Samarra Culture, located near the type site of Samarra.

Tell Madhhur An exceptionally well-preserved example of a late Ubaid dwelling, near the Diyala River north of Baghdad.

Temper Nonplastic material that is combined with clay before it is fired. Temper reduces the risk of cracking as a clay vessel dries, and it counteracts shrinkage.

Tenochtitlán The Aztec capital, located on an island in Lake Texcoco in the Valley of Mexico, established in the fourteenth century.

Teosinte Teosinte (*Zea mexicana*) is a wild grass that is closely related to maize and appears to have been its wild ancestor.

Teotihuacán The city in the Valley of Mexico that was the political, economic, and religious capital of the valley from 200 B.C. to 700 A.D.

Terra Amata A beachfront early Acheulian open site, now in the city of Nice, France. A series of superimposed huts have been claimed as the earliest evidence for structures in Europe.

Teshik-Tash A Middle Paleolithic site in Uzbekistan that included a child's grave surrounded by a ring of wild goat horns, providing clear evidence for intentional burial of Neanderthals with grave goods.

Test trench A small excavation, often 1 by 1 m, designed to reveal the nature and depth of archaeological deposits.

Thermoluminescence (TL) dating An absolute dating method related to electron spin resonance (ESR) dating, based upon the measurement of energy trapped in the mineral crystals of a sample. The energy is measured as light, which is released when the sample is heated. The method is suitable for dating sites of the Lower Paleolithic period and later.

Thomsen, Christian J. (1788–1865) First curator of the Danish National Museum of Antiquities. Thomsen grouped the objects in the museum according to the material from which they were made and asserted that they represented three successive ages: the Stone Age, the Bronze Age, and the Iron Age. This organizational scheme is known as the Three Age System.

Three Age System A system initially developed by C. J. Thomsen as a way of organizing the collections in the Danish National Museum. He sorted the tools according to the materials they were made of—stone, bronze, and iron—and suggested that they represented three successive ages: the Stone Age, the Bronze Age, and the Iron Age.

Tikal A major Maya urban center in Guatemala that has been the focus of intensive archaeological research since the 1950s. At its height in Late Classic times, Tikal was home to 62,000 people.

Tiwanaku The capital of the Tiwanaku state, located 15 km (9 mi.) from Lake Titicaca in Bolivia, which controlled the southern highlands between about 400 and 1000 A.D.

Torralba and Ambrona Nearby sites in central Spain where Acheulian artifacts have been found among the bones of numerous elephants, horses, deer, wild cattle, and other large animals. Many of the animals were clearly butchered; whether they had been hunted or scavenged is not known.

Trihedral picks Large, thick bifaces with sharp points and triangular cross-sections, characteristic of the Early Acheulian industry.

Trinil Site on the Solo River of Java where in the 1890s Eugene Dubois found the fossils that he named "Pithecanthropus erectus" and that are now assigned to *Homo erectus*.

Tybrind Vig A submerged late Mesolithic (ca. 5500–4000 B.C.) site located on the island of Fyn in Denmark. Underwater excavations carried out at the site have produced well-preserved wooden artifacts, including boats and paddles, as well as evidence for intensive fishing.

Type site The site after which an archaeological occurrence, such as a stone industry, is named.

Typology The systematic classification of artifacts according to their shape or form.

Ubaid period The earliest manifestation of classic Mesopotamian civilization (ca. 6200–4000 B.C.), named after the small village site of Al Ubaid but found in the lowest levels of the tell sites of many Sumerian cities, notably Ur, Uruk, and Eridu.

'Ubeidiya A site in the Jordan Valley of Israel, dated to approximately 1.4 million years ago, with an Early Acheulian industry. 'Ubeidiya is one of the earliest archaeological sites outside of Africa.

Unifacial flaking The preparation of a stone artifact by the removal of flakes from only one side of a stone core (or larger flake).

Uniformitarianism The view of Earth's geological history, introduced by James Hutton and further developed by Charles Lyell, that states that the geological processes that operated in the past were similar in nature to those observable today.

Upper Paleolithic   A term used to describe the late Pleistocene (ca. 40,000 to 10,000 years ago) industries of Europe, the Near East, and North Africa. These industries are generally characterized by a high proportion of blade tools.

Upper Swan   A site near Perth in southwestern Australia where charcoal associated with stone tools has been dated to 38,000 years ago.

Vallonet   A cave site near Nice on the southern coast of France, with simple choppers and flakes and early Pleistocene fauna. The actual age of the site is controversial.

Varna   A fifth-millennium B.C. burial ground located near the Black Sea in Bulgaria. Some of the 281 burials included large numbers of copper and gold objects, while others included very few grave goods.

Vindija Cave   A site in Croatia that has yielded a Neanderthal skeleton recently radiocarbon dated to between 28,000 and 29,000 years ago.

Wadi Hammeh 27   A Natufian site located in northern Jordan that has provided evidence for substantial architecture, ground stone artifacts, and human burials. The site and its artifact assemblage show many similarities to the well-known site of Mallaha/Eynan.

Wari   The capital city in the Ayucuchu Valley of Peru from which the Wari state was able to establish political control over a wide area of highland and coastal Peru. The development of an administrative system of labor taxation, as well as the development of new agricultural technologies, may have allowed the Wari state to expand rapidly during the Middle Horizon.

Wattle and daub   A construction technique that uses wicker-work (wattle) for walls. The walls are then plastered with mud (daub).

Windermere interstadial   A late glacial warm period that lasted from about 13,000 to 11,000 radiocarbon years B.P. in Europe.

Worsaae, Jens (1821–1885)   Successor to Christian Thomsen as director of the Danish National Museum. Worsaae is sometimes called the father of modern archaeology; he was the first professional archaeologist. He excavated extensively throughout Denmark and established many of the basic methods used by modern archaeologists.

Xia Dynasty   The earliest dynasty recorded by Chinese historians (ca. 1900–1500 B.C.). Although we have no documents that date from Xia times, later historical sources describe it as China's first dynasty. Today, most archaeologists think that the archaeological materials from the Erlitou period represent the material remains of the Xia Dynasty.

Yangshao period   This period dates from 5000 to 2800 B.C. Yangshao sites are located in the central Yellow River Valley. Most Yangshao sites are permanent villages that were inhabited by farmers who grew millet and raised livestock such as pigs and dogs.

Younger Dryas   The Younger Dryas was a short stadial or cold period that began about 11,000 radiocarbon years ago and lasted for less than a millennium. During the Younger Dryas in Europe, temperatures dropped significantly, and the glaciers began to advance again. Evidence of the Younger Dryas event has also been found in the Near East (Chapters 15 and 16) and in eastern North America.

Zhoukoudian   A cave site near Beijing, China, occupied for about 200,000 years, between 460,000 and 230,000 years ago. The bones of about 45 *Homo erectus* individuals were found there, along with a stone industry without handaxes. Deep layers of ash in the cave have usually been interpreted as indicative of the extensive and prolonged use of fire.

INDEX

Note: Page numbers in *italics* refer to figures. Page numbers in **bold** refer to key terms.

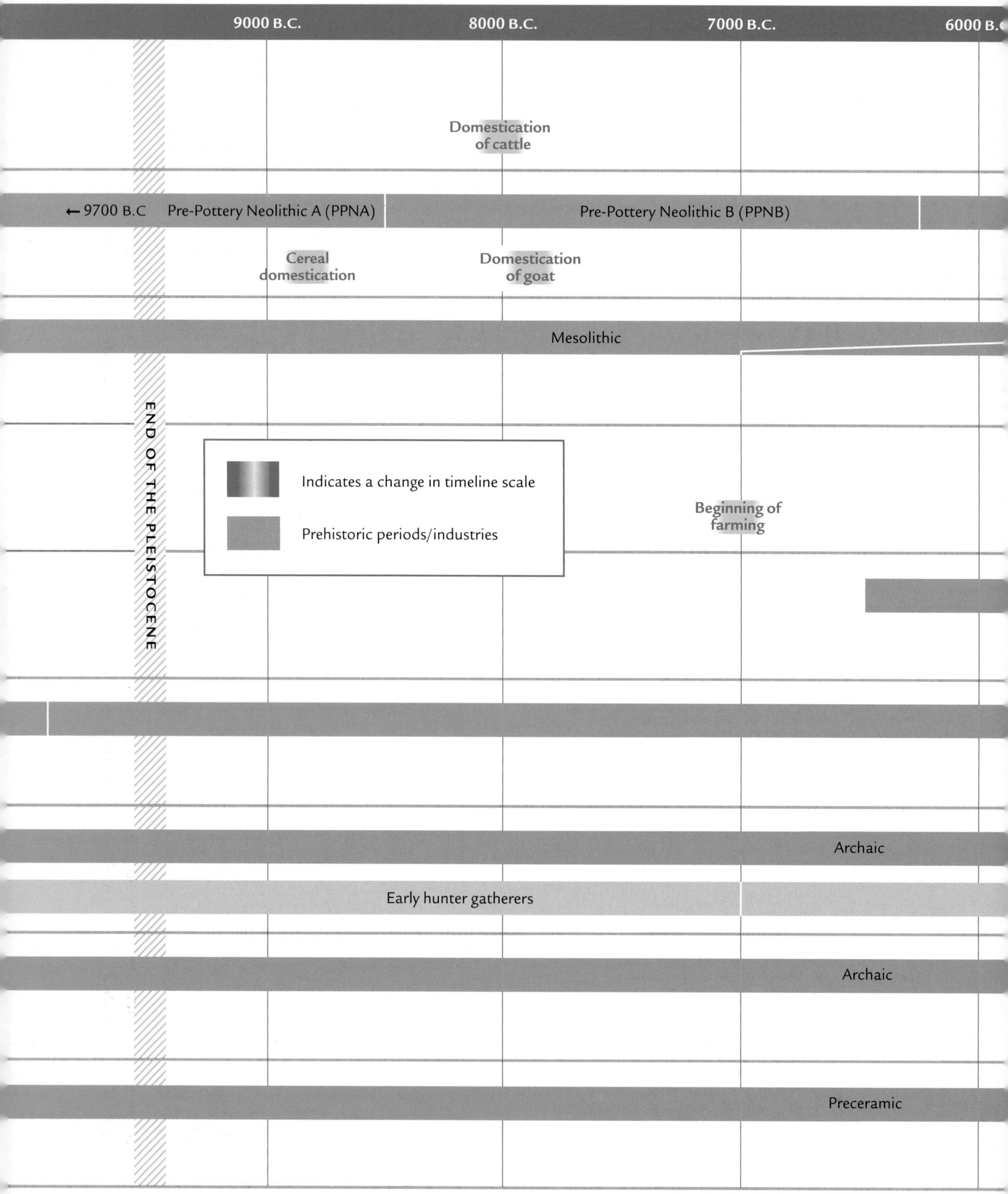

9000 B.C.	8000 B.C.	7000 B.C.	6000 B.C

Domestication
of cattle

← 9700 B.C   Pre-Pottery Neolithic A (PPNA)   Pre-Pottery Neolithic B (PPNB)

Cereal
domestication

Domestication
of goat

Mesolithic

END OF THE PLEISTOCENE

Indicates a change in timeline scale

Prehistoric periods/industries

Beginning of
farming

Archaic

Early hunter gatherers

Archaic

Preceramic

Timeline continues on the next page

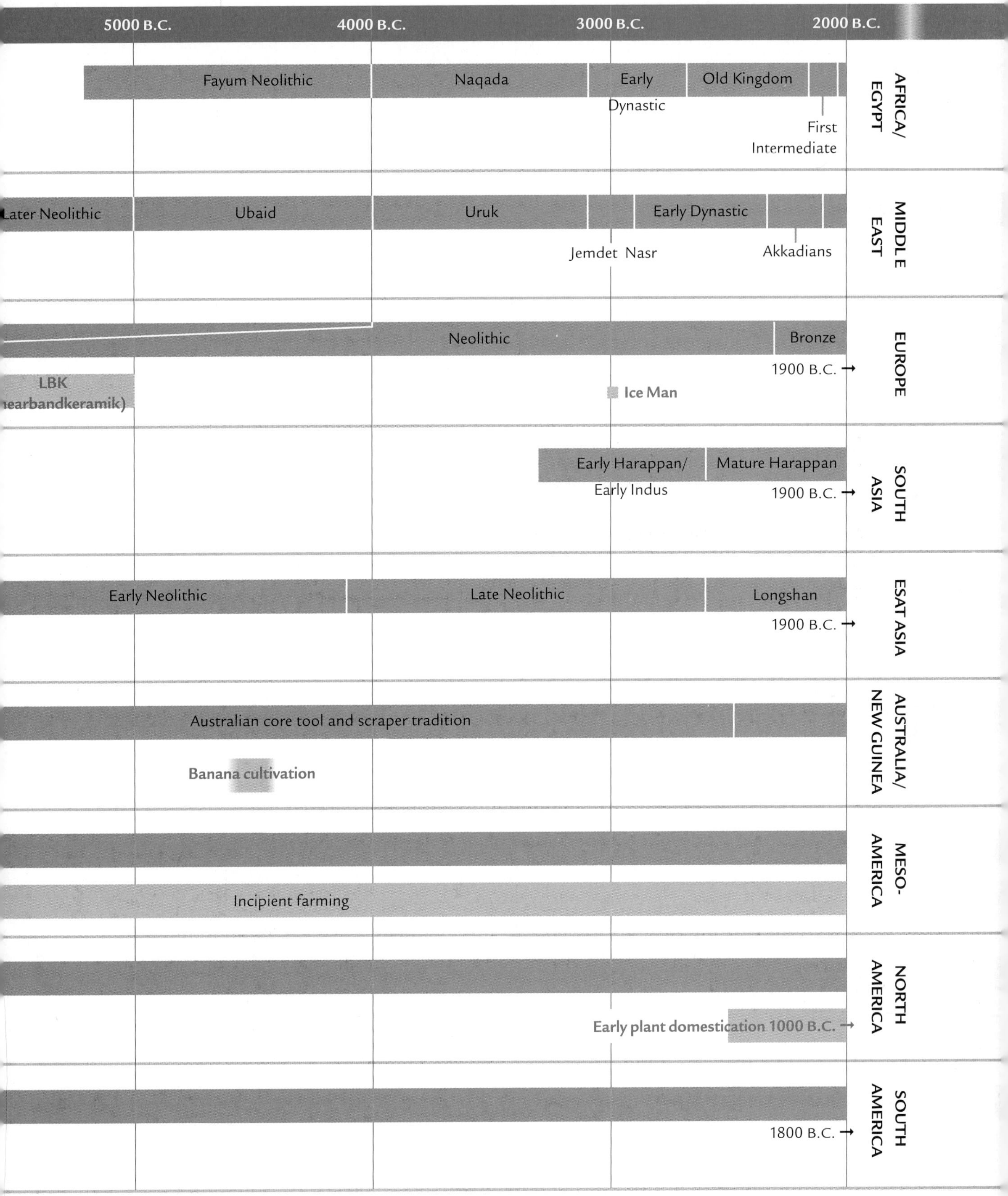

5000 B.C.	4000 B.C.	3000 B.C.	2000 B.C.	

Fayum Neolithic		Naqada	Early Dynastic	Old Kingdom		**AFRICA/ EGYPT**

First Intermediate

Later Neolithic	Ubaid	Uruk	Early Dynastic		**MIDDLE EAST**

Jemdet Nasr   Akkadians

Neolithic	Bronze	**EUROPE**

1900 B.C. →

LBK
(Linearbandkeramik)

▓ Ice Man

Early Harappan/ Early Indus	Mature Harappan	**SOUTH ASIA**

1900 B.C. →

Early Neolithic	Late Neolithic	Longshan	**ESAT ASIA**

1900 B.C. →

Australian core tool and scraper tradition   **AUSTRALIA/ NEW GUINEA**

Banana cultivation

MESO- AMERICA

Incipient farming

NORTH AMERICA

Early plant domestication 1000 B.C. →

SOUTH AMERICA

1800 B.C. →

timeline is continued from previous page

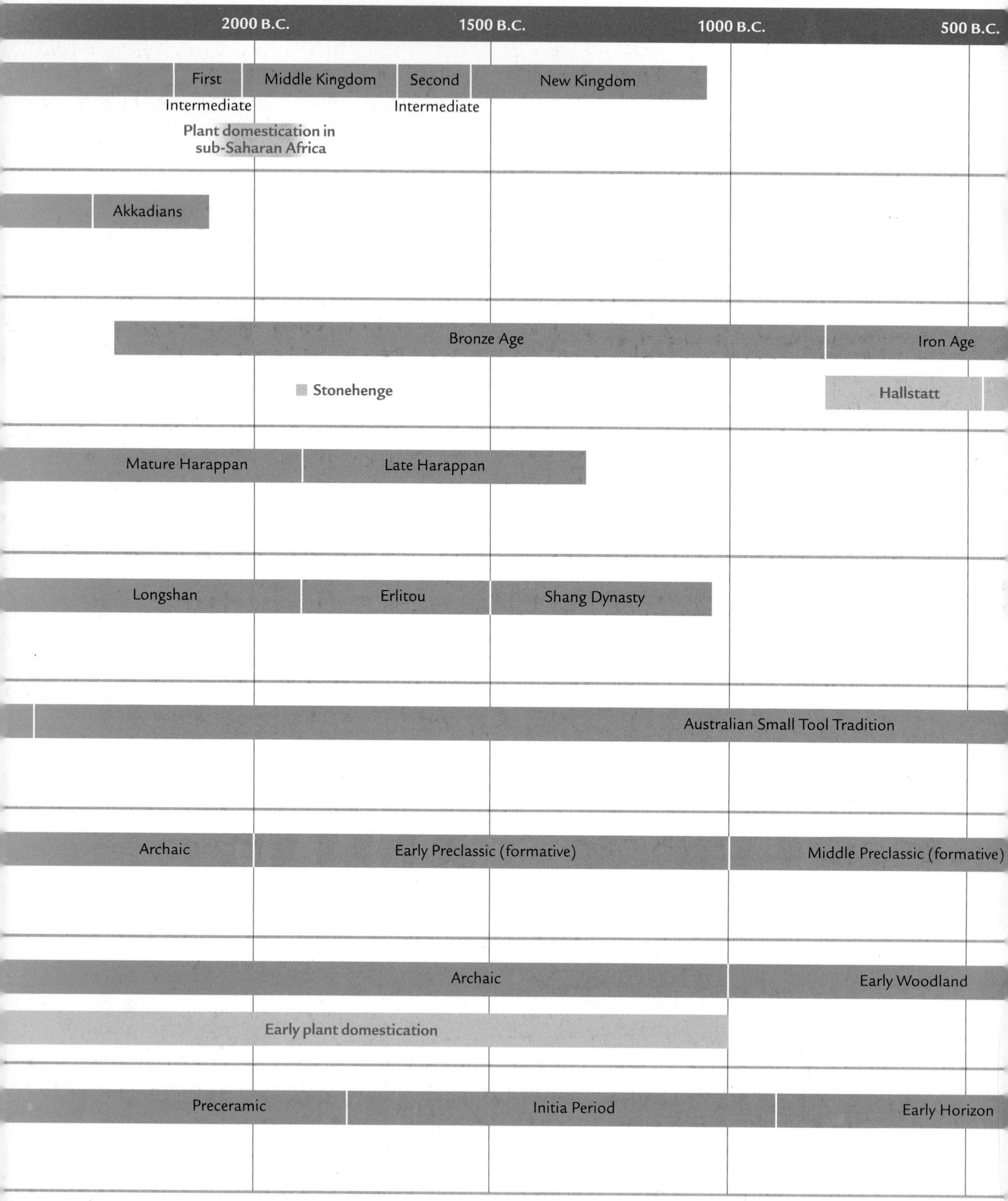

	2000 B.C.	1500 B.C.	1000 B.C.	500 B.C.

First Intermediate | Middle Kingdom | Second Intermediate | New Kingdom

Plant domestication in sub-Saharan Africa

Akkadians

Bronze Age | Iron Age

Hallstatt

■ Stonehenge

Mature Harappan | Late Harappan

Longshan | Erlitou | Shang Dynasty

Australian Small Tool Tradition

Archaic | Early Preclassic (formative) | Middle Preclassic (formative)

Archaic | Early Woodland

Early plant domestication

Preceramic | Initia Period | Early Horizon